Fantasy, Myth, and Reality

Fantasy, Myth, and Reality

Essays in Honor of
Jacob A. Arlow, M.D.

edited by

Harold P. Blum, M.D.
Yale Kramer, M.D.,
Arlene K. Richards, Ed.D.
Arnold D. Richards, M.D.

International Universities Press, Inc.
Madison, Connecticut

Essay Index

Library of Congress Cataloging-in-Publication Data

Fantasy, myth, and reality: essays in honor of Jacob A. Arlow, M.D./
    edited by Harold P. Blum. . . [et al.].
        p.   cm.
    Bibliography: p.
    Includes index.
    ISBN 0-8236-1887-0
    1. Fantasy. 2. Subconsciousness. 3. Identity (Psychology).
    4. Psychology, Pathological. 5. Psychology, Religious. 6. Arlow,
Jacob A. I. Arlow, Jacob A. II. Blum, Harold P.
BF175.5.F36F36 1988
154.3—dc19   88-12766
                                                  CIP

Manufactured in the United States of America

CONTENTS

264148

Part III
UNCONSCIOUS FANTASY: TECHNIQUE

Part IV
UNCONSCIOUS FANTASY: APPLICATIONS

Part V
MYTHOLOGY, RELIGION, AND BELIEF

Part VI
REALITY: SEXUALITY, IDENTITY, AND BIOLOGY

Part VII
PSYCHOPATHOLOGY IN CLINICAL PRACTICE

Part VII
Epilogue

CONTRIBUTORS

SANDER M. ABEND, M.D.
Training and Supervising Analyst, New York Psychoanalytic Institute; Editor-in-Chief, *Psychoanalytic Quarterly*.

FRANCIS BAUDRY, M.D.
Training and Supervising Analyst, New York Psychoanalytic Institute; Fellow, American Psychiatric Association.

MARTIN S. BERGMANN, Ph.D.
Clinical Professor of Psychology, New York University Postdoctoral Program; Faculty Member Emeritus, New York Freudian Society.

ISIDOR BERNSTEIN, M.D.
Clinical Associate Professor of Psychiatry, New York University Medical Center; Training and Supervising Analyst, New York Psychoanalytic Institute.

HAROLD P. BLUM, M.D.
Clinical Professor of Psychiatry and Training Analyst, Psychoanalytic Institute, New York University Medical Center; Executive Director, Sigmund Freud Archives; Past Editor, *Journal of the American Psychoanalytic Association*.

DALE BOESKY, M.D.
Training and Supervising Analyst, Michigan Psychoanalytic Institute; Past Editor-in-Chief, *Psychoanalytic Quarterly*.

CHARLES BRENNER, M.D.
Training and Supervising Analyst, New York Psychoanalytic Institute; Past President, American Psychoanalytic Association.

JANINE CHASSEGUET-SMIRGEL, Ph.D.
Training Analyst, Paris Psychoanalytic Society; Professor, University College London, Freud Chair (1982-1983).

CHARLES FISHER, M.D.
Training Analyst, New York Psychoanalytic Institute; Emeritus Clinical Professor of Psychiatry, Mount Sinai School of Medicine.

J. T. FRASER, Ph.D.
Founder, International Society for the Study of Time.

ELEANOR GALENSON, M.D.
Clinical Professor of Psychiatry, Mount Sinai School of Medicine; Vice President and Member, New York Psychoanalytic Society.

JULES GLENN, M.D.
Clinical Professor of Psychiatry, New York University Medical Center; Training and Supervising Analyst, Psychoanalytic Institute, New York University Medical Center.

WILLIAM I. GROSSMAN, M.D.
Clinical Professor of Psychiatry, Albert Einstein College of Medicine; Training and Supervising Analyst, New York Psychoanalytic Institute.

DONALD M. KAPLAN, Ph.D.
Clinical Professor of Psychology, New York University; Faculty Member, New York Freudian Society.

OTTO F. KERNBERG, M.D.
Associate Chairman and Medical Director, New York Hospital-Cornell Medical Center, Westchester Division; Professor of Psychiatry, Cornell University Medical College; Training and Supervising Analyst, Columbia University Center for Psychoanalytic Training and Research.

YALE KRAMER, M.D.
Clinical Associate Professor, University of Medicine and Dentistry of New Jersey-Robert Wood Johnson Medical School; Assistant Lecturer, New York Psychoanalytic Institute.

BURNESS E. MOORE, M.D.
Geographic Rule Training and Supervising Analyst, Columbia/Emory Center for Psychoanalytic Training and Research; Clinical Professor of Psychiatry, Emory University School of Medicine

PETER B. NEUBAUER, M.D.
Clinical Professor of Psychiatry, New York University.

MORTIMER OSTOW, M.D.
Sandrow Visiting Professor of Pastoral Psychiatry, Jewish Theological Seminary of America; President, Psychoanalytic Research and Development Fund.

LEO RANGELL, M.D.
Past President, American and International Psycho-Analytical Associations; Clinical Professor, University of California at Los Angeles and University of California at San Francisco.

ARLENE K. RICHARDS, Ed.D.
Institute for Psychoanalytic Training and Research; New York Freudian Society.

ARNOLD D. RICHARDS, M.D.
Training and Supervising Analyst, New York Psychoanalytic Institute; Faculty Member, Psychoanalytic Institute, New York University Medical Center.

SAMUEL RITVO, M.D.
Clinical Professor of Psychiatry, Yale University Child Study Center; Training and Supervising Analyst, Western New England Institute for Psychoanalysis.

NATHAN P. SEGEL, M.D.
Training and Supervising Analyst, Michigan Psychoanalytic Institute; Clinical Professor, Department of Psychiatry, Wayne State University, School of Medicine.

THEODORE SHAPIRO, M.D.
Professor and Director, Child and Adolescent Psychiatry, Cornell University Medical College; Editor, *Journal of the American Psychoanalytic Association*.

ROBERT S. WALLERSTEIN, M.D.
   Professor Psychiatry, University of California at San Francisco, School
   of Medicine; President, International Psycho-Analytical Association.

MARTIN WANGH, M.D.
   Clinical Professor Emeritus of Psychiatry, Albert Einstein College of
   Medicine; Visiting Professor, Freud Center, Hebrew University.

MARTIN S. WILLICK, M.D.
   Training and Supervising Psychoanalyst, New York Psychoanalytic
   Institute; Lecturer in Psychiatry, College of Physicians and Surgeons,
   Columbia University.

Part I

JACOB A. ARLOW:
THE MAN
AND HIS WORK

A Tribute to Jacob A. Arlow, M.D.

Harold P. Blum, M.D.

> "That men may know wisdom and instruction, understand words of insight."
>
> *Proverbs I*

Jacob A. Arlow is renowned throughout the psychoanalytic world. His accomplishments are so great, his thinking so profound, his writings so prolific that monographs could be written on Jacob Arlow in each of his several roles: theoretician, researcher, clinician, teacher, lecturer, discussant. Though he is bound by ties of closest affection to his many friends and is the object of their esteem and admiration, not many of his readers know him personally, as a whole person. Jacob Arlow has a rich inner and outer life characterized by familial closeness and long-standing intimate friendships. To know Jacob Arlow is to know a uniquely gifted individual whose dazzling brilliance and unusual capacity for synthesis and organization extend to his personal life. He has the ability to engage in hard work and deep concentration over extended periods, while retaining personal intimacy, close communication, and relationships characterized by true reciprocity. Jack can research and write, work and play, study and investigate with an ease and facility that almost defies description. In his play and recreation he can be passionately involved, an inner freedom showing itself behind the serious, highly regulated exterior. This is apparent everywhere—in his sculpture, his absorption in a play, his concentration on a tennis match.

Neither the vast scope of Jack's contributions, nor their profound depth, tells enough of his method and style. In him a highly refined perceptiveness finds its complement in the masterful way he has of organizing observations and ideas. Jack Arlow is a naturally gifted scien-

3

tist who carefully marshals his evidence and arguments, who can engage in the highest levels of critical thinking, and who can present and explain his findings with a ready elegance. A Jacob Arlow presentation is invariably informed, lucid, and logical, but it involves also an almost poetic selection of word and metaphor, a true feeling for literary aesthetics. In short, he both instructs and delights. Jack's eloquence, erudition, and keenness of perception, combined with an unwavering inquisitiveness and a capacity for creative synthesis, are an Arlow trademark. He has remarked that of the many influences on his prose, the Bible is the most important.

I shall never forget one International Psycho-Analytical Congress where Jack spontaneously discussed from the floor a case that Anna Freud had supervised. The elegance and lucidity of his impromptu speech, the illumination he provided, both of the case and of similar disorders, the novel developmental considerations he introduced, and his deft comparison of the different views represented by the panelists left an indelible impression on everyone present. These extemporaneous remarks were so insightful and erudite, such an original contribution to the topic, as to overshadow many papers prepared long in advance of the Congress.

The author of more than two hundred papers, articles, discussions, and reviews, Jacob Arlow has consistently been recognized as an outstanding psychoanalytic scholar, a leader in the field, and a source of inspiration and guidance for colleagues and students alike. He has always enjoyed teaching and has contributed studies on psychoanalytic education, analytic group process, and unconscious fantasies embedded in the training situation.

As a teacher, Jacob Arlow was noted for his careful methodology and close correlation of clinical material with theoretical concepts. His highly disciplined mind was always ready with the appropriate observations, elaborations, and inferences. He carefully monitored classroom exchanges, chose the most relevant reading assignments, and facilitated his students' critical examination of controversial issues. As unintimidated by challenges or criticism as he was impervious to flattery and attempts at ingratiation, he taught in the best tradition of the psychoanalytic educator—dedicated and helpful, stimulating and organizing without ever being controlling or intrusive.

A most sought after training analyst, supervisor, and teacher, Jacob Arlow has taught at all three New York institutes affiliated with The American Psychoanalytic Association. Though over the years he has been most closely connected with the New York Psychoanalytic Institute, he has also been Clinical Professor of Psychiatry at New York University and has taught regularly at the New York University Psychoanalytic Institute. He has found time as well to give lectures and seminars at the Columbia University Center for Psychoanalytic Training and Research.

His numerous awards and honors include the Heinz Hartmann Award of The New York Psychoanalytic Institute; the Clinical Essay Prize of the British Psycho-Analytical Society for his paper ''Smugness''; and the *Journal* Prize of the American Psychoanalytic Association for his paper ''Psychoanalysis and Time.'' He has delivered the Freud Anniversary Lectures of the New York Psychoanalytic Institute and of the Psychoanalytic Association of New York, as well as the Brill Lecture of the New York Psychoanalytic Society, and has held the Turner Lectureship at the Columbia Psychoanalytic Institute and the Weigand Lectureship at the Department of Philosophy, University of Toronto. This, of course, is only a partial listing. Jacob Arlow continues to this day to be called on to give special lectures, plenary addresses, and keynote speeches at professional meetings and symposia.

An eminent member of the American Medical Association, the American Psychiatric Association, the American Psychoanalytic Association, and the American Psychosomatic Society, Jacob Arlow has rendered distinguished service as president of the American Psychoanalytic Association (1960–1961) and as chairman of its the Board on Professional Standards (1967–1970). He has chaired numerous committees and panels of the Association and of his local societies. He has served also as editor-in-chief of the *Psychoanalytic Quarterly* and continues to serve as an associate editor of that journal. Recently the *Psychoanalytic Quarterly* honored him with a special issue. His collaboration with Charles Brenner bore fruit in 1964 in the famous monograph, *Psychoanalytic Concepts and the Structural Theory*, which remains among the most cited works in the psychoanalytic literature.

For the celebration of the Freud Centennial, Jacob Arlow wrote ''The Legacy of Sigmund Freud.'' He also edited *The Selected Writings of Bertram D. Lewin* and has written numerous introductions for the books and monographs of colleagues. Jack has been extraordinarily generous in giving his time and attention to the profession, to colleagues, and to students; he has helped junior colleagues develop their skills and realize their potential.

For many years after their formal training, Jacob Arlow, David Beres,

Charles Brenner, and Martin Wangh participated in a psychoanalytic study group. They shared their ideas and interests, exchanged views, read drafts of their papers to one another, encouraged and criticized each other's work, and served all the collective functions of a cohesive, productive work group. The experience led to their shared recognition of certain analytic problems and to common research interests. All sought further personal analysis. They have remained close friends yet retain their own analytic pursuits, ideas, and personal interests.

Inwardly motivated and directed, Jack follows his own bent. He still exchanges views with Brenner and remains in touch with Beres, now retired, and with Wangh, now living and working in Israel. He has maintained his intimate friendship with Leo Rangell ever since their youthful, mutually rewarding residency together; their analytic activities and contributions continue to converge, even across a continent.

Jacob Arlow's friendships and collegial ties are rooted in his close-knit family. Blessed with parents who were models of social interest and concern, he grew up with a strong sense of extended family and community obligation. His parents, among the founders of the Pride of Judea Children's Home and of the Home for Incurables (now the Jewish Hospital for Chronic Disease), felt a great sense of obligation toward the poor and the homeless. Born to Adolph Arlow and Ida Arlow, nee Feldman, on September 3, 1912, in New York City, Jack grew up in the city of his birth. His father was in several businesses, and was later associated with the building trades. His mother's involvement in social causes often enough took her away from home during the day, probably contributing to Jack's early independence and spirited self-direction. His brother, five years older, was also a model of activity, a successful accountant and the president of his synagogue. His sister, three years older, typifies the family style in her own social activity.

Frequent childhood illnesses and confinements, combined with his relentless curiosity and superb intellectual endowment, led early on to hours of reading and reflection. For Jack the uses of adversity—recurrent upper respiratory infections, a possible bout of diphtheria, and heart murmurs—surely included mastery through an intensification of his inner life and the refinement of his capacity for abstract thought. Exploratory conquest of the outer world was attained on a mental plane, through wide learning and the acquisition of a deep store of knowledge. As a child Jack read the *Book of Knowledge*, O. Henry's stories, classical and medieval history, Kipling's stories and poems, and the Bible (illustrated by Gustave Dore). Even at a tender age, Jack found a sense of poetry in the Bible that could not easily be shared. He recalls that his paternal grandfather, though not an Orthodox Jew, was deeply appreciative of the Bible as literature and quite fond of quoting Isaiah. Jack's strong sense of Jewish identity and interest in Jewish studies was fostered also by his parents. Though not outwardly very religious or observant, they enrolled Jack in Talmud Torah five days a week; later he attended, simultaneously, both a secular high school and a Hebrew high school. He also came under the influence of Samson Benderly, an outstanding Jewish educator who was concerned with the modernization of Jewish culture, instruction in Hebrew, and the training of future leaders of the Jewish community. Benderly founded and supervised a program for gifted students in which the youthful Jacob Arlow enthusiastically participated through high school and his undergraduate years. He not only studied Hebrew but spoke it in summer camp and with classmates. Today he is fluent in both Biblical and contemporary Hebrew.

Having begun his college studies in the liberal arts, with the idea of possibly becoming an attorney, he underwent a profound change of goals which may well have been associated with an identity crisis. He turned from the humanities to the sciences, with an interest in medicine, and simultaneously fell in love with Alice Diamond, whom he quickly knew he would marry. Soon he was on course to becoming the complete physician-psychoanalyst. Graduating from New York University at the age of twenty, he went on to New York University School of Medicine and married his beloved Alice. In those early years, Alice provided not only loving support and encouragement, but also economic support from her own work. After his internship, the young Dr. Arlow undertook a dual residency program in neurology and psychiatry in the United States Public Health Service at Ellis Island, with further training in neurology at Montefiore Hospital and in psychiatry at the New York State Psychiatric Institute.

His interest in psychoanalysis was predictable, given his early and continued interest in the humanities. He had long before discovered Freud, reading the *Introductory Lectures* while still in high school. Freud's findings struck the adolescent Arlow as correct, a view fortified by his reading of *Totem and Taboo* and other works while studying abnormal psychology in college. Impressed by psychoanalytic teachers during his residency, Jacob Arlow began psychoanalytic training at the New York Psychoanalytic Institute, becoming a graduate analyst in 1947. As a senior candidate, he held a fellowship with Flanders Dunbar in psychosomatics. Having first been an instructor in neurology and then in psychiatry, he became an instructor and lecturer in psychosomatic medicine at the Psychoanalytic Clinic at Columbia University and at the New York Psychoanalytic Institute, School of Applied Analysis.

During these early years, Jack became very friendly with David Beres, Charles Brenner, Bernard Meyer, and Leo Rangell. The pattern of enduring friendships, set so early in his life, remained true for a lifetime. Friends from different stages of development, going back to his youth, are still to be found, and he and his twenty-eight cousins still get together with enduring affection and attachment.

It is impossible to picture Jacob Arlow without his family; they have always been such a vital part of his life. His romance with Alice, which flowered in college, probably had its roots in the Benderly group, in which Alice was a gifted participant. They shared many common interests and activities, ranging from the dance to Jewish culture. Perceptive and empathic, gracious and generous, with refined critical judgment, Alice has complemented Jack with her own special qualities. One cannot think of one without the other. They have four grown sons and are now doting grandparents to their five grandchildren. Their sons have all been successful in their chosen professions. Michael is an engineer who resides in Detroit; Allan a corporate attorney in Chicago; Seth an anesthesiologist in Seattle; and Jonathan a writer in New York. Recently Jack and Alice celebrated their fiftieth wedding anniversary, together with all of their children and grandchildren.

Jacob Arlow is today a revered elder statesman who is regularly consulted on analytic problems, whose opinions are sought in all quarters of the field. His advice and constructive criticism have been influential to a whole era of psychoanalytic education and research. Such recognition, so justly deserved, is reserved for very unique and rare individuals.

2

In the Visions of the Night: Perspectives on the Work of Jacob A. Arlow

Yale Kramer, M.D.

> "And God spoke unto Israel in the visions of the night, and said, Jacob, Jacob. . . fear not to go down into Egypt. . ."
>
> *Genesis 46:2*

INTRODUCTION

The scope of Jacob Arlow's achievements cannot be easily measured or circumscribed. Much of his contribution to the professional life of psychoanalysis and American psychiatry does not reside within the covers of books or journals, but in the minds and memories of those he has treated and taught and in the contributions that his patients and students have in turn made to this and other fields. They are a host of living, breathing contributions and memorials to his skills and understanding.

It is the purpose of this essay to provide a perspective of Arlow's written work—a map of the country, so to speak, identifying its topographical features, its heights and turnings, and the themes that run through it like rivers.

It is uncommon and perhaps unfashionable in psychoanalysis to raise issues of quantity. Partly this is appropriate to a discipline that studies phenomena difficult to quantify; partly, no doubt, this tendency has to do with the fact that the numbers when we do add them up are small and the rate of progress that we observe is invariably slow. There is also something akin to a reverse snobbishness where it comes to quantification—a suggestion that perhaps such an interest represents an immaturity of development.

These attitudes notwithstanding, there are some phenomena that require a quantitative dimension for their fullest appreciation. Works such as the Piazza San Marco, or the golden domes of St. Sophia require the acknowledgement of scale and proportion in order to appreciate the scope of their greatness. And although we will turn to the qualitative aspect of Arlow's work in a moment, it is worth taking note of what he has achieved in purely quantitative terms in order to appreciate the creative powers that have been at work over the past forty years. Since 1944 Arlow has published three volumes and seventy-five original scientific papers, most of which represent major contributions to the literature. In addition he has published approximately thirty educational articles or chapters and thirty-five critical reviews—over one hundred and forty papers in all—enough to fill nine or ten volumes. This canon alone might be the envy of any full-time academician, but all of this was created while at the same time pursuing a full-time psychoanalytic practice, a full measure of family life and, as though two-and-a-half lives were not enough, engaging actively in the work of teacher, educator, and national leader in his profession.

The numbers alone bespeak an astonishing vitality, and yet, as impressive as this scale of publication is, its breadth and scope is equally arresting: Freud, naturally. But what about Yukio Mishima, Antonioni, and the Old Testament prophets? What about cosmology, anthropology, art history, political science, mythology, psychosomatics, finger painting, time, metaphor? Even within the field of psychoanalysis his range of interests has covered every aspect of psychopathology, theory, education, and technique. And in this feast of fresh insights and understanding one senses always that there is a high pleasure value in the work of discovery and learning, and in sharing the discovery.

Refreshing as Arlow's widely ranging exploration may be, to the casual reader there appears to be a lack of coherence in his writings, as though his interests were fickle. Nothing could be further from the truth, and it is the purpose of this essay to demonstrate to those unfamiliar with Arlow's work the organizing principles and abiding themes that inform it.

Since the death of Freud, only a handful of people can be said to have changed the way analysts perceive their patients and think about them. Arlow is one of those. Observing and writing for almost forty-five years, his views have gradually transformed our understanding of the human mind and of what psychoanalysis is.

These transformations, developing slowly at first, reached maturity almost half a generation ago, and by now we take them for granted, and believe that that is the way it has always been. We tend to go on giving Freud credit for what is best in psychoanalysis when in fact it has been refined by two or three analytic generations. I think it is no exaggeration to say that as modern analysts we often think Arlow, talk Arlow, and practice Arlow without altogether knowing it.

Arlow's first paper appeared in 1944. It was one of a series of psychosomatic papers, which, although they were not strictly speaking psychoanalytic, did use analytic ideas as a way of organizing their data. But more important, these early papers, between 1944 and 1952, (Arlow, 1944, 1945, 1948, 1952) demonstrate certain attitudes and habits of mind which have informed all of Arlow's work up to the present time and which, in a sense, have combined to create the profound importance of his achievement.

First and most basic, Arlow sees himself as a physician. Whatever else he may interest himself in, he never leaves his stance as a physician, a problem solver, a therapist, someone concerned with the abnormal.

Related to this physicianly stance is his solidly empirical attitude. When he writes about theory, it is to bring it in line with fact; when he criticizes theory, it is to say that it is too speculative. Furthermore, his empiricism is based on remarkably astute powers of observation. One small example from an early psychosomatic article will demonstrate his unusual capacity for subtle psychological observation and inference. The following brief clinical vignette published in 1948 is from a survey of the diseases of the musculo-skeletal system and their relationship to emotional conflicts (Arlow, 1948). "A middle-aged woman who had undergone a hysterectomy, developed the following postural attitude while discussing her destiny of childlessness; her left knee and ankle were held in extreme tonic flexion. She denied that she was unduly perturbed by her unhappy fate. When the [position] of her musculature was called to her attention, she immediately relaxed her left limb and simultaneously broke into bitter tears'' (p. 279).

His respect for thorough scholarship assures that his contributions are never falsely simple. And his grasp of psychoanalytic history and theory provides perspective and confidence in challenging received wisdom.

This confidence in his clinical observations and scholarship, together with an independence of mind has enabled him to assume a leadership role in the further development of psychoanalytic theory and practice. A rare gift, it was especially valuable in the historical context of post–World War II American psychoanalysis, so dominated at that time by powerful European personalities claiming the mantle of Freud. Perhaps it was the Prophet in Arlow that allowed the Scientist to emerge and present an independent point of view.

Finally it is Arlow's love of stories and symbols that has given his observations profundity about human nature and that, in combination with those habits of mind mentioned above, has led to his most important conceptualization—the theory of unconscious fantasy. His fascination with representations of all sorts—dreams, paintings, fairy tales, novels, films—stories, plots, and scenarios—has been harnessed in the service of science and psychoanalysis.

What a remarkably fortunate combination of personal characteristics, interests, values, and training. The abilities and inclinations of a physician, scientist, scholar, critic, and leader underlie the achievement of Jacob Arlow.

Among these many interests three seem to have played principal roles in Arlow's work from the very start. These are psychopathology and its formation, stories and histories and their psychology, and the structural theory. At first these interests expressed themselves more or less separately, but they gradually became more and more bound up with one another until, in 1969, all three became fused in his theory of unconscious fantasy.

Thus I shall try first to describe the development of Arlow's thought from 1951 to 1969—the phase of discovery—tracing these three themes. Following that I shall try to articulate how during the last twenty years he has changed the way we think about the structural theory and the psychoanalytic method—the phase of elaboration.

THE PHASE OF DISCOVERY — 1949 TO 1969

Arlow's first full-fledged psychoanalytic paper was a brief clinical report of a patient who suffered from feelings of persecution (Arlow, 1949). In it Arlow presented data that suggested that what underlay these feelings were unconscious "masochistic feminine fantasies." It is highly unlikely that what Arlow meant by the term "fantasies" in that paper was identical to his meaning twenty years later. The likelihood is that what he meant by the term "fantasies" at that time was close to what Freud meant in 1908 in his paper on hysterical fantasies—something closely connected to unconscious wishes or impulses. Indeed, the paper is devoid of Arlow's later interest in ego psychology and seems to hark back to an earlier time in which depth psychology was the predominant theory in psychoanalysis.

In 1949 Arlow presented a paper to the New York Psychoanalytic Society (Arlow, 1951) in which he explored the psychology of prophets—individuals who assign to themselves a certain type of moral leadership—and the interplay of dynamic forces between these leaders and the groups they come to represent. The study was a remarkable demonstration of his depth of scholarship in biblical history and sensitivity to symbolism.

In it he describes a prophet as an individual who takes on the role of spokesman of God, focussing his investigation on the hallucinatory experience of revelation which occurs in the writings of a group of Old Testament prophets. This moment of revelation results in the prophet's consecration of his life to God's mission, and precipitates a crucial transformation of his personality. The transformation, in turn, provides the basis for the prophet's mission, making manifest in poetic form a new and higher level of moral demand. Thus, according to Arlow, the prophet gives words to a communal daydream in which superego elements predominate, and which he places before the community for their acceptance.

The paper itself provides illuminating insights into the psychology of certain types of charismatic individuals and their followers, but is of special interest for anyone who wishes to follow the development of Arlow's ideas. It is the first of a series of highly important papers leading to his seminal work in 1969—a transitional work that looks back to the past as well as forward to the future. Arlow generates a number of ideas in it that become the bases of later papers, and yet the informing orientation of the paper is rooted in the depth psychology of the twenties. The terms "ego psychology," "structural theory," even "conflict" are absent, while most of the explanatory concepts are put in terms of instinct theory. The prophet's moment of consecration, for example, is described as a schizophrenoid phenomenon and understood as a manifestation of Freud's decathexis-recathexis theory of psychosis, an idea which Arlow took pains to argue against by 1964 (Arlow and Brenner, 1964).

And yet the paper foreshadows things to come—not in terms of its specific content, but in subtler ways. First of all it heralds Arlow's abiding interest in story and history. The particular stories—those from the Bible—he chose to consider in this paper are ones that partake of story and history, fact and fable, to the degree that it is impossible to disentangle the real from the imagined. As such they represent the perfect exemplifying adumbration of Arlow's later theory of unconscious fantasy, even though the term "fantasy" does not appear in the paper.

Secondly, the paper focusses on the prophet's crucial experience of transformation—a borderline pathological phenomenon. It is neither normal nor is it quite pathological in the ordinary sense of the word—in this case a transitory hallucinatory experience which is "schizophrenoid" but not considered pathological by Arlow or by cultural history. The class of borderline pathological phenomena—clinically real or literary—are of particular interest to Arlow. Masturbation, déjà vu, disturbances in sense of time, temporarily altered states of consciousness are some of the borderline experiences that he focusses on and extrapolates from in both directions to derive greater understanding of both normal and pathological functioning.

Thirdly, the earliest reference to Sachs's concept of the "community of daydreams" or "shared daydreams" appears as a passing footnote (Sachs, 1920). The importance of this notion becomes clear only later and becomes the basis for further development.

In 1953 (Arlow, 1953) Arlow turned his attention to another borderline phenomenon—masturbation. (By "borderline" I mean that the phenomenon is felt, in general, to be neither wholly normal nor wholly abnormal.) Partaking of both normal and abnormal aspects of mental life, masturbation had hitherto been primarily discussed in terms of depth psychology. With this paper Arlow begins his difficult task of bringing depth psychology into the framework of modern psychoanalysis.

In it Arlow turns unambiguously to the structural theory and ego psychology in an attempt to elucidate the relationship between masturbation and symptom formation. It represents an attempt to elaborate Freud's 1908 paper on hysterical fantasies and bisexuality. He suggests, as Freud did, that masturbation and symptoms have much in common. But where Freud thought that symptoms were the result of a compromise between two opposite affective and sexual instincts, Arlow suggests that masturbation and symptoms are *both* manifestations of conflict—that is, compromise formations between instincts, ego, superego and reality demands. Arlow goes further by splitting the masturbatory complex into a fantasy component and an activity component, and shows how each part can be dealt with differently by the ego and recombine in various ways.

Presenting precise and convincing clinical evidence, he demonstrates the link between masturbatory phenomena—actions and fantasy—and symptom formation, one being an egosyntonic, guilt-laden compromise formation, the other an ego-alien pathological compromise formation, both partaking of the various components of a conflict—its instinctual derivatives, defensive reactions, and superego components.

In 1959 Arlow addressed himself to another phenomenon which stands on the border between normal and pathological—déjà vu (Arlow, 1959). Using Lewin's earlier suggestion that it is possible to explore the formal facade of a symptom in the same manner as one would the manifest content of a dream, Arlow presented a case in meticulous detail and demonstrated that there is a specific relationship between the déjà vu experience—a transitory disturbance of cognitive function—and the patient's major conflicts, the precipitating cause of his illness and its psychogenetic roots. He showed that each manifest element in the patient's déjà vu experience was determined by unconscious trains of thought representing defensively disguised expressions of wish-fulfilling fantasies.

Thus, in the déjà vu experience anxiety appears not because the individual was having the feeling of déjà vu but, on the contrary, he was having the feeling of déjà vu in order to fend off anxiety. The déjà vu reaction constitutes a defense against overwhelming anxiety. The defense, however, is only partially successful—some of the anxiety leaks though. The price of the reassuring defense, however, is a transitory, regressive deterioration of a specific cognitive ego function, namely, a sense of reality.

What is important in this paper, in tracing the development of Arlow's ideas, is that for the first time he used structural theory to analyze a paranormal phenomenon, and that this analysis resulted in a parsimonious linkage with the patient's conflicts, symptoms, and dynamic history. Furthermore, the phenomenon itself involved important cognitive functions—perception, a sense of reality, and a sense of time—that regulate adaptive capacities and psychopathology. It is understandable, then, that Arlow discusses *en passant* the relationship between déjà vu and hallucination, illusion and delusion. All of these issues finally come together in an integrated way ten years later in his paper "Fantasy, Memory, and Reality Testing."

Returning again in 1961 to his abiding interest in story and history— the enduring theme in a timeless continuum—Arlow approached myths and mythology from the more complex and clinically sophisticated view of ego psychology (1961).

Starting from Sachs's view (Sachs, 1920) that a myth is a communal experience—a shared fantasy among members of a cultural group with certain common psychological needs—Arlow makes the bridge from shared fantasy to individual fantasy, from communal myth to personal myth. Myth makers like poets and prophets shape the ubiquitous, unconscious fantasy wishes of mankind in communally acceptable ways. They are able to express the guilt-laden private fantasies of individuals in the form of myths which become instruments of socialization.

In the earlier days of depth psychology, psychoanalysis had shown that myths expressed infantile wishes. In this paper Arlow demonstrates how different mythological expressions of the same unconscious infantile wish correspond to differing defensive versions, each consonant with the differing psychological and social needs of a specific culture. He illustrates this thesis with the universal infantile wish to acquire the paternal phallus—a ubiquitous fantasy that finds mythic expression in the fairy tale of Jack and the Beanstalk, the tragedy of Prometheus, and the Biblical legend of Moses receiving the law. In each case the hero ascends to some isolated and/or inaccessible high place and returns with some token of power, wealth, or knowledge from an omnipotent individual who resides in the heavens.

Quite aside from the main point of the paper—a demonstration of the myth-making mechanisms which different cultures use for the resolution of individual instinctual conflicts—almost as a footnote, Arlow turns his attention momentarily to the question of fantasy. Since, according to Sachs, myths are universally shared *fantasies,* he discusses the meaning of the term. His point of departure is Freud's prestructural view of fantasy—the representation of an instinctual wish—but then he adds data from the work of Fisher and Pötzl and within a few sentences states,

> Many illusions and misrepresentations of reality are based upon the
> intrusion of this activity [instinctual wishes] into the neutral function

of checking the raw data of perception. Depending on the nature of the data of perception, the level of cathectic potential, and the state of ego function, different forms of mental function will emerge. It is out of this common matrix of ego activity that dreams, symptoms, fantasies, and myths are created. The pressure of the unconscious fantasy wishes orients one of the aspects of ego activity to be ever alert to. . . integrate. . . or misinterpret the data of perception and the knowledge of the real world in keeping with its pleasure-seeking purpose of discharge [p. 376].

Parallel with this theoretical discussion, Arlow adds an alternative view of fantasy derived from his clinical experience. This, too, is presented in a mere paragraph or two and subordinate to the main point of the paper which of course is cultural psychology rather than fantasy.

He suggests that there is a hierarchy in the fantasy life of each individual in which

unconscious fantasies have a systematic relation to each other. . . . In treating a patient, when we succeed in effecting a genetic reconstruction of the transformations of the childhood instinctual wishes, we are frequently able to trace, in a temporal series, successive editions of the fantasy expressions of these instinctual wishes. Clinical experience demonstrates, furthermore, how one set of fantasies may serve the function of defensively screening out another, repudiated set of fantasies [p. 377].

One can recognize ideas in this statement which will become part of Arlow's theory of unconscious fantasy later—one example of his many footnote insights. (As it happens with some creative individuals, Arlow will often in passing express a flash of insight which he will pick up and develop only years later.) It should be noted, however, that the term "fantasy" in this context is somewhat ambiguous but is used, for the most part, to mean unconscious instinctual wish. The main army of his thinking had not yet quite caught up with the advanced guard.

Thus, in a paper written in 1961, whose main subject is mythology, all of the elements of Arlow's theory of unconscious fantasy begin to come together: conflict, the formation of fantasy, the formation of history—public and private—perception and misperception, past and present, memory and reality, all articulated *en passant* in two or three paragraphs and foreshadowing the work to be published eight years later.

The publication of "Conflict, Regression and Symptom Formation" in 1963 (Arlow, 1963) reflected a major synthesis in Arlow's thinking. It undertook to achieve two major goals. The first was to correct certain tendencies that had crept into psychoanalysis during the post–World War II period—misconceptions concerning the pathogenesis of symptoms and character traits. This had resulted, Arlow suggested, from a theoretical confusion—a tendency to confound earlier psychoanalytic frames of reference with the structural theory. Many analysts, he suggested, were not yet entirely at home with the structural theory, even at that time.

The clarifications Arlow suggests in this paper have important clinical applications and reflect his work with Brenner on the structural theory which was in progress at that time.

The second goal was, in a sense, to bring depth psychology into the twentieth century. Freud had never returned to reconsider earlier formulations of instinct theory after he introduced the structural theory and the concept of signal anxiety. Through his discussion and clarification of (a) the "danger" situation, (b) regression and symptom formation, and (c) the function of fantasy, Arlow does precisely that.

Although the paper is highly integrated and cannot be easily disassembled, for the purpose of this essay I will focus on Arlow's discussion of fantasy.

Using Freud's papers of 1908 (Freud, 1908) and 1915 (Freud, 1915) as his point of departure, Arlow suggests the following elaborations: Each individual has a hierarchy of fantasy formations in his mind and this hierarchy reflects the vicissitudes of his experience and psychic development. Furthermore, these fantasies are grouped around universal infantile wishes, and the same wish may be expressed in different fantasies as the individual matures and the integrative capacity of the ego changes. "The fantasy expression of the instinctual wish grows up, as it were" (p. 21). The same wish may find expression in various fantasies of which some are pathogenic while others may result in no conflict whatever.

The more mature fantasy formations of unconscious wishes are integrated by the ego and appear to be more accessible to conscious awareness. The more primitive fantasy expressions are repressed because they have unacceptable components, and these primitive fantasies are more directly related to the danger situation. But, in any case, each fantasy expresses all the components of conflict.

In another footnote insight, almost as an afterthought, Arlow points out that symptoms may be precipitated by external experiences containing

elements similar to those in the original conflict which had resulted in
the persistent unconscious fantasy.

> This. . . illustrates the reciprocal relationship between the persistent
> unconscious fantasies. . . (which is another way of expressing fixation)
> and the events of the individual's life. Persistent fantasy serves to main-
> tain a constant 'set' which colors the interpretation and the significance
> of external events. External events, on the other hand, provoke,
> stimulate. . . the reemergence of repressed instinctual wishes. The re-
> turning of these repressed instinctual elements may achieve temporary
> discharge in dreams and parapraxes [p. 17].

Thus, by 1963 Arlow's view of fantasy has changed from the simple depth psychological model he held in 1949 to one that includes but
at the same time begins to transcend the structural theory.

1964 produced a major collaboration between Arlow and Charles
Brenner, which stands as a landmark in psychoanalytic theory (Arlow
and Brenner, 1964). If neither had published anything else their place
in the history of psychoanalysis would be assured by their monograph
on the structural theory. It was undertaken by Arlow and Brenner because
of their perception that Freud's two theories of the mind—the topographic
theory and the structural theory—were in many ways mutually contradictory and yet perceived by analysts at that time to be equally valid
and equally useful in understanding clinical data. It was their opinion
that the topographic and the structural theories were neither compatible nor interchangeable. They felt further that the structural theory, the
more modern of Freud's theories was the more satisfactory of the two.
Thus, they undertook in this monograph first of all to characterize each
of these theories in their essential detail, compare the two theories, articulating their differences and similarities, and finally, deal with certain
specific problematical issues—issues which Freud had raised prior to his
development of the structural theory—in order to try to come to terms
with these issues within the context of the structural theory.

Freud had never really readdressed himself to these problems after
the development of the Structural Theory and the Signal Anxiety Theory
of neurosis and so, with this in mind, Arlow and Brenner undertook
to "modernize" the psychoanalytic understanding of dreams, psychosis,
regression, primary process, and the unconscious. Their reconceptuali-

zations of these issues are far reaching, illuminating, and have important clinical and technical implications many of which are further
elaborated by each of them individually.

Lack of space precludes the possibility of summarizing the entire
monograph, and from the point of view of this paper it is only necessary
to see that the 1964 monograph reflects Arlow's belief that the structural theory is the most clinically valid and useful way of approaching
psychopathology and other mental phenomena, and that the practical
consequences of the change from topographic to structural theory are
fundamental.

> The situation may be summarized in the statement that, using the
> structural theory, the very nature of the therapeutic task has changed.
> According to the topographic theory, symptom formation is the result
> of failure of repression. . . . The technical task in therapy is to abrogate
> repression, to recover the forgotten material, in particular the memory
> of childhood traumata. Essentially, the therapeutic task in the
> topographic sense is to make the unconscious conscious [1964, p. 53].

The structural theory, however, taking into account clinical data
which the topographic theory was not able to account for, viewed anxiety not as the result of the leakage of libido from the unconscious, but
as a danger signal that evoked defense mechanisms and symptom
formation.

> . . . moreover, since the defenses themselves are not always accessible
> to consciousness, the analysis of these defenses becomes a part of the
> therapeutic work. . . . The therapeutic task aims at analyzing defenses,
> resolving their automatic operation and permitting the integration of
> previously warded off instinctual derivations and the memories
> associated with them into the normal parts of the ego. . . [p. 53].

In 1966 Arlow demonstrated the clinical power of this expanded
view of the structural theory, by publishing a study of seven cases of depersonalization and derealization (Arlow, 1966b). Based on his previous work
on déjà vu and his and Brenner's discussion of psychosis in 1964, he
demonstrated that these pathological phenomenon are understandable
in terms of intrapsychic conflict.

In the past depersonalization and derealization had been construed as psychotic phenomena, and understood in terms of Freud's decathexis-recathexis theory of psychosis. In this paper Arlow demonstrates beyond any doubt that they occur in normal and neurotic individuals as well, and can be understood within the framework of the more modern structural theory.

Taking as his point of departure Lewin's 1952 paper which demonstrated a connection between phobic symptoms and unconscious fantasies Arlow demonstrates that this relationship also exists with respect to *altered ego states and/or ego regressions.*

> A similar relationship may be demonstrated between altered ego states and unconscious fantasy. . . in these states the fantasy seems to be primarily a defensive one which can be expressed by the words, 'This isn't happening to me. I'm just an onlooker,' in the case of depersonalization, and by, 'all of this isn't real. It's just a harmless dream, or make-believe,' in the case of derealization. The fantasy, however, and especially the reassurance it conveys, does not become conscious as a fantasy. Instead, the patient either experiences a feeling of estrangement from his surroundings, or his surroundings appear unreal to him or both [p. 472].

Arlow is able to demonstrate that the modes of defense employed in these two phenomena have their basis in intrapsychic conflict.

He makes the following technical suggestions in handling experiences of depersonalization or derealization: Analysis should consist of three elements: (1) the phenomenon itself should be treated in the same manner as the manifest content of a dream; (2) the history of these preferred mechanisms of defense should be investigated psychogenetically; and (3) the ego regression should be viewed in the context of anxiety and defense. These technical suggestions are significant because Arlow is generalizing from what was a technique in the analysis of classical symptoms to the analysis of altered ego states, ego regressions, and ego impairments.

Finally, Arlow reemphasizes the importance of understanding these pathological phenomena in terms of intrapsychic conflict and that regression of ego functions are not confined to psychosis. ''They may be observed transitorily in the neuroses as well as in the psychopathology of everyday life'' (p. 473). Prominent among the functions which tend to regress in this fashion are perception, thinking, and reality testing.

In the first issue of the *Psychoanalytic Quarterly* for 1969 Arlow published two papers which articulated his theory of unconscious fantasy in an integrated and systematic form (Arlow, 1969a, 1969b). Although published in 1969, some of his ideas were in sufficiently cogent form for them to be presented as the Abraham A. Brill Lecture before the New York Psychoanalytic Society in 1963. Feeling, however, that they were not yet ripe enough, he delayed publication for six years. Both papers are closely related and are best discussed together.

These papers are, of course, landmark papers in Arlow's collected works and represent important and highly significant contributions to psychoanalytic theory. They are contributions to psychoanalytic theory that are based on all of his previous clinical observations, and most of his work before 1969 foreshadows them. Their focus is unconscious fantasy as a central psychoanalytic concept and Arlow presents a systematic and searching discussion of the nature of unconscious fantasy and its relationship to normal and pathological mental phenomena.

The role of unconscious fantasy in mental life had been recognized early, in fact almost from the beginning, by Freud, and Freud and his early co-workers established beyond any doubt that unconscious fantasies play an important part in symptom and dream formation and parapraxes. Starting where Freud left off, Arlow undertakes to discuss the characteristics of unconscious fantasy itself and its relationship to structural theory.

He starts out by defining unconscious fantasy as akin to a daydream and he suggests that there is no sharp distinction between conscious and unconscious daydreams. It depends essentially on the degree of repression at work at any given moment. Naturally, because of their content, more primitive fantasies tend to be less accessible to consciousness. All fantasies are subject to the ego's synthesizing tendencies and are more or less organized, integrating drive components, defenses, superego components, and reality components.

Arlow prefers the term "unconscious fantasy *function*" to "unconscious fantasy" because it implies a constant process at work. He suggests that we are dreaming all the time, more or less—that there is in all of us a persistent pressure to defy reality, to *not* renounce gratification.

There is a developmental hierarchy of fantasies which are grouped around a relatively small number of infantile wishes. These fantasies represent different "editions"—some normal, some pathological—which appear during various stages of development and result in a "final edition" which integrates all of the different elements of the personality—the drives, defenses, superego, and reality—into a final "identity" and "personal myth."

Although each of these "final" fantasies (actually, composites) is unique and individual, they have universal components. These universal components derive from the biological and developmental bases of human life. It is the universal aspects of these unconscious fantasies, Arlow suggests, that result in the capacity to understand metaphors and symbols. He uses the term "metaphor" in a more general literary sense to include the symbol of, say, Charlie Chaplin's little tramp as embodying an unconscious "waif" fantasy—the small, bewildered, innocent coping with hostile forces in an indifferent world, never quite triumphing but never defeated—a fantasy which is apparently grasped in nearly all cultures. (Another example of one of Arlow's footnote insights. Arlow does not elaborate fully the connections between metaphor, unconscious fantasy, and technique until 1979 [Arlow, 1979a].)

One of the most important and profound aspects of the theory is the reciprocal relationship between unconscious fantasy and external reality. It is at this point that Arlow's ideas transcend psychoanalysis and impinge on epistemology, history, and general psychology.

Unconscious fantasy organizes perception and cognitive functioning in general—making us more sensitive to certain stimuli and less sensitive to others. On the other hand, Arlow suggests that just as day residues—perceptions—may stimulate dream formation, so external reality may stimulate unconscious fantasies—reactivating them to different degrees, depending on the relative strengths of the internal and external factors. Thus, an experience in everyday life which reactivates a core unconscious fantasy may precipitate a dream, or, if the elements of conflict are sufficiently intense, a nightmare or even a symptom.

Memory is organized into schemata centering around childhood wishes, developmental traumata and their compromise formations. "These make up the contents of a continuous stream of fantasy thinking which is a persistent concomitant of all mental activity and which exerts an unending influence on how reality is perceived and responded to" (Arlow, 1969b, p. 29). And the most powerful influence which contributes to the misconception of the present is the intrusion of unconscious fantasy thinking. The present is constantly being misconceived in terms of the content of unconscious fantasy.

When memory and perception offer material which is consonant with
fantasy thinking, the data are selectively perceived and the memories
are selectively recalled and used as material to serve as a vehicle for
the unconscious fantasy. . . . This is not the objective reality which can
be observed by outsiders and validated consensually. [Such objective
reality is]. . . impossible to recollect because what the child experiences
is at the very moment of experience a complex intermingling of perception and fantasy. This complex intermingling is what really happened
as far as the individual is concerned [1969b, p. 39].

For Arlow all memories are essentially screen memories, all clinical
history is clinical myth.

Retaining those concepts from both Freud and the ego psychologists
that have stood the test of time, Arlow departs in varying degrees from
both, providing a more empirically oriented and clinically accurate model
of the mind. Freud understood unconscious fantasy as a derivative of
an instinctual wish, Arlow as a compromise formation. Hartmann suggested that there were ego functions which were autonomous and free
of conflict. Arlow suggests the very opposite, that all of those autonomous,
conflict-free spheres of ego functioning, such as memory, perception, and
reality testing, are constantly intermingled with and participate in conflictual mental processes. Reality and perception are never free of the
impact of wishful thinking and defensive functioning.

It is clear that for Arlow unconscious fantasy is the equivalent of
unconscious conflict and that infantile trauma resulting in fixation means
the formation of one or more stable, organized, unconscious pathogenic
fantasies. Thus the abstract concept of structural conflict becomes the
individualized, fine-tuned unconscious fantasy of Arlow, adding depth,
complexity, and clinical validity to the former.

The path of discovery beginning in 1951 with a loosely organized
set of Arlow's interests—mental phenomena that are neither normal nor
abnormal; the inner tensions and mysteries that exist between history
and myth, fact and fiction; and finally the strengths and weaknesses of
the structural theory—ends in 1969 with all of these interests welded
together in a coherent theory of the mind which, as we shall see, will
shape the theory of psychoanalysis for the next generation and must affect the way scholars and psychologists think about cognition and history.

THE PHASE OF ELABORATION—1970 TO THE PRESENT

Since 1969 Arlow has published thirty-six original papers with his characteristic range, depth, and clinical sophistication. Some continue his interest in psychopathology—tracing in detail, for example, the vicissitudes of conflict from infancy, through adolescence, to final crystalization in adult character (Arlow, 1971a, 1971b). Some explore the relationship between universal fantasy—primal scene fantasy, for example—symptom formation and literary creativity (Arlow, 1978, 1980b). His most important work during this period, however, is represented by two groups of papers—one, a series on technique, and another series on the structural theory—both interrelated and both incorporating the theory of unconscious fantasy. This late work, soundly empirical, suggests a refreshing conceptual streamlining for the next psychoanalytic generation.

THEORY OF TECHNIQUE

In 1966 Arlow and Brenner published "The Psychoanalytic Situation" (Arlow and Brenner, 1966), an effort to correct certain tendencies in clinical theory which had been begun during the forties and fifties by some analysts who viewed the psychoanalytic situation as akin to the infant-mother relationship, and thus saw the therapeutic elements in analysis as attitudinal, educational, and identificatory. That is, if the analyst is loving and accepting enough, then the patient's true self will emerge and grow into maturity. Or, if the analyst's attitude is one of "unconditional kindness," then he will "intuitively" do the right thing in every and any situation that arises in the analysis.

In order to clarify the theoretical basis for this erroneous tendency and the technical mistakes engendered by it Arlow and Brenner reasserted their view that most psychopathology can be best understood as the outcome of intrapsychic conflict and that psychoanalysis aims first to uncover the patient's pathogenic infantile conflicts and second to realign the intrapsychic forces toward a different and more favorable equilibrium.

They assert that in order to accomplish these aims it is necessary to understand the individual components of the conflict: the nature of the defenses, the fears which engender those defenses, the instinctual derivatives from which these fears emerge, and the self-punitive tendencies in the individual.

The goal of psychoanalysis, thus, is the modification of intrapsychic conflict and its method is *insight and understanding* into the components of the conflict.

All of the analyst's interventions, they suggest, are in the service of helping the patient to achieve insight and understanding into his pathogenic conflicts. The difference between psychoanalysis and other forms of therapy, some of which can indeed influence pathogenic conflict, is that in other forms of therapy, modification of conflict does not take place through insight, and thus even partial mastery of the conflict is impossible. "[O]ne must bear in mind that analysis differs from other psychotherapeutic methods or influences in one very important respect: the intrapsychic alterations which analysis aims at producing, are ones which are relatively independent of current external events" (Arlow and Brenner, 1966, p. 33).

The essential point is that technical considerations must be informed by a theory of pathogenesis and Arlow and Brenner's theory of pathogenesis is based on the structural model—intrapsychic conflict causes symptoms—and their theory of treatment is that conflict must be resolved, reduced, or transformed, and that this comes about through understanding the components of conflicts—insight—and not through identification, catharsis, or education. This view articulated at that time remains essentially the same today despite the fact that both Arlow and Brenner have continued to develop their clinical theory along separate but complementary lines.

With this unambiguous theoretical orientation, rooted solidly in the data generated by the Psychoanalytic Situation (a phrase which since 1966 has taken on a more or less technical designation—an ensemble of clinical techniques organized by the principles articulated in the 1966 paper, and elaborated by each of the authors since then), Arlow has expanded and enriched this clinical model.

When pathogenic infantile wishes are identified and acknowledged, anxiety, guilt, and other dysphoric affects can be reduced and thus defensive structures may be altered. Essential therapeutic progress involves such dynamic change—defensive restructuring based on the acknowledgement of unconscious wishes. Whatever other desirable changes occur in the lives and feelings of patients these *dynamic* changes are what Arlow would consider the changes resulting from psychoanalytic treatment.

These changes come about and can *only* come about through insight. It is only by means of a thorough and vivid *understanding* of the specific components of one's pathogenic conflicts—the unacceptable wishes, the fantastic punishments for those wishes, the mechanisms for warding these off—that permanent affective and behavioral relief can occur. It is this notion—that what is mutative and curative is *knowledge* about the deeper emotional aspects of oneself—that makes Arlow's ideas unusual in the climate of psychoanalysis today. This view, of course, we owe to Freud, but what Freud thought was curative—at least when he wrote his papers on technique—was recollections, the knowledge of memories. What Arlow believes is curative is knowledge of conflict—dynamics, how one's terrors actually work. "What is interpreted is the dynamic process and, in this way, the patient comes to understand how his mind works. Recall of forgotten memories is ofttimes the reward for good interpretive work, but it is not the goal of treatment" (1987a, p. 85).

Insight comes about, of course, through systematic interpretations not only of the content of the unconscious wishes and their derivatives and the techniques used to ward off these derivatives, but the ". . . casual links that exist among the various component forces in the conflict . . ." (1987). But his statement is too schematic and summary. What is unique is Arlow's view of how these interpretations originate in the mind of the analyst.

The Psychoanalytic Situation is Arlow's term for an operational definition of the psychoanalytic method itself, the purpose of which is to create a field which is dynamically unstable so that the analyst, from the position of neutrality, may observe the conflictual components as they shift in their unstable equilibrium.

Triggered by the destabilizing stimulus of the fundamental rule, various mental phenomena begin to emerge consisting of a flow of affects, ideation—or rather affectively tinged ideation—and occasional bursts of behavior. Arlow, however, departs from the old concept of free association as primarily a manifestation of instinctual derivatives and suggests that the stream of associations is not free but rather represents a dynamic manifestation of compromise formation. The patient's thoughts, feelings, and actions are a psychological ensemble—a synthesis of unconscious conflict.

Freud's original suggestion—the corollary to the fundamental rule—to the analyst to allow his mind to become a receptive organ which can be stimulated by the patient's associations, results in the appearance of derivatives in the analyst's mind from the patient's unconscious. The mental processes of the analyst thus still remain the prime instrument in the analytic procedure and the inner experience of the analyst remains the focal point of the methodology. The difference, though, between the post-Freudian zeitgeist and Arlow on this issue is the difference, on the one hand, between one generation of analysts mysteriously recognizing empathic "gifts" in the next, and one the other hand a rational, empirically based, demystifying exploration of the processes of empathy and intuition (Arlow and Beres, 1974).

Although the actual processes that occur in the Psychoanalytic Situation are more or less seamless and smooth flowing, apparently effortless or magical—especially with experienced analysts—these processes are not magical and can be articulated. The articulation, however, will appear clumsy and mechanical—like trying to explain the flight of a bird. In any case, in Arlow's view, it works something like this:

The psychoanalytic situation—each individual session and all sessions cumulatively—usually begins as an atunement of the analyst to the patient's verbal and nonverbal behavior. It involves more than listening and is not passive although it may appear so to an outsider. The mental set of the analyst is emotionally neutral, alert to subtle verbal and nonverbal signs.

It is important to understand that the patient's free associations—or rather behavioral flow, since Arlow would prefer to widen the field to include actions and emotional cues such as tone of voice, as well as verbal data—can best be understood as a dynamic compromise formation which is essentially ambiguous and metaphorical. "In reviewing the intermediate steps in the process of arriving at an interpretation, it became clear to me that. . . the inherently ambiguous, metaphorical nature of language as it affects the psychoanalytic situation, has not been fully appreciated. Psychoanalysis is essentially a metaphorical enterprise" (Arlow, 1979b, p. 373). Patients must speak ambiguously because, ". . . at best they experience only a distorted, disguised approximation of what they unconsciously fantasy. Yet, this very ambiguity. . . is unconsciously ordered in the analytic situation as in the aesthetic process, to permit the listener to become a co-creator by completing the unfinished Gestalt. . ." (p. 378). The patient unwittingly speaks metaphorically to the analyst and the analyst listens metaphorically. This is because metaphor is universally used to ward off anxiety by means of the mechanism of displacement—one of the sources of ambiguity in language and in metaphor. "The metaphor, like the repartee at a cocktail party, permits a kind of freedom. . . which is recognized by both parties to be meant and not meant at the same time" (Caruth and Ekstein, 1966, p. 38). And, like repartee and poetic expression, patients' associations can only be understood when context is taken into account. Based on indications from context, contiguity, metaphorical allusions, repetition, and similarity, the hidden meaning of the patient's communications can be divined (Arlow, 1987a).

Metaphorical expressions are, like dreams, conscious compromise formations derived from unconscious fantasies, and thus are particularly susceptible to analysis. "In the psychoanalytic situation, one of the principal functions of the analyst is to interpret to patients certain contents of the patients' productions which are totally *unknown* to them" [Italics mine] (Arlow, 1979b, p. 363). Thus, for Arlow one of the main functions of the analytst is a cognitive one. He must first know what is unknown and then communicate what is unknown to the patient. The metaphor becomes the bridge between emotional understanding and cognitive understanding (Arlow, 1979a, 1979b, 1987a).

Forced by unconscious conflict, patients perceive their lives and experience metaphorically in order to justify and confirm the feelings which compel their behavior. Here the term "metaphor" is used in the broader sense which may include legend-story-scenario-myth—and includes, of course, personal myth. The personal myth like the screen memory both gratifies and conceals at the same time and as such it remains a barrier to insight; and the transference can best be understood as a particularly intense played-out version of the neurotic components of the patient's life-metaphor (Arlow, 1987).

Sometimes large segments of an analysis center around one or two leading metaphors, such as, for example, "pulling something off," which can mean doing something illicit, masturbating, or castrating someone. When analyzed, these metaphors lead to the discovery of an unconscious fantasy typical for the patient. "The unconscious fantasy itself represents a metaphoric apprehension of childhood experience that has remained dynamically active. . ." (Arlow, 1979b, p. 381).

Returning to the Psychoanalytic Situation and the psychological events taking place in the mind of the analyst, in response to the stimulation of a dynamic flow rich with affective and cognitive cues, the analyst becomes aware of mental manifestations stirring in himself. "More often what the analyst experiences takes the shape of some random thought, the memory of a patient with a similar problem, a line of poetry, the words of a song. . . ." (Arlow, 1979a, p. 200). These associative ideas may or may not seem directly pertinent to the material from the patient, but when some thought occurs in the form of a myth, story, fairy tale, or image, the analyst has grasped a clue pertaining to the patient's unconscious fantasy. Indeed, the psychoanalytic situation represents an interaction between analyst and analysand characterized by mutual metaphoric stimulation in which the analyst ". . . in a series of approximate objectifications of the patient's unconscious thought processes, supplies the appropriate metaphors upon which the essential reconstructions and insights may be built" (Arlow, 1979b, p. 381).

It is obvious from the above that Arlow's concept of empathy is more complex than earlier formulations. It is linked to the importance he places on unconscious fantasy as the key to the understanding and resolution of conflict. The purpose of empathy or empathic understanding in the Psychoanalytic Situation is the creation of an intuition about the patient's unconscious fantasy life. Earlier conceptualizations of empathy have emphasized the affective component—to understand how the patient is feeling—as an avenue to the patient's unconscious, i.e., his wishes. Arlow has represented that element—the affective element—as a transient identification. But he adds two other elements—conflict and cognition—to the process. Thus, the conscious manifestations of the analyst's empathic process will include signal affects, images, ideas, metaphorical allusions, which will sooner or later give rise to some partial intuition about the patient's unconscious fantasy.

All of these steps may occur in a silent and effortless way, sometimes subliminally, and may appear instantly as though by magic. This process, Arlow suggests, is similar to the mode of functioning in creative individuals that results in scientific discoveries and artistic innovations.

> The shared intimacy of the psychoanalytic situation, the knowledge of secrets confided and desires exposed, intensifies the trend toward mutual identification in the analytic setting and, in the end, serves to stimulate in the mind of the analyst unconscious fantasies either identical with or corresponding to those decisive in the patient's conflicts and development. Analyst and analysand thus become a group of two sharing an unconscious fantasy in common. . . [Arlow, 1979a, p. 203].

There is, however, a second phase of the interpretive process, according to Arlow, "one that is based on cognition and the exercise of reason. In order to validate his intuitive understanding. . . the analyst must now turn to the data of the analytic situation. He must put his insight to the test of objective criteria in conformity with the data at hand'' (Arlow, 1979a, p. 203). At this juncture his past experience with this patient, with other patients, even his knowledge and understanding of the literature come into play and influence the creation of a technically appropriate interpretation. The timing and wording of the interpretation may include a transient identification with the patient's resistances—tact—if it is done with some degree of conscious awareness. The intuitive and cognitive components of the interpretive work usually do not occur separately and distinctly, but, on the contrary, appear as highly interpenetrating one another.

In summary then, Arlow's clinical theory is a unified one. It emerges out of Freud's structural theory, but is no longer identical to it. His theory of pathogenesis is completely consonant with his theory of cure and treatment, and these are embodied in the clinical evidence he has described. The sources of much adult psychopathology are the universal passions of childhood. These can become problematical when they reach a significant degree of intensity and when the mind of the child becomes sufficiently organized around conflicting childhood wishes and dangers. Here the word "organized" must be emphasized, because it is the existence of a critical degree of mental organization that Arlow believes is required for the development of intrapsychic conflict. This more likely occurs later than earlier, making the critical time frame more likely to be three to five years than one to three years. In any case, when intrapsychic conflict does occur a pathogenic compromise formation may follow. The manifestation of this is a fantasy—or rather a core group of fantasies because there may be several overlapping editions of the fantasy as development progresses—centering around the conflictual wishes. This core of fantasies may become largely unconscious, but its derivatives pervade the structure and functioning of each individual—some pathologically, some nonpathologically.

Although some psychopathology can be influenced to some extent by external forces, relatively permanent change can come only from a realignment of intrapsychic forces—from a diminution of guilt, shame, and anxiety; from a diminution of pathogenic defenses; from a diminution in the need for punishment; from a diminution in the intensity of the yearning for the gratification of impossible infantile wishes. This realignment can result from a clear understanding of all the components in the conflict and their interrelationships, and the medium for understanding is the analysis of the *specific* conscious and unconscious fantasies

that govern each individual's life. It is the specificity and precision that
is important, because it is only the precision that renders the understanding emotionally compelling. Otherwise the insight is abstract and
emotionally meaningless (Arlow, 1979a, 1987a).

The Psychoanalytic Situation is the instrument par excellence for
the resurrection and clarification of unconscious conflict and for the communication of the components of conflict—insight. The apparent constraints and restrictions—analytic neutrality, the frustration of
transference wishes, etc.—of the Psychoanalytic Situation are tailor-made
for the purpose of diagnosing the specific unconscious fantasies—the
specific components of conflict—and for nothing else. Any psychotherapy
which utilizes some other theory of pathogenesis does not require the
Psychoanalytic Situation with its characteristic constraints and restrictions, or even its neutrality (Arlow and Brenner, 1964; Arlow, 1966a).

The Psychoanalytic Situation allows the observation of a set of
dynamic samples of the patient's mind, and the instrument of observation is the resonating, responsive mind of the attentive analyst. Through
a process of mutual mental stimulation which involves affective and
cognitive elements similar to the processes that take place in the creation and re-creation of works of art, an increasingly specific unconscious
fantasy comes to light for both analyst and patient—first analyst, and
then through interpretation the patient—and finally to an unambiguous
unforgettable explication of the patient's pathogenic conflicts.

With this theoretical model of the psychoanalytic method, it is
understandable that Arlow's view of the structural theory is both protective and critical.

THE STRUCTURAL THEORY

Arlow's view of the structural theory has changed gradually in the
course of his work. Hardly referred to at all in his 1951 papers, by 1964
it was the central focus of his and Brenner's attention in their landmark
monograph, asserting its superiority to Freud's earlier model of the mind.

Since that time two separate and unrelated trends have developed
to challenge the usefulness and validity of the structural theory. The first
has been emerging gradually since the death of Freud. A number of
analysts—many with roots in Europe or South America—have developed
a point of view about pathogenesis and treatment which differs markedly
from both Freud's later work and the work of many if not most analysts

practicing in the United States today. The early leaders of this movement were Melanie Klein and Winnicott and, more recently, Kohut.
Although each member of this group—the preoedipal movement, for
want of a better collective term—has a somewhat different set of theories,
they all have in common one or more of the following notions: Their
theory of pathogenesis emphasizes the preoedipal period of development
and tends to minimize the importance of the oedipal crisis. The focus
is on the mother-child relationship and the origins of pathology are to
be found in that relationship. Maternal ambivalence, or insensitivity—the
unempathic, ungiving mother—is the culprit. The most important wishes
of childhood have to do with maternal union, merger, or incorporation,
and, of course, the most important dangers of childhood have to do with
loss of or separation from the "loved object." The most important
mechanisms of defense are introjection, projective identification, and
dissociation (Klein, 1940; Kohut, 1971, 1977; Winnicott, 1953, 1956,
1960).

These motions—one or more—inform the clinical orientation of
the preoedipalists, and thus the model of the treatment situation is based
on the mother-child relationship. Therefore the sensitivity and empathic
capacity of the analyst—like the "good mother" who is attuned to the
needs of her child—becomes the predominant technical value. Knowing the patient's feelings, identifying with them and accepting them is
the curative element in the treatment, just as the "good-enough mother"
accepts and contains her child's bad feelings. But, since the pathogenic
theory is essentially preverbal, little use is made of empathic skills in
the service of divining and articulating the patient's fantasies.

Arlow's criticisms of the preoedipalists are rooted in his empirical
orientation. He finds that their theory of pathogenesis is simplex,
speculative and essentially doctrinaire. They go more by theory than
by clinical data. The clinical facts suggest that psychopathology—
including severe psychopathology—has its origin in conflicts from all levels
of development. And the presumption that pathogenic factors are to be
found chiefly in the first months or years of life precludes the possibility
of any form of validation (except the intuition of the analyst) because
recollection and reconstruction are impossible (Arlow, 1970, 1981, 1986).

Furthermore, since dissociation and projection rather than repression are the main mechanisms of defense, many of the errors in the work
of the preoedipalists are due to a tendency to interpret data superficially
—the manifest content—without reference to psychoanalytic data—free

associations and the allusive contexts in which the manifest phenomena appeared. "A man who dresses up in woman's clothing may have many different unconscious fantasies about the activity while he is practicing it. One can no more deduce the meaning of the perverse behavior and the purpose it serves from the manifest behavior of the pervert than one can interpret the meaning of a dream from its manifest content" (Arlow, 1970, p. 51).

Affects and affectively tinged ideas—such as "I feel like the whole world is coming apart!"—are especially likely to be taken at face value. "Derivative expressions of anxiety that actually reflect the patient's reaction to the danger situation are treated as primary causes in themselves. Thus one deals seriously with such [formulations] as fear of dissolution, fear of loss of ego boundaries, or fear of loss of ego functions" (Arlow, 1970, p. 53).

The most important error, however, is to be found in the relative absence of conflict in the preoedipal model of pathology and treatment. Since inadequate or "unempathic" mothering gives rise to developmental defects, the theory of treatment involves the replacement of bad objects with good objects as distinct from the resolution of conflicts.

All patients tend to experience various aspects of their psychopathology as caused by others, usually love objects. Indeed, such feelings are the commonest components of every patient's personal myth. They tend to see themselves as victims, ". . . as unloved, neglected, abandoned, passed over in favor of some rival, injured, threatened, abused, hurt, misunderstood, poorly fed, poorly clothed, and thrust forth into the world unprepared and incomplete. . ." (Arlow, 1981, p. 504).

In the past one of the aims of psychoanalysis was the recovery of memories of real traumatic events. We know from clinical experience that this rarely happens, and now, in the light of Arlow's theory of unconscious fantasy, it is understandable why. In psychoanalysis we are no longer interested in the individual's objective history because there is none, but rather "in the vicissitudes of the dominant elements of his unconscious fantasy. . . and their effect on his mental functioning and interpersonal relations. What constitutes trauma is not inherent in the actual real event, but rather in the individual's response to the disorganizing disruptive combination of impulses and fears integrated into a set of unconscious fantasies" (Arlow, 1985b, p. 533). All memory is screen memory.

The preoedipalists believe that real events become inscribed in the mind as such, minimizing the role of drive derivatives and defensive distortion that occur in mental activity. They believe in the pathogenic effect of real events.

The second great challenge to the Structural Theory is Arlow himself. In a series of papers over the last decade he has addressed himself to the important issues of object choice, affect theory, psychic reality, and to the structural theory (Arlow, 1977, 1980a, 1985a). While avowing the basic power of the structural theory—its rootedness in clinical observation and its most important concepts: intrapsychic conflict and signal anxiety—he finds the metapsychological superstructure that Freud tried to mix with it abstract, unnecessary, and unverifiable because it is not linked to clinical data (Arlow, 1975, 1982b, 1985a).

But more than any explicit criticism, it is Arlow's work itself that has transformed the structural theory into something quite different from what Freud conceived sixty years ago. Like most good scientific generalizations, elements of it stand more or less unchanged—signal anxiety, for example; and elements of it have withered away—no one talks or writes about THE ego or THE id any more; and elements—like the concept of conflict—have undergone profound transformation under the gradual but persistent impact of more sophisticated practice and more empirically based theory.

In "The Ego and the Id" (Freud, 1923), what Freud meant by conflict was that the forces of the id, instinctual drives, were opposed by the anti-instinctual forces of the ego, defense mechanisms, and that the superego sometimes sided with one force and sometimes the other. This view of conflict and the tripartite model of the mind, to be sure, represented an important advance over Freud's earlier theories of pathogenesis. In 1923 the ego meant anti-instinctual above all else. Only with the emergence of Ego Psychology and the work of Hartmann did the ego become "the organ of adaptation," an organization of functions, one serving defensive purposes, the others—memory, perception, motility, etc.—"autonomous," free of conflict. Defenses, then, were anti-instinctual by definition. The notion of conflict itself meant symptom formation—pathology. In 1923 the classic manifestations of the id were affects, sexual fantasies, hallucinations, delusions, daydreams, dreams; and the superego was conceived of as the heir to the Oedipus complex and the result of parental identifications.

If Sigmund Freud were to return to earth today, he might be surprised to find that affects, mood, sexual fantasies, and most of the other manifestations of what only thirty years ago were thought to be drive manifestations, we understand today as compromise formations. He might be disappointed to find that no one really talks about THE ego any more—at least not in working conferences. And that now we know that any ego function can serve as a defense and no ego function is autonomous—in fact the ego can never be conceived of as anti-instinctual in any sense. In fact no part of the mind can be considered anti-instinctual. In fact it would be more in keeping with our observations and understanding that instinctual derivatives pervade all our mental functioning. In fact it might even be safe to say that there aren't three parts to the mind any more. We have really outgrown that notion. Defenses can be instincts, instincts can be punitive, punishment can be pleasurable. The superego is not merely a set of oedipal identifications but a compromise formation itself that has its own developmental sequence.

But more than anything it is the concept of conflict itself that has changed in the mind of the working analyst, a change brought about by the work of Arlow and Brenner more than any other analysts in the last quarter century. Arlow's ideas have become the leading edge of psychoanalysis. They represent the next stage of the structural theory. At the moment we seem to be in a transitional period, one in which we cannot do without the structural theory, and yet seem to have transcended it. We can no longer think of conflict without understanding that the medium of conflict is unconscious fantasy and that it is through his unconscious fantasy that an individual lives out his life and a patient lives out his neurosis, and his analysis. And that it is through his unconscious fantasy that a patient is understood and that the analyst makes himself understood to the patient. Any interpretation, any insight that is not through the medium of the patient's unique and specific unconscious fantasy is not likely to make much difference to him.

Psychoanalysis has become the science of unconscious fantasy.

REFERENCES

Arlow, J. A. (1945), Identification mechanisms in coronary occlusion. *Psychosom. Med.*, 7:195–209.

———— (1948), Rheumatoid arthritis. In: *Synopsis of Psychosomatic Diagnosis and Treatment*, ed. F. Dunbar. St. Louis: C. V. Mosby, pp. 276–302.

———— (1949), Anal sensations and feelings of persecution. *Psychoanal. Quart.*, 18:79–84.

———— (1951), The consecration of the prophet. *Psychoanal. Quart.*, 20:373–397.

———— (1952), Anxiety patterns in angina pectoris. *Psychosom. Med.*, 14:461–468.

———— (1953), Masturbation and symptom formation. *J. Amer. Psychoanal. Assn.* 1:45–58.

———— (1959), The structure of the déjà vu experience. *J. Amer. Psychoanal. Assn.* 7:611–631.

———— (1961), Ego psychology and the study of mythology. *J. Amer. Psychoanal. Assn.* 9:371–393.

———— (1963), Conflict, regression and symptom formation. *Internat. J. Psycho-Anal.*, 44:12–22.

———— (1966b), Depersonalization and derealization. In: *Psychoanalysis: A General Psychology: Essays in Honor of Heinz Hartmann*, ed. R. M. Loewenstein, et al. New York: International Universities Press, pp. 456–478.

———— (1969a), Unconscious fantasy and disturbances of conscious experience. *Psychoanal. Quart.* 38:1–17

———— (1969b), Fantasy, memory, and reality testing. *Psychoanal. Quart.* 38:28–51.

———— (1970), Some problems in current psychoanalytic thought. In: *The World Biennial of Psychiatry and Psychotherapy*, Vol. I, ed. S. Arieti. New York: Basic Books, pp.34–54.

———— (1971a), Character perversion. In: *Currents in Psychoanalysis*, ed. I. M. Marcus. New York: International Universities Press, pp. 317–336.

———— (1971b), A type of play observed in boys during the latency period. In: *Separation-Individuation: Essays in Honor of Margaret S. Mahler*, ed. J. B. McDevitt & C. F. Settlage. New York: International Universities Press, pp. 157–170.

———— (1975), The structural hypothesis—theoretical considerations. *Psychoanal. Quart.*, 44:509–525.

———— (1977), Affects and the psychoanalytic situation. *Internat J. Psycho-Anal.*, 58:158–170.

———— (1978), Pyromania and the primal scene: A psychoanalytic comment on the work of Yukio Mishima. *Psychoanal. Quart.*, 47:24–51.

———— (1979a), The genesis of interpretation. *J. Amer. Psychoanal. Assn., Suppl.*, 27:193–206.

———— (1979b), Metaphor and the psychoanalytic situation. *Psychoanal. Quart.*, 48:363–385.

———— (1980a), Object concept and object choice. *Psychoanal. Quart.*, 49:109–133.

———— (1980b), The revenge motive in the primal scene. *J. Amer. Psychoanal. Assn.* 28:519–541.

———— (1981), Theories of pathogenesis. *Psychoanal. Quart.*, 50:488–513.

———— (1982), Problems of the superego concept. *The Psychoanalytic Study of the Child*, 37:229–244. New Haven, CT: Yale University Press.

_____ (1982b), Scientific cosmogony, mythology, and immortality. *Psychoanal. Quart.*, 51:177–195.

_____ (1985a), The structural hypothesis. In: *Models of the Mind: Their Relationship to Clinical Work*, ed. Arnold Rothstein. New York: International Universities Press, pp. 21–34.

_____ (1985b) The concept of psychic reality and related problems. *J. Amer. Psychoanal. Assn.* 33:521–535.

_____ (1985c), Some technical problems of countertransference. *Psychoanal. Quart.* 55:164–174.

_____ (1986) The relation of theories of pathogenesis to therapy. In: *Psychoanalysis: A Science of Mental Conflict*, ed. A. B. Richards & M. S. Willick. Hillsdale, NJ: Analytic Press, pp. 49–63.

_____ (1987a), The dynamics of interpretation. *Psychoanal. Quart.*, 56:68–87.

_____ (in press, 1987b), The personal myth.

_____ & Beres, D. (1974), Fantasy and identification in empathy. *Psychoanal. Quart.*, 43:26–50.

_____ & Brenner, C. (1964). *Psychoanalytic Concepts and the Structural Theory*. New York: International Universities Press.

_____ _____ (1966), The psychoanalytic situation. In: *Psychoanalysis in the Americas: Original Contributions from the First Pan-American Congress for Psychoanalysis*, ed. R. E. Litman. New York: International Universities Press, pp. 23–43.

_____ & Dunbar, C. (1944), Criteria for therapy in psychosomatic disorders. *Psychosom. Med.*, 6:283–286.

Caruth, E., & Ekstein, R. (1966), Interpretation within the metaphor: Further consideration. *J. Amer. Acad. Child Psychiat.*, 5:35–45.

Freud, S. (1905), Three essays on the theory of sexuality. *Standard Edition*, 7:125–245. London: Hogarth Press, 1953.

_____ (1908), Hysterical phantasies and their relation to bisexuality. *Standard Edition*, 9:155–166. London: Hogarth Press, 1959.

_____ (1915), The unconscious. *Standard Edition:* 14:159–215. London: Hogarth Press, 1957.

_____ (1923), The ego and the id. *Standard Edition*, 19:12–66. London: Hogarth Press, 1961.

Klein, M. (1940), Mourning and its relation to manic-depressive states. In: *Contributions to Psychoanalysis*. London: Hogarth Press, 1948, pp. 311–338.

Kohut, H. (1971), *The Analysis of the Self*. New York: International Universities Press.

_____ (1977), *The Restoration of the Self*. New York: International Universities Press.

Lewin, B. (1952), Phobic symptoms and dream interpretation. *Psychoanal. Quart.*, 21:295–322.

Sachs, H. (1920), The community of daydreams. In: *The Creative Unconscious.* Cambridge, MA: Sci-Art Publishers, 1942.

Winnicott, D. W. (1953), Transitional objects and transitional phenomena. a study of the first not-me possession. *Internat. J. Psycho-Anal.,* 34:89–97.

———— (1956), On transference. *Internat. J. Psycho-Anal.,* 37:386–388.

———— (1960), The theory of the parent-infant relationship. *Internat. J. Psycho-Anal.,* 41:585–595.

3

From Prophet to Poet: Jacob A. Arlow's
Contributions to Applied Analysis

Francis Baudry, M.D.

The field of applied analysis continues to occupy an important position in the work of many leading analysts despite its status as a less than worthy offspring of the mother discipline. Various reasons have been offered to account for this fact. Some are negative (e.g., the need to find relief from arduous writings on clinical or theoretical issues, the absence of concern about confidentiality, the manifestly greater distance from the analyst's personal dimensions) and some are historical (e.g., the traditional interest of analysis in cultural phenomena as evidence buttressing its findings, the fascination the psychology of creativity has always exerted on psychoanalysts). I would add one additional reason—the delight analysts take in making new connections and relating the works of great masters to details of their personal histories, details often ignored by researchers from other disciplines.

As this review will demonstrate, Jacob Arlow's output in applied analysis is most impressive. In 1951, barely four years after graduating from the New York Psychoanalytic Institute, he published his first full-length paper, ''The Consecration of the Prophet'' (1951a). In the ensuing thirty-five years he produced no fewer than sixteen papers in the field of applied analysis, culminating in ''The Poet as Prophet: A Psychoanalytic Perspective'' (1986a).

I will examine Arlow's output from an historical point of view, inquiring into his influences and placing his ideas among those of his predecessors and contemporaries and from a descriptive point of view, noting recurrent themes in his papers, and how they are expressed, and whether one can detect a thrust in the ideas, concepts, and unconscious fantasies that command his interest. As for questions of method, these are of course the principal difficulties confronting workers in applied analysis, and the absence of a patient would seem to be at their source. Without the analytic interaction, and without the controls of the analytic situation, a dangerous arbitrariness is apt to creep in with regard to interpretation and the selection of explanatory concepts. I hope to indicate, in what follows, the precautions and strategies by which Arlow has avoided these pitfalls.

The late forties and early fifties were a period of great ferment in psychoanalysis; ego psychology was being developed and the so-called conflict-free or autonomous ego functions were being included within its domain. This allowed a more systematic investigation of cultural products. Until Kris's *Psychoanalytic Explorations in Art* was published in 1952, literary texts with rare exception were used primarily to illustrate or buttress a clinical picture or a theoretical concept. Symbolism was a major tool, and the texts were usually treated as barely transformed associations differing little from material presented by a patient on the couch. The goal was to emphasize the pathology of the creative individual, and historical, esthetic, and formal considerations were given short shrift. In their eagerness to confirm the findings of analysis, the early pioneers often ignored issues of method.

Hanns Sachs's "The Community of Daydreams" (1920) was one of the first works to link the mental life of the artist with the community and to apply principles of group psychology to the artistic audience. As this paper is quoted in detail in almost every major paper of Arlow's, a few words about its relevance are in order. The first sentence of the paper clearly had reverberations for Arlow: "All great creators, all those who brought into the world new spiritual values—prophets and poets, philosophers and scientists have been called dreamers" (p. 11). Sachs furnishes us a point of entry into the connection between the private world and the world of creativity. Extending Freud's early paper "Creative Writers and Day-Dreaming" (1908), Sachs studies the social function of art, starting with the notion of mutually shared daydreams. He examines the formal devices that make the transformed daydream acceptable to an audience, thereby allowing the discharge of instinctual drives and the relief of guilt.

Arlow's work has centered on the application and development of Freud's structural theory and the concept of adaptation through the close study of unconscious fantasy and its organizing effect on all spheres of mental activity, including both pathological products (perversion, character abnormalities) and autonomous functions. Key papers on perception, memory, and reality trace out the complex interweaving of inner and outer that creates perceptual reality. The model used by Arlow (1969a) of two projectors on opposite sides of a translucent screen adjoining to create a fused image illustrates this phase of his thinking.

The bulk of Arlow's early papers on applied analysis are devoted to the exploration of religious topics—Judaism, Biblical study, initiation rituals—testifying to a deep and pervasive immersion of the author in Jewish affairs and the history of his people (1951a, 1951b, 1954). The fate of aggression and some of its offshoots in the primal scene is the topic of two later papers, one on the Japanese writer Mishima (1978), the other on the revenge motive in the primal scene, as illustrated by a keen analysis of Antonioni's *Blow-up* (1980). Two key theoretical papers will occupy a substantial part of this review: "Ego Psychology and the Study of Mythology" (1961) and the seminal paper "Metaphor and the Analytic Situation" (1979), Arlow's favorite among his works in the applied field (personal communication). The latter paper will serve as a point of entry into some of Arlow's most recent papers, in particular "Scientific Cosmogony, Mythology, and Immortality" (1982) and "The Poet as Prophet" (1986a). These have a markedly philosophical bent, a tendency often seen in an analyst's work as he gets older.

Unconscious fantasies and their tranformations lie at the core of Arlow's work. If we may broaden the concept of mythology to include religious systems, a consideration of his papers on religion will serve as an apt introduction to "Ego Psychology and Mythology," his first truly theoretical paper.

In "The Consecration of the Prophet" initially presented to the New York Psychoanalytic Society in October 1949, barely two years after his graduation from the Institute, Arlow (1951a) uses Biblical texts to study the consecration experience from the point of view of the relation of son to father. He is aware that we can learn little about the personal biography of the prophets, a fact which limits the psychological data at our disposal. Arlow faces squarely the methodological issues: (1) grave doubts about the existence of some prophets; and (2) questions regarding textual accuracy. He does not attempt the psychoanalytic study of individual prophets but rather proposes the study of a composite type, a person motivated chiefly by his conviction that his spoken words are the words of God. Thus, what Arlow focuses on is a relationship based on a fantasy. He does not study the revelation in its social or historical context; his interest rather is in identifying those elements of the preprophetic personality that give rise to prophecy. These include psychological conflicts, ambivalence in particular.

Arlow suggests a comparison of the prophet with the artist; the terms of this comparison are reversed in his most recent paper, "The Poet as Prophet" (1986a). He described the withdrawal of object libido and the total submission of the prophet to his mission. The main affect coloring the paper is one of awe, both in the relation of the prophet to God and in the relation of the audience to the prophet. The paper ends on a poetic note concerning the true prophet, "who correctly divines and expresses the emergent but still inarticulate dreams and aspirations of his people . . . [a]t the threshold of the ages stands the prophet, midwife of humanity's dreams" (1951a, p. 396).

"The Madonna's Conception through the Eyes" (1964) presents an interesting contrast to "The Consecration of the Prophet." Conception through the eyes may be seen as the female counterpart of the consecration experience. Twelve years have elapsed since the earlier paper, and Arlow's thinking has considerably deepened.

The central myth of the Madonna's conception is seen as a fantasy expression of an oedipal wish to acquire the father's phallus through the process of incorporation through the eyes—a theme parallel to that of the prophet receiving the word of the Lord through the mouth. What is novel about this paper is the addition of a clinical case history illustrating a patient's personal development of a religious myth, a process that involves its regressive reinstinctualization in the service of several aspects of psychopathology, including symptoms, character traits, and masturbation fantasies. Arlow compares mythopoesis with neurosis by centering on a particular unconscious fantasy and showing some of the same mechanisms at work, notably transformation from active to passive and displacement. His understanding of the nature of the underlying fantasy then allows Arlow to turn to cognate myths in religious paintings and to explain some of their details as derivatives of the fantasy. He also stresses the communal sharing of a fantasy or myth via its representatives as allowing the hidden gratification of unconscious wishes with less guilt, a familiar theme in Hanns Sachs's work.

The bar mitzvah paper (1951) deals with a related theme. The initiation rite is a toned-down version of consecration. The representative of God the Father initiates the adolescent boy into adulthood and the moral religious obligations. It is clearly an affect-arousing experience.

Arlow approaches the study of the bar mitzvah rituals from two different routes. First, he carefully examines details of the ritual and draws direct psychological inferences. For example, he mentions the short prayer of five Hebrew words unique in Jewish ceremonials: "Blessed be he who rids me of this one's punishment." The words of the prayer are short, sharp, and impart a definite sense of hostility. Even the name of God is omitted from this prayer, and the word "pator," which means to get rid of, conveys a definite connotation of vexation and distaste. In this prayer no direct reference is made to the son, who is disparagingly referred to as "this one" (p. 357).

The other path Arlow pursues is to produce data both anecdotal and analytic concerning reactions to bar mitzvah ceremonies (both past and anticipated). The reliance on clinical material allows the reader to follow Arlow in the development of his thinking. Again, Arlow focuses on the ambivalence characteristic of the father-son relationship, and on its vicissitudes, through a number of detailed vignettes drawn from his clinical experience.

We now come to the theoretical paper which summarizes and elaborates what has come before, "Ego Psychology and the Study of Mythology" (1961). In this paper, which was delivered as a presidential address to the American Psychoanalytic Association, Arlow establishes a frame of reference within which the psychoanalytic study of mythology may be validated. In contrast to the early topographic point of view and its reductionistic tendencies, Arlow presents a developmental approach integrated with a structural and adaptational perspective; the latter is illustrated through the role myth plays in psychic integration. The emphasis on the adaptive value of a myth is an application of Hartmann's pioneer work, (1939). His concepts were slow to permeate writings on applied analysis, and Arlow was one of the first to deal with this important topic. He shows how the pressure of unconscious fantasies prods the ego to incorporate and integrate the data of perception in keeping with its pleasure-seeking purpose of discharge, and a parallel function and development as regards myth and fantasy. He again returns to one of the fantasies that most intrigues him—that of acquiring the father's phallus by devouring it—and shows how psychoanalysis is in a position to reveal the same deep structure in versions which superficially seem totally different. He groups such unlikely bedfellows as Jack and the Beanstalk, Prometheus, and Moses receiving the law. The difference can be seen as resulting from more or less primitive development of the ego and superego structures. Again, material from patients is presented to illustrate this process.

Arlow further illustrates the hypothesis that a regressive reactivation of instinctual wishes may be permitted following the establishment of certain sublimations. For instance, the sublimation of the religious setting allows the regressive emergence of the incestuous wish for a child as graphically expressed in paintings of the Annunciation. Our understanding of religion is vastly expanded from the narrow view that would liken religious rituals to obsessional neuroses. We can now see how religious observance, like esthetic experience, serves functions beyond that of instinctual discharge.

Another series of papers are united by their attention to the vicissitudes of agression and the primal scene. "Pyromania and the Primal Scene" (1978), commentary on the work of Yukio Mishima, continues Arlow's interest in fire, first elaborated in a brief paper, "Notes on Oral Symbolism" (1955). In the earlier paper, Arlow developed very convincingly, from clinical data, the many connections between the imagery of fire and the various oral drives; being burned to death, he suggested, represented the wish to be united (sexually) with the mother and a fantasy of being devoured and incorporated into her body.

In the Mishima paper, Arlow first isolates the persistent derivative expressions of primal scene fantasies, which abound as barely disguished manifest content. He then observes that fire and pyromania figure prominently as a theme of revenge against parental figures. This connection allows Arlow to comment on pyromania fantasies which can express both agressive and sexual drives (passively or actively). Pyromania, he suggests, is well suited as a vehicle for individuals bent on destructive revenge originating in a primal scene trauma.

Arlow then turns to the life of Mishima. He ventures that "there is sufficient material to say that the primal scene and derivative representations of it constitute a significant and repetitive element in Mishima's writings and accordingly one must conclude, in his fantasy life" (p. 70). The "burning" question for the analyst is, of course, how to connect more specifically the contents of novels with their author. How does one determine the transformations an author's fantasy life undergoes in the process of artistic creation?

At this point Arlow turns to a brief recapitulation of Mishima's childhood, dominated by a sadistic, emasculating, and controlling grandmother who prevented her sickly and unattractive grandchild from playing with boys. Arlow quotes in detail from an autobiographical novel, *Confessions of a Mask* (Mishima, 1949), which is replete with fantasies both sadistic and masochistic. The content of the novel, manifestly confessional in nature, is assumed by Arlow to describe in raw form the author's fantasy life. We are then presented with the real story of Mishima's death, a gory, bloody seppuku ritual in which he disembowels himself and is decapitated by an assistant. Arlow reminds us of the association, documented earlier in the paper, between intercourse and dying/being put to death, and suggests that the dramatic suicide is "a spectacular grandiose acting out of a sadomasochistically conceived, homosexually elaborated primal scene fantasy" (p. 47). As an author with a good sense of the dramatic, Arlow reserves for the final page his evidence for the more specific connections between the life of the author and his novels. It seems that Mishima was a showman who acted out his fantasy life—a pattern, Arlow reminds us, which is characteristic of individuals traumatized by the primal scene. This would be a good example of the content of traumatic experiences affecting the form rather than the content of mental life. The tendency to act out can be considered a character trait. Arlow describes the following event in the novel dating from the narrator's twelfth year. He came upon a picture of St. Sebastian bound to a tree, his body pierced by two long arrows: "the arrows have eaten into the tense, fragrant, youthful flesh and are about to consume his body from within with flames of supreme agony and ecstasy" (Mishima, 1949, pp. 39–40).

Later in his paper, Arlow informs us that four years before his death "Mishima posed for a photograph of himself as St. Sebastian: hands bound, his body pierced with arrows, blood dripping from the wounds" (Arlow, 1978, p. 48). In another novel, the hero commits suicide by seppuku, as Mishima will himself. Once having identified, quite convincingly, the relevance of primal scene motifs in Mishima, Arlow specifically refrains from adressing the question why this motif is so important for this author. To pursue this path would have required an additional paper and data that were simply not available.

The primal scene theme occupies Arlow also in "The Revenge Motive in the Primal Scene" (1980). In this primarily clinical paper Arlow studies two sequelae of the primal scene experience that he feels have been underemphasized: narcissistic mortification and the need for revenge on both parents. I have included it in this review because of an extended commentary on the movie *Blow-up* by Antonioni.

Arlow treats the plot of the movie as if it were a story told by a patient. The criteria he uses in analyzing the details are similar to those applied to clinical material (see Beres and Arlow, 1974): similarity, repetition, and confluence of theme organized by coherence and consistency of the data. These criteria are not limited to psychoanalysis but could apply to any text one might submit to structural analysis. What makes Arlow's approach psychoanalytic is his search for an analogy between the images and stories of the plot and the structure of unconscious fantasies, in this case a primal scene scenario. Arlow does not attempt to attribute motives to the characters. Instead he convincingly identifies similarities between the film's plot, the main characters' behavior, and clinical material, including a dream of a patient in whom the primal scene trauma was reconstructed. Arlow is able to demonstrate the effect of primal scene derivatives not only on the content of the film but on its formal aspects. The film turns out to be "a parable on the functions of memory, on the repression of the traumatic primal scene" (p. 537). This is in line with Arlow's interests in the so-called autonomous function of the ego, which clearly becomes drawn into the conflict.

But if primal scene material pervades the film, what can one say about Antonioni? As with Mishima, Arlow avoids speculating about the psychology of the director. "In imaginative and gifted individuals, the dynamic pressure of the repressed fantasies connected with the primal scene may find expression in sublimated form through works of art. One would expect that this would be particularly true of the motion picture as an art form, centering as it does on the all-intrusive eye of the camera" (1980, p. 530). Arlow has pointed out, in a preceeding sentence, that screen memories apppear regularly as defensive representations of the primal scene.

Arlow's perhaps most profound effort in applied analysis, "Metaphor and the Psychoanalytic Situation" (1979), deserves extended commentary. Presented as a tribute to Rudolf M. Loewenstein in 1977, this paper starts out by describing Loewenstein's views on the central role of speech in the analytic situation. Loewenstein (1957) was interested in exploring how an experienced analyst is able to perceive, in the material presented by a patient, clues that might escape a beginner. He suggested a more systematic study of the implicit method that leads the analyst to draw conclusions from the subtle clues often preconsciously perceived. Speaking of the need to listen, particularly for figurative constellations employed in the patients' language, he indirectly refers to the process of metaphorical expression. Although novel in the terms of ego psychology, the interest in metaphor had already been evident on the continent, in the work of Lacan and even before that in some of Freud's early writings. As early as 1900, in "The Interpretation of Dreams," Freud referred to switch words and verbal bridges. He also compared the process of listening to being on a railroad track. At some point, a word or an image reveals another meaning which allows the therapist to switch to a parallel track. In 1953, Lacan delivered his famous aphorism that the unconscious is structured like a language. In the mid-sixties other writers in France, Laplanche and Pontalis among them, explored the similarity between metaphor and displacement, and metonymy and condensation, pointing out that the two key mechanisms of unconscious mental functioning were closely related to these two fundamental rhetorical devices. They explored further the similar orgins of the words "metaphor" and "transference" in a key article in their *The Language of Psycho-Analysis* (Laplanche and Pontalis, 1967), and Laplanche (1976) took up the question again in his appendix to *Life and Death in Psychoanalysis.*

Arlow believes that metaphor plays a fundamental role in the integration of experience and in the organization of reality. This view is an extension of ideas expressed some ten years earlier in two key papers, "Fantasy, Memory and Reality Testing" (1969a) and "Unconscious Fantasy and Disturbances of Conscious Experience" (1969b). In contrast to the French writers, who often start with theory, Arlow goes back and forth between the clinical data and the theory;

> Focusing in the phenomenon, it seemed to me that metaphor can regularly be seen as an outcropping of unconscious fantasy. Specific associations to the metaphor regularly lead to unconscious fantasy typical for the patient. What was striking about this relationship was the fact that this held true whether the metaphor was vitally innovative and expressive or of a stale cliché quality [Arlow, 1979, p. 370].

Arlow compares the way a patient is able to transmit unconsciously his personal experience in a way that moves the analyst to the way a poet transmits the emotions he experiences via contiguity, repetition, symbolism, allusion, contrast, and, above all, metaphor (p. 373). He then turns to a famous passage from Shakespeare's *Julius Caesar* to demonstrate the latent appeal of metaphor. I will quote the passage in full to illustrate a crucial point, namely, the subjectivity in interpretation and the richness

of Shakespeare's language, which allows several possible meanings to
exist side by side. Which meaning is selected by the reader is a function
not only of conscious purpose but of the reader's sensitivity to different
meanings as a result of personal history. Here is a passage, its context,
and Arlow's commentary:

> In this section, Cassius is appealing to Brutus to join the conspiracy
> to assassinate Caesar and to preserve the republic. Caesar has just
> returned from victories in the field. He is an impressive and awe-
> inspiring figure. Cassius must undermine Brutus' loyalty and at the
> same time dissipate the awe and the fear of retaliation from the ruler-
> father figure. The metaphorical language in which Shakespeare couches
> Cassius' appeal illustrates beautifully the technique by which this is
> accomplished, evoking without articulating the latent oedipal, parricidal
> impulses common to members of the culture.

> For once, upon a raw and gusty day,
> The troubled Tiber chafing with her shores,
> Caesar said to me, "Dar'st thou, Cassius, now
> Leap in with me into this angrey flood,
> And swim to yonder point?" Upon the word
> Accoutred as I was, I plunged in
> And bade him follow: so indeed he did.
> With lusty sinews, throwing it aside
> The torrent roar'd, and we did buffet it
> And stemming it with hearts of controversy;
> But ere we could arrive the point propos'd,
> Caesar cried "Help me, Cassius, or I sink!"
> I, as Aeneas, our great ancestor,
> Did from the flames of Troy upon his shoulder
> The old Anchises bear, so from the waves of Tiber
> Did I the tired Caesar. And this man
> Is now become a god, and Cassius is
> A wretched creature and must bend his body
> If Caesar carelessly but nod on him.
>   [I, 2, 99–117]

   In his interpretation of the passage Arlow stresses the aggression
between the two men. He ends his commentary as follows:

> The final touch in the passage, however, is most telling. Cassius iden-

tifies himself with Aeneas, the heroic progenitor of Rome, and Caesar with Anchises, the father of Aeneas, an impotent figure at the brink of death, soon to be discarded. These metaphors deepen the message contained in the appeal to Brutus. They diminish the image of Caesar's power and stimulate in Brutus latent parricidal wishes toward a father figure in decline and unworthy of respect [Arlow, 1979, pp. 377–378].

In his commentary Arlow omits consideration of the metaphor contained in the last four lines. This reveals the personal animosity of Cassius and may account for his vindictiveness. He contrasts the political power of the physically weaker Caesar with his own reduced condition. Cassius must "... bend his body, if Caesar carelessly but nod on him"; he is reduced to the position of a menial servant who must jump at his master's every whim. He must swallow his pride and forget that at one point the master was desperately dependent on him and would have drowned, had Cassius not rescued him from the raging waters, thus proving his loyalty and love. The sense of unfairness, injustice, and humiliation stand out as particularly poignant. The contrast is even greater if we recall Cassius's immediate response to Caesar's first call: "... Upon the word/Accoutred as I was, I plunged in/and bade him follow. . ." Cassius not only accepts the challenge but takes the lead, in effect daring Caesar to put his words into action. To accept the first challenge is honorable—a test of strength and masculinity which Cassius wins. The reward for his rescuing the physically weaker Caesar is a bitter, demeaning humiliation. The theme of humiliation is found again in a passage spoken by Cassius a few lines further, in which Caesar is compared to a Colossus: "we petty men/walk under his huge legs, and peep about to find ourselves dishonorable graves."

It seems relevant that Arlow's paper on revenge in the primal scene (1980), written at about the same time, stresses the theme of narcissistic rage and injury of a child and his wish for revenge. Is it simply a coincidence that this passage of Shakespeare's was chosen to illustrate Arlow's interest in metaphor? If Arlow's paper on the consecration (1951a) was an illustration of the love of the child and erotic submission to the father, then this passage shows the other side of the ambivalence—the hateful, humiliating submission to a father seen as unjust and arbitrary.

Arlow next relates metaphor to the functioning of the psychic apparatus. The unconscious fantasy itself is a metaphoric apprehension of childhood experience that has remained dynamically active into adult life. Metaphor, as a reliable marker of the past, is intimately related to character, which, as I have suggested can be conceptualized as the enactment of the unconscious beliefs a person holds about himself, others, and their relationships. Metaphor affords us a reliable point of entry into those very personal beliefs so deeply anchored in the past. Metaphor is more than a reflection of the existence of unconscious fantasy. It affords clues to key experiences in the child's development: metaphor "typifies how perception and memory are integrated in terms of similarity and difference"(p. 373).

Metaphor serves as a marker not only in the child's personal development but also in theory building—an apparently remote and unrelated domain. "In recent years such concepts as drives and psychic energy in particular have come under attack as being unscientific," Arlow (1979) writes; "Yet metaphors constitute the only way by which what was hitherto unknown may be organized and conceptualized in a novel way" (p. 383). Although referring to theory, this statement has broad applications to both child development and the analytic situation.

A lovely story illustrating the lack of metaphoric capacity in a two-and-a-half-old is to be found in Alice Balint's *The Early Years of Life* (1959). It concerns a child who was given a large toy elephant as a gift. To the dismay of his parents the child reacted with fear and terror at the sight of the trunk of the animal. Only after his parents moved the trunk up and down, and then moved the little boy's arm up and down, did the child, cautiously at first, look into the direction of the foreign object. One could say that the little boy did not as yet have the capacity to see the world in terms of metaphor. He could not identify the unknown with the known. He could not empathize with the toy animal; the intermediary links had to be provided for him by understanding adults. We do not know what personal meaning the elephant's trunk had for the little boy. Did he, in fact, metaphorically misperceive it? Did he simply react to its strangeness with a generalized fear and anxiety, or did the trunk have a specific meaning? In any case, the parents' intervention may have neutralized the fearsome aspect by substituting a benign object for a potentially malevolent one.

If it is agreed that the capacity to integrate the unknown with the known is central to metaphor and to the formation of psychic structure, then the development of this capacity in children deserves close examination. How do children of various ages understand and create metaphors? The capacity to experience the world metaphorically must be related to the development of symbolic thinking and the concept of space. It also depends on mechanisms such as identification and projection, and on the capacity to grasp analogies. Although I have stressed until now the role of the autonomous functions, the capacity for imagination is influenced also by certain defensive styles—rigidity, fear of letting go, concreteness, and literal-mindedness. Closely related to the realm of imagination, metaphor creation is an offshoot of the capacity for play and illusion. This capacity has its onset somewhere in the second year of life along with the development of speech. Freud's example of the Fort-Da game (1920) reflects an early stage of metaphorization. Gardner and Winnez (1979) distinguished between this phenomenon, which they call metaphoric comprehension, and metaphoric creation, a skill which develops much later. There is considerable variation in the onset of the latter capacity. Sometimes it occurs in children of two and a half, but then, as with artistic ability, it seems to disappear only to resurface at a later date. There is much disagreement on the timing. Those who tend to stress the daringness, spontaneity, and inventiveness involved in the creation of tropes see the years of early childhood as a time of poetic genius (Gardner and Winnez, p. 130). Others question whether the early capacity of the preschool child can really be called metaphoric—that is, whether the child is aware of the conventional extension of the words and of the "mature taxonomic" classification of objects. If not, then the young child creating a metaphor would not be organizing things differently or overriding a customary mode of organization (p. 133).

I will now turn to some aspects of the role of metaphor in clinical work and theory formation. Occasionally when he is listening to a patient, the analyst's associations will turn spontaneously and unexpectedly to a mythological figure, a line of poetry, or an apparently unrelated visual image. Sometimes this phenomenon (described by Beres and Arlow, 1974) is seen as an example of unconscious intuition or empathy, or as the intrusion of primary process; but it can also be understood as a metaphoric bridge creatively synthesized in the analyst's mind in response to the patient's material. The understanding of such metaphors often goes to the heart of the patient's unconscious fantasies.

If it is understood that a patient's view of the world can be considered a "theory" then it becomes natural to study the role of metaphor in theory formation. Much of the controversy over the term "psychic energy" might have been avoided had its second word been understood as a metaphorical expression used to approximate and bring together a number of clinical observations and to reason about them by analogy, with no attempt at reification. The examination of a theory's metaphors can provide information about its gaps, its limitations, and its special articulations with its author's personal interests and unconscious fantasies. Arlow (1986b) has done this in "The Relation of Theories of Pathogenesis to Therapy," and Grossman (1976) has employed the same strategy in an article on Wilhelm Reich.

Metaphors point to the limits of our understanding. Freud implied as much when he referred to metapsychology as our mythology. Metaphor, as Arlow (1979) implies, is where science joins poetry. In this connection, I will now consider two of Arlow's most recent papers. In the first, "Scientific Cosmogony, Mythology, and Immortality" (1982), Arlow expands some of the ideas in the metaphor paper and demonstrates the resemblance of cosmogony to childhood concepts of procreation. His method is not unlike that of Freud (1927) in "The Future of an Illusion." How, he asks, could cosmogony be otherwise? Since facts about the origins of the world are so limited, we have no choice but to fill the gap with fantasies derived from some aspect of our past. Scientific cosmogonies could only develop gradually "out of the matrix of mythological conceptualization" (p. 181). All scientific theories, just as all works of art and all myths, have at least one root in the fantasies of childhood. These fantasies represent a fusion of childhood wishes and fears colored by the child's confused and inadequate grasp of causality and reality (p. 187).

The second paper, Arlow's most recently published, brings us full circle. In "The Poet as Prophet," Arlow (1986a) returns to his early paper, "The Consecration of the Prophet," and to Hanns Sachs's concept of the community of daydreams. He adds the notion that the poet may anticipate change and new directions, particularly in daring to confront themes and images which in the past would have been censored; "for a special group," he remarks, "the work of the poet may. . . make possible the alleviation of pathogenic anxieties" (p. 59).

It is not always easy to distinguish the true prophet from the false. "Only the historical test of mass acceptance and the course of history itself validate the truth of the prophet's vision. The true prophet may be said to be the one who correctly divines and exposes the emergent but still inarticulate dreams and aspirations of his people" (p. 59).

Arlow attempts to relate the poet's creativity and the social function of his art (p. 55). To illustrate the thesis that the efforts of the poet may adumbrate and help bring about change in certain aspects of sexual morality, he chooses a most extreme and provocative example: a play called *The Beard,* given for only six performances in San Francisco and then shut down by the police. The play is a thinly disguised semipornographic encounter between a man and a woman. Arlow was intrigued by the fact that beards do not figure in the play beyond a direction that both characters are to wear paper beards. This anomaly serves as a point of entry for Arlow, who is able to demonstrate that the play functions as a fetish and alleviates castration anxiety through the mechanism of denial in fantasy.

In the final section of this review I would like to emphasize the development of a number of themes over a thirty-five year span as they emerge in the body of Arlow's work.

Going over Arlow's writings I am struck by the frequency with which one particular fantasy recurs: the incorporation by the child of the coveted paternal phallus. This incorporation may be along as many routes as there are bodily orifices. The affect of awe toward the father is part of the total experience, a subject dwelt on in the early papers. Though the fantasy is studied in greatest detail in the case of the little boy, it is clearly applicable to the little girl as well (see Arlow, 1964). The fantasy has a developmental thrust and can assume a variety of cultural forms, in advancing from the most primitive version (e.g., Jack and the Beanstalk) to the Prometheus story and finally the myth of Moses receiving the tables of the law. This last version appears in Arlow's presidential address (1961), while the bar mitzvah paper (1951b) deals with a related theme: the initiation rite in adolescence marking the acquisition of sexual maturity and the right to exercise the religious and sexual prerogatives of an adult (here the gift of the pen symbolizes incorporation of the phallus). Although the Mishima paper (1978) deals with a triadic issue—the primal scene— Arlow stresses the primitive quality of the narrator's reactions. In a regressive way, the child interprets the primal scene in oral terms, conceiving the experience as a form of mutual cannibalism or reciprocal suckling—in one scene a milkman performs cunnilingus on the narrator's wife. In *Confessions of a Mask,* Mishima's narrator expresses the wish to attain his ideal of masculine perfection by murdering and devouring a beautiful youth as part of a struggle against emerging homosexuality. The same content is perversely elaborated in the fantasy of having his body pierced by two lone arrows in identification with St. Sebastian: ''This image aroused within the young Mishima a surge of sexual passion which culminated in his first experience of masturbation and ejaculation'' (p. 45). It is possible to see the fantasy of phallic incorporation either as prelude to a fantasied primal scene or as a negative oedipal fantasy, as in Nunberg's ''Homosexuality, Magic and Aggression'' (1938), which Arlow quotes.

The paper on the revenge motif (1980) adds one further note: the involvement of memory and perception in the conflict, which has as its result the repression of the primal scene and a subsequent return of the repressed. One of the cases presented in the paper on metaphor and the psychoanalytic situation (1979) is that of a patient who had fantasies of acquiring great wealth by robbing or superseding a powerful authority. The same patient also had the wish to be anally penetrated by a powerful father figure whom he would then castrate. The other case, quoted from a student, is that of a woman who is angry at all men because she was born a woman. The beginning of her menstruation is at one point the precepitating cause of a demeaning attack on the analyst. These two examples show that the fantasy of incorporation appears incidentally in what at first would seem unrelated topics. Arlow's selection of this material suggests his special; sensitivity to this particular fantasy.

Methodologically, Arlow is able to avoid many of the pitfalls of applied analysis, primarily because his goal is both well defined and limited. It is well defined in the sense that his main interest is to demonstrate, largely by analogy, the existence in textual material (the Bible, a painting, a novel, a play) of unconscious fantasies, defenses against them, and the effects of both on other functions of the mental apparatus. It is limited in the sense that he does not go beyond the available data and does not pursue the biographical dimensions, no matter how tempting the evidence. He performs his chosen task admirably, with parsimony and the skill of a consummate clinician. His impressive ability to tack between literary text and patient material, enriching our understanding of both, opens new vistas, both for psychoanalysis as a clinical science and for recent attempts at cross-disciplinary cooperation.

REFERENCES

Arlow, J. A. (1951a), The consecration of the prophet. *Psychoanal. Quart.*, 20:374–397.
_____ (1951b), A psychoanalytic study of a religious initiation rite: Bar mitzvah. *The Psychoanalytic Study of the Child*, 6:353–374. New York: International Universities Press.

_____ (1954), Applied psychoanalysis: Religion. *Annual Survey of Psychoanalysis,* 2:538–553.

_____ (1955), Notes on oral symbolism. *Psychoanal. Quart.,* 24:63–74.

_____ (1961), Ego psychology and the study of mythology. *J. Amer. Psychoanal. Assn.,* 9:371–393.

_____ (1964), The Madonna's conception through the eyes. *Psychoanalytic Study of Society* 3:9–25.

_____ (1969a), Fantasy, memory and reality testing. *Psychoanal. Quart.,* 38:28–51.

_____ (1969b), Unconscious fantasy and disturbances of conscious experience. *Psychoanal. Quart.,* 38:1–27.

_____ (1978), Pyromania and the primal scene: A psychoanalytic comment on the work of Yukio Mishima. *Psychoanal. Quart.,* 47:24–51.

_____ (1979), Metaphor and the psychoanalytic situation. *Psychoanal. Quart.,* 48:363–385.

_____ (1980), The revenge motive in the primal scene. *J. Amer. Psychoanal. Assn.,* 28:519–541.

_____ (1982), Scientific cosmogony, mythology, and immortality. *Psychoanal. Quart.,* 51:177–195.

_____ (1986a), The poet as prophet: A psychoanalytic perspective. *Psychoanal. Quart.,* 55:53–68.

_____ (1986b), The relation of theories of pathogenesis to therapy. In: *Psychoanalysis: A Science of Mental Conflict,* ed. A. Richards & M. Willick. Hillsdale, NJ: Analytic Press, pp. 49–63.

Baliant, A. (1959), *The Early Years of Life.* New York: Basic Books.

Beres, D., & Arlow J. A. (1974), Fantasy and identification in empathy. *Psychoanal. Quart.,* 43:26–50.

Freud S. (1900), The Interpretation of Dreams. *Standard Edition,* 4/5. London: Hogarth Press, 1953.

_____ (1908), Creative writers and day-dreaming. *Standard Edition,* 9:143–153. London: Hogarth Press, 1959.

_____ (1920), Beyond the pleasure principle. *Standard Edition,* 18:7–64. London: Hogarth Press, 1955.

_____ (1927), The future of an illusion. *Standard Edition,* 21:5–56. London: Hogarth Press, 1961.

Gardner, H., and Winnez, E. (1979), The development of metaphoric competence: Implications for humanistic disciplines. In: *On Metaphor,* ed. S. Sachs. Chicago: University of Chicago Press, pp. 121–141.

Grossman, W. (1976), Knightmare in armory: Reflections on Wilhelm Reich's contributions to psychoanalysis. *Psychiatry,* 39:376–385.

_____ & Simon, B. (1969), Anthropomorphism: Motive, meaning and causality in pychoanalytic theory. *The Psychoanalytic Study of the Child,* 24:78–111. New York: International Universities Press.

Hartmann, H. (1939), *Ego Psychology and the Problem of Adaptation*. New York: International Universities Press.

Kris, E. (1952), *Psychoanalytic Explorations in Art*. New York: International Universities Press.

Laplanche, J. (1976), Appendix: The derivation of psychoanalytic entities. In: *Life and Death in Psychoanalysis*. Baltimore: Johns Hopkins University Press, pp. 136–138.

———— & Pontalis, J. B. (1967), *The Language of Psycho-Analysis*, trans. D. Nicholson-Smith. New York: Norton, 1973.

Loewenstein, R. M. (1957), Some thoughts on interpretation in the theory and practice of psychoanalysis. *The Psychoanalytic Study of the Child*, 12:127–150. New York: International Universities Press.

Mishima, Y. (1949), *Confessions of a Mask*, trans. M. Weatherby. New York: New Directions Publications, 1958.

Nunberg, A. (1938), Homosexuality, magic and aggression. *Internat. J. Psycho-Anal.*, 19:1–16.

Sachs, H. (1920), The community of daydreams. In: *The Creative Unconscious*. Cambridge, MA: Sci-Art, 1942, pp. 11–54.

Part II

UNCONSCIOUS FANTASY: THEORY

4

Roots and Derivatives of
Unconscious Fantasy

Leo Rangell, M.D.

The unconscious fantasy is an intermediate product. It stands at the same level intrapsychically—between drives and final psychic outcomes—as unconscious affect, an unconscious symptom, or any other compromise formation or more direct instinctual derivative that remains suspended in a repressed form in the dynamic unconscious. Unconscious fantasies have roots and derivatives, input and output, psychological forces that go into their formation, and psychic products deriving from them that become operative in conscious behavior.

When unconscious fantasies play a part in the psychoanalytic search for understanding, they serve as way stations in one of two directions. In the original and progressive development, they play a role, either transiently or in a more enduring form, in the dynamics of character development and symptom formation, as well as in external action and behavior. In a regressive direction, they come to serve in a significant way in the retrogressive unfolding of this developmental sequence during the therapeutic procedure of the psychoanalytic process.

Definitionally, fantasy, whether conscious or unconscious, is complex, variable, and multidetermined. In one colloquial definitional meaning, fantasy connotes an unrealistic wish, approaching the pure wish fulfillment dreams of early childhood cited by Freud (1900). Arlow (1969) uses fantasy in the sense of the daydream. From the adjective "fantastic," meaning too good to be true, to the noun form meaning elaboration unrestrained by truth, wish rather than reality, the connotation of instinctual wish, the wish component of drive is hard to avoid. However, the operation of defenses upon the wishful drives is shown by the fact that the fantasy is repressed (we are speaking mainly of unconscious fantasy) or that, if admitted to consciousness, it remains suspended within the thought processes rather than being translated into action.

A patient's close friend was dying of cancer and also facing bankruptcy. This friend, whom the patient loved and admired, had referred the patient for analysis, for which the patient was grateful. Concerned now for the friend's wife and children, the patient asked the friend, whom he also idealized, "How could you do it?" "F.F." replied the friend, by which he meant, the patient explained to me, "fuckin' fantasy." Long after his own analysis, the friend had come to live according to resources as he wished they were, not as they were in reality.

HISTORICAL

In the second half of the psychoanalytic century, analysts began to look beyond the presenting symptom to another group of unconscious products, also definitive in their construction, that can serve as well, or even better, in leading the way back to the etiological origins of a patient's condition. Following an initial interest in exposing drive derivatives and seeking the discharge of repressed drives, Freud in the second half of his creative life elaborated, among other topics, the workings of the unconscious ego (1920, 1923) and the signal theory of anxiety (1926). His addition of the definitive structural point of view to the topographic one—while some jettisoned the latter entirely, Freud, Anna Freud, and others did not—led to inclusion of the ego's unconscious activities in formulating the genesis of behavior, abnormal and normal, and in conducting the psychoanalytic uncovering process. Secondary process ego activity in the unconscious, which Freud (1915) had noted descriptively even during the period in which he advanced topographic explanations, was now made more explicit from the vantage point of structural theory.

Following Freud's own contributions on the subject of unconscious secondary process functioning, psychoanalytic writers explored various aspects of this unconscious ego activity. First to attract attention was the operation of unconscious defense, a topic elaborated by Anna Freud (1937). Next Hartmann (1939) introduced the concept of the conflict-free sphere of the ego. Rapaport (1951a, 1958) followed this with his descriptions of autonomous ego functioning, presented as a relative concept within the confines and restrictions of drives and reality. Jacobson (1964) delineated the formation of self- and object representations within the ego, using the structural theory to illuminate the achievement of object relationships. Finally, I developed the concept of the "executive functions of the ego" (Rangell, 1971, 1986), evidenced in decision making leading to action, a concept couched within the structural theory, in contrast to Schafer's action theory (1976), which stands outside of psychoanalytic metapsychology.

The development of this theoretical scaffolding for understanding the interactions between id, ego, and superego led to an interest in the psychic formations resulting from these interactions. Jacobson (1953), Rapaport (1953), and others analyzed the composition and vicissitudes of affects and moods, both unconscious and in their progression toward conscious experience. In a series of papers, I described the "intrapsychic process" (Rangell, 1963a, 1963b, 1969), a microdynamic series of sequential steps before and after signal anxiety, leading to the spectrum of psychic outcomes in human behavior. This process encompassed affective and cognitive elements in both separate and fused form, which occur first unconsciously, then to proceed through the preconscious to conscious life.

Of the various forms of unconscious mental activity resulting from these forces and their interaction, the one that has elicited the most interest is the unconscious fantasy. The contributions of Arlow (1961, 1963, 1969) on the status of unconscious fantasy in psychic life and its role in the psychoanalytic process have securely established the significance of unconscious fantasy in psychoanalytic theory and technique. Others have written on the relation of unconscious fantasy to specific subjects and to other closely related forms of unconscious ego functioning. Beres (1960, 1962) stressed the role of the synthetic and organizing functions of the ego in creating the complex structure of unconscious fantasies; he also contributed the idea of fantasy formation, a ubiquitous human psychic function, as a manifestation of imagination. The imaginative process is the human capacity to evoke an image or an idea in the absence of a direct perceptual stimulus. Rosen (1960), also writing on the psychology of imagination, pointed out the origins of this capacity in the development of object constancy reactive to the stimulus of vanished objects. The progression from image formation to concept formation, according to Rosen, requires a synthesis of projected mental contents (fantasy) with an introjection of percepts of external objects. Sandler and Nagera (1963), in a careful study of the metapsychology of fantasy, in a formulation similar to my own, describe the components of which fantasies are composed, and differentiate fantasy from other mental products, including "nonfantasy derivatives," which are alternatives to fantasy. Abend (see chapter 9), in a clinical-theoretical contribution, discusses the role of unconscious fantasies in a specific stage of the psychoanalytic process, the termination phase.

ROOTS

Unconscious fantasy, the most formed and accessible of unconscious mental products by virtue of its central use of secondary process functioning, has become pragmatically the most common product of repression sought by psychoanalysts in the pursuit of the goal of undoing defenses and uncovering drives and their derivative affects and motivations. The psychoanalytic interest in fantasy life, conscious and unconscious, however, should not be pursued as a goal in itself, but for the leads that fantasies provide, and the openings they produce, toward the etiological and neurosogenic roots that went into their formation. Fantasies, however simple or complex, have roots, contents, and derivatives. Their roots, which we direct ourselves to uncover in the psychoanalytic process, consist of instinctual impulses, ego defenses, and contributions from the superego and the external world. Embedded among the contents of fantasies, these early elemental determinants fill the interstices and make up the substance of the complex derivative fantasies to which they give rise.

Unconscious fantasy, which is so stressed today, is always preceded by the ongoing background "intrapsychic process" I have described. Entering into their composition are all the stages of this unconscious process and what their dynamic activation leaves behind—distillates of preliminary instinctual discharges, anxieties experienced, dangers feared, defensive operations instituted, intended actions (usually aborted, inhibited, and modified), and necessary concessions to restricting agencies, within and without. Through interactions with self- and object representations within the ego, issues relating to both self and object are involved during the trial actions of the intrapsychic sequence. Objects are sampled for their reactions to intended discharge, and the self is tested for the experience of either a feeling of anxiety presaging danger, or one of safety and likely mastery. Of the many stages and complex derivatives of this ubiquitous background mental activity, one universal outcome is the construction of fantasies, conscious and unconscious.

FORMS, STRUCTURE, AND FUNCTIONS

Unconscious fantasies are of every degree of complexity and completeness, from unformed to formed, from transitory to stable and enduring, from partial to more complete, from simple flashes of an idea to a linear scenario approaching a dramatic performance. Unconscious fantasies are not solitary or permanent, but multiple, relatively fluid or structured, and changeable. Those which have reached more structured and thereby enduring states are the most fully formed of all unconscious mental products. The roles these play and the influence they exert are of interest for the understanding of both neurosogenesis and normal behavior. The same repetitive unconscious fantasy results if the same neurotic intrapsychic sequence prevails.

Fantasies are formed or potential, or exist in partially developed and incompletely structured frameworks. Additional elements are filled in and integrated in accordance with the needs of the particular intrapsychic moment. There may be an opening at the time for drive derivatives to be added, for sexual or aggressive impulses to find their way into a nascent or otherwise in completely formed fantasy. Or the realities of the internal and external conditions at a time of contemplated action may call for the addition of defensive maneuvers to deflect or distort instinctual wishes in the service of preventing anxiety, depression, shame, or guilt. The ego is inventive within the limits of its possibilities.

With reference to the linkage between the cognitive and the affective, fantasies are cognitive products designed to produce a wished-for affective result. The aim is to produce pleasure and safety, while keeping anxiety or any other form of unpleasure at bay. While still unconscious, they share the characteristics of a dream, with condensation, displacement, and reversal into the opposite, as well as all defensive operations that occur in outer behavior. Appropriate affects may accompany action, be absent, or be dissociated and displaced as in a dream. The closer to consciousness the fantasies are allowed to proceed, the more they acquire a realistic quality. In the end they appear consciously after having undergone the same secondary revision as is applied to the dream.

In common with a symptom, or with any outer and conscious form of behavior, the unconscious fantasy, in its more advanced and total form, is a compromise formation, containing within it derivatives of instinctual drives, effects of ego defenses, restrictions imposed by the superego, and requirements and limitations of the external world. Cognitive pro-

cesses and accompanying affects are combined. Self- and object representations enter into their formation, and object relations, consonant with
their level of integration and completion, are expressed in their contents.
Grossman (1982) writes of the concept of the self—the same would apply
to the object—as fantasy, theory, or myth, although these serve "both
subjective, conflict-resolving aims, and objective, reality-orienting aims"
(p. 923).

Unlike parallel formations, however, which are admitted to consciousness, unconscious fantasies in their totality still remain sufficiently undisguised so as not to be permissible beyond the censorship of unconscious ego defenses. They can be compared to a dream in this respect,
before secondary revision refines the latter for external consumption.
Although sharing in common with the dream the separation from reality, fantasy is closer to reality and secondary process than is the inchoate
dream, requiring more realistic, though still fantastic, characteristics,
and more rational and secondary process traits than does the dream.
Secondary revision, which is called upon only at the final moment of
dream formation—during the rendition of the dream into the waking
state—operates more continuously during the formation and construction of unconscious fantasy life.

A final and probably more energetic revision, however, may indeed
occur as the fantasy becomes conscious during psychoanalysis or in everyday life. Emerging unconscious fantasies can become daydreams—still
fantasies, not action. Their function, both in conscious and unconscious
form, is to perform a holding operation, providing partial or uneven
satisfactions, while remaining within the confines dictated by defenses.
I have described a spectrum of such "imaginary" mental products as
they exist during the twenty-four hour sleep-waking cycle under varying dynamic conditions of drive-defense relationships (Rangell, 1986).
Such psychic formations, both partial and more complete, traverse and
range from the dreams of sleep to the organized complex daydreams of
waking life. Arlow (1961, 1963) speaks of a hierarchy of fantasies. "No
sharp line of distinction," he writes (Arlow, 1969), "can be made between conscious and unconscious fantasies" (p. 25).

While I have been describing secondary process operations in the
unconscious, the opposite is also the case, that at times and under certain
conditions, there are residuals and derivatives of primary process activity
actively operative during conscious life. People drift, daydream, fantasy
when awake, just as they can create, be on guard, and solve problems

while asleep. There is a spectrum from the dream (and even here between deep dream states and REM dreams), hypnopompic hallucinations between sleep and waking, primary and secondary process operations during the day, waking fantasies, alert states, daydreams, and hypnagogic phenomena as one is falling asleep again (Isakower, 1938). All of these mental products, at all stages, night and day, are treated by secondary revision as they approach first the preconscious and then the conscious and alert state. And all are composites of cognitive and affective contents, derivatives of drives and defenses, miniature or intermediate stages of compromise formations, brought together into one running thought or image as a final, more macroscopic compromise formation.

Unconscious fantasies exist in every stage of their development, from transient elements in statu nascendi, to more structured, fixed, and enduring states. They vary from fluid and changeable, to relatively stable, to more structured in form, duration, and tenacity. There may be a passing or abbreviated thought with or without affect, or the reverse, a fleeting affect with or without an accompanying cognitive element. Pulver's description (1974) of potential affects existing in the unconscious, which in effect means channels ready for affective discharge, have wider implications. Fenichel (1945) speaks of "readiness for affect," accustomed neural pathways prepared and sensitized for psychic affective discharge when activated by an appropriate, even minimal, stimulus. Both may apply as well to potential cognitive formations, and also to the more complete fantasies resulting from the combinations of these elements. Fantasies in habitual existence, whether in unconscious or in conscious life, lie in readiness for a stimulus to set them off. The repetition compulsion is the best known form of this dynamic state. Long-lasting experiences, from chronic environmental conditions, internally and externally, and their compulsive repetition in fantasies and trial actions, come to facilitate pathways for psychic and their underlying neural discharge.

There are unformed or preformed fantasies (Freud, 1900; Arlow, 1969) waiting to be finished. These are usually characteristic, of long standing, and developmentally and experientially determined. A patient revealed, after resistances were removed, a fact he had been ashamed to admit, that he could not resist making a certain detour on his way to the analyst's office. The patient was in a protracted period of presumably terminating an extramarital affair he had carried on for years. His girlfriend had told him that a lady friend of hers had taken in a young college student as a boarder who would occupy one of her unused bedrooms. On his way to the analyst early that morning, the patient had driven a half mile out of his way to pass the house of this friend of his girlfriend. The motive was to see either whether his girlfriend's car was parked there or whether there was another car, which he would check for later in his girlfriend's driveway. He wanted to see whether his girlfriend, in separating from the patient, had started an affair with this young student. There was no reason in reality to support this thought. The patient was attempting to construct a piece of reality that would facilitate the stability of a potential and habitual fantasy of his, for the psychic effects it would produce in him. Only some of these were conscious; the bulk of the sustaining mechanisms were not. These, and their developmental and etiological determinants, became known and were brought under greater ego control during the analysis.

CONTENTS

All intrapsychic elements, cognitive and affective, find a place or play a part in the construction of the final unconscious fantasy. As instinctual impulses are filtered through the ego in a tentative trial action to test for signal anxiety, memories are scanned for previous indications of safety or danger. The fantasies which emerge following these trial actions take into account and contain within themselves any or all elements of the results of the scanning processes which preceded them. Memories are righted, i.e., carried to further success than they were originally. Accompanying affects are integrated, filtered, or defended against, and become part of the total unconscious product. Self- and object representations also participate and are grist for the mill. They too are elaborated, worked upon, and utilized in the unconscious fantasies which result.

Fantasies contain, in distorted and undistorted form, the memories brought forth during the intrapsychic scanning for signal anxiety. The memories embedded in the contents of fantasy, extracted from the store of memories, are added to, modified, distorted, and refashioned in accordance with current instinctual wishes within the confines permitted by defenses. Memories which are not traumatic or forbidden can retain their actual or close-to-actual forms. Traumatic memories of minor degree which the ego feels capable of mastering can also be admitted within the scanning process, as close to actuality as possible, until the traumatic effects are mitigated and repetition rendered no longer necessary. Distortions of memories in fantasy come about when the traumatic experience which accompanied them are beyond the ego's capacity to manage. More accurate memories may also be contaminated by previous fantasy formations having acted upon them at earlier stages. Memories brought up at any particular moment are thus a composite of already-distorted subjective products.

More direct derivatives of instinctual wishes also constitute part of the data and contents of unconscious fantasies. In some instances transient and occasional, in others more frequent and habitual, "Walter Mitty" type fantasies have been written about and almost institutionalized as a symbol of the most complex wishful fantasy thinking. Drive and wishful aspects of fantasies can be seen in masturbation fantasies, with special prognostic and diagnostic import, as when described as pathognomonic during adolescence (Laufer, 1976; Laufer and Laufer, 1984).

The same applies qualitatively on a wider scale to sexual fantasies throughout life. Not only can a sexual fantasy during a heterosexual act reveal a diagnostic homosexual impulse, but the nature of heterosexuality itself may be revealed through the route of conscious and unconscious fantasies. A patient, while having intercourse with a "nice wifely woman" by whom he is not turned on, fantasizes another female who combines the voluptuous, "dirty" sexiness necessary for his sexual turn-on, along with soft, buxom maternal qualities. The particular combination points clearly to his historical experience with his oedipal mother. His memories of "intoxicating" sexual feelings while in his mother's bathroom, feeling and smelling her undergarments, became part of his forbidden oedipal sexual life relegated to fantasy and never to be fulfilled. In life he lived and portrayed the common split between the sexpot and the Madonna.

The same applies within the homosexual spectrum. Anna Freud (1951) and Arlow (1969) note that the specific fantasies entertained during homosexual sex are more indicative of sexual orientation and drive-wishes (i.e., receptive-masochistic or active-sadistic) than what the partners actually do with each other. For example, a patient is not only poised between heterosexuality and homosexuality but has another crucial dichotomy within the latter. Within his homosexuality, the patient has a fantasy of "going down" on his partner, performing fellatio and anilingus, assuming the female role to the male. When he actually comes to perform sexually, however, he automatically reverses roles, discards the fantasy, and requires his partner to do to him what he would in fantasy do to the other. Analysis brings out the unconscious anxiety responsible for the switch in roles. The fantasied role is abandoned not because of a change in desire but because of castration anxiety. The fantasy in action would leave him without a penis. Analysis further points to the historical fact that the fantasy itself was adopted during his early adolescence, or younger, as a solution to still deeper unconscious anxiety. The reasons for this resided in his oedipal wishes.

These variations on both sides of the sexual border, and within each side as well, are intermediate products which have at their base a forbidden oedipal impulse accompanied by severe castration anxiety, which also typically rest on a pregenital base. The sexual fantasies, in their varied and complex forms, operate from the unconscious, as a result of which the drive to heterosexual achievement is repressed and forbidden.

The contents of the superego, as of instinctual wishes, may also be expressed in cognitive form. Representatives of both are present in various forms in the fantasy, either directly, distorted, or within compromise formations. As repositories of object relations, fantasies also reveal determining object choices of the ego at the particular intrapsychic moments of their origin or during their extant states. Every shade of conflict is represented within the makeup of the fantasies—heterosexual, pregenital and oedipal, latent homosexual and subtle variations within each. Partial impulses and tentative defenses, interchanges between all psychic structures, combinations of cognitive elements, experimental actions, and tentative affective accompaniments are extracted, distilled, and synthesized within the unconscious fantasy. Memories, wishes, self- and object representations within the ego, superego contents, and associated external perceptions are all reintegrated—by secondary revision—in the unconscious fantasy as in the dreams of sleep.

DEVELOPMENTAL ASPECTS

Unconscious fantasy, like any other mental constellation, undergoes its own developmental history and vicissitudes. It probably begins with the hallucination of the lost object, as Rosen (1960) notes with regard to imagination, or before that of the partial rather than whole object (i.e., the absent breast), as Rapaport (1950, 1951b, 1953) describes the models for thought and affect. Such fantasies can be seen forming and can also be inferred from direct and observed behavior during the progress of early life. As with sexual fantasies, many other fantasies crucial to later life may be actualized in late adolescence (Laufer, 1976; Laufer and Laufer, 1984). One sees the face, as also the character, become relatively final at that age. Blum (1985) describes the role played by shared fantasies between mother and child throughout the child's developmental process, as well as the many instances of reciprocal influences on shared fantasies in object relationships in later life.

Childhood fantasies, such as those often subsumed under the concept of the family romance, can take root at an early age and last throughout a life, greatly affecting it. I have seen them exert their effects through generations. One patient grew up in a ghetto behind her father's meager tailor shop. Her mother constantly berated and humiliated the passive, kind father. Unable to conceive, the mother went to a gynecologist for help. According to the patient's reality-fantasy-history, the physician helped the mother by impregnating her himself. When the patient was about five, her mother imparted this information to her during one of her stormy and derisive attacks against the father. The story was repeated periodically during the patient's childhood and became a fixed and intrinsic part of the patient's fantasy life.

The patient once came upon the mother kissing and embracing a neighbor in the kitchen. Shortly afterwards, following the birth of a younger brother, the mother told the patient, again after an argument with the father and by way of belittling him, that the brother was fathered by still another neighbor. The patient thus grew up with two mental fathers, the "Papa" whom she loved and protected, and the image of a tall, elegant physician rich and socially prominent, who had sired her and watched over her (in fact, she had never met or even seen him).

Hard-working, dreaming, and ambitious, the patient pulled herself out of her deprived life by dressing elegantly and standing tall. She became a model, developed an affected manner of speech, and placed herself in positions where she might find a husband comparable to her ego ideal father. With her fantasy success she would also take care of Papa. She came close but failed to marry a tall doctor, but did marry a wealthy and socially prominent man in a closely related profession. A son later fulfilled her fantasy more precisely, and became the tall, good-looking, suave, and successful physician her fantasied biological father had been.

An early fantasy can exert a positive motivational function or a negative and inhibiting one. One patient, brought up by a good mother and a destructive stepfather, was told by her mother at an early age that she had married this man, whom they both grew to hate, to give the little girl a father. Whatever the mother intended by imparting this information—she may have meant to express her love for the child for whom she had sacrificed her own happiness—the patient grew up feeling that she was responsible for their mistreatment. A sense of guilt and a feeling of unworthiness were combined, and constituted the unconscious affect behind much of her inner fantasy life, as well as her attitudes, behavior, and decisions in life. Another patient, whose father left his mother when she was pregnant with him, was told by his mother as early as he could remember, that the mother had married the father, whom she always spoke of in damning tones, only in order to have her son. The patient grew up with the feeling of being both special and especially deprived. His physical and emotional closeness to his mother, and the ever-present and continuously elaborated image of the absent, uncaring father, led to a self-representation, and to a confusion and pathology of sexual identity, which have been at the center of his neurotic and uneven bisexual life.

Many things happen to influence and direct the course of a life. The purpose of these brief vignettes is not to deny this complexity but to point up instances of the effects of pervasive lifelong fantasy, early incorporated, of origins and destiny. Here can be found the origins of ambition. Arlow (1969) describes how unconscious fantasies can intrude into conscious experience, not only affecting dreams, symptoms, and the pathological behavior of everyday life, but becoming a constant feature of mental life and of the psychoanalytic process as well. Grossman (1982) remarks that our concept of fantasy should not be a static one, and should play a more important role in our "complex structures that have an affect on mental organization as well. They are both an aspect of mental organization and have an effect on it" (p. 926).

DERIVATIVES

Combinations of unconscious fantasies become the anlagen and background for character, i.e., for predictable behavior. Coherent groups of chronic fantasies, which may play a major role in determining character formation, are responsible for a readiness for relationships to external objects and the outer world, what the character will be expected to perceive from the latter, and how it will act toward them. Unconscious fantasies are intrapsychic trial actions formed and organized and extended over time. Unstable and transient, even for long periods, eventually they lead to derivatives. As substitutes for action, they last so long as defensive action, and the prevention of outer behavior, remain necessary.

Enduring fantasies become part of character. Chronic, they can be structuralized psychologically or even somatically. An individual of rigid and unbending character may reflect the same characteristic in the somatic posture of spondylosis. Character traits emanating from unconscious fantasies can be displayed in habits, mannerisms, small actions, and "characteristic" behavior. One person reveals a chronic structured stinginess—based on an unconscious fantasy of preserving and withholding—by a quick impulsive action to be the first to tip in a restaurant, although the amount is always conspicuously insufficient. Another, through a similar reaction-formation, displays an exhibitionistic generosity and an automatic expression of concern and kindness which palls on the recipient, and unmistakably conveys an underlying hostility and withholdingness.

One patient of mine has, built in to his self- and object representational world, a visual fantasy that is an intrinsic part of his characterological attitudes: the concept of his father having big, broad wrists. This anatomical "memory" is elaborated, in the patient's object representation of his paternal introject, into the fantasy concept of his father as huge and powerful, next to whom the patient is of course puny and impotent. This fantasy of himself as castrated, which comes out clearly in associations, lives chronically within him. It remains unaffected by the fact that the patient is a foot taller than his father, weighs more, and is a superior athlete. His father is in fact undersized and physically weak. Nevertheless this memory-fantasy of his father's broad and powerful wrists maintains the patient's perception of himself as inferior and castrated.

In another instance, two close sisters have maintained their perceptions of each other for life. Now seventy-five to her sister's eighty, the younger, still stately and beautiful, cringes before her pudgy older sister, before whom she has always felt small and ugly. Identifying these unconscious fantasies embedded chronically within characterological attitudes, and separating them from reality, is a distinct advance during the course of psychoanalytic treatment.

From these intermediate mental products, the further course of the intrapsychic process, brought about by continuing impulsion toward action and by an instability in the relations among id, ego, superego, and external world, leads to the variety of behavioral outcomes that make up the lives of human beings, individually and in groups. Unconscious fantasies, temporary in nature, may precede symptom formation or, in the absence of symptoms, may issue in distorted and inhibited action. A common outcome, one seen since the advent of psychoanalysis as almost intrinsic to the conduct of complex human life, is psychoneurosis.

Derivatives of unconscious fantasy are in a state of constant formation, with an ongoing interplay between inner and outer. If, at the moment stimuli to action impinge from the outer world, discharge from within is unimpeded, external action may result. External moods are another kind of derivative, and may also be accompaniments of unconscious fantasies. In more complex situations, with instinctual pressures continuously being exerted from within, and defenses against them proving insufficient, symptom formation is an outlet. An ego-syntonic intrapsychic fantasy is then superseded by an ego-dystonic external symptom. The latter can be stable or can itself be in a state of partial or complete decompensation, in either instance resembling certain dream states; e.g., an unstable symptom break down into an anxiety state as a dream can fail and end up as a nightmare.

TREATMENT

Psychoanalytic treatment, when it deals with the analysis of unconscious fantasies, works through these mental products, as with symptoms or dreams, toward the psychic elements that cause them. The psychoanalytic process proceeds from the surface through the various strata of intermediate products—which include the unconscious fantasies and unconscious affects of earlier developmental stages—toward their origins in the bedrock of infantile neurosis. As an ego-syntonic psychic formation, unconscious fantasy is more resistant to exploration and exposure than is the ego-alien symptom, but at the same time it can be more revealing of undisguised wishes and successful defense. Closer to the unconscious and to developmental origins, it can also be more indicative of the etiology and conflicts of preliminary solutions.

Today a trend is discernible toward misuse of the insights afforded by unconscious fantasies. Too often psychoanalysis is viewed as directed mainly or solely to uncovering these unconscious products, which are seen as ends rather than as way stations toward earlier formative forces and events. The role of unconscious fantasies, either in the part they play in the psychoanalytic process, or as a determinant of behavior in general or neurosogenesis in particular, should not be reified. Beres (1962) felt it necessary to protect the concept "from becoming a cliché or an item of technical jargon" (p. 309). Beyond psychoanalysis proper, the idea of unconscious fantasy has captured the popular imagination and spawned such extra-analytic versions as "games people play" (Berne, 1964). Projective identification has suffered such a fate, as did earlier the concept of identity crisis. Early enthusiasm leads to overuse, distortion, and misapplication. This can happen to useful formulations and authentic mechanisms as much as to spurious ones. For instance Mahler's discovery (1972) of the important role of rapprochement conflicts tends currently to produce explanations of the most complex later behavior as linked automatically to a presumed crisis in early childhood.

For a final example of how the psychoanalytic process retrogressively pursues the development of fantasies, and through them the origins of neurosis, I will return to the case of the patient, referred to above, who drove out of his way in an attempt to confirm in reality a sexual fantasy of his girlfriend with another man. Throughout his entire affair with the woman, the patient had struggled with the thought of whether his wife knew. It also came out in the analysis that he and his wife had evolved, as central to their own sexual life, a story they made up together, which was erotically stimulating to both of them, of another woman being present during their lovemaking. The patient's affair was a living out in action of this conscious fantasy, the unconscious aspects of which were repressed.

This ménage à trois fantasy was structured but the identities of the dramatis personae, and even their sexes, were fluid and could be filled in. With his girlfriend the patient was curious to the point of obsession about her other relationships, fantasying her with her lover, with himself as onlooker or participant. The unconscious homosexuality fluctuated between the two males, the patient and his male rival, or two females, his wife and the fantasied female onlooker-partner together. Voyeurism, exhibitionism, and homosexuality played various roles in both constellations.

When the patient found himself compulsively turning off course on his way to analysis, he was unaware of being pulled by his unconscious fantasy. He was just "checking up." By increments of insight, he came to understand first that he was jealous, and then that he had himself created the conditions for his jealousy; for example, he had once introduced his girlfriend to a potential husband, presumably so he could the more easily end the affair. With further insight the full triadic fantasy emerged into conscious awareness. The patient realized the connection of his voyeuristic jealously with previous situations. Every time his girlfriend began a serious relationship which might conceivably lead to marriage, a prospect to which the patient consciously gave support, his possessiveness and his sexual interest in her would flare up anew. And when suitors were not actually available, he would suspect their presence, creating them out of thin air, as in the present instance.

This complex had a long developmental history, with roots in early childhood. Between then and the present, several crucial experiences occurred. One was his being cuckolded by his first wife twenty years previously. For five years she had engaged in extramarital affairs, toward which he was extremely tolerant before finally leaving her. Another episode was in adolescence, when he gave his athletic medal to his first serious girlfriend. One day he saw that she was no longer wearing it. He was crushed; it meant she had given him up for another. Now, in his current conduct, he was converting passive into active, doing to his present wife what had been done to him in at least two instances.

Both of these experiences were intermediate to an earlier decisive period. As a child he was the only boy living with three grown women— his mother, his grandmother, and a maiden aunt—and an ineffectual father they all disparaged. The women doted on the patient and appeared before him in seductive carelessness, often sitting on his bed in their nightgowns. He could remember intense sexual excitement as well as the imperative need to conceal any external sign of it. Castration anxiety, along with a deep sense of phallic inferiority, in relation even to the depreciated father, overlay a preexisting and equally strong sense of stimulation, frustration, helplessness, and danger stemming from the preoedipal period.

Analysis traced the historical connections between these pervasive early feelings and the series of unconscious fantasies and external actions described in this patient's case history. Fantasies—their formation, existence, perseverance, and repetition—are a fertile vein for exploration, as their dissolution or change in character is an indication of the effects of the therapeutic process or other influencing events of life. Changes in fantasies, conscious and unconscious, including their disappearance are a measure of the changed intrapsychic conditions which bring them about.

REFERENCES

Arlow, J. A. (1961). Ego psychology and the study of mythology. *J. Amer. Psychoanal. Assn.* 9:371–393.

———— (1963), Conflict, regression, and symptom formation. *Internat. J. Psycho-Anal.*, 44:12–22.

————(1969), Unconscious fantasy and disturbances of conscious experience. *Psychoanal. Quart.*, 38:1–27.

Beres, D. (1960), Psychoanalytic psychology of imagination. *J. Amer. Psychoanal. Assn.*, 8:252–269.

———— (1962), The unconscious fantasy. *Psychoanal. Quart.*, 31:309–328.

Berne, E. (1964), *Games People Play.* New York: Grove Press.

Blum, H. (1985), Shared fantasy and reciprocal identification: Psychoanalytic studies and *Macbeth*. Freud Anniversary Lecture, the Psychoanalytic Association of New York, April 29.

Fenichel, O. (1945), *The Psychoanalytic Theory of Neurosis.* New York: Norton.

Freud, A. (1937), *The Ego and the Mechanisms of Defense.* Rev. ed. New York: International Universities Press, 1966.

———— (1951), Some clinical remarks concerning the treatment of cases of male homosexuality (abstract). *Bull Amer. Psychoanal. Assn.*, 7:117–118.

Freud, S. (1900), The interpretation of dreams, *Standard Edition*, 4/5. London: Hogarth Press, 1953.

———— (1915), The unconscious. *Standard Edition.* 14:166–215. London: Hogarth Press, 1957.

———— (1920), Beyond the pleasure principle. *Standard Edition*, 18:7–64. London: Hogarth Press, 1955.

———— (1923), The ego and the id. *Standard Edition*, 19:12–66. London: Hogarth Press, 1951.

———— (1926), Inhibitions, symptoms and anxiety. *Standard Edition*, 20:87–174. London: Hogarth Press, 1959.

Grossman, W. (1982), The self as fantasy: Fantasy as theory. *J. Amer. Psychoanal. Assn.*, 30:919–937.

Hartmann, H. (1939), *Ego Psychology and the Problem of Adaptation.* New York: International Universities Press, 1958.

Isakower, O. (1938), A contribution to the pathopsychology of phenomena associated with falling asleep. *Internat. J. Psycho-Anal.* 19:331–345.

Jacobson, E. (1953), The affects and their pleasure-unpleasure qualities, in relation to the psychic discharge processes. In: *Drives, Affects, Behavior*, Vol. 1, ed. R. Loewenstein. New York: International Universities Press, pp. 38–66.

———— (1964), *The Self and the Object World.* New York: International Universities Press.

Laufer, M. (1976), The central masturbation fantasy, the final sexual organization, and adolescence. *The Psychoanalytic Study of the Child,* 31:297–316. New Haven, CT: Yale University Press.

_____ & Laufer, M. E. (1984), *Adolescence and Developmental Breakdown.* New Haven, CT: Yale University Press.

Mahler, M. (1972), Rapprochement subphase of the separation-individuation process. *Psychoanal. Quart.* 41:487–506.

Pulver, S. (1974), Can affects be unconscious? *Internat. J. Psycho-Anal.,* 52:347–354.

Rangell, L. (1963a), The scope of intrapsychic conflict: Microscopic and macroscopic considerations. *The Psychoanalytic Study of the Child,* 18:75–102. New York: International Universities Press.

_____ (1963b), Structural problems in intrapsychic conflict. *The Psychoanalytic Study of the Child,* 18:103–138. New York: International Universities Press.

_____ (1969), The intrapsychic process and its analysis: a recent line of thought and its current implications. *Internat. J. Psycho-Anal.* 50:65–77.

_____ (1971), The decision-making process: A contribution from psychoanalysis. *The Psychoanalytic Study of the Child,* 26:425–452. New York: Quadrangle.

_____ (1986), The executive functions of the ego: An extension of the concept of ego autonomy. *The Psychoanalytic Study of the Child,* 41:1–37. New Haven, CT: Yale University Press.

Rapaport, D. (1950), On the psychoanalytic theory of thinking. *Internat. J. Psycho-Anal.,* 31:161–170.

_____ (1951a), The autonomy of the ego. *Bull. Menn. Clin.* 15:113–123.

_____ (1951b), *Organization and Pathology of Thought: Selected Sources.* New York: Columbia University Press.

_____ (1953), On the psychoanalytic theory of affects. *Internat. J. Psycho-Anal.,* 34:177–198.

_____ (1958), The theory of ego autonomy: A generalization. *Bull. Menn. Clin.,* 22:13–35.

Rosen, V. (1960), Imagination in the analytic process. *J. Amer. Psychoanal. Assn.,* 8:252–269.

Sandler, J., & Nagera, H. (1963), Aspects of the metapsychology of fantasy. *The Psychoanalytic Study of the Child,* 18:159–194. New York: International Universities Press.

Schafer, R. (1976), *A New Language for Psychoanalysis.* New Haven, CT: Yale University Press.

5

The Unconscious and Unconscious Fantasy: Language and Psychoanalysis

Theodore Shapiro, M.D.

Unconscious fantasy has been a core concept in psychoanalysis from the very beginning. The interpretive aim of making the unconscious conscious was, along with the discharge of affects, a key to insight and cure in early Freudian practice. This approach, of course, was based upon topographic theory and the model of repression. The system Ucs. was described as governed by the economic principle of primary process and mobility of cathexis. It was seen also as the receptacle of unconscious psychic contents. Thus, the unconscious had status as a *noun*. However, it also had to obey the functional imperatives of drive theory and permit peremptoriness and displaceability in order to account for transformations into the various representational forms known as derivatives.

This early theory permitted an adequate description of how the human psyche represented and symbolized, but it did not address the contradiction implied in cathectic mobility and stable unconscious structures that repeatedly sought emergence into consciousness. However, it did provide for a system where a few fixed forms expressing the rock bottom needs of the person could be transformed into innumerable and varied fantasies that could be interpreted in the analytic situation. Thus, fantasy, symptom, dream, and symptomatic action could individually and together represent but a few deep fantasies residing in a potentially realizable mental organization.

This contradiction between infinite variability and structured unconscious was addressed by Klein (1970) in the idea that Freud espoused two theories, one biological and the other psychological. The contradiction accounts in part for the sanction of authority claimed for the recent shift in emphasis by psychoanalysts from drive theory towards a hermeneutic approach, concentrating on systems of meaning whereby patients' stories are viewed as analogues of written narratives (Spence, 1983).

Jacob Arlow has concentrated on the role of unconscious fantasy in mental life and on explicating Freud's structural theory and its ramifications for ego psychology. He, along with Brenner, showed the psychoanalytic world the virtue of shifting from a noun concept of the unconscious to an adjectival form of descriptive unconscious (Arlow and Brenner, 1964). Fantasies were no longer to be classified with respect to presumed residence but rather with respect to their representability in consciousness. From this perpective, Arlow and Brenner suggested that the topographic notion of the preconscious is superfluous and moved seriously to consider how fantasies are represented and which ego functions are operative in the formation of compromise. Nowhere in the psychoanalytic literature is Anna Freud's reminder (1937) of our empirical clinical stance more prominent than in Arlow's work. That reminder is that we never see the id in its pure form, but always through the filter of the ego. Arlow confronts the tendency to reify theoretical structure full face, forcing us to reconsider the idea that our work proceeds from surface to depth rather than from concept to data. That is, our work model is to listen to patients, watch patients, and hear verbal productions that can then be reduced for understanding to a few paradigmatic formats that cohere with a continuum of universal circumstance that make up the human condition. Thus, our work is designed to permit data reduction to a few deeper structures that give meaning and cohesion to protean representations. Patients' productions and actions are thereby rendered recognizable in new formats rather than obscured in the seemingly unconnected actions and words that otherwise might strike the untrained observer as a jumble of confusion.

Arlow's "Masturbation and Symptom Formation" (1953) is an exemplary clinical exercise in understanding representability and the drivenness and need for symbolic representation over the life span. He did not respond to the rather fruitless arguments raging then over the reality or verifiability of drives, but instead used the concept of conflict representation and the notion of the body as the source of the work the mind has to do in order to show clinicians the central assumptions that underlie psychoanalytic work. Arlow's contributions, based solidly in Freud's work, are nonetheless original in their integration of new observations into well-formed concepts. In 1969 he cited an important and forward-looking observation from Freud's "The Unconscious" (1915):

> Among the derivatives of the Ucs. instinctual impulses . . . there
> are some which unite in themselves characters of an opposite kind.
> On the one hand, they are highly organized, free from self-
> contradiction, have made use of every acquisition of the system Cs.
> and would hardly be distinguished in our judgement from the forma-
> tions of that system. On the other hand they are unconscious and are
> incapable of becoming conscious. Thus, *qualitatively* they belong to the
> system Pcs, but *factually* to the Ucs.
>   Of such a nature are those fantasies of normal people as well as the
> neurotics which we have recognized as preliminary stages in the for-
> mation of both dreams and of symptoms and which, in spite of their
> high degree of organization, remain repressed and therefore cannot
> become conscious [pp. 190–191].

Arlow (1969) considered these remarks a prescient statement of the structural hypothesis, noting that accessibility to consciousness is not a reliable
criterion for the selection of material with which to erect psychic systems.
The fantasies mentioned by Freud, he wrote, "have inner consistency,
i.e., they are highly organized" (p. 3). In a more recent paper on psychic
reality, Arlow (1985) addressed the organization of inner experience, again
elaborating his view of unconscious fantasy. He characterized the
psychoanalytic view of mind as a psychology of conflict and the analytic
situation as one skewed in the direction of facilitating the emergence of
derivatives of unconscious conflicts originating during childhood. Thus,
unconscious resolutions of conflict in fantasy reside as anachronistic
residues in the mental life of individuals and are expressed in various
experiences explored in the analytic situation.

In a lesser known work Arlow (1977), discussing papers by ex-
perimentalists, stated, "If some mode of study could be envisioned which
would enable the observer to link the simple word units of metaphorical
significance with the inferrable context of meaning, we would have a
most useful instrument for studying communication in a therapeutic relationship" (p. 444); "for the interpretation to be valid and meaningful,"
he continued, "the intuitively derived conclusions must be subject to
a cognitive matching with the material, to a conscious organization of
the evidence into meaningful relationships" (p. 445).

With these words Arlow brings himself well into line with the notion that understanding unconscious fantasy is essential to the psychoanalytic process and method and that the continued interpretation of conscious derivatives in the analytic situation is the medium by which our work is distinguished from other therapies even during the 1980s. Moveover, Freud's paper on the unconscious (1915) harks back to his earlier work on aphasia (1891) and "The Interpretation of Dreams" (1900), in which he struggles to bring together the notions of thing presentation and word presentation. These concepts provide an essential continuity in his thought regarding the task of analyzing and verbalizing the unconscious fantasy. My focus on unconscious fantasy should not be taken to mean that I discount the analysis of defense and resistance; if the latter two concepts are neglected here, it is done simply in the interest of economy of exposition.

Insofar, then, as the analytic task and the aim of theory are advanced by the interpretation of unconscious fantasy, we must know how such interpretation is possible, and how it comes about. It is in this light that our interest in symbol formation, the linguistic mode of expression, and the mechanisms underlying these processes must be considered. I will argue here, as I have elsewhere (Shapiro, 1970, 1979, 1983, 1986), that it is useful for analysts to consider unconscious fantasy as a universal disposition that underlies behavior and thought and is organized in a linguistic format. Indeed the very format of language, its formal structure and its capacity to represent agency, action, and object, past and future potentiality, and conditionals—provides the only means by which analysis can take place as a rational enterprise undertaken by analyst and analysand. However, the conceptual link between drive and the insistence toward representation in the various enactments of unconscious fantasy as formed dispositions must be clarified in order to undo some theoretical confusions.

In this vein, both Freud (1915) and Schur (1966) considered unconscious fantasies to be modifiable. They considered the id to be a metapsychological entity that allows for adaptive response to external influences, though traditionally we view adaptation as a function restricted to the ego. A central proposition of this chapter, then, is that inborn propensities mark the human mind as a symbol-forming organ constrained by determinate limits. In addition, the evolution of the mental apparatus from childhood into adulthood is subject to variation due to experience, perception, and the organization of meaning, which is the most developed faculty of the human species. I hold, with Arlow, that unconscious fantasies are sequestered from awareness because of defensive fuctions and that they are formed in early childhood. Moreover, the link between repetitive adult action and thought deriving from the past provides a key to our understanding of how analysts proceed and even of how analysis works. I will argue that the format of interpretation in language is the only conceivable formal organization whereby such complex ideas may be communicated to patients. As such constructions serve to broaden the ego's scope in achieving its dominance over the id, it is useful to look at what is known about language acquistion as an aid to defining the limits within which we can understand human fantasies as they persist or are formed in adults.

THE LIMITS OF HUMAN EXPRESSION
IN LANGUAGE

Wittgenstein (1921) ended his impressive tract on philosophical logic with the eminently quotable, "What we cannot speak about we must pass over in silence" (p. 151). This text has been variously understood, but it can most parsimoniously be viewed as a comment on the limits imposed on human communication by the constraint of verbal formats. While various modes of nonverbal communication and nonrational communions have been described (see James, 1902; Stern, 1985), we must be able to express relationships of any complexity in oral or written formats if we are to consider them common property whether for scientific exchange by large audiences or in two-person dialogues. Language is our most parsimonious and pragmatically functional medium for the communication of experiences whether of the outer or the inner world. Yet language is thought to be a social enterprise and therefore an aspect of ego functioning that serves not only in adaptation but in the apprehension of external reality. How does this skill emerge, and what competence does it presuppose?

During the earlier part of this century, a controversy developed between Piaget (1934) and Vygotsky (1934) that is worth reviewing here, as it mirrors a problem that Freud (1915) struggled with and that Schur (1966), Arlow (1969) and Beres (1962) have also addressed. If unconscious functioning is closer in its organization to organismic neural structures, and if preconscious and conscious thought are influenced by adaptation to the external world, how is it that fluidity of action among these systems is possible? The controversy between Piaget and Vygotsky evolved in the following manner. Piaget described the earliest expressions of children's language as at first egocentric, only gradually turning toward socialized expression. Against this conception Vygotsky argued that it is difficult to conceive of the formed speech that we consider the earliest expression of language as having originally been egocentric, as it is learned in communities within cultures. While there is evidence of prelinguistic thought, language formats are learned in a social environment and then internalized. Once thought is linked to language, grammatical and logical organizations take hold of our thought organizations, constraining them inextricably. These formats then become the dominant mode of human communication. Socialized language is social at the outset, but it is mapped onto a preformed native competence in the individual.

There is some similarity between this view and Freud's suggestion (1911) that as thought becomes increasingly dominated by secondary process organization a portion of our thought continues to obey the rules of primary process and wish fulfillment; this portion he called fantasy. Although Freud did not examine the source of language, he did refer to the kind of thought that precedes and influences the linguistic format. Even fantasies have grammatical form; Arlow's conception that daydreaming is more closely linked to unconscious functioning than to conscious thought is an analogous idea. Nonetheless, both daydreams and more logically organized thought are finally represented and communicated in verbal formats, as are well-structured interpretation. Indeed, even as the analyst gathers the various experiences that he reduces to what we call an unconscious fantasy, he is formulating the multiplicity of individual experience into the manageably small units of language we call interpretations (Shapiro, 1970). Indeed, we ordinarily reserve the word ''interpretation'' for a specialized format whose structure points to unconscious conflict. The general form of conflict interpretation must include an agent, opposing forces, and an explanation of these to the effect that the expression of the ideas represented is compromised because they are intolerable to consciousness or to the civilized sensibilities of others. The classical interpretation can be stated in the following general form: You (the patient) wish either to receive or to do something that is opposed by a judgment that such a wish is unacceptable, either to you or to others, because of varying social conventions or personal ideas of prohibition (an id wish is compromised by an ego mechanism at the behest of a superego prohibition). An extension of this basic format is that the wish that cannot be expressed was formed during childhood in accord

both with the way in which the immature mental apparatus apprehended the world and with the social judgments deriving from that period.
Thus, unconscious fantasies become unacceptable to awareness because
at the time of formation the individual was ignorant of restraints to be
exercised later in life. Because with development surplus meanings (and
therefore prohibitive aims) accrue that were not evident when the wish
was formed, it occurred to Freud that an unconscious fantasy is stimulated
only by circumstances that later in life serve as metaphoric entrepreneurs
of the idea.

A recent emphasis on the hermeneutic understanding of
psychoanalysis, including Schafer's promulgation of action language as
an extension of psychoanalytic theory (1976), brings us full circle to
another reformulation. The analyst could not state or communicate an
interpretation were the central premise that unconscious fantasies are
organized in linguistic formats not accepted. Wittgenstein may be correct that science or for that matter thought of any sort, even psychoanalysis, cannot move beyond the language that is available to express
its most concise formulations. Could this be what Lacan (1956) meant
when he suggested that the unconscious is organized like a language,
the discourse of the Other? And is this not also Vygotsky's contention
that the continuing impact on the rationality of our thought is derived
from socially communicative sources?

From a developmental viewpoint, there is a long preverbal period
in which the innate competence for linguistic formats is not evident. Could
this be the basis of Freud's assertion concerning the tendency to refor-
mulate preoedipal wishes via regressions from oedipal fantasies and Anna
Freud's assertion that the preverbal period is a psychoanalytic ice age.
That is, we formulate these early tendencies only after language can
encode them. Prior to that time they are not apprehended in such precise
terms. If we had no words with which to communicate, we would certainly be left in a quandary as to how to interpret early experiences.
Arlow's thought (1985) extends this notion, identifying regressions from
oedipal constellations as the central mechanism through which unconscious aims and fantasies are understood. However, Arlow (1977) has
also suggested that if we take into account the context of meaning with
the patient, and use the analyst in the transference as a symbolic foil
for earlier wishes, we have an arrangement in which it is possible to find
not only redundancy in content but in interpersonal constellations. These
constellations become alive again in the psychoanalytic situation:

I frequently cite the experience of a patient who began her session by speaking slowly, promising to discuss a dream, finding reasons why she should not present it, then intellectualizing at great length about whether the dream was a defense, a resistance to the investigation of our problem, a combination of both or a further expression of the difficulties which had been under consideration. She returns to her intention to tell the dream, but finds reasons for not doing so at the particular moment. She thinks she could be responding in this way because of what she had learned recently in her treatment, but then again, she is not sure that this is so. The patient continued in this vein for most of the session, finally describing a portion of the dream, apologizing for not giving all of it, explaining that she could not complete the presentation of the dream, and returning to the kind of communication reported earlier in the session. When I used this material for teaching purposes, I asked the class to describe their own affective responses to the material. After a momentary silence, what usually followed was a spontaneous, contagious, outburst of laughter as the individuals in the group sensed their relief upon discovering that the other members of the group had felt the same sense of boredom, irritation, and impatience which they had experienced individually. They had all felt frustrated. To continue with the report: it took several sessions for this patient finally to get around to completing the presentation of her dream. The content of the dream expressed the wish to frustrate the therapist, making him feel incompetent and impotent to deal with her resistances. But this idea had already been communicated in the first ten or fifteen minutes of the session by the form of her presentation. The analysis of the form was as sure a guide to the content the patient meant to communicate as the analysis of the dream could have been. Actually, by the time the total dream was presented, the dream was superfluous for either purposes of communication or interpretation [Arlow, 1977, pp. 445-446].

Arlow offers the interpretation that the disguised wish to defeat and bore the analyst is tantamount to the desire to undermine his competence, to castrate him, a purpose that is expressed in at least two ways: once in the interaction, and once in the content of the dream. No doubt at other times in the analysis it has found expression in other communicative vehicles. This redundancy of expression and vehicular fluidity is intriguing from the standpoint of the integration of knowledge in linguistic form.

THE DEVELOPMENT AND FORM OF
LANGUAGE EXPRESSION

Linguists have long had their differences regarding the most useful approaches to studying language. Roughly speaking, they divide their enterprise into considerations of (1) grammar and syntax, (2) semantics and reference, and (3) pragmatics or interactional rules. Beginning in 1957, Chomsky created a revolution in linguistics by focusing on generative grammar, a development addressed only cursorily by analysts (Shapiro, 1970, 1979; Rosen, 1977). Edelson (1972) thought that the idea of deep and surface structure in Chomsky's model bears an important relation to the psychoanalytic distinction between manifest and latent dream content. These notions, though not readily adopted by analysts, provide a systematic formulation of the analytic suggestion that the great number of possible sentences, ideas, and images may be accounted for on the basis of a few formats or paradigms already available in deep structural organizations as a native competence rooted in either the hard wiring of the human nervous system or in evolutionarily selected response systems. This approaches the idea that there are very few universal fantasies and only one oedipus complex, but that their derivatives may form an infinite variety of conscious fantasies, enactments, dreams, and symbols.

The second linguistic area, that of semantics, concerns itself with the ways in which words refer to things and ideas, and with the polysemantic nature of verbal presentations. This approach to language has drawn attention from a number of analysts in the last two decades (Edelheit, 1969; Rosen, 1977; Shapiro, 1979). Rosen addressed the question of representability in varying conditions of pathology, Edelheit concentrated on primal scene representations, and I considered the interpretation of unconscious fantasy as a naming procedure. Freud's (1900) own work on thing presentation and word presentation is of great relevance to the concepts of meaning and representability.

The third area of linguistics, pragmatics, has been relatively neglected by analysts, but has lately drawn more attention from practical linguists. Pragmatics addresses the formats of dialogue, not just kinesics, but the ways in which people create and sustain conversation, take turns, express intentions, and even mimic the structure of sentences, verbalizations, and agency in their interaction (Bates, 1976). Workers in this area argue that there exist inborn propensities not only for formatting, but for the erection of *specific* formats and *idiosyncratic* formats in accord with cultural and personal history. Arlow's patient (1977) presents an apt example of the redundant need to express her wish both in the transferential ambience and in the content inferable from the pictorial dream.

Developmental psychologists such as Bruner (1975) have suggested that the structure of sentences reflecting agent, action, and object (the "I am doing x, y or z to somebody") is already available in the preverbal period, in innumerable experiences between babies and their mothers. Games of giving and taking, as well as turn-taking routines, are present very early on, as is attunement to a topic. The ball that is given and taken, the rattle that is exchanged for a ball, and the car that is rolled back and forth are readily available examples. In all these exchanges the action is implied and then learned as a verb. Bruner notes that there is a stage of development where mother and child looking at a book together can be viewed as paradigmatic of the beginnings of joint attention and dialogue making. In fact, there is a set of warm-ups that take place between a young toddler and mother that requires both attunement to the same external observable—a ball—and the convention of turn-taking in addressing this object of scrutiny. Approximating the format of naming at this juncture, the mother asks, "What's that?" in response to which the baby points and utters a protosymbolic "Da." The mother then says, "That's right, it's a ball." This reciprocal verification in patterned repetitive sequences leads ultimately to the intention to influence. The intentions may then become unconsciously related to wishes which are subsequently to be suppressed or which await the acquisition of guilt as an inciter of repression in the inner dialogue between internal agencies.

These formats are disrupted when the person, now an analysand, is asked to provide a monologue in a traditionally dialogic situation. It is hoped that in the analytic situation the wish that has been repressed will repeatedly show itself, even through the resistive disguise, so that it may be interpreted. The analyst as observer then uses his interpretive grasp to uncover the unconscious fantasy underlying the expression, and the therapy advances. Thus, in Arlow's example there is both an enactment and a dream presenting redundant expressions of a singular meaning; the patient expresses herself over and over again using whatever expressive vehicle is at hand. The dialogic frustration she imposes on the analyst is a pragmatic representation, whereas the dream operates on a more directly semantic level.

It can be argued that these formats are realized within analysis and have long been recognized without the use of linguistic terminology and theory. This may well be so. It is probably true that most analysts do this kind of unraveling without going into technical explanations. However, it seems to me characteristic of Freud, and I think also of Arlow, that he availed himself of help from other disciplines wherever possible. If we make sense of what initially seems uncanny, unfathomable, or unreasonable, we have increased the sway and scope of the ego. What happens between patient and analyst should be examined in as many aspects as possible in order to achieve the best and fullest description of the process. Moreover, such elucidation enables us to understand nonanalytic linguistic exchanges that may in turn enrich our analytic understanding.

A recent controversy in the philosophy of language may usefully be incorporated into our discussion of how it is that we communicate with each other in a way that makes a difference. The recent emphasis on meaning analysis, or hermeneutics, has come up against an old problem that may be formulated as the Cartesian conundrum of how minds can have knowledge of things. In more technical language, how can a res extensa prehend a res cogitans? Descartes resorted to the idea that there is a preformed symmetry between things and concepts, and he could not believe that God would act as an evil genius in order to confuse us. His assumption about minds knowing other minds involves similar faith. Kant, following Descartes' unsatisfactory resolution, suggested that the categories employed by mind reside not in nature but in man. Thus, knowledge of things and minds are preformed. A recent rendition of Wittgenstein's early work may offer a more adequate answer. Davidson (1983) notes that interaction between minds is possible because the vehicle of that interaction is linguistic. Insofar as we can describe the world, it is in words, and insofar as we can understand unconscious fantasy, it too is in words. Einstein, when asked whether geometry accurately describes the world of matter, answered that insofar as mathematics describes the world we are uncertain, but insofar as we are certain (i.e., by using an a priori system such as mathematics) we cannot be sure that geometry describes the world. A similar argument would suggest that the limits of expressibility are precisely the limits to which we can proceed in knowing things, including unconscious fantasies.

Language, in the first instance, is a social vehicle of expression, and insofar as we can discourse about minds, it is in terms of language. I do not know that Arlow would go as far as I do in this integration of language theory and the psychoanalytic consideration of unconscious fantasy. Nonetheless, it seems appropriate that psychoanalysis seek congruence with the theoretical systems and empirical observations of other disciplines, if only to sharpen its understanding of elusive concepts. Unconscious structures are a central construct of linguistic formats at the syntactic, semantic, and pragmatic levels. The dynamic unconscious of psychoanalysis should exhibit similar formal features while adding a motivational and conflictual accompaniment that is the unique contribution of Freud. Unconscious fantasy, seen as a small number of formats that reduce data, is compatible not only with the experience of analysts but also with the theoretical formulations I have offered in relation to language theory as applied to the psychoanalytic concept of unconscious fantasy. Many derivatives emerge at the surface, while we infer a few sources in a limited array of unconscious fantasies.

REFERENCES

Arlow, J. A. (1953), Masturbation and symptom formation. *J. Amer. Psychoaml. Assn.* 1:45–58.

⸺ (1969), Unconscious fantasy and disturbances of conscious experience. *Psychoanal. Quart.*, 38:1–27.

⸺ (1977), Issues posed by Section VI. In: *Communicative Structures and Psychic Structures: Psychoanalytic Interpretation and Communication,* ed. N. Freedman & S. Grand. New York: Plenum, pp. 441–450.

⸺ (1985), The concept of psychic reality and related problems. *J. Amer. Psychoanal. Assn.*, 33:52–53.

⸺ & Brenner, C. (1964), *Psychoanalytic Concepts and the Structural Theory.* New York: International Universities Press.

Bates, E. (1976), *Language and Context: The Acquisition of Pragmatics.* New York: Academic Press.

Beres, D. (1962), The unconscious fantasy. *Psychoanal. Quart.,* 31:309–328.

Bruner, J. (1975), The ontogenesis of speech acts. *J. Child Lang.,* 2:1–19.

Davidson, D. (1983), The coherence theory of truth and knowledge. In: *Treatment and Interpretation: Perspectives on the Philosophy of Donald Davidson,* ed. E. LePore. Oxford: Basil Blackwell.

Edelheit, H. (1969), Speech and psychic structure. *J. Amer. Psychoanal. Assn.* 17:381–412.

Edelson, M. (1972), Language and dreams: Interpretation of Dreams revisited. *The Psychoanalytic Study of the Child.* 27:203–82. New York: Quadrangle.

Freud, A. (1937), *The Ego and the Mechanisms of Defense.* Rev. ed. New York: International Universities Press, 1966.

Freud, S. (1891), *On Aphasia.* New York: International Universities Press, 1953.

———— (1900), The Interpretation of Dreams. *Standard Edition,* 4/5. London: Hogarth Press, 1953.

———— (1911), Formulations on the two principles of mental functioning, *Standard Edition,* 12:218–226. London: Hogarth Press, 1958.

———— (1915), The unconscious. *Standard Edition,* 14:166–215. London: Hogarth Press, 1957.

James, W. (1902), *The Varieties of Religious Experience: A Study in Human Nature,* New York: Longmans, Green.

Klein, G. (1967), Peremptory ideation: Structure and force in motivated ideas. In: *Motives and Thought; Psychoanalytic Essays in Honor of David Rapaport,* ed. R. Holt. Psychological Issues Monograph 18/19. New York: International Universities Press, pp. 80–128.

———— (1970), *Perception, Motives, and Personality.* New York: Knopf.

Lacan, J. (1956), The function of language in psychoanalysis. In: *The Language of the Self,* ed. A. Wilden. Baltimore: Johns Hopkins University Press, pp. 1–87.

Piaget, J. (1934), Comments on Vygotsky's critical remarks concerning *The Language and Thought of the Child.*

Rosen, V. (1977), *Style, Character and Language,* ed. M. Jucovy & S. Atkin. New York: Aronson.

Schafer, R. (1976), *A New Language for Psychoanalysis.* New Haven, CT: Yale University Press.

Schur, M. (1966), *The Id and the Regulatory Principle of Mental Functioning.* New York: International Universities Press.

Shapiro, T. (1970), Interpretation and naming. *J. Amer. Psychoanal. Assn.,* 18:399–421.

———— (1979), *Clinical Psycholinguistics.* New York: Plenum.

———— (1983), The unconscious still occupies us. *The Psychoanalytic Study of the Child,* 38:547–567. New Haven, CT: Yale University Press.

———— (1986), On neutrality. *J. Amer. Psychoanal. Assn.* 32:269–282.

Spence, D. (1983), *Narrative Truth and Historical Truth: Meaning and Interpretation in Psychoanalysis.* New York: Norton.

Stern, D. (1985), *The Interpersonal World of the Infant.* New York: Basic Books.

Vygotsky, L. (1934), *Thought and Language.* Cambridge, MA: M.I.T. Press, 1962.

Wittgenstein, L. (1921), *Tractatus Logico-Philosophicus,* trans. D. Pears & B. McGuinness. London: Routledge & Kegan Paul, 1961.

6

Subliminal (Preconscious) Perception: The Microgenesis of Unconscious Fantasy

Charles Fisher, M.D.

In his seminal articles of 1969, Jacob Arlow (1969a, 1969b) prefers to speak not of unconscious fantasies but of unconscious fantasy function:

> fantasy activity, conscious or unconscious, is a constant feature of mental life. In one part of our mind we are daydreaming all the time, at least all the time we are awake and a good deal of the time when we are asleep [1969b, p. 5].
>
> . . . Every instinctual fixation is represented at some level of mental life by a group of unconscious fantasies. The specific expressions in conscious mental life of a fixation or of a repetitive trauma may be traced to the ever present, dynamic potentiality of the specific details of an individual's unconscious fantasy activity to intrude upon its ordinary experience and behavior [1969b, p. 6].
>
> . . . Derivatives of fantasies may influence ego function, interfering with the neutral processes of registering, apperceiving, and checking the raw data of perception. Under the pressure of these influences the ego is oriented to scan the data of perception and to select discriminatively from the data of perception those elements that demonstrate some consonance or correspondence with the latent preformed fantasies.
>
> Situations of perceptual ambiguity facilitate the foisting of elements of the life of fantasy upon data or perception. This plays a very important role in such experimental situations as the Rorschach test and subliminal sensory stimulation (Fisher, 1954) [1969b, p. 8].

Arlow (1969a) undertakes to demonstrate that "how reality is experienced depends for the most part on the interaction between the

93

perceptions of the external world and the concomitant effect of unconscious fantasy activity'' [p. 29].

> Memory recording conflicts, traumata, vicissitudes of the drives and
> of development are organized in terms of the pleasure-unpleasure prin-
> ciples into groups of schemata centering around childhood wishes.
> These make up the contents of a continuous stream of fantasy think-
> ing, which is a persistent concomitant of all mental activity and which
> exerts an unending influence on how reality is perceived and responded
> to [p. 29].

In the interplay of forces the perpetual apparatus of the ego operates
simultaneously in two different directions:

> One part looks outward responding to the sensory stimuli of the
> external world of objects. The other part looks inward reacting to a
> constant stream of inner stimulation. The organized mental represen-
> tations of this stream of inner stimulation is what I call fantasy think-
> ing. It includes fantasies and the memory schemata related to the
> significant conflicts and traumatic events of the individual's life. Fan-
> tasy thinking may be conscious or unconscious. It is a constant feature
> of mental life. It persists all the time that we are awake and most of
> the time when we are asleep [pp. 29–30].

I began this chapter with Arlow's comment that because fantasy
activity, conscious or unconscious, is a constant feature of mental life,
it is preferable to speak not of unconscious fantasy but of unconscious
fantasy function. Though agreeing with his assessment of the ubiquity
of fantasy in mental life, I am not sure his use of the term ''daydreaming'' is very apt, as the formal characteristics and the state of consciousness
of daydreaming are not strictly comparable to those of unconscious
fantasy.
   Some thirty years ago a great deal of work was being done by a
small group of analysts and analytically trained psychologists on
subliminal (or preconscious) perception in relation to the formation of
dreams and images. This work was initiated by the successful repetition
and validation of the famous Pötzl experiment, along with the
simultaneous confirmation of Allers and Teler's work on imagery (Fisher,
1954, 1956, 1957, 1960). The Pötzl experiment demonstrated that visual
stimuli presented tachistoscopically for a hundredth of a second underwent

perceptual registration and transformation into memory trace. The crux of the experiment was that parts of the stimulus picture that were not consciously seen on exposure appeared in the manifest content of the dream. Thus there appeared to occur what could be called unconscious cognition without awareness. Similarly, Allers and Teler were able to demonstrate that mental imagery elicited after tachistoscopic exposure to visual stimuli contained parts of the stimulus picture that had not consciously been perceived.

Further work on these experiments supports the suggestion that unconscious fantasy pervades mental life, both waking and sleeping. This work indicates that the dream process begins during the day, as the unconscious wish and the fantasies associated with it transfer their intensity onto the day residue. It is suggested further that the dream work continues throughout the day, as further day residues are drawn into the dream process. Finally at night, there is a second activation of the unconscious wish, eventuating in the manifest dream. It can be shown that the daytime fantasy material is a preliminary stage in the formation of the final nocturnal dream.

A COMBINED DREAM/IMAGERY EXPERIMENT

We have found that in conducting these experiments it is better to use simple geometrical forms than complex pictures, as the former can be made totally subliminal, that is, kept completely below the threshold of conscious experience. In the experiment to be reported the subject was an intelligent professional man. The experiment was carried out by my secretary-assistant, a middle-aged woman. The circumstances of the experiment are important because, as will be seen, the subject interpreted the experimental situation as one of placing himself in an inferior and submissive role in relation to a dominant woman.

A six-pointed star (see Figure 1) was exposed through a tachistoscope for one hundredth of a second. The subject could not identify the star: he perceived only a flash of light. He was then asked to close his eyes and produce an image, and to describe and draw it. In a period of forty minutes after this single exposure to the star, the subject produced, drew, and described 29 images.

The great majority of these images resulted from fragmentation of the star, which can be thought of as composed of different kinds of geometrical forms, e.g., (1) six acute angles attached to one another in a circular pattern; (2) six overlapping X's arranged in a circular pattern; or (3) six ordinary capital M's overlapping and arranged in a circular pattern. Of the 29 images, 10 were based on the acute angles, 5 on the X figures, and 5 on the M's.

I will discuss a few of each type. Image 14 was said by the subject to represent the spread thighs of a vague hermaphroditic genital. This image, derived from a point of the star that through sheer accident had a tip missing, is one of many that was produced having voyeuristic content relating to childhood memories of watching someone urinate. This particular image was associated to a childhood memory from the age of three or four, when the subject watched a little girl spread her thighs and urinate. Hermaphrodism and the "missing point" connect to the subject's observation of the absence of a penis in the little girl and to his confusion about this.

Image 12, derived from the combination of a point and an X figure, is a tepee with Sitting Bull squatting in the opening. This was another urinary image, the word "tepee" containing a pun on the word "pee" and Sitting Bull having an association with a recently heard toilet joke.

Image 8 is derived from an M figure. Early in the period of free imagery the subject wrote the word "Mother" in block capitals. He then wrote "something blocking me." Up to this point the subject had felt blocked and had produced images only with great difficulty. From here on, however, his inhibition seemed to disappear, a veritable flood of urinary images ensued, fourteen appearing in rapid succession. At the same time, the song beginning "M is for the many things she gave me" began to run through his mind in a perseverating manner.

Image 27 was seen as two people urinating in such a manner that their streams of urine crossed. It is striking that the subject did not draw human figures but represented them in the shape of the letter M, the crossing middle bars—an X— indicating the streams of urine.

Image 28 is of a lawn sprinkler. As the subject drew it, he became aware that his drawing was not a very good representation of a sprinkler but more closely resembled a menorah, a candelabrum used by Jews for ceremonial purposes. This image is probably as close as the subject came to producing the original figure, the six-pointed Star of David generally being found on menorahs in some decorative pattern.

As I have indicated, 20 of the 29 images were derived from fragmentation of the six-pointed star. Several of the remaining images were

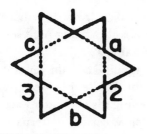

NO. 14 HERMAPHRODITE
(POINT MISSING)

NO. 12 TEPEE

SITTING BULL

MOTHER

NO. 8 M IS FOR THE MANY THINGS
SHE GAVE ME

NO. 27 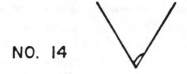 TWO CROSSING STREAMS

NO.28  SPRINKLER
(MENORAH - STAR OF DAVID)

Figure 1. Images produced after the exposure to the six-pointed star (Fisher, 1957).

transformations of preconscious percepts taken from the environment of the experimental situation, a number possibly being representations of the facial profile of the secretary-assistant.

If the 29 images are thought of as a totality, certain general trends can be noted in their order of development. While they were produced as a discontinuous series, the subject opening his eyes after each image to draw and describe it, they nevertheless show certain patterns of meaning. The first 13 contain many phallic representations and appear to relate to fears of castration as does the hermaphroditic image. During the period in which the first 14 images were produced the subject appeared blocked. At the end of this period he wrote down the word MOTHER and indicated that something was inhibiting him. He then produced, in rapid succession, 14 images relating to the act of urination. There developed first the image of a toilet and memories of being in the bathroom watching his mother urinate. This was followed by images and memories of watching horses with their "gigantic" penises urinate in the street. The image of Sitting Bull, as we have seen, referred to urination and sitting on a toilet. All these images seem to refer to the idea of a dominating phallic mother-figure able to produce a large stream of urine. At least one image was derived from the secretary-assistant's profile, indicating a displacement of the phallus on to the nose. A striking feature is the large amount of voyeuristic material that emerged during the imagery period.

When the imagery experiment was completed, we proceeded with the Pötzl dream experiment. The same subject was instructed that if he had a dream that night he was to write it down and report it to the experimenter the next day. The next morning the subject reported the following dream:

> The dream took place in a library. I was looking to see what manuscript *he* had. I do not know to whom the "he" refers. I was looking through some sort of large glass window at the librarian, who was sitting in a chair in front of a desk upon which lay a manuscript. The librarian said, sarcastically, "Is this the one you want?" I said, "Yes." I looked at it and it was not the right one; it had printed on it the word "Diabetes." I had expected something else to be written there. I had the feeling that I had seen a second manuscript that also had something written on it and I believed that this was the one that I wanted."

The subject made a drawing of his dream, showing the librarian sitting on a chair at her desk (Figure 2). On the desk he made a square indicating a manuscript and put next to it the letters MMS. Note that he wrote the abbreviation for manuscript incorrectly, that is, mms. instead of ms. To the left he drew a second square indicating a manuscript and wrote on it "Diabetes." The drawing of the librarian sitting on the chair is of great interest. The legs of the librarian and the legs of the chair are drawn in such a confused way that it is difficult to tell which is which. The figure was drawn without arms or features but has a long bifurcating snout attached to the head. Below the figure of the librarian the subject drew a structure representing the window through which he was looking at the librarian; he indicated his own position by the word "me." When he had finished this, he had the impulse to write the word "amblyopia," which seemed to come into his head out of nowhere.

Associations to the dream. The librarian in the dream brought to the subject's mind two girls he had known years before, both of them librarians. Both were small in stature, like the secretary-assistant, and all three stood for his mother, who was also quite small. Despite their diminutive stature, however, the subject unconsciously viewed these figures from the point of view of a small child; he perceived them as large, dominating, efficient, and aggressive.

The subject pointed out some very interesting features of the drawing of his dream. First, he thought of the curved line emerging from the librarian's body not as a leg but as a stream of urine. Second, he pointed out the peculiar protruberance he had attached to the head and said that it represented the phallus, with a bifurcating stream of urine. Third, he stated that he thought of diabetes as a urinary disease. He had in fact had a childhood constriction of the penile meatus that produced a urinary defect which he somehow related to the word "diabetes." The penile defect brought about both a blocking of the urinary stream and its bifurcation and spraying. This constriction was surgically corrected when the subject was seven. The many sprinkler and spraying images he had were related to the idea of the powerful urinary stream produced by the fantasied phallic mother. Fourth, he thought that the M's in the dream had the same meaning as the M figures that appeared in his imagery. That is, they were symbols of a urinating penis and also representations of the penis of the fantasied phallic mother. Fifth, he stated that the word "amblyopia" was a play on words and really meant to him M-blyopia, meaning a dimness of vision for M's. This referred to the

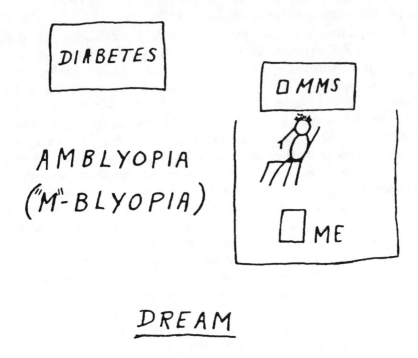

Figure 2. Subject's drawing of his manifest dream image (Fisher, 1957).

voyeuristic aspects of the dream, which begins, "I was looking to see what manuscript *he* had." In the dream the subject is looking through a window at the librarian, and the drawing indicates that he was watching her urinate. The "he" in the sentence quoted is obscure but perhaps relates to the subject's confusion about gender. The reference to the amblyopia probably relates also to the idea of tachistoscopic exposure and to the child's visual confusion when glimpsing the female genital. Sixth, the subject pointed out that he had indicated his own position in the dream by the word "me," itself containing an M.

It is evident that the manifest dream images incorporate some of the same preconscious visual aspects that had arisen during the daytime imagery experiment. The M figures of the six-pointed star played a special role and were elaborated as we have seen. In addition, the displacement of phallus to nose took place both in the dream and in several of the images.

Interpretation of the dream. Both the imagery and the dream were stimulated by certain unconscious fantasies aroused in the subject by the fact of placing himself in the role of subject in relation to a woman. This evoked the childhood fantasy of a submissive, castrated little boy in relation to a dominating phallic mother. This fantasy aroused both infantile conflicts centering around the subject's childhood urinary difficulties and intense voyeuristic wishes directed toward the unconsciously fantasied phallic mother. Above all, the dream expresses the wish to obtain the *right* manuscript from the mother, that is, the right penis rather than the defective one. Behind this is an accusation that his mother had given him the wrong organ, a defective one. The song about Mother— M standing for "the many things she gave me"—is an ironic comment on his mother's deficiencies in giving. The dream revives the infantile trauma. He had expected something else to be written on the manuscript but instead was given the one labeled "Diabetes," which symbolically represented the organ with the urinary disease. All this was expressed by the transformation of the M fragment of the star into a phallic symbol.

The morning following the dream, the subject was repeatedly exposed to the star, the duration of the exposure being gradually increased until, at a duration of one second, the figure was recognized. The original exposure had been one hundred times shorter.

Comment. It would appear that a good part of the manifest dream content was adumbrated by images developed during the imagery experiment earlier that day. The most striking adumbration was the appearance of the M fragment of the star in both the images and the manifest dream. It must be emphasized that while the subject was producing these images he had no idea they were derived from the six-pointed star. He became aware of this only at the very end of the experiments, during the reexposure, when he himself related his images to the different components of the six-pointed star.

Almost the entire manifest dream can be traced to preconscious visual residues of the day before. The librarian sitting at the desk was derived from the memory of the secretary sitting at the desk during the experiment. The secretary was transformed into the librarian by virtue of the fact that she was thought of as someone who "prepares manuscripts." The M fragment was mobilized by symbolic transformation of the manuscript because of its associative connection to the conceptual series secretary-librarian-mother. The window through which the dreamer was looking at the librarian was probably derived from a one-way viewing screen in the wall of the room in which the experiment was conducted. The word "amblyopia" had preoccupied the dreamer the day before. It appears that his consciously perceived and remembered word was fused in some manner with the preconsciously perceived M fragment. The snout-like structure on the face of the librarian was probably derived from the appearance of the tachistoscope.

It is an interesting feature of these experiments that some of the latent content of the dream emerges and becomes evident in the process of drawing the dream. It is very likely that this content would not become evident were the dream recorded only verbally. One might easily overlook the significance of the M's if one depended solely on the verbalization of the word "manuscript." The snout on the librarian's face was not visualized, and the face itself was vague in memory. Only while drawing the figure was the snout quite unconsciously attached to the face. There is no doubt that because dreams are largely visual in structure a purely verbal analysis may obscure significant latent content. This fact was known by Freud (1900, p. 356), who in the 1914 edition of "The Interpretation of Dreams" commented on the work of Marcinowski (1912) on the drawn dream; the latter noted the appearance of concealed latent content in the landscape and castles in drawings of dreams.

Raw material for the subject's dream appears to be present in images developed shortly after tachistoscopic exposure. Not only the visual material but a good part of the unconscious fantasy content of the subsequent dream can already be detected. For example, the vast amount of urinary material in the images was connected with the manifest dream content of the bifurcating snout, the word "diabetes," and the curved line suggesting the urinating librarian. The idea of the mother who gives something appeared in the dream's latent content.

A striking feature is that the images developed in the imagery experiment appear to be less significant and closer to the unconscious content than do the manifest dream images derived from them. In the subject's written version of the dream, its phallic and urinary content, and the latent wish expressed by it, were completely concealed. The previous night, during the second activation of the dream work (the first was seen in the imagery experiment), at which time the unconscious wish was again transferred onto the preconscious day residue, the raw material of the dream was subjected to further distortion, censorship, and compromise formation, that is, to defensive processes on the part of the ego. During the night, additional memory content was drawn into the dream work from both preconscious and unconscious sources. In contrast to the evidently sexual unconscious content of the images, the manifest dream was subjected to secondary revision, and appeared to deal with the innocent problem of obtaining a manuscript from a librarian. Although the images from the experiment appear to constitute the raw material of the dream, they are by no means equivalent to the dream in their formal characteristics.

DISCUSSION

By "microgenesis" I mean the detailed and structured imagery developed during the course of the dream's generation—from the transference during the day of the unconscious wish onto the day residue, to the delayed delivery during the night of the secondarily revised content into consciousness as the manifest dream. This course illustrates the organizing function of unconscious fantasy in the process of dream formation and confirms Arlow's contention that unconscious fantasy is ubiquitous, occurring both day and night, and is organized and structured rather than random.

Stages of the Dream Process

At this point I would like to spell out in greater detail the relation of the images and associated fantasies to the different stages of dream formation.

First stage. Freud stressed that the dream process begins during the day. We have shown that subliminal percepts play an important role in dream formation. Some of these percepts attain registration and become preconscious memory images. These events take place during the day in close temporal association with the day residue experience. Simultaneously, the unconscious wish transfers its intensity onto these memory schemas, which now undergo distortions of a primary process nature. At this point we have not a dream but simply its preliminary stage. Memory images such as those developed in the imagery experiment are formed by the same mechanisms as are the manifest dream images and can be shown to be associated with the same unconscious content and to be composed, as are the latter, of a fusion of memory images of the preconscious registrations with old memory pictures associated with the unconscious wish. We may assume that the elaboration of these images continues all through the day and into the night.

Second stage. Here the dream itself arises, consequent on a second activation of the unconscious wish during sleep, its transference onto the day residue, and the arousal of the memory images laid down during the day. These, in a sense, form the raw material of the dream's sensory structure. But the memory images of the preconscious registration are delivered into consciousness in a delayed manner, now aroused to hallucinatory intensity, and make up the manifest pictures of the dream. These pictures, too, are composed essentially of the memory images of preconscious registrations fused with infantile memory images associated with the unconscious wish and associated fantasies.

Third stage. Recent research has given us evidence of a sleep cycle unknown in Freud's time. It is now clear that there are two kinds of sleep, REM (rapid eye movement) sleep, during which dreaming occurs, and non-REM sleep (non-dreaming), alternating periods of which make up a ninety-minute cycle that is built into the central nervous system and is subject to physiological, neurophysiological, and neurochemical regulation. In both biological and psychological structure the two sleep states show specific differences. We now know that the mind never rests, as Freud (1900) suspected; mental activity proceeds all night long regardless of the stage of sleep. However, REM sleep, as contrasted with non-REM, is much more primary process in nature, more visual and sensory, more bizarre, more emotional, and more related to past events. But unconscious fantasy may be said to go on throughout the night. A stream of day residues appears to be present during non-REM sleep and, with the onset of each REM period, is transformed by primary process mechanisms into the manifest dream. Thus, the hallucinatory dream does not arise fortuitously, as Freud believed, but must await the onset of activated REM sleep within the ninety-minute cycle occurring four or five times nightly. The onset of the dream and its associated unconscious fantasies occurs at the interface where non-REM sleep gives way to REM and it seems probable that the hallucinatory nature of the dream, long considered a mystery, is brought about by the powerful neurophysiological and neurochemical activation that characterizes REM sleep.

Fourth stage. As noted, a striking feature of the imagery experiment described above is that the images developed there appeared to be less disguised and close to the unconscious content than the manifest dream images derived from them. The process by which the former are subjected to distortions, censorship, and compromise formation by the ego's defense mechanisms is known as secondary revision, the fourth stage of dream formation.

Two Conceptual Problems

Unconscious fantasies, Arlow (1969b) writes, "embarrass our methodology. It is clear that they do exist but it is difficult to place them precisely in our conceptual frame of reference. What is their nature and in what form do they exist? How high a degree of organization can we ascribe to unconscious fantasy?" (p. 4).

The nature of fantasy. With regard to the form in which unconscious fantasies exist, Freud was ambiguous and presented several formulations, often seemingly contradictory.

Arlow raises important questions about the form of fantasy thinking and how highly structured and organized it is. He notes that some authors have rejected the suggestion that unconscious fantasies may have complicated organizations or that they contain elements of imagery that are visually represented. "My own experiences," he counters (Arlow, 1969a), "led me to the conclusion that fantasy thinking has a quasi-visual structure in that it is easily transformable into visual representations" (p. 47).

This stress on the visual nature of unconscious fantasy finds support in Freud's most cogent formulation on the subject (1900):

If we now bear in mind how great a part is played in the dream-thoughts by infantile experiences or by phantasies based upon them, how frequently portions of them re-emerge in the dream-content and how often the dream-wishes themselves are derived from them, we cannot dismiss the probability that in dreams too the transformation of thoughts into visual images may be in part the result of the attraction which memories couched in visual form and eager for revival bring to bear upon thoughts cut off from consciousness and struggling to find expression. On this view a dream might be described as a *substitute for an infantile scene modified by being transferred on to a recent experience.* The infantile scene is unable to bring about its own revival and has to be content with returning as a dream [p. 546].

Freuds' discussion (1915) of *word* presentation and *thing* presentation indicates the emphasis he placed on the sensory character of the latter:

what we have permissively called the conscious presentation of the object can now be split up into the presentation of the *word* and the presentation of the *thing;* the latter consists of the cathexis, if not the direct memory-images of the thing, at least of remoter memory-traces derived from these. We now seem to know all at once what is the difference between a conscious and an unconscious presentation. The two are not, as we supposed, different registrations of the same content in different physical localities, not yet different functional states of cathexis of the same locality; but the conscious presentation comprises the presentation of the thing plus the presentation of the word belonging to it, while the unconscious presentation is a presentation of the thing alone [p. 201].

The thing presentation, then, consists of visual or other sensory images, or "at least of remoter traces derived from these, though," it is not altogether clear what Freud means by "remoter" in this instance.

Finally, Rubovits-Seitz (1986) has taken the position that despite

Lacan's views notwithstanding, the repressed unconscious is probably not like a language in content or structure; rather it appears to consist of preverbal, nondiscursive, illogical, infantile, imagistic mental activity, the construing and understanding of which is made possible not by linguistic or communicative concepts but, if anything, by the opposite—that is, by the capacity to transcend the constraints of language, speech, and communication in order to think nonverbally, nondiscursively, nonlogically, and imagistically [p. 38].

While in general agreeing with this statement, I believe that the role of verbal elements (e.g., tepee, M-blyopia) in primary process thought needs further consideration. The primary process is not given all at once at some point in the preverbal stage but continues its development for years. According to Holt (1967), the primary process is still manifest near the end of Piaget's sensori-motor period, time when language, evocative memory, mental representation, and symbolism are developing.

The Organization of fantasy. Arlow has suggested that unconscious fantasies have a complicated organization. The work presented here demonstrates how important a role visual imagery, especially that derived from subliminally registered percepts, plays in dream formation and unconscious fantasy. It has been shown how recent preconscious percepts determine the form in which infantile visual memory appears in consciousness. I have also noted the remarkable fact that the images produced during the imagery experiment may be derived almost exclusively from the tachistoscopically exposed picture, as if the preconscious percept of this picture holds the imagery process in a vise and determines the way in which recent and remote memory images are incorporated into the imagery. The question of structure and organization raised by Arlow must be answered in the affirmative; preconscious percepts are worked over and organized by the imagery process in a highly complex form. The same perceptual content may be used over and over again with different images. The degree of unity attained by the images is very striking, as is the extent to which they center around a single unconscious tendency dominant at the moment of the experiment and activated by the transference relationship between subject and experimenter. A similar degree of unity may be assumed to occur outside the experimental situation, in the transference relationships of patients in therapy.

A FINAL REMARK

Arlow (1969a) proposed a cinematic analogy to illustrate the interaction between fantasy and reality in mental life. Suppose two motion picture projectors are flashing two different series of images simultaneously from opposite sides onto a single translucent screen. Imagine that on that screen there are two centers of perceptual input—introspection and exterospection—supplying data from the inner eye and from the outer eye (the two projectors). This model can be used equally well to demonstrate the interaction between preconscious perception and unconscious fantasy. Just as in its original application it is the function of a third agency of the ego to integrate, correlate, judge, and sift out the competing data of experience, so here must these ego functions influence the final judgment as to what is real and what is unreal.

REFERENCES

Arlow, J. A. (1969a), Fantasy, memory, and reality testing. *Psychoanal. Quart.*, 38:28–51.

———— (1969b), Unconscious fantasy and disturbances of conscious experience. *Psychoanal. Quart.*, 38:1–27.

Fisher, C. (1954), Dreams and perceptions. *J. Amer. Psychoanal. Assn.*, 2:389–445.

———— (1956), Dreams, images, and perception. *J. Amer. Psychoanal. Assn.*, 4:5–48.

———— (1957), A study of the preliminary stages of the construction of dreams and images. *J. Amer. Psychoanal. Assn.*, 5:5–60.

———— (1960), Introduction. In: *Preconscious Stimulation in Dreams, Associations, and Images*, by O. Pötzl, R. Allers, & J. Teler. Psychological Issues, Monograph 7. New York: International Universities Press, pp. 1–40.

Freud, S. (1900), The interpretation of dreams. *Standard Edition*, 4/5. London: Hogarth Press, 1953.

———— (1915), The unconscious. *Standard Edition*, 14:166–215. London: Hogarth Press, 1957.

Holt, R. R. (1967), The development of the primary process: A structural view. In: *Motives and Thoughts: Psychoanalytic Essays in Honor of David Rapaport*, ed. R. R. Holt. Psychological Issues Monograph 18/19. New York: International Universities Press, pp. 344–383.

Marcinowski, J. (1912), Gezeichnete Träume. *Zentralbl. Psychoanal.*, 2:490.

Rubovits-Seitz, P. (1986), Clinical interpretation, hermeneutics and the problem of validation. *Psychoanal. & Contemp. Thought*, 9:3–42.

Part III

UNCONSCIOUS FANTASY: TECHNIQUE

7

Criteria of Evidence for an
Unconscious Fantasy

Dale Boesky, M.D.

> Come again!
> Sweet love doth now invite,
> Thy graces that refrain,
> To do me due delight,
> To see, to hear, to touch, to kiss, to die,
> With thee again in sweetest sympathy.
> Come again
> That I may cease to mourn . . .
>
> —John Dowland

> We can die by it, if not live by love,
> And if unfit for tombs and hearse
> Our legend be, it will be fit for verse;
> And if no piece of chronicle we prove,
> We'll build in sonnets pretty rooms . . .
>
> —John Donne, from The Canonization

In Clements's commentary (1966) on Donne's famous poem we are told that "in Donne's time, to 'die' was slang for consummating the sexual act, and it was believed that this act reduced one's life span" (p. 6). The epigraph from the song by Dowland, Donne's contemporary, attests this as well. Benedick told Beatrice in *Much Ado About Nothing*, "I will live in thy heart, die in thy lap, and be buried in thy eyes" (V, 2, 104–105).

This chapter is a revised version of the Freud Lecture presented to the Psychoanalytic Association of New York on April 28, 1986.

Lear swore, "I will die bravely, like a smug bridegroom" (IV, 6, 201). The recent controversy at Oxford over the attribution to Shakespeare of the poem "Shall I Die" is a reminder of the prevalence of this equation of orgasm and death in Elizabethan literature. In fact, the notion that orgasm shortens life is ancient and near universal. The French call orgasm "le petit mort." In this chapter I wish to report a clinical observation of a patient who not only equated orgasm and death but also believed in his unconscious fantasy that the successful termination of analysis would mean just such a lethal orgasm. I will use this clinical report to clarify certain methodological issues relating to recent challenges to the assumption that data gathered in the psychoanalytic situation can be considered scientifically valid (Spence, 1982; Grunbaum, 1984). As this is my focus, I will ignore the complex topics of termination and the psychology of orgasm, topics otherwise relevant to the clinical material.

That sexual intercourse and death may be extensively associated has long been known to psychoanalysts. The sexual meaning of dying together was discussed by Ernest Jones (1911, 1912), while Calef and Weinshel (1983) have reported the link between the meaning of psychoanalytic termination and the thwarted desire for sexual consummation of transference wishes.

The patient to be reported here was enuretic until the age of eighteen. As with the orgasm-death equation, the sexual meaning of enuresis has long been recognized. Freud (1905, p. 190; 1924, p. 175) observed that continued bed wetting was equated with the emissions of adults and was linked to the child's masturbation. Abraham (1917, p. 281) linked premature ejaculation to conflicts about urination and noted that ejaculatio praecox has two components: it is ejaculation with regard to substance but is like urination with regard to experience. What is distinctive about my patient is that his fantasy was that the termination of his analysis would be a *destructive* ejaculation and orgasm.

I will introduce the patient by summarizing the unique interweaving in this man's mental life of his conflicts about orgasm with the issues of death, object loss, castration, bisexuality, enuresis, and a tortured, ubiquitous dread of losing control of his emotions, a dread which pervaded his sexual and aggressive conflicts at every developmental level. Then, in the two analytic hours to be reported in detail, his thoughts about death, water, explosive discharge, and orgasm will be revealed as so coherently linked that it is possible to infer a specific unconscious fantasy that successful termination means orgastic death.

THE PATIENT

The patient originally sought help for a serious but not psychotic depression which had begun insidiously about six months prior to his first consultation. He was born and raised on the East coast in an Orthodox Jewish family and moved with his wife and children to the midwest to pursue an advantageous professional opportunity. He was obsessed by fears of financial collapse although he had done very well in his career and was in no real financial danger. He had no idea why he had become depressed but felt it had all started with the suicide of two of his friends just a few months apart. As an aside he added that his twelve-year-old son Robert had just recovered from his second and final surgical correction for hypospadias.

Depression meant not wanting to get out of bed in the morning and the worried, pessimistic fear that his business would fail. There was a cold, dark, empty feeling, often located in his stomach. He had to drag himself around and often just shuffled papers at his desk. During his analysis he suffered terrible despair and intense psychic pain; there were times when he spoke of suicide, but I never felt it necessary to suggest hospitalization or to introduce parameters.

The patient had been a bed wetter from his earliest memory. He had no bladder or neurological abnormalities and never lost bladder control during the day. The analysis was pervaded with moist metaphors and various allusions to water—e.g., he often thought he should "liquidate" his business. Once, right before I was to go on vacation, he canceled a few sessions before I left to go on a whitewater rapids trip. The first memory he had of meeting his wife was when they were both camp counselors and she was wearing a yellow rain slicker and comforting a crying child. He was obsessed with the dangers of losing control of his emotions, which unconsciously entailed terrifying fantasies of catastrophic incontinence of all his body sphincters. He therefore had always to avoid the expression of strong emotion of any kind. In the sessions his eyes watered, but not until rather late in the analysis did he ever cry. Genuine sexual excitement was impossible for him at the outset. He was passive with his wife, usually kept her waiting for sex because he was tired or had overeaten, was never passionate, and experienced mostly flowing premature ejaculations rather than orgasm, again until the later stages of the analysis. He had conscious memories of stool retention when he was about three, of his mother's struggles to get him to move his bowels, and of sometimes plugging up the toilet with the huge amount of his retained feces. He associated this with his wife's praising him, when they did have sex, for filling her up with so much semen. He recalled setting fires in alley garbage cans as a boy and once set fire to the seat of his mother's armchair. His father, interestingly, was an air raid warden who carried sand in his car for extinguishing fires. His childhood was haunted by his bed wetting; he carried it with him as a horrible secret that might some day be discovered by his friends. His enuresis was a nightly occurrence during grade school. Like those mothers of enuretic children who covertly encourage their children to wet the bed (Blum, 1970), his mother never once in all those years asked him to take any responsibility for changing his urine-soaked sheets, even when he reached adolescence. It is noteworthy that in no other way was he a spoiled child; in fact, he was literally self-supporting from the age of thirteen. Thus, there was a very telling specificity to this collusive agreement with his mother, a tacit arrangement clearly linked to the collusion whereby he would watch her naked when he was in grade school. This repetitive and traumatic exposure of her body occurred over several years. Here, as with the enuresis, each pretended that nothing was going on. Yet a third collusion involved his behavior in school. By the time he was in the third grade he was the smartest boy in his class in math, but he was also an attention-seeking, disruptive clown. When finally his mother was summoned to the school, she had a different view than the teacher, telling her that just because her husband was away in the service was no reason to pick on her son. That was that. This memory was representative of his view of himself as an exception by virtue of his dependent attachment to his mother. She was a very clever, peppy, and socially skilled person who knew how to handle people. She usually didn't offend them by acting bossy, she just knew how to get her own way, making them love her in the bargain. She was charming and so was he. As her little "pisher" (a child who isn't bladder trained), he could do as he pleased, and of course so could she. She kept two sets of books in the family store, one accurate and one for the IRS. This was exactly how the patient ran his own business, and it was no surprise that it was also how he wished to conduct the analysis. For instance, he consciously withheld important information in the analysis, especially regarding his sex life.

THE MOTHER

The patient's mother suffered the death of her own mother when she was a child and there was clear evidence in the analysis that she suffered consequently from significant conflicts related to her developmental incapacity to adequately mourn the death of her mother at that early age. One aspect of this was her clear need to infantilize the patient and to embroil him in her own unfulfillable longings for her mother by mothering aspects of herself vicariously in her relationship with the patient. She was the center of everything that happened in the family. Just as she would ask her husband if he thought he could drive after drinking so much, so she would ask the patient if he thought he should stay overnight at a friend's house, as he'd probably wet the bed.

The patient's most traumatic sexual experience occurred when he was thirteen, during the first of his father's two psychiatric hospitalizations for psychotic depression. One night he had been worried about something, and his mother, always the one to reassure him, came into his bedroom in her nightgown and climbed into bed with him. He then did something that haunted him the rest of his life. He reached out and touched her breast. She gently pushed his hand away and got out of the bed. He was overcome with horror about the awful thing he had done. There was also strong evidence of primal scene experiences at a younger age, consisting of his hearing the noises of his parents having intercourse.

THE FATHER

His father, too, suffered serious conflicts over mourning and object loss. During his son's infancy he had made a trip to Eastern Europe just before Hitler's invasion of Poland; as far as anyone could tell, he had made no active effort to get his parents and other relatives to leave while there was still time. After his return, they perished in the Holocaust. The patient felt that the death of his grandparents caused his father so much pain that he was never able to discuss them.

It seems plausible to conclude that in the patient's early development he had abundant opportunity to be influenced by conflicts over mourning in both of his parents. This was an important basis for the pathological mourning reaction he himself experienced in response to the death of his own parents, both of whom had died before his analysis was undertaken. After their deaths the patient did not cry, felt little awareness of grief, and with an attitude of resignation carried on business as usual.

THE FIRST HARRY

This characteristic denial of object loss and conflict over mourning, separation, and loss in his parents' attitudes was repeated fatefully in the manner with which they dealt with the death of their firstborn. The patient was the youngest of four boys. He was especially close to his oldest brother Harry. Only when the patient was in grade school did he discover from Harry that there had been another baby named Harry, and that this baby had been killed several years prior to the birth of the second Harry, obviously a replacement for the first one. When the patient was about nine or ten Harry showed him a creased and yellowed news clipping which gave a few sketchy details concerning the baby's death. The facts were unclear, but it seemed an electrical appliance had fallen into the baby's bath when his mother had her back turned for a moment. The baby was about one year old when he was electrocuted.

After the birth of so many boys the patient believed his mother had eagerly hoped that he would be her long wished-for daughter. With the birth of the second Harry, his father got his son again. Before the patient's birth, therefore, his mother had eagerly waited the arrival of a little girl. But though convinced she had wanted him to be a girl, the patient had numerous memories of his mother's later pride in him. She loved to show him off to friends and relatives. With gusto, pride, and a proprietary flourish she would pull down his swimming trunks when he was four or five and tell him to show everyone his "difference"—the sharp margin between his white buttocks and his tanned torso. We learned later that for the patient "difference" meant also the difference between males and females.

During the analysis important homosexual conflicts emerged in a brother transference. When he was younger he loved to be with Harry and his friends. One of the games they played was to have Harry pick him up from behind, around the waist, and swing him around in circles until he felt pleasantly dizzy and excited, falling almost into a faint. Many years later, as the patient arose to say goodbye during a hospital visit to his dying father, he felt exactly the same woozy, dizzy feeling. When the patient got married, he missed the plane for his honeymoon by dawdling over brunch at Harry's house.

HARRY

When the patient was younger he envied and idolized his oldest brother, and his father too, because they could hold their urine so long that it turned dark yellow. He thought that this dark urine was the special juice that fathers gave mothers to make babies. He also thought that erections were caused by accumulated urine, because when he woke up in the morning with an erection he also had a full bladder. The patient displaced many other important aspects of his oedipal conflicts about his father onto Harry. As an adult the patient could not urinate in a public toilet if others were present, and he suffered from premature ejaculations, as I have noted. When he was about twelve and his mother didn't come home to make dinner, Harry would beat up on him if he refused to make him something to eat. As a teenager he envied Harry's self-proclaimed reputation as a lover. Harry could go for hours and the girl couldn't "bust his nuts," but the patient couldn't hold it. Extensive analytic attention centered on sadistic homosexual conflicts about Harry. When they were kids Harry would pin him down and drool saliva on his face, or would tickle him in his armpits until he screamed for release. When the patient was fifteen he was big enough to beat Harry in a fist fight, and that put a stop to Harry's bullying.

THE PARADIGMATIC RESISTANCE

I have selected one type of resistance to document the overdetermined links between the patient's fantasy that termination would mean orgasm and death, for both himself and the analyst, and his conflicts over mourning, object loss, and sadistic sexual fantasies. It was a resistance present almost from the beginning of the analysis, but which became fully visible only after several years. This is the form it took. The patient made a special issue about his activity and responsibility in the analysis and made repeated and highly communicative attempts to show how passive he was as a patient and that all progress would depend on the analyst. This composite summary of his resistance is based on a highly diverse group of manifest behaviors. He might, for instance wonder what I thought about what he was saying. What did it all mean? His physical posture at such times might be that of a man relaxing in a hammock. Typically there would be a more or less visible element of teasing and provocation. If he thought I would want to know his associations to a dream, he would instead report a brief and vividly detailed manifest dream and then ask me to tell him what it was all about. Finally, in the most fully developed and ultimate form of the resistance, the patient expressed a depressed and angry sense of futility about the analysis, asking repeatedly, "So when are you going to throw in the towel?" This challenge to me in the transference was of course also a moistly ironic indicator of the entire enurectic constellation in the transference.

For several years he jeered at my reluctance to throw him out of the analysis. He and his wife had a friend, Roberta, whose name was the feminized version of his second son's name—the son whose hypospadias was corrected just before the original consultation. Roberta's analyst could do nothing more for her. He told her that her resistances were simply too strong to yield to analysis. The patient thought that I, like the mother who changed his sheets, would feel obligated to cure him without his having to go through the pain of talking about his sexual problems so that I could show off his "difference" the way she did. This time it would be the before and after analysis difference, and I would be the one humiliated in the event of failure. He wanted us to reestablish the collusion he shared with his mother so that both of us would need to conceal our deficiencies. Forced to deny his mother's death because he required the fantasy that he was a phallic extension of her, he believed very literally that separation from her meant both object loss and castration. His entire sense of narcissistic balance depended in his fantasy on her evaluation of him and his attachment to her. Thus he was driven to convince both of us that I, like his mother, wanted him to remain a dependent enuretic extension of me. This in turn related to his overwhelming dread of the dangerous preoedipal mother who would destroy him if he ever defied her, just as the baby Harry had been killed. By keeping me a pregenital and phallic mother he also defeated me in the father and brother transferences. The collapse of his father just as he entered adolescence led him to view certain important failures of later male rivals as the actualization of parricidal fantasies and barred his path to masculine sexual functioning. The successful surgical correction of his son's hypospadias, which had helped bring on the depression that motivated the patient to seek treatment, had occurred at about the same age for his son as his father's first psychotic depression had for him. The correction of Robert's hypospadias confronted the patient with the threat of a nonenuretic son, as if his father had been reborn and now sought retribution. To avoid the risk that his patricidal and fratricidal victories might be repeated in a male identification he defeated me instead in a feminine identification (e.g., with Roberta, the woman whose name linked her to his son). His resistance expressed the idea that I would not be man enough to bring the female part of him to successful climax, or to help him learn to do it as a man. Just as he was defeated by his wife when he ejaculated prematurely, so I would "throw in the towel" and climax the analysis prematurely and unsuccessfully. In turn, by not terminating or climaxing with me, he castrated me as a father, preserved me as a mother, and punished himself by sexual defeat and an interminable analysis.

It should be noted that in his complex conflicts over termination he made use of identifications with his parents' pathological mourning and denial of death. This was epitomized by his long-standing inability to allow himself to mourn for his analyst. His emerging ability to grieve over the prospect of losing me through termination coincided with the improvement in his sexual symptoms that occurred later in the analysis.

It is important to understand that though his fantasy that termination meant a destructive orgasm became visible only when termination became an issue, it was not an entirely new formation. Rather, it was itself a continuation of a major oscillation throughout the analysis between two ambivalent transference configurations: the father as an envied, defeated, vengeful, and sadistic rival and the mother as a nurturing, seductive, man-hater who would love him only if he was an enuretic little boy. He struggled with the danger of his father's vengeance if he grew into a man and the regressive tug of his mother's siren call to remain a child. His unstable compromise was the negative oedipal position he unconsciously assumed in the transference. At the level of the behavioral derivatives of these conflicts, he behaved with me in one major position as though he were the aggressive mother and I either the father, his brother, or his own childhood self. In another position I was the mother who entered into collusive arrangements with him in order to keep him a child. We need now to clarify the differing versions of his fantasy about termination as orgasm.

First we must distinguish between the fantasy orgasms associated with unsuccessful and successful termination, my throwing in the towel or a mutually gratifying agreement to terminate the analysis successfully. My throwing in the towel had the following meanings for the patient. In the father transference I would be forced to ejaculate prematurely, with a small, flowing discharge; in his feminine identification with his mother, I would be scorned and castrated. But because I was the one who "came first" I couldn't punish him. After all, he was perfectly willing to stay with me forever, engaging in pregenital foreplay and sadistic teasing. It wasn't his fault I "ejaculated" prematurely. By telling him to quit, I would be the one to lose control, so why should he be punished? In the mother transference, and again with an unsuccessful termination, he could remain with me as a "little pisher" in an eternal, mutually stubborn, pregenital and phallic-oedipal stalemate. If he could make me throw in the towel we could die a little flowing urinary death together, a dying together that would mean eternal union in the hereafter. A successful termination, by contrast, meant he would have the capacity for lethal and sadistic sexual assaults against his mother, would replace me as a father, and would then be punished with abandonment, castration, and death. In addition to these fantasies about termination causing death as a consequence of orgasm, it was of course true that termination, even without its sexual meanings, was directly experienced by the patient as a threat of abandonment and object loss. In fact, that was a very important aspect of his conflicts over termination. I simply choose to ignore it in this discussion in order to focus on his distinctive fantasy equation of termination and orgasm.

Following are detailed reports of certain hours occurring shortly before my annual December interruption. By now the patient had just begun to resume his masturbation and to bring this into the analysis in a manner justifying its description as a therapeutic return of masturbation. He divulged for the first time a masturbation fantasy centering on his mother-in-law. More important, the patient reported an unusual piece of progress in a most revealing manner. In a session shortly before my Thanksgiving holiday, which entailed several canceled hours, he said he had forgotton the dates of the hours I had canceled; in practically the same breath he reported that he had had a simultaneous orgasm with his wife the night before. Actually, his orgasm had occurred a few seconds after hers. He had never enjoyed sex so much, he said; it had been a real orgasm, maybe the first in his life. It was striking to note that his mood prior to sharing this good news had been somber. He had begun the session complaining angrily about why he still had to be in analysis. We were able to link his anger not to his disappointment in analysis but to his fear that coming together with his wife meant that he would no longer have me as his analyst. The spirit and tone of the patient in the two weeks after that session was one of strengthening resolve to finish his analysis. He *was* going to make it; he *could* do it.

The mood of both the patient and analyst in the two weeks after that session was one of optimism. In fact during the period in which the two sessions that I shall report in detail occurred it had seemed likely that termination would be possible soon. Although that proved later to be untrue, the recognition of his fantasy that termination would mean a fatal orgasm proved to be clinically useful. Each of the two hours reported occurred late in the analysis and shortly before canceled hours; the hours took place about one month apart.

HOUR ONE

The patient was briefly silent. He wondered if he was scared to speak because in a few days I'd be starting my vacation. As though it meant a separation. Nah. He was just talking. But Oh! What were those dates again that I had canceled? He had again forgotten the dates. He made two errors trying to remember the dates, then canceled two sessions for business the following month. He had dinner with friends last night. They told a story about a pre-wedding party for their daughter. Both grandmothers showed up in the same dress. His friend's wife was so aggravated. Big deal. Her mother is at least alive. His own mother was seventy when she died—but she wasn't really old. Look at his mother-in-law now. She's a sharp lady—a vibrant woman. I asked if it didn't make him sad to miss his mother and said we had often seen him trying to avoid that sadness. He said, "I wouldn't touch grief with a ten-foot pole." I said, "Maybe you'd have less trouble with your pole if you understood your grief about her better." He then remembered for the first time to say that he had masturbated the night before. But he then provocatively avoided any further reference to that and conveyed the impression that he was now changing the topic by starting to discuss the possibility of reorganizing his firm with his partner Ron.

He just hadn't been working in his firm. Would he let it die? Work is manly stuff like hunting and fucking. He did screw up the dates that I would be away. So what. He then tried to minimize his feelings about my going away by confusing the dates of my canceled hours with his own travel arrangements. I said it seemed he wanted me to do the work, to push him to discuss his masturbation, because it meant a loss to him of his valuable image of being so manly that he wouldn't need to masturbate. He would have to grieve over that loss. He said he wanted me to get mad about it, get riled up like a scolding mother. First confess to me that he masturbated and then get me to make him talk about it for his own good. Then he did an imitation of a scolding mother: "When will you *listen* to me?"

The same lady who told the story of the two grandmothers wearing the same dress told another story. She got a replacement dog when her dog died last month. They loved their dog beyond words. They go to a summer resort every year, where the condominium rules, in order to keep down the number of pets, allow them only if the owners had one at the time of original purchase. So she got a dog exactly like the dog that died and even gave it the same name. By next summer, they thought, it would be big enough that no one would notice the difference. I said, "Harry was a replacement, too." He said, "Harry never had a chance"—an allusion to Harry's unsuccessful career. He then recalled the often told story of an accident somewhat differently. He and Harry had been in the backseat of the car, his father driving and his mother in the front passenger seat. He was about ten. In previous versions of the story his father was sideswiped by a drunk driver who veered into their lane, almost hitting them head-on. This time, however, he recalled how skillful his father had been in averting disaster, at the last second quickly turning the wheel. Although they went into a ditch, he had saved their lives. This account was unusual for the patient, who throughout the analysis had idealized his mother, who could never do anything wrong, and derogated his father, who could never do anything right.

When I mentioned the variation in this version of the accident, he denied there was any difference. I said maybe it seemed that way because it would be painful to feel gratitude now and realize that it was too late. "Like the way I feel about you helping me," he said. "I want to be your friend. Do something nice for you." He noticed I had the humidifier turned on in the office. It looked to him like it was too close to a nice table, that the water might spoil the finish. Well, he said, he hadn't really talked about his masturbation. There used to be a joke when he was a kid. The guys would say about some kid, "His dick is so small he needs a magnifying glass to jack off." He didn't even know what masturbation meant until he heard kids at a bus stop asking, "Did you ever peel your banana?" He had had wet dreams. Wetting the bed was a relief because it washed away the semen stains. Then he said that even though he doesn't tell me what he is thinking when he masturbates I don't push him or argue with him. The session ended.

Discussion. The salient features of the hour are as follows. The patient struggled with his conflict over the impending separation from me. He could say he feared speaking about it, but he also forgot the dates I would be away and chose this moment to "remember" to cancel some hours himself. Then followed the story of the two grandmothers dressed alike. If you can't tell the difference between two mothers you needn't fear losing yours. The look-alike grandmothers foreshadow the look-alike dogs later in the hour, and both are related to the two Harrys. Mothers, children, and analysts can be replaced easily. There is no loss or death. Further, this denial was an identification with his parents' denial of their own parents' deaths and that of their first child. But as soon as I linked his denial of grief to his sexual conflicts he instantly remembered that he had masturbated the night before. He then tried to get me to pry further information out of him. He wondered why he was so passive with his partner. When I asked if he feared losing a precious defensive image of himself as a nonmasturbator, he resumed his wish for me to be a scolding mother. When I linked the replacement dog to his brother, he experienced a déjà raconté and felt sure he had already given me the correct version of his father's having saved the family from a head-on collision. That led him to advise me on how to avoid water damage from the humidifier. This was the offering of a gift. A second gift was his willingness now to discuss his masturbation. As a teenager he had welcomed wetting his bed as a way of washing away semen stains, just as he now washed away his angry feelings toward me with his warning about water damage, and as his father had in his son's fantasy extinguished fires in air raids. These associations suggest extensive connections linking separation, object loss, mourning, and denial of grief with enuretic masturbatory fantasies, a yearning for perpetual union with the mother, a fear of male rivalries, and the fantasied destructive effect of ejaculation.

HOUR TWO

This session occurred one week before a scheduled interruption. As the hour began the patient said he really wanted to finish up his analysis, but again he found himself uninterested in sex. His wife was menstruating just then, but that was no excuse. She also had a little cold. Before that they had had really good sex. Funny. That was the title of that TV show with Dr. Ruth—"Good Sex." He had read an article by a lady psychologist. She said that depressed people blame themselves while nondepressed people blame others. His partner Ron always ignored his opinions. He'd been trying to tell him for months to change their procedures for hiring new associates. But if someone else told Ron the same thing he would listen. Like I've been telling him for years that he's so guilty about his father and brother and he's ignored me. I'll be starting my vacation next week. Will he be upset? Will he miss me? Then he sneezed. Loudly, vigorously. It was a trumpet of a sneeze. He paused. I asked if he had any thoughts about sneezing. He laughed with disparagement at my dumb question. A sneeze yet. It was merely a sneeze. He finally got his weight down from 195 to 180 but he had gained back five pounds. Then he was silent. I said, "If I ask you about your sneeze it's one thing, but if someone else asked you it would be worthwhile?" Then he said that sneezing reminded him of Chaim, a friend of his parents he had mentioned a while back.

His parents had been so close to Chaim and Sally. Chaim had loved Yiddish literature and did a wonderful imitation of a character who is always sneezing in one of Shalom Aleichem's stories. It was the way the man sneezed in the story that gave away something important in his character. A sneeze is such a funny gesture. It's the anguish of the person trying not to sneeze. Chaim would drink a glass of something, and with a mouth full of water a person can't let himself sneeze. Like he'd grab quickly for his handkerchief—a big build up—the gestures and animation. Chaim did it so comically. He was a lovable guy. Never did make any dough. But a real character. Sold door to door, took long lunches, and spent hours prowling around the bookstores. Lucky thing his rich brother-in-law gave him a little steady income from his business. Had he ever told me he used to play cards with Chaim after the old guy had a heart attack? The patient was maybe ten, and Sally didn't want to leave Chaim alone if she went to a movie with the patient's parents. And since his mother didn't want to leave him alone either, they'd bring the patient to Chaim's place and he and Chaim would play gin rummy. When he dealt the cards the first time, Chaim grinned and said, "Now what?" Could you believe it? The man had never played cards before in his life. Chaim's daughter Ethel used to rave about the patient's mother. Ethel's young cousin would be marrying the daughter of his friend who committed suicide. Chaim's wife Sally used to bother him. She would bite him, bite him right on the arm when he was just a little kid. It hurt plenty. Chaim loved Yiddish literature and his wife Sally bit him. He asked his mother why Sally did that. And now there was no more contact with anyone. After his parents died he lost touch with everyone. Ethel said it was his mother who really got everyone together. She was the catalyst. Then he laughed aloud. "Can you imagine that a sneeze would remind me of all that? Chaim, Sally, my parents and their friends, my past." I said, "Maybe it was easier to sneeze than to cry." He replied "Cry? Why cry? It's past. Fond memories."

He had watched a TV show last night: "A girl with two deaf parents who marries. Her mother resented the hearing world. The daughter confronts her parents. She said when my brother died I was only ten and you made me buy the coffin. Every single time I signed with you I spoke out loud too. I hated the silence." I then said, "You had to buy coffins too." He said "I bought the coffin, but I waited to have the feelings." I said, "So you can wait to have feelings about my going away. Like sneezing—it doesn't mean anything." He said "I made it through the last time you were gone—funny choice of words though, 'made it through.'" Then he was silent a moment. As he resumed he said he had just taken off away from here. He had been thinking about work. There's something about dotting all the i's and crossing all the t's that—and he didn't complete his thought. "I don't finish it up. When I get near the end of a project I want to make a change." I said, "Finishing is really hard for you." He said "It's an ending. Like ending a life. Dying is my parents and brothers. Cutting it loose. Wrapping it up. The book is closed and all that's left is the aftermath. The bomb was dropped and then the fallout came and did more damage. But the fallout did good too." I asked what good. He said, "The family fallout is me. I'm all that's left. I'm the product. So it wasn't all bad." Since on several previous occasions the patient had used the word "fallout" to allude to the withdrawal of his penis after premature ejaculation. I said: "And after orgasm the penis falls out?" He then repeated a joke he was fond of telling. What do you do in case of fallout? Put it back in and shorten your stroke. Some joke. He had suffered plenty from the fear of losing his erection. Up and in—can't keep it up. Embarrassed because he was starting to get hard right then. Tough to talk about. Then he was silent.

I asked which part was the tough feeling, and at precisely that point he sneezed for the second time, again very loudly and vigorously. He laughed heartily, itself unusual in this man who for many years had limited himself to a grin at best. He had been feeling the buildup to a sneeze. Should have left well enough alone. Don't stir things up. Did I do any cooking? He said he did a lot. "When you cook a heavy soup with a

lot of filling in it, things tend to settle. If you let it settle and the bottom
burns you have to leave it there. Don't stir it up or you'll contaminate
the rest of the soup. It happens when the cooking fire is too hot. Then
it's too late to fix. You'll only spoil the rest. Just pour it off the top.
I then linked this burned bottom to our earlier work around his having
set fire to the seat of his mother's armchair: "It sounds like ending the
sex act had the meaning for you of exploding like an atom bomb." He
agreed "Like Hiroshima." I then said that exploding, coming in sex,
and saying goodbye were all mixed together for him. I may add that
two months later he explained his superstitious belief that a series of four
sneezes would be fatal. This was expressed in an old Yiddish joke:
"Zugesunt! After the first sneeze one says 'To your health!' After the
second and third sneeze one says 'Zu leben und zu lange yahren' (To
life and to longevity). But after the fourth sneeze one should say 'Gay
in drerd, du hast schon ein kalt' (Drop dead! You have a cold)."

   Discussion. The primary features of this second session are as follows.
As did the first hour, about a month previous, the second preceded some
hours canceled by the analyst. Sex was bad because of blood coming
from his wife's genitals and mucus from her nose. The analyst's sexual
advice wasn't much better than that of Dr. Ruth, a television mother
figure. Like his partner, who prefered to be blind, he had ignored my
statements about his guilt with regard to his father and brother. But would
he miss me when I was gone? His answer was the sneeze—an explosive,
watery, nasal ejaculation which also served to identify him with his wife,
who had a cold. He then recalled the beloved Chaim, a Yiddish Falstaff
who did a comic rendition of a man desperately trying to delay the explosive nasal orgasm. Chaim was linked in prior work to the homosexual transference. Better to be passive like Chaim if all women were like
Sally, who had terrified him with her sharp teeth. Next he started to
cry for his mother but stopped himself. Then, in order to deal with his
conflicts over competition with male rivals, he identified with the girl
in the television drama. This feminine identification was the principal
source of his depressive affect. He then said that he would delay having
feelings about the analyst's being away. He couldn't dot the i's and cross
the t's or finish the analysis or the sex act because finishing anything
meant the death of his parents. Then he spoke of a catastrophic fallout,
equating his orgasm with the destruction of the world, the sexual murder
of his mother, and the annihilation of his oedipal enemies—father, brother,
partner, analyst. "Fallout" thus condensed the drive derivative of lethal

orgasm and the related symptoms of premature ejaculation and impotence. But to counter the dangers of castration he defensively needed the reassurance of an erection; no sooner was he aware of his erection than he had to sneeze again. One can see clearly here the to-and-fro anguish he suffered in struggling with these polarized derivatives of his active-passive, male-female, child-adult, libidinal-sadistic, and progressive-regressive conflicts. He turned from the sneeze to the subject of cooking and the danger of stirring up the excremental dregs at the bottom of the pot. This alluded also to his childhood memory of having set fire to the seat of his mother's armchair. The solution to burning the soup was to pour off unburned soupy liquid at he top—still another return to the enuretic solution and his "shallow" orgasms. "Soupy" was also the derisive nickname his brother used for him when he forced the patient to cook for him. The evidence thus substantiates the inference that the idea of explosive, lethal discharge in orgasm was mixed in with his conflicts about death, separation, and object loss to produce his fantasy about successful analytic termination.

METHODOLOGICAL ISSUES

The clinical report presented here may be considered a specimen of a genre of clinical writing that purports to tender evidence supportive of the inference of an unconscious fantasy. I wish to examine this specimen with an eye to refining the methodology of psychoanalytic evidence, a task which is today a most pressing one. We are living in an era of empirical relativism and polemics in which several rival "schools" claim superior clinical results. Interminable debate over these matters arrives at no decisive conclusions, and many analysts have long agreed that the literature is too often illustrative rather than scientifically convincing. Indeed, Spence (1982) and Grunbaum (1984) question (on very different grounds) whether there is even a possibility of obtaining scientifically valid data within the psychoanalytic situation. In my opinion, Arlow (1979) has provided the most comprehensive and valid description of the criteria provided by the structural theory to detemine whether clinical data constitute supportive evidence for an interpretation or clinical level inference:

Most important is the context in which the specific material appears. Contiguity usually suggests dynamic relevance. The configuration of the material, the form and sequence in which the associations appear represent substantive and interpretable connections. Other criteria are to be seen in the repetition and the convergence of certain themes within the organized body of associations. The repetitions of similarities or opposites is always striking and suggestive. Material in context appearing in related sequence, multiple representations of the same theme, repetition in similarity, and a convergence of the data into one comprehensible hypothesis constitute the specific methodologic approach in psychoanalysis used to validate insights obtained in an immediate, intuitive fashion in the analytic interchange [p. 203].

Arlow has always insisted in his writings (e.g., Arlow and Beres, 1974) that the empathic and intuitive responses that arise in the analyst's mind must be subjected to disciplined validation. Spence (1982) rejects Arlow's criteria of evidence, claiming that context and continuity are unreliable criteria because the search space is infinitely expandable. Any theory can be claimed true if one is allowed to search indefinitely for evidence confirming it. Spence's hermeneutic alternative is essentially a neotopographical view. Whereas the topographic model required that the unconscious become conscious, Spencean hermeneutics requires that the unexpressed be expressed. The satisfaction of this requirement provides narrative rather than historical truth. Grunbaum rejects the hermeneutic argument but on epistemological grounds concludes that it is impossible to gather scientifically valid data from the psychoanalytic situation. There is no way, he argues, to confirm the truth of interpretations of external historic events. In this misconception Grunbaum thoroughly ignores modern structural theory. Edelson (1984, 1986) has mounted a sophisticated epistemological rebuttal of both the Spence and the Grunbaum arguments, one rooted in modern views of the philosophy of science. Edelson also provides arguments for the scientific validity of single case research of the sort reported here. Neither Spence nor Grunbaum presents any sustained consideration of the criteria of evidence concerning resistances in smaller units of psychoanalytic work. Rather, their discussion is far removed from the type of data we are considering.

I have adduced data of four types to support my assertion that it was clinically useful to infer that the patient was influenced by an unconscious fantasy equating termination, orgasm, and death: (1) examples from literature; (2) a biographical summary of the patient's earlier life; (3) a condensed account of one of his central resistances over a lengthy period of the analysis, a resistance viewed as generating the specific fantasy appearing in the late stages of treatment; and (4) a report of two analytic hours. My purpose was to highlight the relation between a protean resistance, one spawning other fantasies earlier in the analysis, and detailed data from the two hours. It is my hope that this method will allow any analyst reading this report to understand how the data was gathered and to draw his own conclusions.

The neglected status of reporting full individual hours in the literature should be remarked. As analysts we use the hour as the unit of psychoanalytic observation in our most important educational and evaluative efforts. It is the sine qua non for supervision, for evaluation of a candidate's progress, for certification, for appointment as a training or supervising analyst, and for the various study groups that have so enriched the science of psychoanalysis. Although we often refer to the "good" or "bad" analytic hour, it is rare that we find a paper that uses the individual hour as a data base. One has only to try to write one to discover some of the reasons for this. Without the benefit of summarized data from earlier sessions, the reader would be swamped in a sea of concrete details isolated from the context of hundreds of hours of work. Nor is this the only problem. The summarized data is itself a mosaic from all of these earlier hours and is compiled with a bias toward validating the inferences the author wishes to make. By summarized data I mean, in the present instance, both the biographical summary and the condensed description of a paradigmatic resistance. Yet when an experienced psychoanalyst summarizes his report of a clinical experience he is doing far more than attempting to persuade his reader or listener as to the validity of his conjectures. The summarizing process itself reflects a highly complex organization of the clinical material by the working ego of the psychoanalyst. When this work of integration has gone reasonably well, a quality of coherence results that is recognized by other analysts, particularly by close colleagues. The summarized material, together with a report of selected individual hours, conveys a sense of fit between the two types of data, the summarized and the detailed. I wish here to emphasize the neglected question of the nature of this fit between these two levels of organizing and reporting our clinical experience. It seems useful to propose that where a persuasive sense of fit occurs it arises because a dynamic congruence has been demonstrated among childhood conflicts, adult symptoms, and the key resistances seen in the transference. The nature of the fit between these two levels of reporting seems too often in the literature to be merely assumed as given; to my knowledge it has rarely been discussed, let alone systematically examined.

Finally a second issue should be touched on, if rather more briefly. Most critical discussions of our literature speak globally about the task of improving our methods of reporting. I wish to be quite explicit in stating that clinical reporting cannot and should not be compressed into a single genre. The kinds of fit required between theoretical assertions and supportive evidence are complex and diverse, far too heterogeneous to be embraced by any single method, including the one I have used and espoused here. We require different varieties of evidence for different levels of inference. Both hostile and sympathetic critics of psychoanalytic methodology too often seem to assume that if their various criticisms (some quite valid) were remedied and suggestions implemented that the new clinical literature would be homogeneously rehabilitated. Such a literature, however, is neither possible nor desirable. Most experienced analysts agree there should be a variety of genres of clinical writing, even if the urgent problem of clarifying the evidential criteria approriate to each remains open. The refinement of analytic methodology of evidence will be furthered when better methods are devised whereby small units of clinical work may be submitted to the probative challenge of a convincing integration of the smaller unit with the major manifestations of transference and resistance.

REFERENCES

Abraham, K. (1917), Ejaculatio praecox. In: *Selected Papers on Psycho-Analysis*. New York: Basic Books, 1960, pp. 280–298.

Arlow, J. A. (1979), The genesis of interpretation. *J. Amer. Psychoanal. Assn.*, 27:193–206.

_____ & Beres, D. (1974), Fantasy and identification in empathy. *Psychoanal. Quart.*, 43:26–50.

Blum, H. (1970), Maternal psychopathology and nocturnal enuresis. *Psychoanal. Quart.*, 39:609–619.

Calef, V., & Weinshel, E. (1983), A note on consummation and termination. *J. Amer. Psychoanal. Assn.*, 31:643–650.

Clements, A. L. (1966), *John Donne's Poetry*. New York: Norton.

Edelson, M. (1984), *Hypothesis and Evidence in Psychoanalysis*. Chicago: University of Chicago Press.

—————— (1986), Causal explanation in science and psychoanalysis: Implications for writing a case study. *The Psychoanalytic Study of the Child*. 41:89–128. New Haven, CT: Yale University Press.

Freud, S. (1905), Three essays on the theory of sexuality. *Standard Edition*, 7:125–248. London: Hogarth Press, 1953.

—————— (1924), The dissolution of the Oedipus complex. *Standard Edition*. 19:173–182. London: Hogarth Press, 1961.

Grunbaum, A. (1984), *The Foundations of Psychoanalysis*. Berkeley: University of California Press.

Jones, E. (1911), On 'dying together,' with special reference to Heinrich von Kleist's suicide. In: *Essays in Applied Psycho-Analysis*, Vol. 1. London: Hogarth Press, 1964, pp. 9–15.

—————— (1912), An unusual case of 'dying together.' In: *Essays in Applied Psycho-Analysis*, Vol. 1. London: Hogarth Press, 1964, pp. 16–21.

Spence, D. (1982), *Narrative Truth and Historic Truth*. New York: Norton.

8

Unconscious Fantasies:
The Hidden Agenda in Treatment

Nathan P. Segel, M.D.

Since Freud first approached the subject of fantasies, conscious and unconscious, in his 1899 paper on screen memories the elaboration of this theme in the literature has paralleled its ubiquity in the consulting room and in the symptoms of our patients. As usual, his genius provided the first important insights into the seminal aspects of the concept, leaving to others the task of fleshing it out, resolving possible contradictions, or transporting it from the land of the topographical to that of the structural hypothesis.

Because the content of his papers on this subject is well known, I will briefly allude to some highlights. Already in 1899 he saw the compromise formation inherent in dealing with disturbing elements in memory and the forces repressing it, while yet allowing indifferent elements "something in the neighborhood" (p. 308) to be remembered. In discussing his own screen memories he was struck by the fact that his daydreams were not so much about the future, as they were a wish to improve the past. It is this element in particular that is one important aspect of what I will later attempt to elaborate. Even then he stressed that we don't get memories from childhood, but only those related to childhood which have been processed over the years and reflect our adult view of them.

In 1908 we were introduced to family romances as the disappointed or slighted child repaired the indignities of his present circumstances by the fantasy that he was an adopted child whose real parents were of noble or even royal birth. As an additional benefit it could lessen the anxiety connected with incestuous or parricidal wishes. Freud felt that it also reflected the child's yearning for the "happy vanished days when his father seemed to him the noblest and strongest of men and his mother the dearest and loveliest of women'' (p. 240). We would now suspect that even those days were more psychic reality than objective reality and hence contained a large dose of fantasy. In the Introductory Lectures (1916–1917) he was to make this even stronger in postulating that childhood memories were compounded of truth and falsehood, of events and fantasies and if anything ''we gradually learn to understand that in the world of the neuroses it is psychical reality which is the decisive kind'' (p. 368). The classical fantasies referred to then included observation of parental intercourse, seduction by an adult, and the threat of being castrated. Even as late as 1925 he was to repeat his conclusions on realizing that memories of seduction were really fantasies, ''that the neurotic symptoms were not related directly to actual events but to wishful fantasies, and that as far as the neuroses were concerned psychical reality was of more importance than material reality'' (Freud, 1925, p. 34). While the importance of psychic reality is generally accepted it is also possible to go too far in this direction. Certainly we recognize that the significance of any trauma or ''real'' event is influenced by the developmental stage and existing intrapsychic conflicts, as well as their associated unconscious fantasies created at the time of the trauma as well as the cumulative effects of later life experiences. However, Sachs (1967) and Blum (1979) are among those who have addressed themselves to redressing the balance on this issue. Thus Blum stated ''Today, I believe we are inclined to give much more weight to the organizing and disorganizing effects of real trauma and to attempt to differentiate between incestous fantasies and actual seduction in the primal scene exposure'' (p. 40). Both Sachs and he see greater sequelae more likely to occur in relation to real trauma that may variously include greater tendencies to act out, creation of altered ego states, such as derealization and interference with adequate reality testing, and superego formation, among others.

Those who enriched our clinical understanding in this area include Kris (1956a) in his elaboration of ''The Personal Myth'' and his other paper (1956b) on recovering childhood memories that called to our attention that even where there has been seduction, the so-called facts are often overlaid with its aftermath of guilt, terror, and thrill, all elaborated in fantasy. This paper also pointed to the remolding of fantasies throughout life and the telescoping effect of condensing multiple small traumas.

As our subject is seen to have greater complexities, we have Beres

(1962) first alone, and later with Arlow (1974), formulating important metapsychological aspects of this concept but always returning to the clinical soil from which their ideas sprang. Sandler and Nagera (1963) painstakingly traced the origins of Freud's thinking on fantasies from the topographical through the structural hypothesis in the process of outlining a more coherent and consistent metapsychological profile. In a parallel fashion and true to his own unique union of theoretical framework amply clothed with clinical illustrations, Arlow was turning out a series of papers that first clarified the structural aspects of unconscious fantasies (1969a). They also dealt with fantasies on the basis of their having unique effects in producing various clinical symptoms (1961, 1969a, 1969b), or else reflected situations where two or more individuals shared aspects of the fantasies (1960, 1981). In the former category were included illusions, parapraxes, misconceptions, distortions of perception, memory and reality testing. In one paper (1969b) he described dominant unconscious fantasy systems which regularly affected the perception of reality, and, as always, illustrated this clinically. In the category of shared fantasies, as in any area when he came upon a paper, which by its excellence further stimulated his own creativity, he acknowledged its virtue and then wrote a separate paper extending and refining the issues. This happened after he read Abend's (1979) paper in which among other things, the latter wrote how unconscious fantasies can creep into even strictly scientific papers, and went on to illustrate how this has affected therapeutic theories in our own field. Arlow (1981), in agreeing with this observation, noted further that many of our patients seek from therapy actualization of the very unconscious fantasies which also produced the original distress and guilt. What was then developed was the degree to which various theories of therapy indicate that the therapist's own unconscious fantasies not only match the wishes and needs of their patients but are paralleled in the theories which they promulgate. This notion of shared unconscious fantasies appears in many of his other papers (Beres and Arlow 1974) where its role in empathy is described; (1961) where the myth was defined as a communal or shared fantasy based on common needs to ward off guilt and anxiety, as well as aiding in the formation of the superego. His shared unconscious fantasies included the relationship between artist and public, author and his readers, and leaders and their groups. In a separate paper (1960) it explored the effects of ambivalence on the shared fantasies of twins.

If proof were needed of the international flavor of the interest in unconscious fantasies, it would be afforded by the Symposium on Fantasy in Stockholm in 1963. The six papers published (1964), in the opinion of the Chairman Kohut, were striking for what he saw as the relationship between the authors' views on fantasy and their preference for certain specific theoretical positions. It was divided essentially between those who subscribed to Kleinian or object relations theories, and those who took an essentially structural hypothesis viewpoint, with special emphasis on the importance of the preexistence of adequate ego development and self-object differentiation, before we could appropriately talk of the complex unconscious fantasies that are so much a part of our clinical work. Rosen who discussed the papers, criticized those who placed the fantasy too directly and too early in the role of psychic representations or mental expressions of instincts prior to the existence of any but the most primitive mental structures. Although not a part of this Symposium, but similar in nature to some of the theorists, Gaddini (1982) carried the concept back even further and saw the earliest fantasies as defensive psychophysiological syndromes that could manifest themselves as rumination or mericism at eight weeks, dermatitis at six months, or asthma by the end of the first year.

Although other papers will also be referred to in relation to the clinical material that will follow, I would like to close this section by alluding to a brilliant poetical-philosophical paper of Schafer (1970). Even though he felt he was describing in an hierarchical fashion, from primitive to most sophisticated, his views of what he felt were psychoanalytic views of reality, I would feel it could as readily have been described as an hierarchical view of the unconscious fantasies as we see them in our patients from their earliest to their most mature forms. The various levels in ascending order of complexity and maturity are called successively the comic, the romantic, the tragic and the ironic views of reality. It is typical of the comic view that the "past can be redone if not undone" (p. 282) while the romantic vision seeks a lost golden age. Certainly most of our therapeutic energy is spent uncovering and hopefully modifying derivatives of both of these central unconscious fantasies. Like many others he insists "that the analytically created life history, while not fictive, is also not what one might call the absolute truth." It is a joint creation of patient and analyst and hence "being subject to a degree to the limitations, individualities, and visions of the two participants in the analytic process" (p. 292).

This brings me to my own longstanding interest in unconscious fantasies and most especially to my gradual realization of how often they can constitute a "hidden agenda" in the patients' unconscious treatment goals that are far different than any they, or we, are cognizant of early in the analysis. Ticho (1972) addressed himself to one aspect of this problem when he suggested that a patient's treatment goals be explored with him at the outset and kept in mind throughout the treatment. It was clear that he recognized how little this might tell us when he said, "changes in the patient's treatment goals will occur during the course of the analysis as the patient becomes aware of the unconscious goals which are closely connected with his neurosis" (p. 315). I believe it will become clear that I feel this is a rather optimistic view of the total picture and that in a varying proportion of instances, we fall far short of achieving this ideal goal.

In the same year I published two papers (1969a, 1969b) that each dealt with the clinical importance of unconscious fantasies connected with the primal scene, but differing in that one group seemed related to real events in the past while the other group did not, and yet both had important consequences. In the first paper (1969a) I cited examples of patients reenacting fantasies connected with real primal scene experiences, whether in dreams or in acting-out behavior, where instead of being the passive viewer excluded from the active drama, he or she was now an active doer or participant while the passive role was assigned to someone else. In the second paper (1969b) in a panel on narcissistic resistance, three clinical illustrations were given as possible explanations of the frequency and intensity of narcissistic resistance in relation to essentially oedipal material. At various times and from the various sources, their associations suggested that the patients had witnessed a parent of the opposite sex betraying them sexually with an adult who was not a parent. When I referred to this later (1981) I wrote

I have wondered if these might not be creations out of whole cloth similar in structure to Kris' "personal myth," arising from a preference for fantasied betrayal. In this latter case, the onus would be on the betraying parent, a reflection that would spare the patient the narcissistic injury connected with the anatomical, physiological and chronological facts that they could not be, and had not been as children, seriously considered as a sexual partner by the desired parent. And if this is true, we must recognize the implications for the patient that a successful analysis would reveal that there had been no real betrayal

—but only a sadly deflated child, and this is what they strive so
arduously to avoid repeating in the transference [p. 473].

Arlow in a related theme (1980) stressed the rage and revenge motives
stirred up in some children exposed to primal scenes.

The above material, and other experiences not necessarily related
to the primal scene, brought home to me again and again that one of
the greatest therapeutic obstacles occurs when the unconscious goal of
the patient is not to recall and then gain understanding of his history,
with all its traumatic and frustrating experiences, but to rewrite history
as he would have wished it to be and often still insists it must be. It is
when we uncover this goal that we recognize that for varying periods
of time we have been struggling with what I have come to think of as
the "hidden agenda" as reflected in one or a series of important unconscious fantasies. It would seem appropriate here to insert a comment
by Arlow (1964) as part of his summary of a discussion, "I did not intend to give the impression that the unconscious mental life of the particular individual is dominated by only one set of fantasies; what I have
meant is that there are many basic conflicts over repressed, instinctual
wishes and that many different sets of fantasies cluster around each of
these wishes" (p. 170). What must be added is that since, as with all
other mental products, these fantasies reflect compromises between id,
ego, and superego derivatives, any given fantasy while containing elements
of all the above, may still individually reflect primacy of the instinctual,
defensive, or punitive functions.

While I cannot conceive of an analysis that does not deal with the
uncovering of unconscious fantasies among other tasks, not all unconscious fantasies reflect the specific characteristics of those I would
like to isolate as reflecting a "hidden agenda." Whether as a result of
fixation, excessive trauma, marked narcissistic coloration, intensity of
the instinctual impulses, or unempathic or inadequate early object relations, the unconscious fantasies I am referring to take on an almost structural rigidity and driven quality that occasionally are not responsive to
the most tactful and repetitive interpretive efforts. It will be seen from
some of the clinical material I will refer to that several of my patients,
after a first analytic experience with me of from four to seven years duration with varying degrees of partial or minor changes, returned to me
a second time for some additional years of analysis. Fortunately several
of them were able to achieve some ultimate degree of fundamental change

but even then this was not always the outcome. Sandler (1976) stressed the frequency with which patients attempt to actualize in the transference their unconscious fantasies. He was essentially focusing on their attempts to restore situations that paralleled past solutions that gratified needs for security and safety but now with the analyst as the object, as in the past it had been with their mother. While I am certain that such devices often occur in treatment, I would only add that a patient may seek out such a relationship with the analyst regardless of whether the desired security reflected a real or fantasied relationship with the mother. Further, this is but one of a large of number of possible gratifications of old fantasies that patients may seek to actualize in the transference whether or not they had been successful in childhood. It is not necessary here to emphasize the potentials for countertransference present with patients who obsessively seek actualization of their fantasies in their relationship with their analyst. Freud (1920) was well aware of what they could evoke in us when he said, "They contrive once more to feel themselves scorned, to oblige the physician to speak severely to them and treat them coldly" (p. 21). And here he was only talking of negative transferences and not of the equally prevalent seductions attempted by patients in a host of subtle or overt forms.

Calef (1971) in his summary of a panel on the transference neurosis stated that after considerable analytic work "the patient experiences the analyst as a new and different person, not identical to his conceptions of his parents and his relationships to them, but much more like his fantasies and wishes dictate them to be. At that point the analyst is a potentially different object of love who promises, he believes, to satisfy his every fantasy" (p. 93). It would be my belief that these fantasies have existed from the beginning of analysis even though it may well take a considerable period of time before they emerge in recognizable form. Blum (1980) in delineating limitations to reconstructions, said, "There are ever present dangers of re-writing history and enlarging legend" (p. 41). He was expressing appropriate concern that we not add "analytic myth" to the patient's personal and familial myths.

CLINICAL MATERIAL

In presenting clinical vignettes to illustrate any issue or concept, one is always aware one is tearing out of the matrix of a long and involved analysis only selected segments. This must of necessity leave many unanswered questions for any sophisticated observer. Yet in order to give some idea of the variety and forms the fantasies connected with hidden agendas may assume, no other course is available.

While all of us can cite numerous examples of female patients who deal with relatively mild forms of penis envy by dreams of cars which they have temporarily lost or misplaced, or by a tendency to lose and rediscover their keys or fountain pens, this is not what I am referring to in case 1 of a number of cases that extend over the total period of my professional life as an analyst.

Case 1

This woman's essential complaints on entering analysis the first time were related to her dissatisfaction with her original profession as a teacher and the panic she anticipated at the idea of going back to graduate school to prepare for any other profession, since it would involve having to stand up and answer questions in class. As the work progressed she produced memories of sex play with an older brother and later of feeling her father's erect penis at times when she would be sitting on his lap. Her most important relations were with her mother and often involved her intense rage at feeling that her brother and father were preferred to her. This was eventually expanded to the whole society which would never allow a woman to achieve any real success and doomed her as well to be my least preferred patient. What emerged ever more clearly, first in dreams and ultimately in her associations, was her almost psychotic fantasy-based insistence that somehow, some day, some way she would get the missing penis back. Although other issues were also uncovered, the first analysis with me ultimately foundered after several years. She did come back into analysis after an interval and at least worked through the paralyzing inhibition against exhibiting herself in class. In fact she did quite well in completing her training for a profession where public speaking was an essential part of her work and even achieved considerable gratification from it. It is quite relevant to note that she had shifted from a profession where the majority of practitioners were women, to one where the majority were men. While this was hardly a total resolution of her major conflicts, she was making an adaptation on a personally more gratifying level.

Case 2

For this patient the central problem that reverberated throughout her two courses of analysis with me had to do with the fact that somewhere between the ages of five to severn years she learned that she was an adopted child. There were unconscious fantasies at various times of idealized or degraded biological parents. In her life activities she tried variously to achieve a reunion with an all-powerful, all-good, all-caring mother by trying to become part of institutions that she saw as in some way omnipotent and enduring. When she stopped the first time, she later revealed to me that she had seen me as the bad biological mother who sent her away and the coming back was like having a "second chance" to get a permanent relationship with the good adoptive mother (Wieder, 1977). She long had fantasies that if she were good enough her real mother would return and often expressed fantasies that someday I would allow her to live in my office between sessions. It was only near the end of her second analysis that she could even allow herself to seek what information was available about her biological mother, who she learned had died by that time. When expressing her wish that I would let her be a part of my family she added wistfully, "You were designated for that role." When the second analysis was ending, she seemed to have come to grips with reality which included the fact that she was married and functioning on a high level in her professional work, but still was aware of a sadness that she was indeed stopping for good now and would be seeking no further miracles from me again, or from any other analyst. While Blum (1969) spoke of potentially adaptive aspects of adoption fantasies, he had no illusions about the impact of real adoption. "They take on an especially profound importance when they are supported by reality" (p. 897).

Case 3

This young man was quite intelligent and yet sought analysis primarily because he was having difficulty completing his work for an advanced graduate degree. In addition, he was troubled by his overt homosexual activities and hoped he could be helped to make a heterosexual adjustment. Like the previous patients his analysis came in two phases and ended the second time when he quit permanently. In his homosexual activities it became clear that he was identified with his preferred lovers, namely adolescent boys who were physically very attractive. It was part of an unconscious fantasy where he identified with a very attractive and musically talented mother, or else he was a phallic extension of her. He was thus the mother who sought a union with an idealized aspect of himself. The father during this prolonged phase was demeaned as crude and generally inferior to the patient or his mother. The patient had heard that after his birth, his father essentially lost sexual interest in the mother. If so, this may well have thrown them even closer together. Yet ultimately, it was unearthed that the father had been away in the service for the first three to four years of his son's life and during that period the patient had come across his mother and a Rabbi, who was also a close family friend, in what has euphemistically been described as a "compromising position." So his homosexuality, and the fantasies associated with it, served the purpose of denying the fact that even in father's total absence he was not his mother's choice of lovers. It also helped avoid the marked castration anxiety he had in relationship to mother having exposed and then spread her labia for him, when as a child he asked for some sexual information. This would also seem to fit with Arlow's (1981) feeling that it was practically a universal fantasy to attempt separation from oedipal defeats with a fantasy "of the endless yearning to reexperience the primordial state of bliss, of reunion with the mother" (p. 504). Although he did finish his graduate work and got married, he never really worked through his oedipal problems and had to quit while seeing me as the ineffective father who had also failed to protect him from faithless and hypocritical women.

Case 4

This patient who had been a child of immigrant parents had through her own intelligence and hard work achieved an important academic position and recognition as a scholar in her area of expertise. But personal happiness was not among her accomplishments. As with the other patients mentioned to this point she was a returnee to analysis when her marriage was collapsing. An important aspect of her character and symptomatology was her attempt to live out her unconscious fantasies with all the important people in her life based on her relationship with her mother. The latter, who late in life became psychotic, had infinite faith in the efficacy of enemas to rid the body of all potential harm. Although a younger brother, relatively early, protested the enemas and then refused them altogether, my patient submitted to them almost to puberty. This became a model for all object relationships, including of course the transference. She was either the victim of a sadistic, intrusive mother/analyst whose interpretations where therefore assiduously avoided, thereby ensuring the need for repetition, or else she played her mother's role in her intrusive behavior into her husband's professional work or into the lives of her children. Abend (1979 p. 582) could well have been thinking of her counterpart when he cited Applebaum (1972) that some patients "have unconscious wishes to defeat, undermine, and ridicule the would-be-helpers in some patients' responses to analysis." Their fantasies then convert the gratification they get in treatment into all they desire for treatment and so perpetuate treatment while blocking all progress or change.

Case 5

An obsessive compulsive male patient with almost overwhelming castration anxiety fantasies based on extremely seductive behavior by his mother with ample opportunity to visit the parental bedroom used the "conditional voice" (Arlow, 1969b) as a device not to see anything too clearly in the analysis, lest he see the unwanted facts about a woman's genitals. He, of course, had many unconscious fantasies of women having penises. He never gave a direct comment about any of this thoughts, feelings or observations without first modifying them with a conditional word like some, a little, maybe, possibly, or perhaps. He might suddenly notice items that had always been in my office after years of coming there as though to prove how easily he could overlook objects that did exist. In the transference for a long time he had a way of warding off my interpretations and denying their reality by assigning to me unwanted aspects of his own thoughts as though he literally heard me saying them, while ignoring what I did say. Although there was no question of his being even remotely psychotic, he used this regressive defense of a merging with self-object mother as though we were one and the same, to defend against the much more frightening oedipal mother, or me as a separate therapist.

Case 6

One of my first analytic cases was a young woman, who early in her analysis suddenly began making rather dramatic writhing movements on the couch that showed no apparent relationship to her free associations. When I finally asked if she were aware of her movements, she acted surprised but never repeated them. It was some three years before we were to recover the memory of an older brother who under the guise of wrestling with her at age five or so had pinned her down and touched her genitals. It became clear that assuming the horizontal position on the couch had stirred up unconscious fantasies based on her wish/fear that I, like her brother, would take advantage of her position on the couch to use her in the same way. It certainly seems an excellent example of Beres and Arlow's (1974) reference to a nonverbal communication of a fantasy through motor activity.

Case 7

The last case that constraints of space allow could actually be a condensation of several women patients I have seen who lived out the unconscious fantasy that they never initiated any activity and only reacted to the behavior of others, or were totally unaffected by what others did to them on the outside, or in treatment. This was a vehicle of denying they had exhibited themselves to adults in childhood or had in any way behaved seductively. It also denied the guilt they felt, even if an adult had initiated the sexual activity, of their having enjoyed it, or responded to it with excitement.

But the patient I would like to describe in more detail here is one whose unconscious fantasies led her to adopt sadomasochistic behavioral activities that were as harmful and painful to herself as they were to others. As part of her neurotic and overdetermined need to deny any sexual interest in all men, including her husband, she had to take on an excessive amount of weight and neglect her personal hygiene. So the first part of her analysis dealt largely with her marked oral needs and feelings of having been the child most neglected by her mother. But even then we were struck with the pas de deux she was involved in with her first child, a daughter with whom she clearly identified in various ways. She would regularly provoke this daughter to attack her verbally in language that became increasingly salty as the daughter got older. This continued even after the daughter got married and left home. If things were peaceful between them for a short time the patient would soon again find some excuse for provoking her daughter in some needlessly intrusive fashion, after which my patient clearly suffered intense pain. While it soon became evident that she was enacting an unconscious fantasy where a bad mother is being severely punished by a daughter who is entitled to self-righteous indignation, it was several years before we could discover why. It is first important to stress that one of her most enduring character traits was the perpetual need to deny she had ever started any quarrel, whether with her husband, her daughter, her boss, or her friends. At the very most, she only reacted to what others started. Finally, and extremely gradually, she began to deal with material hinting that something sexual had occurred between herself and her father, when she was three or four and mother was out of town a few days. For a long time it was presented with the implication that father had her take a nap with him during which time he had done something sexual to her. What finally emerged in a dream and was tearfully corroborated by her was that father had been napping in bed when she joined him. He may have been partially exposed. At any rate she became very curious about his penis, examined and fondled it, and apparently wound up inserting it in her mouth. She was later terrified about what her mother might do to her when she returned. It was now clear that the fantasy she acted out with her daughter totally denied any guilt on her part, especially that she, the daughter, would ever start anything bad, or if anything, it was the absent mother who was the bad one and regularly deserved punishment and abuse from the innocent daughter.

DISCUSSION AND SUMMARY

Although this by no means exhausts the clinical illustrations I might have reported, it is, I trust, sufficient to illustrate a range of unconscious fantasies that can act as a hidden agenda to thwart the conscious goals of the patient seeking analysis and render our own therapeutic efforts either ineffective or requiring considerably longer periods of application.

We have in passing mentioned some of the possible reasons why these types of fantasies can temporarily, or permanently, render our work more or less fruitless and would expect that the answer or answers are multifaceted. One of the things frequently mentioned as capable of producing unconscious fantasies and hence a hidden agenda most difficult to cope with has been that associated with childhood traumas and especially childhood seduction. But my material underlines not only the importance of the role played by "real" and repeated seductions, but the equally devastating effects that can be produced by the guilt arising from "real" sexual activities initiated by the child—as demonstrated by my last clinical example and other patients I have analyzed.

Certainly the more narcissistically tinged the object relationships, the more difficult it may be to use the interpretation of the transference to encourage more adaptive behavior in our patients. In this regard, I found a relatively recent contribution of Ikonen and Rechardt (1984) challenging. Although there are aspects of Kleinian theory in their views, which I cannot ascribe to, I found much of what they say worth noting. They start with the basic assumption that primal scene fantasies are part of the important organizing fantasies in psychosexual development. It further is an intersecting point between narcissistic and oedipal problems. This is one area where the child doesn't learn by experiencing the active help of an instructive parent. Rather, by being excluded from the adult sexual functions, and often even being made to feel inferior or shameful, it affects not only object relations but self-esteem or self-cathexis as well. To be excluded then may lead one to feel one is nothing, while inclusion is an important achievement for both self-worth and positive object relationships. Like any other factor, even if valid, this would hardly account for the vicissitudes encountered in the total variety of fantasies found functioning as hidden agendas. Yet because of the ubiquitous nature of unconscious fantasies, any additional light we can shed on those that act as major obstacles to therapeutic success warrant our full and continued interest.

REFERENCES

Abend, S. M. (1979), Unconscious fantasy and theories of cure. *J. Amer. Psychoanal. Assn.*, 2:579–596.

Applebaum, A. (1972), A critical re-examination of the concept 'motivation for change' in psychoanalytic treatment. *Internat. J. Psycho-Anal.* 53:51-59.

Arlow, J. A. (1960), Fantasy systems in twins. *Psychoanal. Quart.*, 29:175–199.

———— (1961), Ego psychology and the study of mythology. *J. Amer. Psychonanal. Assn.*, 9:371–393.

———— (1964), Symposium on symptom formation and character formation: Summary of discussion. *Internat. J. Psycho-Anal.*, 45:167–170.

———— (1969a), Fantasy, memory, and reality testing. *Psychoanal. Quart.*, 38:28–51.

———— (1969b), Unconscious fantasy and disturbances of conscious experience. *Psychoanal. Quart.*, 38:1-27.

———— (1980), The revenge motive in the primal scene. *J. Amer. Psychoanal. Assn.*, 28:519–541.

———— (1981), Theories of pathogenesis. *Psychoanal. Quart.*, 50:488–514.

Beres, D. (1962), The unconscious phantasy. *Psychoanal. Quart,* 31:309–328.

—— & Arlow, J. (1974), Fantasy and identification in empathy. *Psychoanal. Quart.*, 43:26–50.

Blum, H. P. (1969), A psychoanalytic view of *Who's Afraid of Virginia Woolf? J. Amer. Psychoanal. Assn.*, 17:888–903.

—— (1979), Concept and consequences of the primal scene. *Psychoanal. Quart.*, 48:27–47.

—— (1980), Reconstruction in adult psychoanalysis. *Internat. J. Psycho-Anal.*, 61:39–52.

Calef, V., rep. (1971), Concluding remarks. *J. Amer. Psychonal. Assn.*, 17:89–97.

Freud, S. (1899), Screen memories. *Standard Edition*, 3:301–322. London: Hogarth Press, 1962.

—— (1908), Family romances. *Standard Edition*, 9:235–241. London: Hogarth Press, 1959.

—— (1916–1917), Introductory lectures on psycho-analysis. *Standard Edition*, 15–16. London: Hogarth Press, 1963.

—— (1920), Beyond the pleasure principle. *Standard Edition*, 18:1–64. London: Hogarth Press, 1955.

—— (1925), An autobiographical study. *Standard Edition*, 20:1–39. London: Hogarth Press, 1959.

Gaddini, E. (1982), Early defensive fantasies and the psychoanalytic process. *Internat. J. Psycho-Anal.*, 63:379–388.

Ikonen, P., & Rechardt, E. (1984), On the universal nature of primal scene fantasies. *Internat. J. Psycho-Anal.*, 65:63–72.

Kohut, H. (1964), Some problems of a metapsychological formulation of fantasy. *Internat. J. Psycho-Anal.*, 45:199–202.

Kris, E. (1956a), The personal myth. *J. Amer. Psychoanal. Assn.*, 4:653–681.

—— (1956b), The recovery of childhood memories in psychoanalysis. *The Psychoanalytic Study of the Child*, 11:54–88. New York: International Universities Press.

Rosen, V. (1964), Contribution to the discussion. *Internat. J. Psycho-Anal.*, 45:195–198.

Sachs, O. (1967), Distinctions between fantasy and reality elements in memory and reconstruction. *Internat. J. Psycho-Anal.*, 48:416–423.

Sandler, J. (1976), Actualization and object relationships. *J. Phila. Assn. Psychoanal.*, 3:59–70.

—— Nagera, H. (1963), The metapsychology of fantasy. *The Psychoanalytic Study of the Child*, 18:159–194. New York: International Universities Press.

Schafer, R. (1970), The psychoanalytic vision of reality. *Internat. J. Psycho-Anal.*, 51:279–297.

Segel, N. (1969a), Contribution to panel on narcissistic resistance, rep. N. Segel. *J. Amer. Psychoanal. Assn.*, 17:941–954.

_____ (1969b), Repetition compulsion, acting out, and identification with the doer. *J. Amer. Psychoanal. Assn.*, 17:474–488.

_____ (1981), Narcissism and adaptation to reality. *Internat. J. Psycho-Anal.*, 62:465–576.

Ticho, E. (1972), Termination of psychoanalysis: Treatment goals, life goals. *Psychoanal. Quart.*, 41:315–333.

Wieder, H. (1977), The family romance fantasies of adopted children. *Psychoanal. Quart.*, 46:185–200.

9

Unconscious Fantasies and Issues of Termination

Sander M. Abend, M.D.

That the analysis of a patient's unconscious fantasies about the meaning of termination is a significant analytic task is an observation made frequently by analysts over the years. However, it is not often their principal topic; more often, it appears as a remark subsidiary to exposition of other termination issues (for a notable exception, see Boesky, Chapter 7).

Credit for first calling attention to the importance of analyzing unconscious fantasies about seemingly realistic termination issues might well be attributed to Hermann Nunberg (1926), whose paper ''The Will to Recovery'' elucidated the vital role played by unconscious fantasies about the meaning of cure in determining the course and outcome of analytic treatment. Many, though not all, types of fantasy about termination turn out to be variants of fantasies about how analysis works, and about the meaning of cure through analysis. Others express something about the relationship between analyst and analysand, or about the termination of that relationship and of the treatment itself.

My own interest in this question is an outgrowth of previous work (Abend, 1979) on the connection between unconscious fantasies and the theories of cure held by patients or analysts. In the present work I intend to examine some ways in which patients' unconscious fantasies about termination may affect the termination phase, and to consider how analysts' theories about the analytic process and its termination may influence their management of termination issues.

It is probably best to begin by examining the sorts of fantasies that may arise in patients, and the role these can play in the technical management of termination issues. In the illustrative material I will of necessity condense and simplify complex analytic issues in order to highlight the impact of the relevant fantasies and their practical consequences. Perhaps the most frequently occurring instance involves the emergence of a desire to terminate analysis prematurely because of the upsurge of an unconscious fantasy, or set of fantasies.

Ms. A. entered analysis in her early twenties, primarily because of an unsatisfactory pattern of short-lived love relationships in which she invariably felt herself exploited, mistreated, or otherwise disappointed. Her masochistic character structure contributed to severe difficulties in the expression of aggression; the persistence of a resentfully submissive attitude toward parents, siblings, employers, and friends; inhibition of achievement; and a generalized diminution of conscious pleasure and satisfaction from activities and relationships. During the course of her analysis steady improvement was made in all areas of functioning, although the influence of her character pathology on the transference led her to experience the analysis as in general an unpleasant task that she carried out conscientiously, and the analyst as a powerful taskmaster to whom she had to submit. There was only intermittent recognition of the unconscious gratifications that accompanied these surface attitudes.

In the seventh year of analysis she became pregnant, having by then been satisfactorily married for about a year and a half. She soon began to speak of a wish to interrupt her analysis for an indeterminate period after the birth of her baby. This was an intense wish, despite her opinion that there remained important problems requiring further analytic work.

Over a series of sessions she elaborated the fantasies about interrupting treatment. At first she complained about the inconvenience of a fixed analytic schedule, even though she had selected her hours as optimal from the standpoint of her personal and professional commitments. Of course, she added, no other hours would be any more convenient. If only she did not have to come every day, but only when she chose—a multifaceted, overdetermined wish that had surfaced often earlier in the analysis. She worried that adequate care could not be arranged for her baby when she attended sessions, though she fully intended to keep on running her successful business. Finally she brought up the idea that she intended to breast-feed the child on demand, and worried what might happen if the baby became hungry while she was away. Thus there emerged the unconscious fantasy of providing for her baby the totally available, totally gratifying mother, whose undivided attention the infant was entitled to. This corresponded to her own infantile wishes with respect to her mother, and represented in part a vicarious undoing of severe disappointments. She imagined becoming a reproachful example to her mother of what a real mother should be like. Complaints about her mother's self-absorption and lack of genuine devotion had been a major theme in her analysis. Although these were rooted in a consistent and presumably accurate depiction of her mother's character, the grievances also expressed an intense jealousy and envy of the attention and love her mother bestowed on others, especially Ms. A.'s younger sister. The analysis of many conflicts about this and many other rivalries for her mother's affection had been an important part of the treatment all along.

The fantasy, or rather fantasies, of devotion also expressed an unconscious homosexual current in her emotional life; the analyst, standing for her baby's father, would be shunted aside while she gave her love exclusively to the child, who she said was certain to be a girl.

This material was apparently quite convincing to Ms. A., who soon commented on the impossible, even harmful consequences that might follow if she actually attempted to institute so indulgent a relationship with her baby. Nevertheless, her wish to leave analysis in order to care for her baby persisted. Further associations indicated that this was an unconsciously determined attempt to deny any connection between the analyst and the baby. This was a defense against acknowledging yet another unconscious fantasy, one attributing the child's paternity to the powerful analyst-father. We then added to our understanding of her reactions the fact that unconsciously she thought of this baby as the fulfillment of a forbidden oedipal triumph over her mother. The guilt attendant on this required that she sacrifice her relationship with the analyst, the gratifying aspects of which were usually expressed only in the concealed form of masochistic, obligatory submission. After this work, her idea about interrupting the analysis subsided, and the analysis moved on to other issues.

In summary then, her wish to terminate the analysis prematurely arose from a network of unconscious fantasies, the analysis of which averted its enactment and preserved the analysis, a technical matter of the greatest practical importance. In other cases, comparable fantasies prove resistant to analytic efforts, or fail to emerge with sufficient clarity, and termination under less than optimal circumstances cannot be prevented. When that is the outcome the analyst can hardly be certain that he is altogether aware of all the pertinent fantasies, but their presence can often be inferred.

One young man, in analysis for three and a half years for profound sexual inhibitions, had made sufficient progress to become passionately involved with an attractive and suitable woman. One day he arrived for his session, sat in a chair rather than going to the couch as was usual, and announced that the previous evening he had proposed marriage to her and she had accepted. He had therefore reached the decision to terminate his analysis that very day. He had given no warning whatsoever that this sudden turn of events had been on his mind. He remained in the office just long enough to bring forth some associations to thoughts of his father's death, and some vaguely worded references to worries about what he imagined were the analyst's reactions to his decisions, but the analyst was unable to arouse in him sufficient interest in examining the meanings of these interconnected themes and concerns to prevent the abrupt and untimely foreclosure of the analysis. Though not always so dramatic, unsatisfactory premature terminations of a similar nature, and for comparable irrational reasons, occur more often than we might wish.

Here is an example of another type of termination issue, in relation to which the analysis of unconscious fantasies is of considerable practical significance. I have in mind the problem of evaluating the timeliness of the decision to terminate in cases in which analysis has gone on for many years, with evidence of steady and continuing improvement, but with much residual difficulty. In such cases the relationship with the analyst has often become an important source of gratification that the analysand, consciously or unconsciously, is reluctant to surrender. I do not intend to take up the general question of the appropriate criteria for termination, but instead to indicate how the analysis of relevant unconscious fantasies can contribute to clarifying the issues involved in arriving at a determination in certain difficult cases. In contrast to the previous illustration, in which the pertinent material emerged in the course of a week or so of analysis, in the next case the fantasies about termination or continuation emerged over the course of many weeks.

Ms. B., after the divorce of her parents when she was four years old, was shuttled back and forth between her well-to-do European mother, an unstable, jet-set type, and her expatriate American father. She had several years of productive analysis while in school in Switzerland as a youngster; this had helped her to attain a measure of emotional independence and stability, and to decide on the direction her life would take. She then moved to the United States, where her father had resumed living, and took up a professional career. After her marriage, however, internal conflict involving the prospect of motherhood versus the appeal of continuing her successful career led her to seek further analysis.

I will omit even a summary of the issues with which the analysis dealt in the several years of work before the question of termination arose, but it is accurate to say that slow, sustained progress in many areas of her life was evident, although it was equally clear that residual manifestations of her conflicts persisted in troublesome ways, both in the conduct of her life and in her behavior in sessions. She tentatively brought forward the question of whether we had accomplished as much as we were likely to achieve, if not all she had hoped for. As together we began to contemplate the implications of this question, including her reactions to the possibility of ending the analysis, an uncharacteristic amount of domestic friction arose in her life, and this claimed our attention during her hours. It soon became evident that this served to express her profound unwillingness to give up the analysis and the analyst.

Attention to her reluctance to consider termination seriously first made it clear that she unconsciously regarded the analyst as the benign, omnipotent, and attentive mother she had always wanted. She longed for a magical protector against the vicissitudes of fate, in contrast to her real mother, who had repeatedly failed to provide elementary care and concern even in circumstances when she might reasonably have done so. This aspect of the gratifying transference soon gave way to yet another, more subtle transference motive for continuing the analysis indefinitely. It turned out that the combination of serious application to the analytic work, marked by quite real productivity and dedicated cooperation, coupled with the apparently never-ending necessity for still more analytic work perfectly expressed an aspect of this woman's lifelong relationship with her father. Separated from him by virtue of her parents' divorce when she was a child, she had nevertheless succeeded in establishing a unique bond with him that persisted into her adult years. Despite his two subsequent marriages, and the numerous other offspring that resulted, she had made herself special to him by choosing his profession as her own, by intellectual achievement, productivity, and an essentially cooperative attitude toward him and his preferences, all of which gave him great satisfaction, as she had always realized. She saw to it that their common interests served to cement their mutual attachment. His continuing special interest in her had seemed literally life-saving during her early years, when the environment provided by her mother was chaotic and unreliable. This very real need and attachment also served as the vehicle for more irrational, repressed oedipal longings that had been brought to light by the analysis. Thus the ongoing transference situation neatly replicated the consciously acceptable positive tie she had forged with her father; to bring the analytic work to a successful conclusion would mean surrendering once and for all the childhood romantic wishes and fantasies that were its unconscious accompaniments. To end analysis could in that sense hardly be regarded as satisfactory, but rather as the acceptance of painfully finite limits, of severe disappointment, of inferiority to successful rivals for the analyst-father's love, and of permanent unhappiness. So long as she continued to improve, however, her unconscious view was that she improved her chances of ultimate satisfaction of her oedipal dreams. This unconscious conviction reinforced her reluctance to accept the disappointment associated with the realistic limitations of the treatment process.

The pragmatic issue of arriving at a mutually acceptable estimate of what analysis can be expected to achieve, never easy to resolve in cases such as this one, was complicated here by the fact that she was unconsciously motivated to maintain quite genuine analytic progress while at the same time retaining unyielding islands of resistance that appeared to justify a continuation of the analysis. Once this aspect of the clinical situation was clarified, an extended period of work on the various unconscious meanings of termination ensued. In the course of months of analysis a number of fantasies about termination emerged: termination as death of the analyst, as castration of the analyst and/or the patient, as surrender of her hopes for perfection and omnipotence, as irrevocable loss and loneliness, and as punishment for a variety of unconsciously desired transgressions.

I am not in a position to suggest that in all cases of prolonged analytic treatment one is likely to find unconscious fantasies like the ones described. In this case attention to the possibility of termination brought them to light, and clarified both the course this analysis had taken and the patient's unconscious contribution to it. This increased understanding served to illuminate the practical decision with which the analyst and analysand were faced.

What constitutes the termination phase is a matter of dispute among authors holding different fundamental assumptions regarding the analytic process. Even so, most recent discussions are consistent with Firestein's proposal (1978) that the termination phase be considered to begin when the subject is introduced, whether by the analyst or by the analysand,

and is regarded by both as a real possibility. A second stage of this phase commences when a definite decision to terminate has been reached, and a date has been selected. With some patients, fantasies about the meaning of termination make their appearance early in the course of analysis, but even in treatments where this is not a prominent feature, the serious introduction of the topic serves to mobilize fantasies, the analysis of which constitutes an important aspect of the analytic work of this period. Some fantasies, not previously mentioned, may come forth only after the actual setting of a date.

I believe it is always potentially disadvantageous for analysts to think in terms of typical fantasies or issues, as this may serve to inhibit the sort of open-minded receptivity to the uniqueness of each analytic unfolding that characterizes the optimal analytic attitude. The questions that arise in each analysand's termination phase are highly specific, not only in their minute details, but in their broad thematic organization as well. Arguing against the then prevalent supposition that all analytic termination phases necessarily involve reactions of mourning-separation from the primary (maternal) caretaking figure, Arlow and Brenner (1966) presented data illustrating other varieties of termination fantasies. At the same time, Rangell (1966) independently proffered a warning against any stereotyped way of looking at the problems of this phase and noted that the overt separation "can represent any threat and can reawaken any form of anxiety" (p. 153).

The termination material presented in the literature suggests that while the fantasies that emerge may cluster about a recurrent set of manifest general themes and preoccupations, the unconscious meanings of these fantasies are not always easily to be inferred from their surface appearance. The reader is usually obliged to rely, with more or less confidence, on the writer's conclusions regarding the primary significance of the fantasies encountered. In Firestein's material, for example, in five of the eight cases described, important fantasies about a postanalytic relationship with the analyst, fantasies using an hypothesized, superficially plausible ongoing professional tie as a vehicle for maintaining the contact, were encountered. To what extent these served to deny irrevocable separation and loss, to what extent they represented rationalized derivatives of oedipal wishes of some sort (whether in the form of insufficiently attenuated variants of identification with the analyst, or in other forms of unwillingness to surrender infantile wishes for fulfillment)— these are determinations that cannot always be made from the presentations.

The same might be said for fantasies on the theme of pregnancy, birth, or rebirth, another commonly encountered variety of termination fantasy. Birth and rebirth fantasies often express omnipotent wishes to undo the disappointments of childhood; they may arise in connection with patients' theories, conscious or unconscious, about how analysis will provide a cure for their emotional problems. However, birth and rebirth fantasies may also serve to undo or deny frightening ideas of separation and loss in preoedipal terms, as well as to convey elements of the wishful, conflicted material of the oedipal phase.

Just as fantasies about mourning, separation, and loss can communicate unconscious ideas stemming from any level of aggressive or libidinal development, and are therefore capable of expressing all varieties of instinctual conflict, the same may be said of fantasies involving issues of omnipotence, limitations, and control. It is indisputably true that the ending of an analysis always means facing the inevitable loss of a significant relationship, and whatever unconscious significance that may have in a given individual's emotional life. It also necessarily has the meaning of surrendering, yet again, certain important infantile wishes, whatever these may be in a given case. Kramer (1986) refers to "the renunciation and grief following the recognition that we can never have what we always wanted" (p. 349). Wishes for omnipotence, for control over others and over events are psychological issues related not merely to preoedipal object relations or narcissistic development, but to all aspects of childhood mental life. Their significance as themes of termination fantasies are not limited to conflicts over separation anxiety in the earliest phase of development, as Miller (1965) has suggested, but can express aspects of central oedipal fantasies as well (see Loewald, 1962; Hurn, 1971).

It follows that the ultimate practical consequence of analyzing the unconscious fantasies mobilized by termination is furtherance of the analytic work. Whatever form these termination fantasies take, they express compromise formations derived from the central instinctual conflicts of each analysand's psychological makeup. Many authors (e.g., Freud, 1918; Orens, 1955; Miller, 1965; Schmideberg, 1938; Hurn, 1971; Boesky, Chapter 7) have illustrated the fact that some important fantasies critical to the resolution of patients' neurotic difficulties may emerge only in the context of termination, and consequently are able to be fully clarified only in the course of analyzing the unconscious reverberations of the idea of termination. In some cases the termination phase may in fact assume a dramatic appearance that seems to justify regarding it as the culmination of the entire analytic experience. This is a somewhat deceptive way of looking at things, however. In all cases, whether or not demonstrably new or dramatic material is forthcoming during termination, analyzing the unconscious significance of whatever fantasies are called forth by the idea of termination cannot but advance the analyst's and the patient's understanding of crucial aspects of whatever led the patient to seek analysis in the first place.

If an analyst's theoretical preconceptions lead him to expect that certain issues will invariably arise during termination, or that certain themes and problems must always be faced and dealt with during termination, he may be predisposed to regard material that he encounters during the termination phase in accordance with those views. As I have stated, many fantasies of the termination phase have multiple meanings, and their most important unconscious significance is often far removed from their manifest appearance. It is a simple matter for analysts to agree in principle that all analytic data should be analyzed without prejudice, but theoretical convictions at times act as subtle funnels for channeling analysts' comprehension in the direction of their expectations.

Consciously held theoretical beliefs can influence analysts' handling of the termination phase disadvantageously in ways other than a selective focusing on the aspects of conflict they expect to encounter. I will omit a consideration of individual countertransference difficulties, although it has long been recognized that potentially troublesome countertransferences can be mobilized by impending termination (for a succinct review, see Viorst, 1982).

I regard it as inescapable that the unconscious fantasies and predilections of analysts will to some degree influence their theoretical preferences and convictions. This fact does not of itself speak to the question of the validity of the theories held, though it may in some cases handicap the objective assessment of data. It is, however, only the careful accumulation of good clinical data that ultimately determines the validity of explanatory hypotheses in psychoanalysis. In examining the relation between analysts' theoretical beliefs and issues of termination, I shall concentrate on analysts' explicit or implicit conceptualizations of analysis, insofar as these may influence their understanding and management of termination.

We may well begin with Freud (1918), whose decision arbitrarily to impose a time limit on the Wolf Man's analysis in order to overcome entrenched resistance was demonstrated to have been of more dubious benefit than he believed at the time. This technical device, however, has influenced subsequent generations of analysts faced with difficult or unusually protracted analyses. Freud's tactic was perfectly consistent with the opinion he held at the time that it was both necessary and desirable for the analyst to exercise his influence to persuade the analysand to overcome his resistances. Such is the compelling power of Freud's famous example that in clinical presentations one still encounters the rationale that only the imposition of a definite ending will mobilize certain crucial material. However, there is certainly nothing in our current theory of technique that supports the idea that powerful resistances should or will be curtailed by the exercise of the analyst's authority, or that analysands' attempts to retain transference gratifications can be arbitrarily prohibited without adversely affecting the analytic climate. The tactic of suggesting or imposing termination in order to bring out important issues should be discarded as anachronistic and technically unsound.

A selective survey of the literature will illustrate how analysts' different conceptualizations of the analytic process and its termination can at least in part determine what they are primed to attend to in the analytic material, what they think must be accomplished during the termination phase, what their criteria are for concluding that termination is timely and how that decision is implemented, and whether or not they manage the termination phase any differently from other aspects of the analysis.

Glover (1955) saw the termination phase in classical analysis as devoted primarily to transference weaning and ego readaptation, bringing to an end the state of regression that marks the transference neurosis. According to Glover, the analyst, not the patient, must decide when termination is indicated. Most analysts today would be more likely to hope that in the best cases the decision to terminate would be a mutual one, arrived at after appropriate discussion between the two participants. Goldberg and Marcus (1985) have gone so far as to describe a technical maneuver in which no mutually agreed upon date is ever set, the actual choice being left entirely in the hands of the analysand. Whether the adoption of such a self-consciously nonauthoritarian stance has any real advantage over what it was designed to correct is questionable.

Annie Reich (1950) believed that the gratifications inherent in the analytic situation can never be entirely resolved by interpretations alone, and that therefore, some pressure from the analyst for the analysand to accept termination will nearly always be required. Miller (1965) has suggested that only in the termination period can separation anxiety from the earliest phase of development be worked through; he regards this as a specific task of termination. Loewald (1962) has stated that "ideally termination should culminate in or lead into a genuine relinquishment of the external object (the analyst) as an incestuous love object and, in the transformation of the external relationship into an internal relationship within the ego-superego system" (p. 488).

Hurn (1971) has suggested that a termination phase "begins with the appearance of evidence that the patient has significantly accepted the impossibility of obtaining infantile gratifications from the analyst . . ." (p. 346). He thinks that although separation-mourning reactions derived in part from the realistic collaboration with the analyst as a real person are to be expected, they do not require special technical management. This latter question has at times been a subject of some controversy, as witness the American Psychoanalytic Association Panel discussion reported by Robbins (1975).

Karl Menninger (1966), in a succinct discussion of Rangell's excellent survey of termination issues (1966), makes the observation that analysts' models of psychoanalysis have a bearing on their concepts of termination. Among those he enumerates is the parent-child model, in which "the idea [is] . . . that the parent guides the child less and less and expects emancipation to occur in adolescence as a natural growth" (p. 169). Menninger himself prefers the model of visiting an art gallery, where the "law of diminishing returns" might serve as an indicator for termination.

Derivatives of what Menninger labeled the parent-child model of analysis are not hard to detect in the literature. Buxbaum (1950), writing on the technique of termination of analysis, states that technique should be adapted to fit the particular needs of each analysand. Which course of action is adopted by the analyst depends on an assessment of what will most likely promote the patient's independence and well-being; this cannot be accomplished, in her opinion, by interpretation alone. In a clinical example she employs a tactic in the termination phase designed to demonstrate to the analysand that he could act independently, "and also [to demonstrate] . . . the analyst's faith in his ability to do so and her permission [for him] . . . to be independent" (p. 186). She does not appear to have considered that reaching these assessments and adopting tactics accordingly might themselves constitute maintaining a parental attitude, rather than an analytic one, toward the patient. It may be more accurate to say that Buxbaum regards it as proper for the analyst to have a parental attitude toward patients, as long as that attitude leads the analyst to behave like a better, more health-promoting parent than were the real parents. This conceptualization bears a certain correspondence to the wishes of many patients, as expressed in their theories of cure, especially those based on rebirth or adoption fantasies. For that reason it may well become an issue for any analyst whose theoretical views or personal predilections incline him toward that model of the psychoanalytic relationship.

Novick (1982) has noted parallels between termination phase processes in satisfactory analyses and normal adolescent maturational processes. He believes the imposition of a termination date may be necessary to provide the impetus for work essential to a proper termination, which should include (following the template of adolescent development) experiencing disappointment in the formerly idealized analyst, and mourning the loss of the real relationship with the analyst.

Shane and Shane (1984) are among those influenced by a developmental point of view, and thus their criteria for termination include an assessment, for which they present clinical guidelines, of the analysand's manifest capability for autonomous functioning. They also hold that it is essential to analytic work in the termination phase that the patient anticipate and mourn the impending separation from the analyst, as both transference object and real person.

In contrast to emphases on the transference or developmental criteria, consider the point of view expressed by Kramer (1986). According to him, the goal of analysis centers on the clarification of core conflicts and their registration on the analysand. Speaking of the analyst, Kramer says, "He can clarify for himself and interpret to the patient over and over again so that it becomes unambiguously clear and indelibly permanent what the patient's unacceptable wishes are and what his defenses against these are, and how they are connected with his symptomatology" (p. 348). Included in this conception is the idea that any resolution of conflict, and any change resulting therefrom, is entirely a function of the patient's inherent psychological capabilities and conscious choices. The task of the analyst is conceptualized as a purely technical one, and when it is achieved to the best of the analyst's ability, termination is in order. No special tasks are attributed to the termination phase except that of dealing analytically with whatever reactions to termination may arise.

It follows from Kramer's view of the analytic process that the analyst's technical stance, incorporating the familiar tenets of abstinence and neutrality, and confining interventions to the task of interpretation, will remain unchanged throughout the entire termination phase, right up to the very conclusion of each analysis. This view contrasts with that of such analysts as Glover, who view the termination phase as a period during which the regression that accompanies the transference neurosis is expected to be reversed. Some of these analysts have developed a rationale for adopting a modified technical posture toward their patients during the termination period. A relaxation of the principle of abstinence and its accompanying constraints, in favor of permitting some measure of interaction on a more personal level, along with accepting an increased focus on the realistic aspects of the relationship between analyst and analysand, and on the analysand's current and future realistic concerns, might well characterize their technique during the termination phase. At present very few analysts advocate a radical shift in technique to facilitate termination, but residues of older viewpoints are sometimes seen in the acceptance of a shift of emphasis onto aspects of the real relationship with the analyst, as distinguished from the transference relationship (Robbins, 1975).

Although the present generation of analysts no longer uses marked technical shifts to assist satisfactory termination, the various conceptualizations of analysis still contribute to significant differences among analysts with respect to other termination issues. The many discussions of criteria for termination to be found in the literature attest to the difficulty analysts encounter in arriving at this crucial practical judgment. This is all the more true in analyses, like the one described earlier, in which productive work goes on for a number of years but important symptomatic and characterological problems persist. Arriving at a determination about ending such treatments is never easy for analyst or patient. The analyst's own criteria must guide him, if not necessarily in the categorical fashion described by Glover (1955).

Shane and Shane (1984) have described the effort to identify signs of improved autonomous functioning in patients; Novick (1982) seeks evidence of a full-blown oedipal transference; Hurn (1971) looks for signs that the analysand sees the impossibility of achieving satisfaction of infantile needs; Rangell (1966, 1982) would like to see that the analysand has succeeded in incorporating certain aspects of the analyst's analytic mode of thought into his own mental armamentarium; Miller

(1965) seeks evidence of the confrontation with early separation anxiety; and Kramer (1986) emphasizes only the accomplishment of successfully understanding the crucial elements of the patient's conflicts and communicating them to him. In addition, these authors and others might differ in their expectations as to the nature of the material to be encountered during the termination phase.

In assessing the analytic material generated by their patients, analysts cannot but employ clinical yardsticks derived from their own conceptual preferences, and cannot help scanning the data in search of content that their particular expectations lead them to believe is important. A potential source of difficulty rests in the fact that most if not all analysands take on to some degree the clinical vocabulary employed by their analysts. When material is presented to the analyst in terms that approximate his own intellectual framework, he is perhaps a bit less likely to examine it critically, or to examine it for concealed transference expressions or subtle manifestations of resistance than might otherwise be the case (for a description of one variety of this complication of analysis, see Stein, 1981). The tendency to find confirmation of the analyst's own views with respect to the criteria for termination, as well as to expected reactions to the prospect of termination, is probably harder to overcome in such situations.

To the extent that any of this is true in an analytic situation, the ongoing analytic work of the termination phase is potentially compromised by the influence of the analyst's preferred theories, and any unconscious fantasies he may have that support those theories. Since thorough analysis of all the patient's unconscious fantasies about any aspect of termination is an important part of the analytic work, any constriction of the analyst's sensitivity to the unconscious meaning of analytic material is a definite handicap. Perhaps the best corrective available is to enjoin ourselves to maintain a certain degree of open-minded skepticism regarding our own theories, particularly when our patients seem to confirm them too explicitly.

CONCLUSIONS

I have cited a number of opinions (often quite contradictory) about how and when termination is to be induced, the nature of the termination phase, the kind of material one expects to encounter there, what is to be accomplished in it, and how it should be managed. My own experience suggests that deciding when to terminate an analysis is never cut and dried. In some cases it may seem relatively simple, but in many others it is extremely difficult. It may be the most problematic evaluation we face, especially in protracted or atypical cases. I believe that most analysts rely much more on their clinical judgment than checklists of specific criteria. This statement is not, and ought not to be, reassuring; we must in the end trust to our clinical judgment, while acknowledging that its very subjectivity renders it suspect. I recall one colleague who told me that five years was about as long as he would work with any patient. After that, he felt, he'd lost the ability to see things from a fresh perspective; since the patient had gotten all of worth that he was likely to get by that time, he would be better off with a new analyst. I admired my colleague's honesty, but not necessarily his clinical judgment. I respect the efforts of those who have tried to codify and objectify their bases for reaching clinical judgments about termination, but I think the subjective element here is unavoidable. Imperfect as individual clinical judgments may be, they are still the best tool we have available for this task.

I also believe that whenever the analyst comes to the conclusion that he must impose a termination decision on a reluctant patient, there is an implicit recognition that the analyst has encountered problems that are unanalyzable, at lease in his hands. To be sure, an imposed termination decision may bring forth important new material that can be advantageously analyzed. Even so, the rationale that the analyst has taken the step of enforcing termination as the only way to bring forth hitherto undisclosed material and thereby carry the analytic work to a satisfactory conclusion is theoretically unfounded, and is potentially disadvantageous to the patient. This is not to say that everyone and everything can be successfully analyzed if one works long enough; obviously there are real limitations in even the best of analyses. I am quite certain that enforcing termination will bring forth patients' reactions to enforced termination. To think it can do anything else, it seems to me, is to invite patients to join in their analysts' rationalizations, and that is contrary to the intent of the analytic enterprise.

Another source of potential disadvantage to the patient arises from analysts' expectations of what termination entails. Any theory that leads analysts to believe that certain kinds of material must emerge during termination, or that certain issues and conflicts must be dealt with, can selectively narrow the analyst's field of view. As I have tried to indicate, commonly occurring themes reported during termination can have multiple meanings. An analyst who is convinced that mourning must take place, or devaluation of the analyst appear, or primitive separation anxiety be worked through, or cherished oedipal wishes be definitively surrendered, has unwittingly set a program for the termination phase. Some patients he sees will seem to fit it naturally and easily, but others will not. The consequences of his theoretical beliefs, insofar as they affect his technique, may not be beneficial for the latter group. The sole task of the termination phase is to analyze the analysand's reactions to termination, along with any other material that comes forward, in the most thorough fashion possible. Intentionally or unintentionally adopting selective foci, or other programs to be accomplished during termination, does not provide the optimum milieu for achieving that goal. Jacob Arlow was once asked by a neophyte about his technical management of the end of an analysis. He replied in words to this effect: "You analyze—up to the very last minute of the very last hour." That recommendation, of course, is no less an outgrowth of Arlow's theory of analysis than is any alternative stance an outgrowth of some other theory. And since it happens to be the theory that I espouse, it also informs my technical management of the termination phase.

REFERENCES

Abend, S. (1979), Unconscious fantasy and theories of cures. *J. Amer. Psychoanal. Assn.,* 27:579–596.

Arlow, J., & Brenner, C. (1966), The psychoanalytic situation. In: *Psychoanalysis in the Americas,* ed. R. Litman. New York: International Universities Press, pp. 23–43.

Boesky, D. (in press). Termination as orgasm.

Buxbaum, E. (1950), Technique of terminating analysis. *Internat. J. Psycho-Anal.,* 31:184–190.

Firestein, S. (1978), *Termination in Psychoanalysis.* New York: International Universities Press.

Freud, S. (1918), From the history of an infantile neurosis. *Standard Edition,* 17:7–122. London: Hogarth Press, 1962.

Glover, E. (1955), *The Technique of Psychoanalysis.* New York: International Universities Press.

Goldberg, A., & Marcus, D. (1985), "Natural termination": Some comments on ending analysis without setting a date. *Psychoanal. Quart.,* 54:46–65.

Hurn, H. (1971), Toward a paradigm of the terminal phase: The current status of the terminal phase. *J. Amer. Psychoanal. Assn.*, 19:332–348.

Kramer, Y. (1986), Aspects of termination: Theory and practice. In: *Psychoanalysis: The Science of Mental Content,* ed. A. Richards & M. Willick. Hillsdale, NJ: Analytic Press, pp. 321–351.

Loewald, H. (1962), Internalization, separation, mourning and the superego. *Psychoanal. Quart.*, 31:483–504.

Menninger, K. (1966), Discussion of Rangell's "An overview of the ending of an analysis." In: *Psychoanalysis in the Americas,* ed. R. Litman. New York: International Universities Press, pp. 168–170.

Miller, I. (1965), On the return of symptoms in the terminal phase of psychoanalysis. *Internat. J. Psycho-Anal.*, 46:487–501

Novick, J. (1982), Termination: Themes and issues. *Psychoanal. Inquiry,* 2:329–365.

Nunberg, H. (1926), The will to recovery. In: *Practice and Theory of Psychoanalysis.* Vol. 1. New York: International Universities Press, 1948, pp. 75–88.

Orens, M. (1955), Setting a termination date: An impetus to analysis. *J. Amer. Psychoanal. Assn.*, 3:651–665.

Rangell, L. (1966), An overview of the ending of an analysis. In: *Psychoanalysis in the Americas.* ed. R. Litman. New York: International Universities Press, pp. 141–165.

——— (1982), Some thoughts on termination. *Psychoanal. Inquiry,* 2:367–392.

Reich, A. (1950), On the termination of analysis. In: *Annie Reich: Psychoanalytic Contributions.* New York: International Universities Press, 1973, pp. 121–135.

Robbins, W. (1975), Panel report on termination: Problems and techinques. *J. Amer. Psychoanal. Assn.*, 23:166–176.

Schmideberg, M. (1938), After the analysis. *Psychoanal. Quart.*, 7:122–142.

Shane, M., & Shane, E. (1984), The end phase of analysis: Indicators, functions and tasks of termination. *J. Amer. Psychoanal. Assn.*, 32:739–772.

Stein, M. (1981), The unobjectionable part of the transference. *J. Amer. Psychoanal. Assn.*, 29:869–892.

Viorst, J. (1982), Experiences of loss at the end of analysis: The analyst's response to termination. *Psychoanal. Inquiry,* 2:399–418.

Part IV
UNCONSCIOUS FANTASY: APPLICATIONS

10

Twinship Fantasies in the Work of Mark Twain

Jules Glenn, M.D.

Mark Twain's preoccupation with twins and its influence on his creativity deserve examination in the light of psychoanalytic knowledge. In this chapter, as I suggest childhood and adult determinants of this preoccupation, I will attempt to extend our understanding of twinship fantasies through the medium of applied analysis (Glenn, 1974a, 1974b, 1986). A number of scholars have commented on Twain's interest in twins and dualities (Wecter, 1949; Cardwell, 1953; Barrett, 1955; Duckett, 1964; Kaplan, 1966, 1974; Geismar, 1970), but they have not sufficiently spelled out its manifestations and functions.

Twins appear in Twain's *The Prince and the Pauper* (1882), *The American Claimant* (1892); *The Tragedy of Pudd'nhead Wilson* (1894a); *The Comedy Those Extraordinary Twins* (1894b), based on a sketch called ''Personal Habits of the Siamese Twins,'' in turn inspired by a newspaper story (Kaplan, 1966); ''An Encounter with an Interviewer'' (1895); *Tom Sawyer, Detective* (1896) and ''Was It Heaven? Or Hell?'' (1902); and *The Gilded Age* (Twain and Warner, 1873). In addition, twinship manifests itself in disguised form in other works we will discuss.

The fantasy of having a twin is quite different from the experience of having one. *Actually* being a twin impedes differentiation of self- and object-representations and facilitates intense libidinal and aggressive attachments and particular defensive configurations (Arlow, 1960; Glenn, 1966; Joseph, 1975). The *fantasy* of twinship, although based on observations of twins, is intended to provide certain gratifications and protections that I will detail below.

As Freud (1908), Sachs (1942), and Arlow (1961) have emphasized, creativity involves the production and display by the artist of a personal fantasy or fantasies which move the audience. Their public sharing of the private fantasy, which is artistically presented and aesthetically disguised, permits gratification while alleviating guilt. Arlow (1961) has shown that myths and other creative products serve multiple purposes. They strengthen the group bond and fortify the ego ideals and superegos of the members of the society in which they are produced. In addition, they support and modulate the superego of the individual artist. They can provide author and audiences with new solutions for conscious and unconscious conflicts (Barchilon, 1971). The study of creativity involves understanding the characteristics of the artist, the fantasies he shares with the public, and the reactions of the audience. In the case of fiction and drama, it involves also a study of the author's characters as if they were real persons, an amalgam of fantasies and of traits observed in real people.

As a backdrop to the discussion, I will present a summary of Twain's life (Paine, 1912; DeVoto, 1942; Allen, 1954; Neider, 1959; Kaplan, 1966, 1974). Born Samuel Langhorne Clemens in 1835 in Florida, Missouri, then a frontier area, he was the sixth of seven children, three of whom died in childhood. His mother, Jane, was a down-to-earth, jovial, and perceptive woman who loved and protected her children and home. His father, John Marshall Clemens, a hardworking, dour, unsmiling, compulsively honest lawyer and merchant, did not do well financially, even when the family moved forty miles to Hannibal to improve their lot. When Samuel was eleven, his father died, leaving the family very little. Shortly after, the boy left school to become a printer's apprentice. After a few years his older brother Orion bought a newspaper, which he and Samuel printed and published. Sam's writing ability, not yet fully developed, was not exploited.

The future Mark Twain, at seventeen interested in broadening his scope, went east. At twenty-two he resolved to master the art of navigation and became a Mississippi River pilot. Having encouraged his younger brother Henry to take to the water as well, he was filled with horror and self-recrimination when the young man died in a boiler explosion.

In 1861 the Civil War erupted and closed the Mississippi. After a brief and unsuccessful stint as a Confederate irregular, Clemens traveled west. He mined in Nevada and embarked on a literary career. His story about a jumping frog whose athletic abilities were brought to an end by a gambler's ruse became very well known. He became a reporter and editor for the Virginia City paper in the Nevada Territory. When he was twenty-eight he appropriated the pen name Mark Twain. Later he traveled to many areas of the world, including Hawaii, Europe, and Palestine, and wrote about his experiences. In 1868, at the age of thirty-three, having established himself as a writer and lecturer with a fair but not consistent or fully adequate income, he toured the east, making his headquarters in Hartford, Conn., and Elmira, N.Y., the latter to be near Olivia Langdon, the delicate and protected daughter of a wealthy family, whom he loved. He married Livy, as she was called, when he was thirty-four, on February 2, 1870. They could wed only after his first book, *The Innocents Abroad* (1869), became a best seller and provided him sufficient money. He continued to earn a livelihood as an author and lecturer. His tours as a humorous speaker were immensely successful, as were his literary works. Among his books during this period were *Roughing It* (1872), *The Gilded Age* (1873), *The Adventures of Tom Sawyer* (1876a), *Old Times on the Mississippi* (1876) (later incorporated into *Life on the Mississippi* [1883]) and *A Tramp Abroad* (1880).

Things went reasonably well for many years after an initial depression following the death of Livy's father and Livy's subsequent illness. Although the couple's first child died at two years of age, three others survived. Twain expanded his vistas as he attempted to write serious as well as humorous works. He published *The Prince and the Pauper* in 1882, *Huckleberry Finn* in 1885, *Pudd'nhead Wilson* in 1894, and *Those Extraordinary Twins,* published at the same time. He became extremely popular and highly honored.

Then, to his dismay, he lost vast amounts of his and his wife's money when he invested in a printing machine that failed. In 1894 Twain at fifty-nine had to declare bankruptcy. Encouraged by Livy's stern morality and his financial adviser's practical suggestions, vowed to pay his creditors completely. With this in mind, he embarked on a world lecture tour which enabled him to pay his debts fully by 1900.

Other tragic events aggravated Twain's distress. His beloved daughter Susan died of meningitis in 1896. Another daughter, Jean, developed epilepsy and passed away in 1909. His wife become ill and eventually died of heart failure in 1903. Fortunately the second of his three daughters, Clara, survived her father.

During this catastrophic period, Twain's writings became more openly bitter. A disdain for humanity and the evil forces in the universe became more prominent. The "dream stories" he wrote revealed depression, dismay, and a sense of duality already implicit in his pen name. In 1910 Samuel Clemens/Mark Twain died quietly at the age of seventy-four of a coronary occlusion.

Let us now turn to Clemens's fantasies as they appear in his writing. *The Prince and the Pauper* incorporates two fantasies commonly used to overcome disappointment with one's family and oneself (Freud, 1909; Burlingham, 1952). In the family romance fantasy (Freud, 1909) the child imagines that his true parents are royal and that he has been adopted by the poorer and lesser people with whom he lives. In the fantasy of having a twin, the child fortifies himself against the frustrations of life in his family by inventing an imaginary companion identical with himself. The family romance also defends against incestuous attachments and the punishment which may ensue. The twinship fantasy allows the child to reassure himself that he is not defective or weak and will survive if injured, even if he harbors forbidden wishes. Since he has an alter ego, he need not fear death and disappearance. Further, the imagined twins can act as a team to ward off enemies. They can also represent different aspects of the personality.

In *The Prince and the Pauper,* Tom Canty lived in a poor section of London with his father, mother, grandmother, and fifteen-year-old twin sisters, Bet and Nan. The family's environment was disappointing indeed. In a "foul little pocket called Offal Court, . . . it was small, decayed and rickety, but it was packed full of wretchedly poor families" (p. 16). Tom's father, John, and his grandmother were "a couple of fiends" (p. 17). John was a thief, the mother and children beggars. Father and grandmother were drunkards who fought with each other. When Tom failed to make enough money begging, his father and then his grandmother would beat him, after which his starving mother would mercifully slip him a scrap of food. Tom was able to tolerate his life because, encouraged by Father Andrew, a local priest, he developed and enacted a form of family romance. He "soon forgot his aches and pains in delicious picturings to himself of the charmed life of a petted prince in a regal palace" (p. 18). "By and by Tom's . . . dreaming about princely life wrought such a strong effect upon him that he began to *act* the prince unconsciously" (p. 18). The fantasy that he was royal soon become conscious. "Privately, after a while, Tom organized a royal court! He was the prince; his special comrades were guards, chambermaids, equerries, lords- and ladies-in-waiting and the royal family" (p. 19).

Tom Canty had developed a family romance. Consciously he thought he was a prince, and therefore not a member of his poor and corrupt family. There is, however, no mention of the belief that he was adopted by the father and mother he lived with. We may also assume that Mark Twain too harbored a family romance, which revealed itself in the story he told, and that the book's popularity derives in part from the readers' recognition of the family romance which they too enjoyed and shared with the author.

The twinship theme, which supplements the family romance, appears early. Tom Canty was born on the same day that an actual prince, Edward Tudor, Prince of Wales, was born. The two boys, although totally unrelated biologically, were identical in appearance. To fortify the twin imagery in the reader's mind, Twain arranges it that Tom's sisters are twins. Perhaps it is also relevant that the name Thomas means twin (Barrett, 1955). Again we see the author imposing his fantasy on the audience, stirring resonances of their own unconscious wishes.

As the story proceeds, Tom and Edward meet and, astounded by their identical appearance, change clothers and compare themselves. "The two stood side by side before a great mirror, and lo, a miracle: there did not seem to have been any change made!" (pp. 25-26). The prince, angered by the fact that one of the soldiers had bruised his double, impulsively leaves the palace ground to chastise him. However, since he is dressed in rags, the guards and crowd outside the palace do not recognize him. He finds himself pursued and persecuted. The rest of the book follows the adventures of Tom Canty, now misidentified as the Prince of Wales, and Edward, thought to be a pauper.

Those who hear their protests and explanations believe each of the boys is mad. The royal household cannot believe that Tom is not the prince. They attribute to insanity his failure to know his regal duties and his objections that he is not the king's son. He is pressed to act the prince in order to hide his supposed madness and thus preserve the empire. Tom decides it is best for him to cease declaring his true origins. He learns and enjoys the role of prince and when Edward's father, Henry VIII, dies, he is ready to be enthroned as king.

Twain does not abandon the family romance theme, but he does concentrate on the adventures of Edward, who keeps insisting he is prince (and when Henry VIII dies, king), thus evoking the scorn and skepticism of those about him. Twain makes use of Edward's adventures to expose the injustices of the British authorities, both royal and nonroyal, and to demonstrate the evils of human nature and institutions. Later in his life, Twain's bitterness will come to dominate his thought and work. In *The Prince and the Pauper,* however, his rancor is modulated by the fact the king will eventually right many of the wrongs.

The king manages to get back to his palace on coronation day, is recognized by Tom and restored to the throne in the nick of time. As Edward VI, he honors Tom Canty and corrects many of the injustices he has seen.

Tom's daydreams come true. He attains a kind of royal status, realizes his family romance fantasy in a saga of twinship. Edward affords him "the throne's protection . . . the honorable title of the King's Ward" (p. 202). Oedipal wishes are gratified more directly as well. Edward sentences Tom's father to hanging and finds shelter and bounty for Tom's mother and sisters. Tom's father manages to escape, thus damping patricidal gratification and assuaging the collective conscience.

The twinship fantasy appears again in two intertwined novels, *The Tradegy of Pudd'nhead Wilson* and *The Comedy Those Extraordinary Twins.* The fantasy reveals itself in both form and content. Twain originally wrote the two stories as one, but found the result an unsatisfactory mixture of the serious and the comic. In order to give each story an identity and coherence, he divided the novel in two. We may say that Twain split a Siamese twin into two similar but contrasting individuals, a major theme of *Those Extraordinary Twins.* Twain (1946) wrote of the original that "it was not one story, but two stories tangled together; and they obstructed and interrupted each other at every turn and created no end of confusion and annoyance"; realizing that it was "two stories in one," he "pulled one of the stories out by the roots, and left the other one—a kind of literary Caesarean operation" (p. 135). This mixed metaphor reveals Twain's conception of the story as akin to two fused persons who had to be separated.

The chief characters of *Those Extraordinary Twins* are Counts Angelo and Luigi, joined so that they share a trunk and two legs while having separate heads and two arms each. Like many ordinary twins, Angelo and Luigi have both shared traits and contrasting characteristics, want to be both individuals and part of the twin unit, and both love and hate each other.

Nature has made them alternate their control of their lower extremities, lest they be paralyzed by their contrasting wills. Angelo is the more virtuous twin; blue-eyed and blond, he is sensitive and religious, a teetotaler. Luigi is darker, aggressive, freethinking, brave, and hard drinking. Although the twins are mutually antagonistic, Luigi is the more hostile, causing Angelo all sorts of humiliation and discomfort. He accepts a challenge to a pistol duel which Angelo declines and thus endangers his brother's life; Angelo is wounded and almost dies. Further, the alcohol Luigi drinks enters his brother's body and intoxicates him at crucial times, as when he attends a temperance meeting or a Baptist service. When the two run against each other for town council, Luigi, who is little affected by alcohol, drinks and thus makes Angelo look bad. Luigi wins the election, but a humorous dilemma occurs. Only Luigi is allowed to attend council meetings, but he cannot do so without Angelo. The Council cannot make any decisions until this problem is solved. In the end Luigi is hanged, and presumably Angelo dies as well.

Pudd'nhead Wilson resembles *The Prince and the Pauper* in that an upper-class child is again interchanged with a lower-class child, while the twin theme reappears through the presence of actual twins. In *Pudd'nhead Wilson* a slave, Roxana, who is the caretaker for her own child, Chambers, and for her master's son, Tom, both born the same day, exchanges the two so that her child will have greater advantages. Wilson, playing detective, proves that the switch took place. The actual twins in the story are more prominent than those in *The Prince and the Pauper,* in which Tom Canty's sisters play a minor role. They are Luigi and Angelo, but in the final version they are ordinary twins, not Siamese. Whereas in the earlier novel Tom is the poor child who becomes king, in *Pudd'nhead Wilson* the wealthier boy possesses the name which, as I have noted, means twin.

The family romance fantasy is implied in the elevation of the Negro slave child into the wealthy white family and the demotion of the white infant to slave status. It appears more directly when Roxana justifies her action. She says to herself: " 'Tain't no sin. . . . De queen she lef' her baby layin' aroun' one day, en went out callin'; en one o' de niggers rou' 'bout de place dat was 'mos' white, she . . . put her own chile's clo'es on de queen's chile en put de queen's chile's clo'es on her own chile . . . en nobody ever foun' it out, en her child was de king bimeby" (pp. 31–32).

Roxana's fantasy is a variant of the family romance. There is a switching of children, but not adoption by the socially inferior family. Nor does the royal child, living with the lower class family, return to his regal status.

Adoption appears in *Pudd'nhead Wilson* in another context. The Negro changeling who is raised as Tom loses his white "parents," but his white "uncle" and "aunt" rear him and make him their heir. The child turns out to be greedy and weak of conscience, a gambler and an alcoholic, but his uncle adores him. As Wilson states: "a devil adopted by an old couple is an angel to them, and remains so through thick and thin. Tom is this man's angel; he is infatuated with him" (p. 165).

Toward the end of the story "Tom" kills his "uncle" while attempting to rob him. In determining who the murderer is, Wilson, through a study of fingerprints, proves that "Tom" did it. He also discovers the secret interchange of Tom and Chambers. The true Tom attains his rightful position but his lack of education and Negro dialect make life difficult for him.

The twin fantasy appeared in Twain's life. When he once went on a lecture tour teamed with George Washington Cable, the two of them were billed as the "Twins of Genius" (Cardwell, 1953; Kaplan, 1966). And of course it appeared also in the pen name he selected. Mark Twain, a pilot's term used in reporting soundings, means "two fathoms deep," twain meaning "two" or, as a noun, "couple" or "pair." Further, a humorous story reveals that Twain's thinking encompasses the association of twins and a mark. In a mock interview the interviewee replies to a question: "You see, we were twins. We got mixed up in the bathtub when we were only two weeks old, and one of us was drowned. But we didn't know which. Some think it was Bill. Some think it was me." When the questioner asks "What do *you* think?" the interviewee replies, ". . . I will tell you a secret now, which I never revealed before." One of us had a peculiar mark—a large mole on the back of his left hand; that was *me*. That child was the one that was drowned! . . . I don't know how they could ever have been such a blundering lot as to go and bury the wrong child" (Twain, 1895, p. 414). That Twain associates to the duality implicit in his pen name is attested further by a joke of his reported by Barrett (1955): "Since England and America have been joined in Kipling," he quipped, "may they not be severed in Twain" (p. 434).

The taking of the name Mark Twain reveals his ambivalence toward an older man who died. His assuming the name, I suggest, was an expression of his anger at, and an attempt to become one with, another older man who died, and whom he held in awe: his father. (Perhaps one function of his fascination and identification with twins is that it softened the blow his father's demise dealt him.) Twain told the following apocryphal story, which he repeated many times. Samuel Clemens was an expert river pilot. One Isaiah Sellers, and elder captain, was a writer who had published informative articles about the river under the name of Mark Twain. When Clemens burlesqued one of his articles, Sellers was deeply offended. After the captain died, Clemens adopted his name, "laid violent hands upon it without asking permission of the proprietor's remains" (Twain quoted in Fatout, 1967, p. 161).

The story, it happens, is untrue. Sellers did in fact write, and Clemens did satirize his articles in 1859, but there is no evidence that Sellers called himself Mark Twain, and there is proof that Clemens used the name in 1863, a year before Sellers's death at the age of fifty (Fatout, 1967). Whether Twain invented this story or misremembered it, the appearance of the fantasy later does not detract from our thesis. Indeed there is support for the hypothesis that Twain associated Sellers with his father. The captain's surname and at least an echo of his given name appear in *The Gilded Age,* a novel about Colonel Beriah Sellers, whose character was consciously based on Twain's mother's cousin, a fanciful but impractical and unsuccessful man. Twain's father, John Marshall Clemens, though far from identical with Sellers, shared these traits with this cousin. Both Samuel Clemens and his brother Orion adopted their father's ineptness, but Samuel was in the long run successful. Samuel could earn (and squander) money and eventually succeeded economically after serious financial miscalculations.

Additional evidence for the twinship fantasy thesis, though less compelling, is the fact that Twain wrote a number of works in collaboration with another author: *The Gilded Age* with Charles Dudley Warner, *Ah Sin* with Bret Harte, and the unproduced play *Colonel Sellers as a Scientist,* later called *The American Claimant,* with William Dean Howells. Indeed, all (or most) of his work required collaboration in the sense that his wife Livy, William Dean Howells, and others read and edited them.

A letter to Livy when Twain and she were engaged suggests a twin fantasy frequently encountered in married couples. "I am happy as a king now that it is settled and I can count the exact number of days . . . before we are married. . . . This 4th of February will be the mightiest day in the history of our lives—for it makes of two fractional lives a whole; it gives to two purposeless lives a work, and doubles the strength of each whereby to perform it . . ." (Wecter, 1949, pp. 109–110).

Mark Twain's twin fantasy, as we have seen, is intertwined with a family romance fantasy serving complementary and overlapping functions. We find a clue to another determinant of Mark Twain's preoccupation with twinship and the family romance in that the former is associated with the switching of children, as occurs in *The Prince and the Pauper* and *Pudd'nhead Wilson*. In the latter novel, Roxana, the Negress who had interchanged her son and the white boy she tended, begs her son to sell her into slavery in order to pay his gambling debts. The man who purchases her then sells her down the river to the deep South, where a slaves lot was generally a good deal worse and mistreatment rampant. Similar events occured in Mark Twain's childhood (Wecter, 1952; Allen, 1954). When Samuel was five the family's slave, Jennie, who served as the children's mammy, begged that she be sold to William Beebe who had convinced her he would improve her life. The family must have realized the sale would help their shaky finances. Reluctantly, they agreed, though they grieved at the loss, "for the woman was almost like one of the family" (Twain, quoted by Wecter, 1952). Then, going back on his word, Beebe sold Jennie down the river. Another detail supports the hypothesis that Twain associated Roxana and Jennie: he wrote that Jennie, seen years later, was a chambermaid on a steamboat, a position that Roxana held in *Pudd'nhead Wilson*.

I suggest that, as was true of many children brought up in slaveholding society, Samuel was confused as to his mother's identity. A mammy, as Hardin (1985) has observed of surrogate parents, can become a primary object—loved, hated, and feared—as well as a displacement object. I suggest further that, as a derivative of this uncertainty, an identity confusion occurred which resulted in the fantasy that appeared in *Pudd'nhead Wilson* and *The Prince and the Pauper*: a slave child and a white child—or a poor child and a royal child—were interchanged. There may well be a wishful element in this fantasy of being a Negro. Barchilon and Kovel (1966) argue that there is "a typical unconscious fantasy of Southern children: to possess the warmth, nurture, and instinctual gratification offered by a Negro mammy" (p. 803; see also Kramer, 1986).

Having a mammy facilitates the development of an affection toward blacks as well as antagonism, in part defensive. In Mark Twain's case, I suggest, closeness to blacks, his understanding of them, and his violently antiracist feelings can be attributed in part to his relation to Jennie. The feeling of kinship—twinship perhaps—between Huckleberry Finn and Jim, the escaped slave, as they raft down the Mississippi together is an indicator of Twain's attachment. The reader will recall that Huck and Jim share a common condition—each has escaped from home to seek a freer life, different from the restrictive, punitive one he has left behind.

Barchilon and Kovel (1966) suggest that Huck and Jim represent brothers but don't speak of twinship. However, they later state that an escape scene in the novel suggests "a birth of three helpless babies" (p. 802)— Huck, Jim and Tom Sawyer are in effect triplets!

Mark Twain employed twins or twinlike figures to symbolize the conscience. In "Was It Heaven? Or Hell?" a pair of twin sisters are extremely strict and rigid in their morality. They believe one should tell the truth no matter what the consequences. They forbid even white lies. When a little girl lies and confesses it, they insist her mother, who is dying of typhoid, be told so that she can chastise her daughter. A physician criticizes their inflexibility which has its ill effects. Despite their initial protests, the twins moderate their behavior and ease the death of mother and daughter, the child having caught the disease from her parent.

The internal struggle with a cruel superego is picturesquely drawn in "The Facts Concerning the Recent Carnival of Crime in Connecticut" (Twain, 1876b). Twain's "worst enemy," his conscience, appears before him in the form of a three-foot-tall creature who looks and talks like the author. Twain berates his conscience for its attacking him no matter what he does, whether he tells a white lie to protect someone or tells the truth boldly and hence hurts someone, whether he feeds a derelict or turns him away. The conscience then confesses his mischievous sadism and disruptive behavior. Still, it appears that a conscience serves a good purpose in preventing thievery and murder. In the end Twain kills his conscience and, on a rampage, slays many of his enemies.

In real life, Twain had a painfully powerful conscience. As a child he blamed himself for the death of a drunkard who died in a jail fire after young Samuel had given him matches. Later, as we have seen, he blamed himself for his brother Henry's death in a steamboat explosion, after he had helped him get a job on the ship. (In "Carnival," his conscience tortures him for teasing and tricking this brother when they were children.) Even as an adult he suffered from his conscience's damning him. In 1894, bankrupt and furious at the ravenous and unreasonable demands of his creditors, he nevertheless determined to pay each of them in full. To this end he embarked on a world lecture tour which, along with the sales of a book describing his travels, accomplished this goal by 1900. Typically, he blamed himself for the death of his daughter Susan, whom he considered his most talented child, the one most like himself, of meningitis in 1896 while he was in Europe. He suffered horribly from the loss and wrote feverishly to stem his sadness. Soon thereafter Jean, another daughter, became epileptic, underwent a personality change, and later required years of hospitalization. To make matters worse, his wife Livy fell ill with heart disease, a condition which necessitated full-time nursing care. She was so severely ill that for more than a year the doctors prohibited Twain from entering his wife's sickroom for more than a few minutes a day. Devoted, he placed notes to her under her door, or worked in an adjacent room with the door ajar.

During this time Twain suffered not only from rheumatism and bronchitis but also from his most serious mental disturbances. His rage at the "damned human race" became more vociferous and his awareness of dualities most intense. He wrote "dream stories" which he did not publish, and became confused as to what was real and what was not. In the "dream stories" the author perceives that each individual possesses two types of mind: a dream state which he is unaware of ordinarily, and a waking state. The dream state contains forbidden thoughts, thoughts that may be disgusting to the individual. This hidden, forbidden mind conflicts with the conscious mind, as does the conscience—two inter-related sets of dualities.

Twain's writings became more bitter and biting, more openly hostile and sarcastic during this period of tragedy. True, attacks on human nature, societal injustice, and the oppression of minorities and masses had appeared in the earlier works (Allen, 1954), but the hatred became more overt, his attacks on man and God more openly virulent once fate had repeatedly struck at the Clemenses (Brooks, 1920; DeVoto, 1942; Kaplan, 1966, 1974).

Not that Twain had become completely bitter or humorless. In "Extract from Captain Stormfield's Visit to Heaven" (1907) he twits human egocentrism and superstition in a delightfully funny story far lighter than his attach on mankind in the earlier *The Prince and the Pauper*. Misanthropy appears more viciously in *The Mysterious Stranger* (1916) and "The Man That Corrupted Hadleyburg" (1899). In the latter a seemingly honest community is revealed as not merely dishonest, but corrupt to the extreme.

During the tragic years between 1897 and 1905 Twain wrote at least four drafts of *The Mysterious Stranger*, but published none of them. A. B. Paine and F. A. Duneka combined the versions into a novel which they published in 1916 without informing the public that they had created an abbreviated composite work and had even added to the story. In 1969 the final draft, which Twain had completed and called *No. 44, The Mysterious*

Stranger, was published (Gibson, 1969; Twain, 1982).

In the 1916 composite version the author expresses acrimony and also creates a comforter, in the person of the angel Satan. Geismar (1970) considered Satan a twin imago, possessing two sets of characteristics, as if he were two persons in one. Like Samuel Clemens/Mark Twain, he has two names—Satan and Philip Traum (Dream), his assumed name. In the eerie story the narrator, Theodor Fischel, and his friends run into a charming young man who possesses magical capabilities. Although the town, indeed the world, is obsessed with seeking out witches and revealing the devil's influence, it only momentarily occurs to them that Satan may not be an angel, as he says he is, but a seductive devil. Although Satan's angelic identity remains intact throughout the tale, he shows rather mephisthophelean traits. Under the guise of helping people he causes all sorts of trouble.

An astrologer (an evil priest in other drafts) frames a good priest, Father Peter, so that he loses his position and livelihood. Then, when his house is about to be possessed, Satan arranges for him to find gold coins of considerable value. The priest's explanation of how he acquired the money arouses skepticism and ends in tragedy when the astrologer claims the priest stole it from him. Eventually Father Peter is exonerated, again through Satan's influence. Then to assure that the priest will be happy throughout his life, Satan drives him mad. Only the insane are happy, he says, for they don't recognize reality.

Satan attempts to ameliorate lives by arranging for people to die rather than suffer illness and poverty, much to the dismay of Fischel, who writes, "He didn't seem to know any way to do a person a favor except by killing him or making a lunatic out of him" (p. 1245).

Although Satan helps humans, he claims to be totally indifferent to their fate. Humans cause difficulty through their "Moral Sense." They kill each other in witch-hunts and in wars. Satan, being an angel, is above all that. Animals, having no "Moral Sense," are superior to man. Twain's bitterness reveals itself as Satan describes the horrors of humankind. It appears also in Satan's indifference to man's plight. He creates a group of miniature men and then destroys them without caring. We can imagine Twain's rage at the deity that created and killed Susan and made Jean and Livy suffer so. Indeed one character, when her daughter dies, states that she will never again pray to God: "In His hard heart is no compassion. I will never pray again" (p. 1230).

But despite the horror of what Satan has done, the reader, along with the characters, finds him a charming companion. He talks to Fischel, takes him to China, India, and other exotic climes.

I am emphasizing the two sides of Satan's personality, as if he were two people with opposite traits. Satan is charming, friendly, helpful, generous. He is moral despite his denunciation of "Moral Sense." At the same time he is destructive, murderous, vengeful, amoral—a creature of those impulses that appear during the dream states suffered by Twain in his later years. Satan is a creature of fantasy, a mythological figure who bears traits of the author. At the end of the story Satan, before leaving the narrator forever, informs him that he, Fischel, alone exists, and that even he is but a thought. All else is but a figment of the imagination including Satan himself.

Gibson (1969) has adduced additional evidence that Satan represents both a twin and Mark Twain himself. In the final draft the Satan figure is named No. 44. Gibson notes a joke which seems to cast light on the meaning that number held for Twain. In a newspaper letter entitled "A Mystery" written probably in 1868, Twain complains that his "Double" is wandering about misbehaving and harming his reputation. He then quips, "I am fading . . . [I]f my distress . . . continues, there may be only four of us left." Twain then explains that Twain is two, his "Double is Double-Twain, which is four more; four and two are six; two from six leaves four" (p. 473). Gibson suggests that "in a punning non-mathematical sense 44 might be Twain twice doubled" (p. 473).

Further evidence appears in *No. 44, The Mysterious Stranger* (Twain, 1982) when 44 explains his production of "Duplicates," "Twins" of the workers in a printing plant. "You know, of course, that you are not one person, but two. One is your Workaday-Self, and 'tends to business,' the other is your Dream-Self . . . and cares only for romance and excursions and adventure" (p. 97). Later August Feldner, the narrator, says of his Duplicate:

> To me he was merely a stranger; in all our lives we had never chanced to meet until 44 had put flesh upon him; . . . whenever one of us was awake the other was of necessity asleep and unconscious . . . [I]t was not until my Dream-Self's fleshing that he and I met and spoke. . . Although we had been born together, at the same moment in the same womb, there was no spiritual kinship between us; spiritually we were a couple of distinctly independent and unrelated individuals, with equal rights in a common fleshy property . . . . [p. 125].

Twain believed then that all people are composite twins, each individual containing two independent persons within the same body. He stated this explicity in 1897, when he examined these psychological concepts in his notebook (Paine, 1935); in his notebook and in *No. 44, The Mysterious Stranger,* he also described a third self, the Soul.

The twinlike unitary figure of Satan, in some ways an alter ego of Twain, results, I believe, from the externalization of the split self-representations Twain was experiencing at the time, including representations of id, ego, and superego. In a secondary maneuver, Twain has called upon his twinship fantasy to deal with his sorrow. Satan (as well as 44) serves as an imaginary companion to comfort him. Twain also expresses his profound ambivalence toward God and mankind as Satan plays a peculiar conscience, both vicious and benign. The story likely reveals also his wish that his daughter would return, his certainty, she would not, and his hope that life is but a dream (DeVoto, 1942).

Twain, we have seen, used twins and twinlike figures to represent the conscience. He possessed a potent superego which he could control through creative activity. In his stories he could mollify, modulate, or destroy his conscience, but it remained always a source of inner turmoil. For Mark Twain, the conception of himself as a double resulted from his awareness of intense inner conflicts, as Kaplan (1966, 1974) has demonstrated. Living at a time when Freud was developing his revolutionary theories, Clemens conceived of and experienced a personality structure similar to the one Freud discovered (Gibson, 1976), but did so in a less systematized way and with much less observational basis. He consciously recognized both an id-like dream state, during which his basic drives expressed themselves, and a more civilized ego-like waking state influenced by his conscience.

Man's fascination with twins provides a basis for the aesthetic appeal of Twain's works involving real and disguised twins. It also enables the author to enter the mind and soul of the reader and there to influence his moral activity. Although at times antirepublican, Twain was generally a liberal who wanted to combat tyranny and promote freedom. He was opposed to prejudice against blacks and Jews, to dictatorship and war, and to the evils and irrationality of religion. Many of his stories carry messages, sometimes embedded in humor, often cushioned in artistic expression, but sometimes blatantly stated. He sought to solidify the group bond, its ego ideal and conscience, as Arlow (1960) suggests the myth does, while fortifying and alleviating his own superego and finding release for the antagonism of the dream states he experienced.

His audience was the world, the vast number of people who loved
and emulated him, who devoured his books and crowded the lecture halls
to hear him. He was sensitive to their needs and aware of the financial
rewards this brought. He thus barred from publication some of his boldest
writings. His audience also included those "secret sharers," those alter
egos that Meyer (1972) has shown us authors create for. His wife read
and censored all his work, acted as the twinlike external superego that
protected him from publishing words and works that were not sufficiently
in tune with the mores of the day. So too did William Dean Howells,
his collaborator on *Colonel Sellers as a Scientist,* play an encouraging but
cautionary role.

REFERENCES

Allen, J. (1954), *The Adventures of Mark Twain.* Boston: Little, Brown.
Arlow, J. A. (1960), Fantasy systems in twins. *Psychoanal. Quart.,* 29:175–199.
———— (1961), Ego psychology and the study of mythology. *J. Amer. Psychoanal.
    Assn.,* 9:371–393.
Barchilon, J. (1971), A study of Camus' mythopoetic tale, *The Fall,* with some
    comments about the origins of esthetic feelings. *J. Amer. Psychoanal. Assn.,*
    19:193–240.
———— & Kovel, J. (1966), Huckleberry Finn: A psychoanalytic study. *J. Amer.
    Psychoanal. Assn.,* 14:775–814.
Barrett, W. (1955), On the naming of Tom Sawyer. *Psychoanal. Quart.,* 24:424–436.
Brooks, V. W. (1920), *The Ordeal of Mark Twain.* New York: Dutton, 1970.
Burlingham, D. (1952), Twins: A study of three pairs of identical twins. New
    York: International Universities Press.
Cardwell, G. (1953), *Twins of Genius.* East Lansing: Michigan State University
    Press.
DeVoto, B. (1942), *Mark Twain at Work.* Cambridge, MA: Harvard University
    Press.
Duckett, M. (1964), *Mark Twain and Bret Harte.* Norman: University of Oklahoma
    Press.
Fatout, P. (1962), Mark Twain's non de plume. In: *Mark Twain: A Profile,* ed.
    J. Kaplan. New York: Hill & Wang, pp. 161–168.
Freud, S. (1908), Creative writers and day-dreaming. *Standard Edition,* 9:143–153.
    London: Hogarth Press, 1959.
———— (1909), Family romances. *Standard Edition,* 9:237–241. London: Hogarth
    Press, 1959.

Geismar, M. (1970), *Mark Twain: An American Prophet*. Boston: Houghton Mifflin.

Gibson, W. (1969), *Mark Twain's Mysterious Stranger Manuscripts*. Berkeley: University of California Press.

———— (1976), *The Art of Mark Twain*. New York: Oxford University Press.

Glenn, J. (1966), Opposite sex twins. *J. Amer. Psychoanal. Assn.*, 14:736–759.

———— (1974a), The adoption theme in Edward Albee's *Tiny Alice* and *The American Dream*. *The Psychoanalytic Study of the Child*, 29:413–429. New Haven, CT: Yale University Press.

———— (1974b), Anthony and Peter Shaffer's plays. *American Imago*, 51:270–292.

———— (1986), Twinship themes and fantasies in the work of Thornton Wilder. *The Psychoanalytic Study of the Child*, 41:627–651. New Haven, CT: Yale University Press.

Hardin, M. (1985), On the vicissitudes of early primary surrogate mothering. *J. Amer. Psychoanal. Assn.*, 33:609–629.

Joseph, E. (1975), Psychoanalysis—science and research: Twin studies as a paradigm. *J. Amer. Psychoanal. Assn.*, 23:3-31.

Kaplan, J. (1966), *Mr. Clemens and Mark Twain*. New York: Simon & Schuster.

———— (1974), *Mark Twain and His World*. New York: Harmony Books.

Kramer, S. (1986), Identification and its vicissitudes as observed in children: A developmental approach. *Internat. J. Psycho-Anal.*, 67:161–172.

Meyer, B. (1972), Some reflections on the contribution of psychoanalysis to biography. *Psychoanal. & Contemp. Sci.*, 1:373–391.

Neider, C., ed. (1959), *Mark Twain's Autobiography*. New York: Harper.

Paine, A. (1912), *Mark Twain: A Biography*. New York: Harper.

———— (1935), *Mark Twain's Notebooks*. New York: Harper.

Sachs, H. (1942), *The Creative Unconscious*. Cambridge, MA.: Sci-Art Publishers.

Twain, M. (1869), *The Innocents Abroad*. In: *The Unabridged Mark Twain.*, Vol. 1, ed. L. Teacher. Philadelphia: Running Press, 1976, pp. 11–389.

———— (1872), *Roughing It*. In: *The Unabridged Mark Twain*, Vol. 2, ed. L. Teacher. Philadelphia: Running Press, 1979, pp. 551–899.

———— (1876a), *The Adventures of Tom Sawyer*. In: *The Unabridged Mark Twain*, Vol. 1, ed. L. Teacher. Philadelphia: Running Press, 1976, pp. 437–585.

———— (1876b), The facts concerning the recent carnival of crime in Connecticut. In: *The Unabridged Mark Twain*. ed. L. Teacher. Philadelphia: Running Press, 1976, pp. 423–435.

———— (1880), *A Tramp Abroad*. Hartford, CT: American Publishing.

———— (1882), *The Prince and the Pauper*. New York: New American Library, 1980.

———— (1883), *Life on the Mississippi*. In: *The Unabridged Mark Twain*, Vol. 2, ed. L. Teacher. Philadelphia: Running Press, 1979, pp. 205–512.

———— (1885), *The Adventures of Huckleberry Finn*. In: *The Unabridged Mark Twain*, Vol. 1, ed. L. Teacher. Philadelphia: Running Press, 1976, pp. 747–956.

_____ (1892), The American claimant. In: *The American Claimant and Other Stories and Sketches*. New York: Harper.

_____ (1894a), *The Tragedy of Pudd'nhead Wilson*. In: *The Unabridged Mark Twain*, Vol. 2, ed. L. Teacher. Philadelphia: Running Press, 1979, pp. 19–133.

_____ (1894b), *The Comedy Those Extraordinary Twins*. In: *The Unabridged Mark Twain*, Vol. 2, ed. L. Teacher. Philadelphia: Running Press, 1979, pp. 135–184.

_____ (1895), An encounter with an interviewer. In: *The Unabridged Mark Twain*, Vol. 1, ed. L. Teacher. Philadelphia: Running Press, pp. 411–414.

_____ (1896), *Tom Sawyer, Detective*. New York: Harper.

_____ (1899), The man that corrupted Hadleyburg. In: *The Complete Short Stories of Mark Twain*. ed. C. Neider. New York: Bantam, 1958, pp. 1253–1289.

_____ (1902), Was it Heaven? Or Hell? In: *The Complete Short Stories of Mark Twain*, ed. C. Neider. New York: Bantam, 1958, pp. 474–491.

_____ (1907), Extract from Captain Stormfield's visit to Heaven. In: *The Complete Short Stories of Mark Twain*. ed. C. Neider. New York: Bantam, 1958, pp. 567–600.

_____ (1916), *The Mysterious Stranger*. In: *The Family Mark Twain*. New York: Harper & Row, 1972, pp. 1181–1249.

_____ (1982), *No. 44, The Mysterious Stranger*. ed. J. Tuckey. Berkeley: University of California Press.

_____ & Harte, B. (1877), *Ah Sin*. Produced at National Theater, Washington, D.C.

_____ & Howells, W. D. (1886), *The American Claimant*. Produced in Hartford, Conn.

_____ & Warner, C. D. (1873), *The Gilded Age*. New York: New American Library, 1985.

Wecter, D., ed. (1949), *The Love Letters of Mark Twain*. New York: Harper.

_____ (1952), *Sam Clemens of Hannibal*. Boston: Houghton Mifflin.

11

Alberto Giacometti's Fantasies and Object Representation

Peter B. Neubauer, M.D.

The invasion of conscious and unconscious fantasies into the object representational world became apparent when I studied patients who suffered from the inability to form or to maintain a visual object representation. In a paper on disturbances in object representation (Neubauer, 1987) I described three patients with this disorder; in the meantime colleagues have found similar pathology in patients belonging to this group.

In most of the cases reported there was an early history of loss of a primary object—a father or mother—which seems to have led to a repression of the visual memory function regarding primary objects. Often this extended to friends and what became important in the analysis—to the analyst. The inability to rely on evocative memory of an important object was at times connected with an absence of recognition memory. This influenced the transference of patients so affected, who tended to demand continuous contact with the analyst. Frequently, they used compensatory mechanisms, such as the sound of his voice, visualizing the office, or smell, in order to achieve a sense of reality and conviction regarding his presence.

The question arose whether the experience of early loss led to an inability to internalize the object, or whether the repression of the memory of the internalized object contributed to the symptom. I have found that this disorder is not particular to one specific diagnosis but rather can appear in various conditions. Thus it became important to discover why visual representation was disordered in these patients, whether it occurred through deficiency in relationships or through an invasion of conflicts in the ego function.

With this in mind I visited an exhibition of Alberto Giacometti in

Zurich. I have always been struck by his representation of the human figure, the dimness of his drawings and the elongation and two dimensionality that characterize his sculpture. There was at this exhibition a videotape presentation in which Giacometti spoke about his constant longing to capture the eye, and his despair that he would never be able to do justice to the visual expression of the people he created. Afterward, in biographies of the artist, I found the most telling expressions of his conflicts, anxieties, and fears in connection with the human object representation.

There is a most revealing photograph of his family, taken when he was about four years old, in which all the subjects face the camera as usual, except that Alberto is seen to focus intensely on his mother's face and she in turn to make equally intense visual contact with him. This is not a psychohistory of Giacometti, an attempt to explain his work by using his life history; instead my focus, rather more narrow, will be on those aspects of his work which reveal the man's relation to his inner world, and to external reality as reflected by object representation.

Let me begin with the most dramatic example from James Lord's *A Giacometti Portrait* (1965). Lord, who was the artist's friend, was posing for Giacometti and later described the following scene:

> He reveals first a great degree of anxiety, agony that the encounter generated in him. When I would arrive at the studio for a sitting, Giacometti would disconsolately occupy himself for a half-hour or more doing odds and ends on his sculpture, literally afraid to start on the painting. When he did bring himself to get into painting, the anxiety became severe. At one point, Giacometti started gasping and stamping his foot, "Your head is going away completely!" "It will come back again," I said. He shook his head, "Not necessarily. Maybe the canvas will be completely empty; then what will become of me? I will die of it." He reached into his pocket, pulled out a handkerchief, stared at it for a moment as though he didn't know what it was, then with a moan threw it on the floor. Suddenly he shouted loudly, "I shriek, I scream!" To talk to his model while he is working distracts him, I think, from the constant anxiety which is a result of this conviction that he cannot hope to represent on the canvas what he sees before him.
>
> So intense is the encounter that he often indentifies the painting on the easel with the actual flesh and blood of the person posing. One day his foot accidentally struck the catch that holds the easel shelf at the proper level, which caused the canvas to fall abruptly for a foot

or two. "Oh excuse me," he said. I laughed and observed that he had excused himself as though he had caused me to fall instead of the painting. "That's exactly what I did feel," he answered.

He often feels that the particular sculpture or painting on which he is working at the moment is the one which will for the first time express what he subjectively experiences in response to an objective reality. He struggled via the act of painting to express in visual terms a perceptual reality. In order to go on to hope, to believe that there is some chance of his creating what he ideally visualizes, he is obliged to feel that it is necessary to start his entire career over again every day, as it were, from scratch [p. 26].

I think we may be allowed the following observation: Giacometti's sense of reality was very fragile; not only could he not capture the object in front of him, but when his anxiety mounted he was unable to maintain a sense of the reality either of his paintings or of his self. The derealization went from the external world to his inner world; in other words, he was unable to maintain an internalized object and so could not achieve even a degree of object constancy. With no secure object representation, even when the object was directly in front of him, he experienced the collapse of reality, encompassing both his own self-representation and the inanimate world. His paintings of the human figure, at least during the period Lord was describing, have a quality of disappearance as they try to assert themselves on us.

The change in his attitude toward the representation of the human body was clearly dated and described by Giacometti. He had attempted to do a bust of his cousin, Bianca, with whom he was in love, though quite one-sidedly. As he started to sculpt her, she was so annoyed with his work that she knocked it onto the floor, smashing it to pieces. Ever after, Giacometti spoke of the incident as having altered his future. He considered it his "expulsion from Paradise," after which his true "creative work" could begin. "Before that," he said, "I believed I saw things very clearly, I had a sort of intimacy with the whole, with the universe. Then suddenly it became alien. You are yourself, and the universe is beyond, which is altogether incomprehensible" (Lord, 1983, p. 15). This incident took place in 1921, when he was twenty years old. Later he distorted the event in characteristic fashion by confusing it with a similar incident four years later; he then told the story saying it was he who had destroyed the sculpture.

Rejection by his beloved and the destruction of his work disorganized his sense of reality. It is important that Alberto considered this the true beginning of his creative work, whose major theme was to be the substitution of his disappearing external reality with his inner fantasy and search for a new psychic reality. For the rest of his life he could not blend the one with the other.

As usual, a traumatic event which, according to Freud's definition, suddenly changes the psychic economy, has its antecedents. At the age of eighteen Giacometti was walking in the street when he saw two or three girls walking in front of him. Suddenly he became frightened; they appeared monumental in size and full of violence. This vivid hallucinatory experience set off in him a deep sense of confusion: "It was like a hole torn in reality" (Lord, 1983, p. 47). In his account of this event he states that afterward the paintings of Tintoretto and Giotto, which had had such an important influence on him, became in his mind small and weak and without consistency.

Although the experience was transient, it had a profound effect on him. What is important here is the changing, threatening size of the objects, human and inanimate, for later in his life Giacometti had a period in which his sculptures were so small as to fit easily into a matchbox.

Sometime after the incident with the three girls, he painted the portrait of a prostitute, after which he had sex with her. He described contradictory feelings regarding this. On the one hand he "exploded with enthusiasm," while on the other he shouted, "It's cold" (i.e., mechanical). While the sexual sensation gave him a sense of orgastic jubilation, from the viewpoint of object relations he felt uninvolved, disappointed, and cold: the phallic experience could not fulfill his wish for closeness with the object, particularly since the female object became frightening to him and potentially violent.

His underlying fear of object loss and castration was exemplified by another event, one which impressed on him the sense of life's meaninglessness and fluidity. He had met, by accident, an older man who invited him to be his traveling companion. The second night out, the man died, and for the first time Giacometti found himself confronted with death. It put him in a state of terror. He could not go to sleep, for he felt he would himself die were he to do so; this was for him further proof, not only of the inconstancy of the object, but of his own existence. Again the self mirrored the object, external and internal reality fused, and reality testing was suspended.

A falling-asleep fantasy which Giacometti maintained for many months allows us to place his conflicts on a developmental line.

> I could not get to sleep at night without first having imagined that at dusk I had passed through a dense forest and come to a gray castle which stood in the most hidden and unknown part. There I killed two men before they could defend themselves. One was about 17 and always looked pale and frightened. The other wore a suit of armor upon the left side of which something gleamed like gold. I raped two women, after tearing off their clothes, one of them 32 years old, dressed all in black with a face like alabaster, the other a young girl around who white veils floated. The whole forest echoed with their screams and moans. I killed them also, but very slowly (it was night by that time) often beside a pool of stagnant green water in front of the castle. Each time with slight variations. Then I burned the castle and went to sleep happy [Lord, 1983, p. 182].

Arlow's comparison of fantasies, dreams, and daydreams (1969a, b) comes to mind here. The falling-asleep fantasy has a specific function; it aims for wish fulfillment in order to soothe anxiety and bring on sleep. In Giacometti's fantasy we see a great deal of oedipal material. The men were killed, but he must have been frightened enough of their power to do it when they were defenseless. Only then did he move to overpower the women sexually, finally destroying them in order to confirm his omnipotence. We see here Giacometti's aggression against men and women; we understand that he perceives both as powerful, monumental in size, and himself as in danger of castration and disorganization.

During this period he became suddenly aware that he could not visualize his father's appearance. He was so upset over this that he burst into tears and screamed, "I can't remember my father's face" (Lord, 1983, p. 227). One can assume that the loss of memory is connected with his oedipal aggression against the male figure.

Recalling the time he made his first sculpture, he explained the experience he had about his work, again documenting his need for complete power. He states, "I drew in order to convince and to dominate. I had the feeling of being able to reproduce and possess whatever I wanted. I became overbearing. Nothing could resist me. My pencil was my weapon" (Lord, 1983, p. 257). We can see here a direct connection between his work and his daydreams, his need for human contact and complete dominance. He wanted to do on canvas and with his sculpture what he could not achieve in life, but the step toward sublimating was incomplete.

We can connect this also to his need to stare at women in such a way that he became immobile, his gaze so intense that he was unaware that it made them uncomfortable. He did this, he said, "because I didn't see whom I wanted to see, as if everything was so confused that I could not decipher what I wanted to see" (Lord, 1983, p. 260). This relates to his work, which he undertook because he understood this mode of representing the outside world "the least" and he could not endure having it elude him completely.

It is not surprising that this inability to capture the outside world led him to sleep with the light burning all through his adolescence. His fascination with capturing the face, the eyes, continued throughout his life, and it may be important to follow his own description in order to understand his struggle and to explain the events that occurred when he did a drawing of James Lord:

> One starts by seeing the person who poses, but little by little all the possible sculptures of him intervene. The more a real vision of him disappears, the stranger his head becomes. One is no longer sure of his appearance, or of his size, or of anything at all. There were too many sculptures between my model and me. And when there were no more sculptures, there was such a complete stranger that I no longer knew whom I saw or what I was looking at [Lord, 1983, p. 269].

Here we find a significant elaboration of his disorder, his inability to maintain an object representation, for he states that the previous sculptures he made now start to interfere with the reality; but without the associative functions there was emptiness. It appears as if the unconscious fantasy that reached visual representation was an essential aid to his achieving contact with the outside world. Later he attempted to help himself by modeling a complete figure, not just a head. He started a figure about a foot and a half high, but as he worked on it the figure became uncontrollably smaller and smaller. He became more and more anxious about it but could not control the shrinking of the figure. Finally it was no larger than a pin. He related this event to his feeling that all living beings are frail, that it takes all of the creature's energy not to collapse.

It is hardly surprising, then, that he was amazed his body could function at all. That he could walk with both feet, that he had a body equilibrium in spite of the lability of his inner life—these to him were minor miracles. Once when he injured his foot in an accident, he was very pleased with the result. Later he could not stop saying how glad he was to be permanently lame. It is perhaps relevant here that Giacometti's standing figures are given oversized, unmodeled feet.

While working he dwelled in a special world in which unconscious fantasies asserted themselves and overwhelmed reality. He would say, "When I'm walking in the street and see a whore all dressed I see a whore. When she's in my room and naked before me I see a goddess" (Lord, 1983, p. 269). At one point, when he was about forty-five he experienced a radical change. He was sitting in a movie and the figures on the screen disappeared for him; they lost all meaning. Then he looked at the people around him and, by contrast with what he saw on the screen, saw for the first time a reality that excited him. Everything became different for him—the space, the object, the colors, the silence. Everything appeared for him now in a different light and in a different dimension. From then on, he said, "I began to see heads in the void, in the space which surrounds them. I trembled with terror as never before in my life . . . it was no longer a living head, but an object I was looking at like any other object but like something *simultaneously* living and dead" (Lord, 1983, p. 279).

After this experience, in which he could at least partially capture a sense of reality, Giacometti swore to himself that he would no longer allow his statues to shrink. Now, however, the taller he rendered his sculptures, the thinner they became. Size, space, and dimensionality were in continuous flux, the only constant the oversized feet of his figures.

Around this time an incident occurred in which his reaction to the death of a person he had met in his youth was repeated. His friend, Tonio Pototsching, died. Giacometti stayed with the body overnight. While dressing the corpse, he felt that Tonio was everywhere outside of the corpse and he was afraid, as in a nightmare, that his icy hand would touch him. It is of interest that Jean Genet (1963) wrote a little book about Giacometti in which he was able to grasp his subject's inner world: "His sculptures give me the feeling that they seek refuge at the last in some secret infirmity which acknowledges their solitude." Genet describes Giacometti's studio:

This studio, moreover, on the ground floor is going to collapse at any

moment. It is made of worm-eaten wood, of gray powder, the sculptures
are of plaster, showing bits of string, stuffing or ends of wire. . . .
all is precarious, on the verge of disintegration. . . . When I have
gone away from the studio, when I am outside in the street, then
nothing round me seems real. Shall I say it? In that studio a man is
slowly dying, consuming himself. . . . Giacometti is not working for
his contemporaries, nor for the future generations: he is creating statues
to at least delight the dead [p. 31].

It is interesting to speculate why Giacometti—who has given form
to a world in which the dead are alive and the living are dead, in which
reality and fantasy are interchangeable, in which the fears of old
nightmares assert their power—has gained such wide acceptance and
admiration as an artist. What is it in his paintings and sculptures that
appeals to the general public? Beyond the aesthetic aspects of his work,
he creates a world that touches on fears that have meaning even to those
who have less than he.

From the disruption of relationships and of reality, Giacometti gained
a sense of his own creativity that allowed him to free himself from the
confines of reality and to accept his preconscious and unconscious life.
Thus, the creative process is for him more than the expression of unconscious fantasies; it is an attempt to repair traumatic injuries by creating
new representations that combine inner images with perceived reality.
Picasso put it this way: "If you give meaning to certain things in my
paintings, it may be very true but it was not my idea to give this meaning.
What ideas and conclusions you have got I obtained too, but instinc-
tively, unconsciously. I make paintings for the paintings. I paint objects
for what they are. It's in my subconscious . . ." (Ashton, 1977). Thus
we cannot understand the work of an artist by reducing it to a single
trauma, or to one theme, idea, or determinant. The organizing fantasies,
preconscious or unconscious, are the product of many factors. Creative
work and the play of children are an attempt to find new solutions. Or,
as Gedo (1981) states, "it is no longer possible for the psychoanalyst to
see the artist as a spinner of fantasies. The artist must be understood
as a specially endowed manipulator of varied perceptual elements."

Arlow (1969a), in his classic "Fantasy, Memory and Reality Testing,"
states: "The predominant role of vision in the totality of human perception can hardly be overstressed. . . . the element of visual representability
of fantasy thinking has an important bearing on psychoanalytic techni-

que'' (p. 48). It is clear that memory is an important factor in the representational world in both the evocative memory and recognition memory. Arlow quotes Nunberg (1951)—'It is as if the analysand was trying to match the construction with a picture of his own'' (p. 6)—and then refers to the joint search by patient and analyst for the picture of the patient's past as a reciprocal process. ''In a sense, we dream along with our patients, supplying at first data from our own store of images in order to objectify the patient's memory into some sort of picture'' (p. 24). This is particularly applicable to the task Giacometti sets himself. He continuously attempted to revive old memories, and to rid himself of them, unable to shake the unconscious fantasies that make reality for him a question of being alternately outside or inside, alive or dead, expansive or shrinked to nothing. We are unable to fix the developmental level at which the trauma occurred or to reconstruct a point of fixation or regression, for Giacometti seems to have carried the fluidity to all levels of psychic organization while focused mainly on the diadic position and the role of the woman. We cannot say that the various traumata in Giacometti's life were the cause of his disorientation and inability to achieve ego integration and mastery. He responded to events in a traumatic way, for early in life he could not achieve self-constancy or ego regulation. We can never say whether the ''real'' external event was experienced as external, because at the same time it was endowed with fantasies that contributed to a sudden economic and structural shift.

From a structural point of view, Giacometti's ego was unable to obtain mastery, to shift to secondary processes, and to synthesize and integrate reality and drive expressions. The memories of his earliest unconscious fantasies were too powerful and so penetrated his reality. As an artist Giacometti attempted to interject another truth, another solution, namely, images on canvas, or the forms he gave his sculptures. In this realm he attempted to find a harmony between his perceptual experiences and his terror-ridden fantasies. As both involve visual sensory modalities, his artistic expression provided him a channel that early in life afforded him some relief from his conflicts. Giacometti's artistic work gives us a visual expression of his difficulties in achieving and maintaining visual object representation. He enlarges our understanding of this disorder and of the many modes of compensatory creative achievement.

REFERENCES

Arlow, J. A. (1969a), Fantasy, memory and reality testing. *Psychoanal. Quart.*, 38:28–51.

_____ (1969b), Unconscious fantasy and disturbances of conscious experience. *Psychoanal. Quart.*, 38:1–27.

Ashton, D. (1977), *Picasso on Art: A Selection of Views.* New York: Penguin.

Gedo, M. (1981), The archaeology of painting: A visit to the city of the death beneath Picasso's "La Vie." *Arts,* 56:116–129.

Genet, J. (1963), *The Studio of Alberto Giacometti (L'Atelier d'Alberto Giacometti).* New York: French & European Publishers.

Lord, J. (1965), *A Giacometti Portrait.* New York: Farrar, Straus, & Giroux.

_____ (1983), *Giacometti.* New York: Farrar, Straus, & Giroux.

Neubauer, P. (1987), Disturbances in object representation. *The Psychoanalytic Study of the Child,* 42:335–351. New Haven, CT: Yale University Press.

Nunberg, H. (1951), Transference and reality. *Internat. J. Psycho-Anal.,* 32:1–9.

12

The Triumph of Humor

Janine Chasseguet-Smirgel, Ph.D.

There are at least two good reasons for comparing and possibly op-posing melancholia—the normal prototype of which is mourning—to humor (whose relations whith mania remain to be studied). These reasons are essentially historical. They concern the evolution of Freud's thought. "Mourning and Melancholia" (Freud, 1917) is very likely an enlarge-ment of the article "On Narcissism: An Introduction" (Freud, 1914); we know that Freud began writing it at about the time he finished the work on narcissism and that it prefigures the introduction of the superego—that is, the introduction of the structural theory of the psychic apparatus. As for humor, the 1927 article on the subject (Freud, 1927b) resumes the discussion of a theme Freud (1905) examined in "Jokes and Their Relation to the Unconscious" from the perspective of the first topographical theory (Ucs, Pcs, Cs); the later work introduces the superego, placing it at the heart of this new investigation.

Linked to this first reason—the existence within the psyche of a moral agency—is the question of evaluating the extent to which this split-off ego agency is separated from the rest of the ego. In his article of 1917 Freud writes:

> let us dwell for a moment on the view which the melancholic's disorder affords of the constitution of the human ego. We see how in him one part of the ego sets itself over against the other, judges it critically, and, as it were, takes it as its object. Our suspicion that the critical agency which is here split off from the ego might also show its independence in other circumstances will be confirmed by every further observation. We shall really find grounds for distinguishing this agency from the

197

rest of the ego. What we are here becoming acquainted with is the agency commonly called 'conscience' [p. 247].

According to the same article, the libido is withdrawn from the lost object and displaced onto the ego. In fact, however, the ego has been modified by narcissistic identification with the object. The ego, merged with the object, is judged by the moral agency (the future superego), as is also (though unconsciously) the object, in regard to which the subject has conflictual feelings owing to an ambivalence: ''an object-loss was transformed into an ego-loss and the conflict between the ego and the loved person into a cleavage between the critical activity of the ego and the ego as altered by identification'' (p. 249). This critical activity of the ego, which is in fact directed against the object, now merged with the ego, leads to a situation in which ''the hate comes into operation on this substitutive object, abusing it, debasing it, making it suffer and deriving sadistic satisfaction from its suffering'' (p. 251), going even to the extreme of murdering the object—that is, as far as suicide. In other words, and leaving aside the question of narcissistic identification, we have here a split-off part of the ego which has set itself as far distant from the ego as is possible, and which is relentlessly engaged in its assault. This moral or critical agency, the future superego, is described by Freud (1923) as in melancholia ''a pure culture of the death instinct'' (p. 53).

In the article ''Humour,'' Freud (1927b) considers the case in which ''a person adopts a humorous attitude towards himself in order to ward off possible suffering'' (p. 164). And he wonders:

> Is there any sense in saying that someone is treating himself like a child and is at the same time playing the part of a superior adult towards the child?
> This not very plausible idea receives strong support, I think, if we consider what we have learned from pathological observations on the structure of the ego. This ego is not a simple entity. It harbours within it, as its nucleus, a special agency—the super-ego. Sometimes it is merged with the super-ego so that we cannot distinguish between them, whereas in other circumstances it is sharply differentiated from it. Genetically the super-ego is the heir to the parental agency. It often keeps the ego in strict dependence and still really treats it as the parents, or the father, once treated the child, in its early years [p. 164; italics mine].

The humorous attitude consists then of withdrawing cathexis from the ego and transposing it onto the superego: "To the super-ego, thus in-flated, the ego can appear tiny and all its interests trivial" (p. 164). *"Humour would be the contribution made to the comic through the agency of the super-ego"* (p. 165). Freud acknowledges that we have had frequent occasion to recognize "the severe master" in the superego, yet, where humor is concerned, it would appear to be saying to the ego: "Look! here is the world, which seems so dangerous! It is nothing but a game for children—just worth making a jest about!" (p. 166). And Freud then concludes: "If it is really the super-ego which, in humour, speaks such kindly words of comfort to the intimidated ego, this will teach us that we have still a great deal to learn about the nature of the super-ego" (p. 166).

The second reason justifying the comparison of melancholia and humor—and the same two texts of 1917 and 1927—concerns narcissism. Melancholia is a sickness of narcissism and, for the melancholic, brings about "an extraordinary diminution in his self-regard, an impoverish-ment of his ego on a grand scale." His ego is "poor and empty" and he proclaims that he is "worthless," "lacking in interest. . . . incapable of love and achievement" (Freud, 1917, p. 246). The patient expresses his "dissatisfaction with the ego on moral grounds" (p. 248). Let us not dwell on Freud's interpretation of these self-accusations—they are in fact aimed at the object with which the ego is identified—and turn our at-tention to the subject of humor. As early as 1905, in "Jokes and Their Relation to the Unconscious," Freud emphasizes the fact that humor permits *an economy in the expenditure of affects,* and in this respect he insists on the *elevated* nature of this intellectual activity and of its effect on author and listener alike. He describes it as "one of the highest physical achievements" (p. 228) and speaks of the *magnanimity* of humor, its *grandeur,* its *grand scale.* On the subject of jokes, which are sometimes difficult to distinguish from humor proper, he writes in his introduction: "A new joke acts almost like an event of universal interest; it is passed from one person to another like the news of the latest victory" (p. 15). Because humor procures a feeling of elation for the ego, whereas in melancholia the ego is crushed,

> the grandeur in it clearly lies in the triumph of narcissism, the vic-torious assertion of the ego's invulnerability. The ego refuses to be dis-tressed by the provocations of reality, to let itself be compelled to suffer. It insists that it cannot be affected by the traumas of the external world. . . . Humour is not resigned; it is rebellious. It signifies not only the triumph of the ego but also of the pleasure principle. . . [Freud 1927b, pp. 162–163].

Once again we find Freud using words such as "grandeur," "eleva-tion," "dignity."

Having stated at the end of the 1927 article that we have a great deal to learn regarding the nature of the superego, Freud adds:

> Furthermore, not everyone is capable of the humourous attitude. It is a rare and precious gift, and many people are even without the capacity to enjoy humourous pleasure that is presented to them. And finally, if the super-ego tries, by means of humour, to console the ego and protect it from suffering, this does not contradict its origin in the parental agency [p. 166].

Here I should like to specify the nature of this consoling parental agency which plays so great a part in humor, to determine whether it is indeed the superego, the inheritor of the Oedipus complex, and to relate the role and nature of this parental agency to the problem of narcissism, which is at the core of both humor and melancholia.

HUMOR AND MANIA

I shall start with a commonplace remark. A very great number of humorists suffer from depression. If one knows nothing of their personal lives one need only turn to the back pages of newspapers for confirma-tion. Does it then follow that humor is the equivalent of a manic defense?

Freud (1927b) has a moment's hesitation when he observes that humor rejects the claims of reality and at the same time contrives to secure the success of the pleasure principle. This seems to place humor rather close to the most pathological regressions. "Its fending off of the possibility of suffering places it among the great series of methods which the human mind has constructed in order to evade the compulsion to suffer—a series which begins with neurosis and culminates in madness and which includes intoxication, self-absorption and ecstasy" (p. 163).

How can the humorous attitude, Freud asks, which insists on the ego's invincibility vis-à-vis the real world, and on its victorious hold on the pleasure principle, be compatible with the preservation of mental health? His reply is the hypothesis that the ego is internally divided into an adult part, identified with the superego, and a part that plays the role of the child being consoled by the well-wishing superego, this consola-tion being accompanied by a shift of cathexis from the ego onto the superego. This new distribution of energy between the agencies, the hypercathexis of the superego to the detriment of the ego, allows the superego to suppress or alter the ego's reactions. In humor, "the super-ego is actually repudiating reality and serving an illusion" (p. 166).

In his text on humor Freud seems to attribute reality testing to the superego, though generally he attributes it to the ego, considering it one of that agency's major functions. (In "Group Psychology and the Analysis of the Ego" [Freud, 1921], written before the introduction of the structural theory, it is attributed to the ego ideal.)

In short, the difference between mania and humor would seem to be that in the former the separation between ego and superego, and between ego and ideal has been abolished. These dualities are united in the festivities, whereas in humor there is no decompartmentalization of the agencies. The hypercathected superego, far from being absorbed by the ego, retrieves a function (namely, reality testing) that originally was delegated at least partly to the real parent, much as a young child might refrain from answering questions about his well-being until he has seen the expression on his mother's face. Nevertheless, there are analogies between humor and the manic state, and the hypotheses formulated in 1927 are not totally convincing. In "Mourning and Melancholia" Freud (1917) writes:

> all states such as joy, exultation or triumph, which give us the normal model for mania, depend on the same economic conditions. What has happened here is that, as a result of some influence, a large expenditure of psychical energy, long maintained or habitually occurring, has at last become unnecessary, so that it is available for numerous applications and possibilities of discharge—when for instance, some poor wretch, by winning a large sum of money, is suddenly relieved from chronic worry about his daily bread, or when a long and arduous struggle is finally crowned with success, or when a man finds himself in a position to throw off at a single blow some oppressive compulsion, some false position which he has long had to keep up, and so on. All such situations are characterized by high spirits, by the signs of discharge of joyful emotion and by increased readiness for all kinds of action—in just the same way as in mania, and in complete contrast to the depression and inhibition of melancholia [p. 254].

One notes from this description that the conditions provoking the typical manic state are a sudden economy of energy, principally of affects.

This is precisely what happens in humor, but on the intrapsychic level. Sudden relief is brought not by some event in the outside world but by the fact that the superego (if we are to follow Freud's thinking) has detached itself from the ego and is serving an illusion. It is tossing coins to the ego (the ''poor wretch''), crowning it with success, ridding it of its heavy obligation, and freeing it of the necessity for further dissimulation. The relation between humor and mania has been pointed out by Kris (1952) ''Ego Development and the Comic'' (in his classification, unlike Freud's, humor is a category of the comic): mania, he writes, ''is to some extent the pathological enlargement of the comic'' (p. 216). We know, however, and Freud emphasizes this many times over, that the discharge humor affords the listener, whose psychic processes are the echo of those at work within the humorist, is feeble in comparison to that afforded him by other species of the comic and, a fortiori, by manic states. Humor generally brings a smile, not laughter, and moves one to admiration of the humorist's narcissistic triumph, his rebellion against exterior reality. Even in his work of 1905 Freud emphasizes that humor may only partly succeed in stopping the production of the painful affect: this is ''the humour that smiles through tears'' (p. 232). And yet despite this the victory won by humor is no less complete. Quite the contrary, in fact. The more aware one is of the tragedy of the situation, the more humor takes a sublime turn. What happens, I suggest, is that the energy economized in the expenditure of affects is correlatively cathected in the ego's feelings of exaltation. In other words, there is little room for discharge. It is a matter of energy being displaced from an affect of helplessness onto an affect of triumph. Moreover, a part of the energy is probably used in an anti-cathexis of the representation linked to the affect of helplessness. The humorist is therefore caught on a tightrope: the mechanism he resorts to is essentially precarious, as this anticathexis is liable to give way at any time, submerging him in suffering. If the comic is a clown, then the humorist is more of an acrobat.

Kris holds that humor prevails over other forms of the comic, and over mania, because the victory won by the ego is not transitory. It results in a real transformation of the ego: ''We begin to realize the value of the humorist's achievement, for he banishes man's greatest fear, the eternal fear, acquired in childhood, of the loss of love'' (p. 216). Although this idea of a permanent transformation of the ego does not, I feel, properly describe what takes place in humor, and (if we pursue Kris's argument) a permanent transformation of the ego should lead from a transitory manic state to permanent mania, I do agree with his idea that at the moment the humorist produces humor, he is protecting himself against the loss of love.

THE TRIUMPH OF LOVE?

In "Inhibitions, Symptoms and Anxiety" Freud (1926) describes the prolonged state of helplessness and dependence in which the human child first finds itself; this he descries as the *biological factor* in neuroses:

> Its intra-uterine existence seems to be short in comparison with that of most animals, and it is sent into the world in a less finished state. As a result, the influence of the real external world upon it is intensified and an early differentiation between the ego and the id is promoted. Moreover, the dangers of the external world have a greater importance for it, so that the value of the object which can alone protect it against them and take the place of its former intra-uterine life is enormously enhanced. The biological factor, then, establishes the earliest situations of danger and creates the need to be loved which will accompany the child through the rest of its life [p. 154–155].

In the same text Freud emphasizes the anxiety attendant on being separated from the mother, the result of the infant's state of helplessness:

> The striking coincidence by which the anxiety of the new-born baby and the anxiety of the infant in arms are both conditioned by separation from the mother does not need to be explained on psychological lines. It can be accounted for simply enough biologically; for, just as the mother originally satisfied all the needs of the foetus through the apparatus of her own body, so now, after its birth, she continues to do so, though partly by other means. There is much more continuity between intra-uterine life and earliest infancy than the impressive caesura of the act of birth would have us believe. What happens is that the child's biological situation as a foetus is replaced for it by a psychical object-relation to its mother [p. 138].

Again in the same text, and obviously influenced by Ferenczi's *Thalassa* (1924), he begins to consider castration anxiety as a variation of the anxiety of separation from the mother, the penis being the organ enabling the boy to unite once again with the mother, or her substitute. The subject then interiorizes the parental agency (the father) from whence arises the threat of castration. Subsequently, this agency become impersonal and the danger less defined. The ultimate form of anxiety is the fear of being punished by the superego and of losing its love. The ego is thus delivered up to the "powers of fate."

Our problem is to determine whether the adult part within the person that produces humor represents the paternal superego or the mother of early childhood who, by the care she gives her infant, by her caresses, her milk, and her love, comes to replace intrauterine life for the child who has been thrown too soon into this world, impotent and helpless.

In a note to "Jokes and Their Relation to the Unconscious" Freud (1905) writes,

> So far as I know, the grimace characteristic of smiling, which twists up the corners of the mouth, appears first in an infant at the breast when it is satisfied and satiated and lets go of the breast as it falls asleep. Here it is a genuine expression of the emotions, for it corresponds to a decision to take no more nourishment, and represents as it were an 'enough' or rather a 'more than enough.' This original meaning of pleasurable satiety may have brought the smile, which is after all the basic phenomenon of laughter, into its later relation with pleasurable processes of discharge [pp. 146–147].

Little does it matter whether Freud was right or not in thinking that the first smile of the breast-fed infant expresses satisfaction. Here I concur with Eisenbud (1964) who noted in "The Oral Side of Humor" that this is the one and only time Freud related the nursing situation to humor and that practically no author since has taken this aspect into account. With the help of delicious examples, Eisenbud demonstrates that "the transformation of a passively endured oral helplessness into some active form of denial or reversal is . . . . one of the more frequent latent situations to be found in humor" (p. 60). Significantly, the clinical illustrations he gives include a *depressed* patient and another, the American humorist Robert Benchley, who is described as depressed, as well as an ardent prohibitionist turned alcoholic. The breast can, after all, be considered an external substitute for the uterus; in French the word "sein" applies to the breast and also to the womb (*sinus*, its Latin root, denotes a cavity). In The Song of Solomon we find this verse: "Thy navel is like a round goblet which wanteth not liquor." (7:2); in the original Hebrew, the word for navel is "beten," which means the inside of the belly.

The hypothesis I wish to advance concerning the adult part of the ego that consoles the child extends beyond the nursing mother or the good maternal breast, although the good breast can symbolize a whole series of satisfying maternal functions, as Green (1983) has shown in his work on the dead mother. I believe that the adult part of the ego in humor represents, in their totality, all the mother's efforts of care and attention, efforts liable to clothe the naked infant with the narcissism she has forfeited in its favor. Little does it matter whether one refers here to Winnicott (1956) on "primary maternal preoccupation" or "holding"; to Bion (1967) on the mother's ability for reverie or the breast as container for projective identifications; to Mahler (1952) on the "symbiotic membrane"; to Grunberger on "narcissistic confirmation" (1956) or "the monad" (1985); or to Didier Anzieu (1986) on the "ego-skin." Not that these theories are interchangeable, but without exception they stress the fundamentally important role of the maternal contribution in the early stages of life. This contribution cathects the infant narcissistically, and when correctly dosed enables it to interiorize the mother's good representation of her child, as well as to integrate the ego. Otherwise the child experiences states of dereliction and identifies—as I have had occasion to show elsewhere (Chasseguet-Smirgel, 1987)—with that part of its mother which she refuses, rejects, and rids herself of, that is, with waste material, this being the prefiguration of depressive, even melancholic self-depreciation, and of fecalization of the ego (see Grunberger, 1966).

It is the mother who consoles the child, taking it in her arms saying, "It's nothing, you'll be better soon," or who blows on a hurt to make the pain disappear, not the oedipal father on whom, in Freudian theory, the superego is founded. In my opinion, it is a precocious lack of maternal care that explains the relation between humor and depression. *The humorist is a person trying to be his own loving mother,* the "good enough mother" he has not known and who assures the child in a state of dereliction that he still is, who pretends "its nothing, you'll be better soon." But this loving mother has never been truly assimilated into the ego. It can be supposed, however, that the child has furtively been able to catch a glimpse (a nurser, a grandmother) of what the "loving mother" might have been, and thus has motives for having prefigured the satisfying narcissistic state (or a return to it). Thus, situations of helplessness will provoke a *splitting of the ego* which does not, in my opinion, detach the superego from the ego, but rather takes place within the ego itself, dividing it. Part of the ego recognizes the situation of helplessness and another part denies it, or rather plays at denying it. In the gallows humor joke reported by Freud (1905), the man being led out to be hanged on a Monday who remarks, "Well, this week's beginning nicely" (p. 229), is in a situation very similar to that of the fetischist. We must remember that Freud's "Humour" (1927b) was written only one week after his article on fetischism (1927a): "He has retained that belief," Freud writes of the fetishist, "but he has also given it up" (p. 154). The condemned man knows he is going to die, but a part of him pretends that this is just another everyday event, that life will continue. Unlike the fetischist, though, he remains in control of his denial. In fact, I venture to say that in certain extreme cases, as in gallows humor, the humorist secretly mocks that part of the ego which is supposedly identified with the loving mother. This comes out, I think, in Freud's other example of gallows humor (1905): that of a man who, likewise being led to the gibbet, asked for a scarf for his throat so as not to catch cold. Is this not a mockery of the maternal recommendations of his childhood?

But only morbid humor is the part of the ego that is identified with the "loving mother" submitted to this attack on the maternal imago. In other forms of humor the subject succeeds in allotting to a part of his ego the role of the mother of whom he has been deprived.

Although humor proclaims the triumph of the ego, like "Beauty [which] is nothing but the beginning of terror that we are still just able to bear" (Rilke, quoted by Segal, 1953), it bears the mark of an underlying terror. In this respect, humor differs from mania; though the defense it deploys against depression is "admirable" (we would not admire it if we did not know that the person producing the humor "knows"), in order to be effective it must be constantly repeated. As when Freud (1914) places the humorist next to the criminal to vaunt "the narcissistic consistency with which they manage to keep away from their ego anything that would diminish it" (p. 89) he has no doubt failed to take into account the humorist's underlying helplessness and terror.

In his essay "The Essence of Laughter" Baudelaire (1855) clearly shows that laughter is always bound up with the tragic; his observations in fact apply mostly to humor. Man laughs because he has lost his paradisiacal state of completeness (the intrauterine life which has not been replaced, even by his mother's love):

In the earthly paradise . . . . that is to say in the surroundings in which it seemed to man that all created things were good, joy did not find its dwelling in laughter. As no trouble afflicted him, man's countenance was simple and smooth, and the laughter which now shakes the nations never distorted the features of his face. Laughter and tears cannot make their appearance in the paradise of delights. They are both equally the children of woe . . . .

Laughter is unknown to God, Baudelaire goes on to explain. The humorist momentarily sets himself up as God to avoid falling into the bottomless pit, the fate that meets the child with no narcissistic maternal cathexis. A theatrical sketch by Raymond Devos, "The Ascensional Fall" (1985), seems to me to reflect this psychic state.

Kris (1952) writes at the end of his article on the comic, "We see man as an eternal pleasure-seeker walking on a narrow ledge above an abyss of fear" (p. 216). From time to time the humorist will drop into the abyss of depression. Then his triumphant ego, shining with the light projected onto it by his "loving mother," will tarnish, and become empty and devoid of interest, worthy only, as the melancholic says, of being swept like rubbish from the face of the earth.

This will perhaps lead us to reply affirmatively to Freud's question (1917) as to "whether a loss in the ego irrespectively of the object—a purely narcissistic blow to the ego—may not suffice to produce the picture of melancholia" (p. 253).[1],[2] Depressions in which object loss is evident, and above all those in which one is able to follow the journey of the object through the digestive tract (see Abraham, 1924), are highly evolved, and access to them within the treatment is relatively easy. On the other hand, even if the loss of an object can be detected (this possibly being figured by an abstraction), a certain number of depressions seem to lead to a "denarcissization" of the ego, to its fecalization (Grunberger, 1966), and not to an introjection of the lost object, as if the object had only been a substitute for the insufficiently present "loving mother" of early childhood, a loving mother who has never been introjected and

----

[1] I cannot go into this theme in detail here, nor it is possible to make the distinction between melancholia and other forms of depression.

[2] Where the person capable of humor is concerned, these remarks on the humorist are an exaggeration. Quite obviously he is not constantly battling against depression. But the mechanisms brought into play are similar, as will be seen.

whose disappearance from the exterior world has left the subject naked, feeling worthless and useless.

This is what happens to the humorist when internal or external factors prevent him from bringing about the "narcissistic rehearsal" he achieves with humor.

As Freud remarks, not everyone is capable of humor. Thinking of the fanatic, it is easy to understand how he would be unable to divide his ego, let along show any measure of indulgence to the child within himself or within others. By definition the humorist is a skeptic. (The title of a book by David Rousset [1949] on Nazism, *"Le pitre ne rit pas,* can be literally translated *The Clown is Not Laughing.*)

Although children react to the comic at quite an early age, they are incapable of humor, as many authors have shown. This is doubtless an attitude that can be assumed only after the child has successfully negotiated the latency period. Likewise, persons directly discharging a great amount of instinctual energy are able to laugh but cannot enjoy or produce humor.

The aptitude for humor then, whether as author or amateur, is related to a certain maturation (e.g., the acquisition of instincts inhibited in their aim, the capacity for sublimation) and hence to the superego, as well as to a certain narcissistic fragility. The superego in fact plays a major role in the psychic organization of the humorist, or of the person with a humorous bent, even if, as I believe, where humor is concerned, the split takes place within the ego rather than between it and the superego. The psychic organization of the humorist, as also of the person with an aptitude for humor, tends toward internalization rather than acting out—yet another reason to set him apart from the criminal. The narcissistic satisfaction that humor procures is the result of an intrapsychic transformation. In his "Ego Psychology and the Study of Mythology," Jacob Arlow (1961) speaks of the conflict of two mythologies in Western culture:

> One mythology, working through established institutions, tries to point in the direction of internalized inhibitions and intrapsychic transformation. Alongside this tendency of the official institutions, however, is the opposing trend toward reinstitutionalization of the ego ideal, in keeping with the intensified narcissistic needs, and tending toward the idealization of grandiosely conceived objects from childhood. With increasing frequency, we see narcissistic character difficulties and nar-

cissistic neuroses, together with patients who cannot contain their conflicts within themselves by the process of symptom formation, but who
are forced to externalize them in various forms of acting out [p. 389].

I think I can safely say that humor is oriented toward the first of these
tendencies, that is, in the direction of intrapsychic transformation.
Moreover, would it not be possible to consider humor as one way of dealing with a primal mythical core: the rescue of the helpless child who has
been abandoned or condemned to die?

As we have seen, in order to produce humor, one must be capable
of moving forward along a tiny ledge with no guardrail, knowing that
there is an abyss below. This is an exploit of which few are capable—
probably only those whose personal lives or collective condition have
forced them to such performances, rather after the fashion of Kafka's
"The Fasting Showman" (1920-1924).

I should like to conclude with a few brief remarks on the subject
of Jewish humor.[3]

The collective characteristics I have mentioned as favoring the
development of a humorous attitude within the individual are, I believe,
found in the Jewish condition.

Within the Diaspora, Jews have been subjected to history rather
than involved in its making. After the Roman conquest and the destruction of the Second Temple, when the Jews were dispersed throughout
the world, they came to be regarded as wanderers and pariahs. In the
lands were they settled they were met with persecution, the Inquisition,
pogroms, or, at best, discrimination and prohibitions of all sorts, the
most widespread of these being the laws forbidding Jewish ownership
of land. To say the least, the Jew's surroundings have never been the
equivalent for him of a "loving" and consoling mother. Separated from
Mother Earth, prevented from establishing within the Diaspora a new
link with the earth, he has been a dependent, naked, and impotent child,

---

[3]Curiously enough, at least where the French language is concerned, one speaks
of *British* humor and *Jewish* humor only. (The French say that they have *wit*.)
Despite the admiration I have for British humor, I do not feel qualified to talk
about it. The Jewish condition is quite specific and so is Jewish humor. However,
there must be some factor that is common to all the soils in which humor
flourishes. Certain historians, certain geographers (André Siegfried for one),
have pointed to the paradox of Great Britain with its harsh natural conditions
which hardly seemed to endow it for the role it was to play in world history.

exposed to every danger. Claude Lanzmann has said that without Israel he would feel "naked." Quite apart from any political ideology, a people without a land is a people without a mother—that is to say, an infant in a state of helplessness.

However, the fact of having been deprived of a "good enough mother" does not automatically turn one into a humorist. In addition, one has to have caught a glimpse of her existence, and to yearn for her. The Jewish religion probably played the part of substitute for the "loving mother," with its affirmation that the Jews are the people chosen by God to receive the Torah, and the Talmud, so very much a part of Jewish religious life, that is, narcissistic achievement through spiritual and intellectual activity. Heine (1833–1850) said the Bible is the portable homeland of the Jewish people. Allied to the constant menace hanging over Jewish life in Europe was the consciousness (on a certain level) of a value—a potential value, at least. The stress laid by the Jewish religion on a moral code woven into the acts of everyday life, thereby affecting the structure of family life, was to favor the institution of the superego.

For Jews it was impossible to show open hostility to the authorities. One had to go about things obliquely. It would be hard to think of a better solution than humor. In "Jewish Humor as Jewish Identity," Kurt Schlesinger (1979) has this very apt formula: "In lieu of the playing fields of Eton, the playing fields of the mind had to be utilized for integrating self-assertion." Here we find the vital need for interiorization and psychic elaboration noted by the Hungarian novelist Anna Lesznai (1985): "The intellect is the only human community into which the Jews have been truly received" (quoted in *The Jewish Question in Central and Eastern Europe,* published in Budapest in 1985 and immediately withdrawn from sale).

Besides being conducive to humor, the domain of intellectual achievement is also a land of refuge, a substitute for the loving and consoling mother ready to help the ego on to triumph.[4]

---

[4]I have not dealt with all the aspects of humor here, in particular the fact that ego mastery must be perfect if the ego is to triumph (Kris, 1952). Jewish humor is in part devoted to self-criticism. This is not masochism, but the pre-emptive strategy employed by Cyrano in the tirade of insults he directs to his nose: "je ne veux pas qu'un autre me les serve" (I would not want another to serve them upon me). When Popeck [a French Jewish humorist] bargains over the price of a train ticket he adopts and caricatures a trait that is attributed to Jews. In so doing he escapes criticism.

Humor at its most sublime is produced in the face of death and in all likelihood one finds death profiled beneath the humor. It is no mere chance that several of the examples given by Freud concern persons who have been sentenced to death. There is also the well-known piece of humor he himself produced, just before leaving Vienna for London in 1938, after the Nazis had forced their way into his apartment and seized the money they found there. The Nazis ordered him to sign a declaration attesting the fact that he had been correctly treated. He did this and is said to have added, "I can heartily recommend the Gestapo to everyone" (Jones, 1957, p. 226).[5]

In analyzing this humor we find a very small ego threatened with total annihilation by a terrible agency, adopting a sovereign position of total domination over both the persecutor and the entire world: "I . . . to everyone." Moreover, it is phrased along the lines of the letters of reference that were given to servants in the Vienna of those days (see Deutsch, 1973). The Gestapo is thus reduced to the level of a domestic servant whom Freud has dismissed with a generous and magnanimous letter of reference. It is turned into its opposite. The bad, all-powerful mother has become an inoffensive and dependent maternal substitute.

Can it not be said that here Freud is identifying not only with the loving mother who is there to console the terrified young child and to help him on to victory over the menacing power, but also with the real mother of his childhood, the mistress of the household who had servants at her command?

REFERENCES

Abraham, K. (1924), A short study of the development of the libido, viewed in the light of mental disorders. In: *Selected Papers of Karl Abraham*. London: Hogarth Press, 1927, pp. 418–501.

Anzieu, D. (1986), *Le Moi-Peau*. Paris: Dunod.

---

[5]In point of fact I know of only one other outburst of humor to reach such heights of the sublime and it was uttered in similar circumstances. During the Occupation of France, Tristan Bernard questioned, "Peuplé élu? . . . . Peuplé en ballotage . . . ." This is impossible to translate into English because of the play on the word "ballotage." It can mean either "People in ballot" or "People being shunted or tossed around like so many packages." ("Peuplé élu" is the French way of speaking of the chosen people.)

Arlow, J. A. (1961), Ego psychology and the study of mythology. *J. Amer. Psycho-anal. Assn.*, 3:371–393.

Baudelaire, C. (1855), L'essence du rire. In: *Oeuvres*. Paris: Flammarion.

Bion, W. (1967), *Second Thoughts*. New York: Aronson, 1977.

Chasseguet-Smirgel, J. (1987), Une tentative de solution perverse et son échec chez une femme. Paper presented at the IPA Congress, Montreal, 1987. In press.

Deutsch, H. (1973), *Confrontation with Myself*. New York: Norton.

Eisenbud, J. (1964), The oral side of humour, *Psychoanal. Rev.*, 51:57–73.

Ferenczi, S. (1924), *Thalassa: A Theory of Genitality*. New York: Norton, 1968.

Freud, S. (1905), Jokes and their relation to the unconscious, *Standard Edition*, 8:9–236. London: Hogarth Press, 1960.

_____ (1914), On narcissism: An introduction. *Standard Edition*, 14:73–102.

_____ (1917) Mourning and melancholia. *Standard Edition*, 14:243–258. London: Hogarth Press, 1957.

_____ (1921), Group psychology and the analysis of the ego. *Standard Edition*, 18:69–143. London: Hogarth Press, 1955.

_____ (1923), The ego and the id. *Standard Edition*, 19:12–66. London: Hogarth Press, 1961.

_____ (1926), Inhibitions, symptoms and anxiety, *Standard Edition*, 20:87–174. London: Hogarth Press, 1959.

_____ (1927a), Fetishism. *Standard Edition*, 21:152–157. London: Hogarth Press, 1961.

_____ (1927b), Humour. *Standard Edition*, 21:161–166. London: Hogarth Press, 1961.

Green, A. (1983), *Narcissisme de vie, narcissisme de mort*. Paris: Editions de Minuit.

Grunberger, B. (1956), The analytic situation and the dynamics of the healing process. In: *Narcissism*. New York: International Universities Press, 1979, pp. 35–89.

_____ (1966), Suicide of melancholic. In: *Narcissism*. New York: International Universities Press, 1979, pp. 241–264.

_____ (1985), Die Monade. *Forum*, 2.

Heine, H. (1833–1850), *De l'Allemagne*.

Jones, E. (1957), *The Life and Work of Sigmund Freud*. Vol. 3. London: Hogarth Press.

Kafka, F. (1920–1924), Un champion de jeune. In: *Récits I*. Paris: Cercle du Livre Précieux.

Kris, E. (1952), Ego development and the comic. In: *Psychoanalytic Explorations in Art*. New York: International Universities Press, pp. 204–216.

Lesznai, A. (1985), *The Jewish Question in Central and Eastern Europe* (in Hungarian). Budapest: Withdrawn from publication.

Mahler, M. (1952), On child psychosis and schizophrenia: Autistic and symbiotic infantile psychoses. *The Psychoanalytic Study of the Child*, 7:286–305. New York: International Universities Press.

Rostand, E. (1897), *Cyrano de Bergerac*. Paris: Fasquelle, 1964.

Rousset, D. (1949), *Le pitre ne rit pas*. Paris: Bourgeois.

Schlesinger, K. (1979), Jewish humor as Jewish identity. *Internat. Rev. Psycho-Anal.*, 6:317–330.

Segal, H. (1953), A psycho-analytical approach to aesthetics, In: *New Directions in Psycho-Analysis*, ed. M. Klein, P. Heimann, and R. Money-Kyrle. London: Tavistock, pp. 384–405.

Winnicott, D. (1956), Primary maternal preoccupation. In: *Collected Papers: Through Paediatrics to Psycho-Analysis*. New York: Basic Books, 1958, pp. 300–305.

Part V

MYTHOLOGY, RELIGION, AND BELIEF

13

A Woman's Fantasy of Being Unfinished: Its Relation to Pygmalion, Pandora, and Other Myths

Isidor Bernstein, M.D.

Ever since human beings became able to think and imagine, they have tried to understand the miracle and mystery of the creation of the world and of its inhabitants, especially themselves. Primitive man's lack of scientific knowledge led him to create fantasies to explain the origin of the earth and the universe in which he lived. Answers were found in supernatural forces in the heavenly bodies, and in such elements as fire, earth, and water. Fantasies led to theories and myths. Even recent scientific theories are based on incomplete data and therefore contain elements of speculation or fantasy. The Big Bang theory, for example, bears a resemblance to myths of creation of the earth and universe from Chaos. As Arlow (1982) has stated, "In these myths, one has to discern that the themes of cataclysmic clash, dawning light, separation of the elements of the cosmos, and the beginning of life have analogous representations in both scientific and mythological cosmogonies" (p. 182).

Myths of different societies reflect shared unconscious fantasies influenced by tradition and cultural attitudes and values. Where woman was seen as the most powerful, she was credited with giving birth to all mankind, as symbolized by her designation as Mother Earth. Freund (1964) states that in most mythologies, and especially in the Mediterranean ones, the Earth goddess or Great Mother is the dominant figure. He refers to *Mother Right*, written by the German philosopher and classical scholar, J. J. Bachofen, who argued that devotion to mother goddesses occurred in societies that were for the most part matriarchal. Other myths depicted multiple gods or a single powerful deity such as Zeus, the Greek father of gods and men. Zeus himself had a father, Cronos,

217

and a mother, Ops. Both belonged to the race of Titans, who were themselves the children of Earth and Heaven and sprang from Chaos.

The majority of myths in Western society including the account in the Bible, attributed the creation of the universe to God, referred to as He. This is a reflection of the partriarchal nature of that society. In such myths, man is created by powerful male figures. The Bible, for example, relates how God created man by breathing life into the dust of the ground. The myth of a male creating man reflects the wishful fantasy of boys and men of being able to bear children and attests to their envy of the awesome generative power of the mother (Jacobson, 1950; Blum, 1976). The sublimation of this wish contributes to male creativity in the form of scientific, literary, and artistic productions—their "brain children."

Greek and Roman myths reflect the diversity of theories regarding birth. In some, king and queen (Jupiter and Juno) have sons and daughters; incest is also permissible. In others, the woman (Venus) alone brings forth her son (Cupid, or Eros). In contrast, Minerva (Pallas Athene), the goddess of wisdom, springs forth from the head of Jupiter (Zeus) without a mother. In these myths, we can see the ignorance or denial of parental sexuality (or both) that is so prevalent in the fantasies of children and in the explanations given them by their parents. For instance, a mother reported how she had given a full factual account to her son of how children are conceived, carried by the mother through pregnancy, and then delivered vaginally. The seven-year-old boy, who had listened attentively until she was finished, then drew himself up to his full height, forthwith declaring, "That's what you say!" He then stalked majestically out of the room.

One of the commonly told stories that parents tell children is that the baby is brought by a stork. This was what Little Hans (Freud, 1909) was told. However, using his own powers of observation and reasoning, he discounted what he had been told. His analysis revealed that "he knew in his unconscious where the baby came from and where it had been before" (p. 129).

The mother of the patient to be described below told her that if you put sugar on a windowsill a bird will take it away and bring back a baby. The woman recalled how, when she was five years old, she would run every morning to see if a baby had arrived.

Children construct their own fantasies and theories regarding how children are born. As Freud (1910) pointed out,

> Under the influence of the component instincts that are active in himself, he arrives at a number of 'infantile sexual theories'—such as attributing a male genital organ to both sexes alike, or supposing that babies are conceived by eating and born through the end of the bowel. . . . The fact of this childish research itself, as well as the different infantile sexual theories that it brings to light, remain of importance in determining the child's character and the content of any later neurotic illness [p. 48].

The theories and fantasies created by children reveal the level of both libidinal and ego development at which they were formed. In oral terms, something is eaten and grows inside the mother's body and exits through the navel or anus. Knowledge of the anatomical differences between the sexes and of sexual intercourse may be denied and repressed in consequence of anxiety caused by incestuous, rivalrous, and hostile reactions to such knowledge. Other factors potentially influencing the content of birth theories and fantasies are the dominance of mother or father in the family and the individual's own self-representation and self-esteem. Changes during development may alter the content of the fantasies and determine the selection of which one will prevail. In reciprocal fashion, the particular fantasy will find derivative expression throughout the individual's maturation, affecting choice of defenses, discharge patterns, and object relations. This process will be illustrated by material from my patient; her anal birth fantasies affected her throughout development and shaped the neurotic symptom and character formation.

Piaget (1951) cites examples from Stanley Hall and others that illustrate children's thinking: "S. (3 yrs. 8 mos.) 'Where is the baby now that a lady is going to have next summer?' Mme. Rasmussen then replied, 'It is inside her.' To this the child retorted: 'Has she eaten it then?'" (p. 362). Piaget considers this evidence of the child's idea that the baby exists independently of the parents; it would be more appropriate, at least from a psychoanalytic perspective, to understand the child's question to denote a fantasy of oral impregnation. Other examples show how the child either denies or is unaware of the parents' role in the baby's creation.

Another childhood theory suggests the creation of the baby from clay. Piaget cites Rene (seven years), who was making plasticine figures when she told him, "Mummy still had some flesh over from when I was born. To make my little sister, she modelled it with her fingers and kept it hidden for a long while'' (p. 364). This older child acknowledges the role of the mother. She regards flesh as clay. This fantasy is close to those myths in which humans are created from clay or from part of another human. Piaget then notes, ''We have found ourselves, in those recollections of childhood we have been able to collect, the ideas well known to psychoanalysis, that the baby came out of the anus and is made from excretum or that it is in the urine or again that birth is due to a special food that mothers consume for that purpose'' (p. 365).

Many myths derive man's origin from earth (e.g., the Genesis story of Adam's creation) or from clay or stones. These materials are all unconsciously (and symbolically) equated with feces. A dream reported by my patient which will be presented later, attests to this unconscious equivalence. In a Greek myth, Zeus told Deucalion and his wife Pyrrha, the sole survivors of a great flood, to take up stones and throw them over their heads. The stones Deucalion threw became men, and the stones Pyrrha threw became women.

There is very little data from observations or analyses of children regarding their ideas as to how boys and girls are made differently. Piaget (1951) describes a child named Clan, who was involved in a struggle against masturbation. Having heard that fathers ''continue in their sons,'' the boy imagined that a son had come out of his father's penis. The denial of the woman's role and that of intercourse is obvious. No comparable fantasy was provided for the birth of little girls.

Feigelson (1977) reports the theory of a six-year-old girl who claimed that the father has nothing to do with the birth of the baby. The mother gets the baby in the hospital; it grows from an egg and the doctor helps the mother get it. She forgot how the baby comes out but knows that the mother looks like she has a basketball in her stomach while the baby is there.

The fantasy of having been born anally, as feces, can find expression in the form of a personal myth. The author of such a myth imagines himself as having been born of poor parents in a humble, even squalid setting. From this fecal environment, this child is rescued and uplifted. An example is cited by Rank (1952):

> Sargon, the mighty king, King of Agade, am I. My mother was a vestal, my father I knew not, while my father's brother dwelt in the mountains. In my city Azupiarani, which is situated on the bank of the Euphrates, my mother, the vestal, bore me. In a hidden place she

brought me forth. She laid me in a vessel made of reeds, closed my door with pitch, and dropped me down into the river, which did not drown me. The river carried me to Akki, the water carrier. Akki, the water carrier, lifted me up in the kindness of his heart, Akki the water carrier raised me as his own son, Akki the water carrier made of me his gardener. In my work as a gardener, I was beloved by Istar. I became the king and for 45 years, I held kingly sway [p. 12].

In this myth, the fecal baby is not flushed away but rather is rescued by a good father. Intertwined with the anal birth fantasy is a family romance in which Sargon becomes the beloved of Istar.

Rank points out the similarity of this myth to the Biblical story of the birth of Moses:

And there went a man of the house of Levi, and took to wife a daughter of Levi. And the woman conceived, and bore a son: and when she saw him that he was a goodly child, she hid him three months. And when she could no longer hide him, she took for him an ark of bulrushes,and daubed it with slime and with pitch, and put the child therein; and she laid it in the flags by the river's brink. And the daughter of Paraoh came down to wash herself at the river; and her maidens walked along by the river's side and when she saw the ark among the flags, she sent her maid to fetch it. And when she opened it, she saw the child, and behold the babe wept. And she had compassion on him, and said, this is one of the Hebrews' children. Then said his sister to Pharaoh's daughter, Shall I go and call to thee a nurse of the Hebrew women, that she may nurse the child for thee? and Pharaoh's daughter said to her, Go. And the maid went and called the child's mother. And Pharaoh's daughter said unto her, take the child away and nurse it for me, and I will give thee wages. And the woman took the child, and nursed it. And the child grew, and she brought him unto Pharaoh's daughter, and he became her son. And she called his name Moses: and she said, because I drew him out of the water [p. 14].

In the Moses story there is then the same theme of humble birth. The fecal origin is suggested by the ark daubed with pitch and slime. The fecal baby is rescued from being flushed away.

Children's toilet fantasies and anxieties are elaborations of anal birth theories. For girls, the story of Cinderella has a similar motif. The girl is treated as a castoff, relegated to menial tasks, and dressed in rags.

The status of maid, an anally degraded woman, is imposed on her by
the bad stepmother and envious stepsisters. (The maid, of course, is required to clean, dust, and wash. Her work involves her with dirt, garbage, and waste matter. It may also bring her into contact with excreta
in cleaning toilets. This messy work inevitably ends with her becoming
soiled and messy.) Through the magical intervention of a fairy godmother
she is transformed into a beauty. Six mice, a large grey rat, and six lizards,
symbolic representations of anally produced children (see Shengold, 1971),
are transformed into horses and attendants fit for a queen. In this story
rescue is effected by the fairy godmother and of course, a prince.

Glenn (see Chapter 10) offers, as an illustration of twinship fantasies, Mark Twain's *The Prince and the Pauper*. Twain describes the family's environment in a "foul little pocket called Offal Court" (p. 16). The
anality colors the degraded and devalued character of the father (a thief),
the mother and children (beggars), and their sadistic behavior. Tom Canty,
the pauper, is the product of these foul surroundings. His daydreams
express his wish to be magically transformed into a prince. The story
relates how he temporarily fulfills his wish through an exchange of roles
with a real prince. The story contains not only the fantasy of anal birth
but also the fantasy that the messy anal child has been left unfinished.
These fantasies can be understood also as allusions to the actual process
of child development, from anal messiness and weakness to phallic splendor and power.

Turning now to myths concerning the creation of women, we find
that in many myths woman is born later than man and is created from
man or by man. The Bible, for instance, tells us that Eve was created
from a part of Adam.

> And the Lord God said: "It is not good that the man should be alone;
> I will make him an help meet from him. . . ." And the Lord God caused
> a deep sleep to fall upon the man and he slept; and He took one of
> his ribs, and closed up the place with flesh instead thereof. And the
> rib, which the Lord God had taken from the man, made He a woman,
> and brought her unto the man [Gen. 2:18, 21–22].

Freund (1964) cites Yeats's translation of the Hindu Brihadaranyka-
Upanishad as follows: "As a lonely man is unhappy, God was unhappy.
He wanted a companion. He was as big as man and wife together; He
divided himself into two, husband and wife were born" (p. 3).

Two myths in particular relate to my thesis that the myths of some cultures reflect the fantasy that women are "unfinished." In one version of the Pandora myth (Bullfinch, (1970), the Titans, a race of giants, are said to have inhabited the earth before the creation of man. Prometheus and his brother, Epimetheus, were responsible for making man. Jupiter made Pandora and sent her to Prometheus and his brother to punish them for stealing fire from heaven. This first woman was Pandora; her name reflects the fact that all the gods contributed something to make her perfect. She was then presented to Epimetheus, who gladly accepted her, despite warnings by Prometheus to distrust Jupiter and his gifts. In his house, Epimetheus had a jar which contained evil things. Although warned not to open this jar (or box), Pandora could not restrain her curiosity. She opened it and let all the plagues—physical (diseases) and emotional (hate and envy)—escape. Although Pandora tried to replace the lid, her effort came too late. Only hope remained at the bottom of the jar. In an alternative version, Jupiter sent Pandora as a blessing to man, as in the Biblical account. She was given a box containing marriage gifts from the gods. Out of curiosity, she opened the box and all the gifts escaped, all except hope. The similarity to Eve's punishment for succumbing to curiosity is obvious.

In this myth, Pandora is represented as unsatisfied despite all the gifts that she has been given. Her curiosity can be understood to derive, in part, from this feeling of being unsatisfied. The society responsible for the myth depicted her as wanting something more, an expression of the woman's feeling of being incomplete or unfinished. The myth reflects the limitations placed on women by that society.

A second myth involving the creation of woman is that of Pygmalion, King of Cyprus and a sculptor, who makes a beautiful statue, the very image of Aphrodite. He falls in love with the statue and prays to Aphrodite to give him a wife as beautiful as the statue. The goddess obliges him by making the statue come to life (Frazer, 1972; Barber, 1979). In a fuller version of the myth, Bullfinch (1970) tells us that Pygmalion found so much fault with women that he resolved to remain a bachelor. However, he sculpted a beautiful ivory statue so perfect that it seemed to be alive. Pygmalion admired his own work so much that he fell in love with it and treated it as his wife. At the festival of Venus, he prayed for a wife like his ivory virgin. Venus heard him and granted him his wish. When he returned home, each time he kissed the statue it became warmer and more lifelike, until finally it came alive.

The story of Pygmalion illustrates the male's envy of the woman's ability to produce a child. Pygmalion, the sculptor, unsatisfied with his lifeless reproduction of a human being, asks Venus, in effect, to lend him her womanly power to bring his statue to life.

In George Bernard Shaw's play (1912) based on this myth, Pygmalion is represented by Professor Higgins, a bachelor expert in linguistics. He finds Eliza Doolittle, a Cockney flower girl whom he describes as "a squashed cabbage leaf," and transforms her into a beautiful, charming, and superficially cultivated woman—a partially finished product. Shaw's conflict about his depreciation of women is reflected in the outcome but is not relevant here (Stein, 1956).

CASE STUDY

The following material from the analysis of a patient illustrates how a woman can develop a fantasy of herself as incomplete or unfinished. It reveals some of the unconscious sources of this fantasy, its functions, and its effects on her development, character, and neurotic symptoms.

A middle-aged woman came to treatment because of unhappiness in her marriage. She described her husband as extremely critical of her, often demeaning her in front of her children and her friends. Her low self-esteem made it very difficult for her to counter his depreciation of her, and at such times she would experience impotent rage followed by hysterical sobbing. She was also sexually unsatisfied because of a lack of vaginal sensation that often approached total anesthesia. Her sexual frustration was intensified by her husband's frequent premature ejaculation.

Her lack of self-worth commands special attention. I will trace its origins and its manifestations throughout development, as these could be reconstructed from the analysis, and will relate it to the unconscious fantasy of the woman as an unfinished person.

The patient was the youngest of three children, the only girl. The brother nearest her in age was several years her senior, the other one a full ten years older. An unplanned child, she had been told by her mother that she was a "mistake." Later, the mother explained this by telling her daughter that the father had failed to withdraw his penis in time, meaning before he had ejaculated. This was typical of the many deprecatory statements the mother made regarding her daughter. For instance, if someone said to the mother, "A. looks like you," the mother would shudder visibly and quickly reply, ''No, she looks like her father.'' When the mother was angry with her husband, she would tell her daughter that he was ugly; saying the girl looked like her father therefore amounted to telling her she was ugly. The representation of herself as physically unattractive was reinforced by the mother's telling the girl, ''You have a big mouth. Don't smile like that.'' Such injunctions caused the child to be acutely self-conscious and socially uncomfortable.

Memories of being left in the care of a strict governess and irresponsible maids bolstered the image of a discarded, neglected, and worthless child. Apparently in an effort to control the girl's masturbation, these caretakers put her to bed at night in tight sheets. Warned against the ''dangers'' of vaginal exploration, she contented herself with clitoral stimulation. Still, the resultant guilt contributed to her feelings of being damaged or defective. As a defense against such guilt, she held on to the idea that she had been born defective and had therefore begun life as a mess. She was ''an accident,'' the product of incontinent parents unable to control their sexuality. As an excretory product she was, in her own estimation, a quite literal mess.

At about five years of age she developed abdominal cramps which were diagnosed as symptoms of colitis. This prompted her mother to administer daily enemas well into the patient's early adulthood.

Menstruation and sexuality in her preadolescent and adolescent years were also linked to being a mess through loss of control. She was frightened of the consequences by a dramatic example provided by a maid who seduced or was seduced by the older of her two brothers. The luckless woman was expelled from the household. My patient's belief that the loss of her virginity would make her a worthless mess to be tossed out like garbage persisted into adulthood. She was terrified lest her husband discover she was not a virgin when he married her; she was convinced that this would cause him to discard her.

Throughout my patient's adolescence, her mother described her husband as selfish and penurious, allowing himself extravagances while begrudging his wife and children essentials for their health and welfare. Her parents had violent quarrels as a result of the mother's nagging and complaining to the point where the father would explode in frustration and rage and burst out of the home, leaving his daughter frightened, confused, and often hoping he would never return. To her unfailing surprise, he would come home in the evening in a calm and often gentle mood. The mother's unceasing manipulations to maintain her daughter's dependence had devastating physical and emotional effects on the girl's development. As already mentioned, the mother continued to give the girl enemas until early adult life; she also pampered her during bouts of "colitis" and frightened her regarding the consequences of uncontrolled sexuality. She further discouraged the girl's interest in young men by making fun of them. But at the same time the mother showed intense interest in the girl's intimacies with young men. The homosexual gratification in all this was both stimulating and frightening to the young woman. She attempted to leave home to attend a college out of town, but the regressive pull was so strong that she was unable to continue and had to return home. Finally, she tried to escape into a marriage. The man she selected was a compulsive and perfectionistic professional. Fairly quickly, she established a relationship with him that in part resembled her relationship with her mother and in part her parents' sadomasochistic relationship.

In the beginning of her analysis, the patient attempted to achieve closeness with me by eliciting my sympathy for the sad plight her husband's sadistic behavior created for her. This was an effort to repeat with me her mother's relationship with her husband. Just as she had cooperated with her mother's separating her from her father, so she used these painful recollections to defend herself against the remembrance of loving and sexual feelings and fantasies vis-à-vis her father. The patient tried to follow a similar strategy in her analysis. Her efforts to establish a mother-daughter relationship with me was a way of defending against the frightening feelings of sexual excitement and her fantasies of divorcing her husband to marry me. A key feature of the defense was the maintenance and reinforcement of the fantasy that she was an unfinished fecal mess. What had taken place intrapsychically was a massive retreat from oedipal- to anal-phase gratifications and defenses. The outcome was a masochistic character structure with an overlay of hysterical symptomatology.

The patient was sexually frustrated by her husband, who would have premature ejaculations or avoid sex entirely by falling asleep immediately upon getting into bed. She attempted to relieve her excitement by masturbating. Her comment about this was: "In my sexual activity, the efforts is as if I'm constipated and trying to go." She reported a dream: "Rockefeller is showing me his collection. Feces drop out of my vagina—like an accident." The feces represented both herself as the baby-accident and the wished-for child from Rockefeller-analyst. The association of "rock" and feces here points to the underlying fantasy of anal birth.

The sexual frustration in her marriage intensified the erotic feelings and fantasies about the analyst. Dreams of being in bed with me alternated with reports of sleeping difficulties. She managed to come late to her analytic hours and recognized the pleasurable aspect of holding back in order to create tension and excitement by feeling threatened. She then reported a dream of having a secret tryst with the husband of a friend. This man made love to her "short of having intercourse," but then they were interrupted by the man's secretary. The patient had often thought how nice it would be to have a man who was as attentive to his wife as her friend's husband was.

She next turned to the theme of disloyalty, declaring that her mother had made her feel guilty about her relationship with her father. Both she and her mother played the part of victims in their marriages, thus preserving the mother-daughter closeness and trying to protect each other from jealousy. As this defense was analyzed, the patient recalled having heard sounds through the wall between her bedroom and that of her parents. Hearing those sounds had created anxious feelings and shortness of breath. She then began to feel "closed in" in the consultation room, finding it stuffy and wishing to escape. She asked for reassurance that the analysis would end—that is, that she would not be trapped. Simultaneously, she expressed wishes to be noticed by me, to be touched, and to have an affair. She then remembered being very attracted to her father when she was ten years old. She had been frightened of those feelings and the threat it posed to her relationship with her mother. Around that age, she developed fears of intruders and would lie terrified in bed, listening to footsteps on the stairs leading to her bedroom. These claustrophobic symptoms were connected to her earlier experiences of having been bound down by bedsheets to prevent masturbation, and to the more recent experience of having been held down while ether was administered for a surgical procedure. Not surprisingly, a set of rescue fantasies complemented these fantasies of being trapped.

The counterpart to her fear of being trapped was that of being unprotected and exposed to the sexual dangers she projected onto the outside world. This resulted in patterns of school avoidance and an inability to remain in college away from home. The two sets of fantasies—of being trapped and of being rescued—and their attendant guilts, anxieties, and defenses were regressively condensed in her self-representation as a fecal mass or mess. To be retained meant to be trapped, unfinished, and unborn; to be expelled as a diarrheal, bloody mess meant she was so much worthless waste. This conflict appeared in the analysis in her wish and fear to remain in analysis forever. To leave would mean she would be unprotected from her sexuality and oedipal wishes, projected onto the outside world. To diminish the danger, she would hold on to her self-representation as a defective and unattractive mess. It was from this dilemma that she realistically needed to be rescued. Throughout the analysis, the declaration that she wanted to ''be finished'' was encountered as a form of resistance. But as termination became more imminent, she stated this desire with increasing frequency. Her repeated statement that she wanted to ''be finished'' or ''get finished'' caught my attention and suggested to me that the anal birth fantasy had influenced her development and had throughout it found expression in derivative form.

For this woman, early feelings of neglect by a narcissistic mother lowered her sense of worth. Subsequently, her comparison of herself with her brothers made her feel unimportant and undeserving of love. The sense of defect was heightened by the talent and accomplishments of the older of her brothers. Comparison with her mature and beautiful mother reinforced the negative self-image. All this found support in the comparison she made during an episode of sexual exploration between her own genitals and those of her other brother. The intense preoccupation with her bowel function, by both her mother and herself, set the stage for the development of anal fantasies regarding her birth, her self-representation, her sexuality, and her relationships. Her inability to deal with and resolve her dependence on her mother and her love for her father trapped her in a morass of preoedipal, especially anal, conflicts. The sad truth was that her development *was* unfinished. The concrete expression of this was her view of herself as an unfinished and unformed anal mess.

Wishes to be transformed into a dazzling, vibrant beauty who could fascinate men were spun from her mother's stories. Her mother had described herself to her daughter as having been a much sought after beauty who had turned down many offers of marriage to marry the father. The young husband was a successful entrepreneur. But when financial difficulties set in, the gay, socially popular, ideal couple was succeeded by a nagging, complaining wife and an irritable, explosive husband. Everything had turned to ashes—a Cinderella fantasy in reverse. The mother behaved at home like a scullery maid, dressing in torn undergarments, scrubbing floors, and engaging in endless household drudgery. In reaction, my patient tried to create her own personal myth. Her story was that she had begun as Cinderella—a neglected and mistreated child and, later, an abused wife. Her fantasy was that a Prince Charming would rescue her and enable her to become a happy, sensual woman—a truly royal ending. The parallel to Eliza in Shaw's *Pygmalion* is striking.

Fantasies of being rescued meant therefore to be finished, reborn, and made into an attractive, desirable woman. In her analysis, she sought to "get past" all of the feelings of worthlessness, defect, and messiness by getting finished—a magical transformation. At different levels, this meant that she was to feel wanted, needed, and loved, to be an effective person, to become sexually free and responsive—in sum, to become a truly feminine adult. The real task of the analysis was to free her from the tenaciously held belief that she was unfinished and defective—an anal mess.

Unconsciously, there was another meaning to being "finished." For her, sexuality would result in premarital impregnation or prostitution and render her worthless. She would end as she fantasied she had begun.

DISCUSSION

Factors that led to this woman's creation of the fantasy that she was "unfinished" included: (1) absence of early maternal care or interest, real or imagined; (2) identification with a mother with narcissistic problems regarding her femininity; (3) prolonged and repeated anal stimulation and erotization; (4) traumatic experiences including surgery and seduction resulting in fantasies of having been damaged; (5) a family constellation and attitude that depreciated the importance of women; and (6) a need to defend against oedipal wishes.

Coen (1986) regards the sense of defect as a fantasy, a compromise formation resulting from intrapsychic conflict. Two of his patients, both male, had insignificant skin lesions which they focused on as a basis for feeling unattractive. A third patient, a woman, had an endocrine tumor which caused neuromuscular symptoms and disfigurement of her face and body. She had been subjected to extensive medical workups, hospitalization, and surgery at the age of five. The outcome of her case is understandable in view of her traumatic childhood experiences, but the situation with the male patients seems more to have been determined by conflicts about the wish to be admired and loved. According to Coen, most of his patients with a sense of defect had a genetic history involving one parent with serious psychopathology, usually narcissistic, depressive, or paranoid. The other parent typically encouraged the child's compliance in denying that anything was wrong. This fits my patient's family background of a mother who suffered from severe depressive illness and was highly narcissistic. My patient's sense of defect was the outcome both of traumatic experiences and of her attempts to resolve intrapsychic conflicts about her wish to be loved. Identification with a "defective" mother greatly influenced her own self-representation as an unfinished mess.

At a preoedipal level she had felt unwanted and uncared for. It is probable that the early deficiency in mothering led to difficulties in the separation-individuation phase, so that unfinished aspects of her development adversely affected the completion of subsequent developmental tasks (Mahler, 1967). This was evident in the quasi-symbiotic relationship this patient maintained with her mother in adolescence and early adult life.

The feeling and the concomitant fantasy of being unfinished as a consequence of incomplete accomplishment of developmental goals is not exclusively a female difficulty. Failure to complete the separation-individuation process or succeeding phase-specific tasks occurs in males as well.

To return to my patient: During the "anal" phase of development, she felt abused and victimized by her mother. A sadomasochistic view of sexuality, with the woman as victim, interfered with the establishment of a positive attitude toward becoming a woman. On a phallic level, her self-representation was that she was lacking and therefore defective, i.e., castrated. The incomplete resolution of her preoedipal and oedipal conflicts found expression in the fantasy of being unfinished. In adolescence and adulthood, this was validated for her by her inability to enjoy sex and to have a vaginal orgasm. Regressive reactions reactivated anal birth fantasies; the organizing fantasy was that she was an unfinished anal product—a mess.

A little girl's feelings of inferiority can be created in a variety of ways, some of which I have described in this account of my patient's development. The resultant fantasy of defect finds expression in physical, intellectual, and social spheres. Social attitudes and patterns, especially in patriarchal, male-dominated societies, will tend to confirm these beliefs in external reality. The Pandora and Pygmalion myths are societal elaborations of the idea that a woman is "unfinished." Despite all the gifts the gods have given Pandora, she opens the box to see what else might be found. Evil things escape, but only hope remains. We may ask, "Hope for what?" The various gifts that were given contribute to feminine beauty and charm—they are narcissistic attributes. What was not given was the freedom to love, to bear children, and to be a loving wife and mother. The fulfillment of that part of femininity was unfinished.

In the Pygmalion myth, the woman is unfinished until the goddess turns the cold stone to warm responsive flesh. Shaw's version of the transformation is the story of a dirty, uneducated flower girl who is made over into a beautiful, polished, and sophisticated woman. To do this, Professor Higgins provides his own "finishing" school.

Psychoanalytic investigation of a woman's fantasy of being unfinished revealed that it played a central organizing role in the development of her personality and neurosis. Her personal myth was seen to be a variant of a number of myths that societies have historically preserved. In particular, the myths concerning the creation and "finishing" of a woman as exemplified by the story of Pygmalion and Pandora illustrated the devaluing attitudes of some societies toward women that paralleled this woman's view of herself.

REFERENCES

Arlow, J. A. (1982), Scientific cosmogeny, mythology and immortality. *Psychoanal. Quart.,* 51:177–195.

Barber, R. (1979), *A Companion to World Mythology.* New York: Delacorte.

Blum, H. (1976), Masochism, the ego ideal and the psychology of women. *J. Amer. Psychoanal. Assn.,* 24:157–192.

Bullfinch, T. (1970, *Bullfinch's Mythology.* New York: Crowell.

Coen, S. (1986), The sense of defect. *J. Amer. Psychoanal. Assn.,* 34:47–68.

Feigelson, C. (1977), Essential characteristics of child analysis. *The Psychoanalytic Study of the Child,* 32:353–362. New Haven, CT: Yale University Press.

Frazer, J. (1972), *The New Golden Bough.* New York: S. G. Phillips.

Freud, S. (1909), Analysis of a phobia in a five-year-old boy. *Standard Edition,* 10:5–147. London: Hogarth Press, 1955.

———— (1910), Five lectures on psycho-analysis. *Standard Edition,* 11:9–55. London: Hogarth Press, 1957.

Freund, P. (1964), *Myths of Creation.* London: W. H. Allen.

Jacobson, E. (1950), The development of the wish for a child in boys. *The Psychoanalytic Study of the Child*, 5:145–152. New York: International Universities Press.

Mahler, M. (1967), On human symbiosis and the vicissitudes of individuation. *J. Amer. Psychoanal. Assn.*, 15:876–886.

Piaget, J. (1951), *The Child's Conception of the World*. New York: Humanities Press.

Rank, O. (1952), *The Myth of the Birth of the Hero*. New York: Brunner.

Shaw, G. (1912), *Pygmalion*. In: *Selected Plays*. New York: Dodd, Mead, 1948.

Shengold, L. (1971), More about rats and rat people. *Internat. J. Psycho-Anal.*, 52:277–288.

Stein, M. (1956), The marriage bond. *Psychoanal. Quart.*, 25:238–259.

14

The Transformation of Ritual Infanticide in the Jewish and Christian Religions with Reference to Anti-Semitism

Martin S. Bergmann, Ph.D.

A special affinity between psychoanalysis and the study of myth has existed at least from the time when Freud named the nuclear conflict in neurosis after a Greek hero. Sophocles made Oedipus say, "Now shedder of father's blood, husband of mother is my name." It was Freud who made this prophecy come true. Freud (1908) regarded myths as the dreams of youthful humanity, the distorted residue of wishful fantasy of whole people representing the strivings of early men. Abraham (1909) called myths collective dreams and dreams private myths, with typical dreams occupying an intermediary position. To a degree that would astonish a contemporary psychoanalyst, Freud and his circle were preoccupied with the study of myth.

Within Freud's work two attitudes toward myth can be differentiated. They correspond to two periods in Freud's creative life. During the first, "The Interpretation of Dreams" (Freud, 1900) was the model; myths were interpreted as collective wish fulfillments. Abraham, Ricklin, Jones, and Rank pursued this line of inquiry. Then, after the publication of "Totem and Taboo" (Freud, 1913), myths were interpreted as distorted memories.

For the ideas expressed in this paper I am responsible. I was, however, stimulated by the discussion that took place in the study group on anti-Semitism sponsored by the Fund for Psychoanalytic Research and Development under the chairmanship of Dr. Mortimer Ostow. I wish to express my gratitude to this group. I also wish to thank Drs. Arlene and Arnold Richards, Dr. Bela Gruneberger, and Dr. Janine Chasseguet-Smirgel for the opportunity to discuss this paper.

233

of the totem feast and the subsequent remorse that seized the band of rebellious sons. Prominent in this line of inquiry were Reik and Roheim (Bergmann, 1966). In this new line of inquiry, myths were interpreted as based on real historical events, as collective screen memories.

Jacob Arlow's presidential address to the American Psychoanalytic Association (1961) marks a turning point in the psychoanalytic interest in this area. In it, Arlow staked out a new field of endeavor for psychoanalysts interested in mythology:

> Psychoanalysis has a greater contribution to make to the study of mythology than demonstrating, in myths, wishes often encountered in the unconscious thinking of patients. The myth is a particular kind of communal experience. It is a special form of shared fantasy, and it serves to bring the individual into relationship with members of his cultural group on the basis of certain common needs. Accordingly, the myth can be studied from the point of view of its function in psychic integration—how it plays a role in warding off feelings of guilt and anxiety, how it constitutes a form of adaptation to reality and to the group in which the individual lives, and how it influences the crystallization of the individual identity and the formation of the superego. Personal dreams and daydreams are made to be forgotten. Shared daydreams and myths are instruments of socialization. The myth, like the poem, can be, must be, remembered and repeated [p. 375, 379].

Earlier, Arlow (1951) viewed religion as an "institutionalized experience by which character structure is shaped in conformity with the demands of a social order" (p. 329). In return, religions give to their devotees freedom from doubt and freedom from ambivalence.

I take as my point of departure that it was no accident that Freud named the oedipus complex after a Greek hero, for Greek mythology abounds in descriptions of open struggle between fathers and sons. Uranus, the sky god, confines his sons, the Titans, to the depths of the earth. Cronus, the youngest of his children, conspires with his mother to castrate him. Cronus, in turn, swallows all his children except Zeus, who as his father was, is aided by his mother. Zeus forces Cronus to disgorge the children and collectively they overthrow his reign. Here cannibalistic themes alternate with the theme of castration. Tantalus, king of Lydia, when allowed to share the banquets of the gods, served up his son Pelops to see if the gods could tell the difference. Pelops' son Atreus, the father of Agamemnon, served his own children to his brother. What matters within the context of this presentation is that Greek mythology did not disguise the hostility of fathers toward their children. It merely relegated this brutality to the distant past, before the Olympians established a postcannibalistic order. Fratricidal strife is not unknown to the Greeks. The sons of Oedipus kill each other, and Romulus, founder of Rome, kills his brother Remus. These fratricidal episodes, however, are comparatively minor in comparison with the hostilities between fathers and their children.

By contrast, instead of a generational conflict, the Bible abounds with examples of deadly sibling rivalry. It begins with the murder of Abel by Cain and reappears in the rivalry between Isaac and Ishmael, Jacob and Esau, Rachel and Leah, and Joseph and his brothers.

The description of the rivalry between Cain and Abel is worth recalling.

> And in the process of time it came to pass, that Cain brought of the fruit of the ground an offering unto the Lord.
> And Abel, he also brought of the firstlings of his flock and of the fat thereof. And the Lord had respect unto Abel and to his offerings. But unto Cain and to his offering he had not respect. And the Lord said unto Cain, Why are thou wroth? and why is thy contenance fallen? If thou doest well, shalt thou not be accepted? and if thou doest not well, sin lieth at the door. And unto thee shall be his desire, and thou shalt rule over him [Gen. 4:7].

The enigmatic nature of the last verse and the unexplained preference for Abel suggest that the passage is of great antiquity, before Yhwe needed to justify his morality to man. The first fratricidal act was the result of an arbitrary and flagrant preference by God for one son over the other.

The special molding of the intergenerational conflict that is characteristic of the Bible is nowhere better expressed than in the story of Jacob wrestling with the angel (Gen. 32:24 ff.). World literature knows many wrestling matches but only the Bible could think of ending such a confrontation with a blessing, that is, with the abrogation of intergenerational conflict.

In "Totem and Taboo" Freud (1913) made no reference to Judaism. The task of filling this gap was taken up by Theodor Reik. In a book first published in 1919, Reik studied the significance of the shofar, which plays so crucial a role in the Jewish high holidays. The shofar, one of

the oldest wind instruments known, is a ram's horn. Reik hypothesized
that the ram was once the totem animal of the Jews. Because God was
once a ram (or a bull), his voice sounds from the horns. When the shofar
is blown, the blower becomes identified with God. In Reik's interpretation, Moses killed Yhwe on Mount Sinai and appropriated his horns.
Similarly, when Moses destroyed the Golden Calf, which Reik thinks
was in fact a young bull, he destroyed Yhwe himself. That Moses gave
the Israelites the melted-down Golden Calf to drink is interpreted by
Reik as referring to the totem feast. The name Moses is derived from
the Egyptian *mesu,* meaning child. The etymology suggested to Reik that
Moses was a rebellious son figure.

The horned Moses has an interesting history (Mellinkoff, 1970)
which emerged as a result of the translation or mistranslation into Latin
by Saint Jerome of a passage in Exodus 34:29. The Hebrew word *karan*
can mean either "horned" or "lit up." It refers to the change in the
face of Moses when he descended from Mount Sinai. The first translation supports Freud's totem idea, whereas the idea of a lit-up face is
closer to the idea of a nimbus.

As to circumcision, Freud saw the custom as pertaining to initiation rites:

> When our [Jewish] children come to hear of ritual circumcision they
> equate it with castration. . . . In primeval times and in primitive races,
> where circumcision is so frequent, it is performed at the age of initia-
> tion into manhood and it is at that age that its significance is to be
> found [Freud, 1913, p. 153].

Reik echoed Freud but went a step further. "We know," he wrote,

> that circumcision represents a castration equivalent and supports in
> the most effective way the prohibition against incest. The fear of castra-
> tion would be stimulated by the unconscious fear of retaliation which
> is felt by the man who has now become a father. . . . he might be the
> object injured at the hands of his own child [Reik, 1919, p. 105].

Later Reik (1959) returned to the theme of Moses in a book entitled *The Mystery on the Mountain.* There he stressed the role of Moses as
the creator of this collective superego of the Israelites. This line of thought
was extended by Ostow (1982), who sees the Jewish God as a projected

superego, which the pagan gods were not. Yhwe frowns on any attempt of a mortal to identify himself with Him. There is no equivalent to the Christian *imitatio Christi* in the Jewish religion. Chasseguet-Smirgel (1985) writes in a similar vein when she quotes the detailed prohibitions against all varieties of incest, adultery, and homosexuality in Leviticus, Chapter 18. Among other prohibitions mentioned there is the prohibition against sacrificing children. It is with this prohibition that we will be concerned.

In contrast to what I will call the Reik-Freud hypothesis, which derives Jewish history from long-repressed events analogous to those described in "Totem and Taboo," some psychoanalytic investigators, notably Wellisch (1954), Lustig (1976), Schlesinger (1976), and Rubenstein (1982) see Judaism as originating in the abrogation of the rite of the killing of the firstborn.

Wellisch cites evidence that infanticide was once common in all parts of the world and that it was generally believed that the killing of a son as a substitute prolongs the life of the father. He quotes the following verse from an Icelandic legend:

> In Upsal's town the cruel King
> Slaughtered his sons at Odin's shrine
> Slaughtered his sons with cruel knife
> To get from Odin length of life.

Frazer (1922) supplies additional details. Odin promised the king that he would live as long as he sacrificed a son every nine years. The king sacrificed eight sons and became increasingly feeble. When he wished to sacrifice his only remaining child, the Swedes rebelled and let him die. Frazer believes that originally the king was himself sacrificed after reigning nine years. Later the son was sacrificed as a substitute, prolonging the reign of the father. The legend is significant because here the process of substitution of the son for the father is clearer than in the other preserved accounts.

Even more common was the idea that the sacrifice of a child can avert famine or bring about military victory. Pausanias, the noted traveler in Greece, reports (1.5.2) that Leos, the son of Orpheus, was told by the Delphic oracle that a famine in Athens would be averted if he would sacrifice his three daughters. The daughters joyfully volunteered, the very models of virtue and patriotism. Agamemnon's sacrifice of his daughter Iphigenia to calm the storm so that the Trojan War could begin is the best known example of such religious killings of a child in Greece.

That the peoples among whom the Israelites lived practiced infanticide is evident from numerous Biblical accounts, although the mightiest neighboring nations, the Egyptians, the Assyrians, and the Babylonians, did not seem to engage in the practice. For example, in II Kings, chapter 3, the King of Judea and the King of Israel are fighting the King of Moab who, when the war goes against him, offers his oldest son as a burnt offering on the wall. It is also recorded that King Saul wanted to kill his son Jonathan to assure victory against the Philistines, but the army rebelled and insisted on saving Jonathan's life. As a result the battle was called off (I Sam. 14:43–46). Well known is the story of Jephtha (Judges, chapter 12), who vowed that if Yhwe granted him victory, he would sacrifice whosoever came forth to greet him. It turned out that it was his daughter, who greeted him with timbrel and dances; she was sacrificed as a burnt offering. He did, however, grant her two months to go up and down the mountain bewailing her virginity. The story is important in this context because the author of the Book of Judges sees nothing wrong in human sacrifice; the act is not considered sinful.

Distorted memories of the sacrifice of the firstborn linger at the core of the two great Jewish holidays: Passover and the high holidays inaugurating the Jewish New Year. Passover celebrates a relatively primitive psychological mechanism. The killing of the firstborn is averted from the Israelites and displaced onto the Egyptians. The interrupted sacrifice of Isaac is psychologically more complex.

THE MEANING OF PASSOVER

The Passover sacrifice reported in Exodus, chapter 12, leaves no doubt that the sacrifice of the lamb is a substitute for the killing of the firstborn. Yhwe commands that the blood of the lamb be smeared on the posts and the lintel of the door. The lamb has to be totally consumed. The lamb is therefore an apotropiac sacrifice. Only when this ritual is observed will Yhwe pass over the houses of Israel and smite the firstborn of Egypt, both men and beasts. In Exodus 4:22–23, we read:

And thou shalt say unto Pharaoh, thus sayeth the Lord, Israel is my son, even my firstborn. And I say unto thee let my son go that he may serve me: if thou refuse to let him go, behold I will slay thy son, even thy firstborn.

Thus, it seems that Israel's election, the designation as Yhwe's firstborn, goes hand in hand with the slaying of the Egyptian firstborn. The sentences that follow have puzzled many students of the Bible because thy represent a non sequitur, an interruption of the narrative:

> And it came to pass by the way in the inn, that the Lord met him, and sought to kill him. Then Zipporah took a sharp stone and cut off the foreskin of her son and cast it at his feet and said, "Surely a bloody husband art thou to me" [Exod. 4:24–25].

This chilling and obscure paragraph leaves much to be desired in clarity. Who was Yhwe trying to kill? Moses or his son? Why? How did Zipporah know that the slaying could be averted by circumcision? The uncanny impact of the scene is enhanced by the fact that immediately afterward the story is resumed as if nothing extraordinary had happened.

It seems likely that we are dealing here with a survival of an earlier belief that could not be censored, according to which God demanded the death of Moses but was satisfied with circumcision. The rite of circumcision is thereby brought into close proximity to the act of killing the firstborn.

The Hebrew term for the ceremony of circumcision is *Brit Mila*, the covenant of circumcision, and what else can the covenant be about except that through circumcision the life of the baby is spared? Psychologically speaking, the circumcision absorbs enough of the father's hostility to make survival possible. It is expected to act as a reminder that worse may follow if the oedipal taboo is not observed. I recall a gentile patient who associated that he preferred a Jewish analyst to a gentile one; the Jewish analyst, he thought, would demand only circumcision, whereas the gentile would sacrifice him. He was born on Christmas Day and lived in fear that because of his strong identification with Christ he, too, would be sacrificed.

Eventually the mezuza replaced the blood on the post of the door as a permanent protection of the Jewish home. One of my Jewish analysands associated that the mezuza contained his foreskin. These associations confirm the degree to which this myth is alive even today in the unconscious of both gentile and Jew.

THE BINDING OF ISAAC

The story of the binding of Isaac, in Genesis, chapter 22, opens as follows:

> And it came to pass after these things, that God did tempt Abraham,
> and said unto him, Abraham: and he said, Behold, here I am.
> And he said, Take now thy son thine only son Isaac, whom thou lovest,
> and get thee unto the land of Moriah; and offer him there for a burnt
> offering upon one of the mountains which I tell thee of [Gen. 22:1-2].

This chapter is greatly admired for its literary style. Auerback (1946)
used it to illustrate the difference between the Biblical and the Homeric
styles.

> This opening startles us when we come to it from Homer. Where are
> the two speakers? We are not told. The reader, however, knows that
> they are not normally to be found together in one place on earth, that
> one of them, God, in order to speak to Abraham, must come from
> somewhere, must enter the earthly realm from some unknown heights
> or depths. Whence does he come, whence does he call to Abraham?
> We are not told. He does not come, like Zeus or Poseidon, from the
> Aethiopians, where he has been enjoying a sacrificial feast. Nor are
> we told anything of his reasons for tempting Abraham so terribly. He
> has not, like Zeus, discussed them in set speeches with other gods
> gathered in council; nor have the deliberations in his own heart been
> presented to us; unexpected and mysterious, he enters the scene from
> some unknown height or depth and calls Abraham.
>
> This becomes clearer still if we now turn to the other person in the
> dialogue, to Abraham. Where is he? We do not know. He says, in-
> deed: Here I am—but the Hebrew word means only something like
> "behold me," and in any case is not meant to indicate the actual place
> where Abraham is, but a moral position in respect to God, who has
> called to him—Here am I awaiting thy command. Where he is actual-
> ly, whether in Beersheba or elsewhere, whether indoors or in the open
> air, is not stated; it does not interest the narrator, the reader is not
> informed; and what Abraham was doing when God called to him is
> left in the same obscurity [p. 8].

What to Auerbach and many other critics appeared to epitomize the Bible's abstract style was revealed by Biblical scholarship to be the result
of its reconciliation of contradictory trends. The noted Hebrew scholar
Spiegel (1967) has pointed out that Genesis 22:1-3 and Genesis 22:19
were written by the Aelohist narrator. It is he who tests Abraham and
demands the sacrifice, while Genesis 22:14-18 belong to the Yhweist narrator. It is the angel of Yhwe who prevents the sacrifice and makes the
subsequent promise to Abraham.

Abraham returns to the menservants waiting for him, but the name of Isaac is not mentioned. The question that troubled the Jewish sages was, Where was Isaac after the interrupted sacrifice? The Aggadah has it that God let him stay in Paradise as a reward for his obediance for three years; another version has it that he was dispatched to Paradise to recover from the wounds inflicted upon him by Abraham. The lonely return of Abraham gave rise to the suspicion that Abraham had sacrificed Isaac after all. Even though scripture leaves us in no doubt, for Abraham is told in unmistakable terms, "Lay not thy hand upon the lad, neither do thou anything unto him" (Gen. 22:12). Spiegel (1967) documented that in flagrant violation of the text, the Aggadah rabbis asserted that "father Isaac was bound on the altar and reduced to ashes, and his sacrificial dust was cast on Mount Moriah, the Holy One, blessed by He, immediately brought upon him dew and revived him" (p. 33).

Such a clear-cut defiance of scripture by rabbis requires a psychological explanation. This situation cries out for a villain, but none is forthcoming. To blame Abraham, the greatest of the patriarchs, is impossible, but to blame God is even worse. How could the Jews live with an image of a God who would demand that a father kill his son? Since psychologically a choice had to be made, it was better to vilify Abraham and protect God. No matter how deep the religious conviction, no son can rejoice in his own sacrifice. In the onlooker or reader the scene must arouse either masochistic or sadistic impulses. The suspended sacrifice allows no outlet for these feelings, hence the attempt of the rabbis to suggest, contrary to holy writ, that Abraham did in fact sacrifice Isaac.

It seems that this was also the interpretation of St. Paul:

> By faith Abraham, when he was tried, offered up Isaac: and he that had received the promises offered up his only begotten son.
> Of whom it was said, that in Isaac shall thy seed be called:
> Accounting that God was able to raise him up, even from the dead; from whence also he received him in a figure [Heb. 11:17–19].

It we step out of Jewish history and assume that Yhwe, like other gods, demanded human sacrifice, and that the binding of Isaac represents the historical moment when an animal was accepted as a substitute for the son, the event on Mount Moriah loses some of its mystery. The God of the Aelohistic tradition demanded that the sacrifice be consummated, but the Yhweistic tradition gave the event a new interpretation. The selection of Mount Moriah for the event is significant because it is there that the temple will be built and it is there that the animal sacrifices will be offered. The Jewish religion could not, by its very structure, acknowledge an evolution within the image of its own deity, and it is out of the inability to come to terms with this fact that the story of the binding of Isaac remains such a mystery. The story makes sense only if we assume that it was God who changed his mind, and that from now on He will abhor this sacrifice.

The practice of infanticide has been recorded in many cultures. What is unique to Jewish history is that the moment of transition from the killing of the firstborn to the substitution of the sacrificial animal was not repressed but celebrated, transformed in such a way that it survived in this altered form at the very core of the two religious holidays. The fact that the memory was not repressed but transformed had far-reaching consequences both for Jewish and Christian theology.

I can come only to the conclusion that Yhwe's predecessor accepted these sacrifices and that the historical Biblical Yhwe emerged out of the struggle to prohibit this practice. Because it was an enormous step in the development of culture, the memory remained enshrined. The covenant with God implied that in return for the meeting of moral obligations one could enjoy the security of a God who in return controlled his own aggression and no longer demanded human sacrifice. From a psychoanalytic point of view, we must emphasize that there is something profoundly disturbing in the image of a father, Abraham, sacrificing his own son, allegedly out of love, even when the life of the son was spared at the last moment. Unconsciously at least, every child who encounters this event asks himself, "Will my father under similar circumstances sacrifice me?" And, on a still deeper unconscious level, is there not something profoundly wrong in a religion that insists that a child man be sacrificed as a sign of love? Anxiety, as well as ambivalence to religion, is the result.

FROM THE SACRIFICIAL VICTIM
TO THE SENSE OF ELECTION

In Leviticus 19:18 we are told:

And ye shall be holy unto me for I, the Lord, am holy and have severed you from other people that ye shall be mine.

To this powerful invitation Jewish liturgy responds with "Us you have chosen and us you have sanctified of all the nations." If we recall that the word sacrifice comes from the Latin *sacer facere*, to make holy, it follows that all that is sacrificed is holy. However, at this great juncture, a major transformation took place. Those who were not sacrificed in Egypt became holy. Sanctification became a substitute for the sacrifice. We may go further and say that to be chosen was a sublimation of the fear of being sacrificed. We will see later how Christianity restored the connection between being holy and being sacrificed and thus undid the separation that Judaism brought about.

After the return from the Babylonian exile, all traces of the ritualistic sacrifice of one's children had been overcome. No new prophet was needed to preach against such practices. However, the repressed returned, in a no less horrifying form. In its new form the sacrifice of children had the full sanction of the religious superego.

The concept of the religious martyr is foreign to the Bible. It seems to appear for the first time in the chronicles of the Hasmonean dynasty. Hannah, the mother of seven sons, refuses to bow to the idol and all her sons are killed. The mother of the seven speaks to Abraham: "You built one altar and did not offer up your son, but I built seven altars and offered my sons on them" (quoted in Spiegel, 1967, p. 15). Two new terms emerge that will have fateful consequences in Jewish history— "sanctification of God's name" and "the unification of the Name." The Jewish martyr is supposed to die with the prayer of Schema. "Hear, O Israel, Yhwe is our God, Yhwe is One." And his soul should expire on the word One. This is the closest that the Jewish religion allows for the *union mystica*. It is from these pre-Christian sources that Christianity inherited the concept of martyrs that was so important in the early history of the Church.

During the Crusades, when in one German town after another Jewish fathers slaughtered their children and wives and committed suicide in order to avoid baptism, the sacrifice of Isaac was interpreted as a consummated sacrifice. The magical belief took hold that God could be forced by the sheer numerical magnitude of the martyrs to hasten the coming of the Messiah.

Throughout Jewish history the martyrs to the faith were called *kdoshim,* those who were santified unto the Lord. Finally, the term "Holocaust" comes from the Greek *holokauston.* It is the Greek translation of the Hebrew word for burnt offering. One cannot help but be awed by the cultural continuity that runs through Jewish history, from Biblical times to our own coinage of the term "Holocaust."

A long historical and moral evolution separates the God who demands the burnt offering of the firstborn from the God whose name is santified and unified when parents kill their children and avoid conversion, but the inner continuity is even more impressive.

During the Holocaust, since Hitler, unlike the Crusaders, offered the Jews no alternative to being killed, all those who were killed became the holy ones. Even personal choice was eliminated from the halo of martrydom.

To the Jewish community the need to remember the Holocaust has become a major obligation. Elsewhere (Bergmann, 1985) I raised the question, To what purpose should the Holocaust be remembered? There I suggested that the original impulse after a major defeat is the wish for revenge. During the years of the Diaspora this need was denied the Jews. Religious Jews therefore assumed that God remembers all the iniquities inflicted upon them and that He remembers in order to punish later. Memory, therefore, was at first in the service of a delayed revenge. But eventually the connection between revenge and remembering was severed—or *almost* severed.

Religions are known to evolve slowly over a long period but also to undergo rapid and radical transformations. The emergence of Christianity as an independent religion out of a Jewish past is an example of the latter, as is also the emergence of Protestantism and Catholic Christianity.

Scholem (1941) differentiated three stages in the evolution of religion: In the first, the mythological, the world is full of gods which men encounter at every step. In the second a gulf opens between humanity and God, who is now conceived as infinite and transcendental, while man is small and finite. Across this abyss the voice of the divine is sometimes heard, but God is never seen. Finally, in the third stage, mystics appear who experience a close and personal contact with the deity.

When Christianity arose, Judaism had reached the second of these states. Jesus, St. Peter, and St. Paul all had mystical experiences, indicating that the third stage of religious evolution had been reached. Christianity developed within the matrix of the strong apocalyptic feelings prevalent in the Jewish community at that time. In the Hellenistic world the pagan gods of Greece, under the impact of rational philosophy, were losing their ability to compel belief. Those in need of religious support were turning toward mystery religions built around initiation rites promising direct contact with a deity and salvation after death. Apocalyptic visions and the rites of those mystery religious were powerful forces shaping Christianity.

CHRISTIANITY

In the New Testament the theme of infanticide returns from repression in two forms: in the "massacre of the holy innocents" and, at the very core of Christianity, in the idea of Christ, the Son of God, as sacrificial victim.

As for the first of these, Matthew, chapter 2, tells the story of the three Magi who came to Herod, King of Judea,

> Saying, Where is he that is born King of the Jews? for we have seen his star in the east, and are come to worship him.
> When Herod the king had heard these things, he was troubled, and all Jerusalem with him [Matt. 2:2-3].

When Herod's efforts to eliminate the Christ child were thwarted,

> Herod was exceedingly wroth, and sent forth, and slew all the children that were in Bethlehem and in all the coasts thereof, from two years old and under [Matt. 2:2-3].

We note that the innocents are killed as substitutes for the Christ child. The motive is oedipal in nature, as Herod fears he will be replaced by a new King of Israel.

Legends associated with the birth of Jesus are not part of the historical Jesus. Some were added to legitimize the claim that he was descended from the royal house of David, a claim contradicted by belief in the virgin birth. Many of the unconscious fantasies typically encountered in doing psychoanalysis (Arlow, 1964) have found their way into the legend of Christ's birth, particularly the wish to be born of a virgin mother, thereby being her sole possessor. Shortly after birth, the Christ child is worshiped by exalted father substitutes, the Magi. Most depictions of the Nativity give to the earthly father, Joseph, an insignificant role. He is usually the servant of the exalted mother and child. Most of the Nativity scenes on the sculpted portals and stained-glass windows of the great cathedrals are joyous in content. Only the murder of the innocents, which is always depicted, strikes a discordant note of aggression in the otherwise festive mood of *venite adoramus*. I have been struck by the fact that in all paintings of this scene, with the single exception of one by Pieter Brueghel the Elder, in which the massacre of the innocents is meant to represent the cruelty of the Spaniards in the wars of liberation of the Low Countries, only the mothers are depicted as defending their infants against the murderous soldiers. It seems likely that the scene reflects the unconscious anger of the father so unceremoniously excluded from the celebration of the apotheosis of mother and infant. Insofar as we are children, we identify with the child who has the total love and worship of its mother, the child now has replaced the father. But insofar as we are fathers whose jealousy is evoked, we identify with the murderous soldiers.

The massacre of the innocents was linked by the Church with Christmas. The first three days of Christmas are devoted to it (Male, 1984, p. 186). In theology the innocents were seen as the first martyrs to the Christian faith. In the language of the unconscious, however, they were sacrifical substitutes.

The art historian Emile Male (1984) notes that some theologians have dated the founding of the Church from the very moment of Christ's birth. Artists traditionally place the newborn Christ in an elevated crèche reminiscent of the sacrificial altar. In the thirteenth century the mother does not envelop him in infinite love as she will later, in the paintings of the Italian quattrocento. Rather, she turns her head away from her son, as if aware of the forthcoming sacrifice. Theologians have speculated that Christ was crucified on the exact spot in which Adam was buried, his blood flowing over Adam's bones. The wood of the cross, they say, was the wood of the tree of good and evil. It is of interest to note that in Roman times crucifixion was not a form of sacrifice but a death penalty imposed on criminals. In the teachings of St. Paul, however, the cross became a substitute for the sacrifical altar.

THE HISTORICAL JESUS

The historical Jesus, insofar as we can reconstruct his original teachings from the New Testament, never intended his ministry to go beyond the boundaries of Israel. His message was strongly apocalyptic. In Mattew 10:5-7 we read:

Go not into the way of the Gentiles, and into any city of the Samaritans
enter ye not:
But go rather to the lost sheep of the house of Israel.
And as ye go, preach, saying, The kingdom of heaven is at hand.

It is likely that Jesus was a follower of John the Baptist and that after
John's imprisonment he took his place as leader. This hypothesis is based
on the fact that he who baptizes is hierarchically superior to the one who
is baptized. Eventually New Testament distortions reversed the roles of
the two men and portrayed John as having prepared the way for the coming of Christ. It seems that Jesus' baptism was the turning point in his
life. Matthew reports (3:13, 16–17):

Then cometh Jesus from Galilee to Jordan unto John, to be baptised
of him. . . .
And Jesus, when he was baptised, went up straightway out of the water:
and, lo, the heavens were opened unto him, and he saw the Spirit of
God descending like a dove, and lighting upon him:
And lo a voice from heaven, saying, This is my beloved Son, in whom
I am well pleased.

These words echo those of Deutero-Isaiah: "Thou art my servant in
whom I will be glorified" (Isa. 49:3). But the difference should be stressed.
It is one thing to be called the servant of God and quite another to be
called his beloved son.

In Christian theology the domination of the law, so characteristic
of Old Testament religion, came to an end with the birth of Christ. On
the stage of history, however, the separation between Church and
synagogue took longer. Around A.D. 49 according to Acts (15:23–29)
a council was held in Jerusalem in which Paul played a major role. The
topic was the conversion of the gentiles; much resentment was voiced
against "the burden of the law." Ultimately, only three things were
demanded in the new faith: abstaining from what was sacrificed to idols;
abstaining from blood and from what is strangled; and abstaining from
unchastity. The final separation between Church and synagogue was
brought about by the abrogation of circumcision.

For he is not a Jew, who is one outwardly: neither is that circumcision, which is outward in the flesh: But he is a Jew, which is one inwardly: and circumcision is that of the heart [Rom. 2:28–29].

There is a Jewish precedent for the conversion of circumcision into a metaphor. In Deuteronomy 10:16 God asks his people to circumcise the foreskins of their hearts and be no more stiff-necked. However, within the Jewish orbit the abrogation of circumcision was anathema, for the whole feeling of election was based on the ritual of circumcision.

SAINT PETER

Of special psychological interests in the description of St. Peter's conversion told in Acts, chapter 10: he falls into a trance and has both a visual and an auditory experience. A vessel descends from heaven filled with animals prohibited by the Jewish dietary laws, and a voice summons him to kill and eat. But Peter resists, saying, "I have never eaten anything that is common and unclean." The voice admonishes him, "What God hath cleansed, that call thou not unclean." He meets the Roman centurion Cornelius and keeps his company, yet another violation of the law. Peter is here referring to the thirteen rules of Rabbi Shamai, which greatly restricted contacts between Jews and gentiles. He now has the insight that "God is no respecter of persons," and Cornelius becomes the first uncircumcised man to be baptised. The event is an interesting example of a transformation occurring in the superego. The God is the same, but the covenant and the previous way of life are abrogated.

SAINT PAUL

As a native of Tarsus in Asia Minor and a Roman citizen, Paul was familiar with the mystery religions of paganism. Unlike Jesus, he was a Hellenized Jew. Hooke (1937) is of the opinion that Paul never ceased to feel and reason like a rabbi; however, his outlook was apocalyptic and his conversion on the road to Damascus shows him to be a mystic. Scholem (1960, p. 16) discovered that the obscure verses of 2 Corinthians 12:2–4 are understandable if we assume that both Paul and the Corinthians were familiar with the esoteric writings of the Hebrew Hekhalot literature.

Many, including Freud (1937), regard St. Paul as the true founder of Christianity. Whether in fact it is the achievement of one man or whether Paul merely headed the expansionist wing of early Christianity is a question that cannot be answered on psychoanalytic grounds. The problem is an important one because at this point Christian theology and Christian history are at odds with each other. Paul showed little interest in the historical Jesus. The crucial events for him were Christ's death and resurrection.

Christianity absorbed the dominant theme of the Near Eastern religions, that of the dying and the resurrected God, but it gave the resurrection a new meaning. What in the Near East was essentially the expression of the cyclical year became in Christianity a way of absolution from guilt. The Church replaced the Jews as the elect of God.

It was St. Paul who introduced into Christianity what Dodds (1965) so aptly called "the fantastic value attached to virginity" (p. 35), an idea which culminated in the famous statement, "If they cannot abstain let them marry for it is better to marry than to burn" (I Cor. 7:9). Thus, Paul not only absorbed the sense of guilt prevalent in his time but added considerably to it by the demand for chastity. Saner men, Dodds points out, took the view that the Church, like Noah's Ark, must find room for both clean and unclean animals, but the sexual fanaticism lingered like a slow poison that was absorbed into the Church's system. The significance of this decision for the future history of Western sexual mores was great. From now on God would be involved in every detail of sexual practices. God would be concerned with masturbation, and with extramarital and premarital sexual relationships. He would be practicularly intolerant of homosexual relationships.

In a language that left its imprint on the Western way of feeling, St. Paul described his intrapsychic battle against sexual temptations.

> For I delight in the law of God after the inward man:
> But I see another law in my members, warring against the law of my mind, and bringing me into captivity to the law of sin which is in my members [Rom. 8:22–23].

The inner battle between superego and id that Freud discovered, St. Paul had already described with great force. This intrapsychic struggle has no antecedent in Jewish history but harks back to the metaphor of the charioteer in Plato's *Phaedrus* (see Bergmann, 1982).

FREUD'S VIEW OF CHRISTIANITY

In "Totem and Taboo" Freud (1913), invoking the law of talion, offered a psychoanalytic interpretation of the basic Christian myth:

There can be no doubt that in the Christian myth the original sin was one against God the Father. If, however, Christ redeemed mankind from the burden of original sin by the sacrifice of his own life, we are driven to conclude that the sin was a murder. . . .

In Christian doctorine, therefore, men were acknowledging in the most undistinguished manner the guilty primaeval deed, since they found the fullest atonement for it in the sacrifice of this one son. Atonement with the father was all the more complete since the sacrifice was accompanied by a total renunciation of the women on whose account the rebellion against the father was started. But at that point the inexorable psychological law of ambivalence stepped in. The very deed in which the son offered the greatest possible atonement to the father brought him at the same time to the attainment of his wishes *against* the father. He himself became God, beside, or, more correctly, in place of, the father. A son-religion displaced the father-religion. As a sign of his substitution the ancient totem meal was revived in the form of communion, in which the company of brothers consumed the flesh and blood of the son—no longer the father—obtained sanctity thereby and identified themselves with him [p. 154].

The Eucharist repeats the totem feast in a symbolic manner, but the sons eat the father not to acquire his potency but rather to obtain his forgiveness. In this version, all aggression toward the consumed father is eliminated from conscious thought.

Because the Eucharist's centrality, Christianity fitted better into the model of "Totem and Taboo" than did Judaism and the hypothetical killing of Moses. Freud attributed the victory of Christianity over competing religions to the fact that it derived its theory from a kernel of historical truth. Although Paul's grasp of original sin was delusional, even this delusional admission Freud regarded as a forward step beyond Judaism (1937, p. 136).[1]

A significant detail in the Catholic communion rite supports Freud's view. Until quite recently, the wafer had to be swallowed but not chewed or bitten, under pain of mortal sin. The bitting symbolizes intended aggression (Karl Abraham's second oral stage). A Catholic analysand of mine recalled how as a child with great trepidation he took courage and bit the wafer, he had been told it would result in instant death. When nothing happened, he lost his faith in religion. Jewish children are known

---

[1] For a discussion of Freud's sense of Jewish identity, see Bergman (1976).

to conduct a parallel experiment, pronouncing aloud the forbidden name of Yhwe, with similar results.

AN ALTERNATIVE INTERPRETATION

Like Freud's, my interpretation is psychoanalytic, but I propose a different origin for the development of the two religions. I have hypothesized, the existence of archaic memories and fears pertaining to ritual, as underlying the two great Jewish holidays, infanticide. Christianity has emerged out of the same unconscious elements but radically recasts them.

Christian liturgy connects Abraham's sacrifice of Isaac with that of Christ, viewing the one as prefiguring the other. In the Anglican Church, scriptural accounts of the two events are read on Good Friday, one after the other. It is significant here that Jesus' last supper was a Seder initiating the Jewish Passover; it is out of the Passover meal that the Eucharist emerged. What is reenacted in the latter, however, is not the substitution of the lamb for the firstborn but rather its symbolic opposite. Christ, God's own firstborn, becomes the *agnus dei*, the sacrificial Lamb of God. It would seem that what was overcome but dormant in Judaism has within a new religious frame of reference been brought to consciousness, in however sublimated a form.

If my argument is valid, Jewish religion developed away from the sacrifice of the firstborn to animal sacrifices as a substitute. After the destruction of the Temple, sacrifices gave way to prayer. Christianity brought about a significant reversal, for it made conscious the symbolic equation between animal sacrifice and crucifixion. Edmund Leach (1986) has published an illuminated twelfth-century manuscript in which under the same arch are depicted two events: on top, Christ is crucified and pierced with lances; below, a man sacrifices a lamb on an altar with a sharp knife. The symbolic equation of the two events is powerfully expressed. But to whom was Christ sacrificed? Throughout history the distinction is made between the sacrificer, the victim, and the God who receives the sacrifice. Only in Christianity does God play the double role of both sacrificer and receiver of the sacrifice. Christian believers are left with a mystery: an all-powerful God can find no other way to absolve us from sin but to sacrifice his own beloved son. The reasons offered for this sacrifice are very different from those given by the pagan kings mentioned earlier, but the act is the same. Freud was right to point out that the return of the repressed plays a crucial role in this theology.

The very fact that the Eucharist has been at the center of so many theological controversies I take as a sign that there remains something disturbing about this rite that cannot be laid to rest. Catholic dogma interprets the Eucharist as a transubstantiation of wafer and wine into the flesh and blood of Christ. The Mass converts the unique historical event of the sacrifice into one that is continually repeated. Lutherans introduced a compromise, speaking not of transubstantiation but of cosubstantiation, while Calvin went a step further, declaring that Christ is only spiritually present in the Eucharist. I interpret the fact that transubstantiation had to be made into Catholic dogma as indicating that it was necessary to quiet doubts associated with cannibalism.

CHRISTIAN ANTI-SEMITISM

We have seen that the separation of Church and synagogue was accomplished rather rapidly, within one or two generations. A sense of rivalry was inevitable, as Christians claimed for the Church the place of election once held by the Jews. Further, that Jesus' own people refused his evangelism seemed a dangerous source of heresy. However, the question that must be answered is why anti-Semitism persisted so long after the Church emerged victorious and the Jews offered no threat to its hegemony. It is here that we must turn to psychoanalysis for a possible answer.

We know that historically Christians have leveled two main accusations against the Jews. The first is that they are "Christ killers." In vain have Jewish apologists tried to show that it was the Romans who were to blame: crucifixion was a Roman punishment for rebels; the Jewish punishment would have been stoning. The tenor of the Gospels is decidedly anti-Jewish, and an attempt is made to whitewash Pontius Pilate, the Roman procurator who ordered Christ's crucifixion.

> When Pilate saw that he could prevail nothing, but rather that a tumult was made, he took water, and washed his hands before the multitude, saying, I am innocent of the blood of his just person: see ye to it. Then answered all the people, and said, His blood be on us, and on our children [Matt. 27:24–25].

Theologically speaking, the sacrifice of Christ is the cornerstone of the Christian religion. This event, of cosmic significance, is thought to have been inevitable. Rather illogically, then, those who call the Jews

Christ killers imply that a necessary event, one that has brought them salvation, should not have occurred and would not have happened at all had the Jews behaved differently. St. Paul's epistles do not mention the betrayal of Jesus. But the Gospels attribute the contradiction to Jesus. For example,

> The Son of man goeth as it is written of him: but woe unto that man by whom the Son of man is betrayed! it had been good for that man if he had not been born [Matt. 26:24].

Immediately after this accusation, the Eucharist is established. There is something inherent in the Eucharist that requires a scapegoat. Deicide requires a culprit if the burden of guilt is not to be intolerable. The situation is similar in the binding of Isaac. And who shall be blamed if God must remain faultless? The film documentary *Shoah* demonstrates the extent to which the belief is alive in contemporary Poland that the Jews killed Christ and so deserved the Holocaust.

The second accusation is that Jews use the blood of Christian children to make matzos for Passover. If my psychological hypothesis is correct, anti-Semites unconsciously understand the latent meaning of Passover. They understand the connection between Passover and the killing of the Egyptian firstborn. However, by an even shorter route they derive the accusation from a projection of the unacceptable aspects of the Eucharist. It was a bold step not to deny cannibalism but to incorporate its dervatives in the communion ritual. But the Eucharist is thereby made subject to the inner accusation of cannibalism, which may in turn be projected onto the Jews.

Islam, like Christianity, is a daughter-religion of Judaism, and yet the fate of the Jews in Islamic countries differed from their fate within Christendom. Though never enjoying equality with Muslims—they were subjected to special taxation and various restrictions—Jews did not arouse in them the special hostility they met in Christian lands. The greater tolerance of the Muslims toward the Jews resulted from the fact that both Christians and Jews were considered "people of the book." Islam did not evolve out of Judaism, the sibling rivalry was therefore muted.

CLINICAL DATA

With reference to the material here presented, a number of analysts have focused attention on the cruelty of parents toward their children. Feldman (1947) offered a psychoanalytic interpretation for the special hatred of fathers for their firstborn. The sin of the firstborn is that at birth he is the first to pass through the genitals of the mother and is therefore guilty of incest. The unconscious, "coming out" and "going in" are equated (p. 181). This hatred was dealt with in the Jewish tradition by an emphasis on the special importance of the firstborn to the father.

Berliner (1958) interpreted masochism as the experience of non-love coming from the person whose love is needed. It is the sadism of the love object fused with the libido of the subject. He emphasized that even within recorded history the custom of killing unwanted children has flourished. Both Oedipus and Moses were unwanted children, and in the infancy of Jesus the threat of death was posed by Herod, a father figure. Berliner concluded that ill treatment of children by parents does not belong to the dim prehistoric past, and that Freud erred when he explained reports of parental cruelty as mere projections of the cruelty of children.

Bloch (1985) has drawn attention to the frequently observed clinical fact that many adult analysands behave as if their life still depended on obtaining the love of the mother. She argues that the fear of infanticide may be the child's universal response to his life situation and the primary motive for his defensive structure. While I am not ready to assign infanticide the primary role in the formation of neurosis, I agree that both historically and clinically the aggression of parents toward children has been neglected by psychoanalysis. Shengold (1978) speaks of parents who interfere with their children's attempts to establish a separate identity and, by doing so, kill their joy in life and their capacity to love. He calls such interference "soul murder." Ross (1982) speaks of the "heart of darkness" hidden in all men to whom little children are entrusted. He believes that all fathers have fantasized some variant on the infanticidal wish. Blos (1985) comments that the father's negative emotions toward his male child, his jealousy and envy, have been studied in psychoanalysis far less than have negative maternal feelings. One might add that infanticidal wishes give rise to severe guilt feelings, and in order to escape from them the father withdraws from the child.

The recognition that aggression is not a one-way street leading from child to parent came slowly to psychoanalysis. But when it finally dawned, it occasioned a reevaluation of the Oedipus myth. Freud had derived the term "oedipus complex" from *Oedipus Rex* of Sophocles, but that tragedy presents only a small segment of the myth. In 1953 Devereux coined the term "Laius complex" to designate the murderous wishes of the father toward his son.

Judaism and Christianity created a loving God, an idealized father image. In both, early murderous wishes remained alive in the unconscious and below the surface of religious worship. To return to Arlow's emphasis, both religions stressed the virtues of sonhood over fatherhood and molded the character of their adherents in this direction. Total submission to that God would become the ego ideal of both religions. In the case of Judaism the claim was made that God did not desire the death of the son but wanted merely to test Abraham's loyalty. In Christianity the sacrifice was rationalized as an act of love. But neither succeeded in creating an image of a wholly loving God or father. It would seem that the actual experiences of children confirm over and over that this ideal is beyond reach.

REFERENCES

Abraham, K. (1909), Dreams and myths: A study in folk psychology. In: *Clinical Papers and Essays on Psychoanalysis.* New York: Hogarth Press, 1955, pp. 153–209.

Arlow, J. A. (1951), Review of *Man's Religion* by J. B. Noss. *Internat. J. Psycho-Anal.,* 32:329

——— (1961), Ego psychology and the study of mythology. *J. Amer. Psychoanal. Assn.,* 9:371–393.

——— (1964), The Madonna's conception through the eyes. *Psychoanalytic Study of Society,* 3:13–25.

Auerbach, E. (1946), *Mimesis.* Princeton: Princeton University Press, 1968.

Bergmann, M. (1966), The impact of ego psychology on the study of the myth. *American Imago,* 23:257–264.

——— (1976), Moses and the evolution of Freud's Jewish identity. In: *Judaism and Psychoanalysis,* ed. M. Ostow. New York: Ktav, 1982, pp. 115–142.

——— (1982), Platonic love, transference love, and love in real life. *J. Amer. Psychoanal. Assn.,* 30:87–111.

——— (1985), Reflections on the psychological and social functions of remembering the Holocaust. *J. Psychoanal. Inquiry,* 5:9–20.

Berliner, M. (1958), The role of object relations in moral masochism. *Psychoanal. Quart.,* 37:38–56.

Bloch, D. (1985), The child's fear of infanticide and the primary motives of defense. *Psychoanal. Rev.*, 72:573–588.

Blos, P. (1985), *Son and Father: Before and Beyond the Oedipus Complex*. New York: The Free Press.

Chasseguet-Smirgel, J. (1985), *Creativity and Perversion*. New York: Norton.

Devereux, G. (1953), Why Oedipus killed Laius. *Internat. J. Psycho-Anal.*, 34:134–141.

Dodds, E. (1965), *Pagans and Christians in an Age of Anxiety*. Cambridge: Cambridge University Press.

Feldman, S. (1947), Notes on the primal horde. *Psychoanal. & Social Sci.*, 1:171–173.

Frazer, J. (1922), *The Golden Bough*. Vol. 1. Abridged ed. New York: Macmillan, 1942.

Freud, S. (1900), The interpretation of dreams. *Standard Edition*, 4-5. London: Hogarth Press, 1953.

―――― (1908), Creative writers and daydreaming. *Standard Edition*, 9:143–153. London: Hogarth Press, 1959.

―――― (1913), Totem and taboo. *Standard Edition*, 13:1–161. London: Hogarth Press, 1955.

―――― (1937), Moses and monotheism. *Standard Edition*, 23:7–137. London: Hogarth Press, 1964.

Goitein, S. (1955), *Jews and Arabs: Their Contact Through the Ages*. New York: Schocken.

Hooke, S. (1937), Christianity and the mystery religions; the emergence of Christianity from Judaism. In: *Judaism and Christianity in the Age of Transition*, ed. W. Oesterly. London: Sheldon Press.

Leach, E. (1986), The big fish in the Biblical wilderness. *Internat. Rev. Psycho-Anal.*, 13:129–141.

Lustig, E. (1976), On the origins of Judasim. *Psychoanalytic Study of Society*, 7. New Haven, CT: Yale University Press.

Male, E. (1984), *Religious Art in France*, 9th ed. Princeton: Princeton University Press.

Mellinkoff, R. (1970), *The Horned Moses in Medieval Art and Thought*. Berkeley: University of California Press.

Ostow, M. (1982), Introduction. *Judaism and Psychoanalysis*, ed. M. Ostow. New York: Ktav, pp. 1–44.

Reik, T. (1919), *Ritual Psychoanalytic Studies*. New York: Farrar Strauss, 1946.

―――― (1959), *The Mystery on the Mountain*. New York: Harper.

Ross, J. (1982), Oedipus revisited: Laius and the "Laius complex." *The Psychoanalytic Study of the Child*, 37:169–200.

Rubenstein, R. (1982), The meaning of anxiety in rabbinic Judaism. In: *Judaism and Psychoanalysis*, ed. M. Ostow, New York: Ktav, pp. 77–109.

Schlesinger, J. (1976), Origins of the Passover Seder in ritual sacrifice.

Psychoanalytic Study of Society, 7. New Haven, CT: Yale University Press.

Scholem, G. (1941), *Major Trends in Jewish Mysticism.* New York: Schocken.

—— (1960), *Jewish Gnosticism, Merkabah Mysticism, and Talmudic Tradition.* New York: Jewish Theological Seminary.

Shengold, l. (1978), An assault on a child's individuality: A kind of soul murder. *Psychoanal. Quart.,* 47:419–434.

Spiegel, S. (1967), *The Last Trial.* New York: Schocken, 1969.

Wellisch, E. (1954), *Isaac and Oedipus.* London: Rutledge & Kegan Paul.

15

The Genetic Sources of Freud's Difference with Romain Rolland on the Matter of Religious Feelings

Martin Wangh, M.D.

A topic much neglected in psychoanalysis is the formation of opinion or belief. It is a field closely related to that of sublimation, which has suffered a similar fate. How, why, and when an individual develops the aesthetic, political, or religious notions he does are matters which, like all psychological phenomenon, are highly overdetermined.

In this chapter I will take for granted the impact on opinion and belief formation of traditional, familial sources, as well as that of the political atmosphere in which a person grows up. My attention will be focused instead on the ontogenetic factors influencing the individual's consciously held opinion or weltanschauung.

I will take as my case in point the friendship between Sigmund Freud and Romain Rolland, and their differences regarding the nature and origin of religious feelings.[1]

The interchange between these two giants of the first third of the present century is rather spare. Only once was there direct personal contact, and that was when Rolland came to see Freud upon the latter's invitation, when he, Freud, was already quite ill. Otherwise we have,

---

[1]During the last few decades, quite a number of scholars, within and outside of psychoanalysis, have become curious about the relationship between Freud and Rolland. The psychoanalysts among them are Harrison (1965, 1974), Kanzer (1969), Schur (1972), Hamilton (1976), and Blum (1977). I have also made much use of Ruth Abraham's article (1982) on Freud's relationship to his mother, Amalia Freud. Among the nonpsychoanalysts, Fisher's research (1976) of the Freud-Rolland interchange was most helpful, as was March's brief biography (1971) of Rolland. The work of the latter two authors may well lay the foundations for an eventual psychobiography of the great poet, dramatist, novelist, musicologist, and intrepid pacifist.

over the space of thirteen years, only sixteen letters from Freud to Rolland, many of them brief notes. Not all the letters from Rolland to Freud are, so far as I know, available.

The central issue in my discussion of opinion and belief formation will be the strenuousness with which Freud opposed Rolland's proposal to consider "oceanic feelings" as fundamental to religious experience. It is puzzling that Freud, who, more than any other man, dared to look into the "underworld" of psychic life, including his own, felt so much stress from Rolland's challenge. On hand of direct and indirect personal data, which Freud himself disclosed to us, I shall try to show why this might have been so.

In this discussion of the *fons et origo* of religious feelings, I will deliberately not engage Freud's concept of the Urvater, which he postulates in "Totem and Taboo" (1912–1913) nor will I extend it to the narcissistic sources of omnipotence and omniscience which swell the stream of religious feelings. To do so would distract from the central dispute between Freud and Rolland.

Ultimately it is to be hoped that observations in regard to the belief formation in one man's life might furnish useful guidelines for research into the development of religious beliefs generally. But for this a collaborative effort of archeosociologists, archeologists, historians of religion, and psychoanalysts would surely be needed.

The most widely read book by Sigmund Freud, rivaled only by "The Interpretation of Dreams" (1900) and "The Psychopathology of Everyday Life" (1901) is "Civilization and Its Discontents" (1930). There is hardly any course in sociology at a university or college in the Western world that does not have this work on its reading list. The book begins with Freud's response to Romain Rolland on the source and cause of religious feelings. By placing this issue at the beginning of "Civilization and Its Discontents," Freud underlines the significance that the subject of religious feelings has for him in a social science context. The very personal style of this first chapter entices one to look for its subjective meaning.

In a letter to Freud dated December 5, 1927, Rolland proposed that the concept of "oceanic feeling" was basic to the development of religion. He wrote this letter after reading Freud's "Future of an Illusion" (1927). (We find the letter, together with others from Rolland to Freud, translated from the French by Fisher [1976, pp. 20-21], in an article entitled "Sigmund Freud and Romain Rolland: The Terrestrial Animal and His Great Oceanic Friend.") I quote:

Thank you very much for having kindly sent me your lucid and valiant little book. . . . it tears the blindfold from eternal adolescents, all of us, whose amphibious mind floats between the illusion of yesterday and the illusion of tomorrow.

Your analysis of religion is fair but I would have liked to see you analyze spontaneous *religious feelings* or, more exactly, religious *sensations.* . . .

I understand . . . the simple direct fact of the *sensation of the 'eternal' (i.e. personal survival) which may very well not be eternal, but simply without perceptible limits, and in that way oceanic.* . . .

I, myself, am familiar with this sensation. Throughout my whole life . . . I have always found it a source of vital renewal. In this sense I am profoundly religious . . . without this constant state (like an underground bed of water which I feel surfacing under the bark) in any way harming my critical faculties. . . .

I add that this 'oceanic' feeling has nothing to do with my personal aspirations. Personally, I aspire to eternal rest; survival has no attraction for me. . . . I have recognized it to be identical (with multiple nuances) amongst numerous living souls, it has allowed me to understand that there was the true subterranean source of religious energy. Please believe, dear friend, in my affencionate respect, Romain Rolland.

Freud, seemingly shocked by the interjection of the concept, did not reply to this so confessional communication for more than a year. On July 14, 1929, he wrote to Rolland as follows:

Your letter of December 5, 1927, containing your remarks about a feeling you describe as "oceanic" has left me no peace. It happens that in a new work "Civilization and Its Discontents" which lies before me still uncompleted I am making a starting point of this remark; I mention this "oceanic" feeling and am trying to interpret it from the point of view of our psychology.

And now I am beset with doubts whether I am justified in using your private remark for publication in this way . . . and if it is even in the slightest degree contrary to your wishes I should certainly refrain from using it. My essay could be given another introduction without any loss [Freud, 1960a, p. 388].

Six days later, July 20, 1929, he sent another letter:

My best thanks for your permission! But I cannot accept it before you have reread your letter of the year 1927. . . .

I was glad to hear that your book [*Essay on Mysticism and Action in Living India*; see Fisher, 1976, pp. 24–29] will appear before my small effort. But please don't expect from it any evaluation of the "oceanic" feeling. I am experimenting only with an analytic version of it; I am clearing it out of the way, so to speak [Freud, 1960a, p. 389].

It may be noted that the German original of this final sentence is much harsher: "ich räume es mir sozusagen aus dem Weg" (Freud, 1960b, p. 385). The German phrasing points to a strong feeling of urgency and annoyance about what appears to be an obstacle.

Fisher (1976, p. 24) comments that Freud then expressed a confused series of thoughts with respect to his correspondence with the French writer. Freud shows "faulty memory," displays "possessiveness," "awkwardness of prose," and an "uncharacteristic lapse of memory"; all suggest "resistance vis-à-vis Rolland's letter . . ." (p. 25). Fisher is absolutely right. Freud was obviously troubled by the injection of the concept of an "oceanic" feeling into his "exposé" of religion as an illusion eventually to be overcome by a matured humanity.

In this first chapter of "Civilization and Its Discontents" Freud clearly vacillated while making a serious attempt to gain access, at least intellectually, to Rolland's concept of the "oceanic" sensation. This sensation was for Rolland "a source of vital renewal" (July 9, 1929) "without in any way harming critical faculties and freedom to exercise them" (December 5, 1927). In response Freud (1930) admitted, in the opening pages of "Civilization and Its Discontents," that

> the views expressed by the friend whom I so much honor . . . caused me no small difficulty but I cannot discover this 'oceanic' feeling in myself. It is not easy to deal scientifically with feelings . . . nothing remains but to fall back on the ideational content which is most readily associated with the feeling. If I have understood my friend rightly, he means the same thing by it as the consolation offered by an original and somewhat eccentric dramatist to his hero who is facing a self-inflicted death 'We cannot fall out of this world.' That is to say, it is a feeling of an indissoluble bond, of being one with the external world as a whole [pp. 64-65].

To be noted here are the awkwardness and circumlocution of Freud's language. He cannot say simply, "To think of merging with nature is desirable in order to avoid the fear of death." Instead he speaks via a dramatic character, while having himself in mind. The dramatist he quotes is Christian Dietrich Grabbe (1801–1836), in whose play *Hannibal* the title character (with whom Freud identified as a boy) says: "Ja, aus der Welt werden wir nicht fallen, wir sind einmal d'rin" (Indeed, we shall not fall out of this world. We are in it once and for all").

As if feeling that he had revealed an emotional affinity for Rolland's ideas, he immediately entered the following, rather ambivalent, disclaimer: "this seems something rather in the nature of an intellec-tual perception which is not, it is true, without an accompanying feeling-tone, but only such as would be present with any other act of thought of equal range" (p. 65). He then asserted once more, "From my own experience I could not convince myself of the primary nature of such a feeling," only again to concede that "this gives me no right to deny that it does in fact occur in other people. The only question is whether it ought to be regarded as the *fons et origo* of the whole need for religion" (p. 65).

In the paragraphs that followed, Freud made an intellectual effort to find a place for an "oceanic" feeling arising in the course of human mental development. Before the establishment of the ego, he noted, the surround and the organism must have been "one"; it was through the arousal of "unpleasure" that the environment (i.e., the object) became discerned as alien (i.e., as "not me").

> some sources of excitation . . . can provide [the infant] with sensa-tions at any moment, whereas other sources evade him from time to time—among them what he desires most of all, his mother's breast—and only reappears as a result of his screaming for help. . . . This [sets up] over against the ego an 'object' . . . which is only forced to appear by a special action [p. 67].

Thus the emergence of the "object" as something alien, outside the "pleasure-ego," occurs within a hostile setting. The "desired" breast, unpleasantly absent (at least momentarily), is eo ipso a "denying breast"; Klein (1952) was later to develop this distinction into a sharp dichotomy— the "good breast" and the "bad breast." Freud (1930) went on:

> Our present ego-feeling is, therefore, only a shrunken residue of a much more inclusive—indeed, an all-embracing—feeling which cor-responded to a more intimate bond between the ego and the world

about it. If we may assume that there are many people in whose mental life this primary ego-feeling has persisted . . . side by side with the . . . more sharply demarcated ego-feeling of maturity . . . the ideational contents appropriate to it would be precisely those of limitlessness and of a bond with the universe—the same ideas with which my friend elucidated the 'oceanic' feeling [p. 68].

While Freud thus allowed that many may possess such feelings, he did so in a slightly deprecatory context: these feeling are like the vanished dinosaurs whose representative, the crocodile, still lives among us, or like the traces of the *Roma Quadrata* and the *Septimontium* which can today still be found under and among the structures of present day Rome. But Freud, first feeling forced to admit that "in mental life nothing . . . can perish "(p. 69), quickly recovered from this concession, as he turned to discuss the body: "The earlier phases of development are in no sense still preserved; they have been absorbed into the later phases for which they have supplied the material. The embryo cannot be discovered in the adult" (p. 71). But soon again he relaxed his negative stance:

> Perhaps we are going too far in this. Perhaps we ought to content ourselves with asserting that what is past in mental life *may* be preserved and it is not *necessarily* destroyed. . . . We can only hold fast to the fact that it is rather the rule than the exception for the past to be preserved in mental life.
> Thus we are perfectly willing to acknowledge that the 'oceanic' feeling exists in many people, and we are inclined to trace it back to an early phase of ego-feeling. The further question then arises, what claim this feeling has to be regarded as the source of religious needs [p. 71–72].

And yet the vacillation continued. "To me the claim does not seem compelling," he wrote in the very next line:

> After all, a feeling can only be a source of energy if it is itself the expression of a strong need. The derivation of religious needs from the infant's helplessness and the longing for the father aroused by it seems to me incontrovertible, especially since the feeling is not simply prolonged from childhood days, but is permanently sustained by fear of the superior power of Fate. I cannot think of any need in childhood as strong as the need for a father's protection. Thus the part played by the oceanic feeling, which might seek something like the restoration

of limitless narcissism, is ousted from a place in the foreground. The origin of the religious attitude can be traced back in clear outlines as far as the feeling of infantile helplessness. There may be something further behind that, but for the present it is wrapped in obscurity.

I can imagine that the oceanic feeling became connected with religion later on. The 'oneness with the universe' which constitutes its ideational content sounds like a first attempt at a religious consolation, as though it were another way of disclaiming the danger which the ego recognizes as threatening it from the external world. Let me admit once more that it is very difficult for me to work with these almost intangible quantities. Another friend of mine, whose insatiable craving for knowledge has led him to make the most unusual experiments and has ended by giving him encyclopaedic knowledge, has assured me that though the practices of Yoga, by withdrawing from the world, by fixing the attention on bodily functions and by peculiar methods of breathing, one can in fact evoke new sensations and coenaesthesias in oneself, which he regards as regressions to primordial states of mind which have long ago been overlaid. He sees in them a physiological basis, as it were, of much of the wisdom of mysticism. It would not be hard to find connections here with a number of obscure modifications of mental life, such as trances and ecstasies [p. 72–73].

Freud then concluded his chapter by exclaiming, "in the words of Schiller's diver, 'Let him rejoice who breathes up here in the roseate light!'" Freud, the discoverer of the human unconscious, was in effect saying, "I cannot deal with these depths of experience."

This long review of the correspondence between Rolland and Freud, and of the form and content of Freud's discussion of Rolland's proposition that an "oceanic" feeling was the basis of religiosity, leave no doubt that Freud did "protest too much." He was compelled in a multitude of ways to assert that this "oceanic" feeling was alien to his experience Yet he admitted that Rolland's proposition "has left me no peace." The intensity, the repetitiousness, and the emotionality of Freud's disclaimer, as well as his intellectual attempts to wrestle with the "obscurity" of the oceanic feeling, arouse both our compassion and our wonder.

Freud postulated that the *fons et origo* of Rolland's religiosity lay in the darkness of the mother-infant relationship, where all infantile helplessness is to be found. It is, according to Freud, this helplessness which evokes both a longing for the father and lifelong fears of the superior power of fate. Man cries out for a father's protection. Hence the need for a father-god.

Intellectually, Freud can name the wish for a "meeting with the universe": it signifies the wish to return to a unification with the mother—to reenter the symbiotic phase, we might say today. Freud can concede that many people the world over may possess, or be possessed by, such feelings, but in his mind these are "regressive" phenomena. Yet by admitting that nothing once in the mind is ever lost, in the course of growth, Freud circuitously includes himself. In himself he cannot plumb any awareness of these regressive perceptions. There is too much "obscurity" in it for him. The author of "The Interpretation of Dreams"—who chose as his epigraph a defiant line from Virgil's *Aeneid:* "Flectere si nequeo superos, Acheronta movebo" ("If I cannot sway the heavens, I will move Hell") falters when it comes to searching out the dim moods of the mother-infant relationship.

The emotionality with which Freud clings to his opinion that man, in being religious, seeks the aid of a god-father against an adversary (female) fate is evident. At times confessions of uncertainty interrupt his assertion of this opinion. In what is to follow, after defining the terms of the Freud-Rolland debate more sharply, I will attempt to elucidate the most decisive ontogenetic factors which in my opinion give rise to Freud's formulations of the source of religious belief.

THE THEMES OF THE CORRESPONDENCE

When the practicing psychoanalyst is confronted with a patient's acute or persistent anxiety state—Rolland's letter "has left me no peace," wrote Freud—he asks himself, and also his patient, questions like these:

When did this anxiety state begin?
What was the patient's personal situation at that time?
What was the general social situation?
What specific ontogenetic data are available; what symbolic data are there?

First formulating a provisional hypothesis, the psychoanalyst will look for validation of it and finally interpret. I will follow a more or less similar procedure, first formulating a few themes from the initial material and then, in the sections to follow, pursuing these questions in greater depth.

Explicit in the exchange between Freud and Rolland during the years

1927–1929 are the themes of the origins of religiosity and of death and dying. We find them joined by Rolland in one negatively formulated sentence: "I add that this 'oceanic' feeling has nothing to do with my personal aspirations. Personally, I aspire to eternal rest; survival has no attraction for me" (quoted by Fisher, 1976, p. 21). For Romain Rolland dying was seen as a peaceful merging with the universe. Not so for Sigmund Freud. By that time already ill with an advancing buccal cancer that would eventually kill him, Freud viewed death and fate as forces to be fought, though intellectually of course he acknowledged the inevitability of the one and the superior power of the other.

In Freud's opinion, religious mankind appeals to a male godhead for protection against a death-dealing fate-Ananke (necessity) or Moira (destiny).[2] Freud considered Rolland, who at death wished to merge peacefully with the universe, a mystic. The conception of an oceanic feeling could, according to Freud, be viewed at best as an expression of man's need for consolation. Man has to be consoled about the loss of his own being, i.e., of his consciousness. Almost to the very end, Freud fought to keep this consciousness alive. Only at the last moment did he ask his physician, Dr. Max Schur, to administer morphine (Schur, 1972, p. 529). Before that, as Dr. Finzi, the radiologist in charge of treating Freud's cancer, wrote, "He absolutely refuses to let us give him any pain-relieving medication except aspirin—and the result is that he has bad nights and gets very weak" (Schur, pp. 525-527).

The Freud-Rolland exchange contains two additional themes, though these are less explicit: (1) Freud's opinion that oceanic feelings are an atavistic remnant of the remote past and the mother-infant dyad—he calls them their "regressive" phenomena and analogizes them to crocodiles, the still persistent descendants of the dinosaurs; and (2) the water imagery (symbolically representing birth) present in the language of both correspondents. For Rolland religious feelings stem from an "oceanic river" (Fisher, 1976, p. 24); religious feelings guarantee him a "constant state (like an underground bed of water which I feel surfacing under the bark)" (p. 21). Freud combines the two themes in allusions to bodies of water like Loch Ness and what lives in them: crocodiles, monsters, and embryos (Freud, 1930, p. 68; 1936, p. 241).

---

[2]While *fatum* and *Schicksal*, the Latin and German words for fate, are grammatically neuter, their representatives are always female. Their names in Greek mythology are Clotho, Lachesis, and Atropos. They spin and determine life's course and cut it off with merciless inevitability (Seiffert, 1957).

In sum, oceanic feelings, death and dying, regression, and birth are the essential themes of the Freud-Rolland interchange.

THE FREUD-ROLLAND FRIENDSHIP

What brought these two giants so close together? What kept them at the same time worlds apart? And at what particular moment of Freud's personal history did their relationship begin?

The two men were near contemporaries. In 1923, when their relationship began, Freud was sixty-seven and Rolland ten years younger. Both had witnessed Europe's vast industrial and colonial expansion and the disastrous world war in which it culminated. The horrors of this war led Rolland to affirm life by becoming a clarion voice for pacifism, while it led Freud to conclude, pessimistically, that the basic conflict within man is between a drive for life-promoting love and a drive toward death: Eros versus Thanatos. Freud and Rolland shared a European cultural background, but there were pronounced differences as well in their personal, linguistic, national, and religious provenance. ''Vast differences separated them,'' writes Fisher (1976),

> and their controversies on religious sensations, or psychoanalysis, and on mysticism . . . sprang partly from divergent cultural and social formations. Central European and Jewish, Freud was heir to the 19th century evolutionary traditions, . . . while Romain Rolland, French and Catholic, was a professional historian and musicologist by training, an artist, novelist, and biographer [p. 2].

Beyond their shared sociohistorical experience and contrasting social milieus were private experiences which, reverberating with these public ones, linked as well as distinguished them.

It is to these personal experiences that I turn now. They seem to me of major significance for the development of their differing views on the essential source of religious feelings. Unfortunately, I cannot pursue these matters in any detail as they pertain to Rolland—this must be left to some future psychobiographer.

The issues of birth and death touched both of them early. Freud was eleven months old when his brother Julius was born and nineteen months old when he died. Rolland was two years old when his sister Madeleine was born and five at the time of her death.

Soon after starting his self-analysis Freud reconstructed that he must have entertained rivalrous and murderous feelings at the time Julius was born. And he recognized even more clearly that when this brother died, eight months later, the first trace of an indelible guilt was laid within him. Schur (1972) cites a letter to Wilhelm Fliess (dated October 3, 1897) as evidence that Freud had discovered in his self-analysis that he had ''greeted the one-year younger brother (who died within a few months) with evil wishes and genuine infantile jealousy, so that his death implanted a seed of self-reproach . . . (p. 164). This ''memory'' had far-reaching repercussions in Freud's life (Schur, 1972, p. 119). One of these was Freud's recurrent attempts to revive this lost brother through a sequence of intense friendships with male companions. He calls them ''revenants,'' a term he first used in ''The Interpretation of Dreams.'' His ''uncle'' John was the first of these figures, his brother Alexander probably the second (and again the very last, at the time of their mother's death). Fliess and Jung were the ''revenants'' of his middle age, and Romain Rolland one of the last.

Rolland, as I have noted, lost his younger sister Madeleine when he was five. The three year difference between his age then and Freud's at the time of Julius's death may well have had a great psychogenetic influence on the development of their different perspectives on life. I have described Freud's affective reaction to his sibling's death. Here is Rolland's, as paraphrased from March (1971).

At the age of five Romain was playing in the sand of Arcachon (near Bordeaux) with some other boys. Worsted by them, he buried his face in the skirt of his little sister, who was sitting in a wicker chair on the porch. She caressed his hair, saying, ''Mon pauvre petit mainmain.'' His tears were dried as if by enchantment, as something greater than themselves seem to pass between the two. That night Madeleine died after a six-hour agony of suffocation.

''To a psychoanalyst this recollection of Rolland's has all the earmarks of a screen memory—which by no means diminishes its significance. ''Scarcely an evening passed,'' wrote Rolland, fifty years later, ''without his thinking of her before he fell asleep'' (March, 1971).

Within a year of Julius's death, Freud's sister Anna was born; within a year of Madeleine's, Rolland's mother bore a new daughter, whom she also named Madeleine. This fact alone shows us how unable she was to complete the mourning.[3]

---

[3]Nagera (1967) and Heiman (1976) describe this phenomenon in regard to Vincent van

At what moment in their lives and in what manner did Freud and Rolland come together? And what held them together? (Unfortunately, this study can answer the latter question only as it pertains to Freud.) The relationship began on Freud's initiative. Fisher (1976) reports:

> The Freud-Rolland relationship began *fraternally* [italics mine] in February 1923. On the 9th of that month, Freud wrote a short letter to the French scientist and mathematician, Edouard-Monod Herzen, thanking him for his expression of 'human sympathy': 'Your recent letter [which has yet to be found] gave me great pleasure. Our times have unfortunately made us so shy and suspicious that we no longer dare take human sympathy in others for granted. Since you are a friend of Romain Rolland, may I ask you to pass on to him a word of respect from an unknown admirer. . . [p. 3].

To this overture Rolland responded immediately, in an extensive and very complimentary letter dated February 22, 1923. In it he called Freud "the Christopher Columbus of a new continent of the mind," remarked that Freud's "subliminal" visions corresponded to some of his own intuitions, and chided Freud a bit for his pessimistic view about this convulsed state of the Western world; he felt confident that "renewal" could come out of it (Fisher, 1976, p. 4). Freud's very prompt answer, dated March 4, begins with extraordinary effusiveness: "That I have been allowed to exchange a greeting with you will remain a happy memory to the end of my days. Because for us your name has been associated with the most precious of beautiful illusions, that of love extended to all mankind" (Freud, 1960a, p. 341). In the very next paragraph Freud presents himself as belonging to a "race which in the Middle Ages was held responsible for all epidemics and which today is blamed for the disintegration of the Austrian Empire and the German defeat. Such experiences . . . are not conducive to . . . illusions. A great part of my life's work (I am ten years older than you) has been spent [trying to] destroy illusions of my own and those of mankind" (p. 341). There follows

---

Gogh, while Niederland (1965) notes it in connection with Heinrich Schlieman. This failure of a mother to complete her mourning for a dead child was of deepest significance for the dead child's sibling in each of these instances. Rolland's mother was a deeply religious woman who forever spun an air of mysticism around the death of the first Madeline. Freud's mother had a daughter, Anna, within a year of Julius's death, then another daughter, Rosa, and then a son, Alexander, who was to become a close traveling campanion to his older brother Sigmund.

a prophetic expression of fear that by "exploiting the great progress made in the control of natural resources for our mutual destruction" "the perpetuation of our species" may be at stake (p. 342). "My writings," he concludes, "cannot be what yours are: comfort and refreshment for the reader" (p. 342).

These are Freud's concerns on a societal plane. What are their unconscious private meanings? At which moment of his personal life does Freud turn to the great peace activist, the reconciler and optimist Romain Rolland? The dates of Freud's approach to Rolland are February 9 and March 4, 1923. Schur (1972) cites a letter from Freud to Ernest Jones dated April 25, 1923:

> I detected *two months ago* [italics mine] a leucoplastic growth on my jaw and palate, on the right side, which I had removed on the 20th. I am not yet back to work and cannot swallow. I was assured of the benignity of the matter but, as you know, nobody can guarantee its behavior if it is permitted to grow further. My own diagnosis had been epithelioma but was not accepted. . . [p. 348; see also Jones, 1957, p. 89].

Thus we see that Freud reached out to Romain Rolland at a personally most stressful time. (The agony was to last for the next sixteen years.)

With this data in mind let us now recall Freud's letter of March 4, 1923. It is a confessional document. The first sentence speaks of the "end of my days." The next praises Rolland for holding out "the most precious of beautiful illusions, that of love extended to all mankind." By contrast he feels himself one of the race "held responsible for . . . epidemics and . . . blamed for . . . disintegration . . . and . . . defeat." Next, in a parenthesis, he emphasizes his age—"I am ten years older than you"—and proceeds to a number of rather gloomy observations which he seems to regard as a source of both pride and self-deprecation.

I have pointed out that Freud, very early in his self analysis, recognized that the death of his infant brother when he himself was under two years old (see Blum, 1977, p. 774) sowed a "seed of self-reproach" in him. Thus in his first letter to Rolland he presented himself straightaway as a Jew blamed for epidemics and defeat. Rolland, it has been argued, became for Freud yet another "revenant" of his brother Julius. This might explain the immediate intimacy and extraordinary effusiveness Freud displayed toward him. In Kanzer's view (1969, p. 235) Freud used Rolland, as he had Fliess, as an auxiliary psychoanalyst, an extension of himself as self-analyst. But Freud also related Rolland directly to his brother Alexander. He himself was surprised at having made this connection, though in fact it was a rather late one. In 1936, when preparing his essay "A Disturbance of Memory on the Acropolis" (which details an event that occurred in 1904 while on a trip to Athens with Alexander) in honor of Rolland's seventieth birthday, Freud (1936) inserted this remark: "My brother is ten years younger than I am, so is the same age as you are—a coincidence which has only now occured to me" (p. 246). How close he felt to Rolland is revealed in a light vein in this inscription to his friend: The Terrestrial Animal To His Great Oceanic Friend (Fisher, 1976, pp. 1, 40).

Perhaps the most intense declaration of intimacy in the scant sixteen letters from Freud to Rolland is made in a letter dated May 1931:

> Approaching life's inevitable end, reminded of it by yet another operation and aware that I am unlikely to see you again, I may confess to you that I have rarely experienced that mysterious attraction of one human being for another as vividly as I have with you; it is somehow bound up, perhaps, with the awareness of our being so different. Farewell! Your Freud [Freud, 1960a, p. 406].

I have already mentioned that throughout the years of his prolonged illness Freud resisted any dimming of his consciousness, refusing any analgesics stronger than aspirin. Until almost his last moment he would not "go gentle into that good night" (Dylan Thomas, 1962). He of course rejected Rolland's mysticism, particularly his vision of a pacific melting with the universe at the time of death. "How remote from me are the worlds in which we move!" he wrote Rolland in 1929, "To me mysticism is just as closed a book as music (Freud, 1960a, p. 389).

Lewin (1973) points out that the "concept of consciousness" evolved from the concept of conscience (in German: *Bewusstsein* from *Gewissen*). In other words, the moral theological concept of conscience takes precedence over that of consciousness which the "great rationalizing French and English thinkers" of the late seventeenth and eighteenth centuries introduced (p. 308). This "consciousness epoch" has a decidedly male orientation. Thus, Freud's immense efforts to keep his "consciousness" alive show him clinging to the masculine and rational. The struggle is then twofold: to avoid "pangs of conscience" and to keep from melting with the mystical, the universe, the feminine—which stand for the maternal.

Throughout world literature, sleep and death have frequently been equated. Perhaps the best known example of this occurs in *Hamlet:*

> To die, to sleep
> To sleep, perchance to dream
> There's the rub
> For in that sleep of death
> What dreams may come
> When we have shuffled off
> This mortal coil
> Must give us pause . . .
>   [Shakespeare, 1623, p. 755]

Hamlet's conscience is troubled; his relationship with his mother is full of rage and irony.

Lewin too links sleep and death. In "Sleep, the Mouth and the Dream Screen" (Lewin, 1973) he reports on a patient whose "neurotic fear of sleeping was based on a fear of death, which warded off a wish to die. The wish to die represented the infantile wish to sleep in union with the dear mother. The prototype of this wish for death is the wish for undisturbed, blank sleep . . . " (p. 98). This blank sleep would be the fulfillment of Freud's presumed wish to sleep. "Strict analytic logic compels us to see in the wish to sleep a wish to be eaten up. Falling asleep coincides with the baby's ingestion of the breast; the result is an identification with what was eaten. . . " (pp. 88–89). According to Lewin the dream screen represents the last vision of the breast—"it flattens out" when one falls asleep. Upon this screen—when thought still persists—a dream is "projected." And if these thoughts are troubled thoughts, sleeping becomes a problem. A German proverb has it that good conscience is a good and restful pillow. Lewin held the opinion that the good sleeper had had a satisfying relationship with the maternal breast. Not so the person who sleeps badly—his nursing experience had surely been unsatisfactory.

A peaceful merging with the universe—Romain Rolland's concept of death—is an unacceptable, unreachable, mystical experience to Freud. We must assume that such a happy, symbiotic reunion was barred to him by sensations of unresolved conflict with the early maternal figure. In his perception, the "desired" breast left him too early, too abruptly, or for too prolonged a time. His mother may have made belated efforts to repair her relationship with her oldest son through possessiveness. But by then such possessiveness was not in synchrony with his development. Blum (1977) renders Freud's own reconstruction of that early period in a generic form:

> Up to your nth year you regarded yourself as the sole and unlimited possessor of your mother. Then came another baby and brought you grave disillusionment. Your mother left you for some time and even after her reappearance she was never again devoted to you exclusively. Your feelings toward your mother became ambivalent, your father gained a new importance for you—and so on [Freud, 1937, p. 261].

Blum sees in these statements Freud's reflections on his own past. Blum goes on to say:

> Sibling birth, death, and new pregnancy are inevitably potential developmental disruptions in the mother-child relationship, and impose special challenges during the child's second year of life. The experience of intrapsychic loss is here compounded, during rapprochement, not only by anal-urethral and continuing oral problems and beginning castration conflicts, but by the real illness and loss of Julius. The proclivity to ambivalence will then be increased with abandonment, anxiety and rage at the object, and possible splitting of the object world (Mahler, 1975, p. 108). Hostility toward the mother may also be displaced and projected onto other objects or turned against the self. Fearful of aggression and retaliation, the child "survivor" may display more intense separation reactions, defensive reliance on denial, reparative undoing, restitutive ambition, and reactive goodness. A basic negative mood will be accentuated by the effect on both the mother and her toddler, of the new baby's birth and death, and the mother's withdrawal, grief, sadness, etc. Mahler (1966) has noted that "a negative-depressive mood may persist or may give way to an unchildlike concern which may indicate a precocity of superego structuralization [1977, pp. 774–775].

We certainly can find such precocity of superego structuralization in Freud's repeated acknowledgment that he greeted the birth of his younger brother Julius with "ill wishes and real infantile jealousy" and that Julius's death within a few months left "a germ of guilt" in him. Freud's conception of superego formation is well known: The superego draws its energy from the identification with the parents' attitude, on the one hand, and from the id, particularly its aggressive component, on the other. The severity of the superego is proportionate to the energy carried forward from these sources and is directed against the self (Freud, 1924). Not only did Freud feel that the birth of the new brother deprived him of his mother's attention, but her mourning for Julius, who died after eight months, surely added to his sense of loss. This additional deprivation could only have augmented his rage, which was directed not only against the intruding brother but against the depriving mother as well. The deficit in attention could in turn be perceived as a parental, specifically maternal punishment for his hostile feelings. The projection of his rage in this early period of life is retained in the monster imagery that frequently emerges in Freud's associations when he discusses the mysteries of life, birth, and death.

FREUD'S RELATIONSHIP WITH HIS MOTHER

We shall now take a more detailed look at the personalities and emotions that might have reinforced the foundations of Freud's severe conscience, a conscience that did not facilitate a Rolland-like libidinous immersion into the mystery of death.

Ruth Abraham (1982), the granddaughter of Karl Abraham, points out that in all of Freud's extensive correspondence, spanning more than sixty years, direct references to his mother "may be counted on the fingers of both hands" (p. 444). She contrasts "his public glorification of the mother" to his "private silence on the subject" (p. 444) and concludes that the figure of the oedipal father, whom Freud seeks to persuade us is the dominant figure in the family constellation, does not at all correspond to the reality of the Freudian family constellation. On the contrary, Freud's father was a weak, ineffectual man while Amalia Freud was an "overwhelmingly powerful, sexual and possessive" (p. 441) person. "While Freud adored and depended on his mother and yearned to approach her for the satisfaction of his needs, he could not help fearing, avoiding and defying her. He was torn by his love and hatred of her. This paralyzing conflict of ambivalence forced an early splitting of his mother's image" (p. 441). Freud's mother loved him, according to Abraham, as her narcissistic extension: "When she was 70 she was still addressing him as 'mein goldener Sigi' and late in life she had a telling dream. She saw herself at Freud's funeral and arrayed around his casket were all the heads of state of the major European nations" (p. 444). Abraham believes that this dream reveals "something about her unconscious ability to sacrifice him to the advancement of her own fame and glory" (p. 444).

Freud's postulation of the universality of the oedipal conflict leaves no doubt that he knew of his sexual, genital, and oral libidinal longings for his mother. The dread bound up with them is mostly, but not entirely, limited to the fear of being castrated by a vengeful, rivalrous father. Abraham argues that this patriarchal dread is in large part defensive. It serves to hide the recognition of the matriarchal dread. Freud certainly dreaded the intensity of his mother's emotion, particularly when it was linked to the process of mourning. Thus he writes on May 19, 1918, to Karl Abraham: "My mother will be 83 this year and is now rather shaky. Sometimes I think I shall feel a little freer after she dies because the idea of her having to be told of my death is something from which one shrinks back. So I really have reached sixty-two . . . . My prevailing mood is powerless embitterment or embitterment at my powerlessness" (quoted by Schur, 1972, p. 315). Twelve years later, when his mother died at the age of ninety-five, Freud expressed himself similarly in a letter to Ernest Jones. He added, somewhat cryptically,

> There is no saying what an effect such an experience may produce in the deeper layers, but on the surface I can detect only two—an increase in personal freedom since it was always a terrifying thought that she might come to hear of my death; and secondly, the satisfaction that at last she has achieved the deliverance for which she had earned a right after such a long life. No grief otherwise, such as my ten years younger brother is painfully experiencing. I was not at the funeral; again Anna represented me . . . [Jones, 1957, p. 152].

A Letter to Ferenczi three days later expressed similar sentiments:

> It has affected me in a peculiar way, this great event. No pain, no grief, which probably can be explained by the special circumstances—her great age, my pity for her helplessness toward the end; at the same

time a feeling of liberation, of release, which I think I also understand. I was not free to die as long as she was alive, and now I am. The values of life will somehow have changed noticeably in the deeper layers [Freud, 1960a, p. 400].

We cannot help but hear that even late in life, in 1918, the cancer-suspecting Freud, and then, twelve years later, the cancer-afflicted Freud, still lives in dread of his mother's possessive emotion. He is not allowed to die before her—and he feels released by her death.

Freud's mother's love was "predatory," Abraham writes (p. 445). "The earliest appearance in Freud's life of the 'predatory mother' is in his first recorded dream from childhood, the dream of the bird-beaked figures. "I saw my beloved mother, with a peculiarly peaceful, sleeping expression on her features, being carried into the room by two (or three) people with birds' beaks and laid upon the bed" (Freud, 1900, pp. 583). The birds are Egyptian vultures. Strachey (1957), in his introduction to Freud's "Leonardo da Vinci and a Memory of His Childhood" confirms that the hieroglyph for the Egyptian word for mother (mut) quite certainly represents a vulture—the griffon vulture, Gyps fulvus (p. 59).

Freud (1910), in this paper on Leonardo, stresses the point that the vulture is an ancient symbol of motherliness (p. 88) and in his discussion of the words "dentro alle labbra" points to the maternal nipple-directed orality from which the fellatio wish is derived (pp. 86-87). Freud also considers the female goddesses from Mut to Isis, to Hator, to Neith of Sais, from whom the Greek Athene was derived, to be androgynous, phallic mother representations (p. 94). And, in addition, the Italian origin of the word vulture (from "avvoltare": to wrap around) clearly connects with the concept of an enveloping mother.

In his paper on female sexuality (Freud, 1931) written a year after "Civilization and Its Discontents," Freud, in a parenthesis, writes as follows: "Hitherto, it is only in men that I have found the fear of being eaten up. This fear is referred to the father, but it is probably the product of a transformation of oral aggression directed to the mother" (p. 237). At an earlier point in this paper, he admits to his limitations in grasping the first attachment to the mother "so grey with age and shadowy and almost impossible to revivify" (p. 226). On the next page, while speaking of "the germ of later paranoia in women," he finds it to be the surprising yet regular fear of being killed (devoured) by their mothers: "this fear corresponds to a hostility which develops in the child towards the mother in consequence of the manifold restrictions imposed by the latter in the course of training . . . '' (p. 227).

Up to this point I have traced, as one possible source of the young Freud's early sense of guilt, the introjection of the controlling, domineering character of his mother. According to Ruth Abraham these traits of Amalia Freud were evident to all who knew her intimately. But another root is likely to have grown from the fury of the toddler, Sigmund, at being abandoned by her too early. Freud's descriptions of what an infant may feel about the arrival of a new sibling are our sources for that. To these we must add the imagery, analogies, and associations to dreams with which he has supplied us. In them we often find representations of monsters, dread, awe, and disbelief (see Harrison, 1979).

I agree with Hamilton (1976), who sees Freud as fleeing from fusion with the maternal object:

> Freud's access to such 'early phase of ego-feeling' could easily have been blocked by the rage he felt towards his mother for having given birth to his brother Julius, which was perpetuated by her subsequent pregnancies (she was pregnant seven times in his first ten years) and for delegating a portion of his care to a nursemaid. When his death wishes towards Julius were actualized, the fear of that happening also to this mother might have rendered the quest for regressive fusion with her less a means of achieving security and more one fraught with 'the terror of nothingness', since destruction of the early nurturing figure prior to separation is tantamount to annihilation of the self. Thus the longing for such a reunion carried with it a considerable fear, forcing Freud to deny any 'oceanic' feelings in himself and to attribute such in others to 'the infant's helplessness and the longing for the father aroused by it' while admitting that 'there may be something further behind that, but for the present it is wrapped in obscurity.' At the same time, Freud tried to cope with wishes for fusion in a concretized manner by suggesting that all living substances eventually revert to the inorganic. One must also consider the likelihood that Freud's mother was depressed and withdrawn after Julius's death and thus not as readily available to her son [p. 150].

Freud's inability to recombine the early split off image of the "good mother" with that of the "dreaded mother" who carries her son to the oblivion of death, persisted to his last days. Schur (1972) described these last days:

The final phase began when reading became difficult. Freud did not read at random but carefully selected books from his library. The last book he read was Balzac's "La Peau de Chagrin" (Wild Ass's Skin). When he finished it, he remarked casually to me: 'This was the proper book for me to read, it deals with shrinking and starvation. . . [Schur explains:] Balzac's hero, Raphael . . . make[s] a pact with the devil. Raphael is given a magic but fatal skin of a wild ass. All his wishes will be fulfilled—but with every fulfilled wish the skin will shrink and along with it his life. Raphael cannot *master* his wishes and tries in vain to deny them. He cannot master his fear of death and dies in a hopeless panic [pp. 527–528].

At the very end Freud reminded Schur of his promise "not to forsake him when life is nothing but torture" (p. 529). Schur, by keeping this promise, spared Freud Raphael's show of panic. Freud died in a "peaceful sleep" assured by a heavy dose of morphine. Schur reports that the request for the fulfillment of this promise was made "without a trace of emotion or self-pity, and with full consciousness of reality" (p. 529).

While Harrison (1979) does not specifically concern himself with the contrast between maternal and paternal elements in religious thought and symbolization, he does hold that "any complete analysis of the oceanic feeling would have to encompass both maternal elements and mystery as they evolve in early development" (p. 416). According to Ruth Abraham, Freud flees to the oedipal complex from the preoedipal, mysterious, threatening mother. Harrison concurs:

The record suggests that the mother-goddess of Freud's unconscious fantasy was . . . all-giving but possessive, mysterious and ultimately devouring and terrifying, and that the idea of death arose during that early period of traumatization. It would mean that the idea of death was originally an undifferentiated rage-dread, with horror of abandonment, and that there was a true awareness of siblings as something occupying his mother and contributing to that abandoment. With the terror of being left and confusion on the question of who was subject and who was object went the raging wish that all sources of such terror cease to be [p. 418].

Hamilton (1976) thinks that Freud "attempted to repress and deny elements of the early relationship with his mother" (p. 161) but that they began to break through while he was on the Acropolis, necessitating more stringent defensive mechanism (such as depersonalization, etc.). We can catch the conscious derivatives of these threatening infantile elements through the displacement and symbolizations Freud uses in his confrontation with them. In the Acropolis episode he uses the analogy of the Loch Ness monster. The strange thought he had when standing on the Acropolis, viewing the landscape (and seascape) was: "So all this really *does* exist just as we learned at school!" (Freud, 1936, p. 241) He compares it to "someone walking beside Loch Ness, [who] suddenly catches sight of the form of the famous monster stranded upon the shore . . . [and who] finds himself driven to the admission 'so it really *does* exist— the sea serpent we've never believed in!'" (p. 241).

The "we" in this episode relates clearly to his brother Alexander, who was his tour companion and who suffered none of the symptoms which took possession of Freud at the time. (Let us remind ourselves again: Alexander Freud and Romain Rolland are closely linked in Freud's associations.) Also, when trying to explain to himself that repressed remnants of the earliest wishes for union with the maternal breast could be the atavistic source of the "oceanic feeling," Freud used the simile of the "Saurians," of which our present-day crocodiles are the representatives. The image of "Saurians" was apparently early connected in Freud's mind with feelings of love and hate. According to Eissler (1978, as quoted by Abraham, 1982, p. 446), in adolescence Freud called Gisella Fluss, his first love (a hometown girl who did not requite his love), an ichthiosaura, i.e., a huge aquatic reptile.

Parallel to the libidinal and oedipal attachment to the mother, we find in Freud a split-off, partially unconscious equation of the mother-concept with a death-dealing Fate. An example of this is the "Knödel Dream":

> I went into the kitchen in search of some pudding. Three women were standing in it; one of them was the hostess of the inn and she was twisting something about in her hand, as though she was making Knödel [dumplings]. She answered that I must wait until she was ready. . . . I felt impatient and went off with a sense of injury. I put on an overcoat. But the first I tried on was too long for me. . . [Then comes an initially troubled encounter with a stranger.] But we then became quite friendly with each other [Freud, 1900, p. 204].

The dream clearly refers to an early feeding situation. It is about love and hunger (having to wait until one gets one's turn), anger with a stranger, and reconciliation with him. Freud's associations lead us in such a direction. He felt robbed. Freud recalls:

> When I was six years old and was given my first lessons by my mother, I was expected to believe that we were all made of earth and must therefore return to earth. This did not suit me and I expressed doubts of the doctrine. My mother there upon rubbed the palms of her hands together just as she did in making dumplings. . . and showed me the blackish scales of *epidermis* produced by the friction as a proof that we were made of earth. My astonishment at this *ocular* demonstration knew no bounds and I acquiesced in the belief which I was later to hear expressed in the words: 'Du bist der Natur einen Tod Schuldig' [Thou owest Nature a death] [p. 205].

Interestingly, Freud has misquoted Shakespeare's *Henry IV, Part I*; the original has Prince Hal saying to Falstaff, "Thou owest *God* a death." The awe and fright inspired in the skeptical young lad (and in his adult successor) by his mother's demonstration are perhaps implicated in this slip. Immediately the three Fates come into Freud's associations: "So they really were Fates that I found in the kitchen" (p. 205). The Fates are for Freud a threat overriding all others and it is against them that he sets a rational, male deity, a father-god. Freud (1930) explains:

> The derivation of religious needs from the infant's helplessness and the longing for the father aroused by it seems to me incontrovertible, especially since the feeling is not simply prolonged from childhood days, but is permanently sustained by fear of the superior power of Fate. I cannot think of any need in childhood as strong as the need for a father's protection. Thus the part played by the oceanic feeling, which might seek something like the restoration of limitless narcissism, is ousted from a place in the foreground. The origin of the religious attitude can be traced back in clear outlines as far as the feeling of infantile helplessness. There may be something further behind that, but for the present it is wrapped in obscurity" [p. 72].

For Freud death is thus closely linked to a woman—the mother, the goddess of death—and for the most part it is a hostile linkage. She is destructive, an image in some measure ameliorated by that of her carrying him—the son, the warrior, the old man—away in her arms as she would an infant.

Rather than cite all of the many references Freud made to this conception of the mother, I will simply present the closing passage of "The Theme of the Three Caskets" (Freud, 1913). Here Freud transmutes Cordelia, the daughter of King Lear, into the "Death-Goddess":

> She is the Death-goddess who, like the Valkyrie in German mythology carries away the dead hero from the battlefield. Eternal wisdom, clothed in the primaeval myth, bids the old man renounce love, choose death and make friends with the necessity of dying. . . . We might argue that what is represented here are the three inevitable relations that a man has with a woman—the woman who bears him, the woman who is his mate, and the woman who destroys him; or that they are the three forces taken by the figure of the mother in the course of a man's life—the mother herself, the beloved one who is chosen after her pattern, and lastly the Mother Earth who receives him once more. But it is in vain that an old man yearns for the love of woman as he had it first from his mother; the third of the Fates alone, the silent Goddess of Death, will take him into her arms [p. 301].

Thus, Freud could find no wish for oceanic merger in himself. It would have presumed a fantasy of a peaceable acceptance of oblivion in the arms of death, and for him to have entertained such a fantasy seems to have meant giving in to the embrace of a mystifying, destructive mother-figure, the inexorable representative of an evil Fate. Against this, his preferred stance was to keep his intellect alert: to remain rational, even when thinking about the mysterious, the uncanny, the telepathic, was Freud's aim.

As I mentioned in my comments on the Freud-Rolland correspondence, the themes of death and religion are central and inseparably intertwined. When Freud felt challenged to rank religion along a developmental scale, he placed a monotheistic, paternally derived godhead at the top. And among these the godhead of the Jews he ranked highest: "The religion of Moses brought the Jews a far grander conception of God, or as we might put it more modestly, the conception of a grander God" (1939, p. 112). "The Moses religion was outdoing the strictness of the ATON religion" because of its prohibition against making an image of God:

> The compulsion to worship a God whom one cannot see, [A God who would] have neither a name nor a countenance . . . meant the

sensory perception was given second place to what may be called an abstract idea—a triumph of intellectuality over sensuality . . . an instinctual renunciation, with all its necessary psychological consequences [pp. 112–113].

An increase in thought was one of them. The omnipotence of thought went hand-in-hand with the develoment of speech: this resulted in such an extraordinary advancement of intellectual activities. The new realm of intellectuality was opened up, in which ideas, memories and inferences became decisive in contrast to the lower physical activity which had direct perceptions by the sense-organs as its content. This was unquestionably one of the most important stages on the path to hominization (p. 113).

Thus thought Freud in his latest work on the subject of religion, "Moses and Monotheism." What seemed to him most praiseworthy was an abstract monotheism that was rational, essentially masculine, and promotive of intellectuality. The closest representative of such a god-head was Yehova. Freud stood against anything that betokened a mystical, oceanic union with an indefinable universe.[4]

REFERENCES

Abraham, R. (1982), Freud's mother conflict and the formulation of the oedipal father. *Psychoanal. Rev.,* 69:441–453.

Blum, H. (1977), The prototype of preoedipal reconstruction. *J. Amer. Psychoanal. Assn.,* 25:757–785.

Fisher, D. (1976), Sigmund Freud and Romain Rolland: The terrestrial animal and his great oceanic friend. *American Imago,* 33:1–59.

Freud, S. (1900), The interpretation of dreams. *Standard Edition,* 4/5. London: Hogarth Press, 1953.

———— (1901), The psychopathology of everyday life. *Standard Edition,* 6:1–279. London: Hogarth Press, 1957.

———— (1910), Leonardo da Vinci and a memory of his childhood. *Standard Edition,* 11:63–137. London: Hogarth Press, 1957.

———— (1912–1913), Totem and taboo. *Standard Edition,* 13:1–161. London: Hogarth Press, 1955.

---

[4]Of course Freud's perspective on Judaism eschewed recognition that in fact a mystical side has always coexisted, covertly or overtly, with the rational aspects of the Jewish religion.

_____ (1913), The theme of the three caskets. *Standard Edition,* 12:291–301. London: Hogarth Press, 1958.

_____ (1924), The economic problem of masochism. *Standard Edition,* 19:159–170. London: Hogarth Press, 1961.

_____ (1927), The future of an illusion. *Standard Edition,* 21:5–56. London: Hogarth Press, 1961.

_____ (1930), Civilization and its discontents. *Standard Edition,* 21:64–145. London: Hogarth Press, 1961.

_____ (1931), Female sexuality. *Standard Edition,* 21:225–243. London: Hogarth Press, 1961.

_____ (1936), A disturbance of memory on the Acropolis. *Standard Edition,* 22:239–248. London: Hogarth Press, 1964.

_____ (1939), Moses and monotheism: Three essays. *Standard Edition,* 23:7–137. London: Hogarth Press, 1964.

_____ (1960a), *The Letters of Sigmund Freud,* ed. E. Freud. New York: Basic Books.

_____ (1960b), *Sigmund Freud Briefe 1873–1939.* Frankfurt a/m: S. Fisher Verlag.

Hamilton, J. (1976), Some comments about Freud's conceptualization of the death instinct. *Internat. Rev. Psychoanal.,* 3:151–163.

Harrison, (1965), A reconsideration of Freud's "A disturbance of memory on the Acropolis" in relation to identity disturbance. *J. Amer. Psychoanal. Assn.,* 14:518–527.

_____ (1974), On the maternal origins of awe. *The Psychoanalytic Study of the Child,* 30:181–195. New Haven, CT: Yale University Press.

_____ (1979), On Freud's view of the infant-mother relationship and of the oceanic feeling: Some subjective influences. *J. Amer. Psychoanal. Assn.,* 29:399–419.

Heiman, M. (1976), Psychoanalytic observations on the last painting and suicide of Vincent van Gogh. *Internat. J. Psycho-Anal.* 57:73.

Jones, E. (1957), *The Life and Work of Sigmund Freud,* Vol. 3. New York: Basic Books.

Kanzer, M. (1969), Sigmund and Alexander Freud on the Acropolis. *American Imago,* 26:324–353.

Klein, M. (1952), Some theoretical conclusions regarding the emotional life of the infant. In: *Developments in Psychoanalysis,* ed. M. Klein, P. Heimann, S. Isaacs, & J. Riviere. London: Hogarth Press.

Lewin, B. (1973), *Selected Writings of Bertram Lewin,* ed. J. Arlow. New York: Psychoanalytic Quarterly.

Mahler, M. (1966), Notes on the development of basic moods: The depressive affect. In: *Psychoanalysis—A General Psychology: Essays in Honor of Heinz Hartmann.* ed. R. Lowenstein, L. Newman, M. Schur, & A. Solnit. New York: International Universities Press, pp. 152–168.

_____ (1975), On the current status of the infantile neurosis. *J. Amer. Psychoanal. Assn.,* 23:327–333.

March, H. (1971), *Romain Rolland.* New York: Twayne.

Nagera, (1967), *Vincent van Gogh: A Psychological Study.* New York: International Universities Press.

Niederland, W. (1965), An analytic inquiry into the life and work of Heinrich Schliemann. In: *Drives, Affects, Behavior,* Vol. 2, ed: M. Schur. New York: International Universities Press, pp. 369–396.

Schur, M. (1972), *Freud: Living and Dying.* New York: International Universities Press.

Seiffert, O. (1957), *A Dictionary of Classical Antiquities.* New York: Meridian.

Shakespeare, W. (1623), *The Tragedie of Hamlet: Facsimile Edition.* New Haven, CT: Yale University Press, 1954.

Strachey, J. (1957), Editor's note to "Leonardo da Vinci and a memory of his childhood." *Standard Edition,* 11:57–60. London: Hogarth Press, 1957.

Thomas, D. (1962), *Collected Poems 1934–1952.* London: Dent.

16

Four Entered the Garden: Normative Religion Versus Illusion

Mortimer Ostow, M.D.

Four entered the garden, namely, Ben Azzai, and Ben Zoma, Aher and Rabbi Akiva. Rabbi Akiva said to them: When you arrive at the [place of the] stones of pure marble, don't say, Water, Water! Because it is said: He who speaks falsehood will not stand before my eyes [Psalms 101:7]. Ben Azzai looked and died. Scripture says about him: Blessed in the eyes of the Lord is the death of his righteous [Psalm 116:15]. Ben Zoma looked and was afflicted. Scripture says about him: If you have found honey, eat [only] your fill, because if you become surfeited, you will vomit [Proverbs 25:16]. Aher cut the shoots. Rabbi Akiva departed in peace.

This terse and intriguing story appears in Chapter II (page 14b) of a section of the Babylonian Talmud called Hagigah. The section deals primarily with the celebration of holidays in Temple worship.

Arrangement of the many subjects discussed in the Talmud follows no systematic rules. Often one section follows another on the basis of some common element that seems of only minor importance. The Talmud scholar may be satisfied to explain proximity on the basis of a common concern with specific subjects, but the psychoanalyst will necessarily wonder whether other shared concerns, ones not explicitly given, may be responsible for the placing together of sections dealing with what are really rather disparate subject matters.

At the level of explicitly given concerns, one may cite at least two reasons why this story is presented in Hagigah. The preceding chapter deals with the rules for visiting the Temple for worship on the occasion of the holidays. The story I have quoted from Chapter II tells of visits to another place, attractive but dangerous in a magical way. Perhaps the juxtaposition of the two subjects invites a comparison between the implications of visiting the two places.

Chapter I ends with the observation that in contrast to some laws, including some just discussed, that have little scriptural basis, others, including laws dealing with forbidden sexual relations, are based solidly on Scripture. Chapter II, in which we find our story, starts with a statement that the laws concerning forbidden sexual relations are not to be discoursed upon in public, and that cosmogony and mystical theory require even greater discretion. If our story is interpreted as dealing with mystical experience, it can be understood as a warning of the consequences of violating the implied injunction against personal involvement. We shall consider a third possibility later.

The same story, with minor modifications, is given in at least three other places in the Talmudic literature—the Palestinian (as distinguished from the Babylonian) Talmud, Ḥagigah 77b; Tosefta Ḥagigah 2:3-4; and Midrash Rabbah to Shir Hashirim (Song of Songs) 1:4. A comparision and contrast of these versions would take us too far afield while contributing nothing of interest to my principal thesis.

The four scholars mentioned in the story, all well-known contributors to rabbinic debate, flourished during the first few decades of the second century. The meaning of the story has occupied many competent scholars, and no consensus has been reached. Rowland (1982) interprets the story as ''a metaphorical description of the consequences resulting from the occupation of four teachers of the early second century in the study of the Scriptures,'' upon which layers of other meanings have been subsequently imposed (p. 339). Medieval Jewish commentators, Hai Gaon and Rashi for example, understood the story to refer to a vision of mystical ascent to heavenly structures where the *merkavah* or chariot (described in Ezekiel, Chapter 1) could be seen, and where one could visualize the seven heavenly palaces or *hekhaloth*. Gershom Scholem (1954), the great modern scholar of Jewish mysticism, sees the story as a warning of the dangers of ecstatic ascent to the hekhaloth. Gruenwald (1980) considers the story one of several mystical speculations regarding ecstatic experiences associated with the illusion of translation to heaven. Halperin (1980) treats the story as one of seven units that together make up what he terms the ''mystical collection.'' The latter conveys the message that ''involvement with esoteric matters, is dangerous and normally to be avoided'' (p. 104). The collection does not distinguish the various forms of mysticism.

If we wish to draw our own conclusions about the story's meaning, we shall have to take a closer look at the details. Who were the protagonists? Ben Azzai's name is not associated with any particular exploit or point of view. Some of the basic data of his life are obscured by paradox and uncertainty. First, although he taught that failure to observe the commandment to procreate is as grave a violation as shedding blood, he himself did not marry, offering as an explanation the fact that he loved the Torah too much. Second, although the story tells us that his death was caused by his entry into the garden, there is another tradition that holds he was slain in the Hadrianic persecutions. Third, although he was revered for both his scholarship and his piety, he was never ordained, so that his name is never preceded by the title Rabbi. In addition, we know that mystical powers were attributed to him (Song of Songs, Rabbah 1:10), and he argued that God showed the righteous their future glory before death, a belief typical of the mystical tradition (Bereshith Rabbah 62:2).

Ben Azzai's failure to marry in an age when marriage and procreation were religious desiderata suggests a disturbance in his sexuality, a disturbance that found some compensation in his mystical endeavors. Among his mystical interests some stand out especially, namely, his interest in the physical appearance of God and man. He argued that not even the immortal angels were permitted to see the divine glory, and that Genesis 5:1 was one of the greatest verses of Scripture: ''This is the record of Adam's line. When God created man, he made him in the likeness of God; male and female he created them.'' Apparently, because Ben Azzai died at an early age, his unexpected death was attributed to his involvement in mystical practice and thought.

In the case of Ben Zoma we encounter a different problem. The story as given says only that as a result of his looking into the garden he was ''afflicted'' (nifga). The affliction is generally understood as a euphemism for mental illness. Scholem (1960) calls attention to a variant of the story given in a Jewish gnostic text, Lesser Hekhaloth, that voices this tradition.

> Ben Azzai beheld the sixth palace and saw the ethereal splendor of the marble plates with which the palace was tessellated and his body could not bear it. He opened his mouth and asked them [apparently

the angels standing there]: 'What kind of waters are these?' Whereupon he died. Of him it is said: 'Precious in the sight of the Lord is the death of his saints.' Ben Zoma beheld the splendor of the marble plates and he took them for water and his body could bear it not to ask them, but his mind could not bear it, and he went out of his mind . . . . Rabbi Akiva ascended in peace and descended in peace [p. 15].

Like Ben Azzai, Ben Zoma never achieved ordination, though his scholarship was proverbial. Of his published comments, some imply a narcissistic orientation, though they explicitly profess reverence for God. Upon seeing a crowd on the Temple mount, he observed that he was fortunate that there were so many people laboring to provide him food and clothing. He taught that man should appreciate how much God does for him and that the world was created only to be of service to him who fears God and respects His commandments. One of his best known aphorisms emphasizes paradox.

> Who is a wise man? He that learns from all men . . . . Who is a mighty man? He that subdues his evil impulse . . . . Who is a rich man? He that is content with his portion . . . . Who is an honorable man? He that honors mankind . . . [Pirke Avoth, 4:1].

The story of the four who entered the garden is followed in Hagigah by the following:

> Our Rabbis taught: Once Rabbi Joshua Ben Hanania was standing on a step on the Temple; mount, and Ben Zoma saw him and did not stand up before him. So [Rabbi Joshua] said to him: Whence and whither, Ben Zoma? He replied: I was gazing between the upper and lower waters, and there is only a bare three fingers' [breadth] between them, for it is said: And the spirit of God hovered over the face of the waters—like a dove which hovers over her young without touching [them]. Thereupon Rabbi Joshua said to his disciples: Ben Zoma is still outside [15-a].

I think it not farfetched to infer, as Rabbi Joshua did, that Ben Zoma was psychotic. But an important question for us is, did he become psychotic, as the story would have it, *because* of his mystical activities, or did his tendency to seek disengagement from the world of reality induce him to attempt the mystical escape?

Aher, the name given to Elisha ben Avuya when he became an apostate, means something different, something other, and is intended to be pejorative. The meaning of the statement that "Aher cut the shoots" is no longer evident, and it is variously interpreted. The best scholarship today understands it as a metaphor for his having denied the basic principles of his religion.

Elisha ben Avuya was well known as a learned scholar, and his apostasy was bitterly resented by his former colleagues. The nature of the apostasy is no longer clear, and many suggestions have been made, including his possible defection to the Greek religion, to Gnosticism, to some other Middle Eastern religion, or to atheism. Louis Ginzberg suggests that he left the Pharisees to become a Sadducee (*The Jewish Encyclopedia*). The Hagigah text itself tells us that he sang Greek songs and secretly read heretical books. It also suggests that he became a dualist, as the Gnostics were. During his mystical ascent, the text reports, he interpreted what he encountered to mean that there might be two domains, a dualistic gnostic conception. It tells us also that he became bitter and resentful. Yet he had friends and supporters, one of whom was his distinguished pupil, Rabbi Meir. They sought to mitigate the general harshness toward him and to find virtue in his impressive scholarship.

The question for us is, did he become an apostate because he engaged in ecstatic mysticism, as the story suggests, or was mysticism attractive to him because he had rejected Pharisaic religion? Certainly nothing in the material that has come down to us excludes the latter possibility.

Rabbi Akiva is generally considered "probably the foremost scholar of his age, patriot and martyr, who exercised a decisive influence in the development of the halakhah" (*Encyclopaedia Judaica*). It is surprising to find him listed among the four who entered the garden, as mysticism plays no prominent role in his recorded activities or remarks. The Hagigah text tells us that during his ascent the angels tried to push him away, but God interceded, saying that Akiva was worthy of enjoying His glory. The text of the story tells us the Akiva departed in peace, and the subsequent discussion, that he ascended in peace and descended in peace, thus confirming the interpretation that the story alludes to the mystical ascent to heavenly realms. However, the text misleads us if it implies that no adverse consequences followed from his flirtation with mysticism. For it may well have led to his readiness to support Simon ben Kozeva, called Bar Kokhba (son of the star), as the Messiah who would liberate Israel from its oppressors. It was Bar Kokhba's revolt in

B.C. 132 that led to the catastrophic slaughter of Jews by Roman troops in the final defeat of 135. Akiva's colleagues did not follow his leadership in this venture. "Grass will grow on the cheeks and the Messiah will still not have come." This comment is attributed to Rabbi Johanan ben Tortha (Lamentations Rabbah II, 2, 4). It is interesting that none of the references to Akiva in the literature of that time takes him to task for his misguided messianism.

What do we learn from the story of the four who entered the garden? It seems evident that the narrator or redactor is telling us that engaging in gnostic, mystical exercises poses danger for the individual: losing one's faith in one case; losing one's mind in a second; and losing one's life in a third. Presumably it was observed that among the adepts of gnostic practice a relatively large number of disturbed or deviant individuals were to be found, and it was inferred that the deviance followed from the mystical practice. We can question this inference, of course, and it is not unlikely that involvement in mystical practice simply gave expression to an already present tendency to deviate. Ben Zoma's neglect of a normal gesture of respect, rising when addressed by one's teacher, and his rumination about the approximation of the upper and lower waters were interpreted by some as the consequence of immersion in cosmogonic speculation. But Rabbi Joshua was probably correct when he said that Ben Zoma was "still outside," that is, psychotic. Involvement in mysticism in the case of Elisha ben Avuya was only one of a number of excursions into heterodoxy, irreligion, and alien cultures and activities. In addition to Greek culture and foreign literature, he showed considerable familiarity with wine, horses, and architecture.

The fantasy of flight through the heavens to a place of comfort and protection occurs not only in gnostic theosophy, but also as the recovery component in apocalyptic fantasies and in the dreams of patients in treatment. Such fantasies and dreams occur especially frequently among psychotic patients, borderline patients, and depressed patients. The classical literary apocalypses have frequently included accounts of celestial journeys, but they are intended to amplify the revelation rather than to repair the apocalyptic damage.

Clinical evidence has led me to believe (Ostow, 1986) that the gnostic journey represents a translation to comfort in physical intimacy with the mother, or with both parents, that is, a return to the inside of the mother's body, to a seat on her lap, to comfort in parental arms, or between the parents in bed. The vehicle itself may signify the proverbial claustrum, as does the chamber that the mystic seeks. In our story it is the garden that signifies the *hekhal* or chamber, the goal of the adept in the *hekhaloth* literature, and it symbolizes the chambers associated with the mother's body. Here are two dreams reported from the same night by a woman who was troubled by her destructive fantasies and chronic, though fairly well controlled anger.

> I was in the woods. A man at the edge was drawing pictures. I was buying toys for a child. I was there more than a day. The woods became wet, swampy, rainy, warm, and dark. It looked so beautiful in the rain, like a jungle. The tree twisted. There were vines and high bushes. One tree started to reach out like an umbrella, down to the bushes which clung to the tree. It was very beautiful. There were many greens. It was so rich. The water rises halfway up the trunk of the tree. After seven days I left the garden. I felt very inspired by its beauty. I was very sad for the lonely man standing outside the garden. He was a lonely bum. I had to go back to my children.

> Mother showed me her vagina. She wanted me to make love to her. I said, "No. It's not right." She said, "Come on." I was repelled by it. It was disgusting. The pudenda, the wetness. It was a long rectangle, not sharp at the end, grayish, darkish, and hairy.

In her associations to the second dream, she told me that as a child she was unhappy about sleeping with her mother, and that her mother had indeed often exposed her pubes to the child.

I would infer then, that the gnostic thought and practice that prevailed in Palestine during the two centuries before, and the first several centuries of the Common Era, attracted individuals who found themselves uncomfortable in the world of reality, and who harbored an unconscious desire to leave it for an illusory haven. Among them I would expect to find psychotics, depressives, and borderlines, as well as those whose external reality was too painful to bear. The various cults and religions that flourished throughout the Middle East at that time attracted such individuals and tempted them to turn their backs on the reality of their own tradition in order to find comfort in the proffered illusions. It is hardly surprising, then, that when these individuals gave evidence of clinical decline the blame was placed on the mystical practice in cart-before-the-horse fashion.

The reader will have observed that not only was the ascent to the garden thought to pose a threat to the mystic; but danger lurked too in the fantasy of the journey. The story of the four who went into the garden includes the warning of Akiva, and the related story adduced by Scholem from the hekhaloth literature describes the danger involved in mistaking the shimmering luminescence of the marble stones for water. Why was that dangerous? Perhaps failure to recognize the heavenly luminescence for what it is, instead interpreting the visual experience as that of shining waters, means that the celestial traveler has not entered completely into the illusion, has not left behind normal reality testing and the categories of logic, as the gnostic journey requires. But there is yet another danger, namely, the opposition of the heavenly host. I have mentioned that Hagigah has it that when Akiva ascended to the divine *hekhal* the angels attempted to eject him, and that he was saved only by divine intervention. Hostile celestial forces, endangering the human traveler, are reported in the gnostic religions, and in their Jewish counterparts as well. But if the purpose of cultivating the illusion is to achieve peace of mind, why are these intrusive elements permitted to spoil it? One could as easily construct an illusion in which the traveler achieves his goal unhindered.

For the solution to this problem we can turn again to clinical experience. When the depressed patient dreams of finding some relief from danger, the achievement of that relief will always be precluded by some interfering influence—an intruder, an unfavorable change of environment, an insuperable obstacle. It is only when the patient is about to recover from depression, or is recovering, that he succeeds in finding comfort. The celestial antagonists encountered in gnostic fantasies play the part of these interfering agents in such dreams. They symbolize the intrapsychic, self-defeating elements that will not be overcome unless the individual is ready to accept salvation. In gnostic theosophy, salvation is to be achieved by gnosis, special esoteric knowledge. It is a self-fulfilling system. If the traveler succeeds in reaching his goal, he did so because his gnosis was adequate; if he does not, it was inadequate. In psychoanalytic practice, "salvation" is to be achieved by special knowledge called insight. The analyst plays the role of the apocalyptic seer who provides the revelation. In the first of the two dreams presented above, "the man at the edge" of the woods "drawing pictures," represents the psychoanalyst who, taking notes, was not appreciated as having helped in the patient's reunion with her mother, and is himself ineligible for admission to the garden. This figure also represents her father, who on occasion intruded himself between the patient and her mother, though in the dream he does not. In fact, then, two kinds of danger are said to threaten the gnostic mystic. First, during the ascent he may be not only deterred but actually destroyed by the heavenly host. Second, as human observers attest, individuals attempting the ascent are in danger of succumbing to a personal catastrophe.

But there is yet a third danger, one mentioned neither in gnostic theosophy nor in the rabbinic response to it. This danger is exemplified in the case of Rabbi Akiva, the hero of the story and of his age. Akiva is not known to have been a Jewish gnostic. I am not aware of a report anywhere in the literature of his involvement in such activity. However, late in life, perhaps in his eighties or nineties, he recognized Simon ben Kozeva as the Messiah and thereby lent his sanction to a catastrophic rebellion against Rome. Messianism must be recognized as a component of the apocalyptic vision. It would seem that Akiva's messianism was not caused by his gnostic experience, but rather that both followed from a readiness to resort to illusion when circumstances justified it. Louis Finkelstein (1936), in his biography of Akiva, describes the incident as follows:

> Akiba himself did not long resist the contagion of messianism. When he saw Roman legions yield to untrained Judean youths, new hope blossomed in his heart. 'Yet once, it will be a little while,' he quoted from Haggai [2:6], and I will shake the heavens and the earth, and the sea, and the dry land.' He went so far as to encourage the popular delusion concerning the miraculous role to be played by the new leader and applied to him the verse [Num. 24:17], 'the star hath trodden forth out of Jacob.' Once he even said outright, 'This is the messianic king.'
>
> The dismal response of one of his friends, 'Akiba, grass will grow out of your jaw and the Messiah will not yet have come!' shows that some of the sages were still sane enough to realize the hopeless inequality of the struggle [p. 269].

The third danger, then, is a danger not to the individual but to the community. When individual suffering is brought on by external circumstances so that a large part of the community suffers, even those whose individual disposition does not favor apocalyptic thinking are attracted by it when they encounter it circulating in society, especially when it is sponsored by a charismatic leader. Since most militant apocalyptic thought arises ultimately from self-destructive impulses, millenarian movements almost always end in the defeat of the community, whether in the case of Bar Kokhba, Nazism, or Jonestown. The most serious danger that arises from indulgence in any of the forms of apocalyptic engagement, whether gnostic, mystic, millenarian, messianic, or utopian, is the possibility that an entire community will be seduced by it and be destroyed. It was in the aftermath of the Bar Kokhba revolt and its catastrophic defeat that some rabbis denounced active military resistance to the dominant empires, and counseled passive accommodation.

> Rabbi Jose son of Rabbi Hanina . . . . said: 'What was the purpose of those three adjurations? One, that Israel shall not go up [altogether as if surrounded] by a wall; the second, that whereby the Holy One, blessed be He, adjured Israel that they shall not rebel against the nations of the world; and the third is that whereby the Holy One, blessed be He, adjured the idolaters that they shall not oppress Israel too much' [Kethuboth 111a].

> Rabbi Jose ben Hanina said: 'These are two adjurations, one addressed to Israel and one to the other nations. God adjured Israel not to rebel against the yoke of the governments, and he adjured the governments not to make their yoke too heavy on Israel, for by making this yoke too heavy on Israel they would cause the end to come before it was due. . . .'

> Rabbi Helbo said: 'Four adjurations are mentioned here. God adjured Israel that they should not rebel against the governments, that they should not seek to hasten the end, that they should not reveal their mysteries to the other nations, and they should not attempt to go up from the Diaspora by force [Song of Songs Rabbah II, 7, 1].

There follows a discussion of four generations that "tried to hasten the end," that is, force the coming of the Messiah, and one of the four is listed as that of Ben Kozeva.

> What did they do? They assembled and went forth to battle, and many of them were slain. Why was this? Because they did not believe in the Lord and did not trust in His salvation, but anticipated the end and transgressed the adjuration [Song of Songs Rabbah, II, 7, 1].

It was the strategy of the reed rather than of the cedar that these scholars promoted, the strategy that characterized Jewish resistance to oppression for seventeen hundred years, and that served reasonably well until the Nazi apocalypse.

The apocalyptic pattern attracts and seduces. By promising salvation following destruction, it offers hope in place of despair. How much of the pattern is constitutionally given and how much learned is not evident. One can easily imagine an inherent tendency to reject, detach, and kill, that of itself would generate both anxiety and an automatic recovery response that gives expression to a conscious hope and expectation of rebirth. The sequence of death and rebirth is displayed fairly consistently in response to major shifts in psychic energies. A sharp increase in psychic energy generates the classic *Weltuntergang* fantasy of incipient schizophrenia, which is then followed by delusional rebirth. A decrease in psychic energy generates fantasies and dreams of destruction, but here rebirth usually fails. The stereotypy of apocalyptic fantasies—the regular inclusion of journeys, vehicles, seers, saviors and antagonists—may be taken as evidence for a constitutional basis for the pattern, but it may also be argued that this stereotypy simply reflects the constants of early infant experience. In any case, the promise of redemption after suffering invites commitment to the illusion.

The tenacity of the apocalyptic vision is remarkable. Its derivatives —mysticism, millenarianism, utopianism, gnosticism, messianism— survive underground for long periods of time, like an infection that has been suppressed but not eradicated, only to spring to life and flourish again when circumstances are propitious. The recent eruption of neo-Nazi *apocalyptic* groups in farm regions of the United States well exemplifies this tendency.

Given the ubiquity and tenacity of these illusions, and the usually disastrous consequences of subscribing to them, at least one deterrent to involvement in the apocalyptic program, or to acting upon it, must be at work if universal destruction is not to ensue. On the individual level, the only one I can see is the function of reality testing and the sense of reality it confers or withholds. That function, however, is easily overridden in most of us at the level of inference, but in psychotics even at the level of perception. The apocalyptic sequence begins with the abrogation of reality testing and a rejection of the real world, a rejection that permits the rest of the sequence to unfold.

Reality testing can be preempted by the group. What the group believes is real—in politics, in culture, and especially in religion. Since groups readily come to grief when they engage in apocalyptic behavior, it becomes necessary for them, for their own survival, to discourage it. The problem is that the apocalyptic claims that his revelation supersedes current group beliefs; he becomes a law unto himself. That is why organized religion fears mystics and condemns them as antinomian. The usual response of organized religion to mystical movements is to co-opt them, creating organizational forms whereby the deviation can be controlled. But if organized religion will not co-opt mysticism, for whatever reason (e.g., fear of being contaminated or diluted), it can nevertheless oppose it openly.

That is what we see in the story of the four who entered the garden, and in fact in the whole of Chapter II of Hagigah. The story is placed there to warn the community that mystical exercises and the induction of trances or states of ecstasy, though often presented as forms of religious experience, are disapproved as dangerous. Note that they are not denounced as antinomian, though the story of Elisha ben Avuya implies that they invite antinomianism. The reason for the warning is that a number of fairly distinguished rabbis and scholars had become involved in mystical practices, and had very carefully dissociated themselves from pagan and Christian gnostics by adhering closely to rabbinic law and values. By excluding anything explicitly antinomian in their teachings, the rabbinic practitioners of throne, chariot, and hekhalot mysticism were able to appeal to a broader segment of the community. The injunctions to avoid militance that were issued after the failure of the Bar Kokhba revolt were intended to deter any further messianic adventures.

Messianism posed a serious problem for the rabbis of that era. The Messiah was anticipated and eagerly awaited by almost all. But since he had not come, there had to be an explanation. A discussion of the problem is to be found in Babylonian Talmud Sanhedrin 97b. There Rabbi Samuel bar Nahmani, in the name of Rabbi Jonathan, curses those who "calculate the end," that is, those who would anticipate the Messiah's advent at a specific time. His reason is that if the Messiah does not come when anticipated, people will lose faith.

Maimonides, the great scholar and physician of medieval Jewry, discussed the advent of the Messiah as an event to be expected, but he saw the messianic world as one free of mystical elements. "Let no one think that in the days of the Messiah any of the laws of nature will be set aside, or any innovation introduced into creation," he wrote; "The world will follow its normal course'' (p. 240). ''Do not think that the King Messiah will have to perform signs and wonders (i.e. miracles), bring anything new into being, revive the dead, or do similar things. It is not so'' (p. 239). Maimonides is here promoting a tempered messianism, one divorced as much as possible from its apocalyptic matrix. Such a view, tending to preserve the optimism of messianism while discouraging messianic activism, may prevail for limited periods of time, but the very concept of messianism would seem to invite activism.

Regarding the role of Rabbi Akiva, Maimonides takes the position that he

> was a great sage, a teacher of Mishnah, yet he was also armor bearer of Ben Kozba. He affirmed that the latter was King Messiah; he and all the wise men of his generation shared this belief until Ben Kozba was slain in (his) iniquity, when it became known that he was not (the Messiah). Yet the rabbis had not asked him for a sign or token. The general principle is: this Law of ours with its statutes and ordinances [is not subject of change]. It is forever and all eternity; it is not to be added to or taken away from. [Whoever adds ought to it, or takes away ought from it, or misinterprets it, and strips the commandments of their literal sense is an impostor, a wicked man, and a heretic.][1] [p. 239].

Here Maimonides is clearly opposing messianism while trying to show respect for the messianic allusions of the Bible and the messianic aspirations prevalent among the people.

I would like to advance the hypothesis that one of the major functions of organized religion is to discourage individual mystical speculation and, more important, to contain apocalyptic and millenarian campaigns at the collective level. Freud spoke of religion as an illusion, but he failed to apprehend that organized religion, by offering an illusion sponsored and controlled by the collectivity, tries to discourage irresponsible and self-defeating mysticism, even though the latter might cloak itself in the terminological trappings of traditional religion. The devastating millenarian movements in history, including for example the Nazi apocalypse, have always rejected the discipline and restraints of organized religion, on their own authority overriding these restraints. Despite the traditional anti-Semitism of most of the organized European

---

[1]The material in brackets appears in a variant manuscript.

churches from the time of the Crusades right through the Holocaust, they attempted much more often than might have been expected, to contain the fury of apocalyptic mobs who were attacking Jews. And this, I submit, is the lesson we can learn from the story of the four who entered the garden.

REFERENCES

Ancient Texts

Hagigah. *The Babylonian Talmud,* Hebrew-English edition, trans. I. Abraham; ed. I. Epstein, London: Soncino, 1984.

Kethuboth. *The Babylonian Talmud,* Hebrew-English edition, trans. S. Daiches & I. W. Slotki; ed. I. Epstein. London: Soncino, 1971.

Lamentations Rabbah. In: *The Midrash Rabbah,* Vol. IV, trans. & ed. H. Freedman & M. Simon. London: Soncino, 1977.

Maimonides. *The Book of Judges,* trans. A. M. Hershman. New Haven, CT: Yale University Press, 1949.

Pirke Avoth. In: *The Living Talmud, the Wisdom of the Fathers, and Its Classical Commentaries,* trans. & ed. J. Goldin. New York: Heritage, 1955.

Sanhedrin. *The Babylonian Talmud,* Hebrew-English edition, trans. J. Shachter & H. Freedman; ed. I. Epstein, London: Soncino, 1969.

Genesis, Rubbah. In: *The Midrash Rabbah,* Vol I, trans. H. Freedman & M. Simon. London: Soncino, 1977.

Song of Songs Rabbah. In: *The Midrash Rabbah,* Vol. IV, trans. H. Freedman & M. Simon. London: Soncino, 1977.

Modern Texts

Encyclopaedia Judaica (1972), ed. C. Roth & G. Wigoder. Jerusalem: Keter.

Finkelstein, L. (1936), *Akiba: Scholar, Saint and Martyr.* New York: Atheneum and the Jewish Publication Society.

Gruenwald, I. (1980), *Apocalyptic and Merkavah Mysticism.* Leiden: E. J. Brill.

Halperin, D. (1980), *The Merkavah in Rabbinic Literature.* New Haven, CT: American Oriental Society.

——— *The Jewish Encyclopedia,* (1906), ed. I. Singer. New York: Funk & Wagnalls.

Ostow, M. (1986), Archetypes of apocalypse in dreams and fantasies and in religious scripture. *Israel J. Psychiat. & Related Disciplines,* 23:107–122.

Rowland, C. (1982), *The Open Heaven: A Study of Apocalyptic in Judaism and Early Christianity.* New York: Crossroads.

Scholem, G. (1954), *Major Trends in Jewish Mysticism*. New York: Schocken.
_____ (1960), *Jewish Gnosticism, Merkabah Mysticism, and Talmudic Tradition*. New York: Jewish Theological Seminary.

Part VI

REALITY: SEXUALITY, IDENTITY AND BIOLOGY

17

The Continuum of Reality, Inner and Outer

Robert S. Wallerstein, M.D.

The guiding thread of Jacob Arlow's impressive life's work, his most significant contribution to the theory and practice of psychoanalysis, has been his elaboration of the abiding importance of unconscious fantasy formations in individual human mentation and behavior, as well as in such social creations as myth, religion and culture. The choice of the title of this volume as the thematic expression in his honor, *Fantasy, Myth, and Reality,* bespeaks a widespread consensus within psychoanalysis on that view of his work.

Of all of Arlow's many publications that bear, either centrally or peripherally, on this issue, the most comprehensive is his oft-quoted 1969 paper, "Fantasy, Memory and Reality Testing." Arlow began that article on a deceptively traditional note:

> Reality testing, one of the most important of the functions of the ego, is relatively easy to define but quite difficult to comprehend. . . . As used in psychoanalysis, reality testing refers to the ability to distinguish between perceptions and ideas. . . .As defined in analytic terms, emphasis is placed upon the differentiation of what is external—of the object world—from representations of what is internal—of the self or of mental life [p. 28].

A little further on, he asserted in the same vein that reality testing "according to Hartmann. . .consists of the ability to discern subjective and objective elements in our judgment of reality. Learning to do this is an unending process. Essentially this is the *principal task* which the analyst poses to his patient" (p. 29; italics mine). From that beginning however,

Arlow went on to develop very persuasively his own individual understanding of the concept of "psychic reality" as an intimate intermingling of external perceptions (outer reality) and unconscious fantasy (inner
reality). Later, in the context of my own overall argument, I will present Arlow's sense of the characteristics of the process of that mode of
construction of our psychic reality.

My own concern with these issues started from the opposite side,
from my efforts to understand the nature of our experience of external
reality as ultimately also a "constructed" reality, and in that sense directly
comparable to the intrapsychic instances (id, ego, and superego) in its
role in mental life, a viewpoint developed in my 1972 Presidential Address to the American Psychoanalytic Association (Wallerstein, 1973).
In this chapter my intention will be to bring these two perspectives—
Arlow's, on the attributes and meanings of inner (psychic) reality, and
my own, on the attributes and meanings of outer (material) reality—
into a common framework that emphasizes their likeness and continuity rather than (as is more traditional) their distinctness and dichotomiza-
tion. The consequence of the latter emphasis is that the "principal task"
posed patients by their analysts is perceived to be the delineaton of this
distinction, i.e., the task of reality testing.

This has indeed been the traditional psychoanalytic perspective on
the problem of reality (as opposed to fantasy) and on the achievement
of the adequately adaptive testing of that reality as a hallmark of the
satisfactorily accomplished analysis. Freud's vision in creating psychoanalysis as a psychology focused on the elucidation of *conflict* in human
affairs—epitomized in Ernst Kris's well-known aphoristic statement that
psychoanalysis is "nothing but" human behavior considered from the
point of view of conflict—was throughout Freud's life expressed in the
various contrapuntal dualisms he successively advanced in his descriptive and explanatory efforts: conscious/unconscious, sexual instincts/ego
instincts, primary process/secondary process, love/hate, masculine/
feminine, active/passive, dependent/independent, id/ego, drive/defense,
oedipal/preoedipal, libidinal drives/aggressive drives, life instinct/death
instinct—these are among the most well known. Among these many
dualisms, the conceptual interplay between psychic reality and material
reality has always had comparable place in fashioning a psychoanalytic
understanding of our inner and outer worlds.

Yet this preference for psychological explanation in terms of polarities
and dichotomies is not a given of nature. Blos (1985) for example, in

his recent *Son and Father,* advances an alternative framework for conceptualizing human interaction and conflict (and not the only alternative framework):

> I mentioned earlier in this essay that the dyadic stage operates in polarities which are reflected in the split into "good" and "bad" objects. The cognitive level of thought, when restricted to the exclusive use of polarities, is of a primitive nature and of limited efficiency because complexities are dealt with in terms of simple dichotomies. The advance to the triadic stage lifts the thought process onto a higher level or, to be exact, it establishes the precondition for this advance. We might say that the triadic complexity of object relations with the implicit rise onto a higher level of conflict formation produces an infinite multitude of possible constellations within its realm; of these, a selected few are retained and stabilized in the process of transcending the triadic stage. The oedipal complexity of interpersonal experiences is reflected on the cognitive level in the emergence of the dialectic process. We recognize in this process the triadic nature of thesis, antithesis, and synthesis. The complexity of this thought process permits, by choice or by fortuity, an endless sequence of possible cognitive combinations or permutations, each pressing forward toward a resolution on a higher level of thought [p. 53].

Nor did Freud always see the distinction between memory and fantasy in the usual clear-cut dichotomous terms. In his early paper on screen memories (Freud, 1899) he asserted that childhood memories are never just simple repetitions of veridically intact earlier experiences.

> In the majority of significant and in other respects unimpeachable childhood scenes the subject sees himself in the recollection as a child, with the knowledge that this child is himself; he sees this child, however, as an observer from outside the scene would see him . . . .Now it is evident that such a picture cannot be an exact repetition of the impression that was originally received. For the subject was then in the middle of the situation and was attending not to himself but to the external world. Whenever in a memory the subject himself appears in this way as an object among other objects this contrast between the acting and the recollecting ego may be taken as evidence that the original impression has been *worked over* [p. 321, italics mine].

It is this diminution of the sharp distinction between memory and fantasy that led Freud to his summation in the final paragraph of the same paper:

> It may indeed be questioned whether we have any memories at all *from* our childhood: memories *relating* to our childhood may be all that we possess. Our childhood memories show us our earliest years not as they were but as they appeared at the later periods when the memories were aroused. In these periods of arousal, the childhood memories did not, as people are accustomed to say, *emerge;* they are *formed* at that time. And a number of motives, with no concern for historical accuracy, had a part in forming them, as well as in the selection of the memories themselves [p. 322].

In other words, the screen memory—or any memory— represents a variable mingling of prior perception with wishful (and/or fearful) emendation.

These early trenchant insights notwithstanding, Freud over most of his scientific lifetime adhered to the dichotomized thinking, psychic reality–factual reality—that expressed his characteristic propensity to see human nature as opposed dualisms in interaction. He devoted little explicit concern to defining what he meant by reality or to distinguishing between outer (or factual) reality and inner (or psychic) reality. Characteristically, he simply took the distinct nature of each to be essentially self-evident. In much the same sense that Hartmann (1960) said of Freud, in relation to moral values, that "he used to quote F. T. Vischer's 'What is moral is self-evident'" (p. 14). This tendency to invoke self-evidence would be especially pronounced in a psychology that tried systematically and self-consciously to exclude problems of philosophy and epistemology from its purview.

Freud's statements in this arena were primarily efforts at semantic clarification which I have reviewed in detail elsewhere (Wallerstein, 1983, p. 132). Briefly, he started with the distinction in the *Project* (Freud, 1895) between "thought-reality" and "external reality" (p. 373), altered the former phrase to "psychical reality" in "The Interpretation of Dreams" (Freud, 1900, p. 613), then counterposed this newer term to "factual reality" in "Totem and Taboo" (Freud, 1913, p. 159), and then finally, in the 1919 edition of "The Interpretation of Dreams" changed the latter term to "material reality" (editor's footnote, p. 620). The final form of the sentence at issue became, "If we look at unconscious wishes reduced to their most fundamental and truest shape, we shall have to conclude, no doubt, that *psychical* reality is a particular form of existence not to be confused with *material* reality" (p. 620).[1] Note Freud's unequivocal "not to be confused with"; this same clear distinctness is underlined in Freud's sentence on fantasy in the Introductory Lectures (1916–1917) "The phantasies possess *psychical* as contrasted with *material* reality, and we gradually learn to understand that *in the world of the neuroses it is psychical reality which is the decisive kind*" (p. 368).

It was Hartmann, who so shared Freud's penchant for dualistic thinking, who in a 1956 paper, "Notes on the Reality Principle," both reemphasized the values in counterposing inner and outer reality and carried the dichotomizing to a further extreme in his conception of *two kinds* of external reality.[2] I have reviewed Hartmann's expansions of Freud's conception of reality in detail elsewhere (Wallerstein, 1983, pp. 134–135). Basically, Hartmann divided outer reality into two entities, the preexistent, invariant physical environment, the reality that is validated objectively by the methods of science, and the man-made[3] and man-thought sociocultural reality, that is, the socialized or conventional knowledge of reality that is intersubjectively accepted. Here Hartmann specified that conforming to the demands of this social reality can mean conforming to a shared distortion of reality conveyed by parents, love objects, and the wider culture.

To quote from my own very condensed statement of Hartmann's views (Wallerstein, 1973),

---

[1] For the further vicissitudes of these terms throughout Freud's subsequent writings, see Strachey's footnote on p. 373 of the *Project* (1895).

[2] This paper of Hartmann's is replete with such dualisms—in addition, he describes two kinds of meaning to *reality-testing* (the distinction between inner ideas and outer perceptions; and also, the ability to discern the subjective and objective elements in our judgment of outer reality); two kinds of meaning to *reality principle* (taking adaptive account of the 'real' features of an object or situation; and also, more narrowly, the tendency to wrest our activities from the dominion of the pleasure-principle); and two kinds of meaning to *reality syntonic* (thought corrosponding to reality, and also thought that leads to successful mastery and acting in regard to reality). Hartmann in his careful exegesis felt that he discerned each of these fine honed distinctions in Freud's corpus, though not in the explicit form that he (Hartmann) gave them. Hartmann also was aware enough that often these careful distinctions are blurred or fudged—for example, in relation to reality testing, "that pleasure premia are in store for the child who conforms to the demands of reality and of socialization; but they are equally available if this conforming means the acceptance by the child of erroneous and biased views which the parents hold of reality" (p. 43).

[3] The word "man" used this way in this essay means human or mankind.

He talks vigorously (but always in contrasting terms) of discerning 'subjective and objective elements in our judgment on reality' (p. 256); of 'socialized reality' validated by 'intersubjective acceptance' (p. 258) and of 'objective reality' validated by the normal criteria of science; of reality within science as against reality outside of science, which latter is 'personal reality,' 'our world,' or the 'world of more immediate experience' (p. 260). He quotes, apparently approvingly, Buytendijk's statement, 'one's world . . . is no system of objective correlations, but a system of meanings and hence of values' (p. 264), but then also seems to say that the world of immediate experience is only a way-station on the way to the world of science, "There is no doubt that the evolving of this world [of immediate experience], though it falls short of exactly reproducing or corresponding to 'objective reality,' is helpful toward developing our relations to it" (p. 263). In all, his position on the world lived in is one of two realities or two kinds of reality in which "The scientific conception of knowledge of reality will never entirely eliminate the other conception except in the case of the scientist, and even here, only as long as he does scientific work. It is not to be forgotten that much of our 'knowledge' of reality is of the socially accepted kind, with most of our actions based on it" (p. 258). In all, an inclusive struggle with a nonresolution through recourse to the dualisms in thinking that always served Hartmann (and Freud) so well in theory construction within psychoanalysis [p. 16].

And of course, as we have seen, this is exactly the kind of nonresolution that beset Freud's conceptualization in the wider arena of the distinction between inner (psychic) and outer (material) reality, starting with his paper on screen memories and taking a different turn in the balance of his writing. Hartmann also came in the same paper to deal with the issues of inner reality (and its testing) as separate from but also related to outer reality and its proper testing, which was his main focus. Toward the very end of his paper he wrote,

About the distorted pictures of inner reality, about typical and individual self-deception, we have learned more from analytic work than from any other source. To account for it, it seems reasonable to speak of a testing of the within, in addition to the testing of the without—that is, to distinguish inner reality testing from outer reality testing. Impediments of inner reality testing are so common that, as to certain functions and contents of the mind, we do not expect much objectivity even in a normal person, except in the course of the psychoanalytic process. These impediments will, of course, sometimes also alter the picture of outer reality, as a consequence of repression, for instance. But in the neurotic, interference with the testing of inner reality is in the foreground. The basic properties of outer reality testing, we know, break down in psychosis only [p. 266-267].

And it was Frosch (1966), in a paper on the concept of reality constancy, who carried Hartmann's (and Freud's) kind of dichotomizing to its logical extension, in amplifying even further Hartmann's conception of the two kinds of external reality, the so-called material (or objectively scientific) reality, and the nonmaterial (or conventionally—and intersubjectively—subjective) reality. Frosch added the counterpart *dual internal reality*, also divided into the "material" and the nonmaterial or "psychic":

> Internal reality. . . includes on the psychic side memories, fantasies, impulses, desires, affects, thoughts, the body image, identity, self-representation, etc. Furthermore, it includes the correlate of material objective reality, namely, material internal reality, such as various somatic phenomena which may be derived from explicable or inexplicable processes. These may include somatic sensations of various sorts—pain, heart rhythm, etc. [p. 352-353].

Clearly, this represents the logical extension and amplification of Hartmann's dualistic and dichotomizing thinking.

It was Loewald who, even before Arlow, set the direction for the consideration of the set of issues I wish to propose: the heuristic and conceptual value of elucidating the likenesses and continuities of the realities, inner and outer, in which we live and to which we adaptively relate via our ego's equilibrating activities. Loewald's position, too, I have reviewed in detail (Wallerstein, 1983, p. 135-136). In his provocative paper, "Ego and Reality," Loewald (1951), quite radically conceptualized the object relationships with the parental figures (the father principle as an awesome and threatening power, representing via the oedipus complex and the castration threat the prototype of the demands of reality, and the mother principle as the tug toward maintenance of the primary unity with the environment) as the field of forces within whose vicissitudes the differentiation and *construction* of the child's developing sense of reality gradually takes place. The crux of Loewald's conception of this process is in this quotation:

> It is important to realize that when we speak of object and ego [outer and inner] at this [earliest] stage of development, these terms characterize the most primitive beginnings of the later structures thus designated. Ego, id and external reality become distinguishable in their most primitive, germinal stages. This state of affairs can be expressed either by saying that 'the ego detaches itself from the external world', or, more correctly: *the ego detaches from itself an outer world.* Originally the ego contains everything [p. 11; italics mine].

In this conception reality is developed two-sidedly, as a precipitate detached from the ego and projected "out there," from where it is then represented in its threatening aspects by the figure of the father interfering with the intimacy of the primordial mother-child dyad. Loewald, that is, conceptualized reality in terms of the constructed and projected precipitates of evolving object relationships. Quite aside from the degree of emphasis that we might ourselves wish to give to the several states of object relatedness in the young child during the course of development of the relatedness to reality, we do have here the (epi)genetic and maturational basis for a conception of reality—or of realities across the proposed continuum of inner and outer—as created and evolved and differentiated out of a more primordial, undifferentiated matrix in the same way that we think of ego and id differentiating out of such a matrix, in the mode already made familiar to us by, actually, Hartmann.

It is on the basis of thinking similar in its construction to this that Arlow could evolve his own interactional conception of the perception of reality. He set this main premise toward the beginning of his 1969 article:

> I hope to demonstrate that how reality is experienced depends for the most part on the *interaction* between the perceptions of the external world and the concomitant effect of unconscious fantasy activity . . . a continuous stream of fantasy thinking, which is a persistent concomitant of all mental activity and which exerts an unending influence on how reality is perceived and responded to [p. 29, italics mine].

The data of external perception are themselves declared to be experienced as an interaction, and

> are not experienced in isolation. They are experienced against the background of the individuals's past development and are checked

against earlier perceptions and the memory traces which they have left. Stimuli are selectively perceived in terms of the mental set operative in the individual at the time. The mental set is determined both consciously and unconsciously, consciously by the nature of the task before the individual, unconsciously by the cathectic level of the dominant unconscious fantasy system. . . . The most powerful influence distorting the image of the past and contributing to the misperception of the present is the intrusion of unconscious fantasy thinking. . . the stream of perceptual data from the external world which passes before the outer eye is paralleled by a stream of perceptual data from the inner world which passes before the inner eye [p. 30-32].

In describing this ubiquitous intrusion of daydreaming into conscious experience and activity, Arlow cites experiences from the daily lives of patients demonstrating that "while the patients were alert and vigorously involved in reality oriented activity, their judgment of reality and their response to it was completely distorted by the intrusion of an unconscious fantasy. Actually, this kind of distortion is one of the essential features of the neurotic process and of the transference" (p. 33). It is "This constant intermingling of fantasy and perception [that] helps make it clear why memory is so unreliable, especially memories from childhood, because in childhood the process of intermingling perception and fantasy proceeds to a very high degree" (p. 37). And this process is brought to exquisite pitch in those nodal "memories" we designate screen memories: "we can understand screen memories as an exquisite example of the mingling of fantasy with perception and memory, the raw material for the construction of the screen memories originating from many periods of the individual's life and rearranged in keeping with the defensive needs of the ego" (p. 38). Here Arlow calls on Freud's early paper on screen memories (1899) to quote Freud's vision of that time (already quoted in their essay) that childhood memories do not "emerge" but are "formed" as they are recounted.

In fact, "What we think was real, or what we think really happened, is a combination or intermingling of fantasy with perception of reality . . . . what the child experiences is at the very moment of experience a complex intermingling of perception and fantasy. This complex intermingling is what 'really' happened as far as the individual is concerned" (p. 39). In summary, "there is . . . a reciprocal interplay between reality and fantasy, selective perception on one side, cathectic intensification

on the other'' (p. 41). This review has built to Arlow's central thesis—
what I regard as its creative reach, and also its limitation.

> External perception and internal fantasy were intermingled at the time
> of the experience and together they formed the reality which to the
> patient was the record of his past. . . . This is what I think is the *proper*
> *understanding of the concept 'psychic reality.'* It is not a fantasy that is taken
> for the real truth, for an actual event, but the 'real' recollection of a
> psychic event with its mixture of fact and fantasy . . . . Subsequent
> events and perceptions of reality are selectively organized into memory
> schema consonant with inner fantasy thinking (p. 43, italics mine).

In accord with this conception, ''The traumatic events of the past
become *part of fantasy thinking* and as such exert a never-ending dynamic
effect'' (p. 44, italics mine). And the individual takes as a task to ''scan
the data of perception of reality to discover reassuring evidence of the
validity of the solution which he arrived at in fantasy'' (p. 45).

Arlow ends his article with a visual model to illustrate this interaction between fantasy and reality. He compares this aspect of mental functioning to the effect that would be obtained if two motion picture projectors were to flash a continuous series of images simultaneously but
from opposite sides onto a translucent screen. By analogy, ''There are
two centers of perceptual input, introspection and extrospection, supplying data from the inner eye and data from the outer eye. It is the
function . . .of the ego, however, to integrate, correlate, judge, and discard
the competing data of perceptual experience. All of these factors influence
the final judgment as to what is real and what is unreal'' (p. 48).

All of this is what Arlow calls ''the connection between fantasy,
memory, and reality'' (p. 50)—as seen from a standpoint of concern with
the nature of the inner world, ''the proper understanding of the concept, *'psychic reality'*'' (p. 43). What Arlow has drawn back from,[4] and this
was my reference to the conceptual limitation of his approach, is the

---

[4]That Arlow does not extend his manner of thinking about inner (psychic) reality equally
comprehensively to our conceptions of outer (material) reality but rather feels that
psychoanalysis has no special contribution to make to our understandings of material
reality (and what he takes to be our consensual scientific Weltanschauung), he made
clear in a recent panel on psychic reality (1985) as follows: ''Implicit in . . . [the] definition of reality testing is the idea that reality, as we understand it, results from how the
mind registers, organizes, stores, and interprets the sensory impressions emanating from
the outside world, that is, outside of the individual, strictly speaking, outside his person

equally uncompromising extension of the same logic to our comprehension of the outer world—external or material reality. It has been from this opposite direction, of concern with the psychoanalytic understanding of outer reality, that I have sought to systematically develop the conception of the full comparability of our experience of the *external reality* to the *intrapsychic instances* (id, ego, and superego), as regards its role in mental life. This is the conceptualization I developed at length in a 1973 paper, "Psychoanalytic Perspectives on the Problem of Reality." To quote the central affirmation of that article:

> It is this way of conceptualizing [outer] reality, derived by Loewald within the fabric of psychoanalytic theory as a consequence of the ontogenetic developmental dynamic itself, that I wish to propose as the basis for the understanding, not only of our interpersonal reality (our 'socialized' or our 'social' reality in Hartmann's sense)—with which I think none would quarrel—but also as the basis for understanding the nature of even that other, that seeming polar opposite, which Hartmann calls the objective or the scientific reality. Because even natural science and its organizing postulates represents but a world view, guided and constrained by human-created methodological assumptions and consensually accepted values. Here I wish to call on the distinguished physical chemist and social philosopher, Michael Polanyi, who so cogently argued in the Lindsay Memorial Lecture of 1958 the role of what he called 'tacit knowledge,' or 'pre-articulate knowledge' or the

---

or body. Psychoanalysis thus offers no special metaphysical answer to the philosophical problems of ontology. As in the physical sciences, it is assumed that our mental apparatus responds to stimuli emanating from matter which is in motion and which exists independently of our apprehension of it" (p. 523).

And further on, "Thus, what informs our fundamental sense of reality is more than an appropriate interpretation of the origin of our sensory impressions. Inherent in the process is some appreciation of a reliable, reproducible, repetitive, seemingly unalterable set of relations among events in the physical world . . . . The degree of reliable, predictable orientation toward the external world of physical objects, the world we learn to designate as real, the world we subject to reality testing, does not apply to our relations with those other occupants of the physical world, that is, to people. People are infinitely more changeable, surprising, and unpredictable. We can apply reality testing to the physical attributes of people, but once we begin to apply the concept of reality to interpersonal relations and to the total social milieu, we introduce variables that are not easily tested, that elude simple, confirmable definition. Psychology, value judgment, tradition, and individual history change the situation entirely" (p. 524). My own differing position, to be spelled out in the next paragraphs, is that, in principle, we are dealing with the same situation in the world of physical reality, with our comprehensions and perceptions there also influenced by "psychology, value judgment, tradition, and individual history."

'personal coefficient of knowledge' as essential ingredients in the creation of that world view represented by natural science.

How this world view is manifest in the very structure of science was stated by William Earle in a review of Polanyi's work in the journal *Science* (Polanyi, 1959) as follows:

How then does the personal factor manifest itself in the very structure of science? Polanyi discovers it wherever there is an act of appraisal, choice, or accreditation. Each science operates within a conceptual framework which it regards as the 'most fruitful' for those facts which it 'wishes' to study because they are 'important,' and it thereby chooses to ignore other facts which are 'unimportant,' 'misleading,' and 'of no consequence.'" That is, when we look at the assumptions or postulational bases of the thought systems of the natural sciences, we are back here, too, ultimately in the realm of belief and value systems, and of meanings, i.e. of realities created by acts of perspective and of interpretation. This Polanyi stated directly as The Theory of Personal Knowledge offers an interpretation of meaning. It says that no meaningful knowledge [not even, that is, in the so-called hard sciences, the physical sciences] can be acquired, except by an *act of comprehension* which consists in merging our awareness of a set of particulars into our focal awareness of their joint significance (p. 44, italics added) That is, even the world of natural science is a man-created reality, a particular way of looking at and giving meaning to the facts of nature.

Implicit in all this is that there is not, then, one large and encompassing reality (or world of reality) that we deal with psychologically, the same and uniform for all, but rather many smaller, varyingly ovelapping and varyingly congruent partial realities, man-constructed realities, to which different men in turn declare varying and differential allegiances. Though clearly also man does not easily abandon the quest for a single overarching reality and for ultimate cosmological answers. Through most of recorded history, religious systems have in fact traditionally filled just that role; in more modern times the role has been accorded to or usurped by science, at least for the Western world [pp. 17-19].[5]

---

[5]I quote also from a relevant footnote from that same 1973 paper. "In fact, psychoanalysis itself, as a thought system and a belief system, has passed far beyond the creation and the genius of its founder to become part of the intellectual heritage of the educated world, and, as such, itself a species of reality or a vision of reality. Schafer, in an extremely

None of which is to deny our notions embedded in both common sense, and in the common presumptions of the sense of science, that there is a reality "out there" which we learn to find, which we learn to test by "refinding" (Freud, 1925, p. 237), and to which we adapt by biologically endowed mechanisms of preadaptedness. But it is to assert that our *experience* of that outer or material reality is neither invariant nor isomorphic—even in the case of the objective scientist engaged in scientific inquiry into the nature of the physical universe—but is always a creative construction of man, evolved through human development and effort, and bent by the human values, predilections, and needs that give it meaning. As Fred Weinstein (1982) has noted, "there are no immaculate perceptions of reality, no perceptions unmediated by memory and experience, and by the need to demonstrate loyalty to some group or principle" (p. 30).

It is just this kind of thinking about the nature of our experience of reality that was given conceptual warrant and was prefigured by Loewald's perspectives (1951) on the evolution of our conception of external reality (reality "out there") out of the interplay of outer experience anchored in internalized object relationships and inner (drive and fantasy powered) responsiveness. In my earlier discussion of Loewald's conceptions (Wallerstein, 1983), I inserted at a comparable point the parenthetical sentence, "Are we so sure any more . . . of the line of demarcation between inner and outer world, inner and outer reality, the place where indeed Freud began?" (p. 136). This was in response to the approach to the problem of reality from the perspective of psychoanalytic

---

illuminating article entitled "The Psychoanalytic Vision of Reality" (1970), an article directly exemplifying the major thesis of my presentation, takes his perspectives from the categories of literary and poetic criticism, and argues persuasively the way that the psychoanalytic vision can be seen from the viewpoint of each of the four component categories of the aesthetic vision, the comic, the romantic, the tragic, and the ironic— all of these clearly in part congruent and overlapping, in part antithetic and oppositional. One needs to refer to Schafer's own article for a detailed explication of which aspects of psychoanalytic thinking fit the requirements of each of these aesthetic categorizations. Here I want only to stress the underlying assumption in Schafer's presentation that each world view, each vision of man and of his relatedness to the world, is an intellectual construct of man's, and Schafer's conviction that the various aspects of psychoanalysis, both conceptual and technical, can be fruitfully considered from the viewpoint of their fit with the aesthetic categories that in their origins go back as far as Aristotle" (p. 19).

consideration of external reality, the starting point of my own inquires. And it is of course the exact counterpart of Arlow's conception of the creation of inner or psychic reality out of the interplay of external perception (of the real) and internal impinging and distorting fantasy—i.e., an approach to the problem of reality from the perspective of psychoanalytic consideration of internal reality.

These two paths of inquiry can now be brought together in the combined statement that there is no pure inner mental stream existing without its constant admixture of selectively fused external perceptions, nor is there—from the point of view of the experiencing human being—a pure outer reality, "out there," unchanging and the same for all; rather, there is a constructed outer reality, given meaning within a framework of man-created perspectives, values, and commitments. This conception I broached in a recent panel discussion (with Arlow among others) as follows:

> I am not arguing the epistemological or metaphysical status of the external world, 'out there,' on philosophical grounds. Rather, I *am* arguing that just as the inner world of mental representations as we experience them is regularly infiltrated by the selectively apprehended impingements from the events and happenings outside, and just as we recognize that inner world as ultimately an act of our construction or our creation out of these admixed stimuli from within and without, so too our knowledge of that so-called material world is always filtered through the guiding assumptions, formulations, and thought conventions we bring to it. Therefore, even the world *as science sees it* is also an act of our (human) mental construction and creation [p. 567-568].

I now propose to designate this understanding as the conception of a *continuum of reality* (inner and outer) as against our more traditional emphasis on the dichotomized distinction between inner and outer reality, not really altering—except in interpretive nuance, which *is* important— our central psychoanalytic task, conceptually and technically, the constant clarification of the inner and outer realms as they fashion our mental life through their interaction. To state this more fully, what I am proposing for the perspectival enlargement of our frame for the proper analytic dialogue is the surmounting of the counterpoint between the view from within (the world of psychic reality) and the view from without (the world of material reality), in favor of a conception of the interplay of multiple perspectives, multiple versions, each its own story, each its own admixture or fusion of drive-dictated fantasy interacting with appropriately selected environmental stimuli or vicissitudes—out of the well-balanced consideration of all of which will come that filled-out rewriting of one's autobiography that we call a completed analysis.

This kind of reframing of traditionally dualistic (and dichotomizing) thought conventions in psychoanalysis is not new to psychoanaltytic thinking. I will close with reference to a very familiar and very powerful example. Nothing seems more central to the evolution of Freud's metapsychology than his development of the structural model of id, ego, and superego, each a distinctive grouping of functions and attributes, out of whose varying interplay the psychic conflicts that are the hallmark of the psychoanalytic conception of mental life derive. Yet in a seminal reappraisal of the conception of the id, Max Schur (1966) took a clear stand in favor of a complexly *structured* id, a structure with adaptive and survival functions, and with certain autonomous apparatuses serving its development (as well as that of the ego). In the foreword to Schur's monograph, the editors state that, "It is out of such an approach to psychoanalytic concepts that there arises the concept of a *continuum* as essential to the understanding of all psychic phenomena" (p. 8, italics mine).

It is this same kind of thinking that informed Merton Gill's reappraisal (1963) of the system ego and the ego-id relationship. From the traditional position of the early differentiated allocation of the drives (the repressed) to the id and of the defenses (the repressing forces) to the ego, he moved to a reconceptualizatn of the hierarchical organization of mental life whereby any mental event or behavior could be viewed from the aspect of its expressive function (as drive seeking adequate discharge and representation against the opposition of controlling, mediating, and modifying forces "above" it); from the aspect of its defensive function (as defense or control mechanism seeking to conform instinctual expression "below" it to the exigencies of reality) as well as of course from the aspect of its adaptive function (as the more or less successful deflection or modification of drive aspect by defense aspect so that a modicum of instinctual gratification is obtained within a context sufficiently ego and reality-syntonic). In this hierarchical reconceptualization of the id-ego relationship, multiply layered and imbricated, the original sharp separation of the repressed and their repressing forces and their assignment to different realms with distinctly different functional characteristics have of course disappeared.

It is this same kind of reconceptualization that I am proposing in our thinking on what I call the continuum of reality, inner and outer. Arlow's many contributions in the realm of unconscious fantasy, myth, and reality have played a signal role in the development of that thinking.

REFERENCES

Arlow, J. A. (1969), Fantasy, memory, and reality testing. *Psychoanal. Quart.*, 38:28–51.

——— (1985), The concept of psychic reality and related problems. *J. Amer. Psychoanal. Assn.*, 33:521–535.

Blos, P. (1985), *Son and Father: Before and Beyond the Oedipus Complex.* New York: Free Press.

Freud, S. (1895), Project for a scientific psychology. *Standard Edition*, 1:281–411. London: Hogarth Press, 1966.

——— (1899), Screen memories. *Standard Edition*, 3:299–322. London: Hogarth Press, 1962.

——— (1900), The interpretation of dreams. *Standard Edition*, 4/5. London: Hogarth Press, 1953.

——— (1913), Totem and Taboo. *Standard Edition.* 13:1–161. London: Hogarth Press, 1955.

——— (1916–1917), Introductory lectures on psycho-analysis. *Standard Edition*, 15/16. London: Hogarth Press, 1963.

——— (1925), Negation. *Standard Edition*, 19:233–239. London: Hogarth Press, 1961.

Frosch, J. (1966), A note on reality constancy. In: *Psychoanalysis—A General Psychology: Essays in Honor of Heinz Hartmann*, ed. R. Loewenstein, L. Newman, M. Schur, & A. Solnit. New York: International Universities Press, pp. 349–376.

Gill, M. (1963), *Topography and Systems in Psychoanalytic Theory.* Psychological Issues Monograph 10. New York: International Universities Press.

Hartmann, H. (1956), Notes on the reality principle. In: *Essays on Ego Psychology: Selected Problems in Psychoanalytic Theory.* New York: International Universities Press. 1964, pp. 241–267.

——— (1960), *Psychoanalysis and Moral Values.* New York: International Universities Press.

Loewald, H. (1951), Ego and reality. *Internat. J. Psycho-Anal.*, 32:10–18.

Schafer, R. (1970), The psychoanalytic vision of reality. *Internat. J. Psycho-Anal.*, 51:79–97.

Schur, M. (1966), *The Id and the Regulatory Principles of Mental Functioning.* New York: International Universities Press.

Wallerstein, R. (1973), Psychoanalytic perspectives on the problem of reality. *J. Amer. Psychoanal. Assn.* 21:5-33.

———— (1983), Reality and its attributes as psychoanalytic concepts: An historical overview. *Internat. Rev. Psycho-Anal.,* 10:125-144.

———— (1985), The concept of psychic reality: Its meaning and value. *J. Amer. Psychoanal. Assn.* 33:555-569.

Weinstein, F. (1982), On interpreting interpretations of reality: The problem of subjectivity in history. Paper presented at Conference on History and Psychology, Stanford University, May, 1982.

18

Shared Fantasy and Reciprocal Identification, and Their Role in Gender Disorders

Harold P. Blum, M.D.

Shared fantasies, though ubiquitous and of great clinical significance, have received scant attention in the psychoanalytical literature. In this chapter I shall review the developmental, clinical, and theoretical importance of shared fantasies. The survey will encompass both clinical observation and other areas of analytic study and inference. Because of special ego and object-related dimensions, shared fantasies form a distinct subgroup of fantasies with special features: (1) The communication of fantasy to an object is part of an invitation toward identification, shared living out, or defense intrinsic to the fantasy. (2) The parent's fantasy shared with the child is part of the child's reality with developmental impact. The child, of course, also influences the caretaker, but the child's situation is not symmetrical because of the child's dependence and the caretaker's far more advanced development. (3) The shared fantasy of the child is anchored in reality and contains more than a grain of historical truth. (4) Shared fantasies may powerfully influence superego development, lending the authority of the parent to particular directives and injunctions, permission and prohibition. (5) Shared fantasies contribute to the formation and structure of certain adaptations and sublimations. (6) Shared fantasies exert a selective influence on the growth and development of personality functions and potentials. They facilitate, impede, or fail to stimulate some lines of development while fostering other potentials and lines of development. The impact of the mother's feelings and

Presented as the Freud Lecture, Part I expansion, Psychoanalytic Association of New York, April 1985. Part II published as "Psychoanalytic Studies and Macbeth: Shared Fantasy and Reciprocal Identification," *The Psychoanalytic Study of the Child*, 41:585–600, 1986.

fantasies will so selectively influence development as to make that child
the child of that particular mother (A. Freud, 1965, p. 86) and culture.
(7) Whether shared fantasies exert unusual developmental influence will
likely depend on the investment and exclusive attachment of the parent,
and the developmental phase, sensitivity, and proclivities of the child.
(8) Shared fantasies tend to subjectively shape personal, familial, and
social history. The personal myth (Kris, 1956) may be overdetermined
and affirmed by shared intrafamilial fantasy such as a child's being chosen
for great deeds to fulfill parental ambition, for a scapegoat function, as
a replacement child, etc.

Freud (1908) introduced shared fantasies in a discussion of aesthetic
communication by poets and artists, and in terms of group psychology.
The poet conveys his daydreams and dreams to the audience, awaken-
ing similar fantasies and inviting identification with the character and
content of his own fantasy creation. Further, myth, legend, and folklore
are shown to converge with the fantasies disguised in literature and art.
The primal fantasies of all cultures (Freud, 1916–1917, p. 371)—the universal fantasies of incest, patricide, matricide, pregnancy, birth, death, castration, omnipotence, etc.—are all shared between writer and reader, artist and audience. Shared fantasies are present also in the psychoanalytic
situation, in the very matrix of the transference-countertransference field.
The patient's erotic transference might meet with a reciprocal countertransference reaction of the analyst based on shared fantasies. Of course,
these fantasies need not be identical in all respects; they may be similar
or complementary, with profound influence on psychic function.

Artistic communication with shared fantasies removes responsibility
from the audience, alleviates guilt, avoids anxiety through transformation and disguise, and "bribes us by the offer of a purely formal, that
is, aesthetic, pleasure in the presentation" (Freud, 1908, p. 153). The
aesthetic experience sometimes attained with interpretation in the analytic
situation may be analogous to the artistic communication of forbidden
fantasy and its shared acceptance.

The disguise and secondary revision of past history are important
aspects of mythology and of group formation and function. Arlow (1961)
showed how each society shapes, interprets, and reinterprets its history
through a mythopoesis subserving sociocultural adaptation. Myths are
not private daydreams, but are meant to be communicated and shared
in a social and socializing process. Identification with mythical heroes
and their idealized qualities leads to appropriate character formation

as well as to selective renunciations and ambitions. Groups are organized not only through identification with an idealized leader, but also on the basis of shared unconscious fantasy. Psychoanalytic groups may have their own mythology, as expressed for example in the overidealization of particular teachers, or tenets, or of psychoanalysis itself. Derivative expressions of unconscious fantasy show the increasing influence of developmental transformation and ego mastery. However, the transformations related to development are also influenced by parental and cultural identifications, with regularities introduced by the inevitables of the human condition and common socialization. The mythic materials are endlessly varied and repeated in fantasy play and conveyed to the child in innumerable verbal and nonverbal communications. These may take the form, in certain instances, of direct communication of dream or daydream between parent and child, of favorite fairy tales, stories, and bits of history told and read to the child. Some parents take pains to choose what the child should read or see on TV. Others leave their pornographic books and magazines, their illustrated erotica, for the child's scrutiny and play.

Shared fantasy may range from a folie à deux to the most intricate forms of "secret sharing" in sublimation and creativity. The fantasy shared by artist and audience may earlier have been elaborated and transformed with a "secret sharer," as in Joseph Conrad's story (see Meyer, 1970), usually an important childhood object and identification. What has been described as folie à deux in terms of the person's adaptation and identification vis-à-vis the stronger individual's fantasy or delusion has implications for much more differentiated relationships. Folie à deux has been explained as depending on persistent symbiotic attachment and identification (Anthony, 1970), but more subtle forms of symbiotic disturbance have been conceptualized (Pollock, 1964). Focal symbiosis was described by Greenacre (1959), a circumscribed area of the child's development in which the child's and parent's needs and sensitivities are interwoven with incomplete separation. In terms of contemporary theory, incomplete separation and narcissistic object relation can coexist with more advanced development, as observed in twins. Fantasies of symbiotic merger are not the same as symbiosis, developmental arrest or malformation, or regressive loss of differentiation. Failure to successfully negotiate separation-individualation (Mahler, Pine, and Bergman, 1975) may result in impairment of self and object constancy without implying an actual symbiotic state.

In its classic form folie à deux is relieved when the healthier individual is separated from the psychotic caretaker on whom he is dependent. In other circumstances, however, the disturbance continues, and separation may result not in the alleviation of symptoms but in an outbreak of disorder. Some patients may fear both symbiosis and separation, so that intimacy and separation may both be feared. In each situation there is a balance between the child's need for independence and autonomy and the mother's willingness to grant and facilitate autonomous independence. We know how often various dimensions of child development meet assistance or resistance from the parent (Sperling, 1959; Levy, 1960). Levy quotes Anna Freud:

> As a child moves forward on the developmental scale, each step demands the giving up of former positions and gains, not only from the child himself but also from the parent. . . . More often, it is one or the other partner who lags behind, the child being unable to free himself from fixations, or the parent clinging to attitudes of protectiveness and mothering, which had become unjustified. In the worst cases, mother and child may join forces in a regressive move" [p. 380].

Not all children succumb to such maternal influence, but where the child's disturbance is influenced by shared fantasies and pathological parental influence, development is likely to be distorted and treatment efforts impeded. Strengths and weaknesses in the personality of parent and child are sometimes interdependent and reciprocal. Of course it makes a difference whether the child contends with *communicated* fantasies or with manifest fantasy *enactments* by the parents (Burlingham, 1955). The shared fantasy itself provides a nidus of reality and a motive force in maintaining parental attachment, affections, and approval (Bergmann, 1982). The work of Spitz (1965) on archaic parent-infant reciprocal identification and the establishment of dialogue, and Mahler's delineation (1967) of mutual cueing illuminate the precursors of shared fantasy.

There are always cues and clues to the transfer of unconscious communication. The child's cry or smile, the caretaker's response, and their circular interaction permit communicative registrations, and the only way later fantasies can be transmitted is through behavioral derivatives. This discounts telepathy, magical thought transference, or empathy without perception, cognition, or affectomotor communication.

Actually, Freud discovered shared fantasies concurrent with his discovery of the oedipus complex and his reconstruction of early parent-child relationships. Writing to Fliess of his self-analysis on October 15, 1897, Freud describes the gripping power of *Oedipus Rex* as having become understandable: the Greek myth "seizes on a compulsion which everyone recognizes because he has felt traces of it in himself . . . . The ideas passed through my head; the same thing may lie at the root of Hamlet" (Freud, 1897–1904, pp. 223–224). Freud had noted that in the Oedipus complex the child's fantasies coincide with parental preferences, preferences based also on the Oedipus complex of the parents. Jocasta might then be regarded as engaging in the reciprocal disguised seduction of her son Oedipus. Incest is followed by blight and plague; Jocasta commits suicide, while Oedipus imposes on himself the lesser sacrifice of his eyes. The mother, then, accepted greater responsibility and punishment than did the child. It would be interesting to study the women in Greek history and drama as well as Shakespeare's female characters in terms of mothering, family structure, and actual child-rearing practices. The concept of borrowed guilt (Freud, 1923) is representative of the child's tendency to identify with the parents' affects in the acquisition and transformation of his own affects, but also to identify with and share parental fantasies, e.g., of being punished for oedipal transgressions. But are these transgressions only fantasies, fantasies accompanying infantile masturbation? Freud never lost sight of the role of actual experience in relation to past infantile masturbation, but also in relation to the parent-child relationship. In a letter of September 21, 1897, in which he revealed to Fliess that he no longer believed in the seduction theory, Freud (1897–1904, p. 215) immediately proceeds to the reconstruction of actual oedipal and preoedipal relationships. In his next letter written October 3, he abandoned the idea of seduction by his father only to proclaim his nursemaid as the "primary originator" of his neurosis; he adds on October 4, that she was his "instructress in sexual matters" and that she once washed him in red water in which she had previously washed herself (p. 220). This "seduction" by his nursemaid is reported just after the seduction theory is disclaimed. Freud, then, relinquished the seduction theory as encompassing all of pathogenesis, but he never denied the importance of seduction or of other forms of actual traumatic experience. In this very same series of reconstructions, which are the "prototype of preoedipal reconstruction" (Blum, 1977), Freud recalled that his nursemaid had encouraged him to steal money for her which he now saw as the germ of a child's compliant acting out of a caretaker's wishes

later in life. Just as the nursemaid had received money for his bad treatment, so he got money for the bad treatment of his own patients. This
is likely a continued reversal into self-accusation of the reproach he wished
to level against Fliess. Fantasies are shared between caretaker and child,
Freud and Fliess. The concept of identification is almost explicit here,
and has already been described by Freud in notes written May 31, 1897,
and sent to Fliess (pp. 207–209). Identification with the delinquent
nursemaid foreshadows identification with the seducer and aggressor.
Fliess instructs Freud in bisexual periodicity; Freud instructs Fliess in
psychosexual matters and in the universal oedipal fantasies dramatized
in *Oedipus Rex* and *Hamlet.*

Several years later, the Dora case (Freud, 1905) revealed a system
of shared fantasies and seductive behavior by Dora, her parents, and
Herr and Frau K. Dora fantasied joining in the affair by being the
bartered bride of Herr K. so that her father might continue his affair
with Frau K. In the treatment with Freud, Dora had similar fantasies
of having been brought by her father to Freud and bartered. Freud likely responded to this transference fantasy with a well-defended oedipal
contertransference. The elucidation of Dora's infantile sexual and aggressive fantasies included, in her case, the shared fantasies and seductive, deceptive behavior by her father and by Herr and Frau K. Again,
the reality of her seduction experience at the lake was reconstructed in
depth and detail, along with an understanding of Dora's intrapsychic
experience and her fantasy elaborations and distortion. There was a continuing interplay of fantasy and reality. It is quite likely that Dora's
enmeshment with her father through shared unconscious fantasy and
reciprocal identification, and her own participation in the intrafamilial
object relations, communications, etc., began very early in life.

Wangh (1962), building on Anna Freud's formulation (1937) of
"altruistic surrender" and the vicarious living out of certain fantasies
through an alternate, developed the concept of "evocation of a proxy."
The proxy allows for vicarious forbidden gratification while defending
against the guilt and anxiety that would arise were the gratification to
be directly obtained. The proxy takes on ego and superego functions
and safely substitutes for the behind-the-scenes partner. This can occur
on the basis of a revival of the parent-child, sibling, or twin relationship, but Wangh noted that it was more likely to occur in individuals
with unresolved symbiotic wishes. Wangh's formulations are closely
related to those of Johnson (1953; Johnson and Szurek, 1952), who shows

how forbidden interests and activities are unconsciously instigated and sanctioned by parents. The parents vicariously gratify their own unconscious wishes and may be punished for them through the punishment and traumatization of the child. Superego lacunae are not mere gaps in the superego system, but rather are based on identifications. For instance, the child might sense his mother's excitement in stories of delinquency or crime, sense her own delinquent interest and proclivities, and sense her fondest hopes and deepest fears. He will respond to parental delegation and involvement, whether in school phobia or enuresis (Blum, 1970), shaping his own fantasies in identification with and adaptation to parental preoccupation. However, the child is not a mere tabula rasa who acts out the parents' fantasy; he has similar fantasies and his own impulses, which are gratified in actuality even as his parents' are vicariously. Pathogenic fantasies tend to be consolidated with the passing of the oedipal phase and with consolidation of the superego, but the psychopathology may in some instances be traced back to earliest development, with continuing pathogenic strain through all subsequent phases. This has been directly confirmed in the simultaneous analysis of mother and child (Sperling, 1950; Hellman, 1960; Levy, 1960). Anna Freud (1967) noted the deficient attachment of "chronic losers" in the primary object relationship. They may later show a double identification: with neglectful parents, and with lost objects symbolizing themselves. Children who get lost rather than feel lost are those with ambivalent or ineffective parental feelings; this paradigm may be recapitulated in analysis, when patients may leave treatment in response to a negative countertransference communication to "get lost."

A mother who thought of her daughter in early infancy as ugly, demanding, and exceedingly difficult to comfort and please later regarded the daughter as a serious oedipal rival, of whom she was intensely jealous. She would attempt to separate the daughter from her father and herself, and intended to send her away to boarding school as soon as practicable. The daughter's oedipal jealousy rivaled that of the mother, but she remained ambivalently fixated to the mother and was afraid to let go rather than moving outward to a more secure and expanded relationship with her father. Again, parents' fantasies and behavior reciprocally influence the child's fantasies and behavior (Rangell, 1955). The father of an adolescent girl may begin an extramarital affair concurrent with his daughter's becoming "sexually active." A woman whose father chose a mistress her own age avoided marriage and awareness of a shared incestuous fantasy. In cases of adoption, analysis may uncover the continued shared denial of sterility and narcissistic injury. The adopted child lives in a family system, with shared fantasies of abandonment and rescue, kidnapping and reunion (Blum, 1983). As indicated earlier, shared fantasy may have a beneficial as well as detrimental influence, and may stimulate and promote talent, accomplishment, and creativity.

The origins of shared fantasy bring us into the preoedipal phase, the dialogue of conscious and unconscious, verbal and nonverbal, communication between parent and child. Early object relations and identifications are on a developmental level very different from that of the parent. The material that follows has a bearing on contemporary interest in preoedipal determinants and distortions of oedipal and later development. While transformed within oedipal development, preoedipal determinants may be found beneath and alongside the oedipal configuration (Neubauer, 1977). The cases to be cited, however, showing major preoedipal determinants of later psychopathology, should not be taken as general indications of the balance of forces in any given case. Later development and structuralization may in the long run prove more decisive. Just as the preoedipal may color or distort oedipal conflict and resolution, so later developmental phases may have a beneficial and corrective influence on persisting antecedent problems. With this in mind, let us look at some disturbances in which the psychopathology appears to derive from early infancy, though continually reorganized and consolidated in the oedipal and later phases of development.

Consider a shared fantasy in which the child is an extension, projection, or proxy of the mother, and the mother remains or is regressively represented as a dyadic narcissistic object. Unresolved problems of the dyadic preoedipal phase will influence subsequent development and fantasy formation. I shall continue with a discussion of a transsexual form of gender identity disorder, drawing on the contribution of Stoller (1968; 1980) and on the relevant concepts of Greenacre (1959), Greenson (1966), and Mahler (1972) Mahler and McDevitt (1980), and Roiphe and Galenson (1982).

While it is necessary to understand three generations in tracing the pathogenesis of transsexualism, I shall concentrate mainly on the central mother-child relationship and the shared fantasy that the child is in certain respects an extension of the mother—specifically, her fantasied penis and idealized narcissistic object. The fantasy system is not meant to be generalized to all cases of transsexualism, and may by applicable only to a specific subgroup, a minority of gender identity disorders. In the adult form of this syndrome, the male may seek bodily sex alteration and reassignment, prefers the female gender role socially, and often chooses a male object. Gender identity is a complex phenomenon with variable conscious and unconscious components. Bisexuality is always found, and there is a particular organization and synthesis of masculine and feminine identifications and dispositions.

A woman who is very uncomfortable with her own femininity, who has wanted very much to have been born a boy, but who simultaneously disparages the penis of the envied male is nevertheless overjoyed to give birth to this one particular son. This future transsexual is given a strongly phallic name—Lance—and seems to be idealized rather than despised by his mother (Stoller, 1968; 1980). The infant is regarded as beautiful and graceful and becomes the idealized phallus for which she has yearned since childhood, a childhood characterized by intense feelings of deprivation and depression. Here a particular child is chosen and idealized in this way, while other sons are spared—a type of child rearing along an extraordinarily deviant developmental line. The mother consciously wanted a boy, and refers to her infant as a son, while rearing the infant as a girl. We may see here in statu nascendi the powerful effect of the mother's unconscious fantasy system on the infant destined to be transsexual. By the time the child is one year old his gender behaviors tend to mirror those of his mother, and he seems to be on the way to fulfilling his mother's wishes that he grow up as a girl. The specific developmental deviation proceeds in accord with the mother's terms, with reciprocal rewards and rudimentary identifications. Some perversions retain the tendency toward archaic imitative identification, lending an "as if" quality to the patient's identity and object relations. Histrionic attitudes and theatricality are also supported by denial and by magical role reversal of male and female, self and object.

In some cases of gender identity disorder, a protracted symbiotic phase may be inferred. There is excessive intimacy with the infant, who is kept in seemingly unending skin-to-skin contact with the mother. The father absents himself or is driven into exile by the mother's hostile antagonism. Unavailable to help the child disengage from the symbiotic orbit, he is passive-aggressive toward wife and son, and is manifestly uninterested in protecting the boy from emasculation. The father is also not available as a model for identification, and neither parent encourages masculinity as a basis for identification. The son is enthralled by the

mother's femininity; the mother is thrilled by his feminine identification while denying that his dress and behavior are inappropriate. The
denial is so powerful and complete that it is not until other mothers,
teachers, etc., complain or intervene that any problem may be acknowledged or any help sought. Nevertheless, these particular cases are not
traumatized children, at least on the surface, but children who enjoy
the soft, warm, cradling of their mothers, with intense exposure to her
behaviors and attitudes. Stoller (1980) suggests that perhaps the chosen
son (in cross-gender rearing) introjects the mother's femaleness in the
touch and gazing reminiscent of adult lovers.

To my mind the preconflictual skewed symbiosis, or the adhesiveness
of this mother-infant dyad, is very important but does not account for
the later fantasy formation and the continuing parental influence on
development. Separation-individuation and then the persisting oedipal
reorganization are major influences in the child's structural development.
Inherent self-righting developmental tendencies, however, may be
submerged by constitutional passivity and the ongoing pathogenic parental influence. In my view the role of conflict, in the parents and in the
child, is very significant. The parents' inner conflicts and rearing determine, together with the child's dispositions and individual organization,
the child's conflicted perverse tendencies. This applies particularly to
sexual and aggressive conflict centering around castration, narcissism,
and envy of such maternal attributes as breast or baby. Maternal repression of hostility leads to a lack of conscious ambivalence toward the infant. The mother's idealized relationship with this son also excludes
awareness of the infant's ambivalence. The idealization of the son seems
to be split from the hateful devaluation of the husband-father. The
mother's denial of the child's true gender is a projection and concretization of her denial that she does not have a penis. The child is created
as a fetish and becomes a living phallic woman, a replication of the
"mother" (as all children are, to some degree, in the parent's unconscious). But this special son becomes a living creation of her idealized self-image as a phallic woman. The disorder of gender identity by
the time the child is two years old mirrors that of his mother's fantasies,
and the son becomes what his mother wished and molded him to be,
with the infant's compliance and the father's collusion. The shared unconscious fantasy is not dependent on assumptions of symbiosis, or global
failure in separateness, and is compatible with preoedipal distortions of
the Oedipus complex, related to the gender identity disorder.

Projection, mutual cueing, and reciprocal identification have been used to shape and misshape her son's gender identity. Just as she once saw herself as a boy in an old prepuberty photograph (Stoller, 1980), so she sees her son as a girl; i.e., both are seen as phallic women. Denial in fantasy has become denial indeed, in the shared creation of a shared fantasy that will be lived out together. The child grows up feeling that he is essentially a woman trapped in a man's body, the mirror of the son trapped in his mother's feminine body, as if never fully sexually differentiated, never fully separate in his identity. He remains fixated or easily regresses to body preoccupation and narcissistic object relationship. He and his mother have a shared fantasy, maintained with implacable conviction: that he is a woman with anomalous male genitals and that she is a woman with male genitals represented by the son, who is a feminine phallic extension of herself and a narcissistic object with whom she is identified. He is reciprocally identified with her attitudes so that what he is and would like to be simultaneously represents his mother's preference.

Communication commences at a prerepresentational, prefantasy period of development, prior to separation-individuation. The future transsexual son engaged in mutual cueing with his mother is already selecting and being guided toward his mother's preferences. Interest in the mother's spectacles—her earrings, necklace, beads, clothes, colors; women's tastes in the broadest sense—is already conveyed to the child, who soon begins to sense what pleases and displeases his mother. Her molding of the perspective child toward a perverse identity continues within and beyond separation-individuation. Between eight months and one year of age Lance is described as cooing with deepest pleasure at photographs of well-dressed, beautiful women or of women cooking. He begins cross-dressing in the first days after he began to walk. His astonished mother is thrilled to report that her son feels compelled to "dress up" for part of each day. The child's discriminations and preferences clearly are his mother's, projected onto the child, but also *communicated* to the child. Imitative compliance with his mother's choices is rewarded, while other choices are discouraged. The primordial imitative identifications, at first perhaps transient and dependent on the presence of the model, eventually become deferred imitation, and are later structuralized with profound influence on the child's self- and object representations and identity. Aggressive confrontations are avoided or unacknowledged so that the child appears to be seduced by blandishments rather than intimidated by threat. As the capacity for fantasy develops, the child's fantasy system emerges in concert with the child's primordial identifications, in reciprocity and complementarity with the mother's mirroring, affirming, and encouraging affectomotor and later, verbal communications. Mother-infant dyads of this sort are highly attuned to each other's thoughts, feelings, and sensitivities. The cross-dressing and choice of girl companions and girl's activities, which are representative of the child's feminine identification and the consolidation toward feminine identity, continue under the mother's guidance and direction. Beginning with the primary identifications, or identification with the primary object (Blum, 1986), and reciprocal, rudimentary identifications with the preoedipal mother, the infant's initial imitative identifications become increasingly structuralized (Kanzer, 1985). The identifications, more selective with developmental advance (Jacobson, 1964), are not only endogenously selected by the child but are preselected and guided by the parent in a process which will proceed to the internationalization of parental rules and regulations in superego formation (Schafer, 1968). The perverse superego may paradoxically accept and even require cross-gender aims, objects, and social roles.

Three other inferences may be drawn. The first is that the son is a concretization of the shared fantasy, of the phallic woman, a fantasy which is now part of his reality and identity and which is believed with an omnipotent denial of reality. His body is a phallus and he is a living fetish, with an evolving female self-representation. He values and prefers femininity. The second inference is that unresolved, predominately phallic oedipal and phallic narcissistic conflict in the mother may in very special circumstances have a predominantly preoedipal initial impact on her infant. Third, the transsexual's later wish to be castrated represents the castrating component of his mother's (and father's) conflicts and his need to harmonize his body and his gender identity. His body may remain or retain an illusory phallus. The shared fantasy of femininity overrides and supplants both constitutional masculinity and castration anxiety. Masculinity and identification with the father's male roles, are latently present, but stunted. The mother's devaluation of masculinity and aggression has been internalized, and the parents have joined in the son's psychological castration. (The surgery might also represent an attempt to achieve separateness and individuation. It would be analogous to the boundary setting function of some forms of self-mutilation and masochistic perversion.)

Feminine identification with the mother is based on the child's and mother's shared fantasies, and not simply the mother's real attributes. The phallic and the castrated mother are fantasy creations. Identification with the loved and hated phallic mother simultaneously defends against separation and castration anxiety, and gratifies infantile wishes (McDevitt, 1985). Some cases of gender identity disorder have a history of infantile traumatization, e.g., protracted separations, object loss, parental nudity and seduction, or surgery. The mother is regarded as both castrator and castrated, and the son identifies with her as both aggressor and victim. The phallic mother maintains a denial of castration and preserves omnipotence. The child with gender identity disorder (a spectrum disorder in which transsexualism is included) will have elaborated many unconscious fantasies of himself and the parent as omnipotent and idealized, castrated and humiliated, so that the manifest picture of unambivalent femininity is drastically incomplete. Perverse femininity may mask and defend against hostility and chronic rage.

Shared bilateral denial of appropriate gender continues to operate along with some ego and identity confusion. The mother's fantasy system continues to impact during later preoedipal and oedipal development, contributing to the creation of her compliant son in her own image. It is a perverse variant of the shared fantasy of Pygmalion and Galatea. Clinically, a particular danger appears in the transference-countertransference when the patient expects magical transformation and the analyst has not relinquished omnipotent fantasies of idealized rebirth and re-creation of self and object. Developmentally, the creation of an effeminate male globally identified with his mother's warped femininity may only intensify later inevitable conflict. Rather than an absence of oedipal conflict, a negative oedipal drama will likely be constructed from a deviant preoedipal foundation. The negative Oedipus complex would be infiltrated by body image confusion and incomplete separation-individuation. Castration conflict is resolved by continued omnipotent denial, preoedipal regression, and an acceptance of castration. Hormonal secondary sex change or the extreme of irreversible surgical transformation may be invoked to harmonize feminine identification and identity. The preoedipal determinants are important in the pathogenesis of the perversion and in the consolidation of later oedipal distortion. The shared fantasies and reciprocal identification with parental attitudes and distorted reality representations confirm the transsexual's conviction of phallic womanhood. The perversion is, in this respect, a personification of a shared personal-parental bisexual myth. The specific shared transsexual fantasy system emerges and becomes an organizing influence for subsequent deviant development, colored by later object relations and identification.

This relatively rare form of perversion was chosen to illustrate the developmental influence of shared fantasy for a particular psychopathology where its importance had not previously been elaborated or emphasized. Aberrant development here invites the investigation of shared fantasy in other perversions, and consideration of the general importance of shared fantasy as a major developmental and clinical issue. It is again noteworthy that shared fantasy is more likely to exert unusual influence where there is special bilateral parent-child investment and rather exclusive parent-child attachment. The emerging shared fantasy system will be molded by phase-specific fantasy and the effect of experience. The parents' reaction to each other, and to their child, and what their child evokes and responds to in the parents are reciprocal developmental influences. The child's individual traits and assertiveness, and parental regard and respect for their child's individuation and healthy development, will be very significant for the final form, content, and fate of shared fantasy.

A reciprocal form of shared mother-son fantasy has been inferred in a parallel study of Macbeth, with hyperaggressive, defensive masculinity.

REFERENCES

Anthony, E. (1970), Folie à deux: A developmental failure in the process of separation-individuation. In: *Parenthood: Its Psychology and Psychopathology*, ed. E. Anthony & T. Benedeke. Boston: Little, Brown, pp. 571–595.

Arlow, J. A. (1961), Ego psychology and the study of mythology. *J. Amer. Psychoanal. Assn.*, 9:371–393.

Bergmann, M. (1982), Thoughts on superego pathology of survivors and their children. In: *Generations of the Holocaust*, ed. M. Bergmann & M. Jucovy. New York: Basic Books, pp. 287–310.

Blum, H. (1970), Maternal psychopathology and enuresis. *Psychoanal. Quart.*, 39:609–691.

———— (1977), The prototype of preoedipal reconstruction. *J. Amer. Psychoanal. Assn.*, 25:757–785.

———— (1983), Adoptive parents: Generative conflict and generational continuity. *The Psychoanalytic Study of the Child*, 38:141–164. New Haven, CT: Yale University Press.

_____ (1986), On identification and its vicissitudes. *Internat. J. Psycho-Anal.*, 6:267–276.

Burlingham, D., et al. (1955), Simultaneous analysis of mother and child. *The Psychoanalytic Study of the Child*, 10:115–186. New York: International Universities Press.

Freud, A. (1937), *The Ego and the Mechanisms of Defense*. New York: International Universities Press, 1966.

_____ (1965), *Normality and Pathology in Childhood*. New York: International Universities Press.

_____ (1967), About losing and being lost. In: *Problems in Psychoanalytic Training, Diagnosis, and the Technique of Therapy*. New York: International Universities Press.

Freud, S. (1897–1904), *The Complete Letters of Sigmund Freud to Wilhelm Fliess*, ed. J. Masson, Boston: Harvard University Press, 1985.

_____ (1905), Fragment of an analysis of a case of hysteria. *Standard Edition*, 7:7–122. London: Hogarth Press, 1953.

_____ (1908), Creative writers and day-dreaming. *Standard Edition*, 9:143–153. London: Hogarth Press, 1959.

_____ (1916–1917), Introductory lectures on psycho-analysis. *Standard Edition*, 15/16. London: Hogarth Press, 1963.

_____ (1923), The ego and the id. *Standard Edition*, 19:12–66. London: Hogarth Press, 1961.

Greenacre, P. (1959), On focal symbiosis. In: *Dynamic Psychopathology in Childhood*, ed. L. Jessuer & E. Pavenstedt. New York: Grune & Stratton, pp. 243–256.

Greenson, R. (1966), A transvestite boy and a hypothesis. *Internat. J. Psycho-Anal.*, 47: 396–403.

Hellman, I., et al. (1960), Simultaneous analysis of mother and child. *The Psychoanalytic Study of the Child*, 15:359–377. New York: International Universities Press.

Jacobson, E. (1964), *The Self and the Object World*. New York: International Universities Press.

Johnson, A. (1953), Factors in the etiology of fixations and symptom choice. *Psychoanal. Quart.*, 22:475–496.

_____ & Szurek, G. (1952), The genesis of antisocial acting out in children and adults. *Psychoanal. Quart.*, 2:323–343.

Kanzer, M. (1985), Identification and its vicissitudes. *Internat. J. Psycho-Anal.*, 66:19–30.

Kris, E. (1956), The personal myth. *J. Amer. Psychoanal. Assn.*, 4:653–681.

Levy, K. (1960), Simultaneous analysis of a mother and her adolescent daughter. *The Psychoanalytic Study of the Child*. 15:378–391. New York: International Universities Press.

Mahler, M. (1967), *On Human Symbiosis and the Vicissitudes of Individuation. Selected Papers*, Vol. II. New York: Aronson.

_____ (1972), Rapprochement subphase of the separation-individuation process. *Psychoanal. Quart.*, 41:487–506.

_____ & McDevitt, J. (1980), The separation-individuation process and identity formation. In: *The Course of Life*, Vol. 1, ed. S. Greenspan & G. Pollock, Washington, D.C.: National Institute of Mental Health. pp. 395–406.

_____ Pine, F., & Bergman, A. (1975), *The Psychological Birth of the Human Infant*. New York: Basic Books.

McDevitt, J. (1985), Preoedipal determinants of an infantile gender disorder. Presented at International Symposium on Separation-Individication. Paris, France. November 3, 1985.

Meyer, B. (1970), *Joseph Conrad: A Psychoanalytic Biography*. Princeton, NJ: Princeton University Press.

Neubauer, P. (1977), Panel: Varieties of oedipal distortions of severe character pathologies, rep. W. Robbins. *J. Amer. Psychoanal Assn.* 25:201–218.

Pollock, G. (1964), On symboisis and symbiotic neurosis. *Internat. J. Psycho-Anal.*, 45:1–30.

Rangell, L. (1955), The role of the parent in the oedipus complex. *Bull. Menn. Clin.*, 19:9–15.

Roiphe, H., & Galenson, E. (1982), *Infantile Origins of Sexual Identity*. New York: International Universities Press.

Schafer, R. (1968), *Aspects of Internalization*. New York: International Universities Press.

Sperling, M. (1950), Children's interpretation and reaction to the unconscious of their mothers. *Internat. J. Psycho-Anal.*, 31:36–41.

_____ (1959), A study of deviate sexual behavior in children by the method of simultaneous analysis of mother and child. In: *Dynamic Psychopathology in Childhood*, ed. L. Jessuer & E. Pavenstedt. New York: Grune & Stratton, pp. 221–242.

Spitz, R. (1965), *The First Year of Life*. New York: International Universities Press.

Stoller, R. (1968), *Sex and Gender*. New York: Science House.

_____ (1980), A different view of oedipal conflict. In: *The Course of Life*, Vol. I, ed. S. Greenspan & G. Pollock, Washington, DC: National Institute of Mental Health, pp. 589–602.

Wangh, M. (1962), The evocation of a proxy. *The Psychoanalytic Study of the Child*, 17:451–472. New York: International Universities Press.

19

Three Commentaries on Gender in Freud's Thought: A Prologue to the Psychoanalytic Theory of Sexuality

William I. Grossman, M.D.
Donald M. Kaplan, Ph.D.

We entitle the following discussion a prologue because we have in mind a series of papers on sexuality as exemplified by female sexuality in psychoanalytic thought. We should note at the outset that we are not preparing to introduce any new findings or concepts with respect to the subject of sex and gender.

Psychoanalysis has at present a surfeit of critiques and proposals from both within and without the field, on the subject of female sexuality. Many of these proposals disregard the way they are to fit within the overall structure of psychoanalytic theory. It is this state of affairs that we plan to redress in a series of reviews of the problem as it turns up in the encounters of recent thinking with Freud's writings on the subject. Examined primarily in the interest of recovering a psychoanalytic thread too often lost in the great flux of controversy, the subject of female sexuality is also an occasion for thinking about psychoanalysis in general—its history, its interests, its procedures. It is our intention to provide a technical, that is, a specifically psychoanalytic perspective on the modifications proposed in recent critiques.

An early diagnostic observation of Freud's (1896) provides an instance of the application of a technical approach. Freud began at that time to distinguish between the psychoneuroses and the actual neuroses, not on a descriptive basis, but on the basis of their responsiveness to one kind of treatment or another, that is, on grounds of analyzability. He noted that a group of cases that initially seemed similar could be differentiated on this basis. "Many cases, which on superficial examination, seem to be common (neurasthenic) hypochondria belong to this group of *obsessional affects;* what is known as 'periodic melancholia' seems in particular to resolve itself with unexpected frequency into obsessional affects and obsessional ideas'' (pp. 171–172). When Freud adds that he found such apparent neurasthenias and depressions treatable by a psychoanalytic procedure, we can say that his subject was no longer the relationship of traits to diagnosis, a subject of "superficial" clinical examination, but rather the relationship of diagnosis to analyzability. In other words, the subject of diagnosis was transformed early on from a problem of appearances to a problem of the analyzability of symptoms in terms of gains from the repression of trauma. Regarding female sexuality, much that has been presented has not been subjected to analysis. Such notions as primary femininity and feminine traits were never assigned definitive roles in unconscious mental process, and in current discussions they are presented as if devoid of vicissitudes.

Our point may come down to little more than the proposition that exposition is technical to the extent that it answers to relevant technical principles. However, a review of the controversies with this in mind promises not only to sort out issues according to their actual or merely ostensible relationship to psychoanalysis, but also to reveal implicit controversies over the technical principles themselves. Now, as in the past, arguments about the very nature of psychoanalysis are often waged in terms of some other subject—borderline pathology, self psychology, object relations theory, or, as with our present case in point, female sexuality (Grossman, 1986a).

To this we must add a proviso. Our aim is not to stifle conversation. If our interest on this occasion is in the technical character of a certain exposition, we do not mean that exposition lacking such character is for that reason alone wrongheaded and unworthy of serious consideration. There are always things worth saying that cannot be said within the stringencies of technicality. For example, the presentation of novel interests to an established structure of thought is a matter not of principle but of decision. Even in as conscientiously systematic a writer as Hartmann certain subjects escaped a technical perspective, as Schafer (1970) observed of Hartmann's biological and cultural interest: "Although . . . Hartmann contributed many acute perceptions, thoughtful differentiations and searching questions, he did not always make it clear when he was working *within* the content of psychoanalytic theory and when he was developing *orienting propositions* to analytic theory as a whole"

(p. 43). Such an observation is even more pertinent to Freud's writings, which are full of provisional and edifying reflections that remain at some remove, indeed sometimes at some variance, from his own technical principles.

With respect to female psychology in particular it is our sense that quite a bit that Freud had to say did not succeed as technical discourse, this in varying ways, with varying import, and with varying awareness on his part. Some of what he had to say was simply nontechnical. His observations of allegedly female traits, which constitute one decided commentary in his writing, are examples of this; their justification had nothing to do with the psychoanalytic method strictly speaking. This is the first commentary we mean to examine, as Freud maintained such views with a conviction that overrode the reservations that often accompanied his assertions about female traits.

Inter alia it is possible to find in Freud certain other nontechnical remarks on female sexuality, in the way of passing exemplificatons of points in his text. Sometimes he gave direct utterance to the biased assumptions of his age, sometimes to observations about female patients that would not survive later improvements in his method and theory. Unlike his commentary of traits, however, these remarks did not coalesce into an organized commentary, which is why we simply make note of them here. An example of Freud's speaking entirely as a nineteenth-century sexologist occurs in the *Three Essays* (1905), where he was discussing the "polymorphously perverse disposition" of children, whom he likened to "an average uncultivated woman," who "may remain normal sexually, but if she is led on by a clever seducer she will find every sort of perversion to her taste, and will retain them as part of her own sexual activities" (p. 191). He then added that the vast inclination of women toward prostitution in all manner of sexual behavior confirms a general disposition to perversions of every kind in adult sexuality. Explicit in this passage is a received notion of women as childlike, impressionable, and corruptible. It is also interesting that Freud here regards engaging in "every sort of perversion" as compatible with remaining "normal sexually"—an important distinction between behavior and diagnosis. To be sure, Freud continued to struggle with his penchant for various of the unquestioned conclusions of nineteenth-century sexology. For example, he later located these notions about women among the infantile mythologies of gender and distinguished such mythologies from a theory that accounts for them. However, to the extent that remnants of such notions survive his theoretical transformations in a persistence of ordinary prejudice, they will work mischief with his later attempts to convince us of the psychoanalytic technicality of the ideas he is advancing. Thus, Freud's eventual claims about something flawed in the superego attainment of women may suffer from too direct and unmodified a descendency from the extrapsychoanalytic notion we have just cited from the Three Essays.

Certain other nontechnical remarks of female sexuality went on to a better fate. They simply faded away in corrections by the psychoanalytic method. A good example occurs in Freud's first paper on the neuropsychoses of defense (1894). In the course of describing the process of defense against an imcompatible idea, Freud interjected the observation that "in females incompatible ideas of this sort arise chiefly on the soil of sexual experience and sensation" (p. 47). His implication was that trauma in males arose in experience other than sexual. At this early stage of Freud's familiarity with the psychoanalytic method one may easily imagine that there were many aspects of his patients' testimony that he still took at face value, such as the manifest differences in the manner in which women and men reported their sex lives and sexual thoughts. In the absence of technical concepts concerning the relation between manifest and latent content, and the myriad means by which sexuality is expressed in the clinical situation, Freud at first took the greater apparent modesty of women as straightforward evidence of their greater problem with sex. However, it was soon apparent that the same formulations could be applied to women as to men, "in spite of the confusion introduced into the problem by all the artificial retarding and stunting of the female sexual instinct" (Freud, 1895, p. 109). It then became clear that the clinical problem was not *whether* a patient's attitude to disclosure entailed sexuality but rather *how* it did. Indeed, as time went on Freud regarded the modesty of women not as a diagnostic issue but as a social convention that created a problem for the analyst (particularly the male analyst) with which he confessed to doing less well than other analysts he could think of (Freud, 1920).

Still, a good deal of this nontechnical commentary on female psychology remained and, moreover, as something more than passing remarks. However, before resuming what we will loosely call Freud's trait commentary, we should mention two additional commentaries.

The first of these might be said to be only partly technical. What we have in mind here are Freud's eventually well-rehearsed narratives of female development, antecedents of the "developmental line." These were put together from observations and reconstructions from the clinical situation. One of the difficulties with such narratives, as we shall show, is that they appear to assume that the discovery of significant nodal points in development is a discovery also of how they are inevitably traversed and of what their consequences must be as regards developmental outcome.

Then there is a third commentary in Freud which acknowledges this difficulty and is, in our view, thoroughly technical. Crucial instances of this commentary occur in Freud's clarifying asides and prefatory remarks to his various excursions into female pyschology. Enjoying technical standing, these moments are of course continuous with the general principles governing Freud's thought even apart from the subject of gender and sex difference. This third commentary retains the dynamics and complexities of a psychoanalysis of development and outcome and thus surpasses the fixed linearity of Freud's narratives of development and the polarization of outcome described as fixed traits.

This commentary, we should add, is relevant also to certain problems in sex and gender research beyond psychoanalysis. In a careful review of a whole decade of such research from many academic quarters, Deaux (1984) concluded that a limitation common to most sex- and gender-difference studies is the "static nature of the assumptions—that sex-related phenomena are best approached either through biological categories, via stable traits, or in terms of relatively stable stereotypic conceptions"; over and against these static considerations, Deaux urges that "one must ultimately deal with the *processes* involved . . . processes through which gender informtion is presented and acted upon" (p. 113). What Deaux is saying about academic psychology corresponds to the view we are taking of psychoanalysis. Static traits and fixed developmental events in the psychoanalytic literature take on a reality as concretizations from an averaging of observations, but the more psychoanalytic theory retains its dynamic as a perspective for such observations, the less stability such static notions will have.

A last point among these preliminaries. In arranging these commentaries according to their ascending degree of technicality, we are preparing to view what may arise at a low degree of technicality as an unavoidable step toward a more advanced conception. For example, despite the limitations of Freud's first commentary, it is descriptive of a subject whose vicissitudes will be given by a more technical commentary. This is not to say that the relationship among the commentaries is one of strictly temporal succession, though at times it may be that an instance of the first (or second) commentary provides a necessary beginning for something to follow. Freud (1919) appears himself to have made this point: "In my description," he wrote, "I shall be careful to avoid being more schematic than is inevitable for the presentation of an average case. If then on further observation a greater complexity of circumstances should come to light, I shall nevertheless be sure of having before us a typical occurrence, and one, moreover, that is not of an uncommon kind" (p. 184). This is one of the reasons that the commentaries we shall be examining often appear side by side in the same work. Since psychoanalysis is concerned with transformations in the mental life, it is necessary to retain ideas about what is typical and common in order to be able to talk about what it is that is being transformed. The danger here is that the need for a point of comparison, an idea that refers to something on the order of an average expectable state of affairs, is too easily mistaken for an inevitable and invariant phenomenon or condition, that is, a rigid category. In other words, the first commentary has a certain kind of value, so long as the distinction between what is categorical and what is on the average expectable is kept in mind. The absence of such a distinction is characteristic of certain stages of thought, both in individual development and in the development of theories.

In summary, our review of Freud's various commentaries on female psychology is not conducted in a spirit of "updating" a psychoanalysis of this subject. It is not the merit of particular ideas that interests us so much as their function in the process of creating a systematic theory. We have no arguments about whether any particular idea is sufficient in its own right, as no idea is. We take it for granted that Freud, read literally, is wrong in many respects with regard to his generalizations, assumptions, and conclusions about women, men, and human nature. However, his analyses of these matters are important for their function in the development of our current understanding of concepts, even if we find the "facts" assumed in Freud's reflections rather questionable. But, then, of course, what we consider factual from our present vantage also needs to be understood critically—not only for its content but also for the way we think about what constitutes a fact.

With these preliminaries concluded, we turn now to a closer examination of Freud's commentaries on female sexuality.

THE FIRST COMMENTARY

What we are calling Freud's first commentary consists of a constellation of traits presented as though they were psychoanalytic findings rather than interests, scientific conclusions rather than problems for further research. As such, this first commentary conveys a normative message in which certain stereotypes encountered among infantile ideals and social conventions are underwritten by psychoanalytic authority. It is certainly possible to say that when Freud characterized femininity as passive and masochistic he had long since entertained gender as a set of mental characteristics not necessarily linked to biological sex. However, there is still something about his presentation of such gender traits that suggests that all women are essentially passive and masochistic and that indeed they should be, as a natural complement to the active and dominating sexual aims of men. Women who do not have these traits are, according to this commentary, unfeminine. A good example of Freud's trait psychology occurs in two papers separated by a six-year span. In his study of narcissism, Freud (1914) took up a stereotypical difference between men and women in love:

> Complete object-love of the attachment type is, properly speaking, characteristic of the male. It displays the marked sexual overvaluation which is doubtless derived from the child's original narcissism and thus corresponds to a transference of that narcissism to the sexual object. This sexual overvaluation is the origin of the peculiar state of being in love, a state suggestive of a neurotic compulsion, which is thus traceable to an impoverishment of the ego as regards libido in favor of the love-object [p. 88].

As for the women in this arrangement, Freud described them thus:

> A different course is followed in the type of female most frequently met with . . . . Women, especially if they grow up with good looks, develop a certain self-contentment which compensates them for the social restrictions that are imposed upon them in their choice of object. Strictly speaking, it is only themselves that such women love with an intensity comparable to that of the man's love for them. Nor does their need lie in the direction of loving, but of being loved; and the man who fulfills this condition is the one who finds favor with them. The importance of this type of woman for the erotic life of mankind is to

be rated very high . . . . It is as if we envied them for maintaining a blissful state of mind—an unassailable libidinal position which we ourselves have since abandoned [pp. 88-89].

Between the lines of these passages one can find an incisive subtext, with a rich psychoanalytic texture, on a number of questions encountered in ordinary life. For example, as regards the male, the characteristic object-choice of the attachment type is regarded by Freud as a form of infantile narcissistic striving. His statement could well be read as a proposition in the psychopathology of object relations rather than as the normative assertion it is commonly taken to be. As regards the female, Freud is clear that he is speaking of a "type of female" whose aims are compensatory for the "social restrictions" that are imposed on women generally. Thus Freud is observing, on the one hand, the compelling passion that can arise, in this case in men, in an envy for what they interpret in another person as expansive self-sufficiency. On the other hand, he observes that social restriction, in this instance on the sexuality and power of women, can be turned into a power play against men, who are imagined by women to be more privileged in the expression and pursuit of their sexual aims. Thus the narcissism of "such women" may be restored in the very act of compliance, when such an act—the withholding of sex—becomes a triumph by virtue of depriving men of the very thing they are privileged to enjoy. Not least, Freud is suggesting that these extreme narcissistic positions exist in a state of mutual dependence: the woman's self-esteem is a function of the man's attachment; the man's attachment a function of the woman's self-containment.

This subtext, however, was never taken up, while the dichotomy it related to was carried forward as though it were an explanation rather than a problem requiring explanation. Freud returned to this dichotomous view of men and women in his paper on a case of homosexuality in a woman (Freud, 1920). In the course of things, he attempted to answer a question about the irreducibly masculine nature of this homosexual patient. He waved aside the possibility that something bearing on this could be detected in her "physical type." He admitted a possibility that her intellectual style—'her acuteness of comprehension and her lucid objectivity'—could be connected with masculinity but dismissed this as well, such distinctions being "conventional rather than scientific." (p. 154). Here, though Freud may be seen to offer his own critique of his first commentary—or at least of one principal aspect of it—he promptly fell back on his dichotomous stereotype:

> What is certainly of greater importance is that in her behavior towards her love-object she had throughout assumed the masculine part: that is to say, she displayed the humility and the sublime overvaluation of the sexual object so characteristic of the male lover, the renunciation of all narcissistic satisfaction, and the preference for being the lover rather than the beloved. She had thus not only chosen a feminine love-object, but had also developed a masculine attitude towards the object [p. 15].

The patient's female lover, it is implied, was a self-sufficient, self-determined, and self-absorbed woman, and therefore a person of extreme feminine attainment.

It does not matter much that this paper plunged ahead into a number of unsettling complications of what is here set down with such aplomb. Such passages as we have just quoted, piled one on the other, acquire the force of a definite commentary that employs a categorization of traits long since familiar. This is the commentary in which masochism is said to be "truly feminine" (Freud, 1933, p. 116)—to which Freud added, with a characteristic ironic flourish, that if we find masochism in men, we call them feminine. In this way, infantile fantasies of what it means to be a woman have been treated as a feminine trait that may also characterize certain men. In other instances of this first commentary, Freud (1925) contrasted the superego of women with that of men regarding its emotionality and personalizations; "the character-trait of jealousy . . . plays a far larger part in the mental life of women than of men" he wrote (pp. 257–258), remarking also that masturbation is far more problematic for women than for men (pp. 254–255).

This commentary was lodged more firmly in the analytic literature by virtue of having been picked up by other analysts, Bonaparte (1953), for example, who made the curious point that "the female organism, quantitatively speaking, is in general more poorly endowed with libido than the male" (p. 66). This commentary survives to the present. One still commonly hears analysts and others taking the position that masochism is more prevalent among women than men, or the reverse, or asserting their equality in this matter.

Rebuttals of Freud's trait psychology, which themselves retain the form of the commentary they address, have only kept things in place. What does it mean that Sherfey (1966) took exception to Bonaparte's observation by insisting that, on the contrary, the female is better endowed with libido than males? Or, as regards the matter of the so-called female superego, does it rectify or advance anything to declare that the female superego is better than was once thought? The problem for psychoanalysis is not whether we have the traits right but rather the very nature of such a commentary.

In our preliminary remarks we characterized this first commentary as nontechnical in the sense that traits, as the ultimate substance of this commentary, are not the formulations of the psychoanalytic method. This is not to say that traits, even poorly conceptualized, have no basis in observation.[1] It is rather that a trait by whatever means formulated is always a preliminary state of knowledge with respect to the aims of the psychoanalytic method. Thus a trait presents itself to a psychoanalytic point of view for the sake of analysis, much as did the diagnostic formulations we cited earlier in Freud—"neurasthenic hypochondria" and "periodic melancholia." Thereafter the problems of categorization are superseded by the problem of analyzability. Left as the stable outcomes of observation with simply categorical aims, traits are holdovers methodologically from all that psychoanalysis transformed for its own purposes of diagnosis and treatment.

In other words, in a psychoanalytic perspective a trait standing by itself fails to convey anything dynamic by which an account can be given of its varying significance and weight in the mental life of the individual in whom it is observed. Like a symptom, a trait is a point of departure into a whole history of conflict and functional outcome. The danger of trait psychology is that it leaves us with only the connotations of the trait rather than with the specification of its meaning in mental organization. Like any particular symptom (Katan, 1937), any particular trait, studied as it appears in the mental life of various patients, will reveal significant variation in its role in individual motive and purpose.

Traits are problematic for psychoanalysis because it lacks a critical

---

[1]We acknowledge a vast academic literature on the problems of observation and conceptualization of traits (e.g., Allport, 1968; Deaux, 1984), but these are not the problems that concern us at the moment. Our problem has to do with the adequacy of any pure trait psychology to represent what is particularly pertinent to a psychoanalytic slant on human affairs.

strategy that might improve on a mere mythology of traits. When Freud (1914) went into the matter of object-choice in men and women, he introduced the difference itself with no reference at all to the method by which he came by the difference. All he said was, that "a comparison of the male and female sexes. . . shows that there are fundamental differences between them in respect to their type of object of choice . . ." (p. 87). This is not unusual for psychoanalytic writing on traits, where the principal support for belief in the existence of a trait seems simply to be consensus among analysts that certain observations are relevant to patients being classified. Such a means of justification is little more than an authorization of common sense, and while this is not necessarily a plunge off the deep end, common sense does not always stand to reason.

Again, take Freud's observation of the categorical difference between men and women in love. How does this treatment of object-choice as a trait square with Freud's observation that women are preponderantly the masochistic sex? Using as a criterion the idea of Krafft-Ebing, and of Freud as well, that enactments and fantasies of sexual bondage are the most crucial aspects of masochism (Grossman, 1986b), which sex in Freud's description of men and women in love is the more masochistic? Which sex better corresponds to the following entry in the 1872 diary of Leopold von Sacher-Masoch?

> I do not wish to be ill-treated by someone who loves me too much but by someone who loves me too little. I find jealousy excruciating and yet I am enraptured if a woman makes me jealous, betrays me and behaves badly to me . . . . I require the woman I love to be superior to me by being in complete control of her own sensuality and subduing me through mine. Consequently, my cruel ideal woman is for me simply the instrument by which I terrorize myself [Cleugh, 1967, p. 96].

This expresses the enlistment of the self-sufficient and sexually aloof woman as a source of gratification that is typically masochistic. In fact, Bloch (1908) noted that women are less likely than men to become masochistic perverts because, like Sacher-Masoch's (and Freud's) ideal women, they have too little sexual desire to become enslaved for it. In this connection, recall also Bonaparte's assertion (1953) that "the female . . . . is in general more poorly endowed with libido than the male"

(p. 66). Thus, in Freud's decription of the categorical difference between men and women in love, what we actually have is a masochistic transformation of the phallic narcissism of the male, which leads in turn to the idea that since the women in Freud's portrayal are less sensual than the men it may be concluded that they are therefore less enslaved to sex and the object. To put it another way, men's overvaluation of women in an ''object-choice of the attachment type'' is equivalent to bondage, and hence to greater masochistic tendency. This shows how inconsistent and arbitrary the traits assignment is apt to be.

Another shortcoming of this first commentary is that it treats behavior that is meaningful only in particular and provisional circumstances, though perhaps these are recurrent, as an enduring trait in mental life. (As we shall see, this is also one of the shortcomings of Freud's second commentary, his narratives of development.) The error is akin to observing men at war and concluding that courage is a fixed characteristic whose presence differentiates soldiers from civilians.

Freud lapsed into something very much like this in a passage in ''Civilization and Its Discontents'' (1930) in which he dichotomized females and males along a line of what he conceptualized as the capacity for sublimation. ''Women represent the interest of the family and of sexual life,'' he wrote:

> The work of civilization has become increasingly the business of men, it confronts them with ever more difficult tasks and compels them to carry out instinctual sublimations of which women are little capable. . . . His constant association with men, and his dependence on his relations with them, even estrange him from his duties as a husband and father. Thus the woman finds herself forced into the background by the claims of civilization and she adopts a hostile attitude towards it [pp. 103–104].

The capacity for sublimation, which is yet another difference between men and women in this commentary, entails a conflict between human and cultural objects. The limited quantity of libido, Freud noted, means that what a man ''employs for cultural aims he to a great extent withdraws from women and sexual life'' (pp. 103-104). The point Freud was making was that women, unperturbed by such a conflict, must lack a capacity for involvement with cultural objects. Here Freud enshrined the idea that women compete with culture for the men in their lives, while men feel conflicted between domestic and cultural demands. However, when Freud categorized the psychological differences between men and women on this basis, he confused the problems of certain specific conditions of life with the psychological capacities that such conditions seem to call upon. It was as though he were saying that a life condition does not call upon but rather *signifies* a particular psychological resourcefulness, a resourcefulness, moreover, that pertains to only one sex. (Yet it was, after all, with respect to men that Francis Bacon observed the conditions brought about by domestic commitment: "He that hath wife and children hath given hostages to fortune; for they are impediments to great enterprises, either of virtue or mischief.")

However, if we discard the pseudoquantitative notions that lead to formulations like more or less sublimation (or more or less libido) and yet still discern a difference *in the way* males and females achieve sublimations, this difference does not necessarily depend upon a capacity, that is, upon a fixed trait. Certainly there are psychological impediments to sublimation that arise in the conflicts of development. But this is a matter that transcends sex difference, even if it is true that certain conditions at certain stages of life may influence one sex differently than the other. We are not claiming that there are no differences between the sexes or that the fact of being one sex or the other has no properties of significance, but only that a trait psychology under psychoanalytic auspices gives a feeble and flawed account of what Freud, speaking on the "riddle of femininity," once called "an interest second almost to no other" (1933, p. 113).

One way of summarizing our concerns with this first commentary on female psychology is by considering what happens to the idea of traits in the clinical situation. Although we may begin by characterizing a patient in terms of traits, what takes their place as psychoanalytic findings proper emerge? This is also to ask, What does it mean to analyze a trait? It cannot mean, of course, confirming or disconfirming the concordances the patient reveals between gender attitudes and biological sex, which is what a trait psychology of the sexes is largely about. The patient's revelations about traits and ideal behavior corresponding to the fact of the patient's sex and its differences from the opposite sex remain simply descriptive data gathered in a "superficial examination," no matter how phenomenologically searching the situation is or how keen a listener and observer the analyst is. Divorced from a full play of the analytic method, such data will add up to mere ad hoc correlations between biological sex and mental traits. To be sure, this leads to a kind of psychology of sex, but one grounded only in an accumulation of testimony from a succession of patients who are heard by the analyst in the guise of a sociologist employing a sampling technique. Such data are then reduced to commonalities among patients. Enlightening as the results may be, they fail as psychoanalytic findings in the technical sense. This sampling technique, it may be added, may have the advantage of going deeper into the unconscious than most, but as an investigational method it is hopelessly flawed. Moreover, should the results be mistaken by the analyst for psychoanalytic findings, certain expectabilities applicable to all patients begin to creep into the analyst's point of view. This is bound to detract from the capacity, difficult enough to maintain in the best of circumstances, for a neutrality consistent with the theoretical and practical matter that there is nothing technically different to be done with the fact that a woman, say, is on the couch, rather than a man.

Whether a particular patient is the same sex as the analyst or the opposite sex are facts presented to the analysis. But how dynamic these facts become depends on what the analyst is prepared to make of them. The subject of the effects of sex similarity and difference between analyst and patient is attracting increasing attention. We can say here only that from the point of view of technique we classify this problem with the other significant differences between therapist and patient. That is, all features of similarity and difference, as regards generation, race, ethnicity, and sex, are invested with intense feelings by all people. Therefore, they are all included among the issues which ordinarily impel and organize transference and countertransference. If sex similarities or differences are given a privileged place among these issues, unwittingly stereotyped attitudes shared by both therapist and patient may invade the analysis. Belief in a bedrock of inevitable attitudes mistakes the obvious physical properties for the very attitudes that require psychoanalytic exploration.

The essential issue for the analysis is what the patient makes of gender and what the analyst makes of the patient's beliefs. A patient may, for example, declare a belief in a gender trait considered concordant with the patient's sex: "Of course, I want to have a child at this point more than my husband does. Parenthood is more important to me, I'm a woman." If the analyst agrees with the patient, it is in the agreement of the participants that significance and meaning reside, not in the concept of gender. Moreover, the value of the agreement is a function of what it promotes or impedes in the analysis. Agreement about any trait would be comparable to a consideration for the narcissistic need of the patient, a provisional acceptance of a viewpoint of the patient for the sake of the analysis. At any such stage in the psychoanalytic dialogue, statements of this kind about gender are preliminaries to an understanding of their development in the patient's mental life, their particular contributions to conflict, and their particular functions in the resolution of conflict in neurosis and character. In other words, if the analyst takes the step of analyzing the significance of a trait to the analytic dialogue—how the patient employs the fact of being the same or different with respect to the analyst's sex—a psychoanalytic finding is pursued having to do with the possible value of the trait in a psychopathology of idealization, seduction, contention, triumph, self-defeat, etc. Moreover, in the aftermath of such an analysis, in a stage of working through, a certain light is shed on the economics of traits, e.g., on the circumstances under which they seem obdurate and deceptively encourage a belief in their "primary" and "fundamental" roles in the personalities of the sexes. Here we are suggesting the perspective of process, of which we spoke earlier, and also of a psychopathology of conformity to sexual stereotypes. Although stereotypes alone cannot fully account for the problem of being one sex or the other in the social order, they are often treated as sufficient descriptions of behavior. Still more problematic, they are offered as explanations of why men and women think and behave as they do in particular situations, as in the example above. One of the reasons, then, that a trait psychology can survive the psychoanalytic situation is that not all matters that arise in that situation are immediately subjected to analysis.

THE SECOND COMMENTARY

One of the lessons of the *Three Essays* is that gender (masculine/feminine) is not entirely concordant with sex (male/female). Statements that take the form "Men are this way, women that way" belong, for better or worse, to social discourse. Psychoanalytic theory does not countenance such categorical absolutes of sex-gender concordance, though it takes such absolutes as an interest because in the course of individual development categorical thinking is a plausible way of reckoning with the biological and social issues of sex and gender. That is, it is plausible for the developing individual but not for the theoretician. Moreover, it is important, as we have said before, to distinguish between interests and findings. Freud (1920) was clear about this: "Psychoanalysis cannot elucidate the intrinsic nature of what in conventional or biological phraseology is termed 'masculine' and 'feminine': it simply takes over the two concepts and makes them the foundation [i.e., the interest] of its work" (p. 171). This is a consequence of his view that if certain aspects of sexuality are considered in a psychoanalytic spirit—specifically, bisexuality, gender attitudes, and kinds of object-choice—their fates in development will be found "to vary independently of one another, and are met with in different individuals in manifold permutations" (p. 170).[2]

One of Freud's remarkable strategies in his approach to sexuality in the *Three Essays* (1905) was to devise a technical terminology that created a new subject out of the sexual phenomena of what he called "popular opinion," opinion that led to "errors, inaccuracies and hasty conclusions." (p. 130). Accordingly, he took the step at the outset of introducing "two technical terms," as he called them, *sexual object* and *sexual aim* (pp. 130–131), to be employed for his ensuing discussion of sexual aberrations. The first of the *Three Essays* is an account of the ubiquity, variability, and significance of sex in human psychology. Though matters of gender figured in this account, these were subordinate to the laying out of a whole psychoanalytic subject and of certain general principles of the origins, substitutions, and transformations of erotogeneity in perversion, neurosis, and normality, which three outcomes were now brought into dynamic interrelation.

A crucial message of the *Three Essays* is that nothing about sexuality should be taken for granted or at face value. In a footnote added in 1915, Freud urged, for example, that as with the sexual attraction felt by one person for another same-sexed person in homosexuality, "the exclusive sexual interest felt by men for women is also a problem that needs elucidating and is not a self-evident fact . . ."(p. 142). From the

---

[2]The appearance of these recommendations for a psychoanalysis of sexuality in the same paper in which we observe Freud's unmodified conclusion (1920) about the categorial difference between the object-choices of men and women in love—'What is certainly of greater importance is that in her behavior towards her love-object she had throughout assumed the masculine part" (p. 54)—illustrates our earlier remarks on Freud's several commentaries existing alongside one another.

psychoanalytic point of view there is no concept of the primary (and therefore no primary femininity or masculinity). Everything "primary" invites analysis and a search for antecedents. This is why Freud concluded the descriptive overview of his first essay with the statement: "Thus our interest turns to the sexual life of children, and we will now proceed to trace the play of influences which govern the evolution of infantile sexuality till its outcome in perversion, neurosis or normal sexual life" (p. 168). It is worth noting in passing that with this step Freud was about to demonstrate how the psychoanalytic method had succeeded in analyzing a "primary" issue like degeneracy into certain psychological components. Thus, infantile sexuality would replace large aspects of heredity in the psychoanalytic scheme of things.

It is in connection with this general strategy of analysis of development that Freud's second commentary on female psychology comes into psychoanalysis. Since this commentary is grounded in the psychoanalytic method as the first is not, it more nearly approaches full technical status. However, in the manner with which Freud went on to present the findings that constitute the second commentary there is a relapse into certain shortcomings of the first commentary, mainly in the way in which he rounded off the diversity inherent in his own view of development. In his presentations, the idea, for example, of "manifold permutations" was not always assuredly in his mind. Here, as in the tendency for traits to become categorical, average expectable developments tend to be treated as fixed programs—not seldom by Freud and quite often by others.

The second commentary addresses the problem of sex difference by constructing various narratives of female development. An early attempt at such a narrative, in terms of erogenous zones, is found in the third of the *Three Essays* "Transformations of Puberty": "If we are to understand how a little girl turns into a woman, we must follow the further vicissitudes of this excitability of the clitoris" (p. 216). Nearly thirty years later, in his 1933 lecture on femininity, he virtually repeats this statement. Dismissing biological and sociological accounts, he states: "psychoanalysis does not try to describe what a woman is—that would be a task it could scarcely perform [So much for the first commentary!] . . . but sets about inquiring how she comes into being, how a woman develops out of a child" (p. 116). He then goes on to give an account that brings in the object relations side of development. It is this account and those like it that we shall later criticize.

However, the account in the *Three Essays* of the fate of clitoral excitability in female development deserves a better critique than it has received, despite crucial limitations in Freud's knowledge at the time of the possibilities of genital experience in maturation and development. Here we are referring to Freud's notorious clitoral-vaginal transfer theory, which has been misread over the years, by both analysts and the public, as prescriptive of the so-called vaginal orgasm (a term we have been unable to find anywhere in Freud's writings, including his letters). In the *Three Essays* this particular developmental narrative is given this way: (1) "the leading erotogenic zone in female children is located at the clitoris"; (2) puberty brings a wave of repression of infantile sexuality that affects clitoridal sexuality; (3) when the sexual act is permitted, the excited clitoris has "the task . . . . of transmitting the excitation to the adjacent female parts, just as—to use a simile—pine shavings can be kindled in order to set a log of harder wood on fire" (an inflammatory metaphor, indeed!); (4) the temporary vaginal anaesthesia often observed in young women "may become permanent if the clitoridal zone refuses to abandon its [exclusive] excitability. . ." (pp. 216–217).

Owing to its quaint simplification and incomplete clinical findings (notably an infantile genital phase that includes vaginal sensation—what is called, in the history of these matters, "the discovered vagina"), this section of the *Three Essays* has been off-putting, to say the least. However, we bring it in because it is an example of a developmental narrative embodying lasting psychoanalytic principles, while fostering nothing that impedes further elucidation of the problem it addresses. One value of this section is the reiteration of the principle of conflict between regression and development. Another is its contribution to an ongoing theory in the *Three Essays* of how and why various bodily functions acquire sexual significance. Since Freud believed that the vagina was what was distinctively female in girls at puberty, while the clitoris belonged to the constellation of childhood zones, a continued erotogenic dominance of the clitoris would exert a regressive pull against the emerging of puberty and adulthood. In this scheme, clitoral sensations, like sensations of other pregential zones, are not marked out for sexual extinction. They retain their responsiveness along with vaginal experience. However, should they contribute to fixation, their satisfaction will be limited by the negative affects of anxiety, disgust, shame, and guilt, or by symptomatic phenomena such as phobias, inhibitions, and compulsions.

Though these ideas do not match the scope of modern discussions, we read such a passage favorably because it locates the problem of female sexuality among certain general principles of sex in development. It is true that Freud's claim in this passage has to do with a developmental event specific to the female; but it is more significant as a set of claims having to do with the vicissitudes of infantile sexuality in the development of genitality. Morever, Freud was talking about the sort of event that transpires with all the variability entertained by his clinical method.

However, as the years went on, Freud collated such bits and pieces about female sexuality and now and again extended them into complex and independent narratives of female development (Freud, 1919, 1925, 1933). Such narratives constitute Freud's second commentary in full bloom.

A repeated shortcoming of this commentary is its universalization of several or even numerous cases in point to a singular history of all women, this in disregard of Freud's own many prefatory and parenthetical remarks explicitly to the contrary. Because of the controversy they provoked beginning in the 1920s, the narratives we refer to are by now well-known and hardly require enumeration. For example, on the subject of the sexual curiosity of children, Freud (1925) revised an opinion he had held once that such curiosity was aroused by the inevitable question of where babies came from, which could be raised in the child's mind, as he said earlier (Freud, 1905), by the birth of a sibling. While he still maintained that this was true of boys, "we now see that, at all events with girls, this is certainly not the case" (1925, p. 252). The inspiration for such curiosity in girls was "the momentous discovery which little girls are destined to make" of the anatomical difference between the sexes, a discovery Freud went on to portray in these now famous lines: "She makes her judgement and her decision in a flash. She has seen it and knows that she is without it and wants to have it" (p. 252).

This would have been fair had Freud presented the girl's discovery of the sex difference as yet a further route to the development of sexual curiosity. Nor did Freud give any reason why he thought that this clinical finding superseded, rather than supplemented, his earlier ones on sexual curiosity. However, in addition to this questionable use of an ordinary clinical finding, there is a fallacy here entailing the confusion of a principle for a determinant. In effect, Freud is saying here that the castration complex is the instigator of sexual curiosity in the girl. However, the castration complex, a major organizing principle in a psychoanalytic version of the development of both boys and girls, is here employed as a fixed determinant predicting the only tale of development Freud believes can be told. As an organizing principle, the castration complex can only organize events; it cannot specify them. There is an associated problem in Freud's insistence that the little girl's discovery of the anatomical sex difference is the inevitable event that motivates her entrance into the oedipal stage. Here, too, a single clinical finding is given an undue exclusivity in the construction of a narrative of development.

The full narrative developed in his 1931 paper on female sexuality is instructive on other counts. It goes somewhat as follows: The little girl enters a phase of clitoral masturbation as the dominant form of libidinal gratification. Then she discovers the anatomical sex difference, regards herself as castrated, and "rebels against this unwelcome state of affairs" (p. 229). Three broad lines of development then appear. The first leads to "a general revulsion against sexuality" based on the little girl's dissatisfaction with her clitoris. This results in a widespread inhibition of sexuality and of other activities regarded by the girl as masculine. A common notion of girls is that only boys masturbate. (Here we see how a piece of a narrative is treated as a sex-related capacity, that is, as a trait: women have more trouble with masturbation than do men.) Another notion related to this is that intellectual activity is masculine, and this often leads to intellectual inhibition in girls. The second line of development involves the refusal to accept castration and leads to what Freud described as a defiant clinging to what the girl conceives as masculinity, including the equation of sexuality with masculinity. Common developments along this line are compulsive masturbation, impulsive symptoms like enuresis, and compulsive habits like nail biting, pulling out hair, and self-mutilating scratching. The third line leads to the "normal female attitude, in which she takes her father as her object and so finds her way to the feminine form of the Opedipus complex" (p. 250). To put it succinctly, one path "leads to sexual inhibition or to neurosis, the second to change of character in the sense of a masculinity complex, the third, finally, to normal femininity" (1933, p. 23). This resolution into inhibition, symptom, character pathology, or "normality" is Freud's often repeated basic scheme for the resolution of infantile developmental conflict. The first path led to massive sexual restraint in women; the second to fantasies of being a man or of pursuing with vengenance and rivalry the prerogatives that men were fantasized as having, leading possibly, Freud thought, to homosexuality; the third was the way to normal adult femininity, which might nevertheless be compatible with deficient resolutions of the oedipus complex. Though the reductionism enabling these hypothetical outcomes is less severe than we saw in the first commentary, it is still too much to allow a reasonable account of the developmental alternatives presented by adult women.

Now, this kind of commentary, though developmental in the sense that it connects a sequence of reconstructed, developmentally significant events, contains yet another fallacy not uncommon in psychoanalytic exposition. This account involves only the specification of reconstructed, typical nodal *events* and the conflicts commonly related to them as they are uncovered in analysis. The notion that they also specify the developmental *process* involves the erroneous assumption that the developmental process of analysis simply recapitulates the process of development (and that events and fantasies are strictly correlated). While there are simlarities between the two kinds of processes—conflict resolution in development and in analysis—the similarities are not sufficient to make the processes identical. In his paper "The Dynamics of Transference," Freud (1912a), takes note of this, remarking that what is most obstinate in the transference at a particular moment in an analysis is not necessarily of an analogous pathogenic importance in development (p. 104). However, in his narrative of female development, a typical version of which we have just given, an identity between development and analysis is forced by oversimplifying individual analyses—divorcing certain few, though repeated, themes from their variegated dynamic contexts in analysis—and then overgeneralizing them into a hypothetical developmental scheme. It is true that all girls develop into women by means of passing through the crises of the various infantile phases; but merely to specify the crises and their chronological order does not sufficiently describe the way in which these crises are traversed. Moreover, analysis reveals that the psychological opportunities that each crisis contributes to developmental outcome are differently weighted and therefore produce different outcomes from individual to individual. The mere specification of a phase and its typical conflicts does not predict outcome. The mere ordering of salient developmental issues cannot embody the causal implications that appear in this second commentary.

In recognition of this, Freud provided a third commentary, though, it is true, he never systematized it.

THE THIRD COMMENTARY

In the course of inveighing against categorical, that is, dichotomous thinking in the analytic situation, Schafer (1983) makes the point that the analyst does not speak of what something "really" means. For to speak of "real" meaning disregards the principles of overdetermination and multiple function.

> That one has discovered *further* meaning, *weightier* meaning, *more disturbing* meaning, *more archaic* meaning, or *more carefully disguised* meaning than that which first met the eye or ear does not justify the claim that one has discovered the ultimate truth that lies behind the world of appearances—the "real" world. . . . The analytic attitude will be evident in the analyst's making a more modest as well as a sounder claim, namely, that a point has now been reached in the analytic dialogue where reality must be formulated in a more subtle and complex manner than it has been before [p. 8].

With respect to the first two commentaries, it is precisely their lack of subtlety and complexity, the result of their categorical fixities, that renders them psychoanalytically limited. Indeed, no matter how cogently they are formulated, these commentaries can never succeed on psychoanalytic grounds because they do not involve themselves sufficiently with psychoanalytic principles. This is why we are not persuaded by a vast literature on development that claims to correct and improve these commentaries by offering alternative stipulations and epitomes of normal developmental lines and their ideal outcomes.

However, in the perspective of the third commentary, which embodies what we have called a technical point of view, the value of child development and child therapy studies for a psychoanalysis of sex and gender is in the data they provide for the possibilities of developmental variability. Since no compelling developmental scheme can be a fixed one, the value of developmental studies is the insight they give into how variations occur in the solutions to ordinary conflict. For example, the discovery of sex differences by children is never an isolated and abstract event. Discovery, of necessity, is a process composed of events. This is our critique of Freud's famous line, "She makes her judgement and her decision in a flash. She has seen it and knows that she is without it and wants to have it." Such occurrences are always related to other events, like the birth of a sibling, childhood illness, toilet training, nursery school and other social experiences, and it is its relation to such other events and the psychological issues associated with them that gives the discovery the variability of meanings we actually discern in the psychoanalytic situation, not only from patient to patient, but within the experience of any individual patient.

Thus, the third commentary is a framework that includes accidental events of significance. The realization of this developmental program does not restrict input, but rather accommodates input in all the variety that gives rise to the individuality that always distinguishes one analysis from another. Moreover, in the third commentary, the accidental events of development acquire their variable meanings in connection with the strength of various factors that accompany the crises created by such events. Among these factors, we include the aggressive and libidinal intensity of significant human relationships, the nature of ego capacities, the problem solving and conflict resolving strategies attained at the stage of development in question. And, not least, as regards the meaning of developmental events, there is also the factor of memory and its retroactively revisional functions in connection with subsequent experience.

Regarding Freud's second commentary, which we have called his developmental narratives, we were critical of the absence of such considerations. Where crucial nodal points of development—e.g., the discovery of the anatomical sex difference, the change of object—are put into a fixed sequence without an account of process, a static linearity occurs that does not correspond to the version of development found under the auspices of the psychoanalytic method.[3]

Emde (1981) makes a similar point about infant studies: "We have probably placed far too much emphasis on early experience itself as opposed to the process by which it is modified or made use of by subsequent experience" (p. 219).[4] It is this that Freud's third commentary redresses.

-----

[3]In connection with this problem, Freud's Outline (1940) contains an interesting statement: "We have no way of conveying knowledge of a complicated set of simultaneous events except by describing them successively; and thus it happens that all our accounts are at fault to begin with owing to one-sided simplification and must wait until they can be supplemented, built on to, and so set right" (p. 205).

[4]Consistent with this view, Emde (1981) deplored the fact that "the oedipal years are still understudied and may be underemphasized" (p. 219). That the oedipal period is so dramatically rich in its modifying processes is our understanding of a crucial reason why Freud put such store by this period as a crucible of sex and gender. In this, Freud

Earlier in our discussion we referred to one of Deaux's conclusions to her survey of sex/gender trait studies (1984), in which she was critical of a paucity among such studies of considerations of the *processes* by which gender actually figures in an individual's life. Without such considerations, the findings of trait studies have been static concretizations by which no subject can be said to live an actual life. Deaux did not specify what she meant by process in her brand of research. In the brief account we have just given of some of the complexities of the psychoanalytic problem of sex and gender, we have been suggesting what the idea of process consists of in psychoanalysis. Moreover, since the processes entailed in the development of sex and gender are involved as well in neurosogenesis, the third commentary could well clarify some of the awkwardness of the gender concept by bringing it into a closer relationship with the less peculiar concept of neurosis. At any rate, what characterizes the third commentary is the full consideration of process.

That Freud was aware of such considerations clinically is clear from his paper on female sexuality (1931a). Speaking of the girl's development from the preoedipal stages to the oedipal situation, Freud wrote that actual analytic examination insists that "our interest must be directed to the mechanisms that are at work in her turning away from the mother who was an object so intensely and exclusively loved. We are prepared to find, not a single factor, but a whole number of them operating towards the same end" (p. 231). Further on, on the subject of the girl's response to the "impression of castration and the prohibition against masturbation," Freud anticipated a certain amount of "confusion and contradiction" (p. 233). The reason he gave was that

> We find the most different reactions in different individuals, and in the same individual the contrary attitudes exist side by side. With the first intervention of the prohibition, the conflict is there, and from now on it will accompany the development of the sexual function. Insight into what takes place is made particularly difficult by the fact of its being so hard to distinguish the mental processes of this first phase from later ones by which they are overlaid and are distorted in memory [p. 233].

---

was to find himself in a controversy with certain of his contemporaries, such as Jones and Horney, who began to take the view that the preoedipal period was more crucial in the development of sex and gender. This is an example of the way the problem for the relationship between earlier and later determinants is converted into a choice between polemical alternatives. It is not uncommon for theory formation to mirror in this way the processes of development it describes.

As good a statement as any of this commentary, now in terms of genetic principles, appears in Freud's paper on homosexuality in a female patient (1920), which we have already referred to for its nice example of his first commentary. Here we give Freud at length, for these passages speak precisely to several points we are about to make. He is discussing the psychoanalysis of developmental outcome:

> So long as we trace the development from its final outcome backwards, the chain of events appears continuous, and we feel we have gained an insight which is completely satisfactory or even exhaustive. But if we proceed the reverse way, if we start from the premises inferred from the analysis and try to follow these up to the final result, then we no longer get the impression of an inevitable sequence of events which could not have been otherwise determined. We notice at once that there might have been another result, and that we might have been just as well able to understand and explain the latter. The synthesis is thus not so satisfactory as the analysis; in other words, from a knowledge of the premises we could not have foretold the nature of the result [p. 167].

Freud then goes on the account for "this disturbing state of affairs":

> Even supposing that we have a complete knowledge of the aetiological factors that decide a given result, nevertheless what we know about them is only their quality, and not their relative strength. Some of them are suppressed by others because they are too weak, and they therefore do not affect the final result. But we never know beforehand which of the determining factors will prove the weaker or the stronger. We only say at the end that those which succeeded must have been the stronger. Hence the chain of causation can always be recognized with certainty if we follow the line of analysis, whereas to predict it along the line of synthesis is impossible [p. 168].

It is evident that these passages reiterate ideas we have already advanced. In addition, they show that Freud was mindful of the difference between development and analysis, between a would-be narrative of events and an account of process seen from the vantage point of the present. Thus these passages dispel any notion that psychoanalysis conveys an outcome of personal history as a chronologically linear succession of events, each adding to the next its own predictable causal effect. On the contrary, in the Wolf Man case (Freud, 1918) is it not the second sexual scene that confers a "causal" effect upon the first? We also find an insistence on a distinction we emphasized previously, between a trait and its actual weight in mental life, which Freud here calls a "quality" and its "relative strength" among etiological factors. This much would be a summary of several principles we found Freud's first two commentaries at odds with.

However, it is crucial to observe here the additional fact that Freud brings in these familiar psychoanalytic principles of neurosogenesis in the course of a discussion largely of female sexuality. Moreover, he does this without construing a need to tailor them for the subject at hand. That these principles serve both the subject of female sexuality and neurosis has a most important implication for the fate of the idea of female sexuality and femininity in this third commentary. We suggested earlier, in connection with the first commentary, that issues of sex-sameness and difference and their gender exponents are best explored analytically rather than merely accepted as part of the descriptive data of the "analytic record." Subjected to analysis, the obvious characteristics of sex and gender lose their stability as descriptive items independent of their functions in the transference and, therefore, in the more general problem of neurosis.

The principles embodied in these passages of Freud's appear, though with varied emphasis, on numerous occasions in his writing. Freud's "The Disposition to Obsessional Neurosis" (1913), for example, can be read as a virtual explication of these passages, emphasizing the factors of fixation and regression with respect to pregenital organization in neurosis. Indeed, it was in this paper that Freud made an incisive observation of great pertinence to our sense of his third commentary. He was yet again lamenting the elusiveness to analysis of the ideas of male and female, which usually he assigned to biological lines of thought, just as he often ascribed the distinctions between masculinity and femininity to social convention. This time, however, he suggested that an analytic slant on the problem of gender includes the idea of a retroactive transformation of the meaning of previously acquired libidinal aims. The point arises in his observing that it was from the point of view of the phallic stage that the active/passive modes of the anal stage *acquired* the significance of masculine/feminine. However, that such matters as these should be pursued in a paper Freud described in the title as "a contribution to the problem of choice of neurosis" reminds us that for psychoanalysis the problem of sex and gender is inseparable from the general problem of neurosis.

This characteristic of the third commentary places certain restrictions on what constitutes a psychoanalytically technical reflection on sex and gender. For one, a psychoanalytic account of sex and gender cannot consist of prescriptive or normative claims. What Freud said toward the end of his life about normality and abnormality pertains as well to sex and gender. "We have seen," he wrote (1940), "that it is not scientifically [psychoanalytically] feasible to draw a line of demarcation between what is psychically normal and abnormal; so that the distinction, in spite of its *practical* importance, possesses only a *conventional* value" (p. 195, italics ours). Despite suggestions to the contrary, including some in Freud's writings, the psychoanalysis of gender has no means for deciding what is optimal among conventional values. From a psychoanalytic point of view, what is conventional in the patient's structure of personal ideals reflects at least two different kinds of relation. The first concerns the encounter between infantile mentality and social relations, an encounter that gives rise to the formation of early infantile mythologies regarding the differences between the sexes. The second is a matter of why and how particular infantile mythologies, still the fabric of gender, go on to select confirmations from among the gender stereotypes in the prevailing social order. The analytic problem of gender then becomes a problem of the psychopathology of conformity. In short, a psychoanalysis of sex and gender involves an understanding of the costs and gains of becoming one sex or the other, along with their conflicted ideals of gender. We might add that, from a clinical point of view, the issue of the significance of the sex of the therapist and the patient is also a question that has great "practical importance" and "conventional value" because of the meanings of gender that the psychoanalytic theory of gender explains. This question itself, however, has not yet been shown to have any *theoretical* significance.

Freud's little paper on libidinal types (1931b) gives a neat critique of a certain kind of trait psychology. Speaking in this instance of erotic, obsessional, and narcissistic types and their combinatory possibilities leading to personal and social advantages and disadvantages, Freud came to the idea that development can lead only to types, never to an absolute norm. Hence he concluded "that the phenomenon of types arises precisely from the fact that, of the three main ways of employing the libido in the economy of mind, one or two have been favored at the expense of the others'' (p. 219). This principle also holds for gender, because in a real sense masculinity and femininity are similar to libidinal types in which some lines of development and conflict resolution have been favored at the expense of others. Thus the type itself, which is a constellation of traits, is an interest of psychoanalysis that, like traits, goes on to become one concern in a whole analysis of psychic processes.

The idea here that the outcome of a type involves a process that favors something at the expense of something else is a corrective to the phallocentric idea that maleness implies sufficiency and femaleness deficiency. Whatever the social valuation of gender, the phallus gives no privilege in the ordeals of development. In this respect, we are distinguishing ideological and psychoanalytic points of view. Insofar as the phallus is a crucial term in any psychoanalysis of gender, the girl will reckon with its significance, as will the boy, who then must struggle to represent its presence in development to no less a degree than the girl, who struggles to represent its absence. We should not lose sight of the fact that Freud's specific comments on female sexuality in the particular division male/female constitute only a portion of a larger canon on the problem of subjecthood. In these other pages, subjecthood is never found to be easier for either sex. The idea that development is easier for one sex or the other belongs to the dichotomous fantasies of sexual rivalries and privilege that are part of the developmental mythologies of gender. In fact, such mythologies of sex advantage and disadvantage constitute a significant anchor for narcissistic resistances in the clinical situation.

This brings us to a proviso contained in the third commentary. If a psychoanalysis of female psychology is to avoid the reduction to sociological and biological claims, the similarity of the models of sexual development and pathogenesis should be taken seriously. Within this model, other factors find their place.

Freud's scheme of pathogenesis, which is the process leading to neurosis as well as to types, is well known and requires only a reminder. In "Types of Onset of Neurosis," Freud (1912b) gives us his original scheme in a terminology close to current psychoanalytic usage. A few remarks from this paper will convey his sense. In connection with the possibility of falling ill from an inhibition in development (a fixation), he writes, "Thus conflict falls into the background in comparison with insufficiency. But here, too, all our other experience leads us to postulate an effort [of the developing ego] at overcoming the fixations of childhood;

for otherwise the outcome of the process could never be neurosis but only a stationary infantilism'' (p. 235). (The idea of a ''stationary infantilism'' is yet another shortcoming of the first commentary.)

Freud went on to observe how readily we might see the factor of developmental defect in isolation from other factors, but this would be a truncated view, and he insisted that the clinician continue to pay attention to the contribution of present circumstance, that is, of frustrations of reality and the dynamics leading to regressions to fixations. Pathogenesis is therefore a ''constellation'' of factors, in which subsequent development must never be overlooked in favor of its antecedents.

Freud ends this paper with a statement on the nature/nurture controversy, a point that he has made several times before in relation to development and will repeat a number of times again: ''Psychoanalysis has warned us that we must give up the unfruitful contrast between external and internal factors, between experience and constitution and has taught us that we shall invariably find the cause of [neurosis] in a particular psychical situation which can be brought about in a variety of ways'' (p. 238).

This in a nutshell is Freud's third commentary. Certainly if one hopes for a psychoanalytic version of female sexuality that consists of an extending list of categorical traits and a more and more polished narrative of the development of the division of the sexes, this commentary is discouraging. Nor does this commentary want to decide the respective weights of social ideals and biological factors in the outcome of sex and gender. Mindful of this commentary, though often only in an implicit way, Freud himself put aside such hopes repeatedly. In 1931, speaking of female development, he interjects a most familiar reservation: ''In truth, it is hardly possible to give a description which has general validity'' (1931a, p. 233). He was quoted has having said a few years earlier that everything about the development of the female seemed to him unsatisfactory and uncertain (Steiner, 1985).

This version of things need not be discouraging, even though it implicates variability at the expense of prediction. This is unsatisfying only to an expectation that a theory should lead to something one can count on as more certain than variable. However, such an expectation is also a matter of value. The fact is that the third commentary is not without a predictive aspect; but what it predicts are particular processes, not certainties of outcome. Being a synopsis of process, this commentary predicts what kinds of problems will be entertained in the encounter of interests and method. As for variability, this does not mean that anything and everything can be expected but only those variable things limited by the specific processes with which the commentary is concerned.

As for the fate of sex and gender in this commentary, with this our discussion tapers off to conclusion. For little more remains to be said than that if the interest of female sexuality and femininity is subjected to a technical point of view, which we ascribe to Freud's third commentary, this interest merges with the general theory of neurosis. This is not to say that for this reason nothing more should be pondered of the subject. Every report on this subject is a case in point of how patients think about experience and interpret existence. Every attempt to relate such thoughts and interpretation to a theoretical framework is a trial of existing theory. What we have meant to convey are criteria for evaluating such attempts. Controversies over female sexuality, like controversies over pathogenesis, are ultimately controversies over theory and what a theory should look like. Our endeavor has not been to still such controversy; for such controversy has no reasonable end. However, in the interest of ongoing conversation, some pause for clarity about what we are talking about seems now and again worth a try.

REFERENCES

Allport, G. (1968), *The Person in Psychology.* Boston: Beacon Press.

Bloch, I. (1908), *The Sexual Life of Our Time in Its Relations to Modern Civilization.* New York: Allied Book Co., 1928.

Bonaparte, M. (1953), *Female Sexuality.* New York: International Universities Press.

Cleugh, J. (1967), *The First Masochist: A Biography of Leopold von Sacher-Masoch.* New York: Stein & Day.

Deaux, K. (1984), From individual differences to social categories: Analysis of a decades's research on gender. *Amer. Psychol.,* 39:105–116.

Emde, R. (1981), Changing models of infancy and the nature of early development: Remodeling the foundation. *J. Amer. Psychoanal. Assn.,* 29:179–220.

Freud, S. (1894), The neuro-psychoses of defence. *Standard Edition,* 3:45–61. London: Hogarth Press, 1962.

———— (1895), On the grounds for detaching a particular syndrome from neurasthenia under the description ''anxiety neurosis.'' *Standard Edition,* 3:90–117. London: Hogarth Press, 1962.

_____ (1896), Further remarks on the neuro-psychoses of defence. *Standard Edition*, 3:162–185. London: Hogarth Press, 1962.

_____ (1900), The Interpretation of Dreams. *Standard Edition*, 4/5. London: Hogarth Press, 1953.

_____ (1905), Three essays on the theory of sexuality. *Standard Edition*, 7:130–243. London: Hogarth Press, 1953.

_____ (1912a), The dynamics of transference. *Standard Edition*, 12:99–108. London: Hogarth Press, 1958.

_____ (1912b), Types of onset of neurosis, *Standard Edition*, 12:231–238. London: Hogarth Press, 1958.

_____ (1913), The disposition to obsessional neurosis. *Standard Edition*, 12:317–326. London: Hogarth Press, 1958.

_____ (1914), On narcissism: An introduction. *Standard Edition*, 14:73–102. London: Hogarth Press, 1951.

_____ (1918), From the history of an infantile neurosis. *Standard Edition*, 17:7–122. London: Hogarth Press, 1955.

_____ (1919), A child is being beaten. *Standard Edition*, 17:179–204. London: Hogarth Press, 1955.

_____ (1920), The psychogenesis of a case of homosexuality in a woman. *Standard Edition*, 18:147–172. London: Hogarth Press, 1955.

_____ (1925), Some psychical consequences of the anatomical distinction between the sexes. *Standard Edition*, 19:248–258. London: Hogarth Press, 1961.

_____ (1930), Civilization and its discontents. *Standard Edition*, 21:64–145. London: Hogarth Press, 1961.

_____ (1931a), Female sexuality. *Standard Edition*, 21:225–243. London: Hogarth Press, 1961.

_____ (1931b), Libidinal types. *Standard Edition*, 21:217–220. London: Hogarth Press, 1961.

_____ (1933), New introductory lectures on psycho-analysis. *Standard Edition*, 22:5–182. London: Hogarth Press, 1964.

_____ (1940), An outline of psycho-analysis. *Standard Edition*, 23:144–207. London: Hogarth Press, 1964.

Grossman, W. I. (1986a), Freud and Horney: A study of psychoanalytic models via the analysis of a controversy. In: *Psychoanalysis: The Science of Mental Conflict: Essays in Honor of Charles Brenner*, ed. A. Richards & M. Willick. Hillsdale, NJ: Analytic Press, pp. 65–87.

_____ (1986b), Notes on masochism: The history and development of a psychoanalytic concept, *Psychoanal. Quart.*, 55:379–413.

Katan, A. (1937), The role of displacement in agoraphobia. *Internat. J. Psyco-Anal.*, 32:41–50, 1951.

Schafer, R. (1970), An overview of Heinz Hartmann's contributions to psychoanalysis. *Internat. J. Psycho-Anal.*, 51:425–446.

_____ (1983), *The Analytic Attitude*. New Haven, CT: Yale University Press.

Sherfey, M. (1966), The evolution and nature of female sexuality in relation to psychoanalytic theory. *J. Amer. Psychoanal. Assn.*, 14:28–128.

Steiner, R. (1985), Some thoughts about tradition and change arising from an examination of the British Psycho-Analytical Society's Controversial Discussions (1943–1944). *Internat. Rev. Psycho-Anal.*, 12:27–72.

20

The Precursors of Masochism

Eleanor Galenson, M.D.

> I can no longer understand how we can
> have overlooked the ubiquity of non-erotic
> aggressivity and destructiveness.
> —Freud (1930, p. 120).

The term *masochism* has been variously used in the psychoanalytic literature to connote a metapsychological construct; actions; attitudes and thoughts; defenses against and expressions of aggression; and defense against an unloving object. While the only feature common to these disparate usages is the element of suffering or renunciation (Maleson, 1984), the clinical material from adult patients with masochistic perversions, as described by Loewenstein (1955), shows striking similarities: the suffering is self-limited in intensity and form; a sexual partner participates in the sexual scene or fantasy—i.e., it is a dyadic interplay; and the threat is always related to castration. Loewenstein postulated that masochistic perversions are modified repetitions of childhood situations in which attempts at sexual rapprochement with the mother were rebuffed by actual or imaginary ridicule, threat, or punishment, the perversion representing an undoing of the rebuff. However, the perversion itself does not appear before the oedipal period. Loewenstein remarked that passivity is a prerequisite of masochism rather than its result, and also pointed out the pregenital features in the sexuality of the masochistic

This chapter was originally presented to the Panel on Sadomasochism in Children of the American Psychoanalytic Association, New York, December 1985.

perversion, in line with Freud's insistence (1924) that fixation at the level of pregenital erotism, usually anal, plays an essential role in the genesis of masochism.

Freud's conceptualizations concerning masochism changed with his development of the structural model; the role of the real object received less emphasis, while conflict was seen to derive in greater measure from the pressure of id forces. However, while Freud recognized that the pressure of internal forces was a major source of the fear of castration, he never abandoned his view of the influence of the external object. Anna Freud (1937) continued this emphasis in her concept of "identification with the aggressor."

In regard to the area of developing object relations, Loewenstein and others have related masochism to an early imbalance between libidinal and aggressive components of the infant's early ties to the mother. They hypothesized that the child's approaches to the mother are met with disapproval or rebuff, together with actual or imaginary ridicule, threat, or punishment. The child then attempts to "seduce the aggressor," thereby averting the catastrophe of loss of love. Thus, libidinal attachment becomes intimately associated with aggression, leading toward a special type of sexuality. As a result of various types of excessive stimulation or other unpleasure induced by the mother, the parent in this interchange has become the "aggressor" and the child the "protomasochist," and the child's potential for investing normal aggression in the parent has been modified. Does this shift lay the basis for the development of masochism, providing a means of survival against the danger of parental aggression? This protodefense, though perhaps prevailing in all infants, would be exaggerated where aggression or anxiety in relation to the mother is more intense than usual.

Other experiences of early childhood, such as separations and serious physical traumas, have been described (Bernstein, 1983; Spitz, 1953; Glenn, 1984a) as setting the stage for masochistic responses through a very early predefense, similar to identification with the aggressor. In this view, such children connect the mother with pain, thereby erotizing suffering and fostering a desire for a repetition of the early painful experiences.

Implicit in Freud's views on masochistic development, as well as those expressed by later authors, is the role of aggression in both child and parent in the development of masochism. Confusion in this area has arisen in part from the difficulty of finding agreement regarding the source and manifestations of aggression in the young child. As Compton

(1983) has emphasized, the theoretical dilemma in the case of aggression may be related to a feature he views as distinguishing libidinal from aggressive development. Compton reminds us that the early somatic referents of aggression, unlike those of libidinally related behavior, consist to a much greater extent of responses to environmental stimuli than of responses to stimuli arising within the infant. Anna Freud's concept of "identification with the aggressor" provides a potent theoretical construct for understanding the process whereby the quality of the parental object may arouse anxiety or other unpleasurable states in the child, particularly in its initial stages. Subsequently, both members of the dyad contribute to the development or maldevelopment of aggression in an interactive manner, as in all areas of early development.

In the first systematic attempt to present a genetic picture of the aggressive drive, Spitz (1953) suggested that aggressive manifestations begin with an early period at about two months, when pleasure and unpleasure (particularly in the form of rage) suggest the onset of drive differentiation. When goal-directed action begins at about three months, angry screaming results when the human caregiver withdraws and the withdrawal of food produces the same behavior. Spitz views this as the beginning of specific resentment which is discharged via the general musculature, but not through specific acts as such. By about six months, aggressive manifestations become specific. Hitting, biting, scratching, pulling, and kicking are used to manipulate things, both animate and inanimate; these acts serve for mastery and to establish relations between the infant and the "thing," including the libidinal object.

Spitz maintained that the collaboration of the aggressive with the libidinal drive is the necessary *prerequisite* for the formation of object relations, and that the nascent object is the target of simultaneous manifestations of both drives. The "I" is thereby gradually distinguished from the "non-I," the animate from the inanimate, and finally, the friend from the stranger.

Spitz agreed with Hartmann, Kris and Loewenstein (1949) that the infant's capacity to bear frustration—or, as Freud (1920) put it, to enforce the postponement of satisfaction—must be achieved before any perception of the object as such can emerge. Increasing frustration tolerance furthers perception and thought, initiating the discharge of both drives into aim-directed activities. As regards aggression, a major aim-directed activity of the second half of the first year is grasping; by eight months, aggression mobilizes the beginning conquest of space, which eventuates in locomotion and the differentiation of things from human beings—i.e., the inception of what Spitz considered full-fledged object relations.

But the aspect of Spitz's contribution that I wish to emphasize here is his formulation that aggressive drive development is released in its relation to the love object (the nursing infant who bites the nipple and grasps with his hands), aggressive and libidinal drives manifesting themselves simultaneously, concomitantly, or alternately in response to a single object—the libidinal object. In Spitz's discussion of anaclitic depression, the result of the infant's being deprived of the libidinal object, he emphasizes that *both* drives are here denied their aim, and the infant then vents his aggression against the only object available, his own body, most often in the form of head banging. If the object returns within a certain time, all the child's functions will expand, but an excess of aggressive manifestations will occur, directed now at others instead of himself. However, if the deprivation continues, aggression turned against the self may eventuate in death or, if the infant survives, in turning the aggression outward at everyone and everything in "objectless destruction."

In a related but somewhat different approach to the development of aggression, Stone (1979) proposed an evolutionary view. He noted that oral cannibalistic fantasies, which begin at least as far back as the onset of teething, are then deployed from the mouth and teeth to the hand, leaving the mouth free for the development of speech. Stone emphasized that the mother is the first object of these devouring "fantasies" and impulses, as of all other important strivings. Aggression in its true sense, he argued, does not appear until the child is aware of the impact of his actions upon the other. Further, he proposed that the prolonged nutritive dependence of the human infant is dynamically related to the intense cannibalistic fantasies and the subsequent incest complex characteristic of human beings. Oral rage is replaced by frustrations related to sphincter control, to be followed by other displacements as development proceeds. The anal sphere and its characteristic mode of functioning, according to Stone, are the source of narcissistic mortification; the specifically human practice of toilet training provides an increment of object-directed anger, a fact particularly significant for structuralization, as the struggle for impulse control is an *internal* one, unlike the feeding interaction.

In summary, Stone derived the development of object-related aggression from the original primacy of the oral sphere, despite the fact that behavioral manifestations of the infant might appear to indicate that self and object have not yet been differentiated. The oral patterning of aggression arises within the feeding situation and persists as one of the earliest and most powerful forces of the human unconscious.

While Spitz accepts the theoretical construct of a primary aggressive drive and Stone does not, both agree that the development of aggression begins during the early oral stage and becomes directed simultaneously with libidinal impulses toward the preobject (or object) and is subsequently deployed along other channels. Stone emphasizes speech and use of the hand as early avenues for the entire bodily deployment of aggression, while Spitz emphasizes the musculature through which the infant discovers the object world.

In McDevitt's contribution to the development of aggression (1983) he describes an increase in angry responses to frustrating outer experiences by about six months, followed shortly by real anger against maternal restraints, as early as eight or nine months, although object-directed aggressive actions without anger (such as biting and pulling the mother's hair) also occur. Anger at the mother is then accompanied by efforts to overcome her restraints or frustrations, and is particularly severe when she is highly stimulating, frustrating, or primitive, as Spitz had observed earlier. McDevitt suggests that it is the attainment of sufficient *self-object differentiation* that is primarily responsible for the emergence of directed hostile behavior, and that such hostile behavior does not occur spontaneously but only in response to frustration. Spitz and Stone postulate simultaneity and a close interrelatedness from the earliest months between the differentiation of libidinal and aggressive behavior, differentiation which complements and is complemented by ongoing self-object differentiation. In contrast, McDevitt distinguishes the hostile aggression that emerges in response to developing object relations from its "precursors," namely, nonhostile aggression. This division tends to blur the continuity of aggressive development from its earliest forms through the multitude of later deployments, a continuity I consider essential for understanding the earliest roots of masochism.

McDevitt describes a normal developmental crisis at nine or ten months, when hostile behavior occurs in response to an immediate maternal frustration and then quickly disappears. This crisis is powerful enough to cause a variety of ego modifications, depending on the particular nature of the dyadic relationship. Our own direct observational data support this finding, and it is precisely at this point in development that the aggressive aspect of the infant's relationship to the mother appears to take a decisive turn. The more adaptive direction in the handling of aggression includes delay, control, mastery, and an admixture of affection toward the mother (such as teasing and playfully attacking her). We believe this adaptive mode is the natural outgrowth of the combined libido and aggression of the earlier part of the first year, when the infant first began to recognize the mother as a special person. However, if aggression has been intensified by early trauma (Bernstein, 1983; Glenn, 1984a), whether physical or psychological, or if the maternal response to the child's normal budding aggression is unduly restrictive and harsh, as in some of the syndromes we have described elsewhere (Galenson, 1986), more ominous tendencies appear: the normal ambitendency early in the second year becomes more heavily weighted with aggression of the hostile variety; intense negativism invades the earlier, more balanced investment of libido and aggression in the mother, and the mother-child relationship is seriously threatened. If the hostility becomes too great, the hostile aggression may then be turned inward against the self, resulting in the child's biting itself, pulling its hair, and the like, or instead massive avoidance of the mother may occur, along with serious regression.

The more adaptive pathway offered by most mothers leads to the usual channeling or modulation of aggressive impulses, and separation-individuation from the mother can then proceed, along with the beginning internalization of the mother's prohibitions and rules of conduct. Unduly intense maternal conflict within the mother concerning aggression interferes with both the modulation of aggression and the normal progression of the separation-individuation process.

As to the changing nature of the drives themselves, Shengold (1985) has characterized the anal period as a time of transformation of the instincts and of complex psychic structuralization; he follows Abraham (1921, 1924) in dividing the anal phase into an earlier period, in which the expelling aspect of the anal sphincter is experienced psychologically as a continuation of earlier oral devouring impulses, and a later period in which the experience of anal contraction contributes to body boundary formation and a sense of containment. This second anal phase, which Shengold calls defensive anality, is crucial for the mastery of aggressively charged anal and urethral drive influences and leads to the transformation of body sensation into thought.

Our direct observational data provide rich material illustrating the complexity of normal anal phase development, in regard both to the behaviors and affects related to anal and urethral sphincter operation and to elaboration of the symbolic function (Galenson, 1984). Where anal phase development is distorted, data derived from our treatment of psychologically deviant infants have led us to understand the severe anal phase distortion involved in such syndromes as infant abuse, very early psychosis, and "failure to thrive" (Galenson, 1986).

Various types of infant psychopathology can be linked to maternal conflicts over aggression (conflicts stemming from the mother's own early traumatic experiences). Extensive intolerance of her infant's normal hostile aggression may lead to excessive teasing, and a type of sadomasochistic mother-child interaction develops which often begins during the child's earliest months, emerging in full force during the second year. The mother appears to be experienced as the "aggressor" with whom the child identifies (A. Freud, 1937; Bernstein, 1983; Glenn, 1984b). If the child's anger becomes too intense, the relationship with the mother is jeopardized and the infant submits to her aggression more and more; eventually the infant becomes more and more passive, inhibited, and regressed. Girls become excessively clinging, anxious, and passive under such circumstances and fail to move ahead into the normal early erotic relationship with their father as part of the normal early genital phase (Galenson and Roiphe, 1971). The relationship with the father becomes excessively passive and eventually assumes a masochistic quality, presaging an oedipal relationship of a similar nature.

The sons of women who themselves are in conflict over hostile aggression tend at first to identify with the mother as the aggressor, but then tend to retreat from the over aggressive maternal identification to a more passive position, thus seriously endangering the active aggressive strivings of normal anal phase development. With the advent of the emerging genital phase, this passivity and regression pose a far more serious threat to boys than to girls (Galenson and Roiphe, 1971, 1980). The sense of sexual identity consequent upon the discovery of the sexual difference is seriously threatened in boys who have already adopted an excessively passive position during the early anal phase. The masochistic development that emerges during the oedipal phase is then inextricably bound up with a basic instability in the sense of masculine identity.

These differing developmental lines in the early genital phases of the two sexes may account for the far greater prevalence of masochism in women. While the retreat to a passive maternal relationship does not endanger the sense of sexual identity of girls, the more passive nature of their object relations leads toward a permanent masochistic distortion of their relationship to the father and later to all men. Boys who have retreated into a more passive early anal position are far more seriously compromised, in that they sacrifice their basic sense of masculine sexual identity (Galenson, Vogel, Blau, and Roiphe, 1975) and develop a far more malignant type of masochism which may include incipient perverse practices.

In summary, masochism, the capacity for experiencing pleasure in unpleasure or pain, is preceded by protomasochistic precursors in the latter part of the first year and particularly during the second year, when oral aggression is normally transformed into anal and urethral patterns of drive discharge and patterning. Internal or external influences that tend unduly to stimulate aggression give rise to an excessively hostile maternal relationship. The defense of identification with the aggressor turns aggression against the self, and passivity and regression may ensue, leading to a protomasochist development as the early genital phase beings to emerge. In girls, this protomasochistic development is more prevalent but less damaging to a developing sexual identity, while boys who become excessively passive during the early anal phase, in the face of intense hostile maternal conflicts, suffer a serious blow to their sense of masculine identity; with oedipal development, their object relationships assume a truly masochistic character which may lead to the emergence of true perversions.

REFERENCES

Abraham, K. (1921), Contributions to the theory of the anal character. In: *Selected Papers on Psycho-Analysis*. London: Hogarth Press, 1927, pp. 370–392.
_____ (1924), A short study of the development of the libido, viewed in the light of mental disorders. In: *Selected Papers on Psycho-Analysis*. London: Hogarth Press, 1927, pp. 418–501.
Bernstein, I. (1983), Masochistic pathology and feminine development. *J. Amer. Psychoanal. Assn.*, 31:467–486.
Compton, A. (1983), The current status of the psychoanalytic theory of instinctual drives, drive concept classification and development. *Psychoanal. Quart.*, 60:612–635.
Fischer, N., rep. (1981), Panel: Masochism: current concepts. *J. Amer. Psychoanal. Assn.*, 29:673–683.
Freud, A. (1937), *The Ego and the Mechanisms of Defense*. Rev. ed. New York: International Universities Press, 1966.

Freud, S. (1919), A child is being beaten. *Standard Edition,* 17:179–204. London: Hogarth Press, 1955.

_____ (1920), Beyond the pleasure principle. *Standard Edition,* 18:7–64. London: Hogarth Press, 1955.

_____ (1924), The economic principle of masochism. *Standard Edition,* 19:159–170. London: Hogarth Press, 1961.

_____ (1930), Civilization and its discontents. *Standard Edition,* 21:64–145. London: Hogarth Press, 1961.

Galenson, E. (1984), Influences on the development of the symbolic function. In: *Frontiers of Infant Psychiatry,* Vol. 2, ed. J. Call, E. Galenson, & R. Tyson. New York: Basic Books, pp. 30–38.

_____ (1986), Some thoughts about infant psychopathology and aggressive development. *Internat. Rev. Psycho-Anal.,* 13:349–354.

_____ & Roiphe, H. (1971), The impact of early sexual discovery on mood, defensive organization, and symbolization. *The Psychoanalytic Study of the Child,* 26:195–216. New York: Quadrangel.

_____ (1980), The preoedipal development of the boy. *J. Amer. Psychoanal. Assn.,* 28:805–827.

_____ Vogel, S., Blau, S., & Roiphe, H. (1975), Disturbance in sexual identity beginning at 18 months of age. *Internat. Rev. Psycho-Anal.,* 2:390–397.

Glenn, J. (1984a), A note on loss, pain, depression and masochism in children. *J. Amer. Psychoanal. Assn.,* 32:65–75.

_____ (1984b), Psychic trauma and masochism. *J. Amer. Psychoanal. Assn.,* 32:357–380.

Hartmann, H., Kris, E., & Loewenstein, R. (1949), Notes on the theory of aggression. *The Psychoanalytic Study of the Child.* New York: International Universities Press.

Loewenstein, R. (1955), A contribution to the psychoanalytic theory of masochism. *J. Amer. Psychoanal. Assn.,* 5:197–234.

Maleson, F. (1984), The multiple meaning of masochism in psychoanalytic discourses. *J. Amer. Psychoanal. Assn.,* 32:325–356.

McDevitt, J. (1983), The emergence of hostile aggression and its defensive and adaptive modifications during the separation-individuation process. *J. Amer. Psychoanal. Assn.,* 31(Suppl.):273–301.

Shengold, L. (1985), Defensive anality and anal narcissism. *Internat. J. Psycho-Anal.,* 66:1:47–73.

Sptiz, R. (1953), Aggression: Its role in the establishment of object relations. In: *Drives, Affects, Behavior,* ed. R. Loewenstein. New York: International Universities Press, pp. 126–138.

Stone, L. (1979), Remarks on certain unique conditions of human aggression (the hand, speech, and the use of fire). *J. Amer. Psychoanal. Assn.,* 27:27–33.

21

Identity, Alienation, and Ideology in Adolescent Group Processes

Otto F. Kernberg, M.D.

Among Jacob A. Arlow's seminal contributions to psychoanalytic theory are his investigations into the psychology of groups. His work on myths as universally shared fantasies has provided him the instruments with which to study a broad spectrum of social and cultural phenomena, including religious initiation rites in adolescence (1951), fairy tales and Greek mythology (1961), and institutional conflicts in psychoanalytic institutes (1972). In what follows, I examine several issues involving shared belief systems in normal and pathologically functioning groups, with particular reference to adolescence. I do so in the spirit of extending our knowledge of the fields opened by Arlow to applied psychoanalytic inquiry.

The proclivity for latency children, as they move into early adolescence, to participate in groups is well known. The retreat of late adolescents from groups to couples, a phenomenon to be examined here, has received less attention. Also to be examined are the ways in which participation in groups temporarily compensates the adolescent with borderline or narcissistic pathology. A study of the interaction between adolescents—both normal and pathological—and groups leads me to emphasize the phenomena of ego identity, alienation, ideology, and the relations between the couple and the group.

IDENTITY CRISIS, IDENTITY DIFFUSION, AND ALIENATION

The physical and emotional changes that come with puberty and

An early version of this paper was presented as the William Schonfeld Lecture at the annual meeting of the American Society for Adolescent Psychiatry, Toronto, Canada, May 16, 1982.

381

early adolescence and the corresponding loss of the congruence between the adolescent's concept of himself and the concept significant others-shave of him bring about a temporary loss of what Erikson (1950, 1956) called the "confirmation" of ego identity by the social group and, with it, an identity crisis. As I have stressed in earlier work (Kernberg, 1976, pp. 185–239), I prefer to restrict the concept of identity crisis to the loss of correspondence between a subjective sense of ego identity and the objective psychosocial environment. Such an identity crisis is indeed a normal development in early adolescence. This identity crisis predisposes the early adolescent to a sense of estrangement or alienation under circumstances of acute discrepancy between his subjective sense of identity and the objective reaction to him of his social environment.

In contrast, the syndrome of identity diffusion, characteristic of borderline personality organization, consists in a lack of integration of the self-concept, a lack of integration in the concept of significant others, and, by the same token, a loss of the sense of continuity, cross-sectionally as well as longitudinally, of the self-concept, and a loss of the capacity for understanding oneself and others in depth. Identity diffusion may be reflected in chronic feelings of emptiness and alienation but, as we shall see, under entirely different circumstances from those activating an acute sense of alienation in normal adolescents.

Even with adolescents in emotional turmoil—far less prevalent than used to be thought (see Offer, Ostrov, and Howard, 1981)—or where relatively rapid shifts in identifications with a social group, an ideology, or a lifestyle are reflected in dramatic changes in external appearance, or when severe conflicts with parents produce regressive behavior, it is possible to differentiate the alienated neurotic or normal adolescent with an identity crisis from the borderline adolescent with identity diffusion.

The normal or neurotic adolescent in an identity crisis maintains the capacity to describe in depth the most significant people in his life—highly idealized teachers, friends, even his parents (with whom he may be having intense conflicts). By the same token, he cares about people and has social and cultural interests, value systems, and intellectual pursuits, beyond the gratification of immediate narcissistic needs. He is also able to experience genuine feelings of guilt and concern for himself and others, which reflects a capacity for experiencing ambivalence and for tolerating superego pressures in addition to the development of a normal ego ideal; all of this reflects a solid ego identity and a corresponding consolidation of the self-concept and of object relations in depth.

This sense of alienation, then, is a normal experience that reinforces the adolescent's need to protect himself from the intensification of emotional interactions with parents and siblings under the influence of reactivated oedipal and preoedipal urges. At the same time, this development fosters the adolescent's tendency to overidentify with his group of peers, and explains the remarkable homogenization of appearance, behaviors, and preferences of early adolescent same-sex groups.

The borderline adolescent usually does not experience this sense of alienation in early adolescence. To the contrary, he or she may externalize intense conflicts around sex and aggression—at home, at school, and within the peer group. Splitting mechanisms, denial, and projective identification permit the rationalization of aggression by attributing its causes to a hostile environment. The same primitive defenses facilitate the expression of sexual urges in temporary sexual experiences that bypass the profound emotional challenge of the couple.

All except the most severe cases of borderline and narcissistic personality manage to go "underground" in early adolescence, precisely because the groups they join provide a social structure that stabilizes their functioning. In middle and late adolescence, however, when normal and neurotic adolescents are moving toward forming couples, those with borderline and narcissistic personalities typically show severe behavior disturbances and a growing subjective sense of alienation.

Once the experience of alienation of the normal adolescent (which occurs in the context of the identity crisis of early adolescence) has been brought under control by adaptation to a conventional peer group, a new development arises, relating to the establishment of sexual couples in middle and late adolescence. The sexual couple always experiences itself, and is experienced by the social group surrounding it, as symbolizing an act of defiance. The group admires and envies the couple and struggles with wishes to both emulate and destroy it. It makes little difference whether, in middle and late adolescence, the formal culture and ideology of the mixed-sex adolescent group is sexually "liberated" or conventionally "puritanical." The sexually promiscuous adolescent groups of the sixties facilitated powerful constraints to sexual intimacy (by subscribing to an ideology that reduced sexual behavior to a mechanical act and eliminated the sense of emotional commitment and responsibility). The constraints were equal to those imposed by the traditional, restrictive attitude toward sexuality of the proverbial small-town social groups, who reinforced social hypocrisy and superego prohibitions against sexual intimacy.

Toward the end of adolescence, the same-sex group of latency and early adolescence, and the mixed-sex group of middle and late adolescence, are replaced by a loosely associated network of couples, signaling the successful transformation of adolescence into adulthood. Now the shared experience of the couple, who are creating a new, private world of sexual intimacy, of emotional experiences and values, and thereby freeing themselves from the conventionality of their immediate social environment, may generate a new sense of alienation. Each member of the couple and both jointly may engage in a new search for emotional understanding, not only of the loved person, but of all human relations, a search for the realization of value systems and ideals they establish in their union.

In order to understand why normal and neurotic adolescents, in contrast to their borderline and narcissistic counterparts, react so differently in groups, it will be necessary to review briefly the psychology of groups, especially the regression they activate.

REGRESSION IN GROUPS

Freud (1921) described the primitive, emotionally driven, unreflective behavior of mobs, and explained the sense of immediate intimacy their members experienced as derived from the projection of their ego ideal onto the leader, and from their identification with him as well as with each other. Projecting the ego ideal onto the leader eliminates individual moral constraints as well as the higher functions of self-criticism and responsibility that are so importantly mediated by the superego. As a result, primitive, ordinarily unconscious needs take over.

Bion (1961) described the regressive processes he observed in small groups in terms of the basic emotional assumptions that determined how the group operated. "Basic assumptions groups" operate on the "fight-flight" assumption, the "dependency" assumption, or the "pairing" assumption. These emotional assumptions constitute the basis for group reactions which exist potentially at all times, but which are particularly activated in unstructured groups or when the task structure, or what Bion calls the "work group," breaks down.

The members of the dependency group perceive the leader as omnipotent and omniscient and themselves as inadequate, immature, and incompetent. Their idealization of the leader is matched by desperate efforts to extract knowledge, power, and goodness from him, but their greed is never satisfied.

The "fight-flight" group unites against what it vaguely perceives as external enemies. The group functioning under this assumption expects the leader to direct a fight against such enemies and to protect the group from infighting. The group, however, cannot tolerate any opposition to the "ideology" shared by the majority of its members, and easily splits into subgroups which fight each other. Small groups of this type, often of mixed sex, may temporarily bind borderline adolescents in an unstable and conflictual social subgroup, very unlike the one-sex conventional group of normal early adolescence. Such fight-flight groups do not usually develop a coherent ideology, although idealization and submission vis-à-vis the leader of a street gang may stabilize the group within a generally chaotic social subculture.

The group operating under the pairing assumption focuses on two of its members—a couple (usually but not necessarily heterosexual)—to symbolize the group's hopeful expectation that the selected couple will "reproduce itself," thus preserving the group's threatened identity and survival. The fantasies experienced about this selected pair express the group's hope that, by means of a magical "sexual" union, the group will be saved from the conflicts attending both the dependent and fight-flight assumptions.

Another psychoanalytic contribution to group psychology derives from the observations of Rice (1965) and Turquet (1975), who studied the behavior of large unstructured groups, that is, groups of from 40 to 120 persons who had no special task to unite them other than that of studying their large group's functioning, in ways similar to Bion's study of small group processes. In such large groups it is impossible for the members to maintain eye-to-eye contact. But, in contrast to the conditions that prevail in mobs, any member of the large group can still be heard and responded to by any other member. The social feedback ordinarily characteristic of verbal communications disappears: nobody seems to be able to listen to anybody else, all dialogue is drowned in the discontinuity of communication that evolves, and efforts to establish small, more familiar subgroups typically fail. Under such conditions, the individual member experiences an immediate and total loss of a sense of identity and a concomitant dramatic decrease in the capacity to evaluate realistically the effects of what he or she says or does within such a group setting. The individual is thrown into a void; projections become multiple and unstable, and the individual tries to find some kind of "skin" by which to differentiate himself from his neighbors.

Any effort to withdraw from such a disturbing social experience to one's own past may control the anxiety produced by the loss of a sense of identity, but at the cost of bringing about a total disconnection from the large group, thus further increasing the sense of isolation and impotence. This sense of impotence may motivate the group member to further withdraw from the group, or to search for something in common with others in the large group that seems unattainable. Clearly, what Turquet described—a loss of the sense of continuity of self and of an integrated conception of significant others—corresponds to the temporary activation of a state of identity diffusion, which is a major part of each member's experience.

Turquet also described a fear of aggression, of loss of control, and of violent behavior, which might emerge at any time in the large group. This fear is the counterpart to provocative behaviors among the individual members, behaviors expressed in part randomly but directed mostly at the leader. The frequency with which members attack, reject, distort, and accuse each other is remarkable, the intensity of their aggression most remarkable. Indeed, those who try to withstand this atmosphere and to maintain some semblance of individuality are the ones most subject to attack. It is as if the large group envied people who maintain their sanity and individuality. At the same time, the group may easily pick up any simplistic generalization or ideology and treat it as absolute truth. In contrast, however, to the simple rationalization of the violence that permeates the mob (a rationalization due to attributing all responsibility to the leader, in the context of the activation of ego-syntonic aggression), in the large group a vulgar or ''common sense'' philosophy functions as a calming, reassuring doctrine that reduces all thinking to obvious clichés. One cannot escape the impression that the large group uses a simplistic, ad hoc ideology defensively against the awareness of aggression, and that aggression in the large group mainly takes the form of envy of thinking, of individuality, and of rationality.

I have suggested elsewhere (Kernberg, 1980) that the conditions that prevail in the large group constitute what both the idealization of the leader in the horde, described by Freud, and the small group processes, described by Bion, are defending against: the principal danger for the individual in a large group is a threat to personal identity linked to a proclivity for group situations to activate primitive, internalized object relations and corresponding primitive defenses, together with primitive aggression.

These processes, particularly the activation of primitive aggression in the context of a loss of a sense of personal identity, cause the individual to feel endangered. The performance of necessary group tasks is also endangered. To blindly follow the idealized leader of the mob reconstitutes a sort of identity by identification with him and with others (Freud, 1921), thus permitting protection from intragroup aggression. The aggression is projected onto external enemies, and dependency needs are gratified by submission to the leader. Thus, to be a member of a mob provides better protection against the painful awareness of aggression than does being a member of a large group, with its undefined external enemies, or of a small group, in which it is hard for members to avoid being aware that the "enemy" is right in their midst.

The question, then, is, Why do unstructured large groups so easily activate a threat to personal identity, in the context of activation of primitive aggression? In essence, the multiplicity of primitive self and object representations that predominate as intrapsychic structures in the small child before the consolidation of ego, superego, and id—and therefore before the consolidation of ego identity—and the regressive features of object relations that evolve when normal ego identity disintegrates, are remarkably parallel to the undifferentiated relationships between all individuals within a large group. The reason is that the large group unexpectedly confronts the individual with a situation that resonates uncannily with experiences of the preoedipal phase of development. The simultaneous presence of numerous individuals who can be perceived only in highly distorted, oversimplified ways given the affective developments in the large group, without the possibility of ordinary social roles being reenacted, evokes the intrapsychic conditions of the part-object relations that prevail before object constancy and identity integration. Then, too, primitive levels of preoedipal aggression threaten to be activated under such circumstances, condensed with the sexual and aggressive aspects of oedipal conflicts that typically are linked to such part-object relations.

The activation of aggression within the large group is associated with the striking tendency in such groups for individuals to project superego functions onto the group as a whole. The aim is to prevent violence and recover ego identity by means of a shared set of values or ideology. In the mob, it is no longer possible to project anything on the group itself, so that the leader of the mob becomes the recipient of such projections. The superego functions projected onto the leader include both the sadistic aspects of primitive superego forerunners and the realistic and protective aspects of more mature superego functioning, with the former predominating. This explains an additional feature, namely, the conventionality of crowds. Childlike generalizations and prohibitions are part of conventional wisdom, in contrast to the differentiated value judgments of the mature individual.

ALIENATION: NORMAL
AND PATHOLOGICAL

The concept of alienation has an important place in recent American psychosocial studies, particularly highlighted in Keniston's *The Uncommitted* (1965), a study of alienated youth in American society. As Keniston himself remarks, however, the meaning of the term has been ambiguous, and historically first acquired a significant sociological meaning in the early writings of Karl Marx.

Marx coined the term *alienation* to refer to the objective estrangement of man from his social reality, and the subjugation of man by his own works, which have assumed the guise of independent things (Ollman, 1976; Kolakowski, 1978).

Erich Fromm, in *The Sane Society* (1955), transformed the Marxist conception of alienation into the ''self-alienation'' of the individual who experiences a lack of contact between his conscious self and his ''productive'' potential, a central characteristic, according to Fromm, of the ''marketing personality'' characteristic of capitalism. In the conception of Fromm and other social psychologists, the subjective experience of alienation from society predominates, in contrast to Marx's stress on the objective nature of workers' alienation.

I see the sense of alienation as a normal basic alarm signal that alerts the member of a large group to the danger threatening his sense of identity, as well as to the dangers derived from the emergence of primitive emotions, particularly aggression, and the primitivization of thinking and judgment that takes over large groups. The pathological, chronic sense of alienation that patients with borderline personality organization and narcissistic personalities may experience under ordinary social circumstances is strikingly similar to that experienced by the normal personality when confronted by the activation of large group processes or, to speak more generally, under social conditions in which ordinary role functions are suspended. A feeling of alienation may therefore be the expression of both severe psychopathology and of the normal response to the threat to individual identity from the regressive effects of large group processes.

I think that this sense of alienation in the large group is responsible for the longing to transform the static nature of unstructured large group processes into the action-oriented horde or mob described by Freud. The immediate solutions provided by the idealization of the leader are amplified by the sense of power and safe gratification of aggression in the mob that has found its external enemy. The large group, in contrast to the mob, propels its members to join in its search for a soothing ideology or the establishment of a rigid bureaucracy that will eliminate its unstructuredness. The control by a leader whose idealization transforms the large group into a mob or horde can also be achieved by the idealization of an ideology and the selection of a leader appropriate to such an ideology. The person who resists this pressure is willing to pay the price of alienation and powerlessness in the mob to maintain a sense of identity.

This sort of alienation, involving an individual with a well-defined identity faced with large group processes and mobs, differs not simply in terms of duration from alienation as the experience of a patient with identity diffusion facing a normal social environment. The temporary alienation of normal people in large groups and mobs in a free society may become more permanent in totalitarian societies. When a society is transformed into one huge regressive mob, the capacity for the subjective experience of alienation may be considered an adaptive warning signal for the protection of ego identity. This brings us to the function of ideology as an expression not only of regressive group processes, but also of normal value systems.

IDEOLOGY IN ADOLESCENCE

I am using the term *ideology* in a broad sense, following a definition proposed by Althusser as found in Green (1969): "An ideology is a system (with its corresponding logic and rigor) of representations (images, myths, ideas, or concepts) that possess a historical existence or function within a given society" (p. 212). Ideology, for Althusser, was an unconsciously determined system of illusory representations of reality. In his view, it derived from the dominant conceptions a social group harbored about its own existence, internalized as part of the consolidation of the oedipal superego.

Two related aspects of ideologies require stressing: the content of the ideology and the nature of the individual's commitment to the ideology. Green suggests that the developmental stages of idealization may provide an important means of determining the degree of psychological maturity involved in ideological commitments. From earliest narcissistic omnipotence through the intermediary stages of idealization of parental objects and the final consolidation of the ego ideal, the nature of the commitment to ideologies would be determined by the extent to which the ideologies reflect the projection of an omnipotent self or the externalization of a mature ego ideal. The nature of the commitment may also influence the type of ideology selected, or the subtype within an ideological spectrum.

I agree with Green that the developmental stages of the mechanism of idealization, from the primitive idealization of good objects split off from bad objects, to the projection of a pathological grandiose self, to the idealization of objects out of an unconscious sense of guilt, and, finally, to the establishment of ideal value systems as a reflection of the consolidation of the ego ideal, determine the level of commitment to ideologies. The incapacity to commit oneself to any value system beyond self-serving needs usually indicates severe narcissistic pathology. The commitment to an ideology that includes sadistic demands for perfection and tolerates primitive aggression or a conventional naiveté of all value judgments indicates an immature ego ideal and lack of integration of a mature superego. Accordingly, to identify with a messianic system and to accept social clichés and trivialities are commensurate with narcissistic and borderline pathology, in contrast to the identification with more differentiated, open-ended, nontotalistic ideologies that respect individual discrimination, autonomy, and privacy, and tolerate sexuality while rejecting collusion with the expression of primitive aggression, all of which would reflect characteristics of the value systems of a mature ego ideal.

An ideology that respects individual differences and the complexity of human relations, and leaves room for a mature attitude toward sexuality, will appeal to those with a more mature ego ideal. Here, the liberation of the late adolescent from group mores, as he or she moves toward couple formation, becomes crucial. The capacity for falling in love and the development of love relations in late adolescence lead the couple to search for a shared system of values, one source of stimulation for the search for an ideology that transcends the group and cements the couple. The romantic attitude of the single adolescent capable of falling in love leads him in the same direction. Thus, the search for an encompassing system of beliefs, and for an ideology the couple can share in middle and late adolescence, compensate for the sense of alienation that arises as the individual and the couple emerge from the group, and links the late adolescent with the cultural and historical values of his society.

Simultaneously, the mutual need of the couple and the group, a need that tends to diminish as the group gradually transforms into a network of couples, also fosters a search for an ideology that is broad and universal, open and flexible, one that respects individual thinking and differentiation, a tolerance for the differentiation of couples within the group, and implies a task-oriented attitude toward society. The development of an ideology within that range fosters maturity of the individual, of couples, and of the group that is shifting from the conventionality of early adolescence to adult responsibility.

Here I am referring to the search for an ideology that is broader and more task-oriented than the beliefs, values, and convictions of the adolescent couple and the romantic adolescent, an ideology that often centers around shared life goals in the arts, science, or social and political areas. It seems to me that the organization of civil defense in London during the air raids of the Second World War, our own Peace Corps, and the organized campaigns for voter registration in the 1960s evidenced such qualities. The ideology represented by this kind of activity is characterized by an open-endedness in values, restriction in its aims, a task-oriented interaction with the environment, and a search for functional leadership. The activities themselves provide a channeling of the sublimatory aspects of the search for new meanings and organization of a world view, for an enrichment of personal identity by placing it in an historical context, and for group cohesion that respects the intimacy of couples; the activities also lead the young adults toward participating in the cultural and political processes in the adult community.

Obviously, the development of this kind of ideology within a group requires a socially propitious atmosphere, society's compliance to adolescent needs, and an intelligent adaptation of adolescent groups to their surrounding society. There are historical moments when an entire country appeals to its youth in the context of a shared task, and there are dramatic moments when a social catastrophe may bring out the best in everybody in the context of such group formation. In contrast, the rigid social structure of totalitarian societies fosters the maintenance of highly bureaucratized group structures that can tolerate only conventional and simplistic ideologies so that adult couples have to go underground, and an Orwellian atmosphere of *1984* prevails. Here the normal individual's and couple's capacity to live in an adaptive tolerance of alienation from the social system may be a painful but necessary price to pay for preserving a sense of personal and moral integrity.

Paradoxically, however, an open society may also foster the development of overconventionalized adolescent groups in two very different ways. One way, already performed in the normal group formation of latency and early adolescence, is represented by relatively unstructured, large group formation such as schools, factories, social organizations, or community clubs, where a tolerance of individuals and of couples is guaranteed by certain rigid social conventions and a simplistic ideology of clichés that provides a minimal sociocultural structure and facilitates the projection of infantile superego features on the leadership at large. This relatively benign type of group—benign in the sense that it tolerates individual freedom and even couples—may become a haven for people with narcissistic personality structure. These loosely structured groups permit individuals to maintain their social adaptation without being threatened by excessive intimacy, and constitute an acceptable solution for a large number of people. Lasch's *The Culture of Narcissism* (1978) describes the dominant ideology of such groups.

The other is the availability of social subgroups or even subcultures that profess a messianic ideology, our next point.

MESSIANIC IDEOLOGIES, GANGS, AND TERRORISM

A messianic ideology is a particularly attractive solution for the experience of alienation of many patients with borderline personality organization, including the subgroup of narcissistic personalities functioning on an overt borderline level.

The borderline personality in late adolescence cannot tolerate the loss of protection of the conventional group as his normal and neurotic peers form into couples. The resulting exacerbation of his interpersonal conflicts, both within his home and his immediate social group may force him into social withdrawal with the experience of severe alienation—or into reorganizing the conventional large adolescent group into a small fight-flight group with antisocial behavior.

Severe feelings of alienation usually emerge in middle and late adolescents with borderline personality organization. Alienation may take the form of schizoid withdrawal; the adoption of a lonely and rebellious stance—"a negative identity" (Erikson, 1956); severe polysymptomatic neurosis; or chronic impulsive "acting out" and self-destructive behavior. Narcissistic personalities may, in addition, arrogantly reject their environment.

An alternative solution is to move into a messianic cult that reinforces as well as controls primitive defense operations, replaces lack of internal controls by firm social control, and gratifies dependency needs by allowing identification with the group and its idealized leader. The extent to which the adolescent can freely express his aggression and the extent to which the messianic group can rationalize it will determine the extent to which the group either legitimizes his sadism and criminality or protects him from them. The channeling of aggression in messianic cults takes various forms: their provision of rationalization for devaluating the parental home and its culture may facilitate the enactment of violent attacks against the parents while masking the aggression; or masochistic submission to cultist demands for obedience, begging in the streets, and the like may foster reaction-formations against aggression. The direct physical attack of enemies of the group socializes primitive aggression in its crudest forms.

Groups that consolidate around a messianic ideology usually present the following characteristics. The group divides the world into good and bad. It promotes splitting of interpersonal relations into good ones (within the group), and bad ones (with members of rejected out-groups). It stresses the totalistic quality of its belief system in the sense that it will resolve either all the problems of the world or all the problems of the particular constituency of its group. The messianic cult promotes an enormous sense of power and meaning by promises for a golden future, and in the meanwhile demands total submission to group rules and regulations in addition to total obedience and submission to the group's leader or his representatives. This kind of ideology requires a total commitment; typically does not tolerate couples that have not been sanctioned and do not submit to the strict regulation of their private life; is often subtly or crudely antisexual in its ideology; and regulates many or most details of the members' daily life.

Messianic group ideologies constitute a closed system of beliefs, binding on all group members, so that all other values are reorganized in terms of their fit with the group's ideology. These messianic ideologies typically condense the personal life with political and ideological endeavors to the extent of eliminating individual boundaries, and they discourage private thinking and acquisition of knowledge that may threaten the belief system.

Such ideologies and their corresponding group formations transform the unstructured large group of social conventionality into the basic assumptions group of fight-flight and/or dependency. If several groups coalesce into a mass movement, they acquire simultaneously the quality of a horde or stabilized mob as well. Propitious social conditions may transform these groups into mass movements with significant historical impact, as happened in the 1920s and 1930s in Germany. It is important to consider the extent to which the ideology rationalizes the use of aggression and actually fosters it against out-groups. When this occurs, as in the Marxist terrorist groups in Western Europe and the Middle East, there is a great need to dehumanize all relationships other than those of the in-group. Hence, the constituency of such groups veers from the ordinary borderline to the outright antisocial. The characteristics of the fundamentalist religion of Jim Jones and the sociopsychological characteristics of SS killers (Dicks, 1972) illustrate the relationship between mass murder and institutionalized dehumanization.

Other groups with totalistic ideologies maintain a relatively firm control over the expression of primitive aggression. Many religious cults in this country, for example, serve as protective havens for adolescents with severe identity diffusion, borderline personality organization, and the incapacity to either maintain relations with a large social group or even to one other person. The religious cult group provides controls over the patient's daily life which improve ego functions and gratify needs for dependency and closeness to others. The need for feelings of power and significance is met through identification with the group's messianic mission. The financial exploitation that motivates the leadership of many cults is usually unknown to the true believer who begs in the streets, and whose self-sacrifice serves sublimatory functions as well as defending via masochistic reaction formations against aggression.

The emotional security provided by a religious cult, its protection against the painful alienation related to identity diffusion, and the denial or restriction of aggression more than compensate some adolescents for what they are renouncing in terms of personal privacy, freedom of thought and gratification that comes from a love relation in depth. Relatively normal adolescents, however, soon find the vague and simplistic ideology of cults an insult to their intelligence, and rebel against the restrictions of their personal freedom and the invasion of their privacy—including their sexual life. Practically all the patients with long-term commitments to religious cults that I have been able to examine presented severe types of character pathology. Because the early adolescent with borderline personality finds it easy to adjust to peer groups, he gives the impression of normalcy. Later on, his succumbing to a cultist ideology may surprise those who knew him.

There are, of course, group-centered ideologies that do not present the totalistic characteristics of religious cults or political terrorism. Street-gang psychology prevails when the group ideology contains a direct affirmation of indiscriminate expression of sexuality and aggression in combination with antisocial behavior. A group bound together by this type of ideology may be socially the most maladaptive, but is one from which a member can free himself most easily. For this type of group simply provides a milieu for its members without compensating for the symptom of identity diffusion, and it tolerates the eruption of primitive sexuality and aggression.

The disappearance of the leader, or the end of the group's illusion of omnipotence, perhaps destroyed behind prison bars, may end the emotional commitment to the group as well. The way in which leftist terrorist groups both here and abroad have disintegrated into bands of ordinary criminals illustrates what can happen when the group's omnipotence is punctured.

ALIENATION, AUTONOMY, AND THE COUPLE

The tendency to join groups in early and middle adolescence, as I remarked earlier, has received more attention than the retreat of late adolescents from groups to couple formation.

In the small group, sexuality emerges in the basic assumption of pairing as one defense against primitive aggression; here the "oedipal couple" represents the longing of a sexual resolution of preoedipal conflicts expressed in the wishes, fears, and fantasies of the dependency and fight-flight groups. In the large group, sexuality is either denied or expressed in sadistically infiltrated sexual allusions. More mature forms of sexuality usually go underground, and secret formation of couples occurs as a direct reaction to and defense against large group processes.

In the horde, unchallenged idealization of the leader is the counterpart of the horde's intolerance of the couple that would attempt to preserve its identity as such. Freud (1921) pointed to the intolerance of couples in the army and the church.

The projection of superego functions and the related submission to the idealized leader protects the large group against violence and against the destruction of couples within it. But this projection is accompanied by infantile prohibitions against both fully developed adult sexuality and the polymorphous perverse infantile sexuality that is either integrated into genital sexuality or threatens to emerge with its constituent pregential aggression in the large group. Thus, group morality veers toward a conventional deerotization of heterosexual relations, toward the suppression of erotic fantasy insofar as it contains infantile polymorphous trends and sensuous eroticism, and toward acknowledging and sanctioning only a strictly delimited "permissible" expression of love relations. The alternative to these defensive efforts—and their miscarriage in repressive ideologies under conditions of authoritarian leadership—is the eruption of crude, particularly anally tinged sexuality in large groups, very reminiscent of the sexualized group formations of latency and early adolescence.

In the large group, the dominant sexual ideology tends to be marked by an excessive projection of primitive superego functions onto the group leader. Two curious alternatives emerge here: a conventional ideology that is sexually repressive, or a propensity to dissociate sexual fantasies from emotional relations and to combine devaluative and aggressive attitudes toward sex with fantasies in which preoedipal forms of sexuality, that is, polymorphous perverse infantile sexual trends, clearly predominate. The psychology of group sex illustrates the latter alternative. Both ideologies are similar, however, in that they produce a conventional morality that is directed against the sexual fulfillment of the autonomous couple. I think it is no coincidence that, historically, there are oscillations between sexually repressive and sexually promiscuous ideologies: both aim to conventionalize and flatten the sexual experience of the couple.

Braunschweig and Fain (1971) have described how furtive sexual play during the oedipal period is replaced by the antisexual groups of latency, where sexuality is tolerated only in a depreciative, "anal" fashion. This depreciation becomes part of the early group mores of adolescent male sexuality. In late adolescence, open, collectively sanctioned affirmation of an aggressive promiscuity replaces the remnants of the depreciatory, despised anal sexuality of early male adolescence. Among girls, the pseudo-maturity of a formal, collectively shared ideology in early adolescence demanding that erotic sensuality be rejected—that is, maintaining the repression of urges for direct sexual encounters with men— contrasts sharply with the simultaneous collectively shared hysteriform idealization of an erotized male figure. Only in the latter half of female adolescence do both of these fantasies break down. The emerging mixed-gender group of late adolescence usually reflects a jointly accepted ideology regarding sexuality.

This adolescent ideology may reflect an identification with the conventional sexual morality of the adult society, as evidenced by the asexual quality of adolescents in certain religious subcultures or in the youth organizations of communist countries. Even when adolescents rebel against this conventional morality and advocate free sex, the rebellion often hides the fear of commitment to a relation between a man and a woman in which eroticism and tenderness are combined.

There is a built-in complex, and fateful relationship between the couple and the group. The couple in isolation can destroy itself because it has no outlet other than itself for the aggression generated in all intimate relations (Kernberg, 1976). Because the couple's stability ultimately depends on its successfully establishing its autonomy within a group setting, it cannot escape from its relation to the group. Because the couple enacts and maintains the group's hope for sexual union and love in the face of the potential destructiveness activated by regressive large group processes, the group needs the couple. However, the group cannot escape its internal sources of hostility and envy toward the couple, which derives, at bottom, from envy of the happy and private union of the parents, and from deep unconscious guilt against forbidden oedipal strivings.

The inevitable conflicts between the couple and the group lead us back to the concept of alienation. Alienation, as we have seen, is both a normal and a pathological phenomenon. The alienated borderline patient has not achieved an integrated sense of identity, and lacks a mature, integrated superego. The establishment of a pathological grandiose self to compensate for this identity diffusion leads to the narcissistic personality. Both identity diffusion of the borderline patient and pathological narcissism lead to a wish to submerge in large groups and mobs, because mobs offer the illusion of power and meaning that patients with these pathological character formation so desperately seek. Their incapacity to achieve a stable sexual union with another, one that maintains firm boundaries separating it from the surrounding social group, complements the pathological alienation of these patients.

But alienation is also felt by the normal individual whose integrated sense of identity and firmly established superego permits him to transcend the conventionality of the group, its restrictions of sexuality, its cultural and intellectual flatness. This normal individual, as we have seen, experiences alienation where the emotionally disturbed person feels relief. The establishment of the autonomous couple that overcomes the oedipal restriction of each of its members transforms the normal alienation of the individual into that of the couple. The achievement of this developmental stage is a crucial indicator of a successful completion of the tasks of adolescence.

REFERENCES

Arlow, J. A. (1951), A psychoanalytic study of a religious intitation rite: Bar Mitzvah. *The Psychoanalytic Study of the Child*, 6:353–374. New York: International Universities Press.

——— (1961), Ego psychology and the study of mythology. *J. Amer. Psychoanal. Assn.*, 9:371–393.

——— (1972), Some dilemmas in psychoanalytic education. *J. Amer. Psychoanal. Assn.*, 20:556–566.

Bion, W. (1961), *Experiences in Groups*. New York: Basic Books.

Braunschweig, D., & Fain, M. (1971), *Eros et Anteros*. Paris: Payot.

Dicks, H. (1972), *Licensed Mass Murder: A Socio-Psychological Study of Some SS-Killers*. London: Heinemann.

Erikson, E. (1950), Growth and crises of the healthy personality. In: *Identity and the Life Cycle*. New York: International Universities Press, 1959, pp. 50–100.

——— (1956), The problem of ego identity. In: *Identity and the Life Cycle*. New York: International Universities Press, 1959, pp. 101–164.

Freud, S. (1921), Group psychology and the analysis of the ego. *Standard Edition*, 18:67–143. London: Hogarth Press, 1955.

Fromm, E. (1955), *The Sane Society*. New York: Rinehart.

Green, A. (1969), Sexualité et ideologie chez Marx et Freud. *Etudes Freudiennes*, 1/2:187–217.

Keniston, K. (1965), *The Uncommitted*. New York: Delta.

Kernberg, O. (1975), *Borderline Conditions and Pathological Narcissism*. New York: Aronson.

——— (1976), *Object Relations Theory and Clinical Psychoanalysis*. New York: Aronson.

———— (1980), *Internal World and External Reality*. New York: Aronson.

Kolakowski, L. (1978), The founders. In: *Main Currents of Marxism*, Vol. 1, New York: Oxford University Press, pp. 154–178.

Lasch, C. (1978), *The Culture of Narcissism*. New York: Norton.

Offer, D., Ostrov, E., & Howard, K. (1981), *The Adolescent: A Psychological Self-Portrait*. New York: Basic Books.

Ollman, B. (1976), *Alienation: Marx's Conception of Man in Capitalist Society*. 2nd ed. New York: Cambridge University Press.

Rice, A. (1965), *Learning for Leadership*. London: Tavistock.

Turquet, P. (1975), Threats to identity in the large group. In: *The Large Group: Dynamics and Therapy*, ed. L. Kreeger. London: Constable, pp. 87–144.

22

On Affects: Biological and
Developmental Perspectives

Burness E. Moore, M.D.

Affects are part of the phenomena of everyday life in ordinary individuals and in the symptomatology of virtually every psychopathological
condition. It is understandable, therefore, that they have an important
place in psychoanalytic theory and practice. Nevertheless, our difficulty
in defining them and in developing a unified, general theory of affects
has been frequently noted. In this chapter I shall (1) briefly review our
progress toward such a theory; (2) bring forward selected biological and
developmental considerations; and (3) comment on their clinical implications with special reference to the differentiation of affect, ideation, and
behavior, and the outcome of therapy.

OBSERVATIONS ON THE DEVELOPMENT
OF AFFECT THEORY

Part of the difficulty in understanding affects is attributable to their
manifold nature (Rapaport, 1953) and the complexity of the underlying
neural and psychic structures. But while it is safe to assume that the
manifest phenomenology is not all of the same nature, the relatedness
of differing aspects must be recognized, and they must be subsumed in
any general theory of affects. Such a theory must also take into account
the physiological and the psychological manifestations of affects; the interrelation of ideation, affects, and behavior; and the function of affects
in normative adaptation as well as in pathological conditions. We must
be able also to resolve the paradox of apparently contradictory research
and clinical findings, each of which have a validity that is convincing:
for example, the innately programmed, universal nature of affects as

described by Izard and Buechler (1980) and the ontogenetic potential in relation to culture and experience that gives a unique, highly individualistic quality to each expression (Brenner, 1974a; Arlow, 1977; Emde, 1980a, 1980b). Analysts are familiar with manifestations of affect observed clinically in their patients, but the genesis, development, and vicissitudes of the phenomena must be taken into account. Forms typical of earlier stages of ego maturation must be consistent though not necessarily identical with later manifestations. As Basch (1983) comments: "the maturational line of affective communication tends to be overlooked . . . and little, if any differentiation is made between affective communication in infancy and its potential complexity in later years" (p. 116). Still another requirement for a unified theory is the need to bring anxiety, which has always seemed to have a special place, into conformity with ideas about other affects.

Another basis for confusion is the fact that discussions of affect have been heavily influenced by the need to delineate the historical development of psychoanalytic theory; they are also constricted by the theoretical orientations of the various discussants, and often reflect a conceptual framework in ascendancy at the time. Green (1977) has surveyed these trends in regard to affects, and both he and Arlow (1977) have reviewed, from their differing perspectives, Freud's contributions on the subject. Earlier, Rapaport (1953) succinctly described three stages in the development of affect theory:

> In the first theory, affects were equated with drive cathexes; in the second theory, they appeared as drive representations, serving as safety valves of drive cathexes, the discharge of which was prevented; in the third theory they appear as ego functions, and as such are no longer safety valves but are used as signals by the ego [p. 187].

However, as early as the Marienbad Congress, Landauer and Brierly stated that "affects exist as primary structures early in development and represent relatively independent qualities of experience and behavior which are not necessarily derivatives of drive" (Emde, 1980a, p. 70). Other aspects of affect theory that have received considerable attention are the tension versus discharge concept (Jacobson, 1953), the pleasure-unpleasure regulation of the organism (Brenner, 1953, 1974a, 1974c; Jacobson, 1953), and the question of the existence of unconscious affects (Pulver, 1971). The papers of the 1977 International Congress broadened the purview to relate conceptualizations of affect to those of developing hierarchical psychic structure within the orienting perspectives of metapsychological theory, and to the transference and counter-transference interaction within the psychoanalytic situation itself (Abrams and Shengold, 1978). Following Freud, though with an elaboration possible only with advances in psychoanalytic knowledge, psychoanalysts have moved beyond his initial preoccupation with drives (an economic theory of affects) to a more genetic, developmental consideration which attempts to unify conceptualization of drives, object relations, and affects (Kernberg, 1976; Lester, 1982). Brenner (1974c) and Arlow (1977), in particular, have emphasized the individuality of each person's affective life, citing the variations of experiences during development from which different instinctual wishes, fantasies, conscious and unconscious ideas, conflicts, defenses and compromise formations contribute to the form of affective expression. In a comprehensive review of theory concerning affects, Emde (1980a) has sketched an emerging organizational model of affects which, in his view, best takes into account the findings of contemporary biology and psychology, as well as facts derived from the psychoanalytic situation. Plutchik and Kellerman (1980) have brought together evolutionary, psychophysiological, and dynamic viewpoints in a volume which contains chapters by, among others, Tomkins, Izard and Buechler, and Pribram. Some of these viewpoints were represented on a panel (Lester, 1982) to which Dahl brought a classificatory approach and Knapp a model based on psychoanalytic and psychosomatic principles for understanding the hedonic, activating, and visceral components of affects.

BIOLOGICAL CONSIDERATIONS

I shall turn now to the main purpose of this chapter: to present certain considerations about the biological matrix in which affects occur and the sequences in their development, building on suggestions I have made previously (Moore, 1968, 1974). Though initially Freud used a stimulus-response model for affects, the biological aspects have been relatively neglected by psychoanalysts; some exceptions are Kernberg's work (1976) and, more recently, that of Schwartz (1987). One reason for this neglect is the belief of many analysts that only data obtained within the psychoanalytic situation are relevant to psychoanalytic theory. While it is true that significant semantic, conceptual, and methodological discontinuities exist between the various related disciplines, Emde (1980),

Pribram (1980), and Reiser (1985) have demonstrated the values to be derived from approaching the interface of psychoanalysis with other domains. With regard to this subject, consideration of the available neurophysiological and developmental data help to clarify the historical development of affect theory as well as the diverse phenomena we observe in adult patients.

It will be useful to begin first with certain anatomical and physiological facts, as lucidly explained by MacLean (1964). In his view, man has three brains, the most primitive corresponding to the reptilian, the next to the lower mammalian, and the third a neomammalian, massive expansion of the cortex, most fully developed in primates. The reptilian brain serves primarily automatic, life-regulatory physiological mechanisms. The lower mammalian brain, now called the limbic system, has been shown to play a fundamental role in emotional behavior. MacLean has compared the function of its cortex to a primitive television screen that gives the animal a combined picture of the outside and inside worlds, with some of the confusion of a double exposure. It is adequate for perceiving olfactory and taste sensations and sensations from the interior of the body. The neocortex, by contrast, gives predominately a picture of the outside world made up of impressions from the eye, the ear, and the body surface. The limbic system, concerned with the two basic life principles of self-preservation and preservation of the species, must be the one most operative in the interaction between mother and infant; and it contributes most to the interaction of drives, affects, and internalized self- and object representations, to which Kernberg (1976) has attributed cathexis as a motivational force. Its functions and limited capacity predispose to the early, and sometimes lasting, unity and confusion of self- and object representations. Only after further maturation and integration with the neocortex and consequent ego development can partial differentiation occur.

MacLean and Ploog (1962) also presented evidence that stimulation of the septum and related structures verifies the fact that penile erection is represented in cortical areas as well as in limbic structures connected with the cortex. Because of the close neural relationship between parts of the limbic system, excitation of one part readily spills over into another. The amygdala and septal pathways for oral and genital responses converge in the region of the hypothalamus that Hess and others have shown to be of central importance in the expression of angry, combative, and fearful behavior. These neurophysiological findings contribute to an understanding of the primitive interplay of oral and genital behavior as well as their connection with aggressive behavior. The relationship is exemplified clinically in the observable association of penile erection with feeding in babies and lower animals. In passing, we may note also that this evidence presents a neurophysiological basis for Freud's theory of instinct fusion, and it has obvious significance for the role of erogenous zones in drive theory and for our views about affects as well. Relevant here is Kernberg's discussion (1976) of the role Lorenz, Tinbergen, and other ethologists adduced for lower and higher level centers which determine "appetitive," exploratory behavior. Through "innate releasing mechanisms" and learning, these centers lead to a hierarchical organization that is reactive to internal factors (such as internal sensory stimuli, hormones, and complex stimuli stemming from the highest levels in the central nervous system), as well as external stimuli in a way that is purposive and adaptive.

FILLING IN SOME DEVELOPMENTAL GAPS

Having provided this background, I return now to the theory of affects. In advancing his unitary theory, Brenner (1974c) notes that "pleasure and unpleasure are, as it were, biological givens in an infant's psychological development. . . [and these sensations] are the undifferentiated matrix from which the entire gamut of the affects of later life develop" (p. 536). "The evolution of affects and their differentiation from one another depend on ego and superego development. . . and constitute a very important measure of the level of ego functioning" (p. 535). Through this development, ideas become associated with sensations of pleasure, unpleasure, or both, which together constitute affects which are differentiated by the nature of the ideas. Thus anxiety is related to anticipation that something bad is going to happen, while depression is a reaction to an unpleasurable event that has already occurred. While Brenner's thesis appears to be contradicted by Izard's observations concerning affects in infants before the development of symbol and speech (Lester, 1982), it must be recognized that Izard's work demonstrates only the existence of the somatic apparatus for an essentially reflex response of the organism, which does, however, communicate specific meaning to adults. Brenner, by contrast, is speaking of the acquisition and differentiation of psychological meanings in response to external and internal stimuli. His viewpoint is consistent with that of Engel and his coworkers (Emde, 1980a), who emphasize the biological underpinnings and the fact that "the complex affect states of anxiety and depression each have their own hierarchical developmental histories, their own propensities for sustained mood, and their own signal affect systems" (p. 72).

Brenner was synthesizing ideas advanced by earlier authors, some of whom (Glover, 1947; Novey, 1959; Lewin, 1961, 1965; Schur, 1969; and Katan, 1974) had been concerned with developmental aspects and the linkage (in the adult) of ideas with affects. Brenner's theory clears up many of the misconceptions arising from the assumption that affects can be understood primarily in terms of psychic energy (Freud's economic concept) and inhibits the tendency to regard affects as constant and identifiable phenomena that can be descriptively differentiated and studied as the same from one individual to another. However, his theory does not attempt to bridge the considerable gaps in our knowledge of ego development in regard to affects. In what follows, I will try to fill these gaps with data presently available, hoping to clarify some of the vicissitudes of affect.

Let us begin with the initial experience of pleasure or unpleasure mentioned by Brenner. Spitz (1963) believed that one cannot speak of emotions in the neonate, but only of excitation, preponderantly of a negative nature, which he called "unpleasure" and equated with an increase of tension. The positive side of the newborn's experience does not, he believed conform to the popular use of the term "pleasure," as it is manifested primarily as quiescence, i.e., inactivity. The only active counterpart to manifestations of unpleasure is the "turning-toward" response to key stimuli. Spitz regarded negative excitation and its counterpart, quiescence, as prototypes or precursors of emotions in the neonate and related them to physiological changes occurring in the birth situation. In this he subscribed to Freud's statement that anxiety, and affects in general, are produced in accordance with an already existing mnemic image, the precipitate of a primeval traumatic experience. These prototypes serve as physiological models for the later establishment of psychological functions and phenomena. In my view, this conclusion is not invalidated by evidence derived from the "increasingly organized complexity of developmental biology"—evidence that demonstrates the need of the young infant for both soothing and arousal and the existence in the newborn of a "multiplicity of clearly circumscribed and highly organized behaviors which are related to internal state" (Emde, 1980b, p. 87).

Few would question Spitz's postulation of the internal excitation of hunger and oral tension as unpleasurable, but how does quiescence progress to the experience of pleasure? The information MacLean adduces about the limbic system suggests to me the possibility that genital excitation during nursing provides an intermediate stage before quiescence that might be prototypical of the pleasurable increase in tension described by Jacobson (1953) as accompanying sexual forepleasure. If so, this would illustrate her concept of the production of pleasure by changes in the level of tension above a certain threshold and would attest the ultimate role she assigned affects, that of expressing "mounting and . . . falling tension, or simply and descriptively, feelings of tension, excitement and relief" (p. 54). In the neonate this is a discharge process involving physiological tension with no psychological content, but in the third month, according to Spitz, the turning-toward response develops into a reciprocity with the adult. Now the infant's smile in response to the adult's face is regarded as the expression of a positive emotion because it ceases to be random and becomes stimulus specific, being linked to stimuli of a pleasurable or gratifying nature, and because the intentional activity of the infant shows the presence of both consciousness and mental operations. What has happened, we assume, is that the gratification of physiological needs by the mother establishes memory traces of the satisfying experience. These are reactivated when hunger tension mounts again, resulting in hallucinatory wish fulfillment of the part-object, the breast, if the mother does not satisfy the need immediately. This progression from appreciation of tension to the psychic state after satisfaction, even when the need has not been met, has the anticipatory quality of a conditioned reflex, but it is believed to be the beginning of fantasy and thought, an idea developed further by Schwartz (1987, p. 472). The mother comes to recognize the meaning of her infant's motor activity and emotions, and her response to these preverbal signals establishes a primitive affectomotor form of communication between them. Stern (1985) has described such interactions between mothers and infants nine to fifteen months old under the felicitous term of "affect attunements."

The significance of this nursing experience as a positive factor, and of other interactions as negative ones, lies in its implications for the establishment of internalized self- and object representations, both good and bad, not clearly differentiated at first, and for the storage in memory of the relations between them. An associative linkage of the erogenous zones with the limbic system, and through it with the hypothalamus and the cortex, is part of a biological apparatus providing a channel for physiological and (later) psychological tension, excitation, and discharge, an apparatus that precedes the differentiation of ego and id from an undifferentiated matrix. In the initial stages just after birth, Freud's original formulation—that affects are to be equated with drive cathexes—might well apply; for a similar view, see Kernberg (Lester, 1982, p. 210). At this time motor activity is mostly limited to nondirected, random behavior in response to overly strong stimulation from outside, or to a turning-toward when the sucking reflex is elicited by internal discomfort. Considerable time must elapse before the skeletal musculature is integrated under the direction of a central steering organization. In this early period, therefore, drive representation (now redefined in terms of inborn, programmable patterns of neural activation) can take the form only of physiological discharge as an affect precursor, while organized motor behavior and ideation lag considerably behind.

Spitz, we have seen, regards the infant's smile at three months in response to the adult's face as the first expression of a positive emotion. Let us now examine his thought with respect to the expression of negative emotion. Attention from the object, in the form of cuddling and other physical contact by the mother as she satisfies the infant's physiological needs and relieves unpleasure, becomes a quasi-need. When this quasi-need is not met, the infant responds as if he were being deprived physiologically. By the fourth month the infant reacts by screaming when the gratification of this quasi-need is withheld. At this stage, Spitz believed, precursors of emotion are transformed into emotions proper. Here he seems to have been thinking of emotion in terms of a subjectively meaningful experience; Izard (1971) has shown that the somatic expression of some emotions is present from birth, and that the signals it conveys are readily recognizable by others. Spitz regarded perception as a psychological function, not present in the neonate, that involves the processing of nervous stimuli with the help of operations that eventually will include symbolization. The infant may be said to have achieved perception when it evinces the capacity to recognize a percept previously experienced or the change that would be brought about by the percept. This achievement occurs, according to Spitz, through the conditioned reflex that processes these exchanges of preobject relations, exchanges that lead eventually to the emergence of consciousness (see Schwartz, 1987).

As an extension of Spitz's line of thought, it seems likely that memory traces of early painful sensory experiences must antedate verbal symbol formation and be represented in visual form. The primitive, archaic symbolization would constitute unconscious ideation with primary process attributes. Izard and Buechler (1980) agree in essence, stating that emotions may be represented independently of thought processes, but that there is a bridging time in development during which emotions are connected to images, thoughts, and memories. The "analysis of dreams and the process of free association may be viewed as attempts to help the individual verbalize and symbolize unlabeled and unsymbolized affects" (p. 208). Bodily tensions and reflex responses to unpleasure also leave mnemic traces. The production of these tensions, their relief by the object, and the infant's anticipatory response form the basis for communication with that outside object, the non-I, who has the capacity to exacerbate or alleviate the unpleasure.

But, as Mahler (1966) points out, some infants have less "sending power" than others, and some mothers are less attuned than others to the infant's primitive emotional needs. Her view is that in such children secondary narcissistic libido is insufficiently available for investment in self and object representations, and too much energy is taken up in warding off a sense of loss and in ambivalent efforts to restore a state of oneness with the object. I would conclude that achievement of a separate sense of identity requires a self sufficiently cathected with positive libidinal energy—as a result of pleasurable attention to its need from the mother—to be stable enough within to withstand the hurts from without. Excessive gratification or frustration (the latter particularly) predisposes to a regressive refusion of self- and object images. Under the influence of libidinal and aggressive drive energies the fused self-object image may be alternately overvalued or devalued, with the reactivation of archaic defenses such as splitting into good and bad objects, primitive idealization, and projection. Hurts to self-esteem may occur throughout life, encouraging a defensive regression to primitive ego states. An early defensive regression of this nature may be observed in some female children who, in reaction to the discovery of the differences between the sexes during the separation-individuation phase, often associate the lack of a penis with object loss of the mother. If a mother manifests loving behavior toward a child but is unconsciously rejecting, what will be internalized is a distorted self-representation. This denies a reflected unacceptability of the self that will perpetuate the individual's unconscious disapproval of himself, which he often attempts to conceal by outward grandiosity and aloofness from objects. Tomkins (1980, p. 155) notes the impact of such internalization of a parent's ideoaffective posture on the formation of character structure.

As I have mentioned, the role of the care-giving object in building up tensions and aiding in their discharge—this involves the stimulation and ultimately the erotization of certain areas—facilitates a differentiation of the self from the non-self viewed as a source of tension and its discharge. Thus a "cause and effect" sequence with respect to a constant object is established. Though early affect forms may exist as physiological manifestations in the narcissistic state (Jacobson, 1964), it is object constancy that contributes to their development into a psychological experience and that will later initiate their control. Object relations therefore contribute as much to the ontogenesis of emotional expression as does maturation, but they are reciprocally influenced by the very development they abet; many analysts have emphasized the importance of affects for object relations and social relatedness, including the analytic relationship (Emde, 1980a). When it becomes possible for the child to anticipate unpleasure upon losing the object, such anticipation acquires a signal function, and its expression as emotion serves the function of communication. There is, moreover, anticipation that this signal communication—crying—will bring relief from the mother. The emotional expression takes on the significance of a primary promise (Schlesinger, 1978). Since of course it is followed by disappointment almost as often as it is by gratification, a cycle of promise, disappointment, reproach, and eventual fulfillment is established very early on in the relationship between mother and child, even before speech. This cycle becomes the basis for communication and part of the bond between infant and object. Mahler (1966) has detailed the affectomotor exchanges between mother and infant through the various phases of separation-individuation; at the end of this period there occurs, through introjective-projective mechanisms, the consolidation of self- and object representations and their relative differentiation. The depressive proclivity originating in the rapprochement phase may give rise, according to Blum (1977), to a structuralized state related to subsequent depression and the differentiation of other affects.

The reflexive turning-toward of the sucking experience and a turning-away in reaction to noxious stimuli lend an intentional quality to the responses of the motor cortex to stimuli. As further maturation permits the assembly of memory traces into ideation, and as previously reflexive phenomena acquire meaning in relation to pleasurable or unpleasurable stimuli, an intimate relation develops between drives and the memory traces of self- and object representations in regard to the sensation produced and the motor response to it; this becomes manifest in the union of affect, cognition, and behavior. What has happened between the infant and the external object is now internalized, and to the affectomotor communication between mother and infant is added the possibility later of an internal dialogue, through affects, between good and bad self- and object representations in relation to wish-fulfilling or defensive unconscious fantasies. Affective states and moods must reflect the libidinal and aggressive energic exchanges between self- and object representations that accompany id, ego, and superego functions and conflicts. Rangell (1968) has noted that signal anxiety represents a discharge into the interior, and Emde (1980b) states that at nine months affect signals to the inside become psychological as well as social. In a sense, this must serve the purpose of an intrapsychic communication to mobilize, against anticipated dangers, object representations having ego defensive functions. This can come about only as the result of ego development whereby essentially reflexive discharges of the psysiological system take on psychological meaning as memory traces of distress or relief brought on by the object. Emde adds that it is at this stage that affective expression leads to behavior.

The role of identifications in the development of ego and superego functions is too well known to need recounting. Suffice it to say that the controls, restraints, and delays in discharge they induce in relation to reality and the superego give rise to inter- and intrasystemic conflicts that alter the perception of affects; their pleasurable or unpleasurable qualities may be modified still further as a result of defensive mechanisms. However, as Jacobson (1953) noted, "affects may, but need not, be expressions of conflict" (p. 47). With the increasing organization of the various ego functions, affects are tamed, some neutralization of energy occurs, and affects become part of the autonomous apparatus of the ego, to be used in meeting adaptive needs or to be bound in complex ways in character structure.

The formulations in the preceding paragraph, and in ones to follow, are expressed in the traditional economic metaphor, to which many analysts now object but which I find heuristically useful. I will use a current metaphor in summing up: in affect formation a genetic splicing occurs whereby pleasurable and unpleasurable experiences are introduced into the psychic structure and thereafter modify the maturation, development, and future functioning of the human organism and its descendants.

AFFECT VICISSITUDES

At this point I would like to relate the previous discussion to the vicissitudes of affect. Until the neural connections have matured and developed sufficiently to provide the possibility of ego control, the overflow of the limbic system when stimulated would tend to perpetuate the undiffertiated character of the drives. Subsequently it would contribute to their fusion in a more organized manner, as well as to the continued mobility of cathexis, easy displacement, and condensation characteristic of the primary process mode of mental functioning. This mode has been related principally to the development of thought processes and has not been considered systematically in respect to action and affects, although Jacobson (1953) and Rapaport (1953) refer to primary process-type affects. There is inevitably a somewhat uneven progression in the emergence of affects, ideation, and action, which probably aids in their differentiation. Regression to an earlier stage, in which this differentiation is less sharp, might help account for some of the disturbances of mobility observed in schizophrenic patients. Consideration of these so-called "drive representations," however, would be greatly enhanced by an adequate definition and theory of action.

Freud's statement (1915a) that affects could not be unconscious was made at a time when defense was for the most part equated with repression. It was not until later that other defense mechanisms, previously advanced in only a sketchy way, were more adequately described. One particularly applicable to a vicissitude of affect is isolation, which Freud (1926) described in discussing the compulsive neuroses, where thinking appears hypercathected and erotized. Undoing and isolation are the means employed to protect against the painful affect of guilt with respect to erotic or aggressive impulses. In both defense mechanisms Freud stresses the motor component. I would suggest that undoing hypercathects action that symbolically expresses the impulse but denies the guilt by an act of reversal. The process might be understood also in terms of a heightened differentiation of drive representations, with attention cathexis focused on the action rather than its affective or ideational accompaniments, the perception of which are relatively decathected. In isolation, by contract, there occurs either a hypercathexis of the ideational representation or a decathexis of the perception of emotional feelings. Freud simply states, at the descriptive level, that the isolation occurs by means of the interpolation of a refractory period following an act, during which no perception is registered and no action performed, thereby stripping the experience of its affective and associative connections. As in undoing, one action—the interpolation of an interval—cancels out the affect that one would expect to find associated with a preceding action. Freud's discussion suggests that there may be varieties of isolation, achieved in various economic ways. In any event, the effect is that the thought may be retained in memory, but dissociated from the other drive representations, action and affect, which would give it a full and meaningful expression subject to conflict. Whether or not affects have been rendered unconscious is perhaps a matter of definition, but their significance has certainly been greatly diminished.

In contrast to the isolation of ideation from affect, relatively little attention has been devoted to a similar phenomenon in respect to action, though it is implicit in Freud's discussion. The isolation of action from affect often occurs via the mechanism of displacement. Confronted with the interpretation that much of her behavior seemed to be consistent with a conflict over masturbation, a female patient demurred, stating flatly that she masturbated frequently and enjoyed all forms of sex without any guilt whatever. It was not until later that this anorexic patient recognized that her guilt had been displaced to her periodic eating binges. By similar means many patients continue to act upon their impulses despite conscious knowledge of the conflicts associated with such action, and despite appropriate expressions of affect within the analytic situation. Of importance here is the degree of integration between sensation, perception, cognition, affect, and action. Changes in the quality of emotions and of conscious experience—changes occurring throughout life as a result of such integration—might help account for the greater meaning (in consciousness) of matters that are acted upon rather than merely thought.

AFFECT FUNCTIONS

It is necessary to take a broad view of the development of affect functioning. Beginning as physiological discharge phenomena, affects undergo progressive maturation and development as increasing structural organization occurs, becoming integrated together with the drives

and with drive, self- and object representations, into the total functioning of the psychic apparatus and giving motivational impetus to its observing, regulatory, and communicatory tasks. This physiopsychological
apparatus has both an afferent and an efferent function, the former dealing with affect perception and the latter with the utilization of the affect
charge. Another affect function is that of being an "indicator" of states
of tension (Jacobson, 1953). Here an efferent function provides the ego
the means for tension regulation allowing build-up or discharge as
necessary to maintain an optimal homeostatic balance. In its totality,
the affective system constitutes a dynamic "feeling image" for the ego,
a frame of self-reference in a time continuum. In the earliest stage of
life it would be the most primitive form of the "self." Ross (1975) has
touched on this concept in his view of affects as an early form of cognition. Izard and Buechler (1980) add another function: "These enduring emotion processes lend continuity to conscious experience, which
contributes stability to the sense of self and self-environmental interaction" (p. 176).

IMPLICATIONS FOR THERAPY

The subjective, conscious phenomena we refer to as moods, feelings, or emotions are compromise formations, like symptoms, reflecting
the interplay between drives and defenses in relation to present-day external objects and their archaic, internalized counterparts, a relation which
can best be understood in the analytic situation through the disclosure
of unconscious fantasies. They represent affect derivatives and are
manifest evidence of complex phenomena in which affect, ideation, and
action (whether physical or psychological) are inseparably associated.
Brenner (1974a, 1974c) and Arlow (1977) have emphasized this repeatedly.
Perhaps it will be useful, however, if I illustrate the point with a brief
clinical vignette.

After a weekend, a college student reported that she had been having a very good time until Sunday, when she had felt unaccountably
depressed. In a long telephone conversation with her boyfriend, who had
graduated and was then working in a distant city, she had been so complaining and dependent that she feared he would want nothing further
to do with her. In earlier sessions she had reported her dissatisfaction
with previous telephone conversations during which her boyfriend had
spent most of the time telling her about his work problems and had made

almost no inquiry about her. I mentioned that she had said that she had been having a good time, and she explained that on Saturday a fraternity brother of her boyfriend had taken her to a party. They had been very compatible. He was interested in her and her activities and she had enjoyed herself immensely. She wondered if he would ask her out again. At this point it became possible to understand her depression. Angry at her boyfriend for his inattention and seeming lack of interest in her, she had unconsciously fantasied dropping him in favor of his fraternity brother. Her aggression toward the boyfriend, and a sense of disloyalty inconsistent with her ego ideal, had led to guilt and—as punishment— the projected fantasy that he would abandon her. Depression was the affect appropriate to such a loss—both of the object and of her own idealized self. Her complaining and dependency were expressions of aggression but asserted at the same time how needful she was of her boyfriend's loving care.

It is an observed fact that patients believe that they are helped most when there is a release of affect. On the assumption that inhibition of affect expression is related to unconscious ideation, we are accustomed in analysis to interpreting unconscious fantasies in the hopeful expectation that the affect will be expressed. There is no question that this often occurs after long and arduous efforts in the interpretation of defenses and in working through. But sometimes we are disappointed. There are patients with chronic affective states who are highly resistant to change. In these patients the affective imprint may have been too strong at the preverbal stage, and the ideation we elicit may be secondary, preselected to express, defend against, or master the affect. In constantly changing situations, the same instinctual urges, conflicts, and defenses, accompanied by the same affect, are persistently experienced. The consequences for therapy are signified in such concepts as repetition-compulsion, moral masochism, and negative therapeutic reaction. As an alternative to failure of technique, I offer as an explanation the proposition that we may be dealing here with a "feeling image," relatively fixed by experiences affecting the limbic system in the distant past and then stored as a memory in the lower mammalian brain, which can only dimly seek ideational association of an appropriate kind. I have epitomized this situation as "the affect in search of an idea" (Moore, 1974). Unquestionably this is a reciprocal process, but in some cases the affect is primary and perhaps modifiable only to a limited degree through verbal approaches. In such intractable patients, I question whether the isolation of affects from ideation is entirely psychological in nature: could it not be the biological result of the existence of separate brains in the human organism, a phylogenetic barrier to the integration of drive representations? Like the stimulus barrier, this barrier too may vary from one individual to another.

Despite my caution that there may be limitations to the effectiveness of approaching the limbic system through the neocortex, I would like to stress that analysis goes beyond that conceptualization, which is the reason it offers the greatest potential for change even in such difficult cases. Rangell (1968) has pointed out that Freud's second, "signal" anxiety theory can be used to explain the anxiety observed in the traumatic situations that gave rise to the first theory. Rangell suggested that the ego, by permitting small, trial discharges of instinctual tension, tests the likelihood of mastery. If a minor traumatic state ensues, the ego may judge the potential consequences of further discharge by comparison of the induced traumatic state with the memory of previous traumas. By such titration the ego becomes aware of danger, which automatically brings on the anxiety signal. I would add that the ego must constantly and repetitively employ such trial discharges. This may be one of the functions of fantasy, e.g., the masochistic fantasies of certain patients. The analytic situation facilitates these trial discharges; the analysis repeats, in essence, the dyadic relationship of mother and infant, offering the possibility for a corrective repetition of childhood development but on a higher level facilitating the integration of affect, ideation, and action. Though the analyst's interpretations are given in verbal form, they have affective nuances. By his empathic responses the analyst restores the projective-introjective communication that occurred between mother and infant, and he creates a situation of object constancy—the basis of differentiation of self- and object representations and the sense of a separate identity. This permits a satisfying affective communication between self- and object representations and enhances the capacity to tolerate aloneness without the eruption into awareness of unpleasant and disruptive affective components. Internalization of the analyst occurs primarily through auditory channels, the route of the superego and reality, but ideally this is accomplished in a situation of benign acceptance of derivatives of id, ego, and superego conflicts and defenses. Such acceptance reduces conflict, frees neutralized energy for the synthetic function of the ego, and aids in the integration of the total personality. The result is a structural modification, a state of greater harmony between the psychic systems. Instinctual discharge may occur in this improved situation with less danger and hence with modulated affect below the danger level.

REFERENCES

Abrams, S., & Shengold, L. (1978), Some reflections on the topic of the 30th Congress: Affects and the psychoanalytic situation. *Internat. J. Psycho-Anal.,* 59:395–407.

Arlow, J. A. (1977), Affects and the psychoanalytic situation. *Internat. J. Psycho-Anal.,* 58:157–169.

Basch, M. F. (1983), Empathic understanding: A review of the concept and some theoretical considerations. *J. Amer. Psychoanal. Assn.,* 31:101–124.

Blum, H. P. (1977), The prototype of preoedipal reconstruction. *J. Amer. Psychoanal. Assn.,* 25:757–785.

Brenner, C. (1953), An addendum to Freud's theory of anxiety. *Internat. J. Psycho-Anal.,* 34:18–24.

———— (1974a), The concept and phenomenology of depression, with special reference to the aged: Some observations on depression, on nosology, on affects, and on mourning. *J. Geriatric Psychiat.,* 7:6–20.

———— (1974b), Depression, anxiety and affect theory. *Internat. J. Psycho-Anal.,* 55:25–32.

———— (1974c). On the nature and development of affects: A unified theory. *Psychoanal. Quart.,* 43:532–566.

Emde, R. N. (1980a), Toward a psychoanalytic theory of affect. I. The organizational model and its propositions. In: *The Course of Life: Psychoanalytic Contributions toward Understanding Personality Development.* Vol. 1. ed. S. J. Greenspan and G. H. Pollock. Washington, DC: National Institute of Mental Health, pp. 63–83.

———— (1980b), Toward a psychoanalytic theory of affect. II. Emerging models of emotional development in infancy. In: *The Course of Life: Psychoanalytic Contributions toward Understanding Personality Development.* Vol. 1, ed. S. J. Greenspan and G. H. Pollock. Washington, DC: National Institute of Mental Health, pp. 85–111.

Freud, S. (1915a). Repression. *Standard Edition,* 14:146–158. London: Hogarth Press, 1957.

———— (1915b), The unconscious. *Standard Edition,* 14:166–215. London: Hogarth Press, 1957.

———— (1926), Inhibitions, symptoms and anxiety. *Standard Edition,* 20:87–174. London: Hogarth Press, 1959.

Glover, E. (1947), Basic mental concepts: Their clinical and theoretical value. *Psychoanal. Quart.,* 16:482–506.

Green, A. (1977), Conceptions of affect. *Internat. J. Psycho-Anal.,* 58:129–156.

Izard, C. E. (1971), *The Face of Emotion.* New York: Appleton-Century-Crofts.

_____ & Buechler, S. (1980), Aspects of consciousness and personality in terms of differential emotions theory. In: *Emotion: Theory, Research, and Experience*, Vol. 1., ed. R. Plutchik & H. Kellerman. New York: Academic Press, pp. 165–187.

Jacobson, E. (1953), The affects and their pleasure-unpleasure qualities in relation to the psychic discharge processes. In: *Drives, Affects, Behavior*, Vol. 1., ed. R. M. Loewenstein. New York: International Universities Press, pp. 38–66.

_____ (1957), On normal and pathological moods: Their nature and functions. *The Psychoanalytic Study of the Child*, 12:73–113. New York: International Universities Press.

_____ (1964), *The Self and the Object World*. New York: International Universities Press.

Katan, A. (1972), The infant's first reaction to strangers: Distress or anxiety? *Internat. J. Psycho-Anal.*, 53:501–503.

Kernberg, O. F. (1976), *Object Relations Theory and Clinical Psychoanalysis*. New York: Aronson.

Lester, E. rep. (1982), Panel: New directions in affect theory. *J. Amer. Psychoanal. Assn.*, 30:197–211.

Lewin, B. D. (1961), Reflections on depression. *The Psychoanalytic Study of the Child*, 16:321–331. New York: International Universities Press.

_____ (1965), Reflections on affect. In: *Drives, Affects, Behavior*, Vol. 2, ed. M. Schur. New York: International Universities Press, pp. 23–37.

MacLean, P. D. (1964), Man and his animal brains. *Modern Medicine*, 32:95–106.

_____ (1969), A triune concept of the brain and behavior. In: *The Clarence M. Hincks Memorial Lectures*, ed. T. Boag & D. Campbell. Toronto: University of Toronto Press, pp. 4–66.

_____ & Ploog, D. (1962), Cerebral representation of penile erection. *J. Neurosphysiol.*, 25:29–55.

Mahler, M. S. (1966), Notes on the development of basic moods: The depressive affect in psychoanalysis. In: *Psychoanalysis—A General Psychology: Essays in Honor of Heinz Hartmann*. ed. R. M. Loewenstein, L. Newman, M. Schur, & A. J. Solnit New York: International Universities Press, pp. 152–168.

_____ (1968), *On Human Symbiosis and the Vicissitudes of Individuation: Vol. I. Infantile Psychosis*. New York: International Universities Press.

Moore, B. E. (1968), Some genetic and developmental considerations in regard to affects. Reported in: Panel on the psychoanalytic theory of affects, rep. L. Lofgren. *J. Amer. Psychoanal. Assn.*, 16:638–650.

_____ (1974), The affect in search of an idea. Reported in: Panel toward a theory of affects, rep. P. Castelnuovo-Tedesco, *J. Amer. Psychoanal. Assn.*, 22:612–625.

Novey, S. (1959), A clinical view of affect theory in psychoanalysis. *Interniat. J. Psycho-Anal.*, 40:94–104.

———— (1961), Further considerations on affect theory in psychoanalysis. *Internat. J. Psycho-Anal.*, 42:21–31.

Plutchik, R., & Kellerman, H. (1980), *Emotion: Theory, Research, and Experience*, Vol. 1. New York: Analytic Press.

Pribram, K. H. (1980), The biology of emotions and other feelings. In: *Emotion: Theory, Research, and Experience*, Vol. 1, ed. R. Plutchik & H. Kellerman. New York: Academic Press, pp. 245–269.

Pulver, S. E. (1971), Can affects be unconscious? *Internat. J. Psycho-Anal.*, 52:347–354.

Rangell, L. (1968), A further attempt to resolve the "problem of anxiety." *J. Amer. Psychoanal Assn.*, 16:371–404.

Rapaport, D. (1953), On the psychoanalytic theory of affects. *Internat. J. Psycho-Anal.*, 34:177–198.

Reiser, M. F. (1985), Converging sectors of psychoanalysis and neurobiology: Mutual challenge and opportunity. *J. Amer. Psychoanal. Assn.*, 33:11–34.

Ross, N. (1975), Affect as cognition: With observations on the meanings of mystical states. *Internat. Rev. Psycho-Anal.*, 2:75–93.

Schlesinger, H. (1978), Developmental and regressive aspects of the making and breaking of promises. In: *The Human Mind Revisited*. ed. S. Smith. New York: International Universities Press, pp. 21–50.

Schur, M. (1969), Affects and congnition. *Internat. J. Psycho-Anal.*, 50:647–653.

Schwartz, A. (1987), Drives, affects, behavior—and learning: Approaches to the psychobiology of emotion and to an integration of psychoanalytic and neurobiologic thought. *J. Amer. Psychoanal. Assn.*, 35:467–506.

Spitz, R. A. (1963). Ontogenesis: The proleptic function of emotion. In: *Expression of the Emotions in Man*, ed. P. B. Knapp. New York: International Universities Press.

Stern, D. N. (1985), *The Interpersonal World of the Infant*. New York: Basic Books.

Tomkins, S. S. (1980), Affect as amplification: Some modifications in theory. In: *Emotion: Theory, Research, and Experience*, Vol. 1., ed. R. Plutchik & H. Kellerman. New York: Academic Press, pp. 141–164.

Part VII

PSYCHOPATHOLOGY IN CLINICAL PRACTICE

23

Mothers, Daughters, and Eating Disorders

Samuel Ritvo, M.D.

An epidemic of eating disorders occurring almost entirely in adolescent and young adult women has been raging for almost two decades. A bewildering array of etiological factors have been proposed. These can be divided into external forces—social, cultural, economic—and internal forces related to the use of food, eating, and body image in the expression of intrapsychic conflict (Ritvo, 1984). Eating disorders, with their depressive and obsessional clinical features, are in vogue today, much as conversion hysteria was in vogue in the 1880s and 1890s. It is an indication of how extensively the psychoanalytic paradigm has pervaded our culture that conversion hysteria is too naive or disingenuous a condition to pass the sophisticated scrutiny of a generation that takes unconscious conflict for granted. For a fuller understanding of the eating disorders, and especially why they occur so preponderantly in women, we must examine the psychosexual development and intrapsychic life of women. Psychoanalysis and psychotherapy of adolescent and young adult women with eating disorders corroborate the view that the relationship with the mother is a major dynamic factor in conflicts with respect to the patient's own body and that of the mother, and that this relationship plays a central role not only in the etiology of eating disorders but in the girl's efforts to achieve greater autonomy and independence.

Several features of the girl's preoedipal attachment to the mother contribute to the girl's lifelong relationship with her mother; in instances where constitution and experience effect a pathogenic combination, these result in severe and protracted conflict which leaves its stamp on the girl's psychosexual development. The most troublesome distortion in this regard occurs in the direction of sadomasochism and the pathological defenses erected against it. The quality and intensity of aggression is a major constitutional variable here; derivatives of the aggressive drive, with the mother as external object and introject, play a leading role in symptom formation, including eating disorders. The girl's conflict over agression toward the mother has its earliest roots in the preoedipal relationship with the mother. The girl's preoedipal attachment to the mother lasts longer than the boy's, which merges much earlier into the oedipus complex (Brunswick, 1940). The girl's preoedipal mother attachment is in some respects similar to the oedipus complex of the boy, with the mother as love object and the father as rival. Out of the castration complex this later gives way to the passive oedipus complex of the girl, with the father as love object and the mother as rival. However, the active oedipal-like tie to the mother persists or can be revived and is a major contributor to the androgynous fantasies which play a dynamic role in the girl's development and in the eating disorders of many women.

The first attachment to the mother derives its strength and tenacity largely from her bodily contact and care, especially the feeding of the child. The child's aggression arises in the same context, as the mother or caregiver has to curb the burgeoning activity of the child, which is both a feature of growth and a defensive overcoming of the earlier passivity. The child's hostility is greatly increased by the inevitable narcissistic injuries experienced as coming from the mother: weaning; the birth of a sibling; the relationship between the parents; and the depreciation of the mother as a result of her fantasied castration (an issue over which the girl turns away from the mother as a love object with an embitterment that becomes a major dynamic force in the girl's ambivalence toward the mother. The libidinal tie to the mother remains, drawing much of its intensity from the girl's being like the mother in body, and in identification with her role and functions, though this identification cannot be fully realized until the girl becomes a mother herself. In all this, the mouth, the gastrointestinal tract, food, and eating are universally available and so are utilized, in accordance with the individual child's needs and disposition for the representation, in fantasy and bodily activities, of drive derivatives, conflict, defense, and compromise formations. These oral themes are especially adaptable to the representation of the incorporative, sadomasochistic strivings which mediate the introjection of ambivalently charged objects. The girl's strong tie to the mother's body from very early on is rooted in a sameness she grasps between her own body and that of the primary nurturing object; this tie contributes in manifold ways to the internalizations on which the identification with the mother is based. This sense of body sameness contributes to fantasies of oneness and merger with the mother, which bring with them the danger of being overwhelmed, engulfed, suffocated. Jamaica Kincaid (1978) expressed this beautifully in the opening paragraph of her story, "My Mother":

> Immediately on wishing my mother dead and seeing the pain it caused her, I was sorry and cried so many tears that all the earth around me was drenched. Standing before my mother, I begged her forgiveness, and I begged so earnestly that she took pity on me, kissing my face and placing my head to her bosom to rest. Placing her arms around me, she drew my head closer and closer to her bosom, until finally I suffocated. I lay on her bossom, breathless, for a time unaccountable, until one day, for a reason she has kept to herself, she shook me out and stood me under a tree and I started to breathe again. I cast a sharp glance at her and said to myself, "So." Instantly I grew my own bosoms, small mounds at first, leaving a small, soft place between them, where, if ever necessary, I could rest my own head. Between my mother and me now were the tears I had cried, and I gathered up some stones and banked them in so that they formed a small pond. The water in the pond was thick and black and poisonous, so that only unnamable invertebrates could live in it. My mother and I now watched each other carefully, always making sure to shower the other with words and deeds of love and affection [pp. 53–54].

This dreamlike paragraph conveys the ambivalence, aggression, and hostility of a girl toward her mother. The death wishes are instantly countered by guilt, affection, and fantasies of love, bodily intimacy, and union, a union so engulfing that it leads to death or suspension of life by suffocation. The girl attempts to deal with the pain of loss in the eventual separation from the mother by her bodily identification with the mother and specifically in the capacity to nurture, a reflection of the actuality that with puberty the girl finally becomes isomorphic with the mother. The bitter, poisonous reservoir between them alludes to hostility and death wishes via ingestion, a figure that brings to mind the fear so frequently experienced by girls of being poisoned by their mothers. The restitution is uneasy, a fragile, wary peace, a love shored up by a reaction-formation—"showering one another with words and deeds of love and affection."

The developmental tasks of adolescence—integration of the sexually mature body into the personality in anticipation of establishing the adult sexual role and the capacity for sustained, intimate heterosexual relationships—require increasing autonomy from the mother. In achieving this, the girl has to make a transition from her mother to a man, from the primary same-sexed love object, her relationship with whom is rooted in the bodily isomorphism, to a heterosexual object. This is quite different from the boy's lateral shift, from his mother to another heterosexual object. Partly because of his bodily difference from his mother, he disidentifies with her early on and makes a strong dyadic tie with the father (Blos, 1985). In adolescence, the boy moves from the primary nurturing maternal object to a heterosexual object with whom he can have direct instinctual gratification, in this way maintaining his tie to the mother. The adolescent girl, by contrast, in a misdirected effort to move away from her mother, often transposes the relationship with the mother onto her first heterosexual relationship; as Freud (1933) pointed out, such attempts may have to be given up as conflicted, displaced repetitions of the struggle to achieve greater autonomy from the mother. Relinquishing the infantile tie and going on to an adult love life may be experienced by the adolescent girl as a forbidden and dangerous surpassing of her mother. On the surface this may appear as oedipal rivalry, but on a deeper level it involves the girl's dread of her hostile and destructive abandonment of the mother, made more difficult because it involves both recognizing and giving up a sadomasochistic tie. We need also to keep in mind that the conflict is not the daughter's alone, but may be the mother's as well. The mother's need to hold on to the daughter, just as she as a young woman had held on to her own mother, may be important in perpetuating the tie, even when the daughter is ready to move away. This is frequently seen in a mother's need to interfere with her daughter's treatment.

Although the young girl's body resembles her mother's, it is only in adolescence that it becomes fully the same. This development tends to accentuate their closeness and oneness at a time when the adolescent needs to achieve greater autonomy, and thereby contributes to the intensity of the ambivalent conflict. Late adolescent and young adult women who come for analysis are still actively, often desperately, engaged in this struggle, one form of which are the eating disorders seen so frequently in young women.

By focusing on eating, the girl takes up an old function, very much connected with the mother and subject to conscious control, in an effort to regulate the internal pressure of the drives. This takes place in the context of menarche which is experienced both as an occurrence out-side of conscious control and as an inner regulatory principle that is reassuring and comforting. In an attack on the internalized maternal object based on the shared body image, the adolescent girl can now turn the hostility she feels toward the mother against her own body. Food and the eating function lend themselves very well to this expression because they are the oldest carriers of instinctual drive derivatives toward the mother, especially oral-sadistic strivings. They also have the economically significant feature that the drive derivatives can be temporarily extin-guished at will, offering the individual the possibility of a measure of drive control.

This turn of events in the girl's intrapsychic life involves her body image and gives expression to bisexual conflict. A frequent fantasy con-scious or unconscious is to make her body distinctly different from the mother's by starving it into a straight, slender form in contrast to the mature, curved, female form—the hated mother's body. At the same time, this fantasy and associated behavior convey the bisexual conflict. The drive toward the masculine and prepubertal feminine form may be a representation of the girl's androgynous fantasies, which can express masculine wishes based on envy but are also an expression of the wish to be her mother's closest partner, yet distinct from her and not swallowed up. The tomboy fantasies and behavior of latency girls contain both these trends. The androgynous fantasies have their forerunners in the early, active side of the preoedipal relation to the mother, which resembles the boy's oedipus complex. A clinical vignette illustrates how this appears in the analytic situation.

Ms. A. came to analysis because of depression and difficulty in ex-periencing pleasure in her body in relationships with men. Her rela-tionship and identification with her mother were conflicted. She loved her beautiful and gentle mother and had always sought and obtained her soothing and comforting attention; but the mother's unvarying goodness made it very difficult for the patient to countenance any hostile or critical thoughts or feelings toward her mother. The patient's feminine identification with her mother was conflicted because of what she per-ceived as the woman's bodily vulnerability, a view organized around her having witnessed while she was in latency her mother's menstruation and bloody miscarriage. Her mother's gynecological surgery and early loss of her own mother made Ms. A's identification with her mother a hazardous one associated as it was with fantasies of losing her mother and dying herself at a young age. Nor did the mother's masochistic suffering in the marital relationship improve the patient's view of the woman's role and position.

Masculine identifications were also conflicted. Until her latency years, Ms. A. admired her father and what he stood for, especially as she was supposed to have been his son. He was her first teacher and the first to appreciate her in what was to be her chosen field. But a fateful shift took place in latency, when her sister was born and her father suffered an illness which became chronic. With the mother fully occupied with baby and husband, the patient felt alone and excluded and consoled herself with eating, taking food and her own body as instinctual objects. She became obese and remained so until puberty, when she made a conscious resolution that she was not going to bleed like her mother. She lost weight until she was quite thin but not anorexic, and eventually succeeded in realizing her fantasy of deliberately interfering with her menstruation, which became irregular, disappearing altogether for extended periods. She was determined that she would not be like her mother, because she was supposed to have been her father's son. If she were a boy, she could keep her pretty mother, but as a girl she would have to lose her and have her chronically ill father instead.

This case illustrates also the persistence of unresolved primitive conflicts expressed through the modality of food and eating, with the mother as both external object and introject. An oral fixation is revealed in the unconscious fantasies of incorporation and introjection expressed in eating symptoms. Ms. A. responded to disappointments in the oedipal relationship with her father through an ambivalence that sought bodily representation and discharge in the vicissitudes of eating.

Another young woman Ms. B., who came to analysis at the age of eighteen because of an obsessive preoccupation with food and with efforts to regulate her eating, demonstrated how food may represent the instinctual tie to the mother. Anticipating a visit with her mother, she was shocked to become aware of a mounting, intense excitement that she identified as sexual. One response was to consider this the analyst's fault, an attempt to disavow the excitement as originating in herself by linking it to the transference. Another response was that she should be able to control the excitement, just as she controlled her eating. But with the mounting excitement, she became apprehensive of going to see her mother, fearing that she would "fuck" the woman, a term she associated with sadistic fantasies of penetrating and being penetrated, fantasies having roots in the aggression connected with her active preoedipal attachment to the mother in the course of development. These fantasies evolved into sadomasochistic beating fantasies, first involving women but later including men. She also had a fascination with the lesbian sadomasochistic literature. She saw the homosexual sadomasochistic couple as mother and child, the sadistic partner being the giving one via the laying of hands, the masochist being the one who takes. Interestingly, this patient's earliest conscious sadomasochistic fantasies dated from when she was five, the year her brother was born. But any hostile feelings toward her brother were severely repressed. The conscious fantasy was of her brother as her male side, like a twin, the side she could not be. Eating the same breakfast food with her brother every morning was like incorporating his body into hers. For her, both eating and talking were aggressive and attacking, making for a particularly difficult transference resistance.

Even as the girl directs her hostility at her mother and her own body, she frequently turns to peers or to an older woman with the positive side of her ambivalence, in this way continuing her developmental progress, eventually finding her way back to her mother in her identification with her as—a mother.

This is illustrated in Ms. C., who came to treatment at eighteen because of severe weight loss and a preoccupation with eating in order not to become heavier, particularly in her hips and thighs. She felt that up to the age of fifteen she had had a "center" within her which focused on her mother. Her own identity was based on what her mother was. Her mother had an active, successful professional career, and the daughter was active in the same field, achieving recognition in her school and some professional recognition. Her place among her peers depended on this internalization of the mother. Her friends, who looked up to her mother, admired and envied Ms. C.'s accomplishments in her mother's field.

This equilibrium began to break when she was fifteen. She felt she had lost her center and her relationship with her mother changed. She became disappointed, annoyed and angry with her mother. One reason for her anger was that her mother gave up her professional work for a time in order to devote herself to the peace movement, which took her away from the family even more than had her work. At this juncture she went in two directions at the same time. On the progressive side she began to have relationships with boys, first with peers and later with a man about ten years older than herself, a teacher in her school. With her mother she felt increasingly distressed and angry. Here we see the flight to the man, driven also by the resurgence of oedipal strivings toward the father, in the setting of the conflict over gaining greater autonomy from the mother.

On the regressive side was the beginning of the eating difficulty, the weight loss, the reaction to fat on her body—i.e., to becoming more like her mother and feeling out of control. A major feature of the eating symptom involves shifting the conflict over control of drive discharge to the eating function. The amenorrhea that ensued upon her weight loss was experienced as the loss of an internal regulator and the threatened loss of a valued potential.

At nineteen she felt she was still trying to find "a new center." In her relationships with peers she lived out the various aspects of her struggle with her mother. With one friend she functioned like a mother. With another, she experienced some features of her tie to her mother. From her she learned to cook, manage an apartment, carry on her work, etc. Ms. C. and another friend, a somewhat older woman who had lost her mother in childhood, alternately played mother and child to one another. With another friend, like herself a young woman precociously successful in her own mother's field, she struggled over a temptation and seduction into a homosexual relationship, a temptation she put in the context of being true to her deep love for the young woman. This temptation, however, was countered by her attraction and excitement with regard to men, though she backed away from establishing lasting relationships because of feelings of inadequacy over her sexually mature body; in addition, she feared being trapped in a relationship with a man, with no avenue of retreat, in contrast to being comfortably alone or with her women friends. Though she desired an intimate, intense relationship with a man, she also dreaded being confined in it with no respite; she could not tolerate what she experienced as a demandingness and neediness of men, whom she likened to children. These feelings came up in the context of her own criticism of what she needed and got from her parents, and established a connection between her dread of male demands and her own aggression and demandingness toward her parents, especially her mother. Conflict over aggression toward the mother, which is central in the eating disorder, is also a major factor in the dread some adolescents have of being involved with children, whose aggression is experienced as a return of their own aggression toward their parents. In the meantime, Ms. C.'s relationship with mother improved. Now she felt comforted and loved by her mother and in turn experienced warm and loving feelings in the other direction. However, when she was preparing to go away alone for six months, she became angry and petulant because her mother's work took her away from home at that time and did not allow her to help with the planning and packing, which would have helped Ms. C. cope with her anger and helplessness over separating. At twenty-one, involved with a young man as needy and demanding as a small child, she felt an acute longing for closeness, for being held by her mother. But when her mother did hug her, she thought her mother had the same need to cling to her. Her mother then told her of a similar crisis in her own life, when a very early marriage had broken down and she had a difficult time establishing herself as an autonomous young adult.

Throughout these developmental struggles, which revolved around the issue of greater autonomy from her mother, Ms. C.'s conflicts were expressed to a large degree in terms of her own body and eating function. Thus, the most primitive mode of representing the vicissitudes of the mental process of introjection, incorporation, and identification continued to be of prime importance in the adolescent stage of development. For Ms. C. the introject of the mother was her center, an internalized object that was not the focus of pathogenic conflict until adolescence required that she move toward greater autonomy. Her dissatisfaction with her sexually mature body and with her mother reawakened in her the old preoedipal currents of hostility toward the mother as the one to be blamed for whatever is wrong.

In Ms. D. the eating disorder was even more vividly connected with ambivalent conflict over achieving autonomy from the mother in the context of adolescent sexual development. Her parents' very unhappy marriage, in which she could see her father's many flaws, and her mother's efforts to enlist the patient on her side left her with a very cynical view of men. At seventeen, while away at summer school, she was upset by the very competitive sexual atmosphere, withdrew from it, and lost herself in the contemporary literature she was studying. She was delighted with her male teacher and felt attracted to him. She had a greater sense of freedom—she could do what she wanted, come and go as she pleased. In this setting she began to feel fat and unattractive. She became concerned with her body and with food and started to run very long distances to drive her weight down and keep her hips and thighs thin and firm. At the end of the summer she cried during the entire trip home with her parents. At home her mother, usually quite gentle, seemed to sense her daughter's moving away from her, and began to pick quarrels, actually engaging her in physical fights and cursing her. Ms. D's severe eating disorder lasted several years before yielding to treatment. In this instance the mother seemed to have as much difficulty as her adolescent daughter in relinquishing the instinctualized bodily tie between them.

Although the focus here has been on the mother-daughter relationship, a girl's relationship to her father is also important to her development, both in the early oedipal period and in adolescence. A father's response to his daughter in the oedipal period is a major determinant in the development of her femininity and the father-daughter relationship in adolescence greatly influenced the outcome of the conflicts described in the cases presented above. In each, the father-daughter relationship was troubled. In the families of Ms. A, Ms. B, and Ms. D, bitter divorces took place in adolescence, culminating long years in which the patient witnessed parental strife in which the mother was seen as suffering, embattled and degraded. Ms. C.'s relationship with her father was more positive, but she felt that he was remote and self-contained with her, though much more responsive to her younger sister.

For many a woman the move away from the mother to a man, the relinquishment of a tie strongly rooted in the bodily isomorphism, is a very difficult task, and is accompanied by symptoms and suffering, which often are not alleviated until the woman becomes a mother herself. Again, Jamaica Kincaid beautifully captures the conflict and the attempt at resolution:

> One day my mother packed my things in a grip and, taking me by the hand, walked me to the jetty, placed me on board a boat, in care of the captain. My mother, while caressing my chin and cheeks, said some words of comfort to me because we had never been apart before. She kissed me on the forehead and turned and walked away. I cried so much my chest heaved up and down, my whole body shook at the sight of her back turned toward me, as if I had never seen her back turned toward me before. I started to make plans to get off the boat, but when I saw the boat was encased in a large green bottle, as if it were about to decorate a mantelpiece, I fell asleep, until I reached my destination, the new island. When the boat stopped, I got off and I saw a woman with feet exactly like mine, especially around the arch of the instep. Even though the face was completely different from what I was used to, I recognized this woman as my mother. We greeted each other at first with great caution and politeness, but as we walked along,

our steps became one, and as we talked, our voices became one voice, and we were in complete union in every other way. What peace came over me then, for I could not see where she left off and I began, or where I left off and she began [pp. 59—60].

The fishermen are coming in from sea; their catch is bountiful, my mother has seen to that. As the waves plop, plop against each other, the fishermen are happy that the sea is calm. My mother points out the fishermen to me, their contentment is a source of my contentment. I am sitting in my mother's enormous lap. Sometimes I sit on a mat she has made for me from her hair. The lime trees are weighed down with limes—I have already perfumed myself with their blossoms. A hummingbird has nested on my stomach, a sign of my fertileness. My mother and I live in a bower made from flowers whose petals are imperishable. There is the silvery blue of the sea, crisscrossed with sharp darts of light, there is the warm rain falling on the clumps of castor bush, there is the small lamb bounding across the pasture, there is the soft ground welcoming the soles of my pink feet. It is in this way my mother and I have lived for a long time now'' [pp. 60-61].

From the viewpoint of the daughter, the mother hands her over to ''the captain,'' connoting permission for the girl to make the transitional journey. She overcomes the longing to turn back with the fantasy of the boat encased in a large green bottle, that is, being once more inside the mother's body and remaining at home on the mantelpiece. Once in the new place she finds the mother again, recognizing her by a body sameness. Peace and calm return with the fantasy of bodily merger with the mother.

In the conclusion to the story, the daughter views the men from the safety of the munificent mother's lap. The mother's body is the ultimate source of peace, calm, and contentment. Contact with it assures fertility, and the prospect of the daughter's being herself a mother makes it possible for the two to live together with a minimum of ambivalence.

The mother's strong bond with the daughter is represented in the myth of Demeter and Persephone (Tripp, 1970), in which food and eating play a central role. Demeter, the goddess of corn and of the earth's fertility, had a daughter, Persephone, by Zeus. Hades, god of the underworld, fell in love with her, but Zeus warned him that Demeter would not approve of her daughter's leaving for such a sunless home in the bowels of the earth. Demeter wandered over the earth, searching for her everywhere, stopping not even to bathe or to eat. In retaliation for the loss of her daughter, she brought famine to the earth for an entire year, threatening the survival of the entire race of men. Defeated in his effort to induce Demeter to relent, Zeus sent Hermes to Hades to fetch Persephone. Hades consented to her leaving, while seductively offering her a pomegranate seed to eat. After a joyful reunion with her mother, Persephone admitted on questioning by Demeter that she had tasted the food of Hades. Demeter realized she had been tricked, for anyone who tasted the food of Hades had to spend at least one-third of the year in the underworld. However, realizing that she would have her daughter with her for two-thirds of each year, Demeter relented and agreed to allow the grain to grow once again.

This myth highlights the difficulty a mother experiences in giving up her daughter to a man. Partaking of the forbidden food, which symbolizes sexual gratification and impregnation, separates mother and daughter, but never completely.

REFERENCES

Blos, P. (1985), *Son and Father: Before and Beyond the Oedipus Complex*. New York: Free Press.

Brunswick, R. (1940), The preoedipal phase of the libido development. *Psychoanal. Quart.,* 9:293–319.

Freud, S. (1933) New introductory lectures on psycho-analysis. *Standard Edition,* 22:1–182. London: Hogarth Press, 1964.

Kincaid, J. (1978). *At the Bottom of the River.* New York: Vintage Books.

Ritvo, S. (1984), The image and uses of the body in psychic conflict with special reference to eating disorders in adolescence. 20:344–364. *The Psychoanalytic Study of the Child,* New York: International Universities Press.

Tripp, E. (1970), *Crowell's Handbook of Classical Mythology.* New York: Crowell.

24

Dynamic Aspects of
Homosexual Cruising

Martin S. Willick, M.D.

Homosexual cruising is a very complex behavior which, although common in our society, has not received a great deal of attention in the psychoanalytic literature. Cruising refers to the practice of wandering about in the streets or in selected public places, either on foot or in a car, in search of partners for a sexual rendezvous. The most common locales are gay bars, the streets of homosexual neighborhoods, gay baths, public bathrooms, parks and beaches. A major characteristic of this activity is the mutual anonymity of the partners. Another important characteristic is the extreme promiscuity of the behavior. Most cruising homosexuals seek a different partner each night, or even a number of partners during the course of a single excursion.

There have been a number of statistical and sociological studies of homosexual males and their behavior (Kinsey et. al., 1948; Hoffman, 1968; Humphreys, 1970; Saghir and Robins, 1973; Bell and Weinberg, 1978). There is general agreement that because there are so many different types of homosexuals, the group as a whole is not easy to categorize. However, despite the many differences, promiscuity seems to be the rule rather than the exception, even for many homosexuals engaged in long-term relationships with a single lover.

The promiscuous behavior is largely achieved through the act of cruising. Just as there are many kinds of homosexuals, so there are many types of cruising, ranging from the cruising that occurs in gay bars and on the streets, which often results in partners spending an entire evening together, to the cruising that occurs in public bathrooms and gay baths, in which a multiplicity of partners and almost complete anonymity are the rule.

The feature of anonymity was emphasized by Humphreys (1970), who studied the cruising that occurs in public bathrooms: "Public restrooms are chosen by those who want homoerotic activity without commitment for a number of reasons. They are accessible, easily recognized by the initiate, and provide little public visibility" (pp. 2–3). He also noted that the activity almost always takes placed in silence, which serves to guarantee the anonymity. He distinguished four types of homosexual men who cruised the "tearooms," as these public bathrooms are called. They range from married men with families who stop at the bathrooms on the way home, to single bisexual men, and finally to committed gay men with no interest in heterosexual experiences.

Like any overdetermined and complicated human action, cruising cannot be reduced to simple explanations. Most discussions in the psychoanalytic literature have concentrated on the dynamics of homosexual behavior in general and have not attempted to delineate the specific dynamics of cruising. The one paper with cruising in its title is a recent one by Calef and Weinshel (1984) entitled "Anxiety and the Restitutional Function of Homosexual Cruising." They corroborate the familiar dynamics of homosexuality, emphasizing the influence of aggressive conflicts, sadomasochism, castration anxiety, and anality. As far as the specific dynamics of cruising are concerned, they stress that it is an attempt to return to the scene of the oedipal crime:

> The cruising, a seemingly casual voyage to encounter strangers, fulfilled narcissistic needs in the expression of altruism and served as a restitution and also a form of integration. Filled with the tenderness and love he could not feel toward those close to him, it permitted him repeatedly to meet substitutes for his father and/or himself at the crossroads and reassure himself that the encounters did not result in injury and death [p. 48].

They also point out that for their patient the cruising scenes in bathrooms were repetitions and expressions of the child's curiosity about the toilet habits of his parents.

In this chapter I will draw on my experience with two analytic patients, as well as on impressions from a few patients treated by psychotherapy, to describe some dynamic aspects of cruising which have not received sufficient attention. One of my patients was a twenty-one-year-old graduate student when he began his analysis. He subsequently went to law school and was in analysis for six years. When he first came to see me, he complained of low self-esteem, painful feelings of rejection from both men and women, and depressive moods. He initially came to see me because he had become terribly anxious about his performance in school. Soon afterward, he revealed that he was concerned about his sexual orientation, although he had only occasional homosexual experiences. Unlike many other homosexuals, his recollection was that prior to puberty he was excited by sexual thoughts toward women, but since early adolescence he had been primarily aroused by males rather than females. When I began to see him, he had had one moderately prolonged relationship with a young woman but was finding it increasingly difficult to be aroused sexually by women. For a number of years his masturbatory fantasies had been almost exclusively homosexual.

Born and raised in a large Southern city, he was second of three children, having a brother two years older and another brother four years younger. His mother was a schoolteacher who had returned to work when he was about eight years old. A loving mother and an introspective person interested in art and literature, she was well known in the area for her literary achievements. His father, a successful businessman with a strong temper, was easily angered when the boys were young. He was athletic and interested in sports but did not like to discuss feelings. He had insisted that his three sons attend a private day school, although they all had preferred to stay in the public school system.

All his life my patient felt that he was much more similar to his mother than to his father or his brothers. The latter were good athletes and more action-oriented, while he was sensitive, introspective, and drawn to his mother's interest in the humanities. He experienced painful feelings at not being a good athlete, but enjoyed the not-so-secret idea that he was "special" to his mother because of his sensitive nature.

Rather than continue his history, I will describe his cruising behavior. This will enable me to interweave into the narrative other important elements of his history and of the course of treatment. I will say first that although he had already had a number of homosexual experiences, the cruising actually did not begin until the third year of a six-year analysis; as one might expect, this behavior was intimately related to the gradual development of the transference.

The patient went to look for sexual partners in three kinds of places. Most common were the bathrooms of the highway restaurants he passed driving to and from my office. He also went to pornographic bookstores that provided stalls for sexual contact and to the library, where contact was made in the stacks.

The patient looked for attractive, masculine men, with manly physiques. He had always considered himself small and skinny, and went through a period when he desperately wanted to build up his body and become stronger. Sometimes a part of the desired object, or of his apparel (e.g., Western boots) would serve as a symbol of masculinity. At times boots were all he saw of his partners, as so many of his contacts were anonymous, occurring as they did between stalls in a bathroom or bookstore. In the latter, the partitions contained holes through which to insert the penis, which often was the sole organ of physical contact. He was very much conscious of his wish to take in the masculinity of his imagined manly partner. Effeminate men did not attract him.

The initial contact was one of the most exciting moments of his cruising. This was the moment at which the patient felt chosen. It meant that his partner, an imagined strong male, would choose him and affirm for him his masculinity. This moment of acquiescence signified to him that he was loved and valued. During this initial contact and afterward, the patient did not imagine himself to be a woman, but rather a young boy chosen to be one of the men.

Although the patient occasionally met someone he invited home and wanted to get to know, the vast majority of his contacts were one-night stands or, perhaps more accurate, one-hour stands. Despite the fact that he longed to be loved and never to be left, he really did not want a long-standing permanent relationship because of his fear of its ending. In addition, he feared that a one-to-one relationship would confirm his homosexuality. He had never lost hope that he could conquer these feelings and become heterosexual. Thus, he never really admitted his homosexual preference to anyone. Despite his rather strong feminine identification with his mother, the patient never consciously felt that he was feminine or like a girl and had no confusion about his gender identity. He was a man, but was not man enough.

Most of his sexual activity consisted of mutual masturbation and fellatio. He was not interested in anal sex, in either the passive or active role. However, he was aroused by fondling his partners' testes and by the sweaty smell of the groin. In the event he could not make a contact, he would almost always masturbate in the stall of the bathroom using homosexual fantasies.

The stimuli which prompted the cruising were as varied as the motives involved in the behavior. When, during the course of treatment, he cruised practically every day, it was not so easy to determine its immediate precipitant. Often the urge to cruise overtook him as a compulsion he could not control. At other times he spent the day fantasizing about it, and could not wait to begin.

The cruising took place in response to a number of determining situations: if he felt rejected by a friend or a teacher, either male or female; if he had become unconsciously frightened or guilty about his success as a man; if he had suffered some blow to his self-esteem, such as a poor grade; if he were feeling depressed for any reason; or if he were aware of becoming very angry. Of course, all of these feelings were dramatically enacted in the transference. The most obvious reactions were to my vacations and weekends, but there were innumerable occasions when it was clear that he was responding to what he felt were slights and disappointments in our relationship. The cruising increased when in the course of the treatment he became seriously involved with a woman and unconsciously feared my retaliation.

The patient was extremely attached, though in an ambivalent way, to his older brother. He had always admired him and longed for his respect. He recalled going to his brother's bed in the middle of the night until, when the patient was in early latency, his brother put an end to it. He never forgave him, and constantly wanted to replay and undo this event. His current friendships were all replicas of the relationship with his brother, complete with all the turmoil of love and hate, despair and joy. One of his cherished adolescent fantasies was to be asked to join a group of adventurous men who were led by an older man and his son, a clear reference to his father and brother. When he began to see me, he and his older brother were still getting into frequent disagreements, arguments, and misunderstandings. My patient felt that he was almost totally helpless in the face of his brother's criticizing or ignoring him.

While his relationship with his mother was characterized by love and devotion, it gradually became clear that he was bitterly disappointed that he did not have the special place in her heart he had consciously imagined. The birth of his younger brother when he was four was to prove a terrible betrayal to him. It was never clear to me whether he had always been uncoordinated and unatheletic, or whether he had turned away from strenuous physical activity a few years after the birth of this brother. For many years into the analysis, the patient was still profoundly jealous of both brothers. He truly wanted to be the only object of his parents' affection and found it very gratifying to spend long hours talking to his parents, particularly his mother, about his many problems.

In "Some Neurotic Mechanisms in Jealousy, Paranoia and Homosexuality" Freud (1922) summarized his original observations from "Three Essays on the Theory of Sexuality" (Freud, 1905) and what he had subsequently learned about the factors contributing to homosexuality. He noted fixation on the mother, identification with the mother, the inclination toward narcissistic object choice, and the high value placed on the male organ. He pointed out important factors associated with the castration complex, such as a depreciation and hatred of women, a fear of the father, and a consequent renunciation of women. What Freud specifically added in this paper, aside from once again stressing an organic factor, was the intense rivalry and jealousy among brothers. This hostile and aggressive attitude toward brothers, he wrote, "yielded to repression and underwent a transformation, so that the rivals of the earlier period became the first homosexual love-objects"(1922, p. 231). Nunberg's important paper, "Homosexuality, Magic and Aggression" (1938), added to Freud's insights by stressing that the aggression toward male rivals is by no means entirely repressed, frequently finding conscious expression in homosexual activity.

My patient's analysis revealed most of the dynamic aspects usually associated with male homosexuality. First was his longing to be loved by his father and his brother, although the latter seemed to be a much more prominent part of his fantasy life. This longing included his yearning to be included as one of "the men" and to have his masculinity validated. He had many painful feelings of being weak and feminine and desperately wanted to incorporate the imagined strength of his partners.

A second important factor was his attempt to deny his hatred and rivalry with men. In his sexual activity he was aware primarily of wishes to love and be loved by his partner. He did not imagine himself to be a woman, but rather a man partaking of a masculine love act. During the course of treatment he had some realization of the hostility in this behavior. He fantasied that bringing his partner to orgasm was to unman him, rendering him totally helpless and weakened. He was also aware of the wish to leave his partner, making him feel abandoned and humiliated.

Another dynamic aspect involved the defensive structure of his homosexuality. This sexual orientation enabled him to deny and defend against positive oedipal wishes, which frightened him and made him feel guilty. He also showed a great degree of reaction-formation against rivalrous wishes. At one point he was unable to borrow his roommate's typewriter to do a résumé because of his fear of showing him up. He had a number of dreams revealing oedipal conflict and castration anxiety. In one, a young gorilla overwhelms and defeats the leader of all the other males, who retaliate by grabbing the interloper's genitals. In another, he steals a treasure chest and is chased by a number of men who are trying to kill him and get the key away from him.

A fourth dynamic factor was his wish for revenge against his mother (and against all women) for not prefering him to all others. His homosexual behavior, a terrible reproach to his mother, was repeated in the transference in numerous unmistakable ways. Finally, his homosexual activity was an attempt to deal with narcissistic hurts and blows to his self-esteem by imagining his being chosen and strengthened by physical contact with other men.

One commonly encountered dynamic factor did not appear clearly in this analysis: the choosing of younger men to represent the patient, while the patient identifies himself with the longed-for mother. Of course, a deep attachment to the mother, and his need and love for her, was expressed in the love he showered upon his male partners. Although he never expressed fantasies of merger, the wish for a blissful, unambivalent and permanent closeness appeared in various oblique ways. Finally, the familiar relationship between the yearning for the breast through incorporation of the penis, though present, did not play a predominant role in his mental life.

The factors enumerated above were all important dynamic aspects of my patient's cruising behavior, as they are in male homosexuality in general. But what I wish to draw attention to here are some additional factors that are responsible for cruising behavior in particular. Why is there such a need for multiple partners? Why the compulsive, almost ritualistic behavior of the cruising? Why is anonymity so frequently an important part of the behavior? The patient's own explanation of the need to cruise was quite straightforward: the points of rendezvous were simply places, freely available and relatively safe, in which to meet other homosexuals. Since in cruising he was not committing himself to a permanent relationship, he could maintain his denial that he was truly homosexual.

I have mentioned that there are almost no papers in the literature devoted solely to cruising. However, many discussions about this often compulsive, driven behavior are to be found embedded in the voluminous literature about homosexuality and other male perversions. All of these perversions are characterized by the intense need to discharge immediately, through concrete action, the enormous sexual and aggressive urges with which the patient is struggling. The perversions also represent attempts to deal with narcissistic vulnerabilities.

Perhaps the most comprehensive account of the dynamic issues involved in cruising is given by Socarides (1978), whose general theoretical position is that there are two types of homosexuality—oedipal and preoedipal—and that homosexuals whose pathology is derived from preoedipal conflict are similar to patients we generally classify as borderline or severely narcissistic. Socarides discusses cruising primarily as an attempt to deal with preoedipal conflicts, though it is clear from his case material that cruising occurs in the so-called oedipal type as well. He specifically mentions the preoedipal anxieties of loneliness and the consequences of aggression. He finds that these patients have a lack of the neutralized energy indispensable for control, postponement, and anticipation of gratification. Socarides believes that cruising is an attempt to deal with disturbances in the sense of self, and that such patients have defects resulting from preoedipal conflict. Cruising, he argues, is indicative also of the impairment of object relations in these patients: "In place of object cathexis, the ego seeks ego gratification in a short circuit act between the self and pseudo-objects. . ." (p. 160). Often there is little reality awareness of the partner or of his feelings: as one of his patients told him, "It's a one-sided deal for each person. You're involved with yourself and satisfying your own needs basically. . . .It's not love. It's very selfish with homosexuals" (p. 516). Socarides quotes Masud Khan, who describes the acting out in perversions as a "technique of intimacy" which always fails, leading to a feeling of emptiness and a compulsion to repeat.

These aspects of the dynamics of cruising were apparent in my patient but deserve further elaboration. One element of this behavior that particularly impressed me was the anonymity of the sexual partners. Here was this young man, desperate to be loved and valued and chosen as special, and yet in each of these brief encounters his partner did not even know him. I gradually came to realize that this was precisely the point. During these moments of anonymous sexual contact the patient could imagine his most intense longing fulfilled. He was loved, valued, chosen, and validated as a man. It was as if these partners really chose him, as a person they knew well.

Through his cruising he had orchestrated a new reality which was not painful to him. In his real life every encounter, with acquaintances as well as close friends, was marked by intense conflict. He constantly felt hurt that his friends did not love and respect him enough. Extraordinarily sensitive to slights, to being ignored or being left, he was extremely jealous of the close relationships of others. He was frequently aware of envy and anger toward his friends and felt very competitive with all of them. All of these painful emotions tortured him, and he was able to eliminate them only in these sexual encounters. During these contacts he could imagine the perfect relationship. The cruising was like a wish-fulfillment dream.

However, like any complicated behavior involving the gratification of sexual and aggressive wishes as well as defensive maneuvers and superego determinants, this one was not entirely successful. Even when cruising he would frequently suffer from the emotions described above. If someone entered the next bathroom stall and no hand reached down under the partition, my patient would feel crushed. At other times, after some brief contact, a partner would leave suddenly and abandon him. He would then feel hurt, angry, and depressed. But the interesting thing about these disappointments was that they were never as bad as in "real life." He could always go to the next stall, or the next cubicle, or drive around some more. Cruising, with its promise of a multiplicity of partners, helped him deny his extreme vulnerability. He was loved, if not by this one, then by the next one.

Just as in a dream a multitude of people represent only one person, for this patient all his partners represented now his mother, now his brother or his father or himself. If he were rejected or abandoned he could look for another partner in a few minutes. The partners were interchangeable and therefore never lost. In this way he could always exercise a degree of control over his fears of being rejected and abandoned. I soon came to realize that the patient was actually cruising all the time. He would go to another law firm or to visit a client, and would continuously scan the bodies and eyes of other men. Would this man be the one who would love him and affirm his masculinity and worth?

Another important dynamic feature was the excitement and fear he felt at the prospect of being caught and punished. Frequently he feared being apprehended by the police. He expressed his defiance in this way, though as a homosexual rather than a true man. He constantly feared that punishment for his sexual wishes would be realized, and that he would be ashamed and humiliated by being arrested.

Another aspect of his cruising was the state of mind that preceded it. I am referring here not to the meanings his homosexuality and cruising had for him, but rather to his state of tension or his mood. While the motivation for his cruising lay in a complex of emotions such as anxiety, guilt, and depression, what was most striking was that he was trying to calm and soothe himself. Frequently he found himself in a distressing state of tension, anxiety, or depression, affects the longed-for sexual contact was meant to relieve. He had to cruise in order to handle these distressing affects; he felt he could not otherwise contain himself. Even when the threat of AIDS became apparent he found it difficult to control himself, although he did begin to change the nature of his sexual activity.

I have mentioned that although the patient came to treatment because of his concern about his choice of sexual object, he did not begin to cruise until the third year of analysis. During the first two years we had grown to understand a number of the dynamic issues I have described. We were also aware of the frequent narcissistic hurts he experienced in the relationship with me. If I left for a vacation or had to cancel a session, he felt unloved. He believed that I removed the napkin at the head of the analytic couch too soon after he arose, thus expressing my wish to discard him.

What I did not realize, until it became apparent in his cruising, was that he was deeply disappointed in our relationship. If fact, he had been living out with me, during these first few years, his love affair with his mother. He had been introspective and insightful, interested in Freud and dreams and dreaming, in art and literature and the unconscious mind. He had unconsciously hoped that he would come first in my heart, ahead of my other patients and my own family.

Gradually, this disappointment turned to anger and to wishes to reproach me and take revenge. He did not need me; he could find other lovers. He would handle his depression by soothing himself and would escape the anxiety about our relationship by turning to others. In this way he denied and defended against his rage toward me, which threatened to destroy our closeness.

The other major precipitating factor in his cruising was his acceptance to law school toward the end of his second year of analysis.

This acceptance occasioned a great sense of triumph over his father and his brother in their rivalry for his mother's admiration and love.. Unconsciously, he feared my anger for this major accomplishment, which he saw as a threat to my superiority over him.

Later in the analysis, as the patient began to improve in many ways, the full effect of the oedipal rivalry became more apparent. He was now able to be aroused by heterosexual fantasies. He began to date and started a long-term relationship with a woman. He became sexually potent with her and more successful and assertive in his work. But he was terrified of "really" becoming a man, and the cruising intensified as his anxiety mounted. This was an attempt to prove, both to himself and to me, that he was still not a man, and that I had nothing to fear from his masculinity. He wanted to stay a young boy, chosen by other, more manly men. During the emotional and physical contact of cruising, all of his conflicts were temporarily suspended, even as they were reenacted. He could live out his fantasies while ignoring reality.

During the entire course of treatment the patient was worried that I was terribly disappointed in him. He wanted to show me that he was a man, but the fear and anger he felt in my regard accentuated his need to seek out homosexual encounters. He wanted me to make him a man and to prohibit his cruising. But he would also be defiant and do as he pleased. One motive for disappointing me and both his parents was to make us feel guilty that we had not loved him enough. He maintained that he did not have conscious homosexual fantasies toward me; he wanted me to love him as a manly son.

Another patient of mine had begun to cruise at the age of thirty-five when his wife severely reproached him for having a low sperm count. He came to see me when he was in his late forties. At that time his cruising was intermittent and sudden and would last a few days. It became quite clear after a while what the precipitating factors were. This man, whose father had committed suicide when he was nineteen, had a close but subservient relationship with a respected older man, a relationship that periodically was disrupted. The two would express their mutual admiration, but soon the patient would suffer some terrible disappointment or slight at the hands of his mentor. My patient would then feel explosive and intense rage and be aware of conscious wishes to humiliate and defame this revered father figure. These feelings would mount in intensity, leading to great anxiety and an unconscious fear of the murderous rage within him. Then, suddenly the rage would disappear and in its place would come the need to cruise, to have a tender, loving relationship, even if only for a few minutes. Often, however, this patient's intense ambivalence would break through and the cruising would end in bitter strife.

At the time I was analyzing the first of the two patients I have described, I was treating a young woman who was bulimic, and could not help being struck by certain similarities between cruising and her condition. Bulimia of course involves compulsive food binges, followed by self-induced vomiting and other means of purging. Both cruising and bulimia are expressions and attempted solutions of complicated and varied conflicts. These compulsive behaviors are overdetermined and involve both oedipal and preoedipal conflicts. Both behaviors are attempts to deal with distressing and painful affects—of anxiety, depression, anger, loss of self-esteem, and fear of loss of love—by indulging in a compulsive, ritualistic activity that is often experienced as uncontrollable.

While oral incorporative fantasies are more obvious in bulimia, they are also an extremely important aspect of cruising, which primarily involves fellatio. In addition, both activities are an attempt to control the object, represented by the penis in one activity and by food in the other. Both syndromes frequently manifest themselves shortly after the onset of puberty, when the issues of sexual identity and object choice come into focus.

Bulimia, of course, is extremely rare in men, while sexual perversions are seldom found in women. Female homosexuality appears to be more object-related than does male homosexuality, which frequently involves hundreds of partners. Both cruising for the male homosexual, and bulimia for the woman, have in common the qualities of addiction. It is not at all unusual, in fact, to see these syndromes associated with drug use serving a similar function.

I realize that analogies may be drawn between any two compulsive, ritualized behaviors meant to reduce tension, anxiety, and depressive feelings. Alcoholism, gambling, drug addictions, compulsive masturbation, nail biting, arm cutting, nymphomania, Don Juanism—all have characteristics in common. But by contrasting a compulsive behavior currently very common in men with one currently very common in women, I hope to point up certain interesting differences between the sexes which evolve in adolescence as solutions to oedipal and preoedipal conflicts. The final form of these behaviors highlights the importance of oedipal conflicts in their pathogenesis.

However, I do not want to overemphasize the similarities. There are important differences. The male homosexual cruiser is very aware of his sexual excitement and his hunger for sexual contact, whereas many young women with bulimia deny feelings of hunger entirely and experience no sexual excitement at all. Their actual sexual life is often inhibited or ungratifying. Often they are out of touch with their feelings and totally unaware of their distress. Other young women, however, complain of feeling empty rather than hungry, and are occasionally aware of feeling very tense and uncomfortable.

Both bulimia and cruising may lead to further feelings of emptiness and self-loathing. I see this more commonly in bulimics, as vomiting is well suited to elicit feelings of both sorts. The irresistible urge to binge as a means of handling overwhelming emotions is followed by a terror of being fat. The vomiting, self-induced, is an attempt to deal with this terror, and serves also to control and eject the fantasied object that the food represents. In my homosexual patient, self-loathing was evident after cruising only when he was rejected and very disappointed.

There is no question that there are significant preoedipal determinants to both syndromes. But analysts who emphasize these factors as invariably predominant leave out of account a number of oedipal and phallic factors that are extremely important, both theoretically and therapeutically. In male homosexuals, the absolute necessity of having the penis in order to incorporate the masculinity of the partner, the need to experience sexual gratification and to consummate the act with ejaculation, and the imperative nature of the attempt to deny castration fears, murderous hostility, and rivalry with men all point to the centrality of oedipal conflicts. In female bulimics there are obvious preoedipal conflicts over separation-individuation; issues of control, and fears of loss of love. However, the fear of becoming a woman with a feminine body, the fear of the protruding stomach associated with pregnancy, and the masturbatory quality of the binges, all point to the importance of oedipal conflicts in this syndrome as well.

Returning briefly to the literature on homosexual cruising, I consider Calef and Weinshel (1984) quite correct in saying that the cruiser attempts to deny and undo his murderous rivalry with the father, and that often he is unable to express his love in a real relationship. I have attempted to add to their findings some important dynamic factors responsible for the promiscuity, anonymity, and compulsive quality of this ritualized behavior.

Socarides (1978) makes the important point, similar to the one I have made here, that cruising is an attempt at true object relationship—an attempt, however, which always fails. He also correctly stresses that this compulsive, ritualistic act shares characteristics in common with all perversions. But while I lack his extensive experience analyzing homosexuals, I prefer not to divide the illness, or even the conflicts precipitating it into cases in which the etiology is primarily preoedipal and those in which it is oedipal. It is true that in any clinical syndrome— homosexuality, phobia, depression, obsessions, compulsions—we can see various degrees of ego pathology, but it is hard to imagine that male homosexuals and cruisers do not also have profound oedipal conflicts.

In conclusion, I would like to emphasize the dynamic aspects of male homosexual cruising that have received insufficient attention. Cruising is overdetermined and serves many functions. In addition to dealing with the conflicts seen in homosexuality, generally it is an attempt to deny the vulnerability of the cruiser to intimate relationships with men or with women. It creates a new and fantasied reality in which the cruiser is never rejected and discovers a new love object each time. This new, imagined reality denies the possibility of strife, rejection. and hostility that might lead to the destruction of relationships. Anonymity and the multiplicity of partners are absolutely necessary in order to deny the yearnings for love and acceptance that are forever plagued by doubt. If the cruiser is not loved by this one, he will be loved by another.

Cruising is also a desperate attempt to deal with the turmoil of oedipal conflict by creating a new scenario. The cruiser feels that he wants to love and be loved by men. He wants to deal neither with the murderous rage derived from his oedipal rivalry nor with the destructive hostility toward his mother that is the consequence of his disappointment in her love. As his anxiety and depression increase in intensity, his need for immediate and concrete action becomes overwhelming. This need then takes on a compulsive and repetitive pattern of the sort seen in various addictions. The partner, like food for the bulimic, resembles a desperately needed object, but is in fact rarely treated as a real object at all. This aspect finds its most dramatic expression when the cruiser sees only his partner's penis through a small hole in a partition.

I cannot at present explain why cruisers and bulimics feel the need to handle distressing affect by means of repetitive and compulsive action. After all, many patients with similar conflicts do not feel driven toward this sort of behavior. I do believe that the etiology of cruising and of male homosexuality in general cannot be attributed primarily to pregenital conflict. The dynamic aspects I have described are part of a complicated, overdetermined character structure and group of symptoms that derive from conflicts at many levels of development. Any discussion of cruising, however, must take into account the specific characteristics of the anonymity and multiplicity of partners and the compulsive, driven, and repetitive nature of the behavior.

REFERENCES

Bell, A., & Weinberg, M. (1978), *Homosexualities: A Study of Diversity Among Men and Women*. New York: Simon & Schuster.

Calef, V., & Weinshel, E. (1984), Anxiety and the restitutional function of homosexual cruising. *Internat. J. Psycho-Anal.*, 65:45–53.

Freud, S. (1905), Three essays on the theory of sexuality. *Standard Edition*, 7:125–245. London: Hogarth Press, 1953.

——— (1922), Some neurotic mechanisms in jealousy, paranoia, and homosexuality. *Standard Edition*, 18:221–235. London: Hogarth Press, 1955.

Hoffman, M. (1968), *The Gay World*. New York: Basic Books.

Humphreys, L. (1970), *Tearoom Trade*. Chicago: Aldine.

Kinsey, A., et al (1948), *Sexual Behavior in the Human Male*. Philadelphia: W. B. Saunders.

Nunberg, H. (1938), Homosexuality, magic and aggression. *Internat. J. Psycho-Anal.*, 19:1–16.

Saghir, M., & Robins, E. (1973), *Male and Female Homosexuality*. Baltimore: William & Wilkins.

Socarides, C. (1978), *Homosexuality*. New York: Aronson.

25

An Object Choice and Its Determinants
In Fantasy, Myth, and Reality

Arlene Kramer Richards, Ed.D.

This chapter will trace some of the vicissitudes of the development of a love based on a problematic object choice: the obligatory choice of a black woman by a white man. In the case of an object chosen because of a difference of race, determinants may include the fantasies of what the person of the other race will be like as well as fantasies of what the chooser will be in relation to the person of the other race.

Lewis Nkosi's recent novel *Mating Birds* (1986) attempts to portray the complexities in the choice of a white woman by the black narrator, who explains his motives this way:

> After all, it was I who chose to run after the girl: out of my own inclination, with no other purpose in mind than to discover the sexual reasons for the white man's singular protectiveness toward his womenfolk, I gradually conceived the idea of attaining knowledge of some willing white woman [p. 66].

The narrator attempts to understand his fatal choice of the absolutely forbidden object by talking to an analyst, a Dr. Dufré:

> Was it possible that someone like Dufré, with his immense skill and powers of analysis, could succeed in uncovering something in my background that would provide a clue to my behavior, something that could endow with meaning my choice of this girl or the passion that with each glimpse of her shadowy form I conceived for her: some defect of my personality perhaps, some mental distortion that would indicate the culmination of a particular history of mental aberration and sexual disorder? [p. 67].

He imagines the object's reciprocal choice of him:

> For in my lust for her, Veronica must have recognized the force of her
> own social existence, the image of her own sexual powers; in the ability
> to arouse unextinguishable desire in others, she must have obtained
> confirmation of her own immense and undeniable necessity in our small
> corrupted universe. Seen in that light, both the girl and I were hooked.
> We were both obsessed with the other's unadmitted presence. To her,
> I dare say, I was as much of a drug as she was to me, the ultimate
> mirror in which she saw reflected the power of her sex and her race
> [p. 74].

The narrator's choice is deliberate. He has selected a trait first: he wants
a white woman. Furthermore, he wants her in order to discover what
white men find so special in their women. The author develops a commonly held myth of the sexual superiority of the other race and shows
how it affects personal fantasy and, through fantasy, behavior.

Object choice has been a focus of analytic interest mainly as a
synonym for falling in love (Arlow, 1980). It has sometimes been seen
as having to do with maturity of object relations (Kernberg, 1980) or
a refinding of a state of infantile bliss (Bergmann, 1980). It has been
related to drives as well as to ego choices (Compton, 1981). The use of
part objects obscures the importance of the loved person (Peto, 1975),
and the intrusion of an image of a part object can make the choice of
another person impossible (Weinberger and Glenn, 1977). Developmental
changes have been shown to create changes in object choice in the descriptive sense, as the drive object changes from one's own anal zone to the
genital of the parent of the opposite sex (Glenn, 1977). Finally, the transfer
of the object choice in the oedipal stage has been shown to be facilitated
by preoedipal nurturance from the father (Andresen, 1980).

Ever since Freud (1905) described object choice as an outcome of
early experience, psychoanalysts have attempted to uncover memories
of this experience in reality. The special vicissitudes of object choice in
a person who has experienced loss of a parent before latency have been
studied by Neubauer (1968) and Orgel (1975). Orgel describes a defensive constellation in which split object choice was used to ward off the
pain of separation and loss and to control dangerous oedipal excitement.
In Neubauer's case, a girl who believed that her father had left her mother
weeks after the girl was born, because he had wanted her to be a boy,

tried to become a boy in order to please her father. As a corollary, she had to love a boy in a narcissistic way. As Neubauer put it, "The father's implicit demand. . . that she would be acceptable to him only as a boy, imposed on her a narcissistic type of object choice (Freud, 1914), to love, in effect, what someone else wanted her to be" (p. 298).

Walters (1965) attributed promiscuity in object choice in adolescent girls to a reenactment of the infantile tie to the mother. Francis (1965) and Orgel (1975) described cases in which actual early life experiences influenced object choice decisively. In Francis's cases, parental seduction led to homosexual orientation, and in Orgel's an experience of having two fathers led to a split object choice in later life. Abend (1984) traced object choice in two cases back to experiences with siblings.

Spruiell (1975) amended Freud's distinction (1914) between anaclitic and narcissistic object choice. According to Spruiell, the child or adolescent "loves anaclitically in ways which are still relatively narcissistic in comparison to the optimal passions of adults" (p. 587). In this view object choice can be *relatively* narcissistic or anaclitic; no neat categorization is possible. Van der Waals (1965) pointed out that the object one chooses *always* affects the self-regard, either by contrast with the object or by identificatiion.

Freud (1910) introduced the idea that the choice of a debased object serves incestuous wishes: the choice of a woman who can represent the mother by being already involved with another man. Winning the debased woman is thus a triumph over the father. Rankin (1962) discussed a form of object choice in which the bebased object, a married woman with many lovers, was attractive because she offered the opportunity for triumph over siblings. Variants of this kind of object choice were described by Haas (1986) and Sachs (1974).

Cultural aspects in the choice of objects have been alluded to by Stoller (1974) and Payne (1977). Conflicts over the choice of an object of the same sex have been explored with particular thoroughness. An interchange between Bieber (1976), Socarides (1976), and Friedman (1976) resulted in an agreement to disagree as to whether the choice of a heterosexual or homosexual object could be predicted from family background. The reality of the family situation was thought to be crucial by Bieber and Socarides but was regarded as only one of many factors by Friedman, who believed that sexual object choice is not determined once and for all by a single fantasy, early experience, or trauma. "However," he noted, "common sense and clinical experience suggest that the age range during which sexual object choice crystallizes is protracted and therefore individual differences with regard to predisposing influences toward erotically stimulating objects are probably numerous.''

Similar mechanisms have been thought to account for object choice in interracial marriage. Lehrman (1967) explained such a choice by the following possibilities: incest phobia, debasement, hostility because of an incestuous impulse which has been disappointed, exaggerated narcissism, exhibitionnism, conviction that one is an exception, and attitudes defending against castration anxiety. Steg (1971) rejected the absolute influence of any of Lehrman's factors in favor of an explanation by central fantasy. In the realm of object choice as it relates to sex of object, race of object, and to narcissism and identification, the issue has been whether a central fantasy or various specific determinants best account for object choice.

CLINICAL CASE

In the case of a white professional man who required a black woman for sexual potency and eventually married one, the issue of object choice was central for the last eight years of his ten-year, five-times-a-week analysis. He came for analysis at the age of twenty-six because he had been depressed and unable to work since the breakup of his marriage a year earlier. He was in the profession his father had unsuccessfully attempted. Although he was intellectually capable, he had done so poorly in the past year that he was in danger of being fired. The marriage had been an unhappy one, but then he had been unhappy all his adult life.

In his last year of high school he had impregnated his white middle-class girlfriend. His father had insisted that the child be given out for adoption and had discouraged him from continuing the relationship. His mother, whom he described as an unassertive woman, had gone along with his father's decision. He believed that he had never actually penetrated his girlfriend and that the child would break the hymen at birth. The fantasy, of which he had been unaware at that time, had been to give his parents a child of virgin birth. Later in the analysis this fantasy was explored. Virgin had meant to him uncastrated, as she had suffered no bloody attack. It also indicated loyalty to his father, who believed in the virginity of the Madonna. Finally, it meant an *anal* baby, not begotten in the ordinary genital way. He became aware in the analysis that he believed his father had wanted many children but that his mother had wanted only him. He had believed that his father deserved many children and that the close mother-son relationship was what made his mother want only one child. He felt guilty toward his father for having destroyed the father's potential babies. The child was thus a partly unconscious gift to his father, made to replace himself when he went off to college. As it turned out later in the analysis, his love for his father was strongly colored by negative oedipal wishes for anal penetration and fantasies of an anal baby. Thus, for this patient the child had been a love gift to his very religious father.

In college the patient engaged in antisocial acts of a sort likely to get him punished, though in fact he had always escaped with impunity. Upon finishing college, he had married a woman he had known in high school, the bossiest girl in their circle and, like the girl who had borne his child, white. That choice, based on his then still unconscious need for punishment, had resulted in a five-year marriage. He had been unable to maintain an erection after the first few weeks, but tried to appease his wife through various forms of sex play. His own pleasure was obtained through visits to pornographic movies, reading pornographic literature, and occasional visits to black prostitutes. This pattern continued after his divorce.

He had been unable to maintain a sexual relationship with any woman. For him, the choice of an object now posed a classical problem (Freud, 1910). If he respected a woman and enjoyed her company, he could not get an erection with her. But when he could get an erection with a woman—who could conceivably fit his representation of a debased object—getting to know her as a person destroyed the illusion. As the woman became a human being with admirable qualities in addition to the debased one, he lost potency. His solution for several years was to find a woman corresponding to the debased object, have as little contact with her as possible outside of the sexual encounter, and either pay her if she was a prostitute or, if she was not, leave expensive gifts as if to pay her. As he became aware in the analysis of the anal meanings this behavior had for him, it became less satisfying to him. He then had a black mistress for several years whom he was able to tolerate because he believed her to be stupid and abject. Shame and guilt ostensibly related to her debasement were then seen to stem from his feelings about the sex act itself.

The analysis focused for a time on his need for a black woman.

The idea of black skin being like feces in color and the idea of black people as carefree, earthy, and real were elaborated. When the woman moved in with him and they began to make plans for marriage, he became impotent with her, broke off their relationship, and returned to his previous pattern.

He then recovered a memory of his maternal grandmother showing him a picture of herself as a very young child with a little black girl of the same age. He recalled his grandmother telling him that they used to play their little games in the dirt, but that she had gotten too grown up for that shortly after the picture was taken. He also recovered a memory of his grandmother's garden helper, a large, strong black woman he had thought was a man. This woman had worked for his grandmother while he and his mother lived with the maternal grandparents. His father was away in military service until the patient was twenty months old, at the height of the anal period, when separation issues would have been paramount. His most important discovery in this regard was a reconstruction of an anal game his mother had played with him when he was recalcitrant about defecating on the toilet. To counter his fear of having his feces flushed away, she would let him watch her defecate, show him her product, let him flush it, and then put him on for his turn. The little boy stood facing his mother, thus seeing her exposed genital rather than the actual stool. He recalled a similar game she had played to coax him to eat food he didn't like: a bite for you and a bite for me. In that game, mother ate a bite, baby ate a bite, and they both enjoyed eating as a social experience. Evidently, his mother had decided that what worked for the oral stage had possibilities for the anal stage as well. The toilet game had continued for years. Knowing this, he could see how his father's rejection of his child had seemed to him a castration, as had his mother's flushing away of his feces.

When a black woman at a bordello he used became especially interested in him, he began an affair with her. She told him of her deprived past, of her failed family, of her own degradation. She was like a Scheherezade for him, fitting herself into the picture of a degraded object in many different ways. Her crucial attraction for him only became clear several months into their affair, when he announced in an analytic session that she was pregnant and intent on keeping the baby. While he had much earlier hinted that she had a secret she made him promise not to talk about in analysis, he now admitted that this was the secret.

He had agreed to father a child for her. The child was a continuation of the cycle that had begun in his adolescence.

The analysis of this action produced new understandings. Now he would keep this new child, thus legitimating in his mind the sexual union that had produced it. Now he would be aggrandized rather than humiliated, because now he could support both child and mother, he could make his own decisions rather than go along with what he believed the analyst thought prudent, and he could defy both parents' overt prohibitions against intermarriage. Although initially chosen as a degraded object, the woman now became indispensable to him as the mother of his child.

At this point he had a dream. He was walking with a woman. A roadblock appeared on the sidewalk. He had to show his identification. Instead of his proper credentials, all that came out of his wallet were pornographic photos of himself as he had had sex with various black prostitutes over the years. The woman with him turned out to be not so beautiful. She had smaller breasts than he liked and was fatter than he liked his women to be. His associations began with the idea that in order to become the mother of his child, his girlfriend had to go through pregnancy. Her abdomen had swelled and he began to worry about the stretch marks on her belly. Appearance meant so much to him, how could he tolerate a woman with stretch marks? The conflict resurfaced. Even though she was black and his mother white, plump while his mother was thin, uneducated while his mother was highly educated, if she got stretch marks she would be like his mother, who had a surgical scar on her abdomen. He recalled one of his favorite jokes, in which a little boy asks his father about the terrible gash his mother has between her legs. The father tells him he made that with an axe. "Oh, good shot," says the son; "you got her right in the cunt." Related to this was a screen memory of his father telling him that if he hung around with his mother he'd become a momma's boy rather than a real man like his father. For him this remark was transformed into a castration threat: too much closeness with mother and you will get the axe also. The inference may also have been taken that to have intercourse with a woman would castrate her, and that somehow he too would then be castrated.

In the transference he was showing me his sexual prowess through the pornographic images. This turned the passive viewing of the mother's genital as she was seated on the toilet into an active display of his genital to me. The dream represented the overcoming of his fear by the use of pornography. Looking at pictures of men engaging in all sorts of sex acts with women without losing their genitals protected him from his castration fears. The choice of a woman who had been with many men before him also insured him against castration—she hadn't castrated them. No avenging male had come to protect her from them. She was safe. Not even years of his own sexual activity had castrated him. Both the small breasts and the overweight were overtly disappointing, yet reassuring. The woman was neither as voluptuous as his mother had seemed to him when he was small nor as slim as she had seemed to him for the rest of his life. He once again faced the issue of how to remain excited and potent with a woman who seemed to him an equal. His dilemma took the form: if she is not like my mother, she is not exciting; if she is like my mother, I will be castrated for having castrated her. It was especially difficult for him to find his way out of the dilemma because of several episodes of an overtly seductive nature in which he had been alone with his mother for long periods in early adolescence. These interludes recalled the toilet game. He also suffered because of his perception of his father as aloof and forbidding, a perception related to his father's early absence when away in the military, and to the disappointment of the negative oedipal wish. The patient's choice of object was thus an attempt at reparation. The relationship exacerbated his castration fears. Thus, object choice and object relations worked antithetically and the best solution available for this man turned out to be a normalization of his use of pornography, and fantasies about voluptuous virgins in order to maintain his potency with his ultimate partner, the mother of his child.

The patient reported another dream later in the analysis in which he poignantly depicted the resignation involved in this compromise:

> I was in the Army to defend the U.S. against terrible yellow enemies. The Germans were doing the planning. They sent me a uniform but it was all creased, especially the pants, in front. I thought, the Germans don't do such good planning. They are supposed to be in charge, but they are messing up. I woke and tried to fall asleep again to finish the dream, but I couldn't start it up again.
>
> I realized it was the same creases in my pants I get when I go to the porn club. The girls sitting in my lap crease my pants. You remember I told you I have to send them to the cleaners every time I go. The Germans are like my father. It is trying to live up to his ideals

that I land in the porn club. I think P. is my defiance of him. But it works out for me. She is a nice person. I think I love her. I already love our baby. The baby was the only way I could get out of this. Out of his plan for me.

I got off his lap by having a woman on mine! But P. is not just a kid on my lap. She's real. She's worked hard in her life, had some tough breaks, but it didn't make her bitter. She says I'm another person now. I used to drink hard to be naughty. This weekend I didn't want any. It is tragic that I had to do it this way. [Tragic?] Tragic for everybody. But this is the best I can do.

Analysis of his impotence led to recall of what was possibly a screen memory. His mother took him along to her gynecologist when he was in late latency. She complained that her husband had lost interest in her sexually and was advised to go to bars to pick up men. As the patient understood it then, this meant that his father's sex life was confined to reading the pornographic magazines the patient had seen him buying. He had elaborated his earlier fantasy (of being castrated if he stayed with his mother) in such a way that he would be safe from castration only if he were like his father. But his father was impotent, and the son could find no way to be a man.

His solution was found years later, during his first marriage. Again he recalled it as being prompted by a chance remark. A black co-worker had told him that certain black women have very large clitorises, as large as a white man's penis. He was potent with black women from then on. At last he had found a way to be with a woman without the risk of castrating her. If black women had the equivalent of a penis, being with them and risking becoming like them involved no risk of losing his penis. This culminated in his ultimate object choice, his second wife. It was notable that in the process of the gradual deepening of his relationship with her, different aspects of her personality were seen to fit his picture of the ideal object. Especially salient were her capacity for nurturance and protection of her infant, her contentment with the baby's demands, her reluctance to have him listed on the baby's birth certificate as the father, and her ability to satisfy herself sexually by masturbating when he did not want sex. Her capacity for financial independence appealed to him, as did her willingness to give that up for a time in order to be a full-time mother.

DISCUSSION

The variety of paths to the analysis of this man's unconscious fantasies followed a map provided by Arlow (1969).

> Mythology is thus a culturally organized, institutional form of communal daydreaming. The same is clearly true of many aspects of religious and artistic experience. A person's favorite joke or the kind of humor he generally prefers usually leads directly to the nature of his fantasy thinking inasmuch as every instinctual fixation is represented at some level of mental life in the form of a group of associated unconscious fantasies [p. 36].

His fantasy corresponded to a religious myth discussed by Arlow (1965) and by Jones (1951). According to Arlow, the Madonna's impregnation guards against the dangers of injury to either the man or the woman, the fear of which makes infantile fantasies of intercourse so frightening. The mother's virginity was part of the mythology of sexual life in many of the religions discussed by Jones. Myths of the black virgin and of Magdalene, a prostitute who became the most beloved of all of Christ's disciples (Begg, 1985), also have parallels in this patient's fantasy. His adolescent fantasy gift of a child to his father is similar to the fantasy reported in adolescent mothers of a reparation to the parent who will be lonely when the adolescent leaves home to live a separate life (Sugar, 1979). Kaplan (1984) described adolescent development as ending in a wish to care for a new generation, which Kaplan believes operative in both women and men. If the patient could be a father himself and give his parents a child for whose sake they would stay together, he would be free to go off to college and live as a separate, potent adult. With the disappointment of that wish, his character underwent the marked change of his college years. And it was only with this failure that his ultimate object choice was limited to that of a black woman who was the mother of his child, yet capable of making and carrying out her own decisions.

Character has been long thought to take decisive shape in adolescence. According to Anna Freud (1937), the newly passionate and evanescent object relations of adolescence give rise to ideals of everlasting friendship and loyalty. She believed (A. Freud, 1958) that faithfulness to a love object corresponds to a change of person chosen as the embodiment of this object. As she saw it, adolescent defenses are not so much defenses against conflict as defenses against oedipal and preoedipal object ties.

The new finding in the choice of object in this case seems to be that the person chosen corresponded to a figure in a fantasy consolidated in late adolescence. Although it was possible to trace this event back as far as its determinants in early adolesdcence, the oedipal phase, and preoedipal (especially anal) phases, it was the specific traumatic event of late adolescence, the pregnancy and loss, which, drawing together the strands of earlier development, gave decisive shape to the fantasy. And the particular fantasy determined the eventual choice of the person who could play the major role in it.

Freud (1925) saw the adolescent conflict in terms of the clash between infantile incestuous wishes and the morality, shame, and disgust built up during infancy, with nonincestuous object choice the ideal outcome. This was an elaboration of the typology (Freud, 1914) which led to the belief that object choice depends on a trait rather than on an evolving complex of traits and relationships woven into a central fantasy. Buckley (1985) has pointed out that reconciliation requires at least a partial confirmation in reality of commonality of identity and purpose with the other. Similarly, I believe, successful object choice requires a partial confirmation in reality of the traits which form the basis of the choice. If the real person is too different from the image, or if the real person cannot tolerate being seen as the lover needs to see the beloved, the relationship breaks down.

The first object choice for the patient was a white middle-class virgin. The failure of his fantasy of producing a holy infant to give his father doomed the adolescent relationship with that woman. The next object choice, his first wife, was based on a fantasy of punishment and renunciation, again in the service of winning his father's love. He abandoned that relationship when he recognized that the fantasy had failed. In the end, he was able to find an object meeting his need for punishment while allowing him to retain his father's love and his belief in his genital integrity, as well as the anal wishes so important to him.

When a person chooses another, the process of getting acquainted allows comparison between the traits of the object image and the traits of the person. A complex matching process goes on with the comparison of object to elements of fantasy as well. As Arlow (1980) puts it:

Clinical experience underscores the fact that in every love relationship the individual acts out some form of complicated unconscious fantasy rooted in early vicissitudes of drive and object experience, a fantasy that ultimately determines, *but only in part,* the pattern of loving and the specific person or types of persons that will correspond to the object choice [p. 127].

CONCLUSION

The case presented here adds to Arlow's formulation the idea that the fantasy itself, while rooted in early life, may take decisive shape during late adolescence. It shows how fantasy, myth, and reality interplay to determine object choice initially and how they recombine to influence later choices. The central fantasy of providing an anal baby to the father in a negative oepidal constellation was bolstered by both myths and realities. The religious myth of the birth of a child to a virgin figured in the man's attempt to negotiate adolescence, as did the myth of the hypersexuality of members of another race. The way in which bits of reality—the mother's anal game, her display of her scars, her complaint of her husband's inability to satisfy her sexually—were woven into the central fantasy of an anal baby from an uncastrated woman-man was also crucial. The traumatic effect of the reality of the rejected baby depended on how it fit into the fantasy as elaborated up to that time. In the end, it was the first baby and the finality of its loss that seem to have shaped the patient's adult fantasy life and his object choice.

In the complex tangle of fantasies constructed at various stages of development, the later combine with the earlier levels in ways we cannot predict. Elements from reality, myth, and personal fantasy are involved, and the development of the fantasy may be altered at later stages of development to accommodate experience. The object choice is most clearly at issue when the person choosing is aware of some specific trait that is required in order for the object to be attractive. Specific traits range from the superficial and innocuous to the tangled, deep, and sometimes fateful, but awareness of them always entails a sense of constraint.

REFERENCES

Abend, S. (1984), Sibling love and object choice. *Psychoanal. Quart.,* 53:425–430.

Andresen, J. (1980), Rapunzel: The symbolism of the cutting of hair. *J. Amer. Psychoanal. Assn.*, 28:69–88.

Arlow, J. A. (1965), The Madonna's conception through the eyes. *Psychoanalytic Study of Society*, 3:9–25.

—— (1969). Fantasy, memory, and reality testing. *Psychoanal. Quart.*, 38:28–51.

—— (1980), Object concept and object choice. *J. Amer. Psychoanal. Assn.*, 28:109–133.

Begg, E. (1985), *The Cult of the Black Virgin*. London: Routledge & Kegan Paul.

Bergmann, M. (1980), On the intrapsychic function of falling in love. *J. Amer. Psychoanal. Assn.*, 28:56–77.

Bieber, I. (1976) Psychodynamics and sexual object choice. A reply to Dr. Richard C. Friedman's paper. *Comtemp. Psychoanal.*, 12:366–369.

Buckley, P. (1985), The determinants of object choice in adulthood: A clinical test of object relations theory. *J. Amer. Psychoanal. Assn.*, 33:841–859.

Compton, A. (1981), On the psychoanalytic theory of instinctual drives: II. The sexual drive and the ego drive. *Psychoanal. Quart.*, 50:219–237.

Francis, J. (1965), Passivity of homosexual predisposition in latency boys. *Bull. Phila. Assn. Psychoanal.* 15:160–174.

Freud, A. (1937). *The Ego and the Mechanisms of Defense*. Rev. ed. New York: International Universities Press, 1966.

—— (1958), Adolescence. *The Psychoanalytic Study of the Child*, 13:255–278. New York: International Universities Press.

Freud, S. (1905), Three essays on the theory of sexuality. *Standard Edition*, 7:130–243, London, Hogarth Press 1953.

—— (1910), A special type of object choice made by men. *Standard Edition*, 11:165–175, London, Hogarth Press 1957.

—— (1914), Observations on transference-love. *Standard Edition*, 12:159–171. London: Hogarth Press.

—— (1925), An autobiographical study. *Standard Edition*, 20:7–70. London, Hogarth Press, 1959.

Friedman, R. (1976), Psychodynamics and sexual object choice: A reply to Drs. I. Bieber and C. W. Socarides. *Contemp. Psychoanal.*, 12:379–385.

Glenn, J. (1977), Constipation is a small girl. *Psychoanal. Quart.*, 46:141–161.

Haas, L. (1966), Transference outside the psychoanalytic situation. *Internat. J. Psycho-Anal.*, 47:422–426.

Jones, E. (1951), The Madonna's conception through the ear. In: *Essays in Applied Psycho-Analysis*. London: Hogarth Press, pp. 266–357.

Kaplan, L. (1984), *Adolescence*. New York: Simon & Schuster.

Kernberg, O. (1980), Love, the couple, and the group: A psychoanalytic frame. *J. Amer. Psychoanal. Assn.*, 28:78–108.

Lehrman, S. (1967), Psychopathology of mixed marriages. *Psychoanal. Quart.*, 36:67–82.

Nkosi, L. (1986), *Mating Birds*. New York: St. Martin's Press.

Neubauer, P. (1968), The one-parent child and his oedipal development. *The Psychoanalytic Study of the Child*, 15:286–309. New York: International Universities Press.

Orgel, S. (1975), Split object choice. *Psycholoanal. Quart.*, 44:266–268.

Payne, E. (1977), The psychoanalytic treatment of male homosexuality. *J. Amer. Psychoanal. Assn.*, 25:183–200.

Peto, A. (1975), The etiological significance of the primal scene in perversions. *Psychoanal. Quart.*, 44:177–190.

Rankin, A. (1962), Odi and Amo: Gaius Valerius Catullus and Freud's essay on "A special type of object choice made by men." *American Imago*, 19:437–448.

Sachs, L. (1974), An unusual object choice during the oedipal phase. *Psychoanal. Quart.*, 43:477–492.

Socarides, C. (1976), Psychodynamics and sexual object choice: A reply to Dr. Richard C. Friedman's paper. *Contemp. Psychoanal.*, 12:370–378.

Spruiell, V. (1975), Three strands of narcissism. *Psychoanal. Quart.*, 44:577–595.

Steg, J. (1971), Determination of object choice in an intraracial marriage. *Bull. Phila. Assn. Psychoanal.*, 21:13–18.

Stoller, R. (1974), Development issues in adolescent motherhood. In: *Female Adolescent Development*, ed. M. Sugar. New York: Brunner/Mazel.

Van der Waals, H. (1965), Problems of narcissism. *Bull. Menn. Clin.*, 29:293–311.

Walters, P. (1965), Promiscuity in adolescence. *Amer. J. Orthopsychiat.*, 35:670–675.

Weinberger, J., & Glenn, J. (1977), The significance of the trifurcation of the road: Clinical confirmation and illumination. *J. Amer. Psychoanal. Assn.*, 25:655–668.

26

Self-Mutilation and Father-Daughter
Incest: A Psychoanalytic Case Report

Arnold D. Richards, M.D.

Self-mutilation by cutting, burning, or other means is a dramatic and troubling symptom encountered in clinical practice, particularly in the treatment of adolescent or postadolescent females. An extensive psychiatric literature on this phenomenon (see Simpson, 1975) draws primarily but not exclusively on hospitalized patients, most of whom are diagnosed as schizophrenic. Reports on patients treated outside the hospital setting are not as common, and case reports of nonpsychotic patients treated psychoanalytically are rare indeed. Two exceptions are several patients included in the report of Friedman, (1972), and a patient of Kafka's (1969) who in a hospital setting began a psychoanalytic treatment of almost five years duration. It is not clear from Kafka's report whether the entire analysis was conducted in the hospital or whether the patient was discharged at some point in her treatment and then analyzed in an office setting.

Despite the paucity of analytic data on self-mutilating patients, clinicians who have encountered such symptomatology have frequently drawn on psychoanalytic concepts to explain the psychology involved. Thus, self-mutilating behavior has been conceptualized in terms of alterego states (Pao, 1969), phallic conflicts involving castration (Novotny, 1972), and compromise formations involving incestuous fantasies (Simonopoulos, 1974). Within their group of self-mutilating and suicidal adolescent analysands, Friedman et al. stressed ambivalent ties to the mother and the wish to destroy the body (or body part) perceived as the source of instinctual urges. The inadequate maternal handling and lack of physical stimulation to which self-mutilating patients are subject in infancy (Graf and Malin, 1967; Pao, 1969; Simonopoulos, 1974), along with a related vulnerability to separation anxiety (Pao, 1969; Asch, 1971; Kwawer, 1980) are threads that run through the literature.

In a recent study of twenty young hospitalized self-mutilators Simpson and Porter (1981) elicited a history of sexual abuse in nine of their subjects, including sexual relationships between the self-mutilating girls and their fathers, sexual fondling during preschool years, and intercourse or rape during adolescence. This recorded incidence of sexual abuse was based on information that surfaced in therapeutic interviews during the patients' hospitalization; the authors believe the actual incidence may have been even greater. This study is a significant emendation of the literature. Earlier studies of self-mutilating did not specifically link such behavior to sexual abuse or incest, though Green (1967) has linked self-mutilative behavior to parental abuse and the reports of Crabtree (1967) and Kwawer (1980) invite the inference of specifically sexual parental abuse. It is striking, then, that the relationship between incest and self-mutilation demonstrated by Simpson and Porter should be borne out in the present psychoanalytic case.

A CASE REPORT

Fran, a married graduate student, was twenty-two years old at the time she was referred for analysis. The referral came from a hospital psychiatrist who had seen her for approximately a year in psychotherapy, first while she was hospitalized, then as a hospital day patient, and finally as an outpatient working and living with a foster family. Her hospitalization at a private psychiatric facility had been precipitated by a pregnancy that occurred at the end of her freshman year at college. She gave birth to a baby girl while hospitalized, and the infant was given out for adoption immediately thereafter. The patient had no further contact with her daughter.

During the course of her three-year hospitalization Fran engaged in both self-destructive and mutilative behavior: she once set her nightgown on fire and on several other occasions inflicted burns on her breasts and genitals. These behaviors abated when a divorced man almost thirty years her senior became interested in her. She improved to the point of discharge, went to live with him in his home, and subsequently married him. Two years after hospitalization she contacted her former hospital psychiatrist in New York (where she had since become a graduate student) because she was again pregnant and did not want to have the baby. Her distress was compounded by the fact that her marriage was now in trouble. She had become involved with another older man and was thinking of leaving her husband. She was concerned that her husband might not be the father of her child. Fran's anguish was resolved by a spontaneous abortion, but her marital problems intensified to the point that she began taking amphetamines and was considering experimentation with LSD. It was at this juncture that her former therapist recommended analysis.

At the first session Fran complained of feelings of anxiety, depersonalization, and an inability to control her self-destructive behaviors. The latter included, by her own admission, promiscuity, drug abuse, and suicidal gestures. She reported a long history of self-inflicted injuries, beginning in early adolescence. She had cut her wrists several times during the latter part of her senior year in high school, when she was living in a home for delinquent girls run by nuns. On these and numerous other occasions the actual cutting was done deliberately and dispassionately, without pain but in response to an inner voice commanding her to so injure herself. She was aware of intense feelings as she observed blood appearing on her skin: the act of cutting was accompanied not by orgasm per se but by a sense of relief, release, and discharge.

The presenting picture was discouraging, to say the least. I nevertheless decided to see her five times a week on the couch, not fully aware of the depth of her pathology. My initial diagnosis of hysterical personality was influenced partly by the fact that she had come with a specific recommendation for analysis. Her condition seemed to exemplify what Glover (1954) and Ticho (1970) have described as the heroic indications for analysis. Though uncertain that she could be helped analytically, I believed that no other form of therapy held a better prognosis.

Background and History

Fran was born in the home of her maternal grandparents, devout Irish Catholics. The product of an unwanted and physically difficult pregnancy, she incurred the resentment of both mother and maternal grandmother even before her birth. She did not nurse and was weaned from the bottle at seven months. During her childhood her mother treated her as a virtual prisoner, rationing her food, restricting her activities, and meting out extreme punishment for minor infractions of family rules. She tied Fran's hands at night to prevent her from masturbating, forced her to use the toilet only at certain times of the day, and locked the kitchen cabinet to make sure that she had no food other than the portions allotted her at meal times. As Fran grew older these restrictions encompassed her playmates and play activities as well. In short, her mother spared no effort to humiliate the patient and to depreciate her every achievement.

When Fran entered puberty her mother actively discouraged her from taking any pride in her blossoming feminine appearance. She prohibited her from wearing a bra or stockings, from shaving her legs, and from wearing lipstick, although these same privileges were accorded her older sisters. On one occasion Fran's mother told her she was "deformed" because she had larger breasts than her sisters had. The mother was joined in these efforts of systematic degradation both by the older sisters and by the maternal grandmother.

At the beginning of analysis many of Fran's early memories concerned traumatizing visits to the maternal grandparents on holidays, when she had invariably been compared unfavorably with her older sisters, excluded from family dramatic and musical performances, and endlessly confronted by her grandmother with pictures of Jesus with a bleeding heart—as testimony to the result of her various misbehaviors ("Look what your're doing to Jesus by being bad"). Fran often became sick, vomiting during these visits and eventually just before them. Fran's relationship with her immediately older sister, Cindy, fared no better. This sister adopted the sadistic bearing of the mother and grandmother, and Fran's envy and hatred of her were enormous. She recalled many battles, and was so furious that she had held a knife to her sister's throat. On one occasion the sister pushed Fran down a treacherous hill on a bicycle; on another she persuaded Fran to crawl into a pipe from which she would not help her extricate herself.

Fran's major solace amid all this suffering was her father's interest. Although he frequently traveled and was generally ineffectual in tempering his wife's abusive regimen, he did spend time with her, teaching her to swim when she was three and to play tennis when she was in grade school. In fact, the father's involvement with all his daughters shaded into unnatural intimacy. When home from business trips, for example, he gave all his daughters baths until they were quite grown. When the father was home, moreover, Fran recalled frequently joining both parents in bed in the morning. This behavior continued until she was eleven, when on one occasion she noticed that her father had an erection. On noting her awareness he told her to leave the bed and never to return to it.

Fran's precocious development was the focus of considerable conflict with her mother. She constantly referred to her daughter as a "cow" because her breasts were large. Her sister Cindy reinforced the mother's sadistic behavior, once giving Fran a ridiculously oversized bra as a birthday present. Predictably, social life and social appearance became sources of chronic conflict, especially after the family moved to another part of the country and Fran began high school. She remembered how her mother refused to allow her to act in a school play because of the "indecent" costume the part required. The mother placed a strict curfew on Fran, which she often violated. She had intercourse for the first time when she was sixteen and recalled coming home with blood on her shorts, which she believed her father noticed. On a subsequent occasion her parents discovered she had climbed out the bedroom window one night to join two boys. On returning, she denied having done anything wrong, but nevertheless begged her father to beat her. Shortly after this incident her father came home from work with a high fever; Fran called a friend and announced that she had made her father ill and was going to leave home. A fight with her mother ensued, the family doctor was summoned, and Fran ended up in the psychiatric ward of a general hospital.

She remained there for two months and, being very rebellious, was placed on what she called "solitary confinement." Though permitted to visit her parents at home, she would not speak to them on these occasions. On one such visit they took her to a nearby beach where she swam out so far that she eventually had to be rescued by a lifeguard. Once she ran away from the hospital, only to be discovered by her father and her doctor in a boyfriend's apartment. They dragged her back to the hospital, where she was physically restrained. At this point her psychiatrist recommended that she be placed in a home for delinquents in order to learn "discipline." She did well at this home in certain respects, teaching tennis, but her behavior remained provocative. It was at this time that she first cut her wrists in a suicidal gesture; in analysis she recovered a vivid memory of blood spurting over the white habit of the nun who discovered her.

After graduating from high school Fran was sent to a small college chosen by her mother. Her psychiatrist referred her to a psychiatrist in that area, and she began psychotherapy. Though she was expelled from this college under unclear circumstances, she continued to see her psychiatrist while auditing courses at a local university. This was her status at the time of her first pregnancy. She recounted her great surprise upon learning she was pregnant; she had never used birth control and yet had never before conceived, though by her estimate she had slept with fifty or sixty men, most of them much older than she. At first she denied the pregnancy, even to herself, but eventually she told her psychiatrist, who in turn informed her parents. Only her father came to see her, as her mother would have nothing to do with her. As the major parental objective was to prevent the rest of the family from learning of the pregnancy, her father made arrangements for a maternity residence. Fran could not understand why she was not permitted an abortion. Her father simply relayed her mother's decision that it was out of the question, that Fran must have the baby "to pay for her sins"; she heard nothing further from her father until he appeared at the maternity residence some time later to relocate her in a psychiatric hospital. During the interval he had apparently been advised to hospitalize her by a colleague whose son had recently committed suicide.

The Analysis

Although the later pregnancy that prompted Fran's referral for analysis was, as noted, resolved by spontaneous abortion, marital problems remained in the forefront for the first several years of the treatment. Extramaritally active during this time, she was now using birth control pills to prevent pregnancy. Shortly thereafter, when her husband, desirous of a child, urged her to discontinue the pill, she complied with his request despite her disappointment at having to forgo extramarital affairs. But in fact her own wish to have a child was increasing, seemingly in response to her growing insight into her relationship with her mother and a corresponding ability to feel less guilty about the hostility she felt toward her. This relationship was the major focus of the analytic work during this phase of the analysis and led to her decision to break off contact with her mother. Previously she had visited her occasionally and had spoken with her frequently by phone.

Shortly before going off the pill she had intercourse with a married college professor fifteen years her senior who, she volunteered, looked like her analyst. Within a matter of weeks she was again pregnant. Although she felt it unlikely that her husband was *not* the father, her single extramarital contact around the time of conception made her uncertain.

She agonized over this issue, alternately considering having an abortion, killing herself, killing the baby, and confessing her indiscretion to her husband.

During this turbulent period of the analysis, Fran frequently expressed the wish to terminate, partly because she did not want me to see her pregnant. Pregnancy was a sign of sin, the very attitude evinced by her mother following her first pregnancy. But eventually Fran gave birth and returned to analysis with only a ten-day interruption. Her pleasure and relief at having given birth to a healthy baby boy, the very image of her husband, was diminished by her anger at my failure to visit her in the maternity ward. Although she had not asked me to visit her, on resuming treatment she confessed that she had assumed I would "read her mind," as her mother had. Her sullen anger at my failure to do so seemed to repeat her angry disappointment with both parents, who had likewise refused to see her during her first pregnancy and subsequent hospitalization. She transformed her passive resentment toward her mother into active measures to keep her from visiting her new grandson.

Her anger was compounded by postpartum depression, which she had attributed to her renewed use of birth control pills, her cessation of nursing after six months, and her continued dissatisfaction with her husband, who, while pleased with the baby, was emotionally unavailable.

Following an unsuccessful Caribbean cruise that was intended to save her marriage, Fran's depression intensified in the wake of my announcement that I would be away all of March. Her depression was accompanied by the return of self-mutilating propensities, which had been in abeyance during her pregnancy and the eight months following her delivery. More alarming still, she now expressed suicidal thoughts of sufficient intensity to make me contemplate hospitalization. As a less extreme expedient, I allowed her to sit up, which she did for about five days before voluntarily returning to the couch. It was in the context of this distressing impasse in the analysis that she described a need to "act" rather than "talk." She acknowledged that this inability to talk about feelings embodied simultaneous wishes to reveal and to conceal. She added, however, that she wanted me to force her to confess.

It took some time to work through the layered meanings of the "secret" that she wanted me to drag out of her. Her first confession was that she enjoyed anal masturbation. In reply to my question, she indicated that she masturbated with her right hand even though she is left-handed. When I pointed out that she also used her right hand to cut herself, she volunteered that she was aware of masturbatory wishes preceding her self-mutilative activities, another of her secrets.

It was at this juncture that she came to a session telling me that she had cut herself again. This episode followed her breaking off the relationship with the professor. She reported that she had made a long cut just below the line of her pubic hair, although she had really wanted to cut a long circle under each breast and an "x" on each buttock. Her associations to these fantasied cuts went back to puberty, when her mother had ridiculed her breasts and prescribed an operation to remove "excess fat." She recalled in this connection that she had always been examined by the family doctor in the presence of her parents, and that this doctor, prior to administering an injection, would trace an "x" and a circle on her buttocks with methiolate, thus creating a bull's-eye for the needle. She remembered her father observing this ritual attentively and, from this memory, associated to her father's general interest in his daughters' pubescent bodies. She remembered that he once pulled down Cindy's pants and administered a spanking, though she was then in late adolescence.

It was now clear that memories involving both parents were implicated in her selection of desired sites for cutting, and it was the transference that provided the impetus for the revelant childhood associations. I had become the sexually prohibitive mother, raising questions about her recent affair, but I was also the father to whom she would expose the site of her fantasied and actual cuts, thereupon exhibiting breasts, buttocks, and pubic region. She acknowledged a wish to be naked on the couch, as well as occasional feelings that she actually was naked.

She reported the following dream. She was in a building that resembled a house or stockade that Indians were attacking. They penetrated the stockade through the back door, and a girl was pierced by an arrow. Ensuing association linked the location of the dream to a trip out west with her father during Easter recess her senior year in high school. He had taken her along on a business trip, to both the chagrin and the relief of her mother, who welcomed the opportunity to be apart from both of them. Fran's father was drinking rather heavily then; she recalled the several bottles of whiskey he had taken on the trip. Then she remembered that she had shared her father's bed in the motels they stayed in. Once she awakened in the middle of the night and "thought" her father was having anal intercourse with her. She was upset and accused him of doing something "bad" to her, but he assured her that she had only had a nightmare. The next morning, she continued, "it was as if nothing had happened." When I commented that anal intercourse represented "penetration" through the back door, as in the dream, she replied that her memory of anal rape must be untrue, that her father didn't do such things. But she proceeded to recall an occasion when she had entered her parents' bedroom and observed her father alone, fondling his penis. He permitted her to stay, but cautioned her not to tell her mother. She left this session visibly shaken.

The next day she reported that she had not wanted to come to her session. After the previous day's session she had become aware of her mother's voice instructing her not to talk to me and to cut herself. Overcoming great resistence, Fran returned to the events recounted the previous day. She remembered that after the trip west she had begun to "really sleep around in earnest." It was in response to this behavior that her parents had first hospitalized her and sent her to the reformatory.

Then, during the winter or early spring of her first year at college, her father came to visit her. He picked her up at her dormitory and took her to his hotel room, where he humiliated her with abusive interrogation regarding the boys she was sleeping with. As she associated to the details of the room, she recalled that she not only spent the night with him, but once again shared his bed. As her regression intensified, she recalled the following sequence of events. In the middle of the night she had had intercourse with her father (the dream image of the girl being pierced by the arrow came to her mind). She had been terrified at her father's initial sexual advance; what made matters "even worse," however, was the sequel. She had awakened later in the night and requested intercourse again. When her father refused to comply, she had become even more terrified, both at her own "wish" and at her father's "rejection." Her terror reached a peak when it occurred to her that her mother would discover everything.

Fran reacted to these recovered memories with a mixture of amazement and disbelief; part of her believed it was "all a fabrication." Her mother, after all, had always accused her of making up stories. How could her father have done such a thing? It should be recalled that all this material emerged in the context of her mounting concern over my impending vacation. Her intense wish that I not abandon her was accompanied by a minor suicide attempt, the superficial cutting of a wrist. On my return she again expressed the desire to leave analysis. Why hadn't I canceled my vacation, given how traumatically upsetting her recent memories had been? I was just as bad as her father: I had forced her to recover memories of "all these terrible secret things" only to go away, just as he had initiated intercourse with her only to decline her advances and then leave her. She recalled that for a week following the seduction she had fantasied that her father, having slept with her, would leave her mother and live with her. Yet he had opted for her mother, just as I had opted for a vacation with my own wife and family.

The negative transference reached such a pitch thereafter that she obtained a referral from her husband's analyst. After a single visit with this senior consultant, she returned, reiterating her desire to quit despite the consultant's recommendation that she continue. When I informed her that the decision was hers to make, she proceeded to bewail her weakness and powerlessness with me. Why couldn't she make me do what she wanted? When I suggested that her wish to leave analysis masked her wish to escape from painful material that remained uncovered, she acknowledged this to be the case. She had recently begun to have sexual fantasies about me, realizing full well that intercourse with the analyst would spoil the analysis. She felt doomed to frustration, feeling I could give her something but had elected to withhold it.

As she left one session she expressed the urge to kick me "in the balls." At the following session she reported cutting herself, but would not tell me where. When I surmised that she had cut her genitals, she admitted I was right. She was doing to herself what she had wanted to do to her father and now, in the transference, to me: cut off the penis and have it for herself. I suggested that having a penis would protect her from sex with her father and at the same time enable her to assume his role as frustrator rather than always being the frustrated one. Following this interpretation she recalled yet another incident of paternal abuse. Shortly after having given birth to her daughter she was in a motel room with her father. He said to her, "Okay, get undressed," and proceeded to inspect her genitals. She believed he wanted to "check her out" following the delivery. The details of this memory seemed quite vivid, but the patient had expressed amazement that she had complied with her father's demand in view of his previous behavior.

As we worked through again and again the events following her seduction by her father, her envy of the male genital and a corresponding dissatisfaction with her own emerged into consciousness and became the focus of our work. A penis became desirable because it was intrusive, enabling men to rape women. Women, she observed, could not rape men.

She then recalled her childhood conviction that women *did* have penises, she alone being the exception.

These memories led Fran to a more realistic assessment of her father as sexually perverse and tragically weak. She recognized that intercourse with her father had preceded her first pregnancy, but was unable to entertain consciously the prospect that he may have fathered the little girl put up for adoption, although the stormy course of events that followed this pregnancy surely alluded to an unconscious awareness of this possibility. In fact, her anxiety about the identity of the father following her second pregnancy was a repetition of the anxiety that followed the first. The dynamic significance of the second pregnancy as a repetition of the first provides an explanation for her anxious concern lest the second child be a girl, i.e., lest it be like the first child, her father's child.

An episode of acting out at this point in the analysis proved illuminating. Having resumed her graduate studies, she was propositioned by a younger classmate. She acceded to his request despite herself, in the manner of a compulsion. But intercourse with him was unsatisfying. She felt that his penis did not "look right." Although she was upset by the encounter and had no desire to see him again, she felt cheated when the young man called her up to cancel a subsequent rendezvous. This transaction repeated yet again the events of her seduction at the hands of her father: initial disgust, unwilling arousal, rejection, and abandonment.

But her promiscuity was by now beginning to diminish. She was propositioned by her thesis advisor and declined him. She told him that their collaboration should be in the classroom and not in the bedroom. She separated from her husband, avoided involvements with men, and concentrated her energies on her graduate work and on parenting her son. Her sexual interest henceforth focused on the analyst. Since I had cured her, I should marry her or, at the very least, initiate an affair with her. Having previously been the bad father who had not only abandoned her for his wife (the vacation) but had refused to authorize the abortion that would have undone the possible consequences of his seduction, I now became the desirable father she longed for. Just as she had believed that but for the controlling mother her father would have chosen to live with her, so she now came to believe that but for our analytic contract I would have initiated an affair. If I would not seduce her because she was my patient, she would leave analysis. If, following termination, I still declined to have intercourse with her, it could only be because she was ugly, undesirable, physically repulsive, and misshapen. Her father had abandoned her because she was ugly and penisless; now I would do the same.

It was in this context that she again fantasized cutting herself and showing me her cuts. We understood this wish to *make* herself unattractive as a safeguard by which she defended against my sexual rejection of her. She would spare herself the narcissistic mortification of further rejection by seeing to it that she would never be sufficiently attractive to me; i.e., she would choose to make herself ugly rather than run the continual risk of being rejected by me or by her father because she was ugly. Ugliness produced by self-cutting was thus overdetermined: it was a defense against the dangers associated with oedipal fantasies, a reenactment of their gratification in adolescence, and a punishment (by her mother or herself as her mother's surrogate) for both the fantasy and the reality.

Fran unconsciously identified with what she perceived as her mother's view of sex as sin. Menstruation was "horrible," large breasts were ugly, and pregnancy was a punishment for intercourse. In this context, blood and self-inflicted bleeding achieved overdetermined symbolic status. There was the bleeding heart of Jesus, menstrual blood, the blood on her shorts "exhibited" to her father after her first intercourse, and the blood "spurting" from her wrists on the nun's white habit. The arrow in her dream "drew blood." Piercing stood for incestuous intercourse—genital or anal rape—and castration. The spurting wound was the castrated genital (as suggested by her menstrual bleeding) or, when displaced elsewhere, stood for its opposite, the penis. Her "spurting" wrists defiled the nun's purity and allowed her a feeling of discharge akin to orgasm in which the passivity associated with incestuous victimization was reversed. In the termination phase, her exhibitionistic wishes not only served actively to repulse the wished-for sexual overtures from the analyst; in addition, these wishes to cut and to exhibit her cuts, to the extent that they remained mere wishes, evidenced symbolic mastery of her equation of penis activity with penis injury. A person without a penis, she learned, can be an active agent, not a mere victim, even one's own.

The case reported here presented an opportunity for follow-up approximately ten years after treatment. Following termination Fran had divorced her husband, remarried, and had a second child. She reported being very happy in her second marriage, with no further recourse to self-mutilating activities. She was on good if somewhat distant terms with her father, who has never commented on his sexual exploitation of her.

CONCLUSION

This cas report presents the analytic treatment of a patient who both demographically and clinically qualifies as a practically perfect "model" self-mutilating patient with respect to age, sex, and other variables cited by Simpson and Porter (1981). The patient exhibited many characteristics of their subjects: drug abuse, suicide attempts, a history of parental physical abuse, and feelings of abandonment, isolation, and unlovableness. Many of the types of mutilation catalogued by Simpson and Porter—arm or wrist cutting, the cutting of breasts and genitals, burning oneself with matches or cigarettes, the "aggravation" of existing sores and injuries—were engaged in by this patient at various times. Moreover, the lack of maternal holding and physical stimulation during the first year of life reported by Graf and Malin (1967), Pao (1969), and Simonopoulos (1974) very likely typified her infancy. During psychoanalytic treatment, at a frequency of five sessions per week, the dramatic recovery of the memory of intercourse with her father during late adolescence, along with memories and reconstructions of other sexual experiences with her father, proved central to the understanding of her self-mutilative behavior and her eventual cure. This case therefore strengthens Simpson and Porter's finding of a significant link between self-mutilation in adolescent girls and earlier incestuous experiences.

REFERENCES

Asch, S. (1971), Wrist scratching as a symptom of anhedonia. *Psychoanal. Quart.*, 40:603–617.

Crabtree, L. (1967), A psychotherapeutic encounter with a self-mutilating patient. *Psychiatry*, 30:91–100.

Friedman, M., et al. (1972), Attempted suicide and self-mutilation in adolescence: Some observations from a psychoanalytic research project. *Internat. J. Psycho-Anal.*, 53:179–183.

Glover, E. (1954), The indications for psychoanalysis. *J. Mental Science*, 100:393–401.

Graf & Malin (1954), The syndrome of the wrist cutter. *Amer. J. Psychiat.*, 124:36–42.

Green, A. (1967), Self-mutilation in schizophrenic children. *Abst. Bull. Psychoanal. Med.*, 7:23–26.

Kafka, J. (1969), The body as transitional object: A psychoanalytic study of a self-mutilating patient. *Brit. J. Med. Psychol.*, 42:207–212.

Kwawer, J. (1980), Some interpersonal aspects of self-mutilation in a borderline patient. *J. Amer. Acad. Psychoanal.* 8:203–216.

Novotny, P. (1972), Self-cutting. *Bull. Menn. Clin.* 36:505–514.

Pao, P. (1969), The syndrome of delicate self-cutting. *Brit. J. Med. Psychol.*, 42:195–206.

Simonopoulos, V. (1974), Repeated self-cutting: An impulse neurosis. *Amer. J. Psychother.*, 28:85–94.

Simpson, M. (1975), The phenomenology of self-mutilating in a general hospital setting. *Can. Psychiat. Assn. J.*, 20:429–434.

Porter, (1981), *Bull, Menn. Clin.*

Ticho, E. (1970), Differences between psychoanalysis and psychotherapy. *Bull. Menn. Clin.*, 34/3:128–138.

Part VIII
EPILOGUE

27

Time: Removing the Degeneracies

J. T. Fraser, Ph.D.

This chapter deals with three topics related to time: time interpreted as a hierarchy of unresolvable, creative conflicts; the relationship of time to personal identity; and the structure of the experience of timelessness. The exposition draws on psychoanalytic insight as well as on understanding derived from different branches of natural science.

As my guide to psychoanalysis I have depended on the writings of Jacob Arlow, whose interest in the experience and idea of time spans the five decades of his professional life. The following is my tribute to his distinguished scholarship, and an all too modest token of appreciation for a life dedicated to the art of healing.

TIME AS CONFLICT

Psychoanalysis may be thought of as human nature seen from the point of view of conflict. The functioning of the human mind reflects the interaction of opposing forces and tendencies. Psychoanalysis places special emphasis on the effects of unconscious conflicts, the interaction in the mind of forces of which the individual is unaware [Arlow, 1978].

The Welsh poet Dylan Thomas gave a summary of the psychoanalytic view of time when he wrote, in "Fern Hill,"

Time held me green and dying
Though I sang in my chains like the sea.

481

To mute a recognition of finality and death and to reconcile it with its dreams of eternity, the human mind creates conscious and unconscious goals. Many of them are socially unacceptable, biologically undesirable, or even physically impossible. These goals are the links in the chain of which Dylan Thomas spoke. The desire to liberate ourselves from the bondage of that chain is, as I see it, at the root of the immense creativeness and destructiveness of our species.

That the human sense of time, that ceaseless concern with the forward motion of change, derives from certain irreducible conflicts of the mind has been implicit in much that has been written about time in the psychoanalytic literature. (For a representative bibliography see Fraser, 1981; also Sabbadini, 1979). The conflicts themselves were identified in Freud's "Beyond the Pleasure Principle" (1920) as follows:

> No substitute of reactive formations and no sublimations will suffice to remove the repressed instinct's persisting tension; and it is the difference in amount between the pleasure of satisfaction which is *demanded* and that which is actually *achieved* that will permit of no halting at any position attained, but in the poet's words, *"ungebandigt immer vorwrts dringt"* [untamed, forever forward presses] [p. 427].[1]

Freud quotes here from Goethe's *Faust,* a drama of the paradigmatic character of Western man. Whether or not psychoanalysis can become a universally acceptable theory of man or will ultimately remain culture- and even class or ethnicity-bound depends, in my view, on whether the "repressed instinct's persisting tension" is indeed a necessary feature of the human mind. Though the myriad forms of meeting the challenges of human time are culturally conditioned, I will assume that the human experienc? of time does derive from certain existential tensions peculiar to and necessary for the human mind, and manifest in all members of our species.

In a metaphysical generalization proposed many years ago and worked out in detail elsewhere (Fraser, 1987), I suggested that the dynamics of nature at large is that of a hierarchy of unresolvable, creative conflicts of which those peculiar to the human mind are only level-specific examples. This generalization, known as the theory of time as conflict

---

[1]German poet Angelus Silesius would have agreed with Freud: "Du selber machst die Zeit: das Uhrwerk sind die Sinnen: / Hemmst do die Unruh' nur, so ist die Zeit von hinnen." (You create time yourself: the mind is (the senses are) the clockwork: / if you inhibit its (their) restlessness, time vanishes.)

or the hierarchical theory of time, permits the integration of the psychoanalytic interpretations of human time experience with understandings of the nature of time derived from other fields of knowledge.

The theory draws attention to the hierarchy of stable organizational levels of nature. Considered along a scale of increasing complexity, these levels may be identified with (1) light (representing, pars pro toto, all speed-of-light particles), (2) all other elementary particles, (3) macroscopic bodies, (4) living organisms, (5) the symbolic structures and processes that constitute the world of the human mind, and (6) society, above a certain level of time-compactness.

The hierarchical theory of time maintains that each of these levels is characterized by certain level-specific, unresolvable creative conflicts; by level-specific lawfulness; and by a level-specific temporality. These conflicts, laws, and temporalities are seen to form a nested hierarchy which, from the evolutionary point of view, is open-ended.

In this statement "conflict" signifies the coexistence of two opposing trends, regularities, or groups of principles in terms of which the processes of the integrative level may be explicable. By "unresolvable" is meant that by means indigenous to an integrative level its conflicts may only be maintained (thereby securing the integrity of the organizational level) or eliminated (thereby collapsing the structures and functions of the level in question into the level beneath it); in no sense may those conflicts be solved (that is, peacefully integrated). By "creative" is meant that during the course of evolution the level-specific conflicts have given rise to structures and processes of increased complexity which, once again, possess their own unresolvable creative conflicts.

Explication, such as that proposed by the theory of time as conflict, assumes a formulator of questions and a seeker of answers. These roles define each other through the mutuality of the knower and the known. This mutuality is handled by the theory through an extension of the umwelt principle, proposed early in this century by the theoretical biologist Jakob von Uexkull as a way of formalizing the dynamics of the internal-external mutuality of living organisms.

Von Uexkull recognized the epistemic significance of the fact that the receptors and effectors of an organism determine its world of possible stimuli and actions. He called this species-specific world the umwelt of the species. What is external to that umwelt must be regarded as nonexistent for the members of the species, therefore the umwelt of a species is its world of reality. In psychology, umwelt is defined as "the circumscribed portion of the environment that is meaningful and effective for a given species and that changes its significance with the mood operative at a given moment'' (English and English, 1958).

In this definition the environment—of which the umwelt of a species is a circumscribed portion—is the umwelt of the human mind. Whereas the umwelts of nonhuman species are rigidly delimited and may be enlarged only through the process of organic evolution, humans can extend the boundaries of their species-specific reality beyond its biological limits.

As a first step of such an extension, our senses may be aided by exosomatic devices, ranging from primitive tools to the instruments of science. For instance, although mammalian eyes are insensitive in the ultraviolet region, we know of ultraviolet patterns on the wings of butterflies because we can make photographic plates sensitive in the ultraviolet range and interrogate them in the visible spectrum. "Visible" means visible to the human eye—that is, existent in our biological umwelt.

The boundaries of human reality may be further extended to those portions of the natural world—the very small, the very large, the very fast, the very dense—that are knowable only through mathematical formalism, derived from theory and tested by experiment. These are symbolic devices, extensions of our senses by abstract means.

Von Uexkull's idea of species-specific universe may now be generalized.

If careful exploration of the umwelt of a class of structures and their functions reveals certain types of temporalities, causations, and conflicts that are always found associated with them, then we may think of these peculiar, level-specific features of nature as real aspects of the processes and structures under study. This inductive enlargement of von Uexkull's idea is the generalized or *extended umwelt principle*.

When the time-related teachings of the different sciences are systematically surveyed and arranged to correspond to the hierarchy of nested organizational levels of nature, then, authorized by the extended umwelt principle, we may identify five distinct temporalities. These are themselves ordered along a scale of complexity in a hierarchically nested fashion. That is, each temporality subsumes the ones beneath it, while adding certain umpredictable degrees of freedom of its own.

Employing the visual metaphor of an arrow drawn on a sheet of paper, let me sketch the nature of the temporalities and mention the appropriate, level-specific conflicts. I will begin with the most sophisticated and most familiar temporality—that of the human mind—and proceed toward the most primitive and least familiar one, that of the speed-of-light particles. In the sketch that follows, each temporality has been reduced to its simplest and clearest form. Together, they constitute the *canonical forms of time*.

Let the image of the complete arrow stand for the ordinary, unexamined idea of time. The head and tail of the arrow, clearly drawn, represent the distinct experiential categories of future and past, recognized by the healthy, mature mind in the structure of the *mental present*. The boundaries of the mental present continuously shift depending on attention and the relative investment of psychic energy among the categories of future, past, and present. The arrow now represents the *nootemporal* umwelt of the mind, the human reality of symbols that make it possible for us to think of events and things not present but in the future or in the past. The characteristic conflict of this integrative level is the Freudian-Faustian tension, the difference between what is imagined and what is available or achieved.

Now let the head and tail of the arrow be ill-defined, amounting to no more than ambiguous boundaries to the shaft. So altered, the picture represents the *biotemporal* umwelt of all nonhuman life forms, of man as far as his biological functions go, and the reality of the human infant before the establishment of its selfhood. Here the mental present reduces to the organic present, a category of time experience more or less identical with a perceptual set with no mental content. The characteristic unresolvable creative conflicts of the biotemporal world are those between instinctual needs and their satisfaction. That those needs demand immediate satisfaction follows from the nature of the biotemporal umwelt: long-term futures do not exist in it, delays amount to complete, absolute, and final refusal. Connections between events are those of final causation, directed toward immediately sensible goals.

If now we imagine both the head and the tail of the arrow to be missing, we are left with a line, an image of *eotemporality*, so named after Eos, goddess of dawn. In its canonical form, this is the time of the physical world of macroscopic, massive bodies. This temporality is nowless (time without a present); it is also directionless (a feature corollary to nowlessness).[2] These curious hallmarks are revealed by the way time enters

---

[2]Time is said to be directed or to have an arrow, if it may be metaphorically described as flowing, as from past to future. But futurity and pastness make sense only by reference to a present. It follows that a temporality without a present is also one without direction.

the equations of the physics of the macrosocopic world. For that reason, eotemporality may be spoken of as "the time of the physicist's t." Connections between events are those of deterministic causation, with causes and effects interchangeable. This is consistent with the undirected nature of eotemporality. The level-specific conflicts of this integrative level are difficult to describe in terms of human experience but may be specified in abstract terms as those between growth and decay. The conflict finds formal expression in the principles that govern entropy increase and decrease in thermodynamically closed and open systems.

The shaft of the arrow may disintegrate into slivers of wood, scattered more or less along a line. The image now represents *prototemporality*. In its canonical form this is the time of the world of elementary particles. In addition to being nowless and undirected, it is also a discontinuous time. Connections between prototemporal events are governed by statistical laws: nothing is ever definitely here or there; no event is definitely now or then. Positions and instants may only be given as average values. The level-specific conflicts of the prototemporal world, again in abstract terms, are those between orderability and disorderability.

Finally, even the fragments of the arrow and, with them, the uncertain trace of a line may be lost. We are left with a blank sheet of paper, an empty set, a symbol of *atemporality*. The concept of atemporality is not that of nonexistence, but that of a reality to which none of our ordinary notions of time may be applied. In its canonical form it is the umwelt of speed-of-light particles in whose coordinates—imagined as traveling with them—everything happens at once.

From the atemporal world, let us climb back to the nootemporal one—and beyond. A good case can be made for *sociotemporality* as the temporality appropriate to a time-compact globe. But the difficulties of delineating the hallmarks of sociotemporality are great. To do so it is necessary to use a language whose vocabulary and syntax derive primarily from social and only secondarily from individual experience. Though such a language seems to be in the making, for the purpose of this paper nothing more will be said about sociotemporality.

When the laws that govern the different integrative levels are arranged along the scale of complexity, corresponding to their domains of validity—from physics to biology, psychology, and sociology—they are found to possess increasingly larger regions of undeterminancy.[3] I mention

---

[3] The principles that govern an integrative level leave undetermined the specifications of higher level principles. Thus, the language (laws) of the physical world leave un-

this epistemic issue here because the increasing degrees of freedom of the subsequent integrative levels is one of the hierarchical properties of the laws of nature, and because I shall have to refer to this hierarhical property later, when discussing reality testing.

The nature of noetic time and of biotemporality are intuitively evident; the experiential dimensions of eo-, proto-, and atemporality are not. But they may be made recognizable, once noted.

Thus, the eotemporal umwelt is the time of rhythmic tensions and relaxations, the universe of heartbeats, of rocking chairs, of repetition-compulsion, of the manifest content of many dreams. The prototemporal umwelt is the reality of certain psychotic states in which the continuity of the self is interrupted but not totally absent, and also that of dream content before secondary elaboration. Atemporality may perhaps be exemplified by the ultimate fugue in senility, an aspect of the cessation of personhood.

The sections that follow employ the canonical forms of time in a multidisciplinary interpretation of personal identity of the experience of timelessness.

TIME AND THE SELF

It is my thesis that depersonalization and derealization may be understood as representing a dissociation of the function of immediate experiencing from the function of self-observation [Arlow, 1966, p. 456].

Clinical material demonstrates that depersonalization may appear when the ego is confronted by a danger which it cannot master. The danger may be a realistic, external one in which instance depersonalization, up to a certain point, may serve an adaptive function [Arlow, 1966, p. 470].

This section proposes to interpret selfhood in terms of an adaptive policy of organic evolution, one that may be traced, in a speculative manner, all the way back to the origins of life. That policy is the externalization of inner functions, as an aspect of the coevolution of all species.

The hierarchial theory of time sees nowness—the organic present—

---

determined the laws peculiar to life, and the language of life leaves undetermined the principles that govern mental processes. *In*determinism means the absence of lawfulness which, at least in principle, could exist. *Un*determinism signifies the impossiblility of formulating (recognizing and expressisng) the laws of a higher integrative level in the language of the lower organizational level.

as having been introduced into the nowless world of nonliving matter by the demand of all life-forms for internal coherence. Specifically, to maintain life, it is necessary that within an organism whatever biological changes must take place simultaneously do, while those that should not take place simultaneously do not. In this view, the life process is identically equivalent to the creation and maintenance of *simultaneities of necessity* in physical structures which otherwise would possess only *simultaneities of chance*. Biogenesis, then, consisted of the coming about of structures whose integrity (whose lives) could be maintained only through instant-by-instant inner synchronization.

If the identification of life with the ability to maintain an organic present is taken as valid, then for the origins of life we should look to the appearance on the biogenetic earth of minature, internally coordinated oscillating systems, or "clockshops." Because of their internal coordination, such clockshops would possess certain selective advantages over other, uncoordinated aggregates. Once created, they may be imagined as having evolved through gradual extension of the spectrum of their cyclic functions. The cyclic order of life, represented by the spectrum of biological clocks observable today, spans a of range of seventy-eight octaves.

The cyclic order remained the only form of life until the early species passed a certain threshold of complexity. Then a new division of labor emerged. It separated somata which die by aging from germ cells which, given the right environment, do not. Henceforth, for sexually reproducing organisms, the responsibility for maintaining the moribund soma and for securing the continuity of life became two distinct, though interdependent functions. I believe that the evolutionary birth of death-by-aging is the earliest source of the profound and complicated relation in human life among sexuality, aging, the certainty of death, and the knowledge of time.

The task of keeping an increasingly more complex clockshop internally coherent has surely demanded the evolutionary development of autogenic control rhythms, whose purpose was to help maintain the organic present. To these internally generated cycles no prior external rhythms had to correspond. In due course some of the autogenic cycles are likely to have become externalized as behavioral cycles.

I would also expect that the increasing engram complements of the brains of animals with central nervous systems demanded the generation of new engrams, whose purpose was to help synchronize the neurological events of the brain. (I am using the concept of engram only faute de mieux.) In due course some of these self-generated engrams are likely to have led to behavior which was not in response to any pre-existing adaptive needs. The internal landscape of the brain thus became filled with images that corresponded to external events and things, and yet other images to which nothing in the external world needed to correspond.

Some time after the appearance of the human brain, one or more forms of genus Homo—the speculation may so continue—learned to handle images of possible events and things not present. From among them, those that related to unfulfilled needs experienced in the present could be separated from those that pertained to fulfilled ones, and the two sets of images assigned to the categories of future and past. Images assigned to the future helped lengthen the periods of bearable frustration, as hope was born; those assigned to the past increased the available storage of learned responses, as memory was born. Both hope and memory must have been of immense advantage in the struggle for survival.

I would imagine that our ancestors then learned to work out future behavioral strategies based on individual past experience and to communicate about them through symbols, as in spoken language. Through language—and art and artifact—it becomes possible to create and accumulate an increasing store of collectively generated knowledge, comprised of acquired characteristics.

I further imagine that, with the increasing complexity of the species, the behavior of advanced organisms became less rigid and hence less predictable. There arose, it seems, the need for a new, internally generated image, an executive agent to help coordinate action and thereby provide flexible responses to the unpredictable behavior of food, friend, and foe. As judged from the wisdom of hindsight, the new image stood for the object whose presence made other organisms display a modicum of predictability in their behavior, such as in acts of approach, escape, or neutrality. I submit that the symbol for this constant companion, and the body's sense impressions of itself, eventually merged into the single symbol of self, which retained the ambiguous aspects of its origins.

As a first approximation, the self is imagined as an object that moves and acts external to the body, sharing the infinity of space with all other structures. But the self is also a feeling, a purely temporal experience to which no spatial structure can correspond. Mediating between (1) the external world of space and physical and biological time and (2) the internal world of noetic time, the self is a mental object of multiple dimensions. It is responsible for the conduct of the body according to communal norms; it is said to have expectations and memory; it faces the certainty of death yet may hope for life everlasting; it is also the executive that works out strategies of behavior and, generally, minds the affairs of the body.

Everything I have listed here as being among the tasks of the self are of a temporal nature. But time comprises a hierarchically nested system of temporalities. I wish to postulate, therefore, that disturbances of selfhood necessarily correlate with disturbances of hierarchical, dynamic balance among the canonical forms of time which—as I shall argue— are always present in the mind, as parts of the mind's store of reality assessments.

Let me restate here what those canonical forms of time are. *Nootemporality* is the umwelt of the mature and healthy human mind: it is characterized by long- term future, long-term past, and the mental present with its changing boundaries. In *biotemporality* the mental present reduces to the organic present with its fixed, species-specific boundaries; long-term future and past reduce to limited regions of immediate future and past. *Eotemporality* is a nowless, directionless but continuous time. *Prototemporality* is nowless, directionless, as well as discontinuous. Finally, *atemporality* is the temporal umwelt of chaos, a form of reality to which none of our time-related notions are applicable.

In "Civilization and its Discontents" Freud (1930) formulated a strong recapitulation principle for the mind. He asserted that whereas in the body earlier evolutionary phases are usually absorbed in and supplanted by later phases, the mind preserves unchanged the stages of its evolutionary development. He added that "we are not in a position to represent this phenomenon in pictorial terms"(p. 71). I would like to rewrite this latter claim by changing "pictorial" to "spatial" and by adding that the phenomenon may, however, be represented in temporal terms. To wit: it is like musical instruments of the same kind but of different vintage playing simultaneously.

All living organisms function in the physical and biotemporal levels of nature; their behavior is governed by the appropriate hierarchy of principles. Humans, in addition, also function in the noetic and sociotemporal levels. Their characteristic behavior is governed by the human brain, which, for the reasons discussed, evaluates all stimuli in terms of archaic as well as more recently acquired reality judgments.

Our bodies may therefore be thought of as organized along a nested hierarchy of temporalities. We live simultaneously in all the temporal umwelts of nature. It should follow that in the human experience of time—a creation of the nervous system whose control functions span all the organizational levels of nature—we should be able to demonstrate the presence of archaic temporalities. This may, indeed, be done in connection with the experience generally described as that of the changing speed of time.

We note first that no clock or clocklike process may in itself be judged as being fast, slow, or accurate. A time measurement, any time measurement, consists in comparing two clock readings, mediated by a belief or theory that assures us that the comparison makes sense. The belief or theory may amount to qualitative comparisons: ''I get hungry each time the sun is high up in the sky.'' Or it may be a quantitative transformation rule between clock readings. In everyday life, if I declare that it is 7:00 a.m., the identity of one of the clocks and the theory that connects the two readings are matters of convention—for that reason, they go unnoticed. In the exact sciences the connecting principles become formalized as laws of nature and the identity of the two clocks that are being compared becomes obvious.

I wish to postulate that the speed-of-time experience is a mental time measurement that comprises unconscious comparisons between archaic and more recent modes of time perception. In a schematic form, I would identify the two clocklike processes with that appropriate for the cerebral cortex, and that appropriate for the mammalian and reptilian brains.

The concerns of the archaic parts of the human brain are those of immediate satisfaction: the furnishings of their umwelts are concrete objects and immediate goals. Selfhood cannot be defined in their world because their capacities for the formation of symbolic continuities are poor or nonexistent. By contrast, the concerns of the neocortex are those of long-term planning, long-term memory, and conscious experience. The furnishings of its umwelt include abstract representations of experience and their combinations, as necessary for selfhood. Behavior under its control may thus be directed to serve symbolic causes.

I assume that the unconscious comparisons between the older and the newer reality assessments of the mind are weighted from instant to instant by the needs, desires, and fantasies that mediate the comparison. Going one step further, I submit that the reason we have experiences describable as that of the flow of time to begin with ought to be sought in the very same comparisons.

If this be the case, then we would have removed a subtle contradiction from the psychoanalytic idea of reality testing. Namely, psychoanalytic theory does not demand an ontology of absolute frameworks given by nature and independent of man, such as a universal flow of time. It requires only an epistemology in which several visions of reality are traditional and useful. Yet psychoanalytic practice has assumed the existence of an objective temporal matrix, an aspect of reality, a feature of the cosmos, in which physical, biological, and psychological processes take place, and to which the patient's subjective sense of time, if disturbed, is gradually attuned through therapy.

The contradiction vanishes if we remember that the more complex the integrative level, and the larger its regions of undeterminacy, the less predictive power its laws have. Thus, objective (intersubjective) opinions on the laws of physics are not difficult to reach: the physical temporalities may be assumed to be features of the universe, independent of both patient and physician. It is legitimate to assume the reality of cosmic time (of three different temporalities), except that none of them may be described as "flowing." But it is not to these temporalities that the patient's behavior must be attuned. He is already a part of the physical world without needing to do anything about it or being able to. The levels of time that are significant to the mind are those of bio-, noo-, and sociotemporality. It is to these aspects of reality that the patient must adapt, and these are increasingly more subjective and conventional in their nature. When it comes to psychology, it is not necessary to reach objective (intersubjective) opinions on governing principles. On the contrary, the principles that govern the physical, biological, and mental worlds must provide for an increasingly greater loss of precision.

The mature adult mind in the waking state seems able to keep the different temporalities of its hierarchical reality in a nested, stable, dynamic balance. I do not know how to describe this balance in detail. But it seems to me that whenever it is disturbed, as when the higher brain functions are short-circuited during sleep, the metaphor of passing time ceases to be useful. But the absence from dreams of a time's flow, comparable to that of conscious experience, does not signify that dream umwelts are timeless. It indicates only that they are not nootemporal. Their realities are those of the lower temporalities, with noetic ordering introduced into dream reports only during the recounting of details.

Let me describe the hierarchical balance as a division of labor. Repairing disturbances in the sense of time may then be interpreted as reestablishing that balance through psychotherapy. The process of healing is not one of adapting an inner sense of time to that of an external, cosmic flow of time, for such a cosmic flow does not exist. It is, instead, a reestablishment in the mind of a working balance and division of labor among old and new forms of reality judgment.

Which of the temporalities of the mind is, so to say, the really real one? Which is the reference time of human time experience?

In scientific measurements of time, the clock selected as reference and judged to be more reliable is usually the one which is better understood. This usually is also the simpler one. That is why we measure the running time of rats by the clock on the wall and the rotation of the earth by atomic clocks, rather than the other way around.

In the continuous comparison among the various clocklike processes jointly responsible for our conscious sense of time's flow, it is probably the process whose reality happens to be invested with the most emotional energy that is taken to be the reference clock. Reasons for preferential cathecting of the archaic or the later clocks may be threats of inner, psychological dangers or physical, biological or social ones. We may speculate that what emerges into consciousness is the end product of an intricate process of comparisons, weighted by conscious and unconscious needs and fantasy. That end product is the feeling that time passes slowly, rapidly, not at all, or at just the right speed. In their turn, these feelings give rise to the infinite variety of metaphors our languages use to describe the passage of time.

In terms familiar to psychoanalytic theory, I would like to identify the functions of the neocortex with the self-observing self, and those of the mammalian and reptilian brains with the participating-acting self. The self-observing self may then be associated with secondary process functions: it prefers to deal with ideational issues; it makes human communication possible through symbolic transformations of experience; its reality includes the well-defined categories of long-term future, long-term past, and the mental present. It may be said to understand time. The participating-acting self may then be associated with primary process functions: it deals with concrete issues; it helps communicate through body language; its reality includes only the immediate future, the immediate past, and a species-specific organic present. It may be said to feel time.

The self-observing and the participating-acting selves may be perceived as jointly responsible for the dynamics of selfhood. Their functions are mediated by conscious and unconscious fantasies that help determine where the major sense of reality is to be placed. It is my guess that under normal conditions the selection is made so as to protect the integrity and executive powers of the ego.

In the presence of overwhelming danger that threatens the integrity of the ego, fantasy seems to cease serving as a mediator and becomes instead a means whereby a split between the two selves is precipitated. The patient then cries out with Hamlet, feeling that ''the time is out of joint; O cursed spite / That ever I was born to set it right'' (1.5. l88)

In sum, the power and vicissitudes of selfhood may be interpreted as phenomenological manisfestations of the dynamic balance, or its absence, among the different temporalities present in the mind. Though this interpretation is only one of many, it has the advantages of offering contacts, as far as their common interests go, between psychoanalysis and other scientific and humanistic disciplines.

TIMELESSNESS

This brought to her mind an experience which she regarded as perhaps the most significant of her life. It was an experience of timelessness, a religious, mystical sensibility which she experienced while giving a concert. . . .

. . . she experienced a sense of timelessnes, a feeling that time and space had ceased to exist and that she was in some kind of eternity [Arlow, 1984, p. 21].

What is it that is missing from experiences that both tutored and untutored subjects tend to describe as those of timelessness, that is, by specifying an absence of time?

Compared with nootemporality, all lower temporalities are deficient in some temporal attributes. It is this relative poverty which, in my view, gives rise to the description of certain experiences as being without, or outside time. Whether the experience is pleasurable or painful does not seem to derive from the feeling of timelessness itself but rather from the conscious and unconscious evaluation of the significance of that experience. I would like to examine the temporal structure of timelessness, using Freud's essay ''The Uncanny'' (1919) as my guide.

Freud found that common to situations that tend to bring forth a feeling of the uncanny was the uncertain position on the scale of reality of the events or things involved. Because of that ambivalence, it is difficult to integrate what a person believes he has observed with what he has learned to judge as real. An organism that may be animal or human, a man who may be alive or dead, a room that looks familiar yet we know we have never seen it before—these tend to generate a feeling of the eerie. In a leap of creative induction, Freud concluded that "the 'uncanny' is that class of the terrifying which leads back to something long known to us, once very familiar" (p. 369).

According to this understanding, the feeling of the eerie may be brought about, for instance, by conditions which seem to confirm that old, repressed beliefs in the nature of reality (once very familiar but now unfamiliar) were, after all, correct. In other words, certain events or things tend to bring unconscious fantasies (such as repressed theories of the nature of reality) into consciousness; the feeling that accompanies the return of the repressed is that of the eerie, the strange, the demonic, the sinister, the concealed—in one word, the uncanny.

Consider next that "the arousing of what is repressed is not left to chance but follows the law of development. Further, that repression proceeds backward from what is recent, and affects the latest events first" (Freud, 1897, p. 248). Whatever was repressed the earliest lies the deepest. It follows that the intensity of the feeling of the uncanny, generated by observed events that do not conform to the noetic sense of time but hark back to earlier assessments of time, indicates the topological position of those archaic temporalities in the structure of the mind.

Judging from this writer's subjective experience and from literary and anecdotal accounts, the intensity of uncanniness attached to claims of noninferential foreknowledge of the future is much greater than the intensity of similar feelings engendered by claims of noninferential knowledge of the past. The feeling of the uncanny is the least intense for alleged knowledge of distant events in the present. Prophets have been praised or abused but seldom neglected. People claiming to know hidden details of the past are interesting but seldom powerful enough to cause the kind of social havoc that prophets can cause. Clairvoyants claiming to have noninferential knowledge of distant current events are often not even noted.[4]

---

[4]In none of these cases is factual confirmation of the divined statements necessary: a prophet does not need to have been right in his predictions in order to be idolized or executed.

Let me assume that the different intensities of feelings attached to plausible noninferential knowledge of (1) the future, (2) the past, and (3) the present are indices of the topological positions in the mind of these categories of time. We may, then, conjecture as follows. In the development of the person, it is thoughts concerning certain possible future events that are repressed first. Foremost among these, no doubt, is the anxiety that always accompanies hope, and the discovery that death is certain. Next, so we may speculate, it is certain events of the past that are repressed. Foremost among these, no doubt, are feelings of regrets in their innumerable guises. Since the sequence of future, past, and mental present is also the order in which the categories of time develop in the child, the sequence of repression as suggested here seems to make sense.

That the topological position in the mind of futurity is the deepest layer of the noetic mind, with pastness at a lesser depth, is a claim consistent with psychoanalytic insight: in order to interpret a patient's attitude toward the future, it is necessary to clear a path to it through the removal of the obstacles of past experiences, operating in the present. The same sequence seems to be a recapitulation of the phylogenetic development of the sense of time. Considered along a scale from the simplest toward the more advanced species, animals appear to be able to adjust their behavior to suit future contingencies long before they can modify their behavior through individually acquired memories.[5]

If the reasoning of this section is correct thus far, then reports on an experience of timelessness may sometimes be interpreted as a report on foreshortened horizons of futurity and pastness. They suggest that a person has withdrawn from the responsibilities of the future and the memories of the past, into biotemporality as the highest form of reality. Psychological dangers, however, are not the only conditions that may promote such withdrawals: the biotemporal is usually the highest form of reality for the hungry and for those in pain.

In the topology of the mind, below the biotemporal level, we should be able to identify the next canonical form of time: a perception of the world with eotemporality as the highest form of reality.

Eotemporality, it will be recalled, is a nowless, directionless time; it is an umwelt wherein cause and effect, as well as beginnings and

---

[5]There are many ways I can tell a dog, "I will feed you," but there is no known sign that could carry the message, "I have already fed you."

endings are interchangeable. The suggestion emerges that some reports of timelessness, of eternity, may be descriptions of states of mind in which the eotemporal evaluation of reality become the dominant form of conscious awareness. Responsibility for the future, regrets and guilt feelings about the past, as well as the heavy labor of individuation in the mental present all recede into the background, there to form a reference matrix. Compared to that matrix of higher temporalities, the experience of presentless, directionless time may appear as a fulfillment, a happy arrival in a never-never land, or as an overwhelming threat, depending on the conscious and unconscious evaluations that mediate the comparison.

The prototemporal should be the next level beneath the eotemporal. If, depending on a myriad variables, the prototemporal incoherence intrudes on the eotemporal abiding present and forces itself upon awareness as the highest level of reality, then the bliss of eternity may change into the torments of chaos. Such "time travel" is often described, and appropriately so, as a bad trip. In the mind, heaven and hell stand in close proximity.

One may ask: What does the interpretation of timelessness offered in this section do to the perennial aspirations of mankind for the eternal, the transcendental, the divine? It can change those aspirations not a whit. The discovery of passage, the immediate reaction-formation to deny it, and hence the search for timelessness are necessary features of the human mind. That search takes the form of human creativity and destructiveness. No scientific identification of its sources can change the experienced intensity of the unresolvable conflicts between what is demanded and what is actually achieved. I do not believe that the role of the healthy human mind in the scheme of nature is that of eliminating those tensions. I would rather think that its role is to create and maintain them, for "a man's reach should exceed his grasp, / Or, what's a heaven for?"

REMOVING THE DEGENERACIES

The intellectual history of the idea of time is intricate, but it does permit certain generalizations. One of these is that since Plato, Western thought has tended to see the world in terms of the dichotomy of time and timelessness. The relation of time to motion, to understanding, to the created universe, and to human experience has been given many different evaluations. But whether time was seen as a mental construct, a form of perception, or an absolute and man-independent feature of the universe, it has generally been agreed that once established as a useful concept it must be taken to subsume equally all features of the world—in other words, that time is a global and homogeneous aspect of the universe in which all the furnishings of nature equally partake, although different of its properties become significant, depending on the character of the system comtemplated.

The title of this section, ''removing the degeneracies,'' is a phrase borrowed from physical science, where it signifies a demonstration that an apparently homogeneous condition possesses a structure.[6] The claim that time has a structure removes the degeneracy from the idea that time is a homogeneous aspect of the universe. In the history of modern thought there have emerged two domains of systematic inquiry which, each in its own way, have begun to reveal that structure.

One set of discoveries came through physical science, notably, through quantum theory, relativity theory, and the reexamination of what Newtonian physics discloses about the nature of time. But such is the power of cultural inertia—a phenomenon of social psychology—that until very recently hardly any working physicist believed what the equations of physics have all along been saying about time.

The other set of discoveries came through psychoanalysis. Freud's bold assertion that the processes of the unconscious are timeless is a form of twentieth-century Platonism and, as I have tried to show, incorrect. But the conclusions drawn from that assertion have led to clinically useful practices and have become, as far as I can tell, part and parcel of the pragmatic view of nature implicit in psychoanalysis.

The hierarchical theory of time was suggested to me many decades ago by the mutually reinforcing views of time in physics and depth psychology. Years of work, drawing on a wide spectrum of the sciences and the humanities, helped me develop the theory in some detail.

The literature on time is massive; learned papers may be counted in the thousands, books in the hundreds (see Fraser, 1979, 1987). However, book-length works from the point of view of psychoanalysis are very few. This writer is aware of only three such volumes.

Irvine Schiffer's *The Trauma of Time* (1978) is an inquiry into the methods the mind employs to silence its awareness of passage. The presen-

---

[6]The term comes from mathematics, where ''degeneracy'' signifies ''the condition in which two characteristic functions of an operator have the same characteristic value'' (Parker, 1984).

tation is woven around the clinical case of a painful but finally successful journey of a female patient from her adolescence in Hitler's death camps to the relative freedom of controlled trauma.

Andrea Sabbadini's *Il Tempo in Psichoanalisi* (1979) is a collection of fourteen psychoanalytically oriented papers published during the period 1939–1978, with a historical introduction by the editor.

Peter Hartocollis's *Time and Timelessness* (1983) is a treatise on the varieties of temporal experience as seen through psychoanalysis. It demonstrates the fruitfulness of interdisciplinary approaches to the study of time through a superb interpretation, in terms of the leitmotifs of time and timelessness, of the work of the Greek novelist Nikos Kazantzakis.

One may hope that with the broad sweep of interest illustrated by Jacob Arlow's essays, and with the work of Schiffer and Hartocollis, the psychoanalytic community will begin to answer, more energetically than it has heretofore, the challenge of integrating its findings about the nature of time with those of other sciences, using the study of time as a common intellectual scaffolding.

REFERENCES

Arlow, J. A. (1966), Depersonalization and derealization. In: *Psychoanalysis—A General Psychology: Essays in Honor of Heinz Hartmann,* ed. R. Loewenstein, L. Newman, M. Schur, & A. Solnit, New York: International Universities Press, pp. 456–478.

———— (1978), Psychoanalysis. In: *Collier's Encyclopedia.* New York: Macmillan.

———— (1984), Disturbances in the sense of time, with special reference to the experience of timelesness. *Psychoanal. Quart.,* 53:13–37.

English, H. B., & English, A. C. (1958), *A Comprehensive Dictionary of Psychological and Psychoanalytic Terms,* New York: McKay

Fraser, J. T. (1981), Temporal levels and reality testing. *Internat. J. Psycho-Anal.,* 62:3–26.

———— (1987), *Time, the Familiar Stranger.* Amherst: University of Massachusetts Press.

————, Lawrence, N., & Park D. (1979), Report on the literature of time: 1900–1980. In: *The Study of Time,* Vol. 4, ed. J. Fraser. New York: Springer Verlag, pp. 234–270.

Freud, S. (1897) Draft M. In: *The Complete Letters of Sigmund Freud to Wilhelm Fliess,* 1897–1904, trans. & ed. J. Masson. Cambridge: Harvard University Press, 1985.

———— (1919), The "uncanny." *Standard Edition,* 17:219–256. London: Hogarth Press, 1955.

———— (1920) Beyond the pleasure principle. *Standard Edition,* 18:7–64. London: Hogarth Press, 1955.

————(1930), Civilization and its discontents. *Standard Edition,* 21:64–145. London: Hogarth Press, 1961.

Hartocollis, P. (1983), *Time and Timelessness: A Psychoanalytic Exploration of the Varieties of Temporal Experience.* New York: International Universities Press.

Parker, S., ed. (1984), *The McGraw-Hill Dictionary of Scientific and Technical Terms.* New York: McGraw-Hill.

Sabbadini, A. (1979), *Il Tempo in Psichoanalisi.* Milan: Feltrinelli.

Schiffer, I. (1978), *The Trauma of Time.* New York: International Universities Press.

28

Of Men and Monuments

Charles Brenner, M.D.

If one were asked who were the greatest scientists in the hundred years between 1859 and 1950, three names would come instantly to mind: Darwin, Freud, and Einstein. Each had a revolutionary effect on the course of scientific thought and development in his field. Each made discoveries which were of fundamental importance and which had profound consquences. Biology could never be the same after the *Origin of Species,* nor psychology after "The Interpretation Of Dreams," nor physics after $E=mc^2$. Here were three men who changed the course of intellectual history on a truly grand scale. As Horace, the great Roman poet, said of his poems, the discoveries of Darwin, Freud, and Einstein are monuments more lasting than bronze, higher than the pyramids, monuments that will endure as long as men and women think and talk about the subjects to which the three devoted their lives.

Freud's contributions to his field are so numerous that it is hard to know where to begin. I shall try, nevertheless, to review in a cursory way those that are most outstanding, the ones on which his fame seems mainly to rest. Surely one of the greatest was his discovery of the extent, variety, and importance of unconscious mental processes. Before his time the prevailing opinion among students of psychology was that only what is conscious is mental. Psychology was understood to be the study of what today we call conscious mental life. Anything inaccessible to consciousness could not be psychic, was the idea. It was Freud who discovered the role of unconscious mental processes in psychopathology, in dreaming, in the slips and errors of daily life, in jokes, and eventually, by extension, in every aspect of mental life. By doing so he was also able to document psychic determinism, which is, in effect, a corollary of the

An earlier version of this chapter was presented as the Freud Memorial Lecture of the Philadelphia Association for Psychoanalysis, April 11, 1986.

importance of unconscious mental processes. He could substantiate the thesis that whatever happens in conscious mental life and overt behavior is causally related to the mental events which preceded it. Whatever we think or do is a consequence of what we were thinking just before. In the many instances where that seems not to be the case, it is because the psychic determinants are unconscious ones. It is only if one ignores unconscious determinants that psychic life ever appers to be discontinuous. If one takes into account what one is thinking unconsciously as well as one's conscious thoughts, psychobehavioral events are as precisely determined by what went before as are any other events of the physical world.

But this was only the beginning of Freud's contributions to our knowledge of the mind. Far greater in its impact was his discovery of childhood sexuality, so much of which is subsumed under the heading the Oedipus complex. Childhood sexual wishes, he found, are the pathogenic factor both in the neuroses and in the perversions, as well as the basis of sublimation and of man's moral sense. The knowledge that children, neurotics, and artists have the sexual wishes that Freud described had a powerful effect on twentieth-century thought, far beyond the field of psychopathology or even psychology proper. In the popular mind, as in the minds of many professionals, psychoanalysis and Freud are synonymous with sex.

Another discovery led to an equally close link of Freud and psychoanalysis with dreams. After millennia during which dreams were either revered as prophecy or dismissed as nonsense, Freud showed that dreams have a meaning that can be discovered in a rational, scientific way. Dreams, said Freud, are linked on the one hand with current concerns and, on the other, with the wishes and cares of childhood. At one stroke he unlocked the secret of a phenomenon that had eluded man's understanding since the beginning of time and made that phenomenon accessible to scientific study. Freud's name is linked as closely in the popular mind with dreams as it is with sex.

By combining what he had discovered about the dynamics and genesis of neurotic symptoms with what he had discovered about the mental processes by which the latent content of a dream is transformed into its manifest content, Freud was able to put forward the first statement of a theory of the mind that he considered worth publishing. He was able to write chapter seven of "The Interpretation Of Dreams." In any history of psychology, what today we call the topographic theory will forever stand out as a towering landmark. Freud himself said of it that, "Insight such as this falls to one's lot but once in a lifetime" (1900, p. xxxii).

To be sure, Freud revised this first draft in later years, the final version being what today we call the structural or tripartite theory. This, too, is certainly one of the great monuments to his fame, as is his discovery of the role of conflict in psychic life, as well as its mode of action there. To those who are interested in mental illness the word "repression" is as closely tied to Freud's name as are dreams and the Oedipus complex.

I need only mention Freud's contributions to the fields of art, literature, anthropology, and history to remind you of their contribution to his fame. For many, the applications of psychoanalysis to fields other than those of mental illness and psychology proper are the most important of Freud's contributions to modern culture. These applications are often grouped under the heading of applied psychoanalysis. They consitute what the findings of analysis contribute to the various disciplines just listed. It is interesting that the original relationship was just the reverse. Freud and his early collaborators were not at first concerned primarily with what psychoanalysis had to contribute to other disciplines. They occupied themselves with art, with literature, with myths, with religion, and with history primarily in order to substantiate the findings of psychoanalysis. They culled evidence from each to show that such things as the oedipus complex, castration anxiety, and sexual symbolism are universal phenomena. Though originally inferred from the symptoms and dreams of neurotic patients, they are not to be dismissed as charateristic only of those who are mentally abnormal, or as phantasms of the analysts who treat them. On the contrary, said Freud, what he had found in the mental productions of his neurotic patients is to be found also in man's cultural achievements throughout the ages. Secondarily, the discoveries of psychoanalysis could be applied to many other areas of study. Primarily, however, these fields were of interest to Freud as sources of confirmation of many of the startling new findings about mental life that derived in the first instance from other sources: from his work with neurotic patients; from the direct observation of children; from clinical psychiatric data; and last, but by no means least, from the analysis of his own dreams, from his self-analysis. To a degree that would seem strange to us today, analysts in the early years analyzed one another's dreams, slips, and errors to convince themselves of the validity of Freud's discoveries of the importance of unconscious mental processes, of psychic determinism, and of childhood sexual wishes.

On what then does Freud's fame rest? What were his great discoveries? Though different answers might vary in emphasis, all would include the dynamic unconscious, psychic determinism, the oedipus complex, dream interpretation, the various theories of the mind and its functioning, and the many applications of analysis to other fields of study. As I noted earlier, Freud himself felt his greatest achievement to be the formulations contained in the final chapter of "The Interpretation Of Dreams," his first publishd theory of the mind. For him, this was the highest, most lasting monument to him and to his work.

No one can doubt the greatness of these achievements, least of all the one which he himself prized most highly. But what I wish to discuss in what follows is a discovery of Freud's I have not yet mentioned. As you will see, it is one intimately connected with all the others. More than that, it is what made all the others possible. It is the psychoanalytic method of investigation. As a tool for the study of the mind, it has as yet no peer. In my opinion it is the greatest mark of Freud's genius.

In every branch of science, methods of gathering data are of the greatest importance. One must not only ask the right questions, as this everyone knows. One must also have some way of getting at the answers to those questions. In the field of psychology that way is the psychoanalytic method. Until Freud devised this method, psychology remained largely a *terra incognita*. Had he not devised the method when he did, psychology would today remain a dark continent.

The separation of science into various branches would seem purely a matter of practical convenience. We have every reason to believe that every aspect of the universe, from the tiniest subatomic particles to the largest of its billions of galaxies, is a manifestation of mass/energy in space/time. It was Newton who first grasped the truly revolutionary idea that the motion of the heavenly planets accords with the same laws as does the motion of bodies on the surface of the earth. It was he who first realized that gravitation is as much a force in the heavens as it is on the earth and that the same hypotheses, the same mathematical equations explain both terrestrial and celestial mechanics. Since Newton's time the idea, prevalent until then, that earth and heaven are two very different sorts of places, has steadily lost ground. No serious scientist today doubts that the earth and the rest of the universe are one. No one doubts, because there is at present no reason to doubt the proposition that all scientists, whatever branch of science they pursue, are studying one or another part of what is, after all, a unified whole.

It accords with this view of natural science that what begin as different branches of science merge into one another in the course of time, as chemistry and atomic physics have done and, more recently, biology and chemistry. Current linguistic usage reflects such mergers. We speak of physical chemistry and of molecular biology. It must not be imagined, however, that dividing natural science into several branches is a mere matter of terminology. Though the reasons for the division are purely practical ones, they are nonetheless compelling. They have to do with the gathering of data on which one can base theories and generalizations that are valid and fruitful.

In every branch of science, data, or facts, take first place. They are of prime inportance. They are the empirical basis for all we try to do. Generalizations, theories, hypotheses, laws—call them what you will—must conform to data. It is true that scientists create theories imaginatively. Every scientific theory, however simple or however complicated, is the product of someone's creative imagination, just as much as is a work of art, a myth, or a religious belief. In fact, the psychology of the creative process that produces scientific theories has been studied psychoanalytically. Analysts have discovered that the creative process is deeply rooted in the wishful world of childhood conflicts. It is from these roots that the theories of empirical science spring, but despite its roots in the conflict-ridden world of childhood, for a scientific theory to be acceptable, it must conform with available data to begin with and must be in accord with new data as these become available. Data—facts—are supreme. In science they are the court of last resort.

Obviously, then, methods of gathering data are of great importance in any scientific enterprise, and different areas of investigation, that is to say, different targets of inquiry, require different methods of data gathering. To put the matter somewhat differently, one must adapt one's method of data gathering to the special requirements of each situation. Each branch of science requires its own special methods of study.

The area of inquiry of psychoanalysis—its object of study—is the mind. The method of inquiry—of data gathering—is the psychoanalytic method. Without this method Freud would have known no more about the human mind, either sick or healthy, than did any other neurologist or psychiatrist of his day. It was the method of investigation Freud devised that made psychoanalysis possible, both as a mode of psychotherapy and as a theory of mental functioning. The psychoanalytic method has proved to be by far the best way of learning about the functioning and development of the human mind.

Freud's method is, on the surface, a very simple one. It seems especially so when one compares it with the methods of data gathering of many other branches of science. It requires no special apparatus, merely two people in a room together. Its essence is simply that, in a setting in which external stimuli are unintrusive, one person tells another whatever comes to mind. The one who is being analyzed agrees to speak without editing. The one who is analyzing agrees to do that and only that. The analysand's role is to speak without reserve. The analyst's role is to try to understand what the analysand is saying, to adopt an analytic attitude, one that precludes being judgmental, directive, demanding, irate, or sexually responsive to anything the analysand might say.

The apparent simplicity of all this is of course misleading. The analytic method is not at all easy to practice skillfully. To become a good analytic observer takes much training and experience, part of which is a personal analysis. Still its basic requirement is a very simple one: it is that one study psychology by listening to everything that is going on in someone else's mind—everything that someone else is thinking and feeling.

Now, the study of psychology has been going on for a very long time. Even its origin as a scientific discipline goes back two thousand years, being attributed, by consensus, to Aristotle. And long before that, as well as long after, mystics, poets, and religious thinkers have speculated on human nature and the soul of man. For thousands of years, then, some of the most brilliant and profound of men have studied human psychology, yet within the lapse of less than a century psychoanalysis has made a greater contribution to the knowledge of the human mind than all their contributions put together.

How was that possible? How could such a simple procedure as the psychoanalytic method be so fruitful? What makes it so superior to any other method yet devised as a way of gathering data about the mind?

These are questions that can be answered only in retrospect, as is so often true in the history of science. To ask them is like asking why the telescope was so fruitful as a method of gathering data in astronomy or the microscope in the study of infectious diseases. In both cases it was because there was so much more to be seen than could be seen with the unaided eye. The ancients thought there was nothing more to be seen in the sky than what was visible to the naked eye, but that there was something special to hear—the music of the spheres, a celestial harmony. Had their belief been correct, a telescope would have been useless to Galileo. He would have needed a telephone, not a telescope; an amplifier of sounds, not a magnifier of images. The telescope gave Galileo access to a wealth of otherwise inaccessible astronomical data, but that is not something he or anyone else could possibly have known in advance. It is only in retrospect that it is clear to everyone that there is so much out there to be seen and that a telescope is what is needed to see it. To Galileo it was a guess he made, something he tried in the hope it would prove useful. And so it did. It justified his hope and more.

A similarly retrospective explanation holds true for the psychoanalytic method. Freud tried it because he guessed and hoped that it would work, and work it did, even better than he dared to hope. The fact is that when a person speaks as freely and as fully as possible, an experienced, open-minded listener can learn a great deal about that person's mental functioning, far more than anyone could have predicted. It is also a fact, however, that any person willing to speak so freely must have some very compelling reason to do so. As we know today, the compelling reason is, usually, a significant degree of neurotic suffering, of neurotic inability to function normally, or both. For the analytic method to be possible an analysand must suffer from a significant degree of a certain type of mental illness.

As it happened, Freud, in his practice, was faced with the necessity of treating just such patients. However, he was not the only neurologist of his day who was faced with that necessity. There were many others. It is a measure of Freud's genius that he alone devised and developed the psychoanalytic method from its origins in hypnosis. It is a method devised to meet a therapeutic need. It has made of a therapeutic situation—the situation between patient and analyst—a source of psychological data whose value is unsurpassed.

It is, however, only part of the story to say that the psychoanalytic method, applied in a therapeutic setting, proved to be incomparably fruitful as a source of the data necessary for the understanding of neurotic psychopathology. There was an additional gain from the application of the psychoanalytic method, a gain Freud had not even thought of at the start. It is that the hidden, otherwise inaccessible wishes, fears, memories, and fantasies that psychoanalysis uncovers in the minds of those suffering from neuroses are present, in one form or another, in the minds of normal persons as well. These phenomena are of great importance in normal psychic functioning and development, just as they are in psychopathology. Psychoanalysis is not merely a psychopathology. It is a psychology of the normal as well.

As to the superiority of the psychoanalytic method over other methods of psychological data gathering, its only serious competitor, either a century ago, in Freud's time, or now, in our own, is introspection. Academic psychology is not a competitor. Insofar as it is independent of psychoanalysis and uninflunced by it, academic psychology is concerned only with what is trivial and unimportant emotionally. Introspection, however, like the psychoanalytic method, attempts to gain access to data regarding what is of major, subjective importance in mental life. The data of both the method of introspection and the psychoanalytic method are wishes, moods, emotions, thoughts, memories, physical sensations, actions, dreams, daydreams—in a word, the very stuff of life. The difference is that the introspective psychologist or philosopher is concerned to observe his or her own thoughts and feelings, while the psychoanalyst is concerned with the thoughts and feelings of another, who reports them in the analytic situation.

A priori, the difference seems unimportant. One might even argue that introspection has the advantage. After all, the report of a mental event can never precisely convey its quality, nor can a report ever have the vividness, the immediacy of the event or experience itself.

Despite its advantage in this respect, however, introspection is far less useful as a means of access to reliable data about the mind than is the psychoanalytic method. Indeed, for practical purposes it is worse than useless. The reason for this is obvious now, in the light of knowledge gained by the psychoanalytic method. We know now that human beings, beginning early in childhood, are at great pains to deceive themselves with respect to many of the most important wishes and other motives of their lives—to ignore them, to forget about them, to repudiate them, to disavow them. The consequence of this is that invariably the data of introspection are systematically falsified by the very person who supplies them—falsified to such a degree as to be worthless for any serious scientific purpose. It is no wonder that the adjective *subjective* was synonymous with unreliable and unscientific as long as introspection was the only means of studying subjective phenomena. An independent observer, particularly one with experience and without too great a personal bias, can, with the help of the psychoanalytic method, gain far more in the way of reliable psychological data than anyone can from introspection.

The psychoanalytic method differs from the methods used for gathering data in other branches of science—physiology or chemistry, for instance. It differs from them because the data to be observed are different. The data of psychoanalysis are verbal reports of every sort of thought, feeling, and memory and the method of observing such data must be suited to the task. However, once the data have been gathered, they are dealt with as any scientist deals with data. An analyst postulates the same kind of cause and effect relationships with respect to psychoanalytic data as a physicist, for example, might postulate with respect to the data available to him or her. Like any other scientist, the psychoanalyst is an empiricist who imaginatively infers functional and causal relationships among data, avoiding, if possible, generalizations which are either inherently inconsistent with one another or incompatible with well-supported conclusions from other branches of science. The hypotheses or generalizations thus formed constitute psychoanalytic theory. Some of its hypotheses are well substantiated by abundant data, some less so, but all are empirically based hypotheses fully comparable with those in any other branch of science. It was to these facts that Freud (1933) referred when he wrote that psychoanalysis has no view of life, no Weltanschauung, other than that of science.

A few additional words are necessary in order to put the matter in the proper perspective. The observable data to which such terms as "the mind," "psychic phenomena," and "psychology" all refer are an aspect of the functioning of the brain. No one can doubt the correctness of this statement who is familiar with the established findings of comparative psychology, neuroanatomy, neurophysiology, and neuropathology. The brain is the organ of the mind quite as much as the heart is the organ of circulation. It is true that there are many things we do not know, and that we would like to know, about the relationship between brain and mind. We know much more about how the heart causes the blood to circulate and how the lungs function in respiration than we know about how cerebral functioning is related to the mind. Nevertheless, despite our many areas of ignorance, we are in no doubt that the brain is in fact the organ of the mind. Persons who maintain that the mind is somehow separate or separable from the body, who maintain that there is a dichotomy between mind and body, are simply out of date. They are, in effect, clinging to the untenable conviction, which men have held for as far back as our knowledge of history takes us, that the nature of man is twofold, that man is made up of a mortal body and an immortal soul or spirit.

To use a simple analogy, the earth looks flat. It *is* flat, as far as the subjective experience of each of us goes. Yet we have no doubt that it is round for all of that. Just so, we all feel that our mind is something separate from our body. We distinguish between the two subjectively, yet just as surely as the earth is round, despite our experience of it as flat, so surely is the mind of each of us an aspect of cerebral functioning, an aspect of bodily processes, despite our experience to the contrary.

All of this relates to my exposition of the psychoanalytic method, for this reason. Some aspects of brain functioning are best studied by the methods of chemistry, of physics, or of physiology. None of these, however, as yet rivals the psychoanalytic method as a means of studying the aspect of brain functioning we call the mind. None yields results as useful as those of the psychoanalytic method. The reason for this is not, as has often been argued, that the mind is different from the body and that physicochemical methods and techniques are therefore inappropriate to its study. Not at all. The mind is an aspect of bodily processes quite as much as every other aspect of bodily functioning. There is no reason *in principle* why the psychoanalytic method is the best method for studying the mind. The reason is one of fact, not of theory. The psychoanalytic method has simply proved itself the best way so far devised in which to study the mind.

The reason is not far to seek. When one is freed from the distraction of external stimuli, the influence of internal stimui is proportionately greater. One's wishes and the conflicts associated with them then dominate and direct one's mental processes in larger measure. It is for this reason that they become apparent to the listener to whom one communicates one's thoughts without reserve. As Freud (1925) put it, as soon as he dispensed with hypnosis he came face to face with his patient's wishes and with the defenses against those wishes—in a word, with his patient's conflicts and resistances.

I have dealt in general terms with the way in which application of the psychoanalytic method leads to generalizations about the psychic apparatus and its functioning. An illustration of this procedure will make matters more concrete and more easily comprehensible. I have chosen for the purpose an aspect of psychonanalytic theory more often criticized and condemned than any other. It is the concept of psychic energy. Since so many critics have given reasons why it should be rejected, I hope by arguing for its acceptance to be able to clarify better the role of the psychoanalytic method in theory formation.[1]

---

[1]The following discussion of psychic energy is adapted from Brenner (1980).

The word *energy* derives from the language of physics. In physics, energy is variously defined. One definition is the capacity to do work. Another definition specifies its dimensions: gram-centimeters, that is, displacement of mass against a constant force, as the force of gravity. Still another specifies its relation to mass, that is, the amount of mass in a unit of energy: $E = mc^2$, and so on. What in these definitions of physical energy can be applied to the concept of psychic energy? Are the two to be understood to be the same? Is psychic energy one of the forms of physical energy, like kinetic energy or potential energy or electrical energy? Or is there no relation between the two at all? Is psychic energy a misnomer perhaps, a bad choice of words that can only be misleading and troublesome?

The answer runs as follows. As Freud gained experience in applying the psychoanalytic method to the study of the nature and origin of neurotic symptoms, he was impressed by evidence that such symptoms are a consequence of repressed sexual wishes. His study of dreams by the same psychoanalytic method led to a similar conclusion: every dream fulfills one or more wishes of infantile origin, in however disguised or distorted a way. He also discovered that if slips, errors, and jokes are studied by the psychoanalytic method, the inference is inescapable that unconscious wishes of childhood play a major role in their genesis. In short, what finally emerged was the familiar theory of instinctual drives, first concerned chiefly with libido and later expanded to include aggression as well.

According to this theory, the drives impel the mind—the mental apparatus, as Freud said—to activity. Hence the very name. A drive is something that drives or impels to activity. And, said Freud, the measure of a drive's capacity to impel the mind to activity—to get it going, so to speak—may properly be called psychic energy by analogy with the definition of physical energy as the capacity to do physical work. It is for this reason that our psychological language has borrowed the word energy from the language of physics.

The meaning of psychic energy, then, should be clearer. It means the capacity of a drive to impel the mind to activity. The question remains, however, as to whether this concept is useful or not; in other words, whether the analogy is apt.

The psychological data that led Freud to the theory of drives were those which gave evidence of conscious and unconscious wishes. To put the matter somewhat formally, the evidential basis for psychoanalytic drive theory is in the conscious and unconscious wishes of patients as revealed by the psychoanalytic method of observation. Each observation, be it noted, is of a particular person's wish for a particular kind of gratification from a particular person under particular circumstances. Each wish, as observed psychoanalytically, is personal and specific. It is not, for example, "an oral wish." It is a wish for gratification of a special kind, say, nursing, or swallowing a penis—a wish that has a uniquely personal history and form for each patient. Similarly, a wish is not just "an aggressive wish." It is always a wish to do something to somebody, again with a special history and form.

If, however, the aggregate of such data from many analyses is surveyed, certain generalizations become possible. One of these is that wishes fall readily into two broad groups, libidinal and aggressive, even though every particular wish appears to contain elements of both. Another is that the history of such wishes goes back to the early years of childhood—they are persistent or modified infantile wishes. Still another is that libidinal wishes often involve pleasurable stimulation of the erogenous zones.

All of these generalizations are expressed succinctly by the psychoanalytic theory of drives, that is, by the statement that there are two basic drives, libidinal and aggressive, that both are active throughout mental life, and that the libidinal drive has a special relation to the erogenous zones. The concept of psychic energy, then, is an extension of this formulation. It denotes the capacity of the drives to impel the mind to activity. As such it contains the idea that some wishes, at a given time, are stronger than others and that wishes vary in strength from time to time. Unless one is ready to assume that the drives never fluctuate in intensity, one must attribute a dimension of magnitude to psychic energy; there must be some quantitative aspect to that part of drive theory which is expressed by the concept of psychic energy.

It may be noted in passing that in the terminology of drive theory any particular wish is a *drive derivative*. A drive derivative is what one "observes" in a patient. It is a particular person's particular wish. The concept of drive is a generalization based on many such observations. The term "drive derivative" refers to particular examples or instances of drive activity.

So much by way of explanation of the meaning of the term "psychic energy," and of its evidential basis. Is it justified and useful as a concept and as a term? I believe so, but not because the word "energy" was appropiated from the language of physics. Rather I believe so because I think that drive theory is a valid and useful generalization or theory about mental functioning and that in that theory there should be some term to designate the concept that drives have a capacity to impel the mind to activity—a capacity that varies in strength from time to time. What that concept is *called* matters not at all, any more than it matters whether one speaks English or some other language in discussing it. Call it psychic energy, motivational impetus, or "abc." The tag is unimportant. It is the concept that matters. If you drop the concept altogether, as many analysts would like to do, you have to discard drive theory as well. But then you have to substitute something for it. Just changing the name from "drive" to, say, "motivation," as some have proposed, changes nothing in the theory. It makes the theory no more "psychological," no less "mechanistic," no more "human," than it was before (see Wallace, 1985, pp. 151-177). What one must decide, if one is to introduce a real change into psychoanalytic theory, is whether one thinks it unjustified to generalize about conscious and unconscious wishes as Freud did, by dividing them into two groups, libidinal and aggressive. Or whether one is prepared to assign to wishes a role in mental functioning altogether different from the role Freud assigned them, and to say that they are not of such fundmental importance in mental activity as psychoanalytic theory assumes them to be. If these questions are answered in the affirmative, important changes in the concept of psychoanalytic theory, not simply in its language, are at issue. One would be proposing something of substance that could be evaluated with reference to the facts, that is, with reference to the data observable by the psychoanalytic method, because that is the basis for proposing the concept of psychic energy in the first place. Psychic energy is a concept based on data made available by the psychoanalytic method, data that it orders and explains as I have indicated. Whatever concept one proposes, whether it be that of psychic energy or some alternative, it must explain those data in a logically satisfactory way.

Psychoanalysis is a relatively new science. Its data are often insufficient and always incomplete. The theories its data have given rise to will undoubtedly be altered in the course of time, as all scientific theories must be. But dissatisfaction with their shortcomings should not be allowed to obscure the fact that at present they are by far the best theories of human psychology available. Nor should one lose sight of the fact that the reason for their superiority over other theories is a consequence of the development of a new method of observing the human mind, namely, the psychoanalytic method. Freud was a keen and bold observer and an outstanding framer of hypotheses. But these qualities of mind do not account for the fact that psychoanalytic theories are superior to competing theories. What accounts in greatest measure for Freud's success as a psychologist is the psychoanalytic method he devised. Without this method, as I have said, Freud would have known no more about mental illness or mental functioning in general than did any neurologist or psychiatrist of his day. With it, he was able to make the most important contribution to the knowledge of human psychology that any man ever made. There are many monuments to Freud's genius. To paraphrase Horace, he erected many monuments, more lasting than bronze and higher than the royal pyramids of Egypt. I suggest that of all the monuments to his fame the greatest is the one least often mentioned, his discovery of the psychoanalytic method.

REFERENCES

Brenner, C. (1980), Metapsychology and psychoanalytic theory. *Psychoanal. Quart.*, 49:189–214.

Freud, S. (1900), The interpretation of dreams. *Standard Edition*, 4/5. London: Hogarth Press, 1953.

———— (1925), An autobiographical study. *Standard Edition*, 20:7–70. London: Hogarth Press, 1959.

———— (1933), New introductory lectures on psycho-analysis. *Standard Edition*, 22:7–182. London: Hogarth Press, 1964.

Wallace, E. (1985), *Historiography and Causation in Psychoanalysis: An Essay on Psychoanalytic and Historical Epistemology*. Hillside, NJ: Analytic Press.

INDEX